# Your All-in-One Resource

On the CD that accompanies this book, you'll find additional resources to extend your learning.

The reference library includes the following fully searchable titles:

- *Microsoft Computer Dictionary*, 5th ed.
- *First Look 2007 Microsoft Office System* by Katherine Murray
- Windows Vista Product Guide

Also provided are a sample chapter and poster from *Look Both Ways: Help Protect Your Family on the Internet* by Linda Criddle.

The CD interface has a new look. You can use the tabs for an assortment of tasks:

- Check for book updates (if you have Internet access)
- Install the book's practice file
- Go online for product support or CD support
- Send us feedback

The following screen shot gives you a glimpse of the new interface.

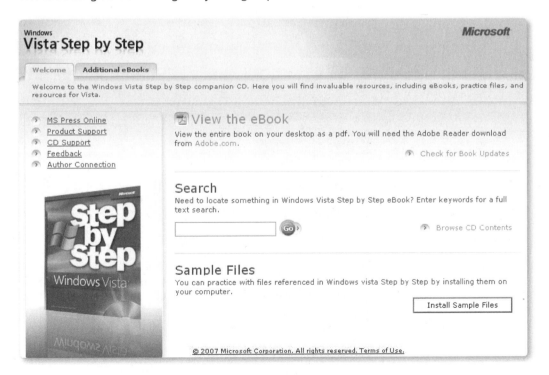

*Microsoft*®

# Step by Step 2007 Microsoft® Office System

*Joyce Cox, Curtis Frye,
M. Dow Lambert III,
Steve Lambert, and
Joan Preppernau,
with Katherine Murray*

PUBLISHED BY
Microsoft Press
A Division of Microsoft Corporation
One Microsoft Way
Redmond, Washington 98052-6399

Library of Congress Control Number: 2006936145

Printed and bound in the United States of America.

2 3 4 5 6 7 8 9   QWT   2 1 0 9 8 7

Distributed in Canada by H.B. Fenn and Company Ltd.

A CIP catalogue record for this book is available from the British Library.

Microsoft Press books are available through booksellers and distributors worldwide. For further information about international editions, contact your local Microsoft Corporation office or contact Microsoft Press International directly at fax (425) 936-7329. Visit our Web site at www.microsoft.com/mspress. Send comments to mspinput@microsoft.com.

**Acquisitions Editor:** Juliana Aldous Atkinson
**Developmental Editor:** Sandra Haynes
**Project Editor:** Lisa Culver-Jones
**Editorial Production:** Carol Whitney and Terrie Cundiff of nSight, Inc.
**Indexer:** Jack Lewis

Body Part No. X12-48777

# Contents

**What do you think of this book? We want to hear from you!**

Microsoft is interested in hearing your feedback so we can continually improve our books and learning resources for you. To participate in a brief online survey, please visit:

**www.microsoft.com/learning/booksurvey/**

## Part IV **Microsoft Office PowerPoint 2007**

## Part V    Microsoft Office Outlook 2007

**What do you think of this book? We want to hear from you!**

Microsoft is interested in hearing your feedback so we can continually improve our books and learning resources for you. To participate in a brief online survey, please visit:

**www.microsoft.com/learning/booksurvey/**

# A Tour of the Office 2007 User Interface

From the moment you launch any of the applications in the 2007 Microsoft Office System, you will notice a dramatic difference: The entire user interface has been redesigned to be more intuitive, easier to navigate, and better suited to the task at hand. When the developers of Office 2007 began brainstorming about the new user interface, they decided to go back to the drawing board and create an interface based on the way people use their computers today. The result is a simplified, smart system that brings you just the tools you need, when you need them. No more clicking through menus, submenus, and nested dialog boxes. Now the commands you need come to you, depending on the type of object you select and the application you are using. This chapter introduces the new elements in the Office 2007 user interface so that you'll recognize the features as you begin to use the applications.

## Using the "Ribbon"

The Office 2007 Ribbon was in the news long before Office 2007 went public. Why? The Ribbon is the dramatic new replacement for the customary menu system in previous versions of Microsoft Office. The Ribbon stretches across the top of the work area in Word, Excel, PowerPoint, and Access, and it appears in selected windows in Outlook, giving you tabs, contextual commands, and more that are related to the current operation you are performing (see Figure I-1).

The Ribbon is actually a collection of several components:

- The Quick Access Toolbar (appears in the top left of the window and contains the Microsoft Office button, which opens the File menu), and the Save, Undo, and Redo icons. (You can customize the QAT to add tools you use frequently.)

- Command tabs (such as Home, Insert, Page Layout, References, Mailings, Review, and View in Word 2007) stretch across the screen just below the window title bar.

- Command sets are the commands available for the selected tab that relate to what you're trying to do. The name of the command set appears below the commands (for example, Clipboard, Font, and Paragraph, in Figure I-1).

- Contextual commands appear only when an object (a table, chart, etc.) is selected.

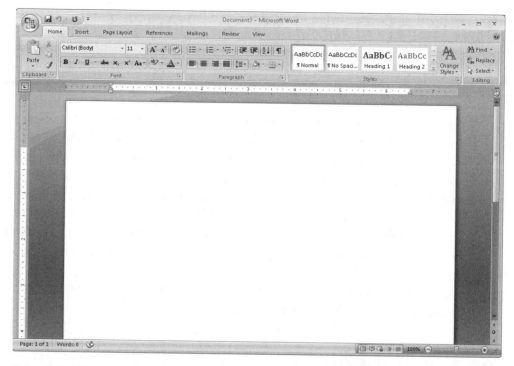

**Figure I-1.** When you click a command tab, the command sets that relate to that tab are displayed in the Ribbon.

## Command Tabs

The command tabs relate directly to the stages of the process you're likely to follow as you create a project in an application. For example, in Office Excel 2007, the command tabs are Home, Insert, Page Layout, Formulas, Data, Review, and View. When you're creating a worksheet, you first need commands related to data entry (Home), editing (Insert), and formatting (Page Layout). Later on in the process, you will want to work with the information on the worksheet by analyzing (Formulas), sorting, filtering, consolidating, and validating it (Data). If you're working as part of a team, you'll want to be able to review the worksheet and share it with others (Review). Along the way, you'll need to be able to modify the ways in which the worksheet is displayed (View).

## Command Sets

Different commands appear in the Ribbon depending on the tab you've selected. If you click the Home tab in PowerPoint 2007, one set of commands appears in the Ribbon;

if you click the Review tab, a different set is displayed. This approach cuts down on the number of menus, commands, and dialog boxes you have to sort through in order to find the items you want. Each command set is grouped according to its function. In Figure I-2, the Page Setup, Themes, Background, and Arrange command sets appear when the Design tab is selected in PowerPoint 2007.

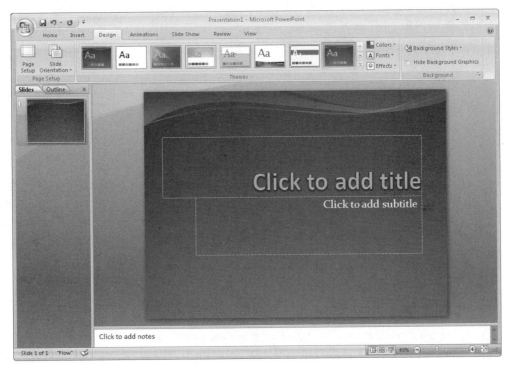

**Figure I-2.** The set of commands displayed in the Ribbon varies depending on the command tab you select.

## Contextual Tools

Contextual tools are different from command sets in that they appear only when you select a specific object in your document. For example, when you create a table in Word, the Table Tools contextual tools appear above the Ribbon. The tool set includes two tabs specific to the selected table: Design and Layout (see Figure I-3). The Design tab includes a variety of command sets that enable you to format a table the way you want it to appear. The Layout tab in the Table Tools contextual commands enables you to choose the way you want data to be positioned and organized in the cells.

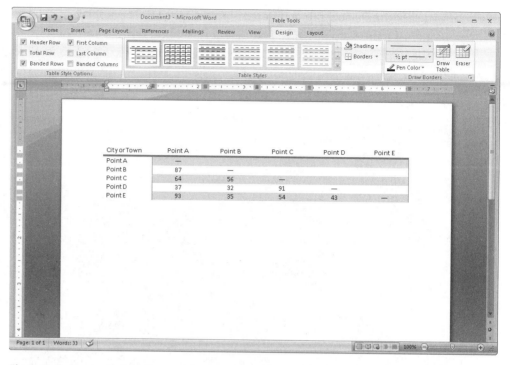

**Figure I-3.** Contextual tools provide you with additional options related to the selected object.

## Dialog Launchers

Some command sets on the Ribbon are also available in traditional style dialog boxes. The presence of a small arrow in the lower right corner of a command set indicates that you can click that "launcher" to display a dialog box containing those commands. For example, if you click the dialog launcher in the Font command set in Excel's Home tab, the Format Cells dialog box appears with the Font tab selected, as shown in Figure I-4.

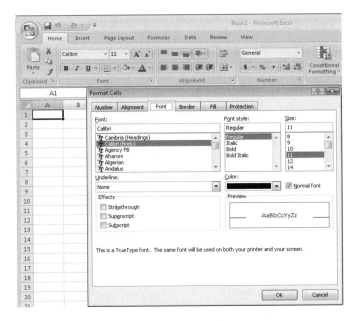

**Figure I-4.** Dialog launchers display some command sets in traditional dialog boxes.

You also will find a dialog launcher available at the bottom of any gallery that shows advanced options. For example, in Word, when you choose the Page Layout command tab and click the Columns arrow in the Page Setup command set, a gallery of column settings appears. Click the More Columns option at the bottom of the gallery to launch the Columns dialog box (see Figure I-5).

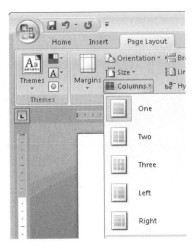

**Figure I-5.** Click the More Columns option at the bottom of a gallery to display a dialog box of additional options.

## Galleries

Galleries are one of the great additions to the design of the new user interface—they make finding the look you want as simple as point-and-click. Office 2007 includes two types of galleries. Galleries with only a few selections are typically shown as part of a command set in the Ribbon; but galleries with multiple selections (such as the Styles, Themes, and Margins in Word 2007) appear as drop-down galleries so that you can make your selection from the displayed group.

When you select a command that has an arrow next to it (which means additional choices are available), the gallery appears (see Figure I-6). You can see at a glance which color combination, format, color scheme, transition, or chart type you want. Just click your choice (or point to it, if you want to use the Live Preview feature) and the setting is applied to the current document or selected object.

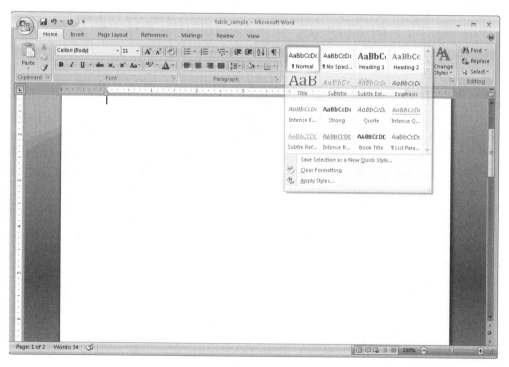

**Figure I-6.** Galleries enable you to easily find and select the choice that's right for your project.

> **Tip** The new Live Preview feature in Office 2007 enables you to see how a style will look before you select it. Simply point to a selection you're considering, and the application will show the effect of the item in the work area. When you find the one you like, click to apply it to your document.

# The New File Menu

The File menu has had a major makeover—instead of the word "File," the Microsoft Office button now marks the spot where the File menu resides. And the changes in the File menu aren't only cosmetic—functional changes help you focus on the file-related tasks you need. The new File menu includes two panels. On the left, you see the major file tasks; on the right, the choices related to those tasks appear when you point to one of the commands on the left. For example, when you position the mouse over Prepare, the options shown in Figure I-7 appear.

**Figure I-7.** The new File menu includes a new design, new organization, and additional commands to expand the way you work with files.

# Quick Access Toolbar

To the right of the Microsoft Office button at the top of the Ribbon you see three familiar tools: Save, Undo, and Redo. These tools are part of the Quick Access Toolbar, which travels with you from application to application. These tools are available in the same spot in all the Office 2007 core applications that have the new user interface. You can customize the Quick Access Toolbar to add other tools you use regularly. For example, you might want to add the Hyperlink tool to the Quick Access Toolbar so it is available in all your applications.

> **Tip** If you put a number of tools on the Quick Access Toolbar, you may want to display it in its own row along the Ribbon. Right-click anywhere on the Ribbon and choose Place Quick Access Toolbar below the Ribbon. To return the display of the toolbar to its original state, right-click the Ribbon a second time and choose Place Quick Access Toolbar above the Ribbon.

## New View Controls

Microsoft Office 2007 moves the View tab to organize the controls you need for viewing your documents. Everything you formerly found in the Window or View menus, you'll now find by clicking the View tab (see Figure I-8). The familiar View tools appear in the lower right corner of the document window, to the left of a handy Zoom tool that enables you to enlarge or reduce the display of your document incrementally while you work.

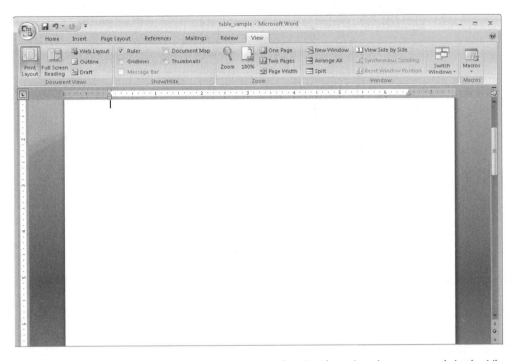

**Figure I-8.** Switch between windows and change the view by using the commands in the View tab.

> **Tip** Included in the back of this book is a four-color poster provided for your reference. This convenient guide points out some of the best new features of the redesigned Office user interface and includes tips to get you started. You will learn about these features and many more while working through this book.

# Key Points

- The Ribbon is available in Word, Excel, PowerPoint, Access, and in some Outlook windows.
- Command tabs replace menus in Office 2007, providing you with selections that follow the lifecycle of your document.
- Command sets are groups of commands that relate to the selected tab in the application window.
- Dialog launchers are available in some command sets and enable you to display a traditional dialog box with additional options related to that command set.

- Galleries display ready-made styles, templates, and content samples that you can add to your document with a click of the mouse.
- The File menu has been redesigned and reorganized. Click the Microsoft Office button to open the File menu.
- The View tab incorporates commands that were formerly found in the View and Window menus of Office 2003 applications.

# Information for Readers Running Windows XP

The graphics and the operating system–related instructions in this book reflect the Windows Vista user interface. However, Windows Vista is not required; you can also use a computer running Microsoft Windows XP.

Most of the differences you will encounter when working through the exercises in this book on a computer running Windows XP center around appearance rather than functionality. For example, the Windows Vista Start button is round rather than rectangular and is not labeled with the word *Start*; window frames and window-management buttons look different; and if your system supports Windows Aero, the window frames might be transparent.

In this section, we provide steps for navigating to or through menus and dialog boxes in Windows XP that differ from those provided in the exercises in this book. For the most part, these differences are small enough that you will have no difficulty in completing the exercises.

## Managing the Practice Files

The instructions given in the "Using the Book's CD" section are specific to Windows Vista. The only differences when installing, using, uninstalling, and removing the practice files supplied on the companion CD are the default installation location and the uninstall process.

On a computer running Windows Vista, the default installation location of the practice files is *Documents\MSP\SBS_Office2007*. On a computer running Windows XP, the default installation location is *My Documents\MSP\SBS_Office2007*. If your computer is running Windows XP, whenever an exercise tells you to navigate to your *Documents* folder, you should instead go to your *My Documents* folder.

To uninstall the practice files from a computer running Windows XP, follow this procedure using Outlook as an example:

1. On the Windows taskbar, click the **Start** button, and then click **Control Panel**.
2. In **Control Panel**, click (or in Classic view, double-click) **Add or Remove Programs**.

3.  In the **Add or Remove Programs** window, click **Microsoft Office Outlook 2007 Step by Step**, and then click **Remove**.

4.  In the **Add or Remove Programs** message box asking you to confirm the deletion, click **Yes**.

> **Important** If you need help installing or uninstalling the practice files, please see the "Getting Help" section later in this book. Microsoft Product Support Services does not provide support for this book or its companion CD.

## Using the Start Menu

Follow this procedure to start a program, such as Outlook 2007, on a computer running Windows XP:

→ Click the **Start** button, point to **All Programs**, click **Microsoft Office**, and then click **Microsoft Office Outlook 2007**.

Folders on the Windows Vista Start menu expand vertically. Folders on the Windows XP Start menu expand horizontally. You will notice this variation between the images shown in this book and your Start menu.

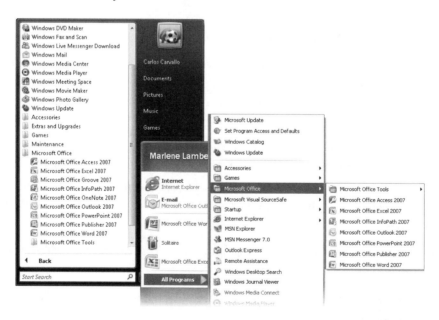

# Navigating Dialog Boxes

On a computer running Windows XP, some of the dialog boxes you will work with in the exercises not only look different from the graphics shown in this book but also work differently. These dialog boxes are primarily those that act as an interface between Office and the operating system, including any dialog box in which you navigate to a specific location. For example, here are the Insert File dialog boxes from Office 2007 running on Windows Vista and Windows XP and some examples of ways to navigate in them.

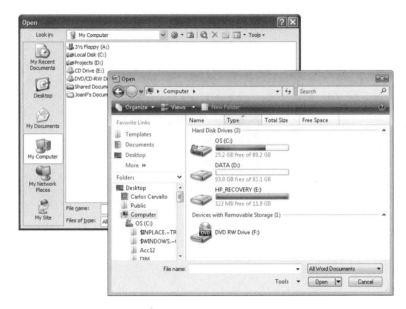

To navigate to the *Chapter01* folder in Windows Vista:

→ In the **Favorite Links** pane, click **Documents**. Then in the folder content pane, double-click **MSP**, **SBS_Office2007**, and double-click **Chapter01**.

To move back to the *SBS_Office2007* folder in Windows Vista:

→ In the upper-left corner of the dialog box, click the **Back** button.

Back

To navigate to the *Chapter01* folder in Windows XP:

→ On the **Places** bar, click **My Documents**. Then in the folder content pane, double-click **MSP**, double-click **SBS_Office2007**, and then double-click **Chapter01**.

To move back to the *SBS_Office2007* folder in Windows XP:

→ On the toolbar, click the **Up One Level** button.

Up One Level

# Getting Help

Every effort has been made to ensure the accuracy of this book and the contents of its companion CD. If you do run into problems, please contact the sources listed below for assistance.

## Getting Help with This Book and Its Companion CD

If your question or issue concerns the content of this book or its companion CD, please first search the online Microsoft Press Knowledge Base, which provides support information for known errors in or corrections to this book, at the following Web site:

*www.microsoft.com/mspress/support/search.asp*

If you do not find your answer at the online Knowledge Base, send your comments or questions to Microsoft Press Technical Support at:

*mspinput@microsoft.com*

## Getting Help with an Office Program

If your question is about a specific program, your first recourse is the Help system in the application. For example, if you're working in PowerPoint 2007, follow the steps and examples here to get help. This system is a combination of tools and files stored on your computer when you installed the 2007 Microsoft Office system and, if your computer is connected to the Internet, information available from Microsoft Office Online. There are several ways to find general or specific Help information:

- To find out about an item on the screen, you can display a *ScreenTip*. For example, to display a ScreenTip for a button, point to the button without clicking it. The ScreenTip gives the button's name, the associated keyboard shortcut if there is one, and unless you specify otherwise, a description of what the button does when you click it.

- In the PowerPoint program window, you can click the Microsoft Office PowerPoint Help button (a question mark in a blue circle) at the right end of the Ribbon to display the PowerPoint Help window.

● After opening a dialog box, you can click the Help button (also a question mark) at the right end of the dialog box title bar to display the PowerPoint Help window with topics related to the functions of that dialog box already identified.

To practice getting help, you can work through the following exercise.

**BE SURE TO** start PowerPoint before beginning this exercise.

Microsoft Office
PowerPoint Help

1. At the right end of the Ribbon, click the **Microsoft Office PowerPoint Help** button. The PowerPoint Help window opens.

2. In the list of topics in the **PowerPoint Help** window, click **Activating PowerPoint**.

PowerPoint Help displays a list of topics related to activating Microsoft Office system programs.

You can click any topic to display the corresponding information.

Show Table of
Contents

**3.** On the toolbar, click the **Show Table of Contents** button.

The Table Of Contents appears in the left pane, organized by category, like the table of contents in a book.

Clicking any category (represented by a book icon) displays that category's topics (represented by help icons) as well as any available online training (represented by training icons).

Category  Topic  Online training

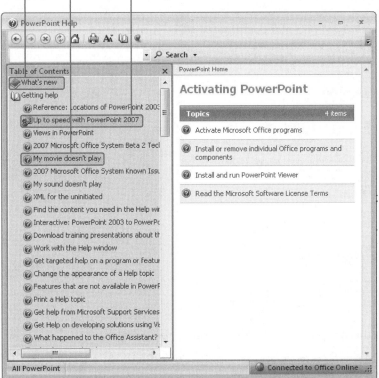

If you're connected to the Internet, PowerPoint displays topics and training available from the Office Online Web site as well as topics stored on your computer.

Back    Forward

**4.** In the **Table of Contents**, click a few categories and topics, then click the **Back** and **Forward** buttons to move among the topics you have already viewed.

Close

5. At the right end of the **Table of Contents** title bar, click the **Close** button.

6. At the top of the **PowerPoint Help** window, click the **Type word to search for** box, type Help window, and then press the `Enter` key.

The PowerPoint Help window displays topics related to the words you typed.

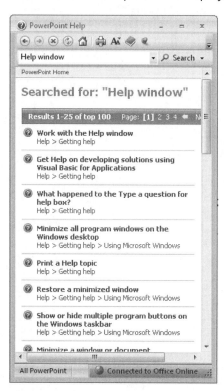

7. In the results list, click **Print a Help topic**.

The selected topic appears in the PowerPoint Help window, explaining that you can click the Print button on the toolbar to print any topic.

8. Below the title at the top of the topic, click **Show All**.

PowerPoint displays any hidden auxiliary information available in the topic and changes the Show All button to Hide All. You can display or hide an individual item by clicking it. When you click the Print button, PowerPoint will print all displayed information.

**CLOSE** the PowerPoint Help window.

# More Information

If your question is about another Microsoft software product and you cannot find the answer in the product's Help system, please search the appropriate product solution center or the Microsoft Knowledge Base at:

*support.microsoft.com*

In the United States, Microsoft software product support issues not covered by the Microsoft Knowledge Base are addressed by Microsoft Product Support Services. Location-specific software support options are available from:

*support.microsoft.com/gp/selfoverview/*

# Using the Book's CD

The companion CD included with this book contains practice files you can use as you work through the book's exercises. By using practice files, you won't waste time creating samples and typing large amounts of data. Instead, you can jump right in and concentrate on learning how to use the programs.

## What's on the CD?

The following table lists the practice files supplied on the book's CD.

| Chapter | Folder\File |
| --- | --- |
| Chapter 1: Exploring Word 2007 | 02_Opening.docx |
| | 03_Viewing1.docx |
| | 03_Viewing2.docx |
| | 05_Printing.docs |
| Chapter 2: Editing and Proofreading Documents | 01_Changes.docx |
| | 02_SavedText.docx |
| | 03_FindingWord.docx |
| | 04_Outline.docx |
| | 05_FindingText.docx |
| | 06_Spelling.docx |
| | 07_Finalizing.docx |
| Chapter 3: Changing the Look of Text | 01_QuickFormatting.docx |
| | 02_Characters.docx |
| | 03_Paragraphs.docx |
| | 04_Lists.docx |
| Chapter 4: Presenting Information in Columns and Tables | 01_Columns.docx |
| | 02_TabularList.docx |
| | 03_Table.docx |
| | 05_Calculations.docx |
| | 05_LoanData.xlsx |
| | 06_Loan.xlsx |
| | 06_Memo.docx |
| | 06_TableAsLayout.docx |

| Chapter | Folder\File |
|---|---|
| Chapter 5: Setting Up a Workbook | Creating\Exception Summary.xlsx |
| | Creating\Route Volume.xlsx |
| Chapter 6: Working with Data and Data Tables | Data and Data Tables\Series.xlsx |
| | Data and Data Tables\2007Q1ShipmentsByCategory.xlsx |
| | Data and Data Tables\Average Deliveries.xlsx |
| | Data and Data Tables\Service Levels.xlsx |
| | Data and Data Tables\Driver Sort Times.xlsx |
| Chapter 7: Performing Calculations on Data | Formulas\VehicleMiles.xlsx |
| | Formulas\ITExpenses.xlsx |
| | Formulas\PackagingCosts.xlsx |
| | Formulas\ConveyerBid.xlsx |
| Chapter 8: Changing Document Appearance | Appearance\VehicleMileSummary.xlsx |
| | Appearance\HourlyExceptions.xlsx |
| | Appearance\HourlyTracking.xlsx |
| | Appearance\ExecutiveSearch.xlsx |
| | Appearance\Dashboard.xlsx |
| | Appearance\CallCenter.xlsx |
| Chapter 9: Creating a Database | 03_TableTemplate.accdb |
| | 04_Manipulating.accdb |
| Chapter 10: Simplifying Data Entry by Using Forms | 01_CreateFormTool.accdb |
| | 02_RefineProperties.accdb |
| | 03_RefineLayout.accdb |
| | 04_AddControls.accdb |
| | 04_CustomersFormLogo.jpg |
| | 05_VBA.accdb |
| | 05_AftUpdate.txt |
| | 06_CreateWizard.accdb |
| | 07_AddSubform.accdb |
| Chapter 11: Locating Specific Information | 01_SortTable.accdb |
| | 02_FilterTable.accdb |
| | 03_FilterForm.accdb |
| | 04_MultipleCriteria.accdb |
| | 05_QueryDesign.accdb |
| | 06_QueryWizard.accdb |
| | 07_Calculate.accdb |

| Chapter | Folder\File |
|---|---|
| Chapter 12: Keeping Your Information Accurate | 01_FieldTest.accdb<br>02_Size.accdb<br>03_Accurate.accdb<br>04_Validate.accdb<br>05_SimpleLookup.accdb<br>06_MulticolumnLookup.accdb<br>07_Update.accdb<br>08_Delete.accdb<br>09_Prevent.accdb |
| Chapter 13: Starting a New Presentation | 01_Creating.pptx<br>03_Converting.docx<br>04_Reusing1.pptx<br>04_Reusing2.pptx |
| Chapter 14: Working with Slide Text | 02_Editing.pptx<br>03_TextBoxes.pptx<br>04_Correcting.pptx<br>05_Spelling.pptx<br>06_Finding.pptx<br>07_Changing.pptx |
| Chapter 15: Adjusting the Layout, Order, and Look of Slides | 01_Layout.pptx<br>02_Rearranging.pptx<br>03_Theme1.pptx<br>03_Theme2.pptx<br>04_ColorScheme.pptx<br>05_OtherColors.pptx<br>06_Background.pptx |
| Chapter 16: Delivering a Presentation Electronically | 01_Adapting.pptx<br>02_Rehearsing.pptx<br>03_NotesHandouts.pptx<br>03_YinYang.png<br>04_Travel.pptx<br>05_Showing.pptx |
| Chapter 18: Sending E-Mail Messages | 03_Attaching.docx<br>03_Attaching.pptx |

In addition to the practice files, the CD contains some exciting resources that will really enhance your ability to get the most out of using this book and Office System 2007, including the following:

- *Microsoft Office System 2007 Step by Step* in eBook format
- *Microsoft Computer Dictionary*, 5th ed. eBook
- *First Look 2007 Microsoft Office System* (Katherine Murray, 2006)
- Sample chapter and poster from *Look Both Ways: Help Protect Your Family on the Internet* (Linda Criddle, 2007)

> **Important** The companion CD for this book does not contain the Office System 2007 software. You should purchase and install that program before using this book.

# Minimum System Requirements

The 2007 Microsoft Office system includes the following programs:

- Microsoft Office Access 2007
- Microsoft Office Communicator 2007
- Microsoft Office Excel 2007
- Microsoft Office Groove 2007
- Microsoft Office InfoPath 2007
- Microsoft Office OneNote 2007
- Microsoft Office Outlook 2007
- Microsoft Office Outlook 2007 with Business Contact Manager
- Microsoft Office PowerPoint 2007
- Microsoft Office Publisher 2007
- Microsoft Office Word 2007

No single edition of the 2007 Office system installs all of the above programs. Specialty programs available separately include Microsoft Office Project 2007, Microsoft Office SharePoint Designer 2007, and Microsoft Office Visio 2007.

To install and run these programs, your computer needs to meet the following minimum requirements:

- 500 megahertz (MHz) processor
- 256 megabytes (MB) RAM
- CD or DVD drive
- 2 gigabytes (GB) available hard disk space; a portion of this disk space will be freed if you select the option to delete the installation files

> **Tip** Hard disk requirements will vary depending on configuration; custom installation choices might require more or less hard disk space.

- Monitor with 800×600 screen resolution; 1024×768 or higher recommended
- Keyboard and mouse or compatible pointing device
- Internet connection, 128 kilobits per second (Kbps) or greater, for download and activation of products, accessing Microsoft Office Online and online Help topics, and any other Internet-dependent processes
- Windows Vista or later, Microsoft Windows XP with Service Pack 2 (SP2), or Microsoft Windows Server 2003 or later
- Windows Internet Explorer 7 or Microsoft Internet Explorer 6 with service packs The 2007 Microsoft Office suites, including Office Basic 2007, Office Home & Student 2007, Office Standard 2007, Office Small Business 2007, Office Professional 2007, Office Ultimate 2007, Office Professional Plus 2007, and Office Enterprise 2007, all have similar requirements.

## Step-by-Step Exercises

In addition to the hardware, software, and connections required to run the 2007 Microsoft Office system, you will need the following to successfully complete the exercises in this book:

- PowerPoint 2007, Word 2007, Excel 2007, and Outlook 2007
- Access to a printer
- 10 MB of available hard disk space for the practice files

# Installing the Practice Files

You need to install the practice files in the correct location on your hard disk before you can use them in the exercises. Follow these steps:

1. Remove the companion CD from the envelope at the back of the book, and insert it into the CD drive of your computer.

   The Step By Step Companion CD License Terms appear. Follow the on-screen directions. To use the practice files, you must accept the terms of the license agreement. After you accept the license agreement, a menu screen appears.

   > **Important** If the menu screen does not appear, click the Start button and then click Computer. Display the Folders list in the Navigation pane, click the icon for your CD drive, and then in the right pane, double-click the StartCD executable file.

2. Click **Install Practice Files**.

3. Click **Next** on the first screen, and then click **Next** to accept the terms of the license agreement on the next screen.

4. If you want to install the practice files to a location other than the default folder (*Documents\MSP\SBS_Office2007*), click the **Change** button, select the new drive and path, and then click **OK**.

   > **Important** If you install the practice files to a location other than the default, you will need to substitute that path within the exercises.

5. Click **Next** on the **Choose Destination Location** screen, and then click **Install** on the **Ready to Install the Program** screen to install the selected practice files.

6. After the practice files have been installed, click **Finish**.

7. Close the **Step by Step Companion CD** window, remove the companion CD from the CD drive, and return it to the envelope at the back of the book.

# Using the Practice Files

When you install the practice files from the companion CD that accompanies this book, the files are stored on your hard disk in chapter-specific subfolders under *Documents\ MSP\SBS_Office2007*. Each exercise is preceded by a paragraph that lists the files needed for that exercise and explains any preparations needed before you start working through the exercise. Here are examples:

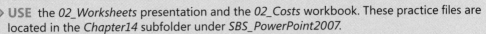

**USE** the *02_Worksheets* presentation and the *02_Costs* workbook. These practice files are located in the *Chapter14* subfolder under *SBS_PowerPoint2007*.

**BE SURE TO** start PowerPoint before beginning this exercise.

**OPEN** the *02_Editing* and *03_TextBoxes* presentation files.

You can browse to the practice files in Windows Explorer by following these steps:

1. On the Windows taskbar, click the **Start** button, and then click **Documents**.

2. In your **Documents** folder, double-click MSP, double-click SBS_Office2007, and then double-click a specific chapter folder.

You can browse to the practice files from a PowerPoint 2007 dialog box by following these steps:

1. On the **Favorite Links** pane in the dialog box, click **Documents**.

2. In your **Documents** folder, double-click **MSP**, double-click **SBS_Office2007**, and then double-click the specified chapter folder.

# Removing and Uninstalling the Practice Files

You can free up hard disk space by uninstalling the practice files that were installed from the companion CD. The uninstall process deletes any files that you created in the *Documents\MSP\SBS_Office2007* chapter-specific folders while working through the exercises. Follow these steps:

1. On the Windows taskbar, click the **Start** button, and then click **Control Panel**.

2. In **Control Panel**, under **Programs**, click the **Uninstall a program** task.

3. If the **Programs and Features** message box asking you to confirm the deletion appears, click Yes.

   **See Also** If you need additional help installing or uninstalling the practice files, see the "Getting Help" section later in this book.

**Important** Microsoft Product Support Services does not provide support for this book or its companion CD.

# Features and Conventions of This Book

This book has been designed to lead you step by step through the most common tasks you are most likely to want to perform in Microsoft Office. If you start at the beginning and work your way through all the exercises, you will gain enough proficiency to be able to create and work on the most common tasks in MIcrosoft Office Word, Excel, PowerPoint, Access, and Outlook. However, each topic is also self contained. If you completed all the exercises and later need help remembering how to perform a procedure, the following features of this book will help you locate specific information:

- **Detailed table of contents.** A listing of the topics and sidebars within each chapter.
- **Chapter thumb tabs.** Easily locate the beginning of the chapter you want.
- **Topic-specific running heads.** Within a chapter, quickly locate the topic you want by looking at the running head of odd-numbered pages.
- **Quick Reference.** General instructions for each procedure covered in specific detail elsewhere in the book. Refresh your memory about a task while working with your own documents.
- **Detailed index.** Look up specific tasks and features and general concepts in the index, which has been carefully crafted with the reader in mind.
- **Companion CD.** Contains the practice files needed for the step-by-step exercises, as well as a fully searchable electronic version of this book and other useful resources.
- **Reference card.** A tear-out guide to the new Microsoft Office system user interface features.

In addition, we provide a glossary of terms for those times when you need to look up the meaning of a word or the definition of a concept.

You can save time when you use this book by understanding how the *Step by Step* series shows special instructions, keys to press, buttons to click, and so on.

| Convention | Meaning |
|---|---|
| (CD icon) | This icon at the end of a chapter introduction indicates information about the practice files provided on the companion CD for use in the chapter. |
| **USE** | This paragraph preceding a step-by-step exercise indicates the practice files that you will use when working through the exercise. |
| **BE SURE TO** | This paragraph preceding or following an exercise indicates any requirements you should attend to before beginning the exercise or actions you should take to restore your system after completing the exercise. |
| **OPEN** | This paragraph preceding a step-by-step exercise indicates files that you should open before beginning the exercise. |
| **CLOSE** | This paragraph following a step-by-step exercise provides instructions for closing open files or programs before moving on to another topic. |
| 1<br>2 | Blue numbered steps guide you through step-by-step exercises and Quick Reference versions of procedures. |
| 1<br>2 | Black numbered steps guide you through procedures in sidebars and expository text. |
| → | An arrow indicates a procedure that has only one step. |
| **See Also** | These paragraphs direct you to more information about a given topic in this book or elsewhere. |
| **Troubleshooting** | These paragraphs explain how to fix a common problem that might prevent you from continuing with an exercise. |
| **Tip** | These paragraphs provide a helpful hint or shortcut that makes working through a task easier, or information about other available options. |
| **Important** | These paragraphs point out information that you need to know to complete a procedure. |
| (Save button)<br>Save | The first time you are told to click a button in an exercise, a picture of the button appears in the left margin. If the name of the button does not appear on the button itself, the name appears under the picture. |
| Enter | In step-by-step exercises, keys you must press appear as they would on a keyboard. |
| Ctrl + Home | A plus sign (+) between two key names means that you must hold down the first key while you press the second key. For example, "press Ctrl + Home" means "hold down the Ctrl key while you press the Home key." |
| **Program interface elements** | In steps, the names of program elements, such as buttons, commands, and dialog boxes, are shown in black bold characters. |
| User input | Anything you are supposed to type appears in blue bold characters. |
| *Glossary terms* | Terms that are explained in the glossary at the end of the book are shown in blue italic characters. |

# About the Authors

## Joyce Cox

Joyce has 25 years' experience in the development of training materials about technical subjects for non-technical audiences, and is the author of dozens of books about Office and Windows technologies. She is the Vice President of Online Training Solutions, Inc. (OTSI). She was President of and principal author for Online Press, where she developed the *Quick Course* series of computer training books for beginning and intermediate adult learners. She was also the first managing editor of Microsoft Press, an editor for Sybex, and an editor for the University of California. Joyce and her husband Ted live in downtown Bellevue, Washington, and escape as often as they can to their tiny, offline cabin in the Cascade foothills.

## Curtis Frye

Curt Frye is a freelance writer and Microsoft Most Valuable Professional for Microsoft Office Excel. He lives in Portland, Oregon, and is the author of eight books from Microsoft Press, including *Microsoft Office Excel 2007 Step by Step*, *Microsoft Office Access 2007 Plain & Simple*, *Microsoft Office Excel 2007 Plain & Simple*, and *Microsoft Office Small Business Accounting 2006 Step By Step*. He has also written numerous articles for the Microsoft Work Essentials web site. Before beginning his writing career in June 1995, Curt spent four years with The MITRE Corporation as a defense trade analyst and one year as Director of Sales and Marketing for Digital Gateway Systems, an Internet service provider. Curt graduated from Syracuse University in 1990 with an honors degree in political science. When he's not writing, Curt is a professional improvisational comedian with ComedySportz Portland.

## Steve Lambert

Steve has written 18 books, most of which are about Microsoft applications. As President of Online Publishing and Programming Solutions, Inc. (OP²S), he has managed the development of many tools for creating and viewing training material. Steve takes advantage of the Internet and computer technology to work from home—a ten-acre horse ranch on the Olympic Peninsula. When not working on technology products, he and his wife Gale spend their time working on the property, training and riding horses, and picking up horse poop.

## M. Dow Lambert III

During 20 years in academia, Dow authored or co-authored 19 social science research publications, developed curriculum and training programs for social services professionals, and managed longitudinal studies of human behavior. In 1995, he moved from academia to the private sector, where he worked for a small company that developed and maintained reservation systems for the travel industry. Here he learned the difference between writing research reports for scientific journals, writing technical specifications for programmers, and writing user guides for the people who actually needed to understand and use the software that his company produced. In his spare time, Dow and his wife Marlene enjoy birding and bird photography.

## Katherine Murray

Katherine Murray is the author of many books on technology, with a special emphasis on Microsoft Office. Her most recent book, *First Look 2007 Microsoft Office System* (Microsoft Press, 2006) is available as a free downloadable PDF on the 2007 Microsoft Office download site. Katherine is also the coauthor of *Microsoft Word 2007 Inside Out* and *MSN Spaces: Share Your Story*. Katherine is a regular contributor to a number of Microsoft sites and publishes a blog called BlogOffice, offering tips, updates, news, and resources related to a variety of Microsoft Office versions and events.

Katherine has been fascinated by computers since the early 80s when her husband brought home one of the first IBM PCs to arrive in the city of Indianapolis. She lives in the Midwest with her three children (one of whom is married and lives a mile away with her husband and newborn daughter, Ruby—Katherine's first grandbaby!) and enjoys many non-technical activities including gardening, cooking, reading, jazz, and playing Trivial Pursuit with the kids.

## Joan Lambert Preppernau

Joan is the author of more than a dozen books about Windows and Office, including the popular *Microsoft Windows XP Step by Step*, and a contributor to the development of the Microsoft certification exams for the 2007 Office system and Windows Vista. Having learned about computers literally at her father's knee, Joan's wide-ranging experiences in various facets of the computer industry contribute to her enthusiasm for producing interesting, useful, and reader-friendly training materials. Joan is the President of Online Training Solutions, Inc. (OTSI) and an avid telecommuter. The power of the Internet and an obsession with technology have made it possible for Joan to live and work in New Zealand, Sweden, Denmark, and various locations in the U.S. during the past 15 years. Having finally discovered the delights of a daily dose of sunshine, Joan has recently settled in San Diego, California, with her husband Barry and their daughter Trinity.

## Online Training Solutions, Inc. (OTSI)

OTSI specializes in the design, creation, and production of Office and Windows training products for information workers and home computer users. For more information about OTSI, visit www.otsi.com

# Quick Reference

## 1  Exploring Word 2007

**To start Word**

→ At the left end of the Windows taskbar, click the **Start** button, point to **All Programs**, click **Microsoft Office**, and then click **Microsoft Office Word 2007**.

**To open an existing file**

1. Click the **Microsoft Office Button**, and then click **Open**.

2. In the **Open** dialog box, navigate to the folder that contains the file you want to open, and then double-click the file.

**To move the insertion point to the beginning or end of the document**

→ Press `Ctrl`+`Home` or `Ctrl`+`End`.

**To convert a document created in an earlier version of Word**

→ Click the **Microsoft Office Button**, and then click **Convert**.

**To view multiple pages**

1. On the **View** toolbar, click the **Zoom** button.

2. In the **Zoom** dialog box, click the **Many pages** arrow, select the number of pages, and then click **OK**.

**To adjust the magnification of a document**

1. On the **View** toolbar, click the **Zoom** button.

2. In the **Zoom** dialog box, click a **Zoom to** percentage or type an amount in the **Percent** box, and then click **OK**.

**To display the Document Map**

→ On the **View** tab, in the **Show/Hide** group, select the **Document Map** check box.

**To display thumbnails of pages**

→ On the **View** tab, in the **Show/Hide** group, select the **Thumbnails** check box.

**To display or hide non-printing characters**

→ On the **Home** tab, in the **Paragraph** group, click the **Show/Hide** ¶ button.

**To display a document in a different view**

→ On the **View** tab, in the **Document Views** group, click the button for the desired view; or

→ Click a view button on the **View** toolbar at the right end of the status bar.

**To switch among open documents**

→ On the **View** tab, in the **Window** group, click the **Switch Windows** button, and then click the name of the document you want to switch to.

**To view multiple open documents**

→ On the **View** tab, in the **Window** group, click the **Arrange All** button.

**To open a new document**

→ Click the **Microsoft Office Button**, click **New**, and then in the **New Document** window, double-click **Blank document**.

**To save a document for the first time**

1. On the **Quick Access Toolbar**, click the **Save** button; or click the **Microsoft Office Button**, and then click **Save As**.

2. If **Browse Folders** is shown in the lower-left corner of the **Save As** dialog box, click it, and then navigate to the location where you want to save the file.

3. In the **File name** box, type a name for the document, and then click **Save**.

**To create a new folder while saving a document**

1. Click the **Microsoft Office Button**, and then click **Save As**.

2. In the **Save As** dialog box, navigate to the folder where you want to create the new folder.

3. On the dialog box's toolbar, click the **New Folder** button.

4. Type the name of the new folder, press [ Enter ], and then click **Open**.

5. In the **File name** box, type a name for the document, and then click **Save**.

**To preview how a document will look when printed**

→ Click the **Microsoft Office Button**, point to **Print**, and then click **Print Preview**.

**To print a document with the default settings**

→ Click the **Microsoft Office Button**, point to **Print**, and then click **Quick Print**.

**To print a document with custom settings**

1. Click the **Microsoft Office Button**, and then click **Print**.

2. In the **Print** dialog box, modify the settings as needed, and then click **OK**.

## 2   Editing and Proofreading Documents

**To select text**

→ Word: Double-click the word.

→ Sentence: Click in the sentence while holding down the Ctrl key.

→ Paragraph: Triple-click in the paragraph, or double-click in the selection area to the left of the paragraph.

→ Block: Click to the left of the first word, hold down the Shift key, and then click immediately to the right of the last word or punctuation mark.

→ Line: Click in the selection area to the left of the line.

→ Document: Triple-click in the selection area.

**To delete text**

→ Select the text, and then press Del or Backspace.

**To copy or cut and paste text**

1. Select the text, and then on the **Home** tab, in the **Clipboard** group, click the **Copy** or **Cut** button.

2. Click where you want to paste the text, and then in the **Clipboard** group, click the **Paste** button.

**To undo an action**

→ On the **Quick Access Toolbar**, click the **Undo** button.

**To move text by dragging**

1. Select the text, and then point to the selection.

2. Hold down the mouse button, drag the text to its new location, and then release the mouse button.

**To save text as a building block**

1. Select the text. Then on the **Insert** tab, in the **Text** group, click the **Quick Parts** button, and then click **Save Selection to Quick Part Gallery**.

2. In the **Create New Building Block** dialog box, type a name for the building block, make any necessary changes to the settings, and then click **OK**.

**To insert a building block in a document**

→ Click where you want to insert the building block. Then either type the name of the building block, and press F3; or on the **Insert** tab, in the **Text** group, click the **Quick Parts** button, and select the building block from the **Quick Part** gallery.

**To insert the date and time**

1. Click where you want the date or time to appear, and then on the **Insert** tab, in the **Text** group, click the **Date & Time** button.

2. In the **Date and Time** dialog box, under **Available formats**, click the format you want, and then click **OK**.

**To use the Thesaurus**

1. Double-click the word you want to replace, and then on the **Review** tab, in the **Proofing** group, click the **Thesaurus** button.

2. In the **Research** task pane, point to the word you want to insert in place of the selected word, click the arrow that appears, and then click **Insert**.

**To research information**

1. On the **Review** tab, in the **Proofing** group, click **Research**.

2. In the **Research** task pane, in the **Search for** box, type the research topic.

3. Click the arrow of the box below the **Search for** box, click the resource you want to use, and then in the results list, click a source to view its information.

**To translate a word or phrase into another language**

1. Select the word or phrase, and then on the **Review** tab, in the **Proofing** group, click the **Translate** button.

2. In the **Translation** area of the **Research** task pane, select the desired languages in the **From** and **To** boxes to display the translation.

**To display a document in Outline view**

➔ On the **View** toolbar, click the **Outline** button.

**To display specific heading levels in Outline view**

➔ On the **Outlining** tab, in the **Outline Tools** group, click the **Show Level** arrow, and in the list, click a heading level.

**To collapse or expand heading levels in Outline view**

➔ Click anywhere in the heading to be collapsed or expanded. Then on the **Outlining** tab, in the **Outline Tools** group, click the **Collapse** or **Expand** button.

**To demote or promote headings in Outline view**

➔ Click the heading to be demoted or promoted. Then on the **Outlining** tab, in the **Outline Tools** group, click the **Demote** or **Promote** button.

**To move content in Outline view**

→ Collapse the heading whose text you want to move. Then on the **Outlining** tab, in the **Outline Tools** group, click the **Move Up** or **Move Down** button.

**To find text**

1. On the **Home** tab, in the **Editing** group, click the **Find** button.
2. On the **Find** tab of the **Find and Replace** dialog box, specify the text you want to find, and then click **Find Next**.

**To replace text**

1. On the **Home** tab, in the **Editing** group, click the **Replace** button.
2. On the **Replace** tab of the **Find and Replace** dialog box, specify the text you want to find and the text you want to replace it with, and then click **Find Next**.
3. Click **Replace** to replace the first instance of the text, **Replace All** to replace all instances, or **Find Next** to leave that instance unchanged and move to the next one.

**To check spelling and grammar**

1. On the **Review** tab, in the **Proofing** group, click the **Spelling & Grammar** button.
2. In the **Spelling and Grammar dialog** box, click the appropriate buttons to correct the errors Word finds or to add words to the custom dictionary or AutoCorrect list.
3. Click **OK** when Word reaches the end of the Spelling and Grammar check, and then click **Close**.

**To remove personal information from a document**

1. Click the **Microsoft Office Button**, point to **Prepare**, and then click **Inspect Document**.
2. In the **Document Inspector** dialog box, select the items you want checked, and then click **Inspect**.
3. In the **Document Inspector** summary, click the **Remove All** button to the right of any items you want removed, and then close the **Document Inspector** dialog box.

**To mark a document as final**

1. Click the **Microsoft Office Button**, point to **Prepare**, and then click **Mark as Final**.
2. Click **OK** in the message box, click **Save**, then click **OK** in the finalization message.

## 3   Changing the Look of Text

**To preview and apply styles**

→ Click the paragraph or select the text to which you want to apply a style. Then on the **Home** tab, in the **Styles** group, click the thumbnail of the style you want to apply in the **Styles** gallery.

**To change the style set**

→ On the **Home** tab, in the **Styles** group, click the **Change Styles** button, click **Style Set**, and then click the set you want to use.

**To apply character formatting**

→ Select the text. Then on the **Home** tab, in the **Font** group (or on the **Mini toolbar** that appears), click the button of the formatting you want to apply.

**To copy formatting**

→ Select the text that has the formatting you want to copy. Then on the **Home** tab, in the **Clipboard** group (or on the **Mini toolbar** that appears), click the **Format Painter** button, and select the text to which you want to apply the copied formatting.

**To change the font**

→ Select the text. Then on the **Home** tab, in the **Font** group, click the **Font** arrow, and click the font you want.

**To change the font size**

→ Select the text. Then on the **Home** tab, in the **Font** group, click the **Font Size** arrow, and click the font size you want.

**To apply text effects**

1. Select the text, and then on the **Home** tab, click the **Font** Dialog Box Launcher.
2. In the **Font** dialog box, under **Effects**, select the check box for the effect you want, and then click **OK**.

**To clear formatting from text**

→ On the **Home** tab, in the **Font** group, click the **Clear Formatting** button.

**To change the color of text**

→ Select the text. Then on the **Home** tab, in the **Font** group, click the **Font Color** arrow, and in the color palette, click the color you want.

**To highlight text with a color**

➡ Select the text. Then on the **Home** tab, in the **Font** group, click the **Highlight** arrow, and click the color you want.

**To select all text with the same formatting**

➡ Click the formatted text. Then on the **Home** tab, in the **Editing** group, click the **Select** button, and click **Select Text With Similar Formatting**.

**To insert a line break**

➡ Click at the right end of the text where you want the line break to appear. Then on the **Page Layout** tab, in the **Page Setup** group, click the **Breaks** button, and click **Text Wrapping**.

**To align paragraphs**

➡ Click the paragraph, or select multiple paragraphs. Then on the **Home** tab, in the **Paragraph** group, click the **Align Left**, **Center**, **Align Right**, or **Justify** button.

**To indent the first line of a paragraph**

➡ Click the paragraph. Then on the horizontal ruler, drag the **First Line Indent** marker to the location of the indent.

**To indent an entire paragraph**

➡ Click the paragraph, or select multiple paragraphs. Then on the horizontal ruler, drag the **Left Indent** or **Right Indent** marker to the location of the indent.

**To increase or decrease indenting**

➡ Click the paragraph, or select multiple paragraphs. Then in the **Paragraph** group, click the **Increase Indent** or **Decrease Indent** button.

**To set a tab stop**

➡ Click the paragraph, or select multiple paragraphs. Then click the **Tab** button until it displays the type of tab you want, and click the horizontal ruler where you want to set the tab stop for the selected paragraph(s).

**To change the position of a tab stop**

➡ Click the paragraph, or select multiple paragraphs. Then on the horizontal ruler, drag the tab stop to the new mark.

**To add a border or shading to a paragraph**

1. Click the paragraph. Then on the **Home** tab, in the **Paragraph** group, click the **Borders and Shading** arrow, and click **Borders and Shading**.

2. In the **Borders and Shading** dialog box, on the **Borders** tab, click the icon of the border style you want to apply, and then click **OK**.

3. In the **Borders and Shading** dialog box, on the **Shading** tab, click the **Fill** arrow, click the shading color you want, and then click **OK**.

### To format paragraphs as a list

→ Select the paragraphs. Then on the **Home** tab, in the **Paragraph** group, click the **Bullets** or **Numbering** button.

### To change the style of a list

1. Select the list paragraphs. Then on the **Home** tab, in the **Paragraph** group, click the **Bullets** or **Numbering** arrow.

2. In the **Bullets Library** or **Numbering Library**, click the bullet or number style you want to use.

### To change the indent level of a list

→ Select the list paragraphs. Then on the **Home** tab, in the **Paragraph** group, click the **Decrease Indent** or **Increase Indent** button.

### To sort items in a list

1. Select the list paragraphs. Then on the **Home** tab, in the **Paragraph** group, click the **Sort** button.

2. In the **Sort Text** dialog box, click the **Type** arrow, and then in the list, click the type of text by which to sort.

3. Select **Ascending** or **Descending**, and then click **OK**.

### To create a multilevel list

1. Click where you want to create the list. Then on the **Home** tab, in the **Paragraph** group, click the **Multilevel List** button.

2. In the **Multilevel List** gallery, click the thumbnail of the multilevel list style you want to use.

3. Type the text of the list, pressing Enter to create another item at the same level, pressing Enter and then Tab to create a subordinate item, or pressing Enter and then Shift + Tab to create a higher-level item.

## 4   Presenting Information in Columns and Tables

### To format text in multiple columns

→ Select the text. Then on the **Page Layout** tab, in the **Page Setup** group, click the **Columns** button, and click the number of columns you want.

**To change the width of columns**

1. Click anywhere in the first column. Then on the **Page Layout** tab, in the **Page Setup** group, click the **Columns** button, and then click **More Columns**.

2. Under **Width and spacing**, change the setting in the **Width** column or the **Spacing** column, and then click **OK**.

**To hyphenate text automatically**

→ On the **Page Layout** tab, in the **Page Setup** group, click the **Hyphenation** button, and then click **Automatic**.

**To insert a column break**

→ Click where you want the column break to appear. Then on the **Page Layout** tab, in the **Page Setup** group, click the **Breaks** button, and then click **Column**.

**To create a tabular list**

1. Type the text of the list, pressing [Tab] between each item on a line and pressing [Enter] at the end of each line.

2. Select the lines of the list, change the **Tab** button to the type of tab stop you want, and then click the horizontal ruler where you want to set tab stops that will line up the items in columns.

**To insert a table**

1. Click where you want to insert the table. Then on the **Insert** tab, in the **Tables** group, click the **Table** button.

2. In the grid, point to the upper-left cell, move the pointer across and down to select the number of columns and rows you want, and click the lower-right cell in the selection.

**To merge table cells**

→ Select the cells you want to merge. Then on the **Layout** contextual tab, in the **Merge** group, click the **Merge Cells** button.

**To add rows to a table**

→ Click in the row above or below which you want to add a single row, and then on the **Layout** tab, in the **Rows & Columns** group, click the **Insert Above** or **Insert Below** button; or select the number of rows you want to insert, and then in the **Rows & Columns** group, click the **Insert Above** or **Insert Below** button.

**To convert text to a table**

1. Select the text you want to convert. Then on the **Insert** tab, in the **Tables** group, click the **Table** button, and click **Convert Text to Table**.

2. In the **Convert Text to Table** dialog box, enter the dimensions of the table in the **Number of columns** and **Number of Rows** boxes, select the type of text separator, and then click **OK**.

### To insert a Quick Table

1. Click where you want to insert the table. Then on the **Insert** tab, in the **Tables** group, click the **Table** button, and then point to **Quick Tables**.

2. In the **Quick Tables** gallery, click the table style you want.

### To apply a table style

→ Click the table whose style you want to change. Then on the **Design** contextual tab, in the **Table Styles** group, click the style you want in the **Table Styles** gallery.

### To total a column of values in a table

1. Click the cell in the table where you want the total to appear.

2. On the **Layout** contextual tab, in the **Data** group, click the **Formula** button.

3. With the SUM formula in the **Formula** box, click **OK** to total the values.

### To insert an Excel worksheet

→ Click where you want to insert the worksheet, and then on the **Insert** tab, in the **Tables** group, click the **Table** button, and click **Excel Spreadsheet.**

or

→ Copy the worksheet data in Excel, and then in Word, click where you want to insert the copied data, and on the **Home** tab, in the **Clipboard** group, click the **Paste** button.

or

1. In Excel, copy the worksheet data. Then in Word, click where you want to insert the copied data, and on the **Home** tab, in the **Clipboard** group, click the **Paste** arrow, and click **Paste Special**.

2. In the **Paste Special** dialog box, in the **As** list, click **Microsoft Office Excel Worksheet Object**, select the **Paste link** option, and then click **OK**.

### To draw a table

1. Click where you want to draw the table. Then on the **Insert** tab, in the **Tables** group, click the **Table** button, and then click **Draw Table**.

2. Drag the pointer (which has become a pencil) across and down to create a cell.

3. Point to the upper-right corner of the cell, and drag to create another cell, or draw column and row boundaries inside the first cell.

# 5    Setting Up a Workbook

### To open a workbook

1. Click the **Microsoft Office Button** and then click **Open**.
2. Navigate to the folder that contains the workbook you want to open.
3. Click the workbook.
4. Click **Open**.

### To create a new workbook

1. Click the **Microsoft Office Button**.
2. Click **New**.
3. Click **Blank Workbook**.

### To save a workbook

1. On the **Quick Access Toolbar**, click the **Save** button.
2. Type a name for the file.
3. Click **Save**.

### To set file properties

1. Open the file for which you want to assign property values.
2. Click the **Microsoft Office Button**.
3. Point to **Finish** and then click **Properties**.
4. Add information describing your file.

### To define custom properties

1. Open the file for which you want to assign property values.
2. Click the **Microsoft Office Button**.
3. Point to **Finish** and then click **Properties**.
4. Click the **Property Views and Options** down arrow.
5. Click **Advanced**.
6. Click the **Custom** tab.
7. Type a property name.
8. Select the type of data contained in the property.
9. Type a value for the property.

10. Click **Add**.

11. Click **OK**.

### To display a worksheet

→ Click the sheet tab of the worksheet you want to display.

### To create a new worksheet

1. Right-click the sheet tab of the worksheet that follows the location where you want to insert a worksheet.

2. Choose **Insert** from the shortcut menu.

3. Double-click **Worksheet**.

### To rename a worksheet

1. Double-click the sheet tab of the worksheet you want to rename.

2. Type the new name of the worksheet and press Enter.

### To copy a worksheet to another workbook

1. Open the workbook that will receive the new worksheets.

2. Switch to the workbook that contains the worksheets you want to copy, hold down the Ctrl key, and click the sheet tabs of the worksheets you want to copy.

3. Right-click the selection.

4. Choose **Move Or Copy** from the shortcut menu.

5. Select the **Create A Copy** check box.

6. Click the **To Book** down arrow.

7. Click the workbook to which you want the worksheet(s) copied.

8. Click **OK**.

### To change the order of worksheets in a workbook

→ Drag the sheet tab of the worksheet you want to move.

### To hide a worksheet

1. Hold down the Ctrl key and click the sheet tabs of the worksheets you want to hide.

2. Right-click any selected worksheet tab and then choose the Hide command.

### To unhide a worksheet

1. Right-click any worksheet tab.

2. Click **Unhide**.

3. Click the worksheet you want to unhide.

4. Click **OK**.

## To delete a worksheet

1. Hold down the Ctrl key and click the sheet tabs of the worksheets you want to delete.

2. Right-click the selection.

3. Choose **Delete** from the shortcut menu.

## To change a row's height or column's width

1. Select the rows and columns you want to resize.

2. Drag a row or column border until it is the desired size.

## To insert a column or row

1. Right-click the column header to the right of, or the row header below, where you want the new column or row to appear.

2. Choose **Insert** from the shortcut menu.

## To delete a column or row

1. Select the row or column you want to delete.

2. Right-click the selection and choose **Delete** from the shortcut menu.

## To hide a column or row

1. Select the rows or columns you want to hide.

2. Right-click a row or column header in the selection and choose **Hide** from the shortcut menu.

## To unhide a column or row

1. Click the row or column header of the row above or the column to the left of the rows or columns you want to unhide.

2. Hold down the Shift key and click the row or column header of the row or column below or to the right of the rows or columns you want to unhide.

3. Right-click the selection and choose **Unhide** from the shortcut menu.

## To insert a cell

1. Select the cells in the spot where you want to insert new cells.

2. Click the **Home** tab.

3. In the **Cells** group, click the **Insert** button's down arrow.

4. Click **Insert Cells**.

5. Select the option button representing how you want to move the existing cells to make room for the inserted cells.

6. Click **OK**.

### To delete a cell

1. Select the cells you want to delete.

2. Click the **Home** tab.

3. In the **Cells** group, click the **Delete** button's down arrow.

4. Click **Delete Cells**.

5. Select the option button representing how you want the remaining cells to fill in the deleted space.

6. Click **OK**.

### To move a group of cells to a new location

1. Select the cells you want to move.

2. Move the mouse pointer over the outline of the selected cells.

3. Drag the cells to the desired location.

### To zoom in or out on a worksheet

→ Click the **Zoom In** control to make your window's contents 10 percent larger per click.

→ Click the **Zoom Out** control to make your window's contents 10 percent smaller per click.

→ Drag the **Zoom** slider control, shown in the figure, to the left to zoom out, or to the right to zoom in.

### To zoom in or out to a specific zoom level

1. On the **View** tab, in the **Zoom** group, click **Zoom**.

2. Select the Custom option.

3. Type a new zoom level in the **Custom** field.

4. Click **OK**.

### To change to another open workbook

1. On the **View** tab, in the **Window** group, click **Switch Windows**.

2. Click the name of the workbook you want to display.

**To arrange all open workbooks in the program window**

1. On the **View** tab, in the **Window** group, click **Arrange All**.
2. Select the desired arrangement.
3. Click **OK**.

**To add a button to the Quick Access Toolbar**

1. Click the **Customize Quick Access Toolbar** button.
2. Click **More Commands**.
3. Click the **Choose Commands From** down arrow.
4. Click the category from which you want to choose the command.
5. Click the command you want to add.
6. Click **Add**.
7. Click **OK**.

**To move a button on the Quick Access Toolbar**

1. Click the **Customize Quick Access Toolbar** button.
2. Click **More Commands**.
3. Click the command you want to move.
4. Click the **Move Up** button or the **Move Down** button.

**To remove a button from the Quick Access Toolbar**

1. Right-click the button you want to remove.
2. Click **Remove from Quick Access Toolbar**.

# 6 Working with Data and Data Tables

**To enter a data series using AutoFill**

1. Type the first label or value for your list.
2. Drag the fill handle to the cell containing the last label or value in the series.

**To change how dragging the fill handle extends a series**

1. Type the first label or value for your list.
2. Hold down the [Ctrl] key, and drag the fill handle to the cell containing the last label or value in the series.

**To enter data by using AutoComplete**

1. Type the beginning of an entry.

2. Press [Tab] to accept the AutoComplete value.

**To enter data by picking from a list**

1. Right-click a cell in a column with existing values and click **Pick from Drop-down List** from the shortcut menu.

2. Click the item in the list you want to enter.

**To copy and paste cells**

1. Select the cell you want to copy.

2. On the **Home** tab, in the **Clipboard** group, click **Copy**.

3. Click the cells into which you want to paste the values.

4. On the **Home** tab, in the **Clipboard** group, click **Paste**.

**To copy and paste a row or column**

1. Select the row or column you want to copy.

2. On the **Home** tab, in the **Clipboard** group, click **Copy**.

3. Click the header of the row or column into which you want to paste the values.

4. On the **Home** tab, in the **Clipboard** group, click **Paste**.

**To find data within a worksheet**

1. Click the **Home** tab.

2. In the **Editing** group, click **Find and Select**.

3. Click **Find**.

4. Type the text you want to find.

5. Click **Find Next**.

6. Click **Close**.

**To replace a value with another value within a worksheet**

1. Click the **Home** tab.

2. In the **Editing** group, click **Find and Select**.

3. Click **Replace**.

4. Type the text you want to replace.

5. Type the text you want to take the place of the existing text.

6. Click **Find Next**. Follow any of these steps:

   - Click **Replace** to replace the text.
   - Click **Find Next** to skip this instance of the text and move to the next time it occurs.
   - Click **Replace All** to replace every instance of the text.

7. Click **Close**.

**To edit a cell's contents by hand**

1. Click the cell you want to edit.

2. Select the text you want to edit in the Formula Bar.

3. Type the new text and press Enter.

**To check spelling**

1. On the **Review** tab, in the **Proofing** group, click **Spelling**. If you are asked whether you want to save your work, do so.

2. Follow any of these steps:

   - Click **Ignore Once** to ignore the current misspelling.
   - Click **Ignore All** to ignore all instances of the misspelled word.
   - Click **Add to Dictionary** to add the current word to the dictionary.
   - Click the correct spelling and then click **Change** to replace the current misspelling with the correct word.
   - Click the correct spelling and then click **Change All** to replace all instances of the current misspelling with the correct word.
   - Click **Cancel** to stop checking spelling.

3. Click OK to clear the dialog box that appears after the spelling check is complete.

**To look up a word in the Thesaurus**

1. Select the word you want to look up.

2. On the **Review** tab, in the **Proofing** group, click **Thesaurus**.

**To translate a word to another language**

1. Select the word you want to look up.

2. On the **Review** tab, in the **Proofing** group, click **Translate**.

**To create a data table**

1. Type your table headers in a single row.
2. Type your first data row directly below the header row.
3. Click any cell in the range from which you want to create a table.
4. On the **Home** tab, in the **Styles** group, click **Format as Table**.
5. Click the desired table style.
6. Verify that Excel identified the data range correctly.
7. If your table has headers, select the **My table has headers** check box.
8. Click **OK**.

**To add rows to a data table**

Follow either of these steps:

→ Click the cell at the bottom right corner of the data table and press [Tab] to create a new table row.

→ Type data into the cell below the bottom left corner of the data table and press [Tab]. Excel will make the new row part of the data table.

**To resize a table**

1. Click any cell in the table.
2. Drag the resize handle to expand or contract the table.

**To add a Total row to a column**

1. Click any cell in the table.
2. On the **Design** tab, in the **Table Style Options** group, click **Total Row**.

**To change the Total row summary function**

1. Click any cell in the table's **Total** row.
2. Click the down arrow that appears.
3. Click the desired summary function.

**To rename a table**

1. Click any cell in the table.
2. On the **Design** tab, in the **Properties** group, type a new value in the **Table Name** box.

# 7    Performing Calculations on Data

**To create a named range**

1. Select the cells you want to name.
2. Click the **Name Box** on the **Formula Bar**.
3. Type the name you want for the range.
4. Press [Enter].

**To create a named range from a selection**

1. Select the cells you want to name as a range. Be sure either the first or last cell contains the name for the range.
2. On the **Formulas** tab, in the **Defined Names** group, click **Create from Selection**.
3. Select the check box that represents the cell that contains the range's desired name.
4. Click **OK**.

**To display the Name Manager**

→ On the **Formulas** tab, in the **Defined Names** group, click **Name Manager**.

**To edit a named range**

1. On the **Formulas** tab, in the **Defined Names** group, click **Name Manager**.
2. Click the named range you want to edit.
3. Click the **Edit** button.
4. Click the **Collapse Dialog** button.
5. Select the cells you want in the range.
6. Click **Close**.

**To create a formula**

1. Click the cell into which you want to enter a formula.
2. Type =.
3. Type the expression representing the calculation you want to perform.
4. Press [Enter].

**To create a formula using the Insert Function dialog box**

1. On the **Formulas** tab, in the **Function Library** group, click **Insert Function**.

2. Select the function you want to use, and click **OK**.

3. Fill in the **Function Arguments** dialog box, and click **OK**.

### To use a named range in a formula

1. Begin typing the formula.

2. Type the name of the named range as a function's argument.

### To refer to a table column or row in a formula

1. Click the cell in which you want to create the formula.

2. Type =, followed by the function to include in the formula and a left parenthesis; for example, =SUM( would be a valid way to start.

3. Move the mouse pointer over the header of the table column you want to use in the formula. When the mouse pointer changes to a black, downward-pointing arrow, click the column header.

4. Type a right parenthesis and press `Enter`.

### To create a formula using Formula AutoComplete

1. Begin typing the formula.

2. Click the desired function from the list that appears.

### To create a formula that doesn't change when copied between cells

1. Begin typing the formula.

2. Precede all column and row references with a dollar sign (e.g., $C$4).

### To create a formula that does change when copied between cells

1. Begin typing the formula.

2. Type all column and row references without a dollar sign (e.g., C4).

### To create a conditional formula

1. Click the cell in which you want to enter an IF function.

2. On the **Formulas** tab, in the **Function Library** group, click **Logical**, and then click **IF**.

3. Type a conditional statement that evaluates to true or false.

4. Type the text you want to appear if the condition is true.

5. Type the text you want to appear if the condition is false.

6. Click **OK**.

**To display cells that provide values for a formula**

1. Click the cell you want to track.
2. On the **Formulas** tab, in the **Formula Auditing** group, click the **Trace Precedents** button.

**To display formulas that use a cell's contents**

1. Click the cell you want to track.
2. On the **Formulas** tab, in the **Formula Auditing** group, click the **Trace Dependents** button.

**To remove tracer arrows**

1. Click the cell you want to track.
2. On the **Formulas** tab, in the **Formula Auditing** group, click the **Remove Arrows** button.

**To locate errors in a worksheet**

1. On the **Formulas** tab, in the **Formula Auditing** group, click the **Error Checking** button.
2. Click the **Edit in Formula Bar** button.
3. Edit the formula.
4. Click the **Next** button to view the next error.

**To step through a formula to locate an error**

1. Click the cell with the formula you want to evaluate.
2. On the **Formulas** tab, in the **Formula Auditing** group, click **Evaluate Formula**.
3. Click **Evaluate** (one or more times) to move through the formula's elements.
4. Click **Close**.

**To watch a value in a cell**

1. On the **Formulas** tab, in the **Formula Auditing** group, click **Watch Window**.
2. Click **Add Watch**.
3. Select the cells you want to watch.
4. Click **Add**.
5. Click **Watch Window**.

**To delete a watch**

1. On the **Formulas** tab, in the **Formula Auditing** group, click **Watch Window**.
2. Click the watch you want to delete.
3. Click **Delete Watch**.
4. Click the **Close** button.

# 8  Changing Document Appearance

**To change a cell's font, font style, font color, or background color**

1. Select the cells you want to change.
2. On the **Home** tab, use the controls in the **Font** group to format the cells.

**To add a border to a cell**

1. Select the cells around which you want to draw a border.
2. On the **Home** tab, in the **Font** group, click the **Border** button's down arrow.
3. Click the type of border you want to apply.

**To apply a style to a cell**

1. Select the cells you want to change.
2. On the **Home** tab, in the **Styles** group, click **Cell Styles**.
3. Click a style.

**To create a new style**

1. On the **Home** tab, in the **Styles** group, click **Cell Styles**.
2. Click **New Cell Style**.
3. Type a new style name.
4. Click **Format**.
5. Specify the formatting you want this style to contain.
6. Click **OK** twice.

**To delete a style**

1. On the **Home** tab, in the **Styles** group, click **Cell Styles**.
2. Right-click the style you want to delete.
3. Click **Delete**.

**To copy a cell's formatting onto another cell**

1. Click the cell that contains the format you want to apply to another cell.
2. On the **Home** tab, in the **Clipboard** group, click the **Format Painter** button.
3. Select the cells to which you want to apply the formatting.

**To apply a workbook theme**

1. On the **Page Layout** tab, in the **Themes** group, click **Themes**.
2. Click the theme you want to apply.

**To change theme fonts, colors, and graphic effects**

Using the **Controls** on the **Page Layout** tab, in the **Themes** group, follow one of these steps:

- Click the **Fonts** button and select a new font.
- Click the **Colors** button and select a new color set.
- Click the **Effects** button and select a new default effect.

**To save a workbook's format as a new theme**

1. Format your worksheet using the colors, fonts, and effects you want to include in your theme.
2. On the **Page Layout** tab, in the **Themes** group, click **Themes**.
3. Click **Save Current Theme**.
4. Type a name for your theme.
5. Click **Save**.

**To create a new table style**

1. On the **Home** tab, in the **Styles** group, click **Format as Table** and then click **New Table Style**.
2. In the **Name** field, type a name for the table style.
3. In the **Table Element** list, click the element you want to format.
4. Click **Format**, and use the controls in the Format dialog box to format the table element.
5. Click **OK**.
6. Repeat as desired to format other elements, and then click **OK**.

**To format a cell value as a phone number**

1. On the **Home** tab, click the **Number** group's dialog box expander.
2. Click **Special**.
3. Click **Phone Number**.
4. Click **OK**.

**To format cell data as a currency value**

→ On the **Home** tab, in the **Number** group, click the **Accounting Number Format** button.

**To select a foreign currency symbol**

1. On the **Home** tab, in the **Number** group, click the **Accounting Number Format** button's down arrow.
2. Click the currency symbol you want to apply.

**To add words to a cell's value**

1. On the **Home** tab, click the **Number** group's dialog box expander.
2. Click **Custom**.
3. Click the format to serve as the base for your custom format.
4. Type the text to appear in the cell, enclosed in quotes (e.g., " cases").
5. Click **OK**.

**To apply a conditional format to a cell**

1. Select the cells you want to change.
2. On the **Home** tab, in the **Styles** group, click **Conditional Formatting**.
3. Click **New Rule**.
4. Click **Format Only Cells That Contain**.
5. Click the **Comparison Phrase** down arrow, and then click the comparison phrase you want.
6. Type the constant values or formulas you want evaluated.
7. Click **Format**.
8. Specify the formatting you want and click **OK** twice.

**To edit a conditional formatting rule**

1. Select the cells that contain the rule you want to edit.

2. On the **Home** tab, in the **Styles** group, click **Conditional Formatting**.

3. Click **Manage Rules**.

4. Click the rule you want to change.

5. Click **Edit Rule**.

6. Use the controls to make your changes.

7. Click **OK** twice to save your changes.

**To delete a conditional formatting rule**

1. Select the cells that contain the rule you want to edit.

2. On the **Home** tab, in the Styles group, click **Conditional Formatting**.

3. Click **Manage Rules**.

4. Click the rule you want to delete.

5. Click **Delete Rule**.

6. Click **OK**.

**To display data bars in one or more cells**

1. Select the cells that contain your data.

2. On the Home tab, in the Styles group, click Conditional Formatting.

3. Point to Data Bars.

4. Click the data bar option you want to apply.

**To display a color scale in one or more cells**

1. Select the cells that contain your data.

2. On the Home tab, in the Styles group, click Conditional Formatting.

3. Point to Color Scales.

4. Click the color scale pattern you want to apply.

**To display icon sets in one or more cells**

1. Select the cells that contain your data.

2. On the Home tab, in the Styles group, click Conditional Formatting.

3. Point to Icon Sets.

4. Click the icon set you want to apply.

**To add a picture to a worksheet**

1. On the Insert tab, in the Illustrations group, click Picture.
2. Double-click the picture you want to insert.

**To change a picture's characteristics**

1. Click the picture.
2. Use the controls on the Format tab to edit the picture.

# 9  Creating a Database

**To open a template and save it as a new database**

1. On the **Getting Started with Microsoft Office Access** page, in the **Template Categories** list, click a category.
2. Click the template icon for the template you want to open.
3. In the **File Name** box, type a new name for the database, and note the default path.
4. Click the **Create** button.

**To open a new blank database**

1. Open Access.
2. On the **Getting Started with Microsoft Access** page, click **Blank Database**.
3. In the **File Name** box, type the name for the database.
4. Click the **Browse for a location** button, browse to the folder where you want to save the database, click **OK**, and then click **Create**.

**To enter information in a database**

→ Click in an empty cell, type your text, and then press Tab to move to the next cell.

**To change a field name**

→ Double-click the field name, and then type the new name.

**To change the data type of a field**

→ In Design view, click in the data type cell you want to change, click the arrow that is displayed, and then click the data type you want to use.

**To change the size of a field**

1. In Design view, click the field name.
2. In the **Field Properties** area, select the current field size, and then enter the new field size.

**To close and save a table**

→ Click the **Close** button to close the table, and then click **Yes** to save changes.

**To create a table by using a template**

→ On the **Create** tab, in the **Tables** group, click the **Table Templates** button, and then click the type of template you want to create.

**To add a new field name to a table and assign it a data type**

1. Click in the first blank **Field** Name cell below the existing field names, type the field name, and then press `Tab`.

2. Click the **Data Type** arrow for the new field, and then click the data type that you want assigned to the field.

**To delete a table row while in Design view**

→ Right-click in the row you want to delete, and then click **Delete Rows**.

**To edit a field name**

→ Select the part of the field name you want to edit, and then type the new information.

**To change the size of a table column**

1. With the table in **Datasheet View**, drag the vertical bar at the right edge of a column header to the left or right until the column is the size you want.

2. To size a column to the minimum width that will display all the text in that field in all records, point to the vertical bar on the right of the column header, and when the pointer changes to a double-headed arrow, double-click.

**To change the height of all rows in a table**

→ With the table in **Datasheet View**, on the left side of the datasheet, drag the horizontal bar between any two record selectors up or down until the rows are the height you want.

**To reset all rows in a table to standard height**

1. With the table in **Datasheet View**, on the **Home** tab, in the **Records** group, click **More**, and then click **Row Height** to display the **Row Height** dialog box.

2. In the **Row Height** dialog box, select the **Standard Height** check box or type in the height you want in the **Row Height** box, and then click **OK**.

**To hide and unhide columns**

1. Click anywhere in the column you want to hide, and in the **Records** group, click **More**. Then click **Hide Columns**.

2. To restore the hidden column, click **More** again, and then click **Unhide Columns** to display the **Unhide Columns** dialog box.

3. In the **Unhide Columns** dialog box, select the check box of the column you want to unhide, and then click **Close**.

**To freeze and unfreeze columns**

1. Drag through the column header of the column or columns you want to freeze.

2. With the columns selected, click the **More** button, and then click **Freeze**.

3. To restore the columns to their normal condition, click **More**, and then click **Unfreeze**.

## 10   Simplifying Data Entry by Using Forms

**To create a form based on a table by using the Form tool**

1. Open the table on which you want to base the form.

2. On the **Create** tab, in the **Forms** group, click the **Form** button.

**To move labels on a form**

→ Select the labels to be moved by dragging through them, drag them to a blank section of the form, and then release the selection.

**To change the font and font size of a label on a form**

1. Open the form in Design View, and click the label (not its text box) you want to change.

2. On the **Design** contextual tab, in the **Font** group, click the **Font** arrow, and then in the list, click the font you want to use.

3. With the label still selected, click the **Font Size** arrow, and then in the list, click the size you want.

**To edit form control properties by using the Property Sheet pane**

1. Open the form in Design view, and if the **Property Sheet** pane is not visible, right-click the desired control, and then click **Properties**.

2. In the **Property Sheet** pane, click the property you want to change, and either type the new value, or click the down arrow and select the value you want. Repeat for all properties that you want to change.

**To edit multiple form control properties at once**

1. Click anywhere in the **Detail** section of the form, and then drag diagonally to draw a rectangle through some portion of all the controls to select them.

2. In the **Property Sheet** pane, click the property you want to change, click the arrow that appears, and then click the option you want. Repeat for all properties that you want to change.

**To set the background properties of all controls on a form**

1. Select all the controls on the form. Then on the **Format** tab of the **Property Sheet** pane, click **Back Style**, and set it to the option you want.

2. Click **Back Color**, and then click the ellipsis button.

3. In the **Color Builder**, click the square of the color you want.

4. Set the **Special Effect** property to the option you want, and the **Border Color** property to the color you want.

**To edit the caption of a form control**

→ Click the label whose caption you want to change. Then in the **Property Sheet** pane, click the **Caption** property, change the text to what you want, and press Enter.

**To change the layout of controls on a form**

→ Drag through all the controls on the form to select them. Then on the **Arrange** tab, in the **Control Layout** group, click the **Remove** button.

**To delete a form control label**

→ Click the label you want to delete, and then press the Del key.

**To select specific control labels on a form**

→ Hold down the Shift key as you click each control or drag through just the labels you want to select.

**To align form controls**

→ Select the labels (but not their corresponding text boxes), and then in the **Property Sheet** pane, set the **Text Align** property to the alignment you want.

**To size form control labels to fit their contents**

→ Select the labels to be sized, and then on the **Arrange** contextual tab, in the **Size** group, click the **Size To Fit** button.

**To insert space between form control labels and text boxes**

→ Select all the text boxes (but not their corresponding labels). Then in the **Property Sheet** pane, click the **Left** property, and then change the setting to the amount of space you want.

**To save the design of a form**

→ On the **Quick Access Toolbar**, click the **Save** button.

**To expand the Detail area of a form**

→ Point to the right edge of the form **Detail** grid, and when the pointer changes to a double-headed arrow, drag the edge of the background to the right.

**To move a label or text box control on a form**

→ Click a label or text box, move the pointer over its border, and when the pointer changes to a four-way arrow, drag it to a new location.

**To create an AutoFormat form template**

1. On the **Arrange** contextual tab, in the **AutoFormat** group, click the **AutoFormat** button.

2. At the bottom of the **AutoFormat** gallery, click **AutoFormat Wizard**.

3. In the **AutoFormat** dialog box, click the **Customize** button.

4. In the **Customize AutoFormat** dialog box, click **Create a new AutoFormat based on the Form** option, and then click **OK**.

5. In the **New Style Name** dialog box, type a name for the new style, and then click **OK**.

6. Click **OK** to close the **AutoFormat** dialog box. Then click the **Save** button, and close the form.

**To add a graphic to a form control**

1. In the **Navigation Pane**, under **Forms**, right-click the form you want to use, and then click **Design View**.

2. On the **Design** contextual tab, in the **Controls** group, click the **Image** button, and then click the area where you want to place the image, drag diagonally to draw a rectangle, and release the mouse button.

3. In the **Insert Picture** dialog box, navigate to the folder where the graphic you want to use is located, and then double-click the graphic.

**To add a caption below a picture**

1. In the **Controls** group, click the **Label** button, and then drag diagonally to draw a rectangle where you want it to appear.

2. In the active label control, type the caption text, and then press `Enter`.

**To size a label control to fit the text**

→ Click the label control, and then on the **Arrange** tab, in the **Size** group, click the **Size to Fit** button.

**To add a combo box control without using a wizard**

1. On the **Design** tab, in the **Controls** group, look at the **Use Control Wizards** button. If the button is active (orange), click it to deactivate it.

2. In the **Controls** group, click the **Combo Box** button, and then drag diagonally in the form to draw a rectangle where you want the combo box to appear.

**To copy the formatting of one control to another**

→ Click the box whose formatting you want to copy, and in the **Font** group, click the **Format Painter** button. Then click the box to which you want to apply the formatting.

**To remove the record selector and scroll bar controls from a form**

1. In Design view, click the **Form** selector (the box at the junction of the horizontal and vertical rulers), and then press [F4] to display the **Property Sheet** pane for the entire form (if the sheet is not already displayed).

2. On the **Format** tab, change **Record Selectors** to **No**, and **Scroll Bars** to **Neither**.

**To create a form based on the fields in a table by using the Form wizard**

1. In the **Navigation Pane**, under **Tables**, click the table in which you want to create the AutoForm.

2. On the **Create** tab, in the **Forms** group, click the **More Forms** button, and then in the list, click **Form Wizard**.

3. With the open table selected in the **Tables/Queries** list, click the **Move All** button to move all the table fields to the **Selected Fields** list, and then click **Next**.

4. On the second page of the wizard, choose the layout of the fields in the new form. On the third page, select a style option.

5. On the fourth page, with the **Open the form to view or enter information** option selected, click **Finish**.

**To create a form and subform simultaneously**

1. On the **Create** tab, in the **Forms** group, click the **More Forms** button, and then click **Form Wizard**.

2. On the first page of the **Form** wizard, in the **Tables/Queries** list, click the table on which you want to base the form. Then click the **Move All** button to include all the table fields in the new form.

3. To create the subform, display the **Tables/Queries** list, and then click the table on which you want to base the subform.

4. In the **Available Fields** list, double-click the fields you want to include in the sub-form to move them to the **Selected fields** list, and then click **Next**.

5. With your primary table and **Form with subform(s)** selected, click **Next**.

6. With **Datasheet** selected, click **Next**.

7. On the last page of the wizard, select a style, and then click **Finish**.

**To add a subform to a form**

1. Open the form in Design view. Then on the **Design** tab, in the **Controls** group, make sure the **Use Control Wizards** button is active (orange).

2. In the **Controls** group, click the **Subform/Subreport** button, and then drag diagonally to draw a rectangle in a section where you want to put the subform.

3. On the **Subform** wizard's first page, with the **Use existing Tables and Queries** option selected, click **Next**.

4. In the **Tables/Queries** list, click the type of item you want to use.

5. Add fields to the **Selected Fields** list by double-clicking each field. Then click **Next**, select the options you want, and click **Finish**.

# 11   Locating Specific Information

**To sort information in one column**

→ Click the arrow at the right side of the column header for the column you want to sort, and then click the direction you want to sort the information.

→ Click the header of the column you want to sort, and then on the **Home** tab, in the **Sort and Filter** group, click the **Ascending** or **Descending** button.

**To sort information in multiple columns**

→ Select the adjacent columns you want to sort, right-click the column header area of your selection, and then click how you want to sort the columns.

**To move a field**

→ Click the column head you want to move, and then drag it to the position you want.

**To filter records by a single criterion**

1. In the field, click any instance of the record you want to filter by.

2. On the **Home** tab, in the **Sort & Filter** group, click the **Selection** button, and then in the list, click **Equals** "[the term you want to filter on]".

**To remove a filter**

→ In the **Sort & Filter** group, click the **Toggle Filter** button.

**To filter records with a text filter**

1. Click the column header arrow, point to **Text Filters**, and then click the criterion you want to filter by.

2. In the Custom Filter dialog box, in the **ItemText begins with** box, type the first few letters of the text you want to filter by. Then click **OK**.

**To filter records with a "does not equal" filter**

→ In the column, right-click any instance of the criterion you don't want to filter, and then click **Does Not Equal** "[the item you don't want to filter]".

**To use the Filter By Form command**

1. In the **Navigation Pane**, under **Forms**, double-click the form you want to search.

2. On the **Home** tab, in the **Sort & Filter** group, click the **Advanced** button, and then in the list, click **Filter By Form**.

3. Click the box you want to search in, type the search criterion, and then press Enter.

4. In the **Sort and Filter** group, click the **Toggle Filter** button.

**To use the Advanced Filter/Sort command to sort tables**

1. On the **Home** tab, in the **Sort & Filter** group, click the **Advanced Filter Options** button, and then in the list, click **Advanced Filter/Sort**.

2. In the field list, double-click a field to copy it to the first cell in the first column of the design grid.

3. In the **Criteria** cell under the field you just copied, type the search criterion, and then press Enter.

4. Repeat Steps 2 and 3 for any other fields you want to filter on.

5. In the **Sort & Filter** group, click the **Toggle Filter** button to view the records that match the criteria.

**To create a query in Design view**

1. On the **Create** tab, in the **Other** group, click the **Query Design** button.

2. In the **Show Table** dialog box, on the **Tables** tab, double-click any tables you want to add to the query window. Then close the dialog box.

3. Drag the fields to be used in the query from the field lists to consecutive columns in the design grid.

4. On the **Design** contextual tab, in the **Results** group, click the **Run** button to run the query and display the results in Datasheet view.

## 12    Keeping Your Information Accurate

**To set the data type for a field**

1. With the table in Design view, click the **Data Type** cell next to the desired field.

2. Click the **Data Type** arrow, and then in the list, click the data type you want.

**To view the properties of a field**

→ With the table in Design view, click the field name to display its properties in the Field Properties area.

**To set the Field Size property for text, number, and autonumber fields**

→ With the table in Design view, click any cell in a field, and then in the **Field Properties** area, change the **Field Size** property to what you want.

**To use the Input Mask wizard**

1. With the table in Design view, select a field, and then click **Input Mask** in the **Field Properties** area.

2. Click the ellipsis button to the right of the cell to start the **Input Mask** wizard. (Click **Yes** if Access prompts you to install this feature.)

3. Select an available mask in the **Input Mask** list, and then click **Next**.

4. In the **Input Mask** and **Placeholder character** boxes, make any changes you want, and then click **Next**.

5. Choose whether to store the data with the symbols, and then click **Finish**.

6. Press [Enter] to accept the mask. Then save your changes.

**To set a field validation rule**

1. With the table in Design view, select a field, and then click in the **Validation Rule** box in the Field Properties area.

2. Type an expression in the **Validation Rule** box, or click the ellipsis button to use the Expression Builder.

3. Press [Enter]. Then save the table.

**To test the validation rules in a table**

→ Open the table in Design view. Then right-click its title bar, and click **Test Validation Rules**.

**To select an entire field**

→ Move the pointer to the left end of a field, and when the pointer changes to a thick cross, click the field.

**To set a table validation rule**

1. Right-click in the table window, and then click **Properties**.
2. Click in the **Validation Rule** box, type the information for the rule, press `Enter`, and then save the table.

**To create a lookup list with the Lookup wizard**

1. Set the data type of a field to **Lookup Wizard**.
2. Select the options you want, and then click **Next**.
3. Continue selecting the options you want, clicking **Next** when you are done with each page. When you are done filling out the wizard, click **Finish**.
4. On the **Quick Access Toolbar**, click the **Save** button.

**To restrict what can be entered in a lookup list**

1. In Design view, in the **Field Properties** area, click the **Lookup** tab.
2. Change **Limit To List** to **Yes**.
3. Change **Allow Value List Edits** to **No**.
4. Save the table.

**To create a multi-column lookup list**

1. Add a new field, name it, and then set the data type to **Lookup Wizard**.
2. Select the **values** option you want, and then click **Next**.
3. Type the number of columns you want, and then enter the data you want in each column.
4. Click **Next**, and then click **Finish**.
5. Save your changes.

**To prevent a column from being displayed in a multi-column lookup list**

→ In Design view, on the **Lookup** tab, in the **Column Widths** box, change the width for the column you don't want displayed to 0. Then save your changes.

**To filter selections in a multi-column lookup list**

1. Right-click any cell in a column you want to filter, point to **Text Filters**, and then click the filter option you want.
2. In the **Custom Filter** box, type criterion you want to filter for, and then press `Enter`.

**To create a select query**

1. You must first create a select query. On the **Create** tab, in the **Other** group, click the **Query Design** button.

2. In the **New Query** dialog box, with **Simple Query Wizard** selected, click **OK**.

3. In the **Tables/Queries** list, click the option you want. Then in the **Available Fields** list, double-click the fields you want to move to the **Selected Fields** list.

4. In the **Simple Query Wizard** dialog box, click **Finish** to create the select query.

### To create an update query

1. First, create a select query that selects the records you want to update.

2. Open the select query in Design view. Then on the **Design** contextual tab, in the **Query Type** group, click the **Update** button.

3. In the design grid, type the expression for your update.

### To create an action query

1. First, create a select query that selects the records you want to manipulate.

2. Open the select query in Design view. Then on the **Design** contextual tab, in the **Query Type** group, click the **Make Table**, **Append**, **Update**, or **Delete** button.

3. Provide the information requested for the specified query type.

### To create a delete query

1. First, create a select query that selects the records you want to delete.

2. Open the select query in Design view. Then on the Design contextual tab, in the **Query Type** group, click the **Delete** button to convert this select query to a delete query.

3. In the design grid, set the delete criteria.

### To back up a database

1. Click the **Microsoft Office Button**, point to **Manage**, and then click **Back Up Database**.

2. In the **Save As** dialog box, navigate to the folder in which you want to store the backup, and then click **Save**.

### To compact a database

→ Click the **Microsoft Office Button**, point to **Manage**, and then click **Compact and Repair Database**. Acknowledge the safety warning if prompted to do so.

### To analyze the performance of a database

1. On the **Database Tools** tab, in the **Analyze** group, click the **Analyze Performance** button.

2. In the **Performance Analyzer** dialog box, on the **All Object Types** tab, click **Select All**, and then click **OK**.

   **3.** Click each result in the **Analysis Results** box to display more information about that result in the **Analysis Notes** area.

**To document a database**

   **1.** On the **Database Tools** tab, in the **Analyze** group, click the **Database Documenter** button.

   **2.** In the **Documenter** dialog box, select the options you want on each tab. Then click **OK** to start the documentation process.

# 13   Starting a New Presentation

**To base a presentation on an example from Office Online**

   **1.** Click the **Microsoft Office Button**, and then click **New**.

   **2.** Under **Microsoft Office Online** in the left pane, click **Presentations**.

   **3.** Scroll the center pane until you find the presentation you want, and then click **Download**.

**To base a presentation on an existing presentation**

   **1.** Click the **Microsoft Office Button**, and then click **New**.

   **2.** In the left pane, under **Templates**, click **New from existing**.

   **3.** Navigate to the folder containing the presentation on which you want to base the new one, and then double-click that presentation.

**To base a presentation on a design template**

   **1.** Click the **Microsoft Office Button**, and then click **New**.

   **2.** In the left pane, under **Microsoft Office Online**, click **Design slides**.

   **3.** In the **Design slides** category list, click the category that you want.

   **4.** Scroll the center pane until you find the template you want, and then click **Download**.

**To add a new slide with the default layout**

   → On the **Home** tab, in the **Slides** group, click the **New Slide** button.

**To add slides with other layouts**

   → On the **Home** tab, in the **Slides** group, click the **New Slide** arrow, and then in the list, click the layout you want.

**To delete a slide**

   → At the top of the **Overview** pane, on the **Slides** tab, right-click the slide, and then click **Delete Slide**.

**To convert a Microsoft Office Word outline into a presentation**

1. On the **Home** tab, in the **Slides** group, click the **New Slide** arrow, and then click **Slides from Outline**.

2. Navigate to the folder containing the Word outline, and then double-click the Word document.

**To save a presentation as an outline**

1. Click the **Microsoft Office Button**, and then click **Save As**.

2. In the **File name** box, enter the name of the outline file.

3. Click the **Save as type** arrow, and then in the list, click **Outline/RTF**.

4. Navigate to the folder where you want to store the outline, and then click **Save**.

**To insert a slide from another presentation**

1. Click the slide after which you want to insert the slide.

2. On the **Home** tab, in the **Slides** group, click the **New Slide** arrow, and then in the list, click **Reuse Slides**.

3. In the **Reuse Slides** task pane, click the **Open a PowerPoint File** link.

4. Navigate to the folder containing the presentation with the slide you want to reuse, and double-click the presentation.

5. In the task pane, click the slide you want to reuse.

# 14    Working with Slide Text

**To create slides, bullet points, and subpoints on the Outline tab**

→ Click to the right of a slide title, and then press F to create a new slide.

→ With the insertion point in a slide title, press D to convert it to a bullet point.

→ With the insertion point in a bullet point, press G+D to convert it to a slide.

→ With the insertion point in the bullet point, press D to convert it to a subpoint.

**To delete and replace a word**

→ Double-click the word to select it, and then press Del or Backspace.

→ Double-click the word, and then type a different word.

**To move text**

→ On the **Outline** tab or the slide, select the text, and then drag the selection to the desired location; or

1. Select the text, and on the **Home** tab, in the **Clipboard** group, click the **Cut** button.

2. Click where you want to insert the text, and then click the **Paste** button.

**To undo or redo editing actions**

➜ On the **Quick Access Toolbar**, click the **Undo** or **Redo** button.

**To select an entire placeholder**

➜ Point to the border of the placeholder, and when the pointer changes to a four-headed arrow, click the mouse button once.

**To create a text box**

➜ On the **Insert** tab, in the **Text** group, click the **Text Box** button, click the slide, and then type the text.

**To rotate a text box**

➜ Select the text box, and then drag the green rotating handle in the direction you want.

**To move a text box**

➜ Select the text box, point to the border of the box (not to a handle), and then drag the box to the desired location.

**To size a text box**

➜ Select the text box, point to one of the square or round handles around its frame, and drag the handle until the box is the size you want.

**To add a solid border to a text box**

1. Right-click the border of the text box, and then click **Format Shape**.

2. In the **Format Shape** dialog box, click **Line Color**, click the line option you want, select appropriate options, and then click **Close**.

**To change the default settings of a text box**

1. Format the text and the text box the way you want all the text boxes you create from now on in this presentation to be.

2. Right-click the border of the text box, and then click **Set as Default Text Box**.

**To add an AutoCorrect entry**

1. Click the **Microsoft Office Button**, click **PowerPoint Options**, click **Proofing**, and then click **AutoCorrect Options**.

2. In the **Replace** box above the table in the dialog box, type a word you commonly misspell, and then press ⎄Tab.

3. In the **With** box, type the correct spelling of the word, click **Add**, and then click **OK** twice to close the dialog box and PowerPoint Options window.

**To correct a word flagged as a misspelling**

→ Right-click the word, and on the context menu, click the correct spelling.

**To mark a non-English word**

1. With the insertion point in the word, on the **Review** tab, in the **Proofing** group, click the **Language** button.

2. In the **Language** dialog box, click the language, and then click **OK**.

**To check the spelling of an entire presentation**

1. With the first slide displayed, on the **Review** tab, in the **Proofing** group, click the **Spelling** button.

2. If the **Spelling** dialog box appears, click the appropriate buttons to correct the errors PowerPoint finds or to add words to the custom dictionary or AutoCorrect list.

3. Click **OK** when PowerPoint reaches the end of the spelling check, and then click **Close**.

**To find a synonym for a word**

1. Select a word (but not the following space). Then on the **Review** tab, in the **Proofing** group, click the **Thesaurus** button.

2. Point to the word you want to substitute for the selection, click the arrow that appears, and then click **Insert**.

**To find and replace a word**

1. On the **Home** tab, in the **Editing** group, click the **Replace** button.

2. In the **Find what** box, type the word you want to replace, and in the **Replace with** box, type the replacement text.

3. If necessary, select the **Match case** or **Find whole words only** check box.

4. Click **Find Next**, and then click **Replace** or **Replace All**.

**To find and replace a font**

1. On the **Home** tab, in the **Editing** group, click the **Replace** arrow, and then in the list, click **Replace Fonts**.

2. In the **Replace** list, click the font you want to replace, and then in the **With** list, click the replacement font.

3. Click **Replace**.

**To hide or display an object on a slide**

1. On the **Home** tab, in the **Editing** group, click the **Select** button, and then click **Selection Pane**.

2. Under **Shapes on this Slide** in the task pane, click the box to the right of the object to hide or display it.

**To change the font size**

→ Select the text, and then on the **Home** tab, in the **Font** group, click the **Decrease Font Size** or **Increase Font Size** button; or

→ Click the **Font Size** arrow, and then in the list, click the desired size.

**To change the size of a placeholder**

→ Point to one of the placeholder's handles, and when the pointer changes to a two-headed arrow, drag to increase or decrease the size.

**To size a placeholder to fit its text**

1. Right-click the placeholder's border, and then click **Format Shape**.

2. Click **Text Box**, select the **Resize shape to fit text** option, and then click **Close**.

**To change text alignment**

→ With the insertion point in the text you want to align, on the **Home** tab, in the **Paragraph** group, click the **Left**, **Center**, **Right**, or **Justify** button.

**To adjust line spacing**

→ Click the paragraph. Then on the **Home** tab, in the **Paragraph** group, click the **Line Spacing** button, and click the spacing you'd like to use;
or

1. Click the paragraph, and then click the **Paragraph** Dialog Box Launcher.

2. Under **Spacing**, in the **Paragraph** dialog box, adjust the **Line Spacing** setting, and then click **OK**.

**To change the text case**

→ With the text selected, on the **Home** tab, in the **Font** group, click the **Change Case** arrow, and then in the list, click the option you want.

**To apply bold or italic formatting to text**

→ Select the text, and then on the **Home** tab, in the **Font** group, click the **Bold** or **Italic** button; or

➡ Select the text, and then on the **Mini toolbar**, click the **Bold** or **Italic** button.

## To change the color of text

➡ Select the text, and then on the **Home** tab, in the **Font** group, click the **Font Color** arrow, and click the color you want.

# 15   Adjusting the Layout, Order, and Look of Slides

### To change the layout of a slide

➡ On the **Home** tab, in the **Slides** group, click the **Layout** button. Then in the **Layout** gallery, click the layout you want.

### To restore the default layout after making changes

➡ On the **Home** tab, in the **Slides** group, click the **Reset** button.

### To collapse bullet points under slide titles

➡ On the **Outline** tab of the **Overview** pane, double-click the title of the slide whose bullet points you want to hide. Double-click again to redisplay them.

### To expand or collapse the entire presentation outline

➡ On the **Outline** tab of the **Overview** pane, right-click the title of a slide, point to **Expand** or **Collapse**, and then click **Expand All** or **Collapse All**.

### To arrange slides in a presentation

➡ On the **Slides** tab of the **Overview** pane, drag slide thumbnails to new positions; or

➡ On the **View** toolbar, click the **Slide Sorter** button, and then drag slide thumbnails to new positions.

### To move slides from one open presentation to another

1. Open two or more presentations in Slide Sorter view, and then on the **View** tab, in the **Window** group, click the **Arrange All** button.
2. Drag slides from one presentation window to another.

### To change the theme

➡ On the **Design** tab, in the **Themes** group, click the **More** button to display the Themes gallery, and then click the theme you want.

### To change the color scheme

1. On the **Design** tab, in the **Themes** group, click the **Colors** button.
2. In the **Colors** gallery, click the color scheme you want.

**To create your own color scheme**

1. On the **Design** tab, in the **Themes** group, click the **Colors** button, and then click **Create New Theme Colors**.

2. In the **Create New Theme Colors** dialog box, select the colors you want, and then click **Save**.

**To change the color scheme of the current slide**

➜ On the **Design** tab, in the **Themes** group, click the **Colors** button. Then right-click the color scheme you want, and click **Apply to Selected Slides**.

**To change a theme's fonts and effects**

➜ On the **Design** tab, in the **Themes** group, click the **Fonts** button, and then click the font combination you want.

➜ On the **Design** tab, in the **Themes** group, click the **Effects** button, and then click the effect combination you want.

**To create a custom font combination**

1. On the **Design** tab, in the **Themes** group, click the **Fonts** button, and then click **Create New Theme Fonts**.

2. In the **Create New Theme Fonts** dialog box, specify the font combination you want, and then click **Save**.

**To add a picture to the slide background**

1. On the **Design** tab, in the **Background** group, click the **Background Styles** button, and then click **Format Background**.

2. In the **Format Background** dialog box, click the **Picture or texture fill** option.

3. Click **File**, navigate to the folder containing the picture you want to use, and then double-click the picture.

4. To make the picture fill the entire slide, select the **Tile picture as texture** check box.

5. To use the picture in the background of the current slide, click **Close**, or to use it in the background of all slides, click **Apply to All**.

**To add a shade or texture to the slide background**

➜ On the **Design** tab, in the **Background** group, click the **Background Styles** button, and then click a shade; or click **Format Background**, and specify a shade or texture in the **Format Background** dialog box.

## 16    Delivering a Presentation Electronically

**To create a custom slide show**

1. On the **Slide Show** tab, in the **Start Slide Show** group, click the **Custom Slide Show** button, and then click **Custom Shows**.

2. In the **Custom Shows** dialog box, click **New**.

3. In the **Slide show name** box of the **Define Custom Show** dialog box, type a name for the custom show.

4. In the **Slides in presentation** list, click the slides you want, and then click **Add**.

**To start a custom show**

→ Display the **Custom Shows** dialog box, select the custom show, and then click **Show**.

**To hide a slide**

→ In the **Overview** pane, on the **Slides** tab, right-click the slide, and then click **Hide Slide**.

→ To display a hidden slide while delivering a presentation, right-click the screen, point to **Go to Slide**, and then click the hidden slide.

**To apply slide timings to all the slides**

1. On the **Animations** tab, in the **Transition to This Slide** group, under **Advance Slide**, select the **Automatically After** check box, and then type or select the time you want the current slide to appear on the screen.

2. On the **Animations** tab, in the **Transition to This Slide** group, click the **Apply To All** button.

**To rehearse a presentation and apply slide timings**

1. With Slide 1 displayed, on the **Slide Show** tab, in the **Set Up** group, click the **Rehearse Timings** button.

2. Rehearse the presentation, clicking **Next** to move to the next slide. To repeat the rehearsal for a particular slide, on the **Rehearsal** toolbar, click the **Repeat** button to reset the time for that slide to 0:00:00.

3. At the end of the slide show, click **Yes** to apply the recorded slide timings to the slides.

**To set up a self-running presentation**

1. On the **Slide Show** tab, in the **Set Up** group, click the **Set Up Slide Show** button.

2. In the **Show type** area of the **Set Up Show** dialog box, select the **Browsed at a kiosk (full screen)** option, and select or clear the **Show without narration** and the **Show without animation** check boxes. Then click **OK**.

**To enter speaker notes**

➔ With a slide selected, in the **Notes** pane, click the **Click to add notes** placeholder, type your note, and then press [Enter].

**To insert a graphic, table, or other object in a note**

1. On the **View** tab, in the **Presentations Views** group, click the **Notes Pages** button.

2. Insert the object the way you would insert it on a slide.

**To customize the layout of speaker notes**

➔ On the **View** tab, in the **Presentation Views** group, click the **Notes Master** button. Then adjust the layout the way you would adjust the layout of a slide master.

**To preview and print speaker notes or handouts**

1. Click the **Microsoft Office Button**, and then click **Print**.

2. In the **Print** dialog box, click the **Print what** arrow, select **Notes Pages** or **Handouts** in the list.

3. In the lower-left corner of the **Print** dialog box, click **Preview**.

4. On the **Print Preview** tab, in the **Print** group, click the **Print** button, and then click **OK**.

**To prepare a presentation for travel**

1. Click the **Microsoft Office Button**, point to **Publish**, and then click **Package for CD**. Click **OK** in the message box that appears.

2. In the **Name the CD** box of the **Package for CD** dialog box, type the name you want.

3. To include embedded fonts, click **Options**. Then under **Include these files**, select the **Embedded TrueType fonts** check box, and click **OK**.

4. Insert a blank CD in your CD burner, and then click **Copy to CD**. Or click **Copy to Folder** instead, and then select the folder in which you want to store the package.

5. When PowerPoint asks you to verify that you want to include linked content, click **Yes**.

**To run a presentation in the PowerPoint Viewer**

➔ If you're running your presentation from a CD, insert the CD into the CD burner, and then in the list of file and folder names, double-click the presentation name.

→ If you're running the presentation from your computer, navigate to the folder where the package is stored, and double-click the package folder. Then double-click **PPTVIEW** to start the Presentation Viewer.

**To navigate by using the keyboard**

→ To move to the next slide, press [Space], the [↓] key, or the [→] key.

→ To move to the previous slide, press the [Page Up] key or the [←] key.

→ To end the presentation, press the [Esc] key.

**To end a presentation without a black screen**

1. Click the **Microsoft Office Button**, click **PowerPoint Options**, and then click **Advanced**.

2. In the **Slide Show** area, clear the **End with Black Slide** check box, and then click **OK**.

**To navigate by using the onscreen toolbar**

→ To move to the next slide, click the **Next** button.

→ To move to the previous slide, click the **Previous** button.

→ To jump to a slide out of sequence (even if it is hidden), click the **Navigation** button, click **Go To Slide**, and then click the slide.

→ To display the slides in a custom slide show, click the **Navigation** button, click **Custom Show**, and then click the show.

→ To display keyboard shortcuts for slide show tasks, click the **Navigation** button, and then click **Help**.

→ To end the presentation, click the **Navigation** button, and then click **End Show**.

**To use a pen tool to mark up slides**

→ Right-click the screen, point to **Pointer Options**, click a pen style, and then use the pen pointer to mark slides. (Change the pointer option to **Arrow** to turn off the pen.)

**To erase all markup from a slide**

→ Right-click the screen, point to **Pointer Options**, and then click **Erase All Ink on Slide**.

# 17   Getting Started with Outlook 2007

**To configure Outlook to connect to an e-mail account**

1. On the **Start** menu, point to **All Programs**, click **Microsoft Office**, and then click **Microsoft Office Outlook 2007**.

2. On the welcome page of the **Outlook 2007 Startup** wizard, click **Next**.

3. On the **E-mail Upgrade Options** page, select the **Do not upgrade** option, and then click **Next**.

4. On the **E-mail Accounts** page, with the **Yes** option selected, click **Next**.

5. On the **Auto Account Setup** page, enter your name, e-mail address, and password in the corresponding text boxes, and then click **Next**.

**To manually configure your Exchange Server account settings**

1. On the **Start** menu, point to **All Programs**, click **Microsoft Office**, and then click **Microsoft Office Outlook 2007**.

2. On the welcome page of the **Outlook 2007 Startup** wizard, click **Next**.

3. On the **E-mail Upgrade Options** page, select the **Do not upgrade** option, and then click **Next**.

4. On the **E-mail Accounts** page, with the **Yes** option selected, click **Next**.

5. On the **Auto Account Setup** page select the **Manually configure server settings** check box, and then click **Next**.

6. On the **Choose E-mail Service** page, select the **Microsoft Exchange Server** option, and then click **Next**.

7. On the **Microsoft Exchange Settings** page, enter the name or address of your Exchange Server and your user name, and then click the **Check Name** button. If the **Connect to** dialog box appears, enter your logon information, and then click **OK**.

8. After your name is underlined, click **Next**, and then on the final page of the wizard, click **Finish**.

**To connect to an additional e-mail account**

1. On the **Tools** menu, click **Account Settings**.

2. On the **E-mail** tab of the **Account Settings** dialog box, click the **New** button.

3. On the **Choose E-mail Service** page of the **Add New E-mail Account** wizard, with the **Microsoft Exchange Server, POP3, IMAP, or HTTP** option selected, click **Next**.

4. On the **Auto Account Setup** page, enter the account display name, the e-mail address, and the password of the account you want to add to your profile. Then click **Next**.

5. Click **Finish** to complete the account setup.

**To create an additional Outlook profile**

1. Exit Outlook if it is running.

2. Display **Control Panel** in **Classic View**, and then double-click the **Mail** icon. In the **User Account Control** dialog box, if you're logged on as an administrator, click **Continue**. Otherwise, enter an administrator password, and then click **OK**.

3. In the **Mail Setup** dialog box, click the **Show Profiles** button.

4. In the **Mail** dialog box, click the **Add** button.

5. In the **Profile Name** box, type a name to identify the new profile, and then click **OK**.

6. On the **Choose E-mail Service** page, with the **Microsoft Exchange Server, POP3, or IMAP** option selected, click **Next**.

7. On the **Auto Account Setup** page, enter the name, e-mail address, and password in the corresponding text boxes, and then click **Next**.

8. After Outlook connects to the e-mail account, click **Finish**.

**To configure Outlook to prompt for a profile when starting**

1. Display **Control Panel** in **Classic View**, and then double-click the **Mail** icon. In the **User Account Control** dialog box, if you're logged on as an administrator, click **Continue**. Otherwise, enter an administrator password, and then click **OK**.

2. In the **Mail Setup** dialog box, click **Show Profiles**.

3. In the **Mail** dialog box, select the **Prompt for a profile to be used** option, and then click **OK**.

## 18   Sending E-Mail Messages

**To check addresses**

→ If a message recipient's address is in your address book, type the person's name and either wait for Outlook to validate the name or press [Ctrl]+[K] to immediately validate it.

**To have Outlook search additional address books**

1. On the **Tools** menu, click **Address Book**. Then in the **Address Book** window, on the **Tools** menu, click **Options**.

2. In the **Addressing** dialog box, click **Add**.

3. In the **Add Address List** dialog box, click the address list you want to add, click **Add**, and then click **Close**.

4. In the **Addressing** dialog box, click **OK**, and then in the **Address Book** window, click the **Close** button.

**To send a courtesy copy of a message**

→ In the message window, enter an e-mail address in the **Cc** or **Bcc** box.

**To display the Bcc field in an outgoing message**

→ In the message window, on the **Options** tab, in the **Fields** group, click the **Show Bcc** button.

**To compose and send a new e-mail message**

1. On the Standard toolbar, click the **New Mail Message** button.

2. In the **To** box of the message window, type an e-mail address.

3. In the **Subject** box, enter the main idea of your message.

4. In the message content area, type the body of the message.

5. When you finish, click **Send**.

**To recall a message**

1. In the **Sent Items** folder, open the message you want to recall.

2. On the **Message** tab, in the **Actions** group, click the **Other Actions** button, and then click **Recall This Message**.

3. Select the option to delete unread copies of the message or to replace them with a new message, and then click **OK**.

**To attach a file to an e-mail message**

1. Display the message window.

2. On the **Message** tab, in the **Include** group, click the **Attach File** button (not the arrow under the button).

3. Browse to the file you want to attach, click it, and then click **Insert**.

**To send a business card**

1. Display the message window.

2. On the **Message** tab, in the **Include** group, click the **Insert Business Card** button, and then in the list, click **Other Business Cards**.

3. In the **Insert Business Card** dialog box, select the card or cards you want to send, and then click **OK**.

**To create a SmartArt diagram within an e-mail message**

1. Click to place the insertion point in the message content area.

2. On the **Insert** tab, in the **Illustrations** group, click the **SmartArt** button.

3. In the **SmartArt** gallery, click the diagram you want to create, and then click **OK**.

**To format the text of an e-mail message**

→ In the message content area, select the text you want to format. Then do one of the following:

- Click formatting buttons on the **Mini toolbar**.
- Click formatting buttons in the **Basic Text** group on the **Message** tab.

**To apply a different theme to an outgoing e-mail message**

1. In the message window, on the **Options** tab, in the **Themes** group, click the **Themes** button.

2. In the **Themes** gallery, click the theme you want.

**To create a signature and insert it in all the new messages**

1. On the **Tools** menu, click **Options**. On the **Mail Format** tab of the **Options** dialog box, click **Signatures**.

2. On the **E-mail Signature** tab of the **Signatures and Stationery** dialog box, click **New**.

3. In the **New Signature** dialog box, type a name for the signature, and then click **OK**.

4. In the signature content area, type a salutation, such as Regards, and a comma. Press the ⌈Enter⌋ key once or twice, and then type your name.

5. Add any other information you want to include, such as a telephone number, legal disclaimer, or link to your organization's Web site, and format the text and paragraphs the way you want them to appear in messages.

6. In the **Choose default signature** area of the **Signatures and Stationery** dialog box, in the **New messages** list, click the name you gave your signature. Then click **OK** twice.

# 19    Managing Your Inbox

**To use Instant Search to locate a specific message**

→ In the **Search** box at the top of the Inbox, type a word contained in the message.

→ To refine the search, click the **Expand the Query Builder** button to the right of the **Search** box, and supply additional information.

→ To expand the search to include all the folders in your mailbox, at the bottom of the Search Results pane, click **Try searching again in All Mail Items**.

→ To remove the search filter and view all messages, click the **Clear Search** button.

**To change the display, arrangement, sort order, and grouping of messages**

→ On the **View** menu, point to **Arrange By**, and then click the command you want; or

➡ Click the column heading on which you want to sort messages. Click it again to reverse the order.

**To expand or collapse groups**

➡ On the **View** menu, point to **Expand/Collapse Groups**, and then click the collapse or expand view you want.

**To filter the Inbox content**

➡ On the **View** menu, point to **Current View**, and then click the view you want. Click **Messages** on the **Current View** list to remove the filter.

**To add and remove fields**

1. On the **View** menu, point to **Current View**, and then click **Customize Current View**.

2. In the **Customize View** dialog box, click the **Fields** button.

3. To add fields, in the **Available fields** list of the **Show Fields** dialog box, click the fields you want to add, and then click **Add**.

4. To remove fields in any list view, drag the column heading downward, and release the mouse button when a large black X appears over the heading.

**To change the order of columns in any view**

➡ Drag the column headings to the locations you prefer.

**To restore the default Inbox settings**

1. On the **View** menu, point to **Current View**, and then click **Define Views**.

2. In the **Custom View Organizer** dialog box, click **Reset**. In the **Microsoft Office Outlook** message box asking whether you want to reset the current view to its original settings, click **OK**.

3. Reset any customized views you want by clicking the view name and then clicking **Reset**. When you finish, click the **Messages** view, and then click **Apply View**.

**To create a custom Search Folder**

1. In the **Navigation Pane**, right-click the **Search Folders** folder, and then click **New Search Folder**.

2. In the **New Search Folder** dialog box, scroll the **Select a Search Folder** list to see the available options, select the option you want, and then click **OK**.

**To make changes to the contents of an existing Search Folder**

➡ Right-click the folder, and then click **Customize this Search Folder**.

**To display the default color categories**

➜ In the Inbox, click a message you want to categorize, and then on the Standard toolbar, click the **Categorize** button.

**To rename categories**

1. On the Standard toolbar, click the **Categorize** button, and in the **Category** list, click **All Categories**.

2. In the **Color Categories** dialog box, click the category (not the check box), and then click **Rename**.

3. Type the name you want, and then press Enter.

**To change the color associated with a category**

1. On the Standard toolbar, click the **Categorize** button, and in the **Category** list, click **All Categories**.

2. In the **Color Categories** dialog box, click the category you want.

3. In the **Color** palette, click the icon of the color you want.

**To create categories**

1. On the Standard toolbar, click the **Categorize** button, and in the **Category** list, click **All Categories**.

2. In the **Color Categories** dialog box, click **New**.

3. In the **Name** box of the **Add New Category** dialog box, type the name you want to give the category. Then if you want, assign a color and a shortcut key.

**To sort the Inbox contents by category**

1. At the top of the Inbox, click the **Arranged By** bar, and then click **Categories**.

2. To the right of the **Arranged By** bar, click the command you want.

**To create a folder**

1. On the Standard toolbar, in the **New** list, click **Folder**.

2. In the **Name** box of the **Create New Folder** dialog box, type the folder name, and then click **OK**.

**To move messages to a folder**

➜ Drag the message to the desired folder in the **Navigation Pane**.

Or

1. Right-click the message, and then click **Move to Folder**.

2. In the **Move Items** dialog box, in the **Move the selected items to the folder** list, click the folder where you want to move the message, and then click **OK**.

**To send the content of an e-mail message to OneNote**

→ Select the message, and then on the Standard toolbar, click the **Send selected e-mail to OneNote** button.

**To set the default automatic archive options**

1. On the **Tools** menu, click **Options**. On the **Other** tab of the **Options** dialog box, click **AutoArchive**.

2. Make the changes you want to your AutoArchive settings, then click **OK** in each of the open dialog boxes.

**To manually archive a folder**

1. Click the folder you want to archive. Then on the **File** menu, click **Archive**.

2. In the **Archive** dialog box, select the **Archive this folder and all subfolders** option, and then click **OK**.

**To set the archive options for an individual folder**

1. Right-click the folder in the **Navigation Pane**, and then click **Properties**.

2. On the **AutoArchive** tab of the **Properties** dialog box, set the archive options you want, and then click **OK**.

# 20   Managing Appointments, Events, and Meetings

**To schedule an appointment**

1. In the Calendar, display the date on which you want to schedule an appointment.

2. Click the desired time slot, type information about the appointment, and then press Enter .

3. To change the end time for the appointment, drag the bottom border of the time slot down to the bottom of the end time.

**To reschedule an appointment**

→ Drag the appointment to a different time slot on the calendar.

**To make an appointment recurring**

1. Open the appointment. Then on the **Appointment** tab, in the **Options** group, click the **Recurrence** button.

2. In the **Recurrence pattern** area of the **Appointment Recurrence** dialog box, select the option that corresponds to the desired recurrence, and then click **OK**.

3. On the **Recurring Appointment** tab, in the **Actions** group, click the **Save & Close** button.

**To schedule an event**

1. In the **Date Navigator**, click the date on which you want to schedule an event, and then in the **Calendar** pane, click the blank space below the day header and above the time slots.

2. Type the name of the event, and then press Enter.

**To make an event recurring**

1. Double-click the event, and then on the **Event** tab, in the **Options** group, click the **Recurrence** button.

2. In the **Recurrence pattern** area of the **Appointment Recurrence** dialog box, select the option that corresponds to the recurrence you want, and then click **OK**.

3. On the **Recurring Event** tab, in the **Actions** group, click the **Save & Close** button.

**To create and send a meeting request**

1. In the **Date Navigator**, click the date on which you want the meeting to occur.

2. On the Standard toolbar, in the **New Appointment** list, click **Meeting Request**.

3. In the **To** box, type the e-mail addresses of the meeting attendees; in the **Subject** box, type the name of the meeting; and in the **Location** box, indicate where the meeting will take place.

4. On the **Meeting** tab, in the **Show** group, click the **Scheduling** button. Then set the meeting time, and click **Send**.

**To manually respond to a meeting request**

1. In the **Date Navigator**, double-click the scheduled meeting.

2. In the meeting request window, in the **Reading Pane**, click **Accept**, **Tentative**, or **Decline**.

3. Choose whether to send a standard response, a personalized response, or no response at all.

**To propose a new time for a meeting**

1. In the **Reading Pane** of the meeting request window, click **Propose New Time**.

2. In the schedule area of the **Propose New Time** dialog box, set the proposed meeting start and end times, and then click **Propose Time**.

3. In the meeting response window that opens, enter a message to the meeting organizer, and then click **Send**.

**To instruct Outlook to automatically respond to meeting requests**

1. On the **Tools** menu, click **Options**. On the **Preferences** tab of the **Options** dialog box, click **Calendar Options**.

2. In the **Calendar Options** dialog box, click **Resource Scheduling**.

3. In the **Resource Scheduling** dialog box, select the **Automatically accept meeting requests and process cancellations** check box.

4. Select the **Automatically decline conflicting meeting requests** and/or the **Automatically decline recurring meeting requests** check boxes if you want Outlook to do this.

5. Click **OK** in each of the open dialog boxes.

# 21  Managing Your Calendar

**To add the holidays of other countries to your calendar**

1. On the **Tools** menu, click **Options**. On the **Preferences** tab of the **Options** dialog box, click **Calendar Options**.

2. In the **Calendar Options** dialog box, click **Add Holidays**.

3. In the **Add Holidays to Calendar** dialog box, select the check boxes of the countries whose holidays you want to add, and then click **OK** in each open dialog box.

**To remove holidays from your calendar**

1. In Calendar view, on the **View** menu, point to **Current View**, and then click **All Appointments**.

2. On the **View** menu, point to **Current View**, and click **Customize Current View**. Then in the **Customize View** dialog box, click **Group By**.

3. In the **Group By** dialog box, clear the **Automatically group according to arrangement** check box if it is selected. Then in the **Group items by** list, click **Location**.

4. Ensure that all the **Then by** lists display **(none)**, and then click **OK** in each of the open dialog boxes.

5. In the **Calendar** pane, collapse the displayed groups or scroll the pane until the **Location** group of the holidays you want to remove is visible. Then do the following:

   ● To remove a specific holiday, click it, and then press `Del`.

   ● To remove all the holidays of the displayed country, click the **Location** group header, and then press `Tab`. If a **Microsoft Office Outlook** message box warns you that this action will apply to all items in the selected group, click **OK**.

**To change your work week**

1. Display your calendar in **Week** view, and at the top of the **Calendar** pane, select the **Show work week** option.

2. On the **Tools** menu, click **Options**. On the **Preferences** tab of the **Options** dialog box, click **Calendar Options**.

3. In the **Calendar work week** area of the **Calendar Options** dialog box, select or clear the check boxes of the days of the week.

4. Set the start and end times, and then click **OK** in the open dialog boxes.

**To change the time zone**

1. On the **Tools** menu, click **Options**. On the **Preferences** tab of the **Options** dialog box, click **Calendar Options**.

2. In the **Calendar Options** dialog box, click **Time Zone**.

3. In the **Time zone** list, click the time zone you want. Then click **OK** in each of the open dialog boxes.

**To simultaneously display two time zones in your Calendar**

1. On the **Tools** menu, click **Options**. On the **Preferences** tab of the **Options** dialog box, click **Calendar Options**.

2. In the **Calendar Options** dialog box, click **Time Zone**.

3. In the **Time Zone** dialog box, select the **Show an additional time zone** check box. Then in the second **Time zone** list, click the additional time zone you want to display.

4. Type a label for each time zone in its corresponding **Label** box, and then click **OK** in each of the open dialog boxes.

**To preview and print your calendar**

1. On the **View** menu, click **Day**.

2. On the Standard toolbar, click the **Print** button. Then in the **Print** dialog box, click **Preview**.

3. On the **Print Preview** toolbar, click the **Print** button to redisplay the **Print** dialog box.

4. In the **Print style** list, click the style of printing you want.

5. In the **Print range** area, set the first and last dates you want to print, and then click **OK**.

**To save calendar information as a Web page**

1. Display your calendar, and then on the **File** menu, click **Save as Web Page**.

2. In the **Save as Web Page** dialog box, enter the start and end dates for which you want to publish calendar information.

3. In the **Options** area, select whether to include appointment details or a background graphic.

4. In the **Save as** area, append a file name (the extension is unnecessary) at the end of the path shown in the **File name** box. If you want, change the title that will be displayed on the Web page and the location where Outlook saves it.

5. With the **Open saved web page in browser** check box selected, click **Save**.

**To embed information about your schedule in an e-mail message**

1. Display your calendar, and then in the **Navigation Pane**, under **Other Calendars**, click **Send a Calendar via E-mail**.

2. In the **Send a Calendar via E-mail** dialog box, in the **Date Range** list, click the command you want.

3. In the **Detail** list, click the option you want.

4. Click **Advanced**, set any options you want, and then click **OK**.

**To link one or more calendar entries to OneNote**

→ Select the calendar item (or items) you want to link. Then on the Standard toolbar, click the **Open or create linked notes in OneNote** button.

**To link to an Internet calendar**

1. In the **Calendar** module **Navigation Pane**, scroll the **All Calendar Items** list to the **Other Calendars** section, and then click **Search Calendars Online**.

2. On the **Internet Calendars** page, scroll to the **Subscribe to a Free Internet Calendar** section, and then click the Internet calendar you want.

3. If an **Internet Explorer Security** message box prompts you to allow Outlook to open Web content, click the **Allow** button.

4. In the **Microsoft Office Outlook** message box asking whether you want to add the calendar to Outlook and subscribe to updates, click **Yes**.

**To view multiple calendars side by side and as a composite**

1. In either the **My Calendars** or **Other Calendars** list in the **Navigation Pane**, select the check box for at least one other calendar.

2. On the title bar tab of a secondary calendar, click the **View in Overlay Mode** button.

3. Click either **Calendar** tab to display that calendar on top of the other calendar.

4. On either of the overlaid calendars, click the **View in Side-By-Side Mode** button to return to the standard display.

**To delegate control of your calendar so that meeting requests can be created and responded to on your behalf**

1. On the **Tools** menu, click **Options**. On the **Delegates** tab of the **Options** dialog box, click **Add**.

2. In the **Add Users** dialog box, click the person you want to delegate control to, click **Add**, and then click **OK**.

3. In the **Delegate Permissions** dialog box, in the **Calendar** list, click the level of permission you want to delegate.

4. Select the **Automatically send a message to delegate summarizing these permissions** check box, and then click **OK** in each of the open dialog boxes.

# Part I

# Microsoft Office
# Word 2007

# Chapter at a Glance

Work in the Word
environment, **page 4**

Display
different
views of a
document,
**page 17**

Preview and
print a
document,
**page 29**

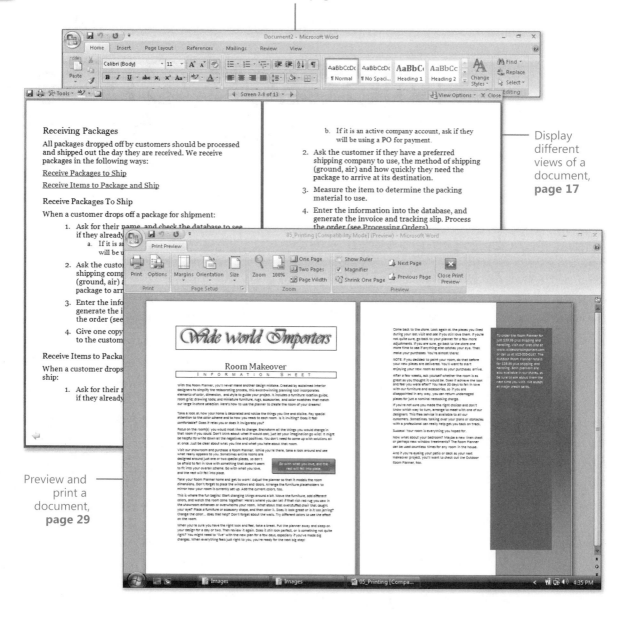

# 1 Exploring Word 2007

---

**In this chapter, you will learn to:**

✔ Work in the Word environment.

✔ Open, move around in, and close a document.

✔ Display different views of a document.

✔ Create and save a document.

✔ Preview and print a document.

---

When you use a computer program to create, edit, and produce text documents, you are *word processing*. Microsoft Office Word 2007 is one of the most sophisticated word-processing programs available today. With Word 2007, it is easier than ever to efficiently create a wide range of business and personal documents, from the simplest letter to the most complex report. Word includes many *desktop publishing* features that you can use to enhance the appearance of documents so that they are appealing and easy to read. The program has been completely redesigned to make these and other powerful features more accessible. As a result, even novice users will be able to work productively in Word after only a brief introduction.

In this chapter, you will first familiarize yourself with the Word working environment. Then you will open an existing Word document, learn ways of moving around in it, and close it. You will explore various ways of viewing documents so that you know which view to use for different tasks and how to tailor the program window to meet your needs. You will create and save a new document and then save an existing document in a different location. Finally, you will preview and print a document.

**See Also** Do you need only a quick refresher on the topics in this chapter? See the Quick Reference entries at the beginning of this book.

> **Important** Before you can use the practice files in this chapter, you need to install them from the book's companion CD to their default location. See "Using the Book's CD" at the beginning of this book for more information.

> **Troubleshooting** Graphics and operating system–related instructions in this book reflect the Windows Vista user interface. If your computer is running Microsoft Windows XP and you experience trouble following the instructions as written, please refer to the "Information for Readers Running Windows XP" section at the beginning of this book.

# Working in the Word Environment

As with all programs in the 2007 Microsoft Office release, the most common way to start Word is from the Start menu displayed when you click the Start button at the left end of the Microsoft Windows taskbar. If Word is the first program in the 2007 Office system that you have used, you are in for a surprise! The look of the program window has changed radically from previous versions.

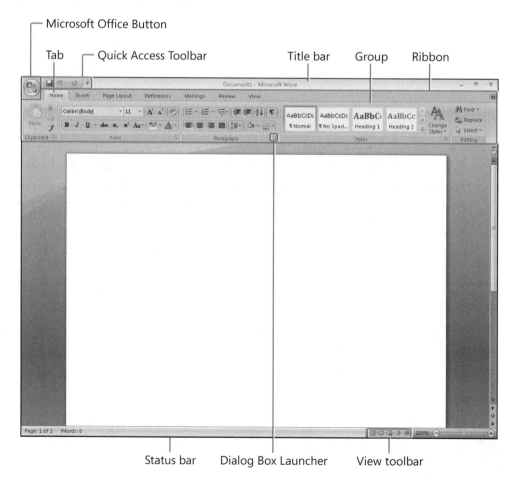

Microsoft Office Button

Tab — Quick Access Toolbar     Title bar    Group    Ribbon

Status bar     Dialog Box Launcher     View toolbar

> **Tip**  What you see on your screen might not match the graphics in this book exactly. The screens in this book were captured on a monitor set to a resolution of 1024 by 768 pixels with the Windows taskbar is hidden to increase the display space.

The new Word environment is designed to more closely reflect the way people generally work with the program. When you first start Word, this environment consists of the following elements:

Microsoft Office
Button

● Commands related to managing Word and Word documents as a whole (rather than document content) are gathered together on a menu that is displayed when you click the *Microsoft Office Button*.

● Commands can be represented as buttons on the *Quick Access Toolbar* to the right of the Microsoft Office Button. By default, this toolbar displays the Save, Undo, and Repeat buttons, but you can customize the toolbar to include any command that you use frequently.

● The *title bar* displays the name of the active document. At the right end of the title bar are the three familiar buttons that have the same function in all Windows programs. You can temporarily hide the Word window by clicking the Minimize button, adjust the size of the window with the Restore Down/Maximize button, and close the active document or quit Word with the Close button.

● Below the title bar is the *Ribbon*, which makes all the capabilities of Word available in a single area so that you can work efficiently with the program.

● Commands related to working with document content are represented as buttons on the *tabs* that make up the Ribbon. The Home tab is active by default. Clicking one of the other tabs, such as Insert, displays that tab's buttons.

> **Tip**  If Microsoft Outlook with Business Contact Manager is installed on your computer, you will have a Business Tools tab in addition to those shown in our graphics.

● On each tab, buttons are organized into *groups*. Depending on the size of the program window, in some groups the button you are likely to use most often is bigger than the rest.

> **Tip** Depending on your screen resolution and the size of the program window, a tab might not have enough room to display all of its groups. In that case, the name of the group resembles a button, and clicking the button displays the group's commands.

Dialog Box
Launcher

- Related but less common commands are not represented as buttons in the group. Instead they are available in a dialog box, which you can display by clicking the *Dialog Box Launcher* at the right end of the group's title bar.

- Some button names are displayed and some aren't. Pausing the mouse pointer over any button for a few seconds (called *hovering*) displays a *ScreenTip* with not only the button's name but also its function.

- Some buttons have arrows, but not all arrows are alike. If you point to a button and both the button and its arrow are in the same box and are the same color, clicking the button will display options for refining the action of the button. If you point to a button and the button is in one box and its arrow is in a different box with a different shade, clicking the button will carry out that action with the button's current settings. If you want to change those settings, you need to click the arrow to see the available options.

- The *Microsoft Office Word Help button* appears at the right end of the Ribbon.

- You create a document in the *document window*. When more than one document is open, each document has its own window.

- Across the bottom of the program window, the *status bar* gives you information about the current document. You can turn off the display of an item of information by right-clicking the status bar and then clicking that item.

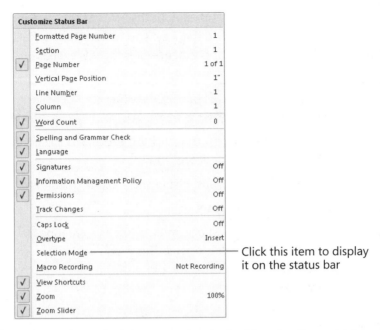

Click this item to display it on the status bar

- At the right end of the status bar is the *View toolbar*, which provides tools for adjusting the view of document content.

**See Also** For information about adjusting the view of a document, see "Displaying Different Views of a Document" later in this chapter.

The goal of the redesigned environment is to make working on a document more intuitive. Commands for tasks you perform often are no longer hidden on menus and in dialog boxes, and features that you might not have discovered before are now more visible.

For example, when a formatting option has several choices available, they are often displayed in a *gallery* of *thumbnails*. These galleries give you an at-a-glance picture of each choice. If you point to a thumbnail in a gallery, an awesome new feature called *live preview* shows you what that choice will look like if you apply it to your document.

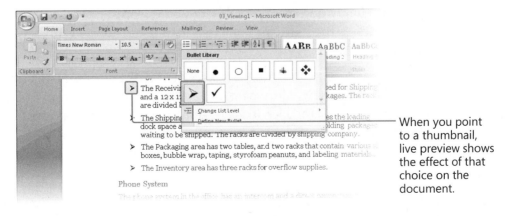

When you point to a thumbnail, live preview shows the effect of that choice on the document.

In this exercise, you will start Word and explore the Microsoft Office Button and the tabs and groups on the Ribbon. Along the way, you will see how to take advantage of galleries and live preview. There are no practice files for this exercise.

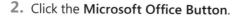
**BE SURE TO** start your computer, but don't start Word yet.

**Start**

**1.** On the taskbar, click the **Start** button, click **All Programs**, click **Microsoft Office**, and then click **Microsoft Office Word 2007**.

The Word program window opens, displaying a blank document.

Microsoft Office
Button

**2.** Click the **Microsoft Office Button**.

Commands related to managing documents (such as creating, saving, and printing) are available from the menu that opens. This menu, which we refer to throughout this book as the *Office menu*, takes the place of the File menu that appeared in previous versions of Word.

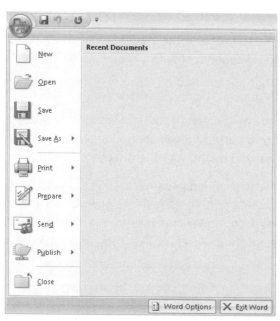

The commands on the left are for tasks related to the document as a whole. After you have worked with a document, its name appears in the Recent Documents list so that you can quickly open it again. At the bottom of the menu are buttons for changing program options and for quitting Word.

**3.** Press the `Esc` key to close the menu.

On the Ribbon, the Home tab is active. Buttons related to working with document content are organized on this tab in five groups: Clipboard, Font, Paragraph, Styles, and Editing. Only the buttons representing commands that can be performed on the currently selected document element are active.

**4.** Hover the mouse pointer over the active buttons on this tab to display the ScreenTips that name them and describe their functions.

> **Important** Depending on your screen resolution and the size of the program window, you might see more or fewer buttons in each of the groups, or the buttons you see might be represented by larger or smaller icons than those shown in this book. Experiment with the size of the program window to understand the effect on the appearance of the tabs.

**5.** Click the **Insert** tab, and then explore its buttons.

Buttons related to all the items you can insert are organized on this tab in seven groups: Pages, Tables, Illustrations, Links, Header & Footer, Text, and Symbols.

**6.** Click the **Page Layout** tab, and then explore its buttons.

Buttons related to the appearance of your document are organized on this tab in five groups: Themes, Page Setup, Page Background, Paragraph, and Arrange.

Margins

Dialog Box
Launcher

**7.** In the **Page Setup** group, display the ScreenTip for the **Margins** button.

The ScreenTip tells you how you can adjust the margins.

**8.** At the right end of the **Page Setup** group's title bar, click the **Page Setup** Dialog Box Launcher.

The Page Setup dialog box opens.

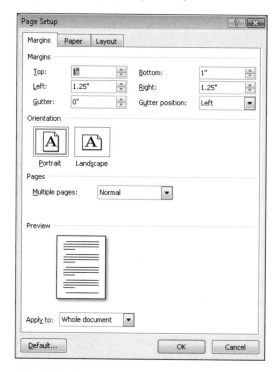

The dialog box provides a single location where you can set the margins and orientation, and specify the setup of a multi-page document. You can preview the results of your changes before applying them.

**9.** Click **Cancel** to close the dialog box.

**10.** In the **Themes** group, click the **Themes** button.

You see a gallery of thumbnails of the available themes.

Themes

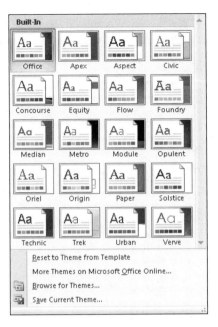

**11.** Press `Esc` to close the gallery without making a selection.

**12.** In the **Page Background** group, click the **Page Color** button, and then in the top row of the **Theme Colors** palette, point to each box in turn.

The blank document page shows a live preview of what it will look like if you click the color you are pointing to. You can see the effect of the selection without actually applying it.

**13.** Press `Esc` to close the palette without making a selection.

**14.** Click the **References** tab, and then explore its buttons.

Buttons related to items you can add to long documents, such as reports, are organized on this tab in six groups: Table Of Contents, Footnotes, Citations & Bibliography, Captions, Index, and Table Of Authorities.

**15.** Click the **Mailings** tab, and then explore its buttons.

Buttons related to creating mass mailings are organized on this tab in five groups: Create, Start Mail Merge, Write & Insert Fields, Preview Results, and Finish.

**16.** Click the **Review** tab, and then explore its buttons.

Buttons related to proofing, commenting, and changing documents are organized on this tab in six groups: Proofing, Comments, Tracking, Changes, Compare, and Protect.

**17.** Click the **View** tab, and then explore its buttons.

Buttons related to changing the view or the display of documents are organized on this tab in five groups: Document Views, Show/Hide, Zoom, Window, and Macros.

# Opening, Moving Around in, and Closing a Document

To open an existing document, you click the Microsoft Office Button and then click Open to display the Open dialog box. The first time you use this command, the dialog box displays the contents of your Documents folder. If you display the dialog box again in the same Word session, it displays the contents of whatever folder you last used. To see the contents of a different folder, you use standard Windows techniques. After you locate the file you want to work with, you can double-click it to open it.

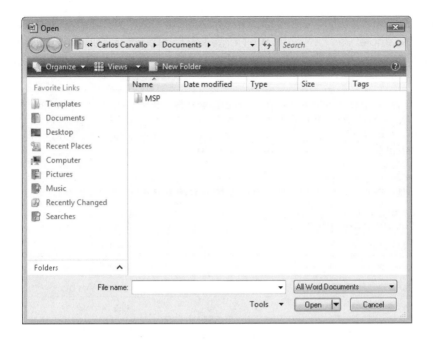

**Tip** Clicking a file name and then clicking the Open arrow in the lower-right corner of the Open dialog box displays a list of alternative ways in which you can open the file. To look through the document without making any inadvertent changes, you can open the file as *read-only*, or you can open an independent copy of the file. You can open an file in a Web browser, or open an XML file with a transform. In the event of a computer crash or other similar incident, you can tell Word to open the file and attempt to repair any damage. And you can display earlier versions of the file.

To move around in an open document without changing the location of the insertion point, you can use the vertical and horizontal scroll bars in the following ways:

- Click the scroll arrows to move the document window up or down by a line, or left or right by a few characters.

- Click above or below the vertical scroll box to move up or down one windowful, or to the left or right of the horizontal scroll box to move left or right one windowful.

- Drag the scroll box on the scroll bar to display the part of the document corresponding to the location of the scroll box. For example, dragging the scroll box to the middle of the scroll bar displays the middle of the document.

You can also move around in a document in ways that do move the insertion point. To place the insertion point at a particular location, you simply click there. To move the insertion point back or forward a page, you can click the Previous Page and Next Page buttons below the vertical scroll bar.

You can also press a key or a *key combination* on the keyboard to move the insertion point. For example, you can press the Home key to move the insertion point to the left end of a line or press Ctrl+Home to move it to the beginning of the document.

> **Tip** The location of the insertion point is displayed on the status bar. By default, the status bar tells you which page the insertion point is on, but you can also display its location by section, line, and column, and in inches from the top of the page. Simply right-click the status bar, and then click the option you want to display.

This table lists ways to use your keyboard to move the insertion point.

| To move the insertion point... | Press... |
| --- | --- |
| Left one character | Left Arrow |
| Right one character | Right Arrow |
| Down one line | Down Arrow |
| Up one line | Up Arrow |
| Left one word | Ctrl+Left Arrow |
| Right one word | Ctrl+Right Arrow |
| To the beginning of the current line | Home |
| To the end of the current line | End |
| To the beginning of the document | Ctrl+End |
| To the beginning of the previous page | Ctrl+Page Up |
| To the beginning of the next page | Ctrl+Page Down |
| Up one screen | Page Down |
| Down one screen | Page Up |

In a long document, you might want to move quickly among elements of a certain type; for example, from graphic to graphic. You can click the Select Browse Object button at the bottom of the vertical scroll bar  and then make a choice in the palette of browsing options that appears, such as Browse by Page or Browse by Graphic.

If more than one document is open, you can close it by clicking the Close button at the right end of the title bar. If only one document is open, clicking the Close button closes the document and also quits Word. If you want to close the document but leave Word open, you must click the Microsoft Office Button and then click Close.

In this exercise, you will open an existing document and explore various ways of moving around in it. Then you will close the document.

**USE** the *02_Opening* document. This practice file is located in the *Chapter01* subfolder under *SBS_Office2007*.

Microsoft Office
Button

1. Click the **Microsoft Office Button**, and then click **Open**.

   The Open dialog box opens, showing the contents of the folder you used for your last open or save action.

2. If the contents of the *Documents* folder are not displayed, in the **Navigation Pane**, click **Documents**.

3. Double-click the **MSP** folder, double-click the **SBS_Office2007** folder, and then double-click the **Chapter01** folder.

4. Click the *02_Opening* document, and then click the **Open** button.

   The *02_Opening* document opens in the Word program window.

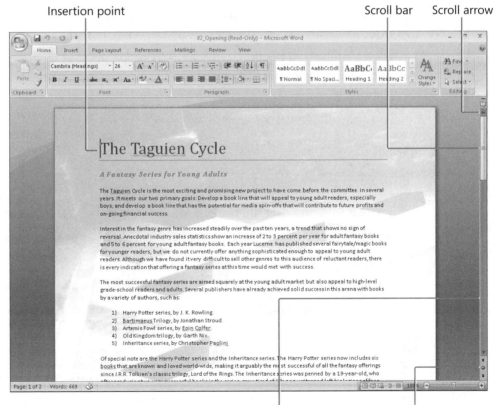

Insertion point · Scroll bar · Scroll arrow · Vertical scroll bar · Select Browse Object button

5. In the second line of the document title, click at the end of the paragraph to position the insertion point.

6. Press the `Home` key to move the insertion point to the beginning of the line.

7. Press the `→` key two times to move the insertion point to the beginning of the word *Fantasy* in the heading.

8. Press the `End` key to move the insertion point to the end of the line.

9. Press `Ctrl`+`End` to move the insertion point to the end of the document.

10. Press `Ctrl`+`Home` to move the insertion point to the beginning of the document.

11. At the bottom of the vertical scroll bar, click the **Next Page** button.

Next Page

12. Click above the vertical scroll box to change the view of the document by one windowful.

13. Drag the vertical scroll box to the top of the vertical scroll bar.

   The beginning of the document comes into view. Note that the location of the insertion point has not changed—just the view of the document.

14. Click to the left of the title to place the insertion point at the top of the document, and then at the bottom of the vertical scroll bar, click the **Select Browse Object** button.

Select Browse Object

   A palette of browse choices opens.

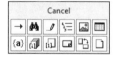

15. Move the pointer over the buttons representing the objects you can browse among.

   As you point to each button, the name of the object appears at the top of the palette.

16. Click the **Browse by Page** button.

Browse by Page

   The insertion point moves from the beginning of Page 1 to the beginning of Page 2.

17. Click the **Microsoft Office Button**, and then click **Close**.

> **Troubleshooting**  If you click the Close button at the right end of the title bar instead of clicking the Microsoft Office Button and then clicking Close, you will close the open Word document and quit the Word program. To continue working, start Word again.

**Compatibility with Earlier Versions**

Word 2007 uses a different file format than previous versions of the program. You can open a document created with previous versions, but the new features of Word 2007 will not be available. The name of the document appears in the title bar with [Compatibility Mode] to its right. You can work in Compatibility Mode, or you can convert the document to the Word 2007 file format by clicking the Microsoft Office Button, and clicking Convert. You can then click the Save button on the Quick Access Toolbar to overwrite the existing document, or click Save As on the Office menu to save the document in the new format as a different file.

You cannot open a Word 2007 document in a previous version of Word unless you install the Compatibility Pack for the 2007 Office system, which is available for free download from Microsoft Office Online. After installing the Compatibility Pack, you can open and work with Word 2007 documents, but you cannot open Word 2007 templates.

# Displaying Different Views of a Document

In Word, you can view a document in a variety of ways:

- *Print Layout view*. This view displays a document on the screen the way it will look when printed. You can see elements such as margins, page breaks, headers and footers, and watermarks.

- *Full Screen Reading view*. This view displays as much of the content of the document as will fit on the screen at a size that is comfortable for reading. In this view, the Ribbon is replaced by a single toolbar at the top of the screen with buttons that you can use to save and print the document, access references and other tools, highlight text, and make comments. You can also move from page to page and adjust the view.

- *Web Layout view*. This view displays a document on the screen the way it will look when viewed in a Web browser. You can see backgrounds, AutoShapes, and other effects. You can also see how text wraps to fit the window and how graphics are positioned.

- *Outline view*. This view displays the structure of a document as nested levels of headings and body text, and provides tools for viewing and changing its hierarchy.

**See Also**   For information about outlining, see "Reorganizing a Document Outline" in Chapter 2, "Editing and Proofreading Documents."

● *Draft view.* This view displays the content of a document with a simplified layout so that you can type and edit quickly. You cannot see layout elements such as headers and footers.

You switch among views by using buttons in the Document Views group on the View tab or by using the buttons on the View toolbar in the lower-right corner of the window.

You can use other buttons on the View tab to do the following:

● Display rulers and gridlines to help you position and align elements

● Display a separate pane containing the *Document Map*—a list of the headings that make up the structure of the document—while viewing and editing its text.

● Display a separate pane containing *thumbnails* of the document's pages.

● Arrange and work with windows.

● Change the magnification of the document.

You can also adjust the magnification of the document by using tools on the View toolbar at the right end of the status bar. You can click the Zoom button and select (or type) a percentage; drag the slider to the left or right; or click the Zoom Out or Zoom In button at either end of the slider.

When you are creating more complex documents, it is easier to place elements exactly if you turn on the display of non-printing characters. These characters fall into two categories: those that control the layout of your document and those that provide the structure for behind-the-scenes processes such as indexing. You can turn the display of non-printing characters on and off by clicking the Show/Hide ¶ button in the Paragraph group on the Home tab.

> **Tip**   You can hide any text by selecting it, clicking the Font Dialog Box Launcher at the right end of the Font group's title bar on the Home tab, selecting the Hidden check box, and clicking OK. When the Show/Hide ¶ button is turned on, hidden text is visible and is identified in the document by a dotted underline.

In this exercise, you will first explore various ways that you can customize Print Layout view to make the work of developing documents more efficient. You will turn white space on and off, zoom in and out, display the rulers and Document Map, and view non-printing characters and text. Then you will switch to other views, noticing the differences so that you have an idea of which one is most appropriate for which task. Finally, you will switch between open documents and view documents in more than one window at the same time.

> **USE** the *03_Viewing1* and *03_Viewing2* documents. These practice files are located in the *Chapter01* subfolder under *SBS_Office2007*.
>
> **OPEN** the *03_Viewing1* document.

1. In Print Layout view, scroll through the document.

   As you can see, on all pages but the first, the printed document will have the title in the header at the top of the page, the page number in the right margin, and the date in the footer at the bottom of each page.

2. Point to the gap between any two pages, and when the pointer changes to two opposing arrows, double-click the mouse button. Then scroll through the document again.

   The white space at the top and bottom of each page and the gray space between pages is now hidden.

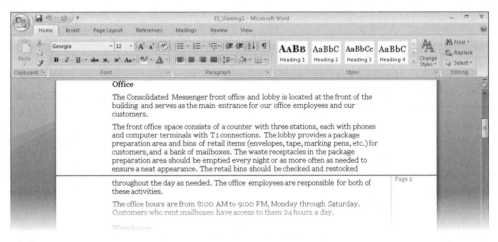

3. Restore the white space by pointing to the black line that separates one page from the next, double-clicking the mouse button.

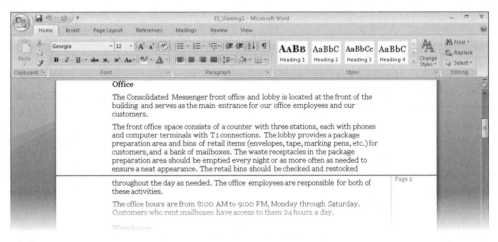
100%

Zoom

4. Press Ctrl + Home to move to the top of the document, and then on the **View** toolbar, click the **Zoom** button.

   The Zoom dialog box opens.

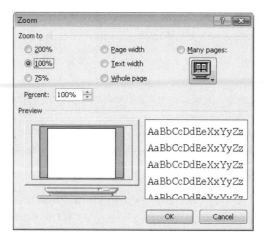

5. Under **Many pages**, click the monitor button, click the second page thumbnail in the top row, and then click **OK**.

The magnification changes so that you can see two pages side by side.

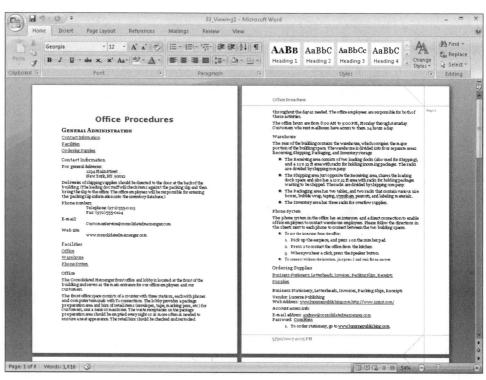

Next Page

6. Below the vertical scroll bar, click the **Next Page** button to display the third and fourth pages of the document.

**7.** On the **View** toolbar, click the **Zoom** button. Then in the **Zoom** dialog box, click **75%**, and click **OK**.

Notice that the Zoom slider position is adjusted to reflect the new setting.

Zoom Out

**8.** At the left end of the **Zoom** slider, click the **Zoom Out** button a couple of times.

As you click the button, the slider moves to the left and the Zoom percentage decreases.

Zoom In

**9.** At the right end of the **Zoom** slider, click the **Zoom In** button until the magnification is 100%.

**10.** On the **View** tab, in the **Show/Hide** group, select the **Ruler** check box.

Horizontal and vertical rulers appear above and to the left of the page. On the rulers, the active area of the page is white and the margins are blue.

**11.** In the **Show/Hide** group, click the **Document Map** check box.

A pane opens on the left side of the screen, displaying an outline of the headings in the document. The first heading on the active page is highlighted.

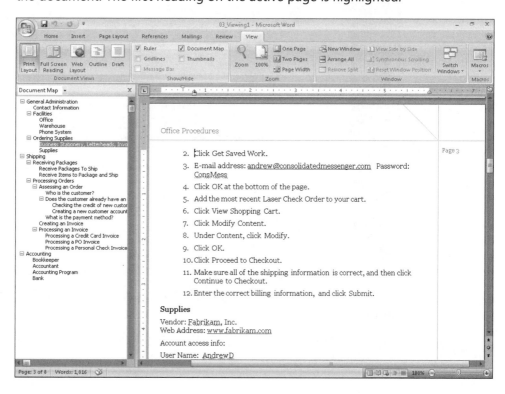

**12.** In the **Document Map**, click the **Shipping** heading.

Word displays the page containing the selected heading.

**13.** In the **Show/Hide** group, click the **Thumbnails** check box, and then scroll the **Thumbnails** pane, and click Page **5**.

Close

**14.** In the **Thumbnails** pane, click the **Close** button.

The pane on the left closes.

Show/Hide ¶

**15.** On the **Home** tab, in the **Paragraph** group, click the **Show/Hide ¶** button.

You can now see non-printing characters such as spaces, tabs, and paragraph marks.

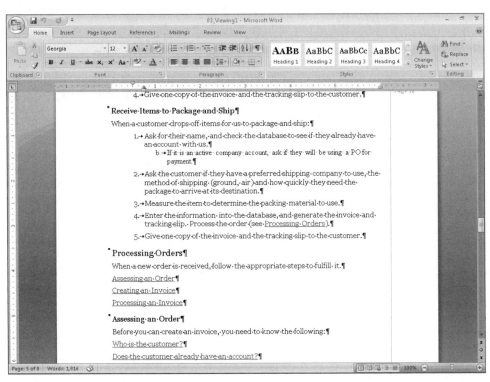

Full Screen Reading

**16.** On the **View** tab, in the **Document Views** group, click the **Full Screen Reading** button.

The screen changes to display the document in a format that makes it easy to read.

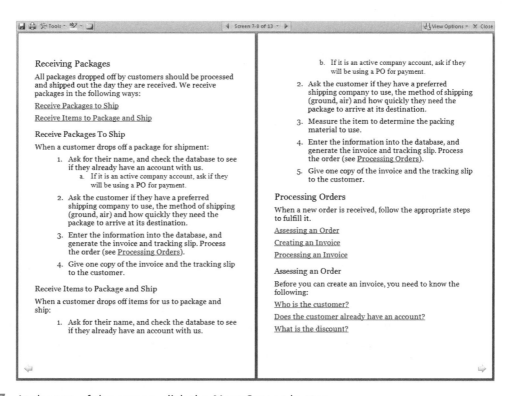

Next Screen

**17.** At the top of the screen, click the **Next Screen** button.

You move to the next two screens of information.

**18.** Explore the other buttons at the top of the Full Screen Reading view, and then click the **Close** button to return to Print Layout view.

Web Layout

**19.** Press Ctrl + Home. Then on the **View** toolbar, click the **Web Layout** button, and scroll through the document.

In a Web browser, the text column will fill the window and there will be no page breaks.

Outline

**20.** Press Ctrl + Home, and then on the **View** toolbar, click the **Outline** button.

The screen changes to show the document's hierarchical structure, and the Outlining tab appears at the left end of the Ribbon.

**21.** On the **Outlining** tab, in the **Outline Tools** group, click the **Show Level** arrow, and in the list, click **Level 2**.

The document collapses to display only the Level 1 and Level 2 headings.

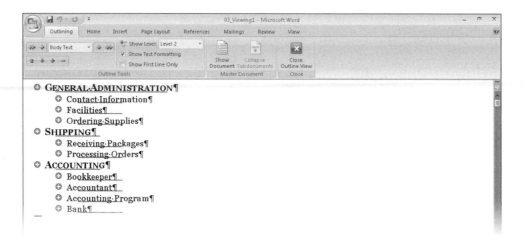

Draft

22. On the **View** toolbar, click the **Draft** button, and then scroll through the document.

    You can see the basic content of the document without any extraneous elements, such as margins and headers and footers. The active area on the ruler indicates the width of the text column, dotted lines indicate page breaks, and scrolling is quick and easy.

23. Click the **Microsoft Office Button**, click **Open**, and then in the **Open** dialog box, double-click *03_Viewing2*.

    The *03_Viewing2* document opens in Print Layout view in its own document window. Notice that the telephone number in the body of the memo has a dotted underline because it is formatted as hidden.

24. On the **Home** tab, in the **Paragraph** group, click the **Show/Hide** ¶ button to turn it off.

    Non-printing characters and hidden text are no longer visible.

25. On the **View** tab, in the **Window** group, click **Switch Windows**, and then click *03_Viewing1*.

    The other open document is displayed in Draft view, with non-printing characters visible.

26. On the **View** tab, in the **Window** group, click the **Arrange All** button.

    The two document windows are sized and stacked one above the other. Each window has a Ribbon, so you can work with each document independently.

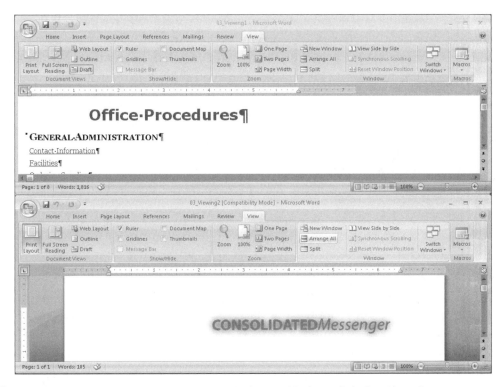

Close

**27.** At the right end of the *03_Viewing1* window's title bar, click the **Close** button.

Clicking the Close button does not quit Word because more than one document is open.

Maximize

**28.** At the right end of the *03_Viewing2* window's title bar, click the **Maximize** button.

The document window expands to fill the screen.

**29.** On the **View** tab, in the **Show/Hide** group, clear the **Ruler** check box to turn off the rulers.

CLOSE the *03_Viewing2* document.

# Creating and Saving a Document

To create a Word document, you simply open a new blank document and type your content. The blinking insertion point shows where the next character you type will appear. When the insertion point reaches the right margin, the word you are typing moves to the next line. Because of this *word wrap* feature, which is common in word-processing and desktop-publishing programs, you press Enter only to start a new paragraph, not a new line.

Each document you create is temporary unless you save it as a file with a unique name or location. To save a document for the first time, you click the Save button on the Quick Access Toolbar or click the Microsoft Office Button and then click Save. Either action displays the Save As dialog box, where you can assign the name and storage location.

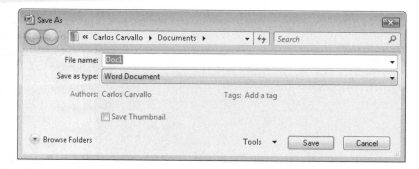

If you want to save the document in a folder other than the one shown in the Address bar, you can click the chevrons to the left of the current folder name and then navigate to the folder you want. You can also click Browse Folders to display the Navigation Pane and a toolbar. If you want to create a new folder in which to store the file, you can click the New Folder button on this toolbar.

After you save a document the first time, you can save changes simply by clicking the Save button. The new version of the document then overwrites the previous version. If you want to keep both the new version and the previous version, click Save As on the Office menu, and then save the new version with a different name in the same location or with the same name in a different location. (You cannot store two files with the same name in the same folder.)

In this exercise, you will enter text in a new document, and you will save the document in a folder that you create. There are no practice files for this exercise.

 **BE SURE TO**   close any open documents before beginning this exercise.

Microsoft Office
Button

1. Click the **Microsoft Office Button**, click **New**, and then in the **New Document** window, double-click **Blank Document**.

   A new document window opens in Print Layout view.

**2.** With the insertion point at the beginning of the new document, type Decorators, Get Ready for Change!, and then press [Enter].

The text appears in the new document.

**3.** Type With spring just around the corner, let's start making those home decor changes you've been thinking about all winter. Let's introduce fresh new color. Let's add some accessories. Let's come up with a great plan for a room to love.

Notice that you did not need to press Enter when the insertion point reached the right margin because the text wrapped to the next line.

> Decorators, Get Ready for Change!
>
> With spring just around the corner, let's start making those home décor changes you've been thinking about all winter. Let's introduce fresh new color. Let's add some accessories. Let's come up with a great plan for a room to love.

> **Tip** If a red wavy line appears under a word or phrase, Word is flagging a possible error. For now, ignore any errors.

**4.** Press [Enter], and then type Here at Wide World Importers, we realize that you need to have the right tools to guarantee a successful room makeover. And with that in mind, we are proud to present the latest addition to our line of decorating tools, the Room Planner.

Save

**5.** On the **Quick Access Toolbar**, click the **Save** button.

The Save As dialog box opens, displaying the contents of the Documents folder. In the File Name box, Word suggests *Decorators*, the first word in the document, as a possible name for this file.

**6.** In the lower-left corner of the dialog box, click Browse Folders.

The dialog box expands to show the Navigation Pane and a toolbar.

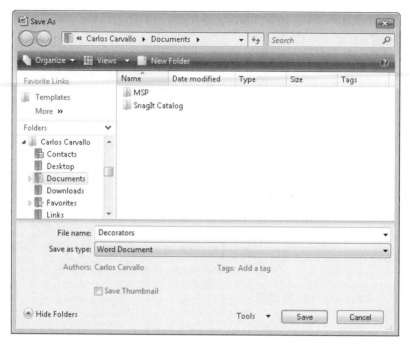

7. Double-click **MSP**, double-click **SBS_Office2007**, and double-click **Chapter01**.

8. On the dialog box's toolbar, click the **New Folder** button, type My New Documents as the name of the new folder, and then press Enter.

   My New Documents is now the current folder in the Save As dialog box.

9. In the **File name** box, double-click the existing entry, and then type My Announcement.

> **Troubleshooting** Programs that run on the Windows operating systems use file name extensions to identify different types of files. For example, the extension *.docx* identifies Word 2007 documents. Windows Vista programs do not display these extensions by default, and you shouldn't type them in the Save As dialog box. When you save a file, Word automatically adds whatever extension is associated with the type of file selected in the Save As Type box.

10. Click **Save**.

    The Save As dialog box closes, Word saves the *My Announcement* file in the *My New Documents* folder, and the name of the document, *My Announcement*, appears on the program window's title bar.

11. Click the **Microsoft Office Button**, and then click **Save As**.

The Save As dialog box opens, displaying the contents of the *My New Documents* folder.

**12.** In the Address bar in the **Save As** dialog box, click the chevrons to the left of *My New Documents*, and then in the list, click **Chapter01**.

The dialog box now displays the contents of the *My New Documents* folder's *parent folder*, *Chapter01*.

**13.** Click **Save**.

Word saves the *My Announcement* file in the *Chapter01* folder. You now have two versions of the document saved with the same name but in different folders.

 **CLOSE** the *My Announcement* file.

> **Tip** By default, Word periodically saves the document you are working on in case the program stops responding or you lose electrical power. To adjust the time interval between saves, click the Microsoft Office Button, click Word Options, click Save in the left pane of the Word Options window, and specify the period of time in the box to the right of the Save AutoRecover Information Every check box. Then click OK.

# Previewing and Printing a Document

When you are ready to print a document, you can click the Microsoft Office Button, point to Print, and then click Quick Print. Word then uses your computer's default printer and the settings specified in the Print dialog box. To use a different printer or change the print settings, you click the Microsoft Office Button, and then click Print to open the Print dialog box. You can then specify which printer to use, what to print, and how many copies, and you can make other changes to the settings.

Before you print a document, you almost always want to check how it will look on paper by previewing it. Previewing is essential for multi-page documents but is helpful even for one-page documents. To preview a document, you click the Microsoft Office Button, point to Print, and then click Print Preview. This view shows exactly how each page of the document will look when printed. Word displays a Print Preview tab on the Ribbon to provide tools for checking each page and making adjustments if you don't like what you see.

By using the buttons in the Page Setup group on the Print Preview tab, you can make the following changes:

- Change the margins of the document to fit more or less information on a page or to control where the information appears. You define the size of the top, bottom, left, and right margins by clicking the Margins button and making a selection from the Margins gallery, or by clicking Custom Margins and specifying settings on the Margins tab of the Page Setup dialog box.

- Switch the *orientation* (the direction in which a page is laid out on the paper). The default orientation is *portrait*, in which the page is taller than it is wide. You can set the orientation to *landscape*, in which the page is wider than it is tall, by clicking the Orientation button and selecting that option.

> **Tip** The pages of a document all have the same margins and are oriented the same way unless you divide your document into sections. Then each section can have independent margin and orientation settings.

- Select the paper size you want to use by clicking the Size button and making a selection in the Paper Size gallery.

You can click buttons in other groups to change the printer options, change the view of the document, and change the mouse pointer so that you can edit the text.

In this exercise, you will preview a document, adjust the margins, change the orientation, and select a new printer before sending the document to be printed.

**USE** the *05_Printing* document. This practice file is located in the *Chapter01* subfolder under *SBS_Office2007*.

**BE SURE TO** install a printer and turn it on before starting this exercise.

**OPEN** the *05_Printing* document.

**Microsoft Office Button**

**1.** Click the **Microsoft Office Button**, point to the **Print** arrow, and then click **Print Preview**.

The window's title bar now indicates that you are viewing a preview of the document, and the Print Preview tab appears on the Ribbon.

**2.** On the **Print Preview** tab, in the **Zoom** group, click the **Two Pages** button.

Word displays the two pages of the document side by side.

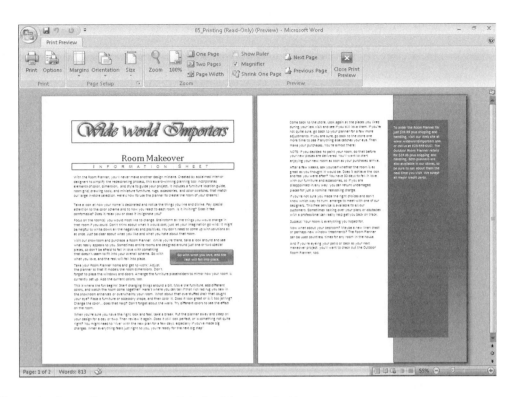

3. In the **Page Setup** group, click the **Margins** button.

   The Margins gallery appears.

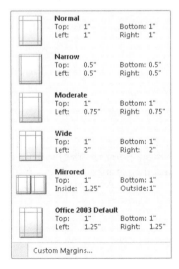

4. In the gallery, click **Wide**.

   The text rewraps within the new margins, and the left end of the status bar indicates that the document now has 3 pages.

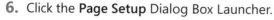

5. In the **Preview** group, click the **Next Page** button to see the last page of the document.

Dialog Box
Launcher

6. Click the **Page Setup** Dialog Box Launcher.

   The Page Setup dialog box opens, displaying the Margins tab.

7. Under **Margins**, replace the value in the **Left** box by typing 1". Then replace the value in the **Right** box with 1", and click **OK**.

   The width of the margins decreases, and the text rewraps to fill 2 pages.

Orientation

8. In the **Page Setup** group, click the **Orientation** button, and then click **Landscape**.

   The pages of the document are now wider than they are tall.

9. Point to the top of the first page of the document so that the pointer becomes a magnifying glass, and then click.

   The first page is magnified. Notice that the Zoom box at the right end of the status bar now displays 100%.

10. Click near the top of the document.

    The Zoom percentage changes, and you now see both pages at the same time.

Close Print
Preview

11. In the **Preview** group, click the **Close Print Preview** button.

    You don't have to be in Print Preview to change the orientation of a document. You can do it in Print Layout view.

 Orientatio

12. On the **Page Layout** tab, in the **Page Setup** group, click the **Orientation** button, and then click **Portrait**.

13. Click the **Microsoft Office Button**, and then click **Print**.

---

**Tip** You can click the Microsoft Office Button, point to Print, and then click Quick Print to print the document without first viewing the settings.

---

The Print dialog box opens.

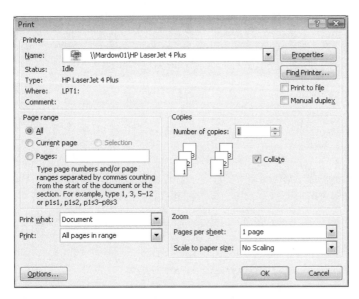

14. If you have more than one printer available and you want to switch printers, click the **Name** arrow, and in the list, click the printer you want.

15. Under **Page Range**, click the **Current Page** option.

16. Under **Copies**, change the **Number of copies** setting to 2, and then click **OK**.

    Word prints two copies of the first page on the designated printer.

**CLOSE** the *05_Printing* document without saving your changes, and if you are not continuing directly on to the next chapter, quit Word.

# Key Points

- You can open more than one Word document, and you can view more than one document at a time, but only one document can be active at a time.

- You create Word documents by typing text at the insertion point. It's easy to move the insertion point by clicking in the text or pressing keys and key combinations.

- When you save a Word document, you specify its name, location, and file format in the Save As dialog box.

- You can view a document in a variety of ways, depending on your needs as you create the document and on the purpose for which you are creating it.

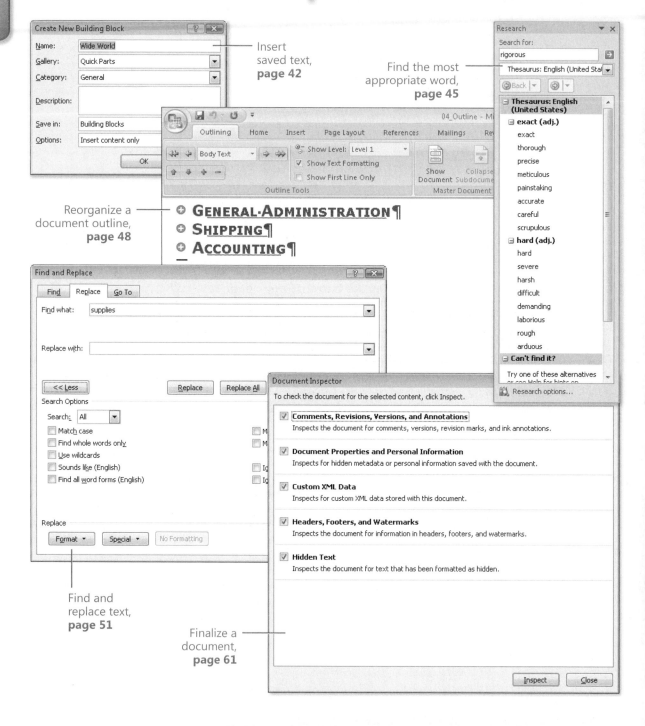

# Chapter at a Glance

Insert saved text, **page 42**

Find the most appropriate word, **page 45**

Reorganize a document outline, **page 48**

Find and replace text, **page 51**

Finalize a document, **page 61**

# 2 Editing and Proofreading Documents

---

**In this chapter, you will learn to:**

✔ Make changes to a document.

✔ Insert saved text.

✔ Find the most appropriate word.

✔ Reorganize a document outline.

✔ Find and replace text.

✔ Correct spelling and grammatical errors.

✔ Finalize a document.

---

Unless the documents you create are intended for no one's eyes but your own, you need to ensure that they are correct, logical, and persuasive. Whether you are a novice writer or an experienced writer, Microsoft Office Word 2007 has several tools that make creating professional documents easy and efficient:

● Editing tools provide quick-selection techniques and drag-and-drop editing to make it easy to move and copy text anywhere you want it.

● The building blocks feature can be used to save and recall specialized terms or standard paragraphs.

● Reference and research tools include a thesaurus that makes it easy to track down synonyms and research services that provide access to a variety of Web-based reference materials.

● Outlining tools allow easy rearranging of headings and text to ensure that your argument is logical.

- Search tools can be used to locate and replace words and phrases, either one at a time or throughout a document.

- The AutoCorrect and Spelling And Grammar features make it easy to correct typos and grammatical errors before you share a document with others.

- Finalizing tools ensure that a document is ready for distribution.

In this chapter, you will edit the text in a document by inserting and deleting text, copying and pasting a phrase, and moving a paragraph. You will save a couple of building blocks, and you'll rearrange a document in Outline view. You will find a phrase and replace one phrase with another throughout the entire document. You'll change an AutoCorrect setting and add a misspelled word to its list. You'll check the spelling and grammar in a document and add a term to the custom dictionary. Finally, you'll inspect a document for inappropriate information and mark it as final.

**See Also**  Do you need only a quick refresher on the topics in this chapter? See the Quick Reference entries at the beginning of this book.

> **Important**  Before you can use the practice files in this chapter, you need to install them from the book's companion CD to their default location. See "Using the Book's CD" at the beginning of this book for more information.

> **Troubleshooting**  Graphics and operating system–related instructions in this book reflect the Windows Vista user interface. If your computer is running Microsoft Windows XP and you experience trouble following the instructions as written, please refer to the "Information for Readers Running Windows XP" section at the beginning of this book.

# Making Changes to a Document

You will rarely write a perfect document that doesn't require any editing. You will almost always want to insert a word or two, change a phrase, or move text from one place to another. You can edit a document as you create it, or you can write it first and then revise it. Or you might want to edit a document that you created for one purpose so that it will serve a different purpose. For example, a letter from last year's marketing campaign might be edited to create a new letter for this year's campaign.

Inserting text is easy; you click to position the insertion point and simply begin typing. Any existing text to the right of the insertion point moves to make room for the new text.

## What Happened to Overtype?

By default, Word is in Insert mode. In previous versions of Word, it was possible to accidentally switch to Overtype mode by inadvertently pressing the Insert key. In Overtype mode, existing text does not move to the right when you type new text; instead, each character you type replaces an existing character.

In Word 2007, you must deliberately switch to Overtype mode if you want to use it. Here's how:

1. Right-click the status bar, and then click **Overtype** to display the Insert mode status at the left end of the status bar.

2. Click **Insert** on the status bar.

   The word *Overtype* then replaces *Insert*. You can click the word to switch back to Insert mode when you have finished overtyping.

By default, pressing the Insert key has no effect on the mode. If you want the Insert key to turn Overtype mode on and off, follow these steps:

1. Click the **Microsoft Office Button**, and then click **Word Options**.

2. In the **Word Options** dialog box, click **Advanced** in the left pane, and then under **Editing options**, select the **Use the Insert key to control overtype mode** check box.

3. Click **OK**.

Deleting text is equally easy. If you want to delete only one or a few characters, you can simply position the insertion point and then press the Backspace or Delete key until the characters are all gone. Pressing Backspace deletes the character to the left of the insertion point; pressing Delete deletes the character to the right of the insertion point.

To delete more than a few characters efficiently, you need to know how to *select* the text. Selected text appears highlighted on the screen. You can select specific items as follows:

- To select a word, double-click it. Word selects the word and the space following it. It does not select punctuation following a word.

- To select a sentence, click anywhere in the sentence while holding down the Ctrl key. Word selects all the characters in the sentence, from the first character through the space following the ending punctuation mark.

- To select a paragraph, triple-click it.

You can select adjacent words, lines, or paragraphs by positioning the insertion point at the beginning of the text you want to select, holding down the Shift key, and then pressing the Arrow keys or clicking at the end of the text that you want to select. If you want to select words, lines, or paragraphs that are not adjacent, you make the first selection and then hold down the Ctrl key while selecting the next block.

As an alternative, you can use the *selection area* to quickly select various items. This is an invisible area in the document's left margin, where the pointer becomes a hollow right-pointing arrow. You can use the selection area as follows:

● To select a line, click the selection area to the left of the line.

● To select a paragraph, double-click the selection area to the left of the paragraph.

● To select an entire document, triple-click the selection area.

The Taguien Cycle
A Fantasy Series for Young Adults

The Taguien Cycle is the most exciting and promising new book project to have come before the committee in several years. It meets our two principal goals: Develop a book line that will appeal to young adult readers between the ages of twelve to fifteen, especially boys; and develop a book line that has the potential for media spin-offs that will contribute to future profits and on-going financial success.

 Each year Lucerne has published several fairytale/magic books for younger readers, but we do not currently offer anything sophisticated enough to appeal to young adult readers. Although we have found it very difficult to sell other genres to this audience of reluctant readers, there is every indication that offering a fantasy series at this time would meet with success.

Interest in the fantasy genre has increased steadily over the past ten years, a trend that shows no sign of reversal. Anecdotal industry sales statistics show an increase of 2 to 3 percent per year for adult fantasy books and 5 to 6 percent for young adult fantasy books

└─ Selection area

After selecting the text you want to work with, simply press the Backspace or Delete key.

**Tip** To deselect text, click anywhere in the document window except the selection area.

After selecting text, you can move or copy it in the following ways:

● Use the *Clipboard* when you need to move or copy text between two locations that you cannot see at the same time—for example, between pages or between documents. The Clipboard is a temporary storage area in your computer's memory. Select the text, and then click the Cut or Copy button in the Clipboard group on the Home tab. Then reposition the insertion point and click the Paste button to insert the selection in its new location. When you cut text, it is removed from its original location, and when you copy it, it also remains in its original location.

**See Also** For more information, see the sidebar entitled "About the Clipboard" later in this topic.

● Use *drag-and-drop editing* (frequently referred to simply as *dragging*) when you need to move or copy text only a short distance—for example, within a paragraph or line. Dragging does not involve the Clipboard. Start by selecting the text. Then hold down the mouse button, drag the text to its new location, and release the mouse button. To copy the selection, hold down the Ctrl key while you drag.

If you make a change to a document and then realize that you made a mistake, you can easily reverse the change. You can undo your last editing action by clicking the Undo button on the Quick Access Toolbar. To undo an earlier action, click the Undo arrow and then click that actions in the list.

> **Tip** Selecting an action from the Undo list undoes that action and all the editing actions you performed after that one. You cannot undo a single action except the last one you performed.

If you undo an action and then change your mind, you can click the Redo button on the Quick Access Toolbar. You can redo only the last action that you undid.

In this exercise, you will edit the text in a document. You'll insert and delete text, undo the deletion, copy and paste a phrase, and move a paragraph.

**USE** the *01_Changes* document. This practice file is located in the *Chapter02* subfolder under *SBS_Office2007*.
**BE SURE TO** start Word before beginning this exercise.
**OPEN** the *01_Changes* document.

Show/Hide ¶

1. If non-printing characters are not visible in the document, on the **Home** tab, in the **Paragraph** group, click the **Show/Hide ¶** button.

2. In the third sentence of the first paragraph, click immediately to the left of the word **between**, hold down the Shift key, and then click immediately to the right of the word **fifteen** (and to the left of the comma that follows it).

Word selects the text between the two clicks.

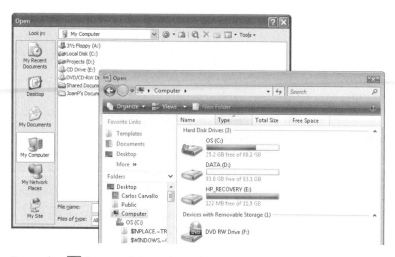

3. Press the ⌈Del⌋ key to delete the selection.

   Word also deletes the space before the selection.

4. Select the word **book** in the first sentence of the first paragraph by double-clicking it, and then press the ⌈Backspace⌋ key.

5. Double-click the word **principal** in the same paragraph, and then replace it by typing primary.

   Notice that you don't have to type a space after *primary*. Word inserts the space for you.

   > **Tip**  Word inserts and deletes spaces because the Use Smart Cut And Paste check box is selected on the Advanced page of the Word Options dialog box. If you want to be able to control the spacing yourself, click the Microsoft Office Button, click Word Options, click Advanced, clear this check box, and click OK.

6. Position the mouse pointer in the selection area to the left of the phrase *A Fantasy Series for Young Adults*, and then click once to select the entire line of text.

Copy

7. On the **Home** tab, in the **Clipboard** group, click the **Copy** button.

   The selection is copied to the Clipboard.

Paste

8. Click the Next Page button below the vertical scroll bar to move to the beginning of the next page, press the ⌈↓⌋ key, and then in the **Clipboard** group, click the **Paste** button (not its arrow).

   The Paste Options button appears below and to the right of the insertion. You can click this button if you want to change Word's default way of pasting, but in this case, you can just ignore it.

Cut

**9.** Return to Page 1, and then in the numbered list, triple-click anywhere in the *Bartimaeus Trilogy* paragraph to select the entire paragraph.

**10.** In the **Clipboard** group, click the **Cut** button.

**11.** Press the ↑ key to move to the beginning of the *Harry Potter series* paragraph, and then in the **Clipboard** group, click the **Paste** button.

The two paragraphs have effectively switched places and the list has been renumbered.

**See Also** For more information about numbered lists, see "Creating and Modifying Lists" in Chapter 3, "Changing the Look of Text."

Undo

**12.** On the **Quick Access Toolbar**, click the **Undo** arrow, and in the list, click the third action (**Paste**).

Word undoes the previous cut-and-paste operation and the pasting of the copied text.

**13.** Press Ctrl + Home to move to the top of the document. Then move the pointer into the selection area adjacent to the paragraph that begins *Interest in the fantasy genre*, and double-click to select the paragraph.

**14.** Point to the selection, hold down the mouse button, and then drag the paragraph up to the beginning of the paragraph above it.

When you release the mouse, the text appears in its new location.

**15.** With the text still selected, press the End key.

Word releases the selection and moves the insertion point to the end of the paragraph.

**16.** Press Space , and then press Del .

Word deletes the paragraph mark, and the two paragraphs are now one paragraph.

¶

The·Taguien·Cycle¶
A·Fantasy·Series·for·Young·Adults¶

¶
The·Taguien·Cycle·is·the·most·exciting·and·promising·new·project·to·have·come·before·the·committee·in·several·years.·It·meets·our·two·primary·goals:··Develop·a·book·line·that·will·appeal·to·young·adult·readers,·especially·boys;·and·develop·a·book·line·that·has·the·potential·for·media·spin-offs·that·will·contribute·to·future·profits·and·on-going·financial·success.¶
¶
Interest·in·the·fantasy·genre·has·increased·steadily·over·the·past·ten·years,·a·trend·that·shows·no·sign·of·reversal.··Anecdotal·industry·sales·statistics·show·an·increase·of·2·to·3·percent·per·year·for·adult·fantasy·books·and·5·to·6·percent·for·young·adult·fantasy·books.·Each·year·Lucerne·has·published·several·fairytale/magic·books·for·younger·readers,·but·we·do·not·currently·offer·anything·sophisticated·enough·to·appeal·to·young·adult·readers.··Although·we·have·found·it·very·difficult·to·sell·other·genres·to·this·audience·of·reluctant·readers,·there·is·every·indication·that·offering·a·fantasy·series·at·this·time·would·meet·with·success.¶
¶
¶

**17.** In the selection area, click adjacent to the paragraph mark below the combined paragraph, and then press [Del].

 **CLOSE** the *01_Changes* document without saving your changes.

---

**About the Clipboard**

You can view the items that have been cut and copied to the Clipboard by clicking the Clipboard Dialog Box Launcher to open the Clipboard task pane, which displays up to 24 cut or copied items.

To paste an individual item at the insertion point, you simply click the item. To paste all the items, click the Paste All button. You can point to an item, click the arrow that appears, and then click Delete to remove it from the Clipboard, or you can remove all the items by clicking the Clear All button.

You can control the behavior of the Clipboard task pane by clicking Options at the bottom of the pane. You can choose to have the Clipboard task pane appear when you cut or copy a single item or multiple items. You can also choose to display the Clipboard icon in the status area of the taskbar when the Clipboard task pane is displayed.

To close the Clipboard task pane, click the Close button at the right end of its title bar.

---

# Inserting Saved Text

To save time and ensure consistency in your documents, you can save any text you use frequently as a *building block*. You do this by selecting the text, clicking Quick Parts in the Text group on the Insert tab, clicking Save Selection To Quick Part Gallery, and assigning the text a name. It then appears under its assigned name in the Quick Parts gallery.

After you have saved the text, you can insert it at any time by clicking Quick Parts to display its gallery and then clicking the building block you want.

> **Tip** You can also type the name of the building block and then press the F3 key to insert it at the insertion point.

In this exercise, you will save the names of a company and a product as building blocks so that you can insert them elsewhere in a document.

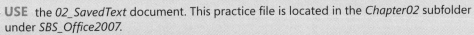

**USE** the *02_SavedText* document. This practice file is located in the *Chapter02* subfolder under *SBS_Office2007*.

**OPEN** the *02_SavedText* document.

1. Toward the end of the first paragraph of the document, select **Wide World Importers**.

2. On the **Insert** tab, in the **Text** group, click the **Quick Parts** button, and then click **Save Selection to Quick Part Gallery**.

   The Create New Building Block dialog box opens.

   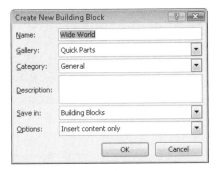

3. In the **Name** box, type www, and then click **OK**.

   Word saves the selection in the Quick Parts gallery.

4. In the third paragraph of the document, select **chimonobambusa marmorea**, and then in the **Text** group, click the **Quick Parts** button.

   Notice that the company name now appears as a building block in the Quick Parts gallery.

5. Click **Save Selection to Quick Part Gallery**, and save the selected text with the name cm.

6. Press ⌈Ctrl⌉+⌈End⌉ to move the insertion point to the end of the document, and then press ⌈Space⌉.

7. Type In particular and a space. Then in the **Text** group, click the **Quick Parts** button, and in the gallery, click the **www** entry.

   The company name appears at the insertion point.

8. Type a space followed by recommends cm.

9. Press the ⌈F3⌉ key, and then type a period.

   Word replaces *cm* with its building block, *chimonobambusa marmorea*.

about anyone who wishes to grow one in their backyard. Some dwarf species include chimonobambusa marmorea, indocalamus tessellatus, and pleioblastus chino vaginatus. Also suitable for the personal garden are those categorized as mid size. Examples of these types of plants are bambusa glaucophylla and otatea acuminata aztectorum. Plant starts and seeds are easier to find than ever, being available at nurseries and through mail order. ¶
¶
Bamboo is quickly becoming an important economic factor in many developing nations. A 60-foot tree cut for marketing can take up to 60 years to replace, whereas a 60-foot bamboo can take as little as 60 days to reach marketability. And the majority of bamboo destined for the world market is harvested by women and children, most of who live at or below subsistence levels in poor nations. So as production increases, so does support for the economies of those countries that produce it. ¶
¶
Choosing bamboo as part of home or garden design makes sense on many levels. Not only does it have an appealing look, but it supports the environment as well as the countries that produce it. In particular Wide World Importers recommends chimonobambusa marmorea. ¶

www       cm

**Troubleshooting** Pressing the F3 key substitutes the corresponding building block only if the name you type contains no spaces. There must be a space to its left, and the insertion point must be to its right.

 **CLOSE** the *02_SavedText* document without saving your changes.

**Important** When you quit Word, you will be asked whether you want to save the Building Blocks template, which by default is where your custom building blocks are saved. If you want to discard the building blocks you have created in this Word session, click No. If you want to save them, click Yes.

### Inserting the Date and Time

One of the easiest ways to insert today's date or the current time in a document is to use the Insert Date And Time button in the Text group on the Insert tab. After you specify the format you want to use, Word retrieves the date or time from your computer's internal calendar or clock. You can insert the information as regular text or as a *field*. A field is a placeholder that tells Word to supply the specified information in the specified way. The advantage of using a field is that it can be updated with the click of a button.

Here are the steps for inserting the date or time:

1. With the insertion point located where you want the date or time to appear, on the **Insert** tab, in the **Text** group, click the **Date & Time** button.

   The Date And Time dialog box opens.

2. Under **Available formats**, click the date and/or time format you want.

3. If you want to insert a date or time field, select the **Update automatically** check box.

4. Click **OK**.

If you selected Update Automatically, Word inserts a Date or Time field depending on the format you selected. When you point to the field, it is highlighted as a unit. You can click the field to select it, and you can click the Update button that appears above it to update the field with the most current information. If you right-click the field, you can click Toggle Field Codes to see the codes that control the field; click the command again to redisplay the date or time information.

You can insert other types of date and time fields, such as a PrintDate field or an EditTime field. Insert a Date or Time field in the usual way, right-click the field, and then click Edit Field. In the Field dialog box, change the setting in the Categories box to Date And Time, and in the Field Names list, click the field you want. When you click OK, the information corresponding to the field type you specified is shown in the document.

# Finding the Most Appropriate Word

Language is often contextual—you use different words and phrases in a marketing brochure, in a letter requesting immediate payment of an invoice, and in an informal memo about a social gathering after work. To help you ensure that you are using the words that best convey your meaning in any given context, Word provides a *Thesaurus* where you can look up synonyms (alternative words) for a selected word. The Thesaurus is one of a set of Research services provided by Word.

To look up alternatives for a word in the Thesaurus, you select the word and then click the Thesaurus button in the Proofing group on the Review tab. The Research task pane opens, displaying a list of synonyms. You then click the synonym that you want to re-place the selected word.

In this exercise, you'll use the Thesaurus to replace one word with another.

**USE** the *03_FindingWord* document. This practice file is located in the *Chapter02* subfolder under *SBS_Office2007*.

**OPEN** the *03_FindingWord* document.

1. Double-click the word **rigorous** in the last line of the first paragraph of the letter.

2. On the **Review** tab, in the **Proofing** group, click the **Thesaurus** button.

   The Research task pane opens, listing synonyms for the word *rigorous*.

**3.** In the task pane, under **exact**, click **meticulous**.

The word *meticulous* replaces *rigorous* in the Search For box at the top of the task pane, and synonyms for *meticulous* are now listed in the task pane.

**4.** Point to the word **thorough**, click the arrow that appears, and then click **Insert**.

The word *thorough* replaces *rigorous* in the document.

**5.** Close the **Research** task pane.

 **CLOSE** the *03_FindingWord* document without saving your changes.

## Researching Information

In addition to the Thesaurus, the Research task pane provides access to a variety of informational resources from within Word. You can enter a topic in the Search For box and specify in the box below which resource Word should use to look for information about that topic. By clicking Research Options at the bottom of the Research task pane, you can specify which of a predefined list of reference materials, such as Microsoft Encarta and various Internet resources, will be available from a list, and you can add your own reference-material sources.

To research information:

**1.** On the **Review** tab, in the **Proofing** group, click the **Research** button to display the Research task pane.

**2.** In the **Search for** box, type the topic you are interested in researching.

For example, you might type *bamboo*.

**3.** Click the arrow to the right of the box below the Search For box, and then in the list, click the resource you want to use to search for information.

For example, you might click MSN Search. When you have made your selection, the Start Searching button to the right of the Search For box flashes, and seconds later, the search results are displayed in the task pane.

**4.** Click any information sources that interest you.

You can click a hyperlink to a Web address to go to the Web to track down further information. You can also select part of a topic, right-click the selection, click Copy, and then paste the selection into your document. Or you can click right-click the selection and click Look Up to research information about the selection.

**Translating Text**

Word now comes with built-in dictionaries for many common languages, so you can easily translate words and phrases from one language to another.

To translate a word into another language:

1. Select the word, and then on the **Review** tab, in the **Proofing** group, click the **Translate** button.

   The Research task pane opens with boxes in which you can specify the source language and the translation language.

2. Under **Translation** in the **Research** task pane, change the settings in the **From** and **To** boxes as necessary.

   The translated text appears under Bilingual Dictionary.

To translate a different word or phrase, you can type it in the Search For box and then click the Start Searching button to the right.

To view the translation of any word you point to, click the Translation ScreenTip button in the Proofing group on the Review tab, and then select the language you want to see. You can then point to any word in a document to display the equivalent word in the language you selected. Click the button again, and then click Turn Off Translation ScreenTip to turn off the translation display.

# Reorganizing a Document Outline

If you are creating a document that contains headings, you can format it with built-in heading styles that include outline levels. Then it is easy to view and organize the document in Outline view. In this view, you can hide all the body text and display only the headings at and above a particular level. You can then rearrange the sections of a document by moving their headings.

To view a document in Outline view, click the Outline button in the Document Views group on the View tab, or click the Outline button on the View toolbar. The document is then displayed with a hierarchical structure, and the Outlining tab appears on the Ribbon.

The Outline Tools group on this tab includes buttons you can click to display only the headings at a specific level and above, to *promote* or *demote* headings or body text by changing their level, and to move headings and their text up or down in the document. The indentations and symbols used in Outline view to indicate the level of a heading or paragraph in the document's structure do not appear in the document in other views or when you print it.

> **Tip** You can click the buttons in the Master Document group to create a master document with subdocuments that you can then display and hide. The topic of master documents and subdocuments is beyond the scope of this book. For more information, see Word Help.

In this exercise, you'll switch to Outline view, promote and demote headings, move headings, and expand and collapse the outline.

> **USE** the *04_Outline* document. This practice file is located in the *Chapter02* subfolder under *SBS_Office2007*.
>
> **OPEN** the *04_Outline* document.

Outline

1. In the lower-right corner of the window, on the **View** toolbar, click the **Outline** button.

    The screen changes to display the document in Outline view, and the Outlining tab appears at the left end of the Ribbon.

2. On the **Outlining** tab, in the **Outline Tools** group, click the **Show Level** arrow, and in the list, click **Level 1**.

    The document collapses to display only level-1 headings.

- GENERAL·ADMINISTRATION¶
- SHIPPING¶
- ACCOUNTING¶

Expand

Demote

Undo

Collapse

Promote

**3.** Click anywhere in the **Accounting** heading.

**4.** In the **Outline Tools** group, click the **Expand** button.

Word expands the *Accounting* section to display its level-2 headings.

**5.** In the **Outline Tools** group, click the **Demote** button.

The *Accounting* heading changes to a level-2 heading.

**6.** On the **Quick Access Toolbar**, click the **Undo** button.

The *Accounting* heading changes back to a level-1 heading.

**7.** In the **Outline Tools** group, click the **Collapse** button.

**8.** Click the **Demote** button.

Again, the *Accounting* heading changes to a level-2 heading.

**9.** Click the **Expand** button.

Because the subheadings were hidden under *Accounting* when you demoted the heading, all the subheadings have been demoted to level 3 to maintain the hierarchy of the section.

**10.** Click the **Collapse** button, and then in the **Outline Tools** group, click the **Promote** button.

The *Accounting* heading is now a level-1 heading again.

**11.** Press Ctrl + Home to move to the top of the document, and then in the **Outline Tools** group, in the **Show Level** list, click **Level 2**.

The outline shows all the level-1 and level-2 headings.

**12.** Click the plus sign to the left of the *Accounting* heading, and then in the **Outline Tools** group, click the **Move Up** button three times.

Move Up

The *Accounting* heading and all its subheadings move above the *Shipping* heading.

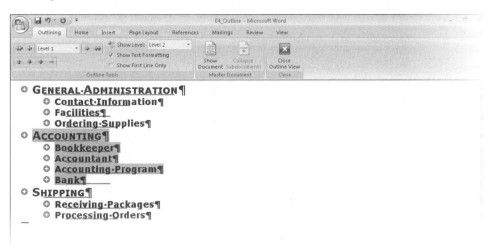

**13.** In the **Outline Tools** group, in the **Show Level** list, click **All Levels**.

You can now scroll through the document to see the effects of the reorganization.

**14.** In the **Close** group, click the **Close Outline View** button.

Word displays the reorganized document in Print Layout view.

**CLOSE** the *04_Outline* document without saving your changes.

# Finding and Replacing Text

One way to ensure that the text in your documents is consistent and accurate is to use the Find feature of Word to search for every instance of a particular word or phrase. For example, if you were responsible for advertising a trademarked product, you would probably want to search your marketing materials to check that every instance of the product's name was correctly identified as a trademark.

Clicking the Find button in the Editing group on the Home tab displays the Find tab of the Find And Replace dialog box. After you enter the text you want to find in the Find What box, you can do the following:

- Click Find Next to select the first occurrence of that text.
- In the Reading Highlight list, click Highlight All to highlight all occurrences.

If you find an error in the document while conducting a search, you can make editing changes on the fly without closing the Find And Replace dialog box. Simply click the document, make the change, and then click the Find And Replace dialog box to make it active again.

If you know that you want to substitute one word or phrase for another, you can use the Replace feature to find each occurrence of the text you want to change and replace it with different text. Clicking the Replace button in the Editing group displays the Replace tab of the Find And Replace dialog box, which is similar to the Find tab. On the Replace tab, you can do the following:

- Click Replace to replace the selected occurrence with the text in the Replace With box and move to the next occurrence.
- Click Replace All to replace all occurrences with the text in the Replace With box.
- Click Find Next to leave the selected occurrence as it is and locate the next one.

You can use other options in the Find And Replace dialog box to carry out more complicated searches and replaces. Clicking More expands the box to make these additional options available.

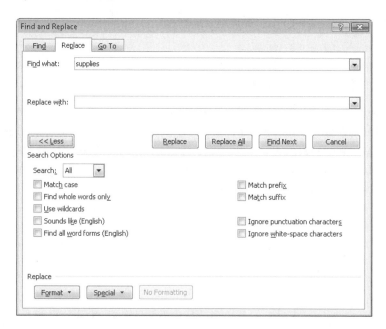

You can make a selection from the Search list to guide the direction of the search. You can select the Match Case check box to match capitalization and select the Find Whole Words Only check box to find only whole-word occurrences of the Find What text. If you want to check that your usage of two similar words, such as *effect* and *affect*, is correct, you can select the Use Wildcards check box and then enter a *wildcard character* in the Find What box to locate variable information. The two most common wildcard characters are:

- The ? wildcard stands for any single character in this location in the Find What text.
- The * wildcard stands for any number of characters in this location in the Find What text.

> **Tip** To see a list of the other available wildcards, use Help to search for wildcards.

Selecting the Sounds Like check box finds occurrences of the search text that sound the same but are spelled differently, such as *there* and *their*. Selecting the Find All Word Forms check box finds occurrences of a particular word in any form, such as *plan*, *planned*, and *planning*. You can match a prefix or a suffix, and you can ignore punctuation and white space. Finally, you can locate formatting, such as bold, or special characters, such as tabs, by selecting them from the Format or Special list.

In this exercise, you will find a phrase and make a correction to the document. Then you'll replace one phrase with another throughout the entire document.

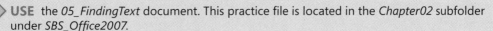

**USE** the *05_FindingText* document. This practice file is located in the *Chapter02* subfolder under *SBS_Office2007*.

**OPEN** the *05_FindingText* document.

 Find

1. With the insertion point at the beginning of the document, on the **Home** tab, in the **Editing** group, click the **Find** button.

   The Find And Replace dialog box opens, displaying the Find tab.

2. In the **Find what** box, type The Taguien Cycle, click **Reading Highlight**, and then in the list, click **Highlight All**.

3. Scroll to Page 2.

   Word has found and selected all the occurrences of *The Taguien Cycle* in the document. (We dragged the title bar of the dialog box to move it to the side.)

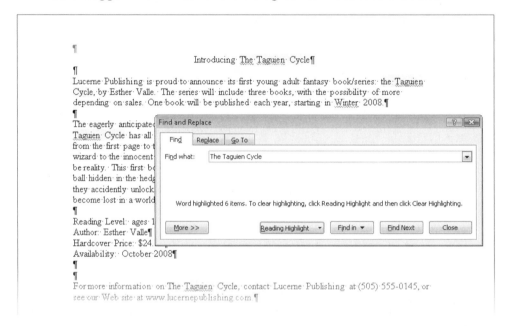

4. Click the document behind the **Find and Replace** dialog box, double-click the word **the** in *the Taguien Cycle* in the first paragraph (not the title) on Page 2, and then type The to correct the capitalization.

5. Press Ctrl + Home to move the insertion point to the beginning of the document.

6. Click the title bar of the **Find and Replace** dialog box, and then click the **Replace** tab.

   The Find What box retains the entry from the previous search.

7. Click the **Replace with** box, type The Taguien Cycle, and then click the **More** button.

8. At the bottom of the expanded dialog box, click the **Format** button, and then click **Font**.

The Replace Font dialog box opens.

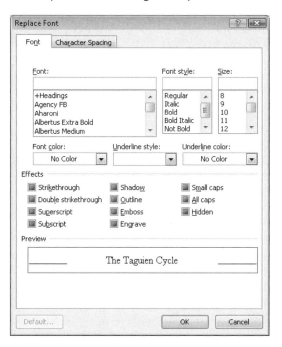

9. Under **Font Style**, click **Italic**, and then click **OK**.

10. Click **Find Next**, and then click **Replace**.

   The selected plain text title is replaced with italicized text, and the next occurrence of *The Taguien Cycle* is selected.

11. Click **Replace All**.

   Word displays a message box indicating that six replacements were made.

12. Click **OK** to close the message box, and then in the **Find and Replace** dialog box, click the **Find** tab.

13. In the **Find what** box, click **Reading Highlight**, and then in the list, click **Highlight All**.

   Word highlights six occurrences of the Find What text.

14. Click **Reading Highlight**, and then in the list, click **Clear Highlighting**.

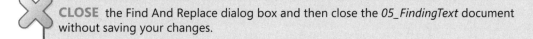

**CLOSE** the Find And Replace dialog box and then close the *05_FindingText* document without saving your changes.

# Correcting Spelling and Grammatical Errors

In the days of handwritten and typewritten documents, people might have tolerated a typographical or grammatical error or two because correcting such errors without creating a mess was difficult. Word processors like Word have built-in spelling and grammar checkers, so now documents that contain these types of errors are likely to reflect badly on their creators.

> **Tip** Although Word can help you eliminate misspellings and grammatical errors, its tools are not infallible. You should always read through your documents to catch the problems that the Word tools can't detect.

Word provides two tools to help you with the chore of eliminating spelling and grammar errors: the AutoCorrect and Spelling And Grammar features.

Have you noticed that Word automatically corrects some misspellings as you type them? This is the work of the AutoCorrect feature. AutoCorrect corrects commonly misspelled words, such as *adn* to *and*, so that you don't have to correct them yourself. AutoCorrect comes with a long list of frequently misspelled words and their correct spellings. If you frequently misspell a word that AutoCorrect doesn't change, you can add it to the list in the AutoCorrect dialog box.

If you deliberately mistype a word and don't want to accept the AutoCorrect change, you can reverse it by clicking the Undo button on the Quick Access Toolbar before you type anything else.

Although AutoCorrect ensures that your documents are free of common misspellings, it doesn't detect random typographical and grammatical errors. For those types of errors, you can turn to the Spelling And Grammar feature for help. You might have noticed that as you type, Word underlines potential spelling errors with red wavy underlines and grammatical errors with green wavy underlines. You can right-click an underlined word or phrase to display suggested corrections.

If you want to check the spelling or grammar of the entire document, it is easier to click the Spelling & Grammar button in the Proofing group on the Review tab than to deal with underlined words and phrases individually. Word then works its way through the document from the insertion point and displays the Spelling And Grammar dialog box if it encounters a potential error. If the error is a misspelling, the Spelling And Grammar dialog box suggests corrections; if the error is a breach of grammar, the Spelling And Grammar dialog box tells you which rule you have broken as well as suggesting corrections. The buttons available in the Spelling And Grammar dialog box are dynamic and change to those most appropriate for fixing the error. For example, for a grammatical error, you are given the opportunity to ignore the rule you have broken throughout the document.

In this exercise, you'll change an AutoCorrect setting and add a misspelled word to its list. You'll check the spelling in the document and add terms to the custom dictionary, and you'll find, review, and correct a grammatical error.

> **USE** the *06_Spelling* document. This practice file is located in the *Chapter02* subfolder under *SBS_Office2007*.
>
> **OPEN** the *06_Spelling* document.

1. Click at the end of the first paragraph in the letter, press $\boxed{\text{Space}}$, and then type in your reserch, followed by a period.

   As soon as you type the period, AutoCorrect changes *reserch* to *research*.

Microsoft Office Button

2. Click the **Microsoft Office Button**, and then click **Word Options**.

3. In the left pane of the **Word Options** window, click **Proofing**, and then on the Proofing page, click **AutoCorrect Options**.

   The AutoCorrect dialog box opens, displaying the AutoCorrect tab.

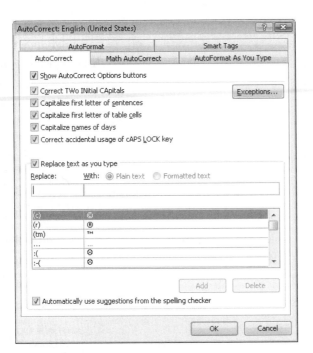

Notice the corrections that AutoCorrect will make. You can clear the check box of any item you don't want corrected. For example, if you don't want AutoCorrect to capitalize a lowercase letter or word that follows a period, clear the Capitalize First Letter Of Sentences check box.

4. Click in the **Replace** box, and then type avalable.

   Word scrolls the list below to show the entry that is closest to what you typed.

5. Press the [Tab] key to move the insertion point to the **With** box, and then type available.

6. Click **Add** to add the entry to the correction list, and then click **OK**.

7. Click **OK** to close the Word Options window.

8. Press Ctrl+End to move to the end of the document, and then in the paragraph that begins *Thank you for your* interest, position the insertion point to the right of the period at the end of the third sentence.

9. Press [Space], and then type Shelly will not be avalable May 10-15 followed by a period.

   The word *avalable* changes to *available*.

10. Press [Ctrl]+[Home] to move to the top of the document, and then right-click *sorces*, the first word with a red wavy underline.

Word lists possible correct spellings for this word, as well as actions you might want to carry out.

11. In the list, click **sources**.

    Word removes the red wavy underline and inserts the correction.

Spelling & Grammar

12. Press $\boxed{\text{Ctrl}}$+$\boxed{\text{Home}}$ again, and then on the **Review** tab, in the **Proofing** group, click the **Spelling & Grammar** button.

    The Spelling And Grammar dialog box opens, with the first word that Word does not recognize, *commited*, displayed in red in the Not In Dictionary box.

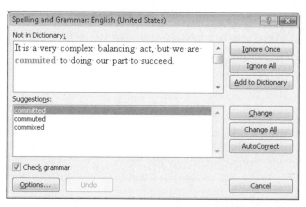

13. With **committed** selected in the **Suggestions** box, click **AutoCorrect**.

    Word adds the misspelling and the selected correction to the AutoCorrect list, so that the next time you type *commited* by mistake, the spelling will be corrected for you as you type. Word then flags *Dyck* as the next possible misspelling.

> **Troubleshooting** If the errors we mention don't appear to be in the practice file, click Options at the bottom of the Spelling And Grammar dialog box. Then in the Word Options window, under When Correcting Spelling And Grammar In Word, click Recheck Document, click Yes to reset the checkers, and then click OK.

14. Click **Ignore All**.

    Word will now skip over this and any other occurrences of this proper noun. It moves on to highlight the duplicate word *for*.

15. Click **Delete**.

    Word deletes the second *for* and then flags a possible grammatical error.

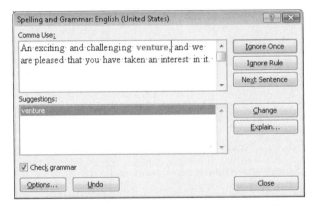

    This grammatical error is identified as incorrect use of a comma. You need to read the sentence and then decide whether and how to correct it. In this case, the error is not related to the comma after *venture* but to the fact that there is no verb in the first half of the sentence.

> **Tip** Word's grammar checker helps identify phrases and clauses that do not follow traditional grammatical rules, but it is not always accurate. It is easy to get in the habit of ignoring green wavy underlines. However, it is wise to scrutinize them all to be sure that your documents don't contain any embarrassing mistakes.

16. Behind the **Spelling and Grammar** dialog box, click the document, double-click the word **An** at the beginning of the sentence with the error, and then type The import business is an.

17. Click the title bar of the **Spelling and Grammar** dialog box, and then click **Resume**.

Word flags *Florian* as a word that it doesn't recognize. *Florian* is a proper noun and is spelled correctly. By adding words like this one to the custom dictionary, you can prevent Word from continuing to flag them.

**18.** Click **Add to Dictionary**.

Word displays a message, indicating that it has finished checking the spelling and grammar of the document.

**19.** Click **OK** to close the message box.

 **CLOSE** the *06_Spelling* document without saving your changes.

---

### Viewing Document Statistics

As you type, Word keeps track of the number of pages and words in your document, displaying this information at the left end of the status bar. To see the number of words in only part of the document, such as a few paragraphs, simply select that part. The status bar then displays the number of words in the selection, expressed as a fraction of the total, such as 250/800.

To see more statistics, you can open the Word Count dialog box by clicking the Word Count button in the Proofing group on the Review tab. In addition to the count of pages and words, the Word Count dialog box displays the number of characters, paragraphs, and lines. It also gives you the option of including or excluding words in text boxes, footnotes, and endnotes.

# Finalizing a Document

When a document is complete and ready for distribution, you typically perform several final tasks. These might include inspecting the document for any remaining private or inappropriate information, restricting access, or adding a digital signature.

Many documents go through several revisions, and some are scrutinized by multiple reviewers. During this development process, documents can accumulate information that you might not want in the final version, such as the names of people who worked on the document, comments that reviewers have added to the file, or hidden text about status and assumptions. This extraneous information is not a concern if the final version is to be delivered as a printout. However, these days more and more files are delivered electronically, making this information available to anyone who wants to read it.

Word 2007 includes a tool called the Document Inspector, which finds and removes all extraneous and potentially confidential information. You can instruct the Document Inspector to look for comments, revisions, and annotations; for any personal information saved with the document; and for hidden text. The Document Inspector displays a summary of its findings and gives you the option of removing anything it finds.

Word also includes another finalizing tool called the Compatibility Checker, which checks for the use of features not supported in previous versions of Word.

After you have handled extraneous information and compatibility issues, you can mark a document as final and make its file read-only, so that other people know that they should not make changes to this released document.

In this exercise, you will inspect a document for inappropriate information and mark it as final.

**USE** the *07_Finalizing* document. This practice file is located in the *Chapter02* subfolder under *SBS_Office2007*.

**OPEN** the *07_Finalizing* document.

Microsoft Office Button

1. Click the **Microsoft Office Button**, point to **Prepare**, and then click **Properties**.

   The Document Information Panel opens above the document, showing that identifying information has been saved with the file. Some of the information, including the name of the author, was attached to the file by Word. Other information was added by a user.

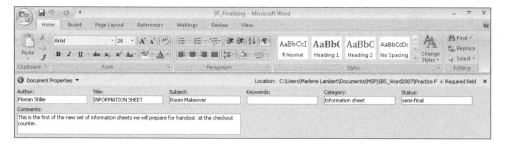

**2.** In the upper-left corner of the **Document Information Panel**, click the **Document Properties** arrow, and then in the list, click **Advanced Properties**.

The Properties dialog box opens.

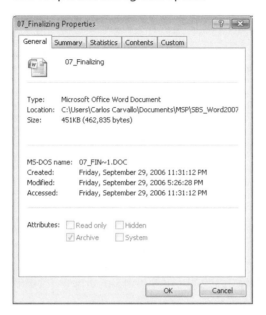

**3.** In turn, click the **Summary** and **Statistics** tabs, noticing that additional identifying information is displayed there.

Close

**4.** Click **Cancel** to close the **Properties** dialog box, and then in the upper-right corner of the **Document Information Panel**, click the **Close** button.

**5.** Save the document in the **Chapter02** subfolder with the name My Information Sheet.

**6.** Click the **Microsoft Office Button**, point to **Prepare**, and then click **Inspect Document**.

The Document Inspector dialog box opens, listing the items that will be checked.

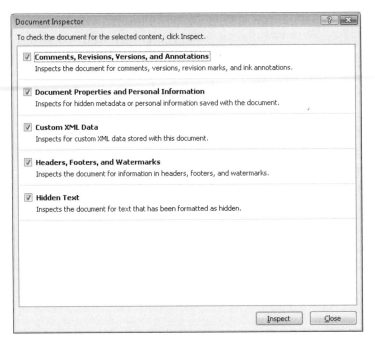

7. Without changing the default selections in the **Document Inspector** dialog box, click **Inspect**.

   The Document Inspector reports the presence of the document properties and personal information that you viewed earlier in this exercise, as well as some custom XML data.

8. To the right of **Document Properties and Personal Information**, click **Remove All**.

   Word removes the document properties and personal information.

9. To the right of **Custom XML Data**, click **Remove All**.

10. In the **Document Inspector** dialog box, click **Close**.

11. Click the **Microsoft Office Button**, point to **Prepare**, and then click **Mark As Final**.

    A message tells you that the document will be marked as final and then saved.

12. Click **OK** to complete the process.

    A message tells you that the document has been marked as final and that typing, editing commands, and proofing marks are turned off.

13. Click **OK** to close the message, and then click the **Insert** tab.

    Most of the buttons are inactive, indicating that you cannot make changes to the document.

**CLOSE** the *My Information Sheet* document, and if you are not continuing directly on to the next chapter, quit Word.

### Adding a Digital Signature

When you create a document that will be circulated to other people via e-mail or the Web, you might want to attach a *digital signature*, which is an electronic stamp of authentication. The digital signature confirms the origin of the document and indicates that no one has tampered with the document since it was signed.

To add a digital signature to a Word document, you must first obtain a digital ID. Certified digital IDs can be obtained from companies such as IntelliSafe Technologies and Comodo Inc. You can obtain the ID and attach it to a document by clicking the Microsoft Office Button, pointing to Finish, clicking Add a Digital Signature, and then following the instructions.

# Key Points

- You can cut or copy text and paste it elsewhere in the same document or in a different document. Cut and copied text is stored on the Clipboard.

- Made a mistake? No problem! You can undo a single action or the last several actions you performed by clicking the Undo button (or its arrow) on the Quick Access Toolbar. You can even redo an action if you change you mind again.

- You don't have to type the same text over and over again. Instead, save the text as a Quick Part and insert it with a few mouse clicks.

- Need a more precise word to get your point across? You can use the Thesaurus to look up synonyms for a selected word, and use the Research service to access specialized reference materials and online resources.

- If you take the time to apply heading styles to a document, you can use the outline to rearrange the document.

- You can find each occurrence of a word or phrase and replace it with another.

- You can rely on AutoCorrect to correct common misspellings. Correct other spelling and grammatical errors individually as you type or by checking the entire document in one pass.

- Before you distribute an electronic document, you can remove any information you don't want people to be able to see.

# Chapter at a Glance

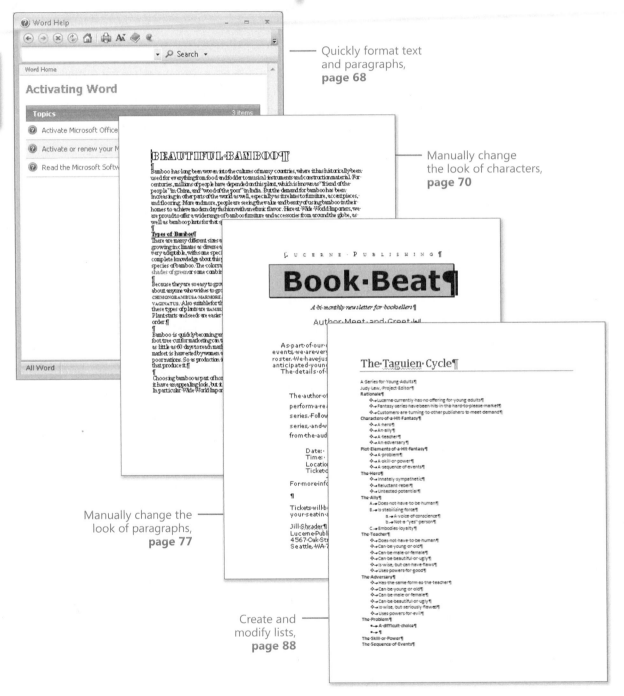

Quickly format text and paragraphs, **page 68**

Manually change the look of characters, **page 70**

Manually change the look of paragraphs, **page 77**

Create and modify lists, **page 88**

# 3 Changing the Look of Text

---

**In this chapter, you will learn to:**

- ✔ Quickly format text and paragraphs.
- ✔ Manually change the look of characters.
- ✔ Manually change the look of paragraphs.
- ✔ Create and modify lists.

---

The appearance of your documents helps to convey their message. Microsoft Office Word 2007 can help you develop professional-looking documents whose appearance is appropriate to their contents. You can easily format your text so that key points stand out and your arguments are easy to grasp.

In this chapter, you will experiment with Quick Styles and then change the look of individual words. Then you'll indent paragraphs, change paragraph alignment and spacing, set tab stops, modify line spacing, and add borders and shading. Finally you'll create and format both bulleted and numbered lists.

**See Also** Do you need only a quick refresher on the topics in this chapter? See the Quick Reference entries at the beginning of this book.

> **Important** Before you can use the practice files in this chapter, you need to install them from the book's companion CD to their default location. See "Using the Book's CD" at the beginning of this book for more information.

> **Troubleshooting** Graphics and operating system–related instructions in this book reflect the Windows Vista user interface. If your computer is running Microsoft Windows XP and you experience trouble following the instructions as written, please refer to the "Information for Readers Running Windows XP" section at the beginning of this book.

# Quickly Formatting Text and Paragraphs

Word 2007 includes a number of new features, as well as enhancements to existing features, that make the process of formatting content effortless. For example, buttons for changing the font size, color, and other character attributes have been gathered in the Font group on the Home tab so that they are all easily accessible. And many common formatting buttons are available on the Mini toolbar that appears when you point to selected text.

**See Also** For information about changing character attributes, see "Manually Changing the Look of Characters" later in this chapter.

However, you don't have to apply attributes one at a time. You can easily change several attributes at once with a couple of mouse clicks by using *Quick Styles*. This powerful tool is available in the Styles group on the Home tab. Quick Styles are galleries consisting of the following:

- *Paragraph styles.* You can use these styles to apply a consistent look to different types of paragraphs, such as headings, body text, captions, quotations, and list paragraphs.

- *Character styles.* You can use these styles to change the appearance of selected words.

All of the Quick Styles in a particular gallery coordinate with each other, lending a clean, consistent, professional look to your documents. You can switch from one set of styles to another by selecting from Quick Styles galleries with names like Traditional, Distinctive, Modern, and Elegant. To help you choose the style you want, you can point to the name of the set to see a live preview of how your document will look with a particular set of Quick Styles applied to it. After you have applied one set of Quick Styles, you can easily change the look of the entire document by selecting a different set of Quick Styles from the Change Styles list.

In this exercise, you will experiment with Quick Styles.

> **USE** the *01_QuickFormatting* document. This practice file is located in the *Chapter03* subfolder under *SBS_Office2007*.
> **BE SURE TO** start Word before beginning this exercise.
> **OPEN** the *01_QuickFormatting* document.

1. With the insertion point at the top of the document, on the **Home** tab, in the **Styles** group, move the pointer over each thumbnail in the displayed row of the **Quick Styles** gallery.

The formatting of the heading changes to show you a live preview of how the heading will look if you click the style you are pointing to. You don't have to actually apply the formatting to see its effect.

Down

**2.** Without making a selection, click the **Down** arrow to the right of the gallery.

> **Tip** This arrow has a dynamic ScreenTip that currently reads *Row 1 of 5*.

The next row of the Quick Styles gallery scrolls into view.

**3.** Move the pointer over each thumbnail in this row of the **Quick Styles** gallery.

More

**4.** In the **Styles** group, click the **More** button.

Word displays the entire Quick Styles gallery. The style applied to the paragraph containing the insertion point is surrounded by a border.

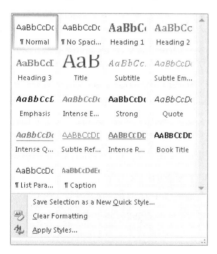

**5.** In the gallery, click the **Title** thumbnail to apply that style to the paragraph containing the insertion point.

**6.** Click anywhere in the **Information Sheet** heading, and then in the **Styles** group, click the **Subtitle** thumbnail.

> **Troubleshooting** If you select text and then apply a paragraph style, only the selected text takes on the formatting of the style. You can simply click again in the paragraph and reapply the style.

Up

**7.** Click anywhere in the **Moving to a New Home** heading, and then in the **Styles** group, click the **Up** arrow, and click the **Heading 1** thumbnail.

8. Apply the **Heading 1** style to the **Staying Healthy** and **Keeping Bugs at Bay** headings.

9. Apply the **Heading 3** style to the **Mites** and **Mealy Bugs** headings.

10. In the **Styles** group, click the **Change Styles** button, click **Style Set**, and then point to each set name in turn, watching the effect on the document.

11. When you have finished exploring, click **Modern**.

The formatting of the document changes and the headings and text take on the look assigned to this set of styles.

 **CLOSE** the *01_QuickFormatting* document without saving your changes.

# Manually Changing the Look of Characters

When you type text in a document, it is displayed in a particular font. Each *font* consists of 256 alphabetic characters, numbers, and symbols that share a common design. By default the font used for text in a new Word document is Calibri, but you can change the font at any time. The available fonts vary from one computer to another, depending on the programs installed. Common fonts include Arial, Verdana, and Times New Roman.

You can vary the look of a font by changing the following *attributes*:

- Almost every font comes in a range of *font sizes*, which are measured in *points* from the top of letters that have parts that stick up (ascenders), such as *h*, to the bottom of letters that have parts that drop down (descenders), such as *p*. A point is approximately 1/72 of an inch.

- Almost every font comes in a range of *font styles*. The most common are regular (or plain), italic, bold, and bold italic.

- Fonts can be enhanced by applying *font effects*, such as underlining, small capital letters (small caps), or shadows.

- A palette of harmonious *font colors* is available, and you can also specify custom colors.

- You can alter the *character spacing* by pushing characters apart or squeezing them together.

After you have selected an appropriate font for a document, you can use these attributes to achieve different effects. Although some attributes might cancel each other out, they are usually cumulative. For example, you might use a bold font in various sizes and various shades of green to make different heading levels stand out in a newsletter. Collectively, the font and its attributes are called *character formatting*.

In this exercise, you will format the text in a document by changing its font, font style, size, color, and character spacing.

> **USE** the *02_Characters* document. This practice file is located in the *Chapter03* subfolder under *SBS_Office2007*.
>
> **OPEN** the *02_Characters* document.

Underline

1. In the *Beautiful Bamboo* heading, click anywhere in the word **Beautiful**.

2. On the **Home** tab, in the **Font** group, click the **Underline** button.

> **Tip** If you click the Underline arrow, you can choose a style from the Underline gallery. You can also change the underline color.

The word containing the insertion point is now underlined. Notice that you did not have to select the entire word.

Repeat Underline Style

3. In the same heading, click anywhere in the word **Bamboo**, and then on the **Quick Access Toolbar**, click the **Repeat** button.

The last formatting command is repeated. Again, although you did not select the entire word, it is now underlined.

4. In the selection area, click adjacent to *Beautiful Bamboo* to select the entire heading.

Word displays a Mini toolbar of buttons that you can use to quickly change the look of the selection.

Bold

5. On the **Mini toolbar**, click the **Bold** button.

The heading is now bold. The active buttons on the Mini toolbar and in the Font group on the Home tab indicate the attributes that you applied to the selection.

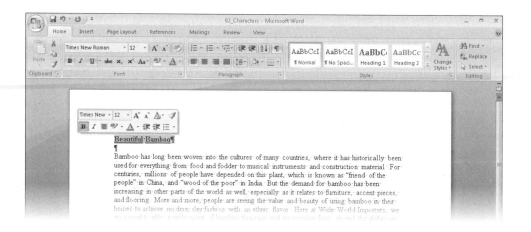

**See Also** For more information about the use of character formatting, see formatting, see what formatting is applied to a selection, see the sidebar entitled "More About Case and Character Formatting" later in this chapter.

Format Painter

**6.** On the **Mini toolbar**, click the **Format Painter** button, and then click in the selection area adjacent to the *Types of Bamboo* heading.

Word "paints" the formatting of *Beautiful Bamboo* onto *Types of Bamboo*.

> **Tip** The Format Painter button is also available in the Clipboard group on the Home tab.

**7.** Select **Beautiful Bamboo**, and then on the **Home** tab, in the **Font** group, click the **Font** arrow, scroll the list of available fonts, and then click **Stencil**.

> **Troubleshooting** If Stencil is not available, select any heavy font that catches your attention.

The heading at the top of the document now appears in the new font.

**8.** In the **Font** group, click the **Font Size** arrow, and then in the list, click **26**.

The size of the heading text increases to 26 points.

> **Tip** You can increase or decrease the font size in set increments by clicking the Grow Font and Shrink Font buttons in the Font group, or by clicking the same buttons on the Mini toolbar that appears when you select text.

**9.** In the **Font** group, click the **Dialog Box Launcher**.

The Font dialog box opens.

Font Size

Dialog Box
Launcher

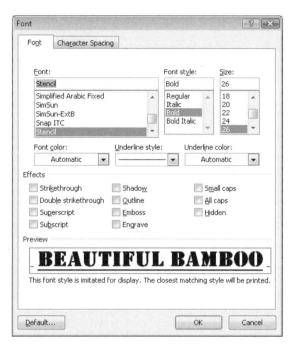

**10.** Click the Underline style arrow, and then in the list, click **(none)**.

**11.** Under **Effects**, select the **Outline** check box.

**12.** Click the **Character Spacing** tab.

13. Click the **Spacing** arrow, and then in the list, click **Expanded**.

14. To the right, click the **By** up arrow until the spacing is expanded by **2 pt** (points), and then click **OK**.

    The selected text appears with an outline effect and with the spacing between the characters expanded by 2 points.

Clear Formatting

15. On the **Home** tab, in the **Font** group, click the **Clear Formatting** button.

    The formatting of the selected text is removed.

Undo

16. On the **Quick Access Toolbar**, click the **Undo** button.

    The formatting of the selected text is restored.

17. In the last sentence of the second paragraph, select the words **light green**.

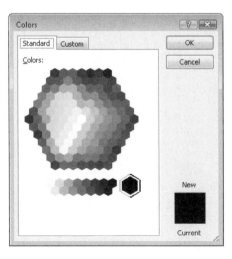

Font Color

18. On the **Home** tab, in the **Font** group, click the **Font Color** arrow, and then under **Standard Colors** in the palette, click the light green box.

    The selected words are now light green. (To see the color, clear the selection by clicking a blank area of the document.)

> **Tip** If you want to apply the Font Color button's current color, you can simply click the button (not the arrow).

19. In the same sentence, select **dark, rich shades of green**, click the **Font Color** arrow, and then below the palette, click **More Colors**.

    The Colors dialog box opens.

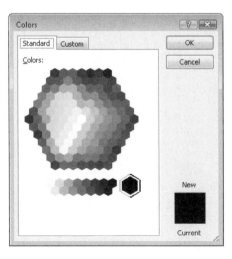

**20.** In the **Colors** wheel on the **Standard** tab, click one of the dark green shades on the left, and then click **OK**.

The selection is now dark green.

Highlight

**21.** Select the phrase **supports the environment** in the second sentence of the last paragraph. Then in the **Font** group, click the **Highlight** arrow, and under **Recent Colors** in the palette, click the green box.

This is the same green that you selected in Step 20. After you select a custom color in one palette, it is available in all the palettes. The highlighted phrase now stands out from the rest of the text.

> **Tip** If you click the Highlight button without first making a selection, the mouse pointer becomes a highlighter that you can drag across text. Click the Highlight button again or press Esc to turn off the highlighter.

**22.** In the paragraph that begins *Because they are so easy to grow*, select the bamboo species name **chimonobambusa marmorea**. Then hold down the Ctrl key while selecting **indocalamus tessellatus**, **pleioblastus chino vaginatus**, **bambusa glaucophylla**, and **otatea acuminata aztectorum**.

**23.** In the **Font** group, click the **Dialog Box Launcher**.

**24.** In the **Font** dialog box, click the **Font** tab, and under **Effects**, select the **Small caps** check box. Then click **OK**.

The lowercase letters in the species names now appear in small capital letters, making those names easy to find in the text.

**25.** Click anywhere in the first species name. Then on the **Home** tab, in the **Editing** group, click the **Select** button, and click **Select Text with Similar Formatting**.

All the species names that have been formatted in small caps are selected.

**26.** In the **Font** group, click the **Bold** button, and then click away from the selection.

The species names are now both small caps and bold.

Types of Bamboo¶

There are many different sizes and varieties of bamboo. It is both tropical and subtropical, growing in climates as diverse as jungles and mountainsides. Actually giant, woody grasses, it is very adaptable, with some species deciduous and others evergreen. Although there isn't yet a complete knowledge about this plant, there are believed to be between 1100 and 1500 different species of bamboo. The color range is from light green leaves and culms (stems) to dark, rich shades of green or some combination thereof.¶

¶

Because they are so easy to grow in such a variety of climates, there is a plant available for just about anyone who wishes to grow one in their backyard. Some dwarf species include CHIMONOBAMBUSA MARMOREA, INDOCALAMUS TESSELLATUS, and PLEIOBLASTUS CHINO VAGINATUS. Also suitable for the personal garden are those categorized as mid size. Examples of these types of plants are BAMBUSA GLAUCOPHYLLA and OTATEA ACUMINATA AZTECTORUM. Plant starts and seeds are easier to find than ever, being available at nurseries and through mail order.¶

¶

Bamboo is quickly becoming an important economic factor in many developing nations. A 60-foot tree cut for marketing can take up to 60 years to replace, whereas a 60-foot bamboo can take as little as 60 days to reach marketability. And the majority of bamboo destined for the world market is harvested by women and children, most of who live at or below subsistence levels in poor nations. So as production increases, so does support for the economies of those countries that produce it.¶

¶

Choosing bamboo as part of home or garden design makes sense on many levels. Not only does it have an appealing look, but it supports the environment as well as the countries that produce it. In particular Wide World Importers recommends chimonobambusa marmoreal.¶

**CLOSE** the *02_Characters* document without saving your changes.

## More About Case and Character Formatting

The way you use case and character formatting in a document can influence its visual impact on your readers. Used judiciously, case and character formatting can make a plain document look attractive and professional, but excessive use can make it look amateurish and detract from the message. For example, using too many fonts in the same document is the mark of inexperience, so don't use more than two or three.

Bear in mind that lowercase letters tend to recede, so using all uppercase letters (capitals) can be useful for titles and headings or for certain kinds of emphasis. However, large blocks of uppercase letters are tiring to the eye.

Where do the terms uppercase and lowercase come from? Until the advent of computers, individual characters were assembled to form the words that would appear on a printed page. The characters were stored alphabetically in cases, with the capital letters in the upper case and the small letters in the lower case.

> **Tip** If you want to see a summary of the formatting applied to a selection, you can display the Style Inspector pane by clicking the Styles Dialog Box Launcher and then clicking the Style Inspector button (the middle button at the bottom of the Styles task pane). You can then click anywhere in the document to see a formatting summary of the word containing the insertion point. To see details about the formatting, you can click the Reveal Formatting button at the bottom of the Style Inspector pane to open the Reveal Formatting task pane.

# Manually Changing the Look of Paragraphs

As you know, you create a *paragraph* by typing text and then pressing the Enter key. The paragraph can be a single word, a single sentence, or multiple sentences. You can change the look of a paragraph by changing its alignment, its line spacing, and the space before and after it. You can also put borders around it and shade its background. Collectively, the settings you use to vary the look of a paragraph are called *paragraph formatting*.

In Word, you don't define the width of paragraphs and the length of pages by defining the area occupied by the text; instead you define the size of the white space—the left, right, top, and bottom *margins*—around the text. You use the Margins button in the Page Setup group on the Page Layout tab to define these margins, either for the whole document or for sections of the document.

**See Also** For information about setting margins, see "Previewing and Printing a Document" in Chapter 1, "Exploring Word 2007."

Although the left and right margins are set for a whole document or section, you can vary the position of the text between the margins. The easiest way to do this is by moving controls on the horizontal ruler. You can indent paragraphs from the left and right margins, as well as specify where the first line of a paragraph begins and where the second and subsequent lines begin.

Setting a right indent indicates where all the lines in a paragraph should end, but sometimes you might want to specify where only a single line should end. For example, you might want to break a title after a particular word to make it look balanced on the page. You can end an individual line by inserting a *text wrapping break* or *line break*. After positioning the insertion point where you want the break to occur, you click the Breaks button in the Page Setup group on the Page Layout tab, and then click Text Wrapping. Word indicates the line break with a bent arrow. Inserting a line break does not start a new paragraph, so when you apply paragraph formatting to a line of text that ends with a line break, the formatting is applied to the entire paragraph, not just that line.

> **Tip** You can also press Shift+Enter to insert a line break.

You can align lines of text in different locations across the page by using *tab stops*. The easiest way to set tab stops is to use the horizontal ruler. By default, Word sets left-aligned tab stops every half-inch, as indicated by gray marks below this ruler. To set a custom tab stop, you start by clicking the Tab button located at the left end of the ruler until the type of tab stop you want appears. You have the following options:

- **Left Tab.** Aligns the left end of the text with the stop.
- **Center Tab.** Aligns the center of the text with the stop.
- **Right Tab.** Aligns the right end of the text with the stop.
- **Decimal Tab.** Aligns the decimal point in the text with the stop.
- **Bar Tab.** Draws a vertical bar aligned with the stop down the paragraph containing the insertion point.

After selecting the type of tab stop, you simply click the ruler where you want the tab stop to be. Word then removes any default tab stops to the left of the one you set. To change the position of an existing custom tab stop, you drag it to the left or right on the ruler. To delete a custom tab stop, you drag it away from the ruler.

To move the text to the right of the insertion point to the next tab stop, you press the Tab key. The text is then aligned on the tab stop according to its type. For example, if you set a center tab stop, pressing Tab moves the text so that its center is aligned with the tab stop.

> **Tip** When you want to fine-tune the position of tab stops, click the Paragraph Dialog Box Launcher on either the Home or Page Layout tab. In the Paragraph dialog box, click the Tabs button to display the Tabs dialog box. You might also open this dialog box if you want to use *tab leaders*—visible marks such as dots or dashes connecting the text before the tab with the text after it. For example, tab leaders are useful in a table of contents to carry the eye from the text to the page number.

In addition to tab stops, the horizontal ruler also displays *indent markers* that are used to control where each line of text starts and ends. You use these markers to indent text from the left or right margins as follows:

- **First Line Indent.** Begins a paragraph's first line of text at this marker.
- **Hanging Indent.** Begins a paragraph's second and subsequent lines of text at this marker.
- **Left Indent.** Indents the text to this marker.
- **Right Indent.** Wraps the text when it reaches this marker.

You can also determine the positioning of a paragraph between the left and right margins by changing its alignment. You can click buttons in the Paragraph group on the Home tab to align paragraphs as follows:

- **Align Left.** Aligns each line of the paragraph at the left margin, with a ragged right edge.
- **Align Right.** Aligns each line of the paragraph at the right margin, with a ragged left edge.
- **Center.** Aligns the center of each line in the paragraph between the left and right margins, with ragged left and right edges.
- **Justify.** Aligns each line between the margins, creating even left and right edges.

> **Tip** If you know that you want to type a centered paragraph, you don't have to type it and then format it as centered. You can use the *Click and Type* feature to create appropriately aligned text. Move the pointer to the center of a blank area of the page, and when the pointer's shape changes to an I-beam with centered text attached, double-click to create an insertion point that is ready to enter centered text. Similarly, you can double-click at the left edge of the page to enter left-aligned text and at the right edge to enter right-aligned text.

To make it obvious where one paragraph ends and another begins, you can add space be-tween them by adjusting the Spacing After and Spacing Before settings in the Paragraph group on the Page Layout tab. You can adjust the spacing between the lines in a para-graph by clicking the Line Spacing button in the Paragraph group on the Home tab.

When you want to make several adjustments to the alignment, indentation, and spacing of selected paragraphs, it is sometimes quicker to use the Paragraph dialog box than to click buttons and drag markers. Click the Paragraph Dialog Box Launcher on either the Home or Page Layout tab to open the Paragraph dialog box.

To make a paragraph really stand out, you can put a border around it or shade its background. For real drama, you can do both.

> **Tip**  A paragraph's formatting is stored in its paragraph mark. If you delete the paragraph mark, thereby making it part of the following paragraph, its text takes on the formatting of that paragraph. If you position the insertion point anywhere in the paragraph and press Enter to create a new one, the new paragraph takes on the existing paragraph's formatting.

In this exercise, you'll change text alignment and indentation, insert and modify tab stops, modify paragraph and line spacing, and add borders and shading around para-graphs to change their appearance.

> **USE**  the *03_Paragraphs* document. This practice file is located in the *Chapter03* subfolder under *SBS_Office2007.*
>
> **BE SURE TO**  turn on the display of non-printing characters for this exercise. Also display the rulers.
>
> **OPEN**  the *03_Paragraphs* document.

Zoom Out

**1.** In the lower-right corner of the document window, click the **Zoom Out** button twice to set the zoom percentage to 80%.

You can now see all the text of the document.

**2.** In the fourth line of the document, click to the left of *Update*, and then on the **Page Layout** tab, in the **Page Setup** group, click the **Breaks** button, and then click **Text Wrapping**.

Word inserts a line break character and moves the part of the paragraph that follows that character to the next line.

**See Also** For information about column breaks, see "Presenting Information in Columns" in Chapter 4, "Presenting Information in Tables and Columns."

Center

**3.** Select the first four lines of the document, and then on the **Home** tab, in the **Paragraph** group, click the **Center** button.

The lines are now centered between the margins. Notice that even though you did not select the fifth line, it is also centered because it is part of the *Author Meet and Greet* paragraph.

Text wrapping line break

Justify

**4.** Select the next two paragraphs, and then in the **Paragraph** group, click the **Justify** button.

The edges of the first paragraph are now flush against both the left and right margins. The second paragraph doesn't change because it is less than a line long.

First Line Indent

**5.** With both paragraphs still selected, on the horizontal ruler, drag the **First Line Indent** marker to the 0.25-inch mark.

The first line of each paragraph is now indented a quarter inch from the left margin.

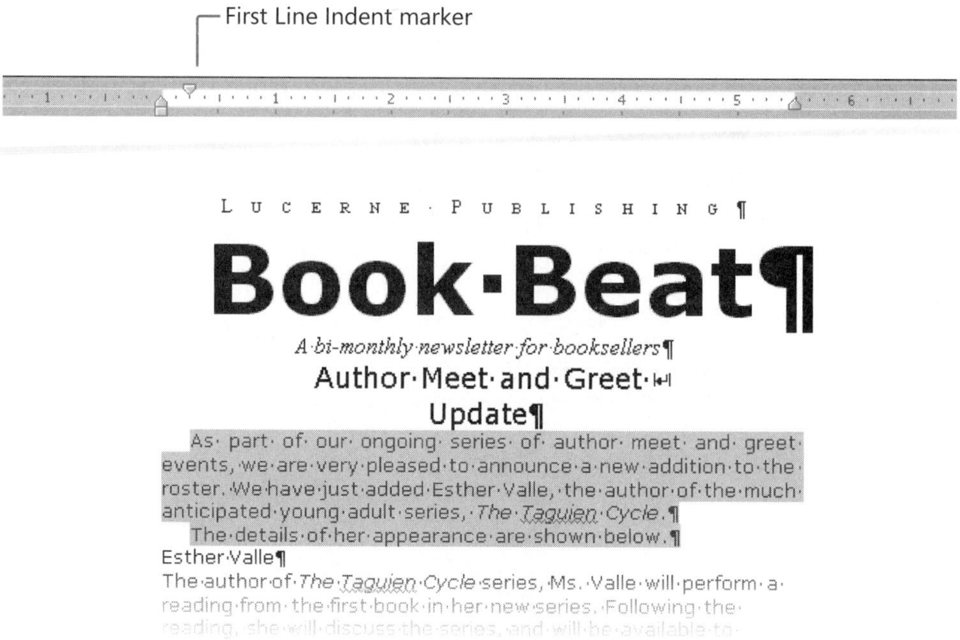

First Line Indent marker

L U C E R N E · P U B L I S H I N G ¶

# Book·Beat¶

*A·bi-monthly·newsletter·for·booksellers*¶
## Author·Meet·and·Greet·↵
## Update¶

As· part· of· our· ongoing· series· of· author· meet· and· greet·
events,·we·are·very·pleased·to·announce·a·new·addition·to·the·
roster.·We·have·just·added·Esther·Valle,·the·author·of·the·much·
anticipated·young·adult·series,·*The·Taguien·Cycle*.¶
The·details·of·her·appearance·are·shown·below.¶
Esther·Valle¶
The·author·of·*The·Taguien·Cycle*·series,·Ms.·Valle·will·perform·a·
reading·from·the·first·book·in·her·new·series.·Following·the·
reading,·she·will·discuss·the·series,·and·will·be·available·to·

**6.** Click anywhere in the *Esther Valle* paragraph, and then in the **Paragraph** group, click the **Center** button.

> **Tip**  When applying paragraph formatting, you don't have to select the entire paragraph.

Left Indent

**7.** Select all the paragraphs below *Esther Valle*, and then on the horizontal ruler, drag the **Left Indent** marker to the 0.5-inch mark.

The First Line Indent and Hanging Indent markers move with the Left Indent marker, and all the selected paragraphs are now indented a half inch from the left margin.

Right Indent

**8.** Drag the **Right Indent** marker to the 5-inch mark.

The paragraphs are now indented from the right margin as well.

Left Indent marker                    Right Indent marker

Increase Indent

**9.** Select the **Date:**, **Time:**, **Location:**, and **Ticket cost:** paragraphs, and then in the **Paragraph** group, click the **Increase Indent** button.

These four paragraphs are now indented to the 1-inch mark.

Left Tab

**10.** Without changing the selection, make sure the **Left Tab** button at the junction of the horizontal and vertical rulers is active, and then click the ruler at the 2.5-inch mark to set a left tab stop.

**11.** Click at the right end of the *Date:* paragraph to position the insertion point before the paragraph mark, and then press the [Tab] key.

Word will left-align any text you type after the tab character at the new tab stop.

**12.** Press the [↓] key, and then press [Tab].

**13.** Repeat Step 12 for the *Location* and *Ticket cost* paragraphs.

All four paragraphs now have tabs that are aligned with the tab stop at the 2.5-inch mark.

Left-aligned tab stop        Default tab stop

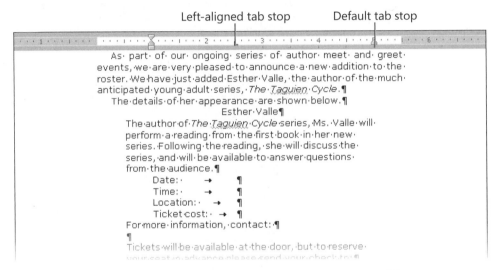

**14.** Without moving the insertion point, type **Adult**, and then press [Tab].

Decimal Tab

**15.** Click the **Tab** button three times to activate a decimal tab, and then click the 4-inch mark on the horizontal ruler.

**16.** Type $10.00, press [Enter], press [Tab] type **Child**, press [Tab] again, and then type $5.00.

The new paragraph takes on the same paragraph formatting as the *Ticket cost* paragraph, and the dollar amounts are aligned on their decimal points.

Decimal-aligned tab stop

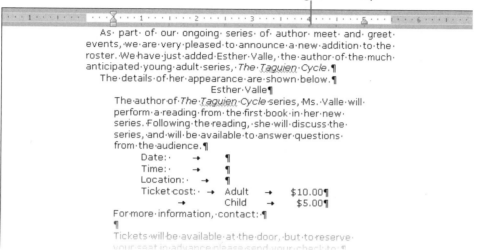

As· part· of· our· ongoing· series· of· author· meet· and· greet·
events,·we·are·very·pleased·to·announce·a·new·addition·to·the·
roster.·We·have·just·added·Esther·Valle,·the·author·of·the·much·
anticipated·young·adult·series,·*The·Taquien·Cycle*.¶
The·details·of·her·appearance·are·shown·below.¶
Esther·Valle¶
The·author·of·*The·Taquien·Cycle* series,·Ms.·Valle·will·
perform·a·reading·from· the·first·book·in·her·new·
series.·Following·the·reading,·she·will·discuss·the·
series,·and·will· be·available·to·answer·questions·
from·the·audience.¶

| Date:· | → | ¶ | | |
| Time:· | → | ¶ | | |
| Location:· | → | ¶ | | |
| Ticket·cost:· | → | Adult | → | $10.00¶ |
| | → | Child | → | $5.00¶ |

For·more·information,·contact:·¶
¶
Tickets·will·be·available· at·the·door,·but·to·reserve·
your·seat·in·advance,·please·send·your·check·to:·¶

17. Drag through any part of the two paragraphs with dollar amounts, and then on the horizontal ruler, drag the decimal tab stop from the 4-inch mark to the 3.5-inch mark.

18. On the **Home** tab, in the **Editing** group, click the **Select** button, and then click **Select All**.

19. On the **Page Layout** tab, in the **Paragraph** group, change the **Spacing After** setting to **12 pt**.

Word inserts 12 points of space after every paragraph in the document.

Line Spacing

20. Click anywhere in the paragraph that begins *As part of*, and then on the **Home** tab, in the **Paragraph** group, click the **Line Spacing** button, and then click **Remove Space After Paragraph**.

21. Select the **Date:**, **Time:**, **Location:**, and **Ticket cost:** paragraphs, and then repeat Step 20.

22. Select the **Jill Shrader**, **Lucerne Publishing**, and **4567 Oak Street** paragraphs, and then repeat Step 20 again.

**23.** Click anywhere in the paragraph that begins *The author of*, click the **Line Spacing** button again, and then click **1.5**.

You have adjusted both the paragraph and line spacing of the document.

Borders

**24.** Click the *Book Beat* paragraph. Then on the **Home** tab, in the **Paragraph** group, click the **Borders** arrow, and at the bottom of the list, click **Borders and Shading**.

The Borders And Shading dialog box opens.

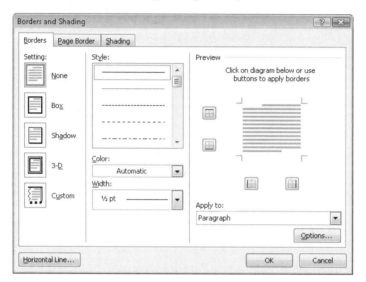

**25.** Under **Setting**, click the **Shadow** icon to select that border style.

> **Tip** You can change the settings in the Style, Color, and Width boxes to create the kind of border you want. If you want only one, two, or three sides of the selected paragraphs to have a border, click the buttons surrounding the image in the Preview area.

**26.** Click the **Shading** tab.

You can use the options on this tab to format the background of the selected paragraph.

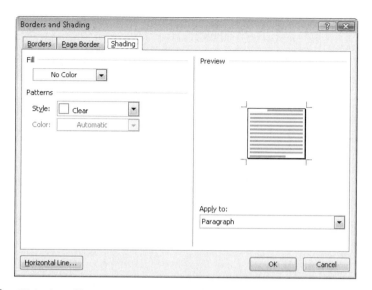

**27.** Click the **Fill** arrow, and under **Theme Colors**, click the second lightest purple box
(**Purple, Accent 4, Lighter 60%**). Then click **OK** to close the **Borders and Shading**
dialog box.

A border with a shadow surrounds the text, and the background color is light purple.

**BE SURE TO** change the Zoom percentage back to 100% before moving on to the next
exercise, and if you want, turn off the rulers.

**CLOSE** the *03_Paragraphs* document without saving your changes.

**Finding and Replacing Formatting**

In addition to searching for words and phrases, you can use the Find And Replace dialog box to search for a specific format and replace it with a different format.

To search for a specific format and replace it with a different format:

1. On the **Home** tab, in the **Editing** group, click the **Replace** button.

    The Find And Replace dialog box opens, displaying the Replace tab.

2. Click **More** to expand the dialog box, click **Format**, and then click **Font** or **Paragraph**.

    The Find Font or Find Paragraph dialog box opens. (You can also click Style to search for paragraph styles or character styles.)

3. In the dialog box, click the format you want to find, and then click **OK**.

4. Click the **Replace with** text box, click **Format**, click **Font** or **Paragraph**, click the format you want to substitute for the Find What format, and then click **OK**.

5. Click **Find Next** to search for the first occurrence of the format, and then click **Replace** to replace that one instance or **Replace All** to replace every instance.

# Creating and Modifying Lists

When you want to present a list of items in a document, you will usually want to put each item on its own line rather than burying the items in a paragraph. When the order of items is not important—for example, for a list of items needed to carry out a task—use a bulleted list. When the order is important—for example, for the steps in a procedure—use a numbered list.

With Word, you start a bulleted or numbered list as follows:

- To create a bulleted list, type * (an asterisk) at the beginning of a paragraph, and then press the Spacebar or the Tab key.
- To create a numbered list, type 1. (the numeral 1 followed by a period) at the beginning of a paragraph, and then press the Spacebar or the Tab key.

In either case, you then type the first item in the list and press Enter. Word starts the new paragraph with a bullet or 2 followed by a period and formats the first and second paragraphs as a numbered list. Typing items and pressing Enter adds subsequent bulleted or numbered items. To end the list, press Enter twice, or press Enter and then Backspace.

> **Troubleshooting**  If you want to start a paragraph with an asterisk or number but don't want the paragraph to be formatted as a bulleted or numbered list, click the AutoCorrect Options button that appears after Word changes the formatting, and then click the Undo option.

After you create a list, you can modify, format, and customize the list as follows:

- You can move items around in a list, insert new items, or delete unwanted items. If the list is numbered, Word automatically updates the numbers.

- You can sort items in a bulleted list into ascending or descending order by clicking the Sort button in the Paragraph group on the Home tab.

- For a bulleted list, you can change the bullet symbol by clicking the Bullets arrow in the Paragraph group and making a selection from the Bullet Library. You can also define a custom bullet by clicking the Bullets arrow and then clicking Define New Bullet.

- For a numbered list, you can change the number style by clicking the Numbering arrow in the Paragraph group and making a selection from the Numbering Library. You can also define a custom style by clicking the Numbering arrow and then clicking Define New Number Format.

- You can create a multilevel bulleted list, numbered list, or outline by clicking the Multilevel List button in the Paragraph group, selecting a style from the List Library, and then typing the list. You press Enter to create a new item at the same level, the Tab key to move down a level, and the Backspace key to move up a level.

  **See Also**  For information about another way to create an outline, see "Reorganizing a Document Outline" in Chapter 2, "Editing and Proofreading Documents."

- You can modify the indentation of the list by dragging the indent markers on the horizontal ruler. Lists are set up with the first line "outdented" to the left from the other lines, and you can change both the overall indentation of the list and the relationship of the first line to the other lines.

In this exercise, you will create a bulleted list and a numbered list and then modify lists in various ways. You will then create a multilevel list with letters instead of numbers.

**USE** the *04_Lists* document. This practice file is located in the *Chapter03* subfolder under *SBS_Office2007*.

**OPEN** the *04_Lists* document.

Bullets

**1.** Select the three paragraphs under *Rationale*, and then on the **Home** tab, in the **Paragraph** group, click the **Bullets** button.

The selected paragraphs are reformatted as a bulleted list.

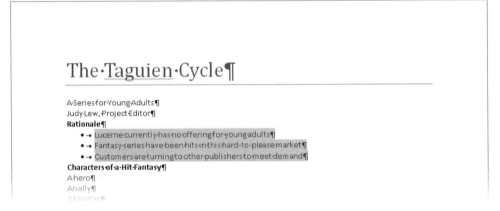

**2.** With the three paragraphs still selected, in the **Paragraph** group, click the **Bullets** arrow.

The Bullet Library appears.

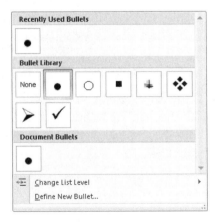

3. In the gallery, click the bullet composed of four diamonds.

   The bullet character in the selected list changes.

4. Select the four paragraphs under *Characters of a Hit Fantasy*, and then in the **Paragraph** group, click the **Bullets** button.

   The new list has the bullet character you selected for the previous list. This character will be the default until you change it.

5. Select the paragraphs under each of the bold headings, and then in the **Paragraph** group, click the **Bullets** button.

6. Scroll to the bottom of the page, select the four paragraphs under *The Sequence of Events*, and then in the **Paragraph** group, in the **Bullets Library**, click **None**.

   The bulleted paragraphs revert to normal paragraphs.

Numbering

7. With the paragraphs still selected, on the **Home** tab, in the **Paragraph** group, click the **Numbering** button.

   The selected paragraphs are reformatted as a numbered list.

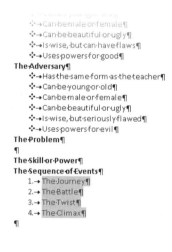

8. In the **Paragraph** group, click the **Numbering** arrow.

   The Numbering Library appears.

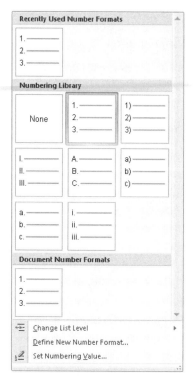

9. In the gallery, click the **A. B. C.** box.

   The numbers change to capital letters.

Decrease Indent

10. With the numbered paragraphs still selected, in the **Paragraph** group, click the **Decrease Indent** button.

    The numbered list moves to the left margin.

Increase Indent

11. In the **Paragraph** group, click the **Increase Indent** button to move the list back to its original indent.

> **Tip** You can also adjust the indent level of a bulleted list by selecting its paragraphs, and on the horizontal ruler, dragging the Left Indent marker to the left or right. The First Line Indent and Hanging Indent markers move with the Left Indent marker. You can move just the Hanging Indent marker to adjust the space between the bullets and their text.

Sort

12. Scroll the document until you can see the bulleted list under *The Hero*, select the three bulleted paragraphs, and then on the **Home** tab, in the **Paragraph** group, click the **Sort** button.

    The Sort Text dialog box opens.

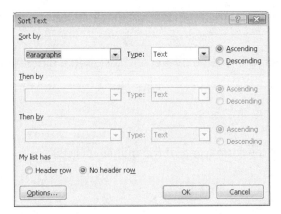

13. With the **Ascending** option selected, click **OK**.

   The order of the bulleted items changes to ascending alphabetical order.

Multilevel List

14. Click the blank paragraph under *The Ally*, and then on the **Home** tab, in the **Paragraph** group, click the **Multilevel List** button.

   The List Library appears.

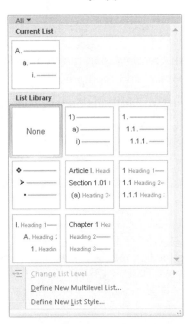

15. In the gallery, click the thumbnail under **Current List**.

   The first item in the new numbered list will have a capital letter as its numbering style.

**16.** Type Does not have to be human, press `Enter`, type Is a stabilizing force, press `Enter`, and then press `Tab`.

The new item is indented to the next level and assigned a different number style.

**17.** Type A voice of conscience, press `Enter`, type Not a "yes" person, press `Enter`, and then press `Shift` + `Tab`.

**18.** Type Embodies loyalty.

Word takes care of all the formatting of the multilevel list.

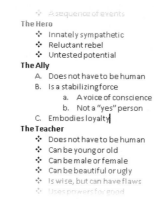

**19.** Under *The Problem*, click to the left of the blank paragraph mark, type * (an asterisk), press `Tab`, type A difficult choice, and then press `Enter`.

Word converts the asterisk into a bullet and formats the next paragraph as a bulleted item.

**20.** Type An injustice, press `Enter`, and then type A quest.

 **CLOSE** the *04_Lists* document without saving your changes.

**Formatting Text as You Type**

The Word list formatting capabilities are just one example of the program's ability to intuit how you want to format an element based on what you type. You can learn more about these and other AutoFormatting options by exploring the AutoCorrect dialog box. To open this dialog box, click the Microsoft Office Button, click Word Options, click Proofing in the left pane of the Word Options window, and then click AutoCorrect Options in the right pane.

On the AutoFormat As You Type tab, you can see the options that Word implements by default, including bulleted and numbered lists. You can select and clear options to control Word's AutoFormatting behavior.

One interesting option is Border Lines. When this check box is selected, you can type three consecutive hyphens (-) and press Enter to have Word draw a single line across the page. Or you can type three consecutive equal signs (=) and press Enter to have Word draw a double line.

# Key Points

- Quick Styles are a great way to apply combinations of formatting to give your documents a professional look.

- You can format characters with an almost limitless number of combinations of font, size, style, and effect—but for best results, resist the temptation to use more than a handful of combinations.

- You can change the look of paragraphs by varying their indentation, spacing, and alignment and by setting tab stops. Use these formatting options judiciously to create documents with a balanced, uncluttered look.

- Bulleted and numbered lists are a great way to present information in an easy to read, easy to understand format. If the built-in bulleted and numbered list styles don't provide what you need, you can define your own styles.

# Chapter at a Glance

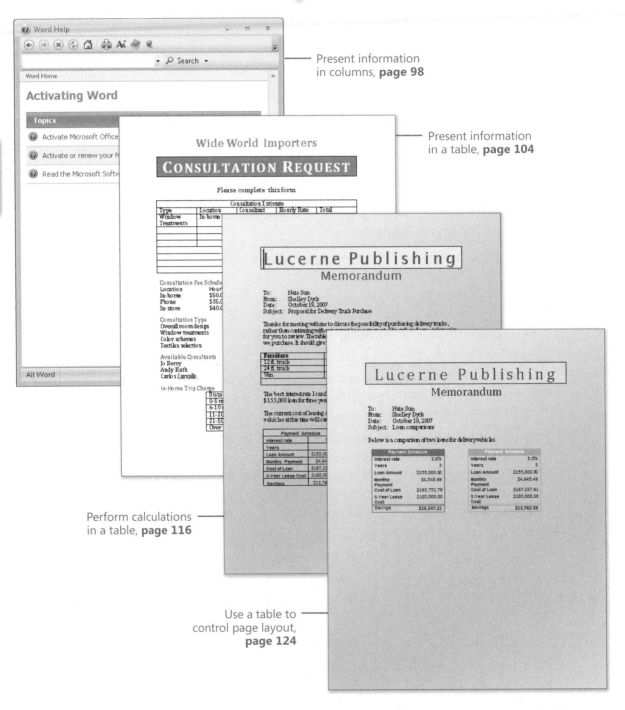

Present information in columns, **page 98**

Present information in a table, **page 104**

Perform calculations in a table, **page 116**

Use a table to control page layout, **page 124**

# 4 Presenting Information in Columns and Tables

---

**In this chapter, you will learn to:**

- ✔ Present information in columns.
- ✔ Create a tabular list.
- ✔ Present information in a table.
- ✔ Format table information.
- ✔ Perform calculations in a table.
- ✔ Use a table to control page layout.

---

When creating a Word document, you might find it useful to organize certain information into columns or tables. Flowing text in multiple columns is common practice in newsletters, flyers, and brochures. After you specify the number of columns, Word flows the text from one column to the next. You can also manually end one column and move subsequent text to the next column.

It is often more efficient to present numeric data in a table than to explain it in a paragraph of text. Tables make the data easier to read and understand. Small amounts of data can be displayed in simple columns separated by left, right, centered, or decimal tab stops to create a tabular list. Larger amounts or more complex data is better presented in a Word table that includes a structure of rows and columns, frequently with row and column headings.

A Word table is useful not only for presenting data but also for providing the structure for complex document layouts. For example, you can set up a table with two columns and two rows to present a set of four paragraphs, four bulleted lists, or four tables in a format in which they can be easily compared.

In this chapter, you will create and modify columns of text, create a simple tabular list, create tables from scratch and from existing text, format a table in various ways, and perform calculations within a table. You will copy and paste worksheet data, link to worksheet data, and create an Excel object. And finally, you will create a table for the purpose of displaying two other tables side by side.

**See Also**  Do you need only a quick refresher on the topics in this chapter? See the Quick Reference entries at the beginning of this book.

**Important**  Before you can use the practice files in this chapter, you need to install them from the book's companion CD to their default location. See "Using the Book's CD" at the beginning of this book for more information.

**Troubleshooting**  Graphics and operating system–related instructions in this book reflect the Windows Vista user interface. If your computer is running Microsoft Windows XP and you experience trouble following the instructions as written, please refer to the "Information for Readers Running Windows XP" section at the beginning of this book.

# Presenting Information in Columns

By default, Word displays text in one *column*, but you can specify that text be displayed in two, three, or more columns to create layouts like those used in newspapers and magazines. When you format text to *flow* in columns, the text fills the first column and then moves to the top of the next column. You can insert a *column break* to move to the next column before the current column is full.

Word provides several standard options for dividing text into columns. You have the choice of one, two, or three equal columns, or two other two-column formats: one with a narrow left column and the other with a narrow right column. No matter how you set up the columns initially, you can change the layout or column widths at any time.

You can format the text in columns the same way you would any text. If you *justify* the columns for a neater look, you might want to have Word hyphenate the text to ensure that there are no large gaps between words.

In this exercise, you will divide part of a document into three columns. You will then justify the columns, change the column spacing, hyphenate the text, and indent a couple of paragraphs. You'll also break a column at a specific location instead of allowing the text to flow naturally from one column to the next.

> **USE** the *01_Columns* document. This practice file is located in the *Chapter04* subfolder under *SBS_Office2007*.
>
> **BE SURE TO** display the rulers and non-printing characters before starting this exercise.
>
> **OPEN** the *01_Columns* document.

**1.** Click just to the left of the paragraph that begins *Take a look* (do not click in the selection area). Then scroll the end of the document into view, hold down the ⎙ Shift key, and click just to the right of the period after *credit cards*.

Word selects the text from the *Take a look* paragraph through the end of the document.

> **Tip** If you want to format an entire document with the same number of columns, you can simply click anywhere in the document—you don't have to select the text.

**2.** On the **Page Layout** tab, in the **Page Setup** group, click the **Columns** button, and then click **Three**.

**3.** Press ⎙Ctrl + ⎙Home to move to the top of the document.

Word has inserted a section break above the selection and formatted the text after the section break into three columns.

Room·Makeover¶

With·the·Room·Planner,·you'll·never·make·a·design·mistake·again.·Created·by·acclaimed·interior· designers·to·simplify·the·redecorating·process,·this·planning·tool·incorporates·elements·of·color,· dimension,·and·style·to·guide·your·project.·It·includes·a·furniture·location·guide;·room·grid;·drawing· tools;·and·miniature·furniture,·rugs,·accessories,·and·color·swatches·that·match·our·large·in·store· selection.·Here's·how·to·use·the·planner·to·create·the·room·of·your·dreams!¶

¶··················································Section·Break·(Continuous)··················································

Take·a·look·at·how·your· home·is·decorated·and·note· the·things·you·like·and· dislike.·Pay·special·attention· to·the·color·scheme·and·to· how·each·room·"feels"·to· you.·Is·it·inviting?·Does·it· feel·comfortable?·Does·it· relax·you·or·does·it· invigorate·you?¶

love,·and·the·rest·will·fall· into·place.¶

Take·your·Room·Planner· home·and·get·to·work!· Adjust·the·planner·so·that·it· models·the·room· dimensions.·Don't·forget·to· place·the·windows·and· doors.·Arrange·the·furniture· placeholders·to·mirror·how·

design·for·a·day·or·two.· Then·review·it·again.·Does·it· still·look·perfect,·or·is· something·not·quite·right?· You·might·need·to·"live"· with·the·new·plan·for·a·few· days,·especially·if·you've· made·big·changes.·When· everything·feels·just·right·to· you,·you're·ready·for·the· next·big·step!¶

Justify

**4.** On the **Home** tab, in the **Editing** group, click the **Select** button, and then click **Select All**.

**5.** In the **Paragraph** group, click the **Justify** button.

The spacing of the text within the paragraphs changes so the right edge of the paragraph is straight.

Center

**6.** Press Ctrl + Home to deselect the text and move to the top of the document, and then in the **Paragraph** group, click the **Center** button to center the title.

**7.** At the right end of the status bar, click the **Zoom** button. Then in the **Zoom** dialog box, click **75%**, and click **OK**.

You can now see about two-thirds of the first page of the document.

**8.** Click anywhere in the first column.

On the horizontal ruler, Word indicates the margins of the columns.

**9.** On the **Page Layout** tab, in the **Page Setup** group, click the **Columns** button, and then click **More Columns**.

The Columns dialog box opens. Because the Equal Column Width check box is selected, you can adjust the width and spacing of only the first column.

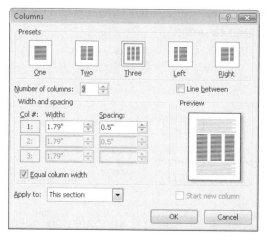

**10.** Under **Width and spacing**, in the **Spacing** column, click the down arrow until the setting is **0.2"**.

Word changes the measurement in the box below and widens all the columns to reflect the new setting.

**11.** Click **OK**.

Word reflows the columns to fit their new margins.

# Room·Makeover¶

With·the·Room·Planner,·you'll·never·make·a·design·mistake·again.·Created·by·acclaimed·interior·designers·to·simplify·the·redecorating·process,·this·planning·tool·incorporates·elements·of·color,·dimension,·and·style·to·guide·your·project.·It·includes·a·furniture·location·guide;·room·grid;·drawing·tools;·and·miniature·furniture,·rugs,·accessories,·and·colors·watches·that·match·our·large·in-store·selection.·Here's·how·to·use·the·planner·to·create·the·room·of·your·dreams!¶

¶·················Section·Break·(Continuous)·················

Take·a·look·at·how·your·home·is·decorated·and·note·the·things·you·like·and·dislike.·Pay·special·attention·to·the·color·scheme·and·to·how·each·room·"feels"·to·you.·Is·it·inviting?·Does·it·feel·comfortable?·Does·it·relax·you·or·does·it·invigorate·you?¶

Focus·on·the·room(s)·you·would·most·like·to·change.·Brainstorm·all·the·things·you·would·change·in·that·room·if·you·could.·Don't·give·a·thought·to·any·financial·considerations;·just·let·your·imagine·go·wild!·It·might·be·helpful·to·write·down·all·the·negatives·and·positives.·You·don't·need·to·come·up·with·solutions·all·at·once.·Just·get·

planner·so·that·it·models·the·room·dimensions.·Don't·forget·to·place·the·windows·and·doors.·Arrange·the·furniture·placeholders·to·mirror·how·your·room·is·currently·set·up.·Add·the·current·colors,·too.¶

This·is·where·the·fun·begins!·Start·changing·things·around·a·bit.·Move·the·furniture,·add·different·colors,·and·watch·the·room·come·together!·Here's·where·you·can·tell·if·that·rich·red·rug·you·saw·in·the·showroom·enhances·or·overwhelms·your·room.·What·about·that·overstuffed·chair·that·caught·your·eye?·Place·a·furniture·or·accessory·shape,·and·then·color·it.·Does·it·look·

just·right·to·you,·you're·ready·for·the·next·big·step!¶

Come·back·to·the·store.·Look·again·at·the·pieces·you·liked·during·your·last·visit·and·see·if·you·still·love·them.·If·you're·not·quite·sure,·go·back·to·your·planner·for·a·little·more·tweaking.·If·you·are·sure,·take·a·look·around·the·store·one·more·time·to·see·if·anything·else·catches·your·eye.·Then·make·your·purchases.·You're·almost·there!¶

NOTE:·If·you·decided·to·paint·your·room,·do·that·before·your·new·pieces·are·delivered.·You'll·want·to·start·enjoying·your·new·room·as·soon·as·your·purchases·

**12.** Click immediately to the left of *Take a look*. Then in the **Page Setup** group, click the **Hyphenation** button, and click **Automatic**.

Word hyphenates the text of the document, which fills in some of the large gaps between words.

**13.** Click anywhere in the *NOTE* paragraph in the third column.

Hanging
Indent
**14.** On the horizontal ruler, in the third column, drag the **Hanging Indent** marker 0.25 inch (two marks) to the right.

All the lines in the *NOTE* paragraph except the first are now indented, offsetting the note from the paragraphs above and below it.

**15.** Click just to the left of *Take your Room Planner home* at the bottom of the first column on Page 1. Then in the **Page Setup** group, click the **Breaks** button, and click **Column**.

The text that follows the column break moves to the top of the second column.

Repeat

**16.** Click just to the left of *If you're not sure* at the bottom of the third column on Page 1, and then on the **Quick Access Toolbar**, click the **Repeat Insertion** button to insert another column break.

The text that follows the column break moves to the top of the first column on Page 2.

**CLOSE** the *01_Columns* document without saving your changes.

# Creating a Tabular List

If you have a relatively small amount of data to present in a table, you might choose to display it in a *tabular list*, which arranges text in simple columns separated by left, right, centered, or decimal tab stops.

**See Also** For more information about setting tab stops, see "Manually Changing the Look of Paragraphs" in Chapter 3, "Changing the Look of Text."

When entering text in a tabular list, people have a tendency to press the Tab key multiple times to align the columns of the list. If you do this, you have no control over the column widths. To be able to fine-tune the columns, you need to set custom tab stops rather than relying on the default ones. When you want to set up a tabular list, you should press Tab only once between the items that you want to appear in separate columns. You can then apply any necessary formatting and set the tabs in order from left to right so that you can see how everything lines up.

> **Tip** In addition to left, right, centered, and decimal tabs, you can set a bar tab. This type of tab does not align text like the others, but instead adds a vertical line to selected paragraphs. This bar can be used to further distinguish the columns in a tabular list.

In this exercise, you will create a tabular list. First you'll enter text separated by tabs, and then you'll format the text and set custom tab stops.

**USE** the *02_TabularList* document. This practice file is located in the *Chapter04* subfolder under *SBS_Office2007*.
**BE SURE TO** display the rulers and non-printing characters before starting this exercise.
**OPEN** the *02_TabularList* document.

**1.** Scroll down to the bottom of the document, click to the left of the paragraph mark at the end of *The Skill or Power*, and then press Enter.

2. Type Self, press [Tab], type Other People, press [Tab], type Nature, and then press [Enter].

3. Add three more lines to the list by typing the following text. Press [Tab] once be-tween each item in a line, and press [Enter] at the end of each line except the last.

   *Transformation* [Tab] *Life/death* [Tab] *Weather*

   *Time travel* [Tab] *Telepathy* [Tab] *Oceans*

   *Visible/invisible* [Tab] *Mind control* [Tab] *Animals*

   The tab characters push the items to the next default tab stop, but because some items are longer than others, they do not line up.

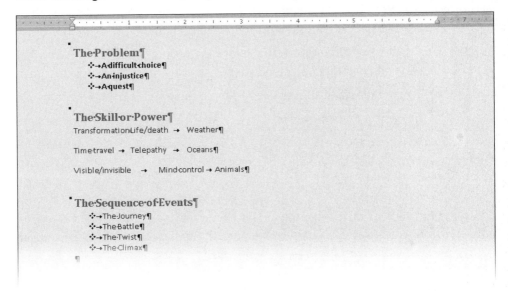

   **See Also** For information about tab stops, see "Manually Changing the Look of Paragraphs" in Chapter 3, "Changing the Look of Text."

**Bold**

4. Select the first line of the tabular list, and then on the **Mini toolbar** that appears, click the **Bold** button.

   > **Troubleshooting** If the Mini toolbar doesn't appear, click the Bold button in the Font group on the Home tab.

Increase
Indent

5. Select all four lines of the tabular list, and then on the **Mini toolbar**, click the **Increase Indent** button.

6. With the lines still selected, on the **Page Layout** tab, in the **Paragraph** group, under **Spacing**, change the **After** setting to 0 pt.

Left Tab

7. Without changing the selection, verify that the **Tab** button at the junction of the horizontal and vertical rulers shows a Left Tab stop (an L), and then click the 2-inch mark on the horizontal ruler.

   Word displays a Left Tab stop on the ruler, and the items in the second column of all the selected lines left-align themselves at that position.

8. Click the **Tab** button twice.

   The icon on the button changes to a Right Tab stop (a backward L), indicating that clicking the ruler now will set a right-aligned tab.

9. Click the horizontal ruler at the 4-inch mark.

   Word displays a Right Tab stop on the ruler, and the items in the third column of the selected lines jump to right-align themselves at that position.

10. On the Home tab, in the Paragraph group, click the Show/Hide ¶ button to hide non-printing characters. Then click away from the tabular list to see the results.

    The tabular list resembles a simple table.

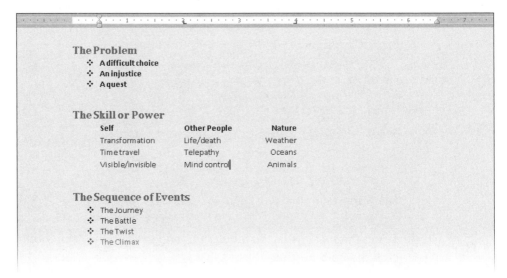

 **CLOSE** the *02_TabularList* document without saving your changes.

# Presenting Information in a Table

Creating a Word table is a simple matter of clicking the Table button and selecting the number of rows and columns you want from a grid. You can then enter text, numbers, and graphics into the table's *cells*, which are the boxes at the intersections of a row and a column. At any time, you can change the table's size; insert and delete columns, rows, and cells; and format individual entries or the entire table. You can sort the information in a logical order and perform calculations on the numbers in a column or row.

Clicking the Table button creates a table with the number of columns and rows you select from the grid, with all the cells of equal size. You can click Insert Table below the grid to open the Insert Table dialog box, where you can specify the number of rows and columns as well as their sizes. You can also create a table by drawing cells the size you want. If the text you want to appear in a table already exists in the document, you can convert the text to a table.

**See Also** For information about drawing tables, see "Using a Table to Control Page Layout" later in this chapter.

A new table appears in the document as a set of blank cells surrounded by *gridlines*. Each cell has an end-of-cell marker, and each row has an end-of-row marker. When the pointer is over the table, the table has a move handle in its upper-left corner and a size handle in its lower-right corner. While the insertion point is in the table, Word displays two Table Tools contextual tabs, Design and Layout.

End-of-row marker

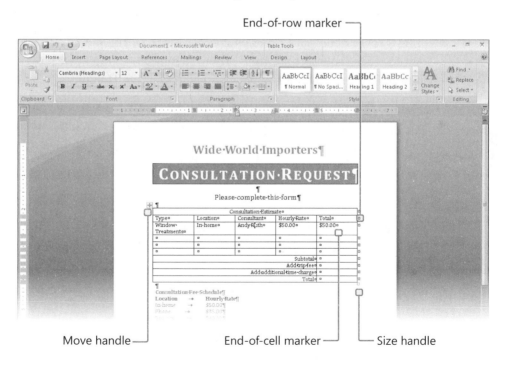

Move handle    End-of-cell marker    Size handle

**Tip** You cannot see the move handle and size handle in Draft view.

After you create a table, you can type text or numbers into cells and press the Tab key to move the insertion point from cell to cell. Pressing Tab when the insertion point is in the last cell in the last row adds a new row to the bottom of the table. In addition to the Tab key, you can use the Arrow keys to position the insertion point, or you can simply click any cell.

You can modify a table's structure at any time. To change the structure, you often need to select the entire table or specific rows or columns, by using the following methods:

- **Select a table.** Click anywhere in the table. Then on the Layout contextual tab, in the Table group, click the Select button, and click Select Table.
- **Select a column.** Point to the top border of the column. When the pointer changes to a black, down-pointing arrow, click once.
- **Select a row.** Point to the left border of the row. When the pointer changes to a white, right-pointing arrow, click once.
- **Select a cell.** Triple-click the cell or click its left border.
- **Select multiple cells.** Click the first cell, hold down the Shift key, and press the arrow keys to select adjacent cells in a column or row.

The basic methods for manipulating tables are as follows:

- **Insert a row or column.** Click anywhere in a row or column adjacent to where you want to make the insertion. Then on the Layout tab, in the Rows & Columns group, click the Insert Above, Insert Below, Insert Left, or Insert Right button. Selecting more than one row or column before you click an Insert button inserts that number of rows or columns in the table.

> **Tip** You can insert cells by clicking the Rows & Columns Dialog Box Launcher and specifying in the Insert Cells dialog box how adjacent cells should be moved to accommodate the new cells.

- **Delete a row or column.** Click anywhere in the row or column, and in the Rows & Columns group, click the Delete button. Then click Delete Cells, Delete Columns, Delete Rows, or Delete Table.
- **Size an entire table.** Drag the size handle.
- **Size a single column or row.** Drag a column's right border to the left or right. Drag a row's bottom border up or down.
- **Merge cells.** Create cells that span columns by selecting the cells you want to merge and clicking the Merge Cells button in the Merge group on the Layout tab. For example, to center a title in the first row of a table, you can create one merged cell that spans the table's width.

- **Split cells.** Divide a merged cell into its component cells by clicking Split Cells in the Merge group on the Layout tab.

- **Move a table.** Point to the table, and then drag the move handle that appears in its upper-left corner to a new location. Or use the Cut and Paste buttons in the Clipboard group on the Home tab to move the table.

- **Sort information.** Use the Sort button in the Data group on the Layout tab to sort the rows in ascending or descending order by the data in any column. For example, you can sort a table that has the column headings Name, Address, ZIP Code, and Phone Number on any one of those columns to arrange the information in alphabetical or numerical order.

In this exercise, you will work with two tables. First you'll create a table, enter text, align text in the cells, add rows, and merge cells. Then you'll create a second table by converting existing tabbed text, you'll size a column, and you'll size the entire table.

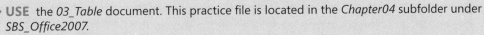

**USE** the *03_Table* document. This practice file is located in the *Chapter04* subfolder under *SBS_Office2007*.

**OPEN** the *03_Table* document.

1. Click in the second blank line below *Please complete this form.*

2. On the **Insert** tab, in the **Tables** group, click the **Table** button, point to the upper-left cell, and move the pointer across five columns and down five rows.

   Word highlights the cells as you drag across them and creates a temporary table in the document to show you what the selection will look like.

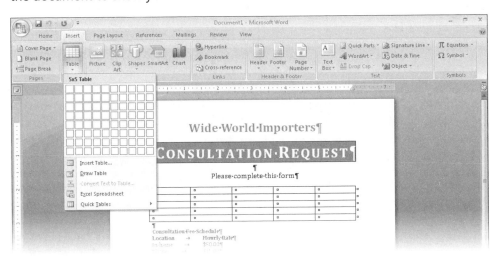

3. Click the lower-right cell in the selection.

Word creates a blank table with five columns and five rows. The insertion point is located in the first cell. Because the table is active, Word displays the Table Tools Design and Layout contextual tabs.

4. In the selection area, point to the first row, and then click to select the row.

5. On the **Layout** contextual tab, in the **Merge** group, click the **Merge Cells** button.

Word combines the five cells in the first row into one cell.

Align Center

6. With the merged cell selected, in the **Alignment** group, click the **Align Center** button.

The end-of-cell marker moves to the center of the merged cell to indicate that anything you type there will be centered.

7. Type Consultation Estimate.

The table now has a title.

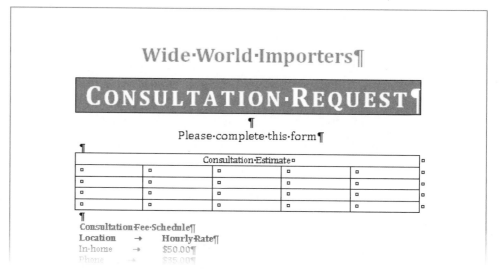

8. Click the first cell in the second row, type Type, and then press [Tab].

9. Type Location, Consultant, Hourly Rate, and Total, pressing [Tab] after each entry.

The table now has a row of column headings. Pressing Tab after the *Total* heading moves the insertion point to the first cell of the third row.

**10.** Type Window Treatments, In-home, Andy Ruth, $50.00, and $50.00, pressing [Tab] after each entry.

You have entered a complete row of data.

**11.** Select the last two rows, and then on the **Layout** tab, in the **Rows & Columns** group, click the **Insert Below** button.

Word adds two new rows and selects them.

**12.** In the last row, click the first cell, hold down the [Shift] key, and then press the [→] key four times to select the first four cells in the row.

**13.** In the **Merge** group, click the **Merge Cells** button.

Word combines the selected cells into one cell.

Align Center Right

**14.** In the **Alignment** group, click the **Align Center Right** button.

**15.** Type Subtotal, and then press [Tab] twice.

Word adds a new row with the same structure to the bottom of the table.

Wide·World·Importers¶

## CONSULTATION·REQUEST¶

¶
Please·complete·this·form¶

| Consultation·Estimate□ | | | | | □ |
|---|---|---|---|---|---|
| Type□ | Location□ | Consultant□ | Hourly·Rate□ | Total□ | □ |
| Window·Treatments□ | In-home□ | Andy·Ruth□ | $50.00□ | $50.00□ | □ |
| □ | □ | □ | □ | □ | □ |
| □ | □ | □ | □ | □ | □ |
| □ | □ | □ | □ | □ | □ |
| | | | | Subtotal□ | □ |
| | | | | □ | □ |

¶
Consultation·Fee·Schedule¶
Location → Hourly·Rate¶
In-home → $50.00¶

**16.** Type Add trip fee, press [Tab] twice to add a new row, and then type Add additional time charge.

**17.** Press [Tab] twice to add a new row, and then type Total.

**18.** Scroll to the bottom of the document, and select the rows of the tabular list beginning with *Distance* and ending with *$20.00*.

**19.** On the **Insert** tab, in the **Tables** group, click the **Table** button, and then click **Convert Text to Table**.

The Convert Text To Table dialog box opens.

> **Tip** To convert a table to text, select the table, and then click the Convert To Text button in the Data group on the Layout tab.

**20.** Verify that the **Number of columns** box displays **2**, and then click **OK**.

The selected text appears in a table with two columns and six rows.

**21.** Click anywhere in the table to release the selection, and point to the right border of the table. When the pointer changes to two opposing arrows, double-click the right border.

Word adjusts the width of the right column so that it is exactly wide enough to contain its longest line of text.

Jo Berry¶
Andy Ruth¶
Carlos Carvallo¶

**In-Home Trip Charge**¶

| Distance | Fee | |
|----------|-----|---|
| 0-5 miles | No charge | |
| 6-10 miles | $5.50 | |
| 11-20 miles | $7.00 | |
| 21-50 miles | $10.00 | |
| Over 50 miles | $20.00 | |

¶

**22.** Point to the In-Home Trip Charge table.

Word displays the move handle in the upper-left corner and the size handle in the lower-right corner.

**23.** Drag the size handle to the right, releasing the mouse button when the right edge of the table aligns approximately with the 4-inch mark on the horizontal ruler.

✕ **CLOSE** the *03_Table* document without saving your changes.

### Other Layout Options

You can control many aspects of a table by clicking Properties in the Table group on the Layout tab to display the Table Properties dialog box. You can then set the following options:

- On the Table tab, you can specify the preferred width of the entire table, as well as the way it interacts with the surrounding text.
- On the Row tab, you can specify the height of each row, whether a row is allowed to break across pages, and whether a row of column headings should be repeated at the top of each page.

> **Tip** The Repeat As Header Row option is available only if the insertion point is in the top row of the table.

- On the Column tab, you can set the width of each column.
- On the Cell tab, you can set the preferred width of cells and the vertical alignment of text within them.

> **Tip** You can also control the widths of selected cells by using the buttons in the Cell Size group on the Layout contextual tab.

- You can control the margins of cells (how close text comes to the cell border) by clicking the Options button on either the Table or Cell tab.

> **Tip** You can also control the margins by clicking the Cell Margins button in the Alignment group on the Layout contextual tab.

If the first row of your table has several long headings that make it difficult to fit the table on one page, you can turn the headings sideways. Simply select the heading row and click the Text Direction button in the Alignment group on the Layout tab.

## Formatting Table Information

Formatting a table to best convey its data is often a process of trial and error. With Word 2007, you can quickly get started by creating a *quick table*, a preformatted table with sample data that you can customize. You can then apply one of the *table styles* available on the Design contextual tab, which include a variety of borders, colors, and other attributes to give the table a professional look.

To customize the appearance of a quick table or a table you have created from scratch, you can use the buttons on the Design and Layout contextual tabs. You can also use buttons in the Paragraph group on the Home tab to change alignment and spacing. You can format the text by using the buttons in the Font group, just as you would to format any text in a Word document. You can also apply character formatting from the Styles gallery.

In this exercise, you will create a quick table and then apply a table style to it. You will then change some of the text attributes and modify the borders and shading in various cells to make the formatting suit the table's data. There are no practice files for this exercise.

> **BE SURE TO** display non-printing characters before starting this exercise.
>
> **OPEN** a new, blank document.

Table

1. With the Zoom level at 100%, on the **Insert** tab, in the **Tables** group, click the **Table** button, and then point to **Quick Tables**.

   The Quick Tables gallery opens.

   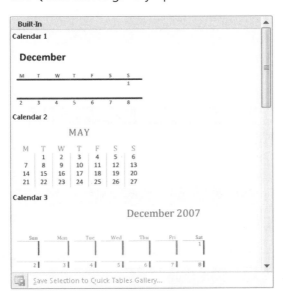

2. Scroll through the gallery, noticing the types of tables that are available, and then click **Matrix**.

   Word inserts the selected table and displays the Design contextual tab . Notice that the table data includes headings across the top and down the left column. Some of the cells are blank, and obviously have less importance than the cells that contain numbers. The table does not include summary data, such as totals.

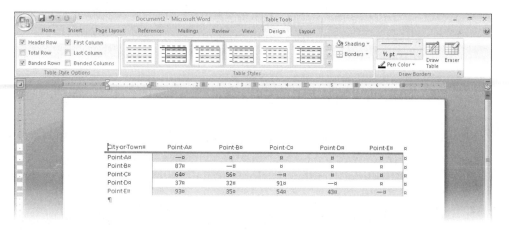

3. On the **Design** tab, in the **Table Style Options** group, clear the **Banded Rows** check box.

More

4. In the **Table Styles** group, point to each style in turn to see its live preview, and then click the **More** button.

   Word displays the Table Styles gallery.

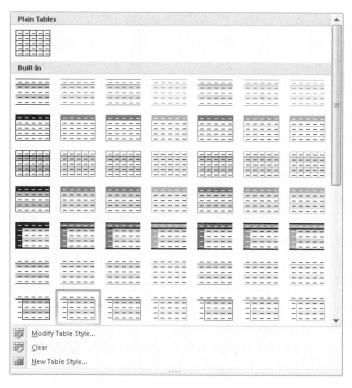

5. Explore all the styles in the gallery. When you finish exploring, click the **Medium Shading 2 – Accent 2** thumbnail.

You need to modify this style a bit, but it is a good starting point.

**6.** Select all the white cells by dragging through them. Then in the **Table Styles** group, click the **Borders** arrow, and in the list, click **All Borders**.

**7.** Select all the cells in the last row (*Point E*) by clicking to its left, and in the **Table Styles** group, in the **Borders** list, click **Borders and Shading**.

The Borders And Shading dialog box opens, displaying the borders applied to the selected cells. The thick gray borders in the Preview area indicate that different borders are applied to different cells in the selection.

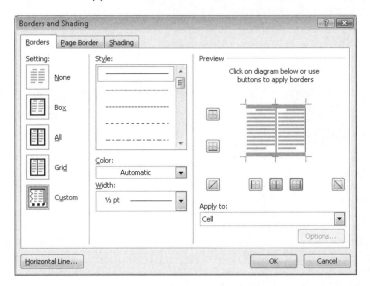

**8.** In the **Preview** area, click the bottom border of the diagram twice to remove all bottom borders.

**9.** Click the **Color** arrow, and then under **Theme Colors**, click the black box (**Black, Text 1**).

**10.** Click the **Width** arrow, and then in the list, click **2 1/4 pt**.

**11.** In the **Preview** area, click the bottom border of the diagram, and then click **OK**.

The table now has the same border at the top and bottom.

**12.** Select the empty cells in the *Point A* row. In the **Table Styles** group, click the **Shading** arrow, and then under **Theme Colors**, click the lightest burgundy box (**Red, Accent 2, Lighter 80%**).

**13.** Repeat Step 12 for all the remaining blank cells in the table.

**14.** Select the dash in the cell at the junction of the *Point A* column and the *Point A* row, hold down the Ctrl key, and select the other four dashes.

**15.** On the **Mini toolbar**, click the **Font Color** arrow, and then under **Standard Colors** in the palette, click the bright **Red** box.

> **Troubleshooting** If the Mini toolbar doesn't appear, click the Font Color arrow in the Font group on the Home tab.

Show/Hide ¶

**16.** Click outside the table to release the selection, and then in the **Paragraph** group, click the **Show/Hide ¶** button to hide non-printing characters.

You can now judge how well the table displays its data.

| City or Town | Point A | Point B | Point C | Point D | Point E |
|---|---|---|---|---|---|
| Point A | — | | | | |
| Point B | 87 | — | | | |
| Point C | 64 | 56 | — | | |
| Point D | 37 | 32 | 91 | — | |
| Point E | 93 | 35 | 54 | 43 | — |

**CLOSE** the document without saving your changes.

# Performing Calculations in a Table

When you want to perform a calculation on numbers in a Word table, you can create a *formula* that uses a built-in mathematical function. You construct a formula by using the tools in the Formula dialog box, which you can access by clicking Formula in the Data group on the Layout contextual tab. A formula consists of an equal sign (=), followed by a function name (such as SUM), followed by parentheses containing the location of the cells on which you want to perform the calculation. For example, the formula =SUM(Left) totals the cells to the left of the cell containing the formula.

To use a function other than SUM in the Formula dialog box, you click the function you want in the Paste Function list. You can use built-in functions to perform a number of calculations, including averaging (AVERAGE) a set of values, counting (COUNT) the number of values in a column or row, or finding the maximum (MAX) or minimum (MIN) value in a series of cells.

## Creating Table Styles

If none of the predefined table styles meets your needs, you can create your own styles for tables in much the same way you create styles for regular text.

To create a table style:

1. On the **Design** tab, in the **Table Styles** group, click the **More** button, and then click **New Table Style**.

    The Create New Style From Formatting dialog box opens.

2. In the **Name** box, type a name for the new style.

3. Click the **Apply formatting to** arrow, and in the list, select the table element for which you are creating the new style.

4. Select the formatting options you want, until the table shown in the Preview area looks the way you want it.

5. If you want the style to be available to tables in other documents based on this template, select that option, and then click **OK**.

To apply a custom table style:

1. Select the table element to which you want to apply the new style.

2. On the **Design** tab, in the **Table Styles** group, click the **More** button, and under **Custom**, click the thumbnail for your custom style.

Although formulas commonly refer to the cells above or to the left of the active cell, you can also use the contents of specified cells or constant values in formulas. To use the contents of a cell, you type the *cell address* in the parentheses following the function name. The cell address is a combination of the column letter and the row number—for example, A1 is the cell at the intersection of the first column and the first row. A series of cells in a row can be addressed as a range consisting of the first cell and the last cell separated by a colon, such as A1:D1. For example, the formula =SUM(A1:D1) totals the values in row 1 of columns A through D. A series of cells in a column can be addressed in the same way. For example, the formula =SUM(A1:A4) totals the values in column A of rows 1 through 4.

When the built-in functions don't meet your needs, you can insert a Microsoft Office Excel worksheet in a Word document. Part of the Microsoft Office system, Excel includes sophisticated functions for performing mathematical, accounting, and statistical calculations. For example, you can use an Excel worksheet to calculate loan payments at various interest rates. You can insert Excel worksheet data into a Word document in the following ways:

- **By copying and pasting.** You can open Excel, enter the data and formulas, and then copy and paste the data as a table in a Word document. The data is pasted as regular text, with the formulas converted to their results.

- **By linking.** While pasting Excel worksheet data into a Word document, you can link the version in the document to the original source worksheet. You can then double-click the linked object in the document to open the source worksheet in Excel for editing. After you edit and save the worksheet, you can return to the document, right-click the linked object, and then click Update Link to display the edited version of the data.

- **By embedding.** You can create an Excel worksheet directly in a Word document by clicking the Table button in the Tables group on the Insert tab, and then clicking Excel Spreadsheet. The worksheet is created as an object with Excel row and column headers, and the Excel tabs and groups replace those of Word so that you can enter data and manipulate it using Excel.

> **Tip** If you change a value in a Word table, you must recalculate formulas manually. If you change a value in an Excel worksheet, the formulas are automatically recalculated.

In this exercise, you will perform a few calculations in a Word table. Then you'll copy and paste worksheet data, link the same data, and enter the same data in an Excel object so that you can see the three different ways of working with Excel data.

**USE** the *05_Calculations* document and the *05_LoanData* workbook. These practice files are located in the *Chapter04* subfolder under *SBS_Office2007*.

**OPEN** the *05_LoanData* workbook in Excel, and then open the *05_Calculations* document in Word.

1. Save the practice file in the *Chapter04* folder with the name My Calculations.

2. In the table displayed in the document, click the cell below the *Total* column heading, and on the **Layout** contextual tab, in the **Data** group, click the **Formula** button.

   The Formula dialog box opens.

3.  Select the contents of the **Formula** box, and then type =C2*B2.

4.  Click the **Number format** arrow, and in the list, click **$#,##0.00;($#,##0.00)**.

5.  In the **Number format** box, delete **.00** from both the positive and negative portions of the format, and then click **OK**.

    You have told Word to multiply the first dollar amount under *Unit Price* by the quantity on the same row and to display the result as a whole dollar amount. Word enters the result, $60,000, in the cell containing the formula.

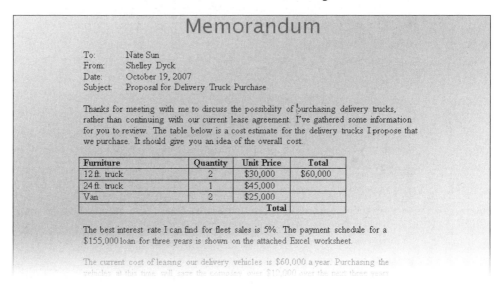

6.  Repeat Steps 2 through 5 for the next two cells under *Total*, adjusting the cell addresses appropriately.

7.  In cell **B4**, change **2** to **3**, right-click the formula in cell **D4**, and then click **Update Field**.

    Word recalculates the formula and enters the new result, $75,000, in the cell.

8. Change the **Unit Price** of the **24 ft. truck** to $42,500, and then update the corresponding total.

9. Click cell **D5**, and in the **Data** group, click the **Formula** button.

10. With **=SUM(ABOVE)** in the **Formula** box, set the **Number format** to whole dollar amounts (following the method in Steps 3 and 4), and then click **OK**.

You have told Word to add the amounts in the *Total* column. Word enters the result, $177,500, in the cell containing the formula.

## Memorandum

To:      Nate Sun
From:    Shelley Dyck
Date:    October 19, 2007
Subject: Proposal for Delivery Truck Purchase

Thanks for meeting with me to discuss the possibility of purchasing delivery trucks, rather than continuing with our current lease agreement. I've gathered some information for you to review. The table below is a cost estimate for the delivery trucks I propose that we purchase. It should give you an idea of the overall cost.

| Furniture   | Quantity | Unit Price | Total     |
|-------------|----------|------------|-----------|
| 12 ft. truck | 2        | $30,000    | $60,000   |
| 24 ft. truck | 1        | $42,500    | $42,500   |
| Van         | 3        | $25,000    | $75,000   |
|             |          | Total      | $177,500  |

The best interest rate I can find for fleet sales is 5%. The payment schedule for a

11. Press Ctrl+End to move to the end of the document, and then on the Windows taskbar, click the **Microsoft Excel** button.

> **Troubleshooting** If you have hidden your Windows taskbar, as we have, point to the bottom of the screen to make the taskbar appear so that you can click the Microsoft Excel button.

Copy

12. On **Sheet1** in the *05_LoanData* workbook, select cells **A1:B8** by dragging through them. Then on the **Home** tab, in the **Clipboard** group, click the **Copy** button.

The worksheet data is copied to the Clipboard. From there it can be pasted into any Microsoft Office program.

Paste

13. Redisplay the *My Calculations* document. Then on the **Home** tab, in the **Clipboard** group, click the **Paste** button.

Word pastes a copy of the worksheet data in the document as a table.

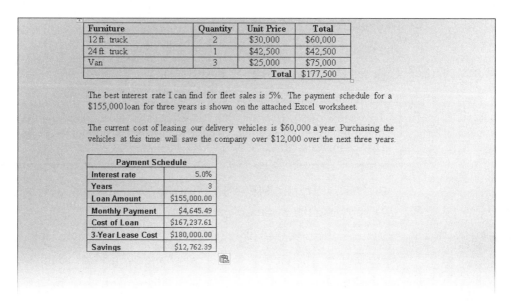

14. Press [Enter], and then in the **Clipboard** group, click the **Paste** arrow, and click **Paste Special**.

    The Paste Special dialog box opens.

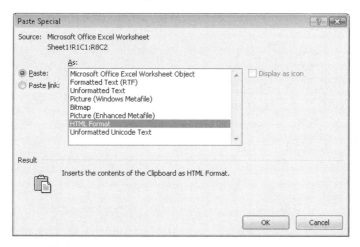

15. In the **As** list, click **Microsoft Office Excel Worksheet Object**, select the **Paste link** option, and then click **OK**.

    Word pastes a second copy of the worksheet data as a linked table on a new page.

**16.** Double-click the new table.

The linked worksheet opens in Excel.

**17.** Click cell **B2**, type 6, and then press [Enter].

> **Troubleshooting** If someone has already worked through this exercise using the practice files on your computer, 6.0% might already appear in cell B2. In that case, change the value to 5.0%.

Excel recalculates the formulas in the worksheet to reflect the new interest rate.

**18.** Save and close the workbook, and quit Excel.

**19.** In Word, right-click the linked table, and then click **Update Link**.

Word updates the table to reflect the change you made to the worksheet data.

**20.** Press [Ctrl]+[End] to move to the end of the document, press [Enter] twice to add some space, and then save the document.

Table

**21.** On the **Insert** tab, in the **Tables** group, click the **Table** button, and then click **Excel Spreadsheet**.

Word inserts an Excel object in the document.

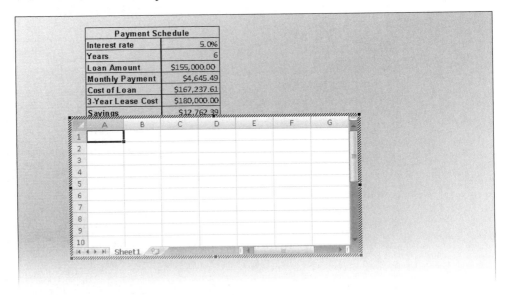

**22.** In row **1**, type Rate, press [Tab], and then type 5%.

**23.** Type the following in rows **2**, **3**, and **4**:

   2    Years [Tab] 3

   3    Amount [Tab] $155,000

   4    Payment [Tab]

**24.** With cell **B4** active, on the **Formulas** tab, in the **Function Library** group, click the **Financial** button, scroll the list, and then click **PMT**.

Excel enters =PMT() in cell B4 and then opens the Function Arguments dialog box so that you can enter the information needed to calculate the monthly payment on a loan of $155,000 at 5% interest for three years.

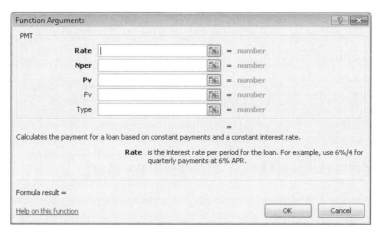

**25.** In the **Rate** box, type **B1/12** (the annual rate per month), in the **Nper** box, type **B2\*12** (the number of years expressed as months), and in the **Pv** box, type **B3**. Then click **OK**.

Excel calculates the formula and enters the result, $4,645.49, expressed as a negative because it is money you are paying out.

> **Tip** To express the payment as a positive, you can insert a minus sign between the equal sign and PMT in the formula.

**26.** Drag the black handle in the lower-right corner of the Excel object up and to the left, until the frame of the object is just big enough to enclose the cells with data in them. Then click a blank area of the page to deactivate the object.

The object appears on the page as a table with barely visible borders around its cells.

| Payment Schedule | |
|---|---|
| Interest rate | 5.0% |
| Years | 6 |
| Loan Amount | $155,000.00 |
| Monthly Payment | $4,645.49 |
| Cost of Loan | $167,237.61 |
| 3-Year Lease Cost | $180,000.00 |
| Savings | $12,762.39 |

| Rate | 5% |
|---|---|
| Years | 3 |
| Amount | $155,000 |
| Payment | ($4,645.49) |

**27.** Double-click the object to activate it in Excel again, change the entry in cell **B1** to 7%, press Enter, and then click a blank area of the page.

The object's formulas have updated the monthly payment to reflect the change.

> **CLOSE** the *My Calculations* document without saving your changes.

# Using a Table to Control Page Layout

Most people are accustomed to thinking of a table as a means of displaying data in a quick, easy-to-grasp format. But tables can also serve to organize your pages in creative ways. For example, suppose you want to display two tables next to each other. The simplest way to do this is to first create a table with one tall row and two wide columns and no gridlines. You can then insert one table in the first cell and the other table in the second cell. These *nested tables* then appear to be arranged side by side.

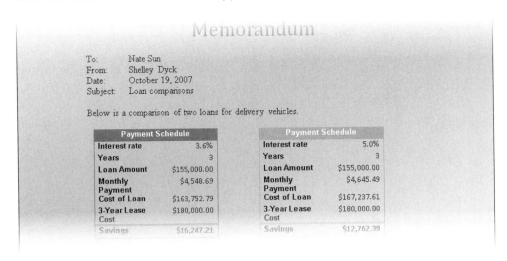

## Deciding How to Insert Excel Data

To decide how to insert Excel data in a Word document, you need to understand how Microsoft Office system programs integrate data from outside sources. Understanding this will enable you to decide how to use information created in any other Office program, not just Excel.

If you don't need to maintain a connection with the source Excel worksheet and the data is simple enough to be edited in Word, you can copy and paste the data.

If you do need to maintain a connection with the source Excel worksheet, or if you need to be able to manipulate the data in Excel after it is incorporated into the Word document, you can use the Microsoft linking and embedding technology to insert an *object* (a file or part of a file) created in Excel into a document created in Word. The object is sometimes called the *source file*, and the document into which you are inserting the information is called the *destination file*. The difference between linking and embedding is the type of connection that is maintained between the source and destination files, as follows:

- A *linked object* is displayed in the destination file, but its data is stored in the source file. If you want to change the data, you do it in the source file. Then when you open the destination file, the linked object is updated to reflect the change.

- An *embedded object* is displayed in the destination file and its data is stored there. If you want to update the data, you do it in the destination file using the source program.

Whether an object should be linked or embedded depends on whether you need the information in the destination file to always be the same as the information in the source file. If you do, it is best to link the object so that you don't have to manually update the data in two places.

As with regular tables, you can create a nested table from scratch, by formatting existing information, or by inserting Excel data. And just like other tables, you can format a nested table either manually or using one of Word's ready-made table styles.

> **Tip** Tables can be used to organize a mixture of elements such as text, tables, charts, and diagrams. For more information, you might want to consult *Advanced Documents Inside Out* (Microsoft Press, 2007).

When creating a table to contain other elements, you might want to take advantage of the Word table-drawing feature. If you click Draw Table below the grid displayed when you click the Table button, the pointer changes to a pencil with which you can draw cells on the page. You can set up the container table visually, without having to fuss with dialog boxes and precise dimensions while you are designing the layout. Then after everything is set up the way you want it, you can use the Table Properties dialog box to fine-tune the table specifications.

In this exercise, you will draw a table to contain two other tables. You will then insert and format the nested tables.

> **USE** the *06_Loan* workbook and the *06_Memo* and *06_TableAsLayout* documents. These practice files are located in the *Chapter04* subfolder under *SBS_Office2007*.
>
> **BE SURE TO** display non-printing characters before starting this exercise.
>
> **OPEN** the *06_Loan* workbook in Excel, and then open the *06_Memo* document and the *06_TableAsLayout* document in Word.

1. Before you begin, save a copy of the *06_TableAsLayout* document in the *Chapter04* subfolder as My Nested Tables.

   > **Troubleshooting** The operations you perform in this exercise use a lot of your computer's resources. You will have better results if you save the My Nested Tables document regularly.

2. In the *My Nested Tables* document, on the **Insert** tab, in the **Tables** group, click the **Table** button, and then click **Draw Table**.

   The pointer becomes a pencil.

3. Point below the last paragraph mark in the document, and drag across and down to create a cell about 3 inches wide and 1 1/2 inches tall.

   > **Tip** The location of the pencil is marked with guides on the horizontal and vertical rulers. You can use these guides to help you draw cells of specific dimensions.

4. Point to the upper-right corner of the cell (you don't have to be precise), and drag to create another cell about the same size as the first.

   When you release the mouse button, Word joins the two cells to create the structure of a table.

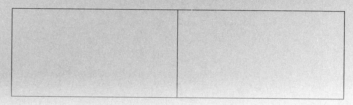

5. On the **View** tab, in the **Window** group, click the **Switch Windows** button, and then click *06_Memo*.

6. Scroll to the bottom of the page, click anywhere in the *Payment Schedule* table, and on the **Layout** tab, in the **Table** group, click **Select**, and then click **Select Table**.

7. On the **Home** tab, in the **Clipboard** group, click the **Copy** button.

8. Switch to the *My Nested Tables* document, right-click the first cell in the table, and then click **Paste as Nested Table**.

   Word inserts the table you copied into the cell and adjusts the size of the container table to fit the size of the nested table.

9. On the Windows taskbar, click the **Microsoft Excel** button to activate Sheet1 of the *06_Loan* workbook, select cells **A1:B8**, and then on the **Home** tab, in the **Clipboard** group, click the **Copy** button.

10. Switch back to the *My Nested Tables* document, click the second cell in the table, and then on the **Home** tab, in the **Clipboard** group, click the **Paste** button.

    Word inserts the worksheet data as a nested table in the cell.

> **Troubleshooting** If the pasted table doesn't appear in the container table, minimize the document window and then maximize it.

Memorandum

To:       Nate Sun
From:     Shelley Dyck
Date:     October 19, 2007
Subject:  Loan comparisons

Below is a comparison of two loans for delivery vehicles.

| Payment Schedule | |
| --- | --- |
| Interest rate | 3.6% |
| Years | 3 |
| Loan Amount | $155,000.00 |
| Monthly Payment | $4,548.69 |
| Cost of Loan | $163,752.79 |
| 3-Year Lease Cost | $180,000.00 |
| Savings | $16,247.21 |

| Payment Schedule | |
| --- | --- |
| Interest rate | 5.0% |
| Years | 3 |
| Loan Amount | $155,000.00 |
| Monthly Payment | $4,645.49 |
| Cost of Loan | $167,237.61 |
| 3-Year Lease Cost | $180,000.00 |
| Savings | $12,762.39 |

**11.** Move the pointer to the selection area adjacent to the container table, and then click to select its two cells.

Borders

**12.** On the **Home** tab, in the **Paragraph** group, click the **Borders** arrow, and then in the list, click **No Border**.

Word removes the borders from the container cells.

**13.** Click anywhere in the left table, and on the **Design** contextual tab, in the **Table Style Options** group, select the **Header Row** and **Total Row** check boxes, and clear all the other check boxes.

**14.** In the **Table Styles** group, display the **Table Styles** gallery, and click the thumbnail of a table style that you want to apply to the nested table.

We used Light List – Accent 4.

**15.** Repeat Steps 13 and 14 to format the right table, perhaps using a similar table style with a different color.

We used Light List – Accent 6.

**16.** Turn off non-printing characters to see the results.

The nested tables now look as shown at the beginning of this topic.

**CLOSE** the *My Nested Tables* document, saving your changes. Then close the *06_Memo* document, and if you are not proceeding directly to the next chapter, quit Word. Finally, close the *06_Loan* workbook without saving changes, and quit Excel.

# Key Points

- To vary the layout of a document, you can divide text into columns.
- If your data is simple, you can create the look of a table by using tabs to set up the data as a tabular list.
- Word comes with quick tables that you can use as a starting point for creating professional, easy-to-read table formats.
- If you have already created a table, you can format it quickly by applying a table style. You can enhance the style by applying text attributes, borders, and shading.
- Formulas that perform simple calculations are easy to build in Word. For more complex calculations, you can create an Excel worksheet and then insert the worksheet data as a table in the Word document.
- Tables are great tools for organizing different types of information on the page. By using tables in creative ways, you can place information in non-linear arrangements for easy comparison or analysis.

# Part II
# Microsoft Office
# Excel 2007

# Chapter at a Glance

Create a workbook, **page 134**

Modify a workbook, **page 138**

Modify a worksheet, **page 141**

Customize the Excel 2007 program window, **page 146**

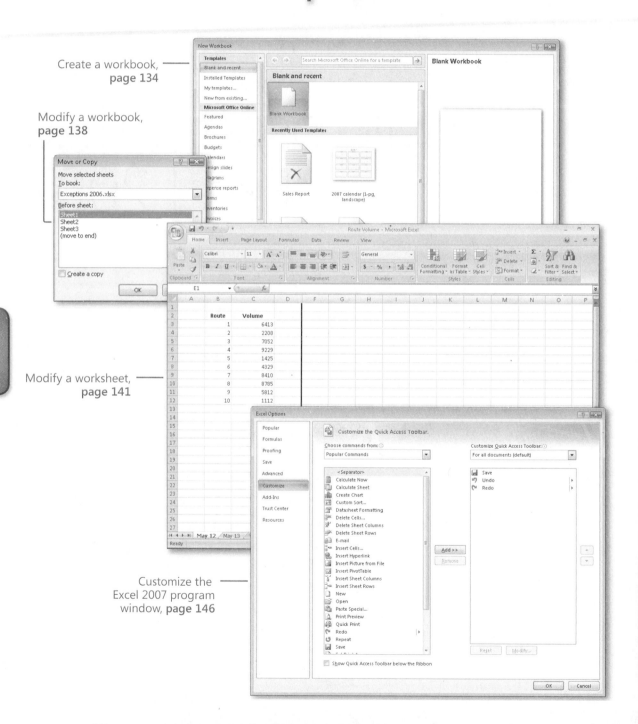

# 5 Setting Up a Workbook

---

**In this chapter, you will learn how to:**

✔ Create a workbook.

✔ Modify a workbook.

✔ Modify a worksheet.

✔ Customize the Excel 2007 program window.

---

When you start Microsoft Office Excel 2007, the program presents a blank workbook that contains three worksheets. You can add or delete worksheets, hide worksheets within the workbook without deleting them, and change the order of your worksheets within the workbook. You can also copy a worksheet to another workbook or move the worksheet without leaving a copy of the worksheet in the first workbook. If you and your colleagues work with a large number of documents, you can define property values to make your workbooks easier to find when you and your colleagues attempt to locate them by using the Microsoft Windows search facility.

Another way to make Office Excel 2007 easier to use is by customizing the Excel 2007 program window to fit your work style. If you have several workbooks open at the same time, you can move between the workbook windows by using the new user interface. However, if you switch between workbooks frequently, you might find it easier to resize the workbooks so they don't take up the entire Excel 2007 window. In that case, you just need to click the title bar of the workbook you want to display.

The 2007 Microsoft Office system design team created the new user interface to reduce the number of places you have to look for commands; if you find that you use a command frequently, you can add it to the Quick Access Toolbar so it's never more than one click away.

In this chapter, you learn how to create and modify workbooks, create and modify worksheets, make your workbooks easier to find, and customize the Excel 2007 program window.

**See Also** Remember, you can get a quick refresher on the topics in this chapter. See the Quick Reference entries **at the beginning of this book.**

**Important** Before you can use the practice files in this chapter, you need to install them from the book's companion CD to their default location. See "Using the Book's CD" at the beginning of this book for more information.

# Creating Workbooks

Every time you want to gather and store data that isn't closely related to any of your other existing data, you should create a new workbook. The default new workbook in Excel 2007 has three worksheets, although you can add more worksheets or delete existing worksheets if you want. Creating a new workbook is a straightforward process—you just click the Microsoft Office Button, click New, and identify the type of workbook you want to create.

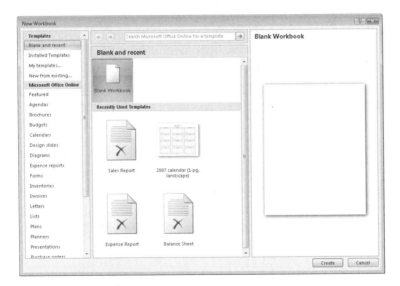

When you start Excel 2007, the program displays a new, blank workbook; you can begin to enter data in the worksheet's cells or open an existing workbook. In the exercises that follow, you'll work with some of the workbooks that have already been created for Consolidated Messenger. After you make any desired changes to a workbook, you should save the workbook to avoid losing your work.

When you save a file, you overwrite the previous copy of the file. If you have made changes that you want to save, but you want to keep a copy of the file as it was previously, you can use the Save As command to specify a name for the new file.

> **Tip** Readers frequently ask, "How often should I save my files?" It is good practice to save your changes every half hour or even every five minutes, but the best time to save a file is whenever you make a change that you would hate to have to make again.

You also can use the controls in the Save As dialog box to specify a different format for the new file and a different location in which to save the new version of the file. For example, Jenny Lysaker, the chief operating officer of Consolidated Messenger, might want to save an Office Excel file that tracks consulting expenses as an Office Excel 2003 file if she needs to share the file with a consulting firm that uses Office Excel 2003.

After you create a file, you can add additional information to make the file easier to find when you search for it using the Windows search facility. Each category of information, or *property*, stores specific information about your file. In Windows, you can search for files based on the file's author or title, or by keywords associated with the file. A file tracking the postal code destinations of all packages sent from a collection might have the keywords *postal*, *destination*, and *origin* associated with it.

To set values for your workbook's properties, click the Microsoft Office Button, point to Prepare, and click Properties to display the Document Properties panel on the user interface. The Standard version of the Document Properties panel has fields for the file's author, title, subject, keywords, category, and status, and any comments about the file. You can also create custom properties by clicking the Property Views and Options button, located just to the right of the Document Properties label, and then clicking Advanced Properties.

On the Custom tab of the advanced Properties dialog box, you can click one of the existing custom categories or create your own by typing a new property name in the Name field, clicking the Type arrow and selecting a data type (for example, Text, Date, Number, Yes/No), selecting or typing a value in the Value field, and then clicking Add. If you want to delete an existing custom property, move your mouse pointer down to the Properties list, click the property you want to get rid of, and click Delete. After you finish making your changes, click the OK button. To hide the Document Properties panel on the user interface, click the Close button in the upper-right corner of the panel.

In this exercise, you will create a new workbook, save the workbook under a new name, assign values to the workbook's standard properties, and create a custom property.

**USE** the *Exception Summary* workbook in the practice file folder for this topic. This practice file is located in the *Creating* folder under *SBS_Office2007.*

**BE SURE TO** start Excel 2007 before beginning these exercises.

**OPEN** the *Exception Summary* workbook.

1. Click the **Microsoft Office Button** and then click **Close**.

   The **Exception Summary** workbook disappears.

2. Click the **Microsoft Office Button** and then click **New**.

   The **New Workbook** dialog box appears.

3. Click **Blank Workbook** and then click **Create**.

   A new, blank workbook appears.

4. Click the **Microsoft Office Button** and then click **Save As**.

   The **Save As** dialog box appears.

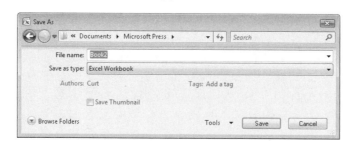

5. Use the navigation controls to display the *My Documents\Microsoft Press\Excel SBS \Setting Up\Creating* folder. In the **File name** field, type Exceptions 2006.

6. Click the **Save** button.

   Excel 2007 saves your work, and the **Save As** dialog box disappears.

7. Click the **Microsoft Office Button**, click **Prepare**, and then click **Properties**.

   The **Document Properties** pane appears.

8. In the **Keywords** field, type exceptions, regional, percentage.

9. In the **Category** field, type performance.

10. Click the **Property View and Options** button and then click **Advanced Properties**.

    The **Exceptions 2006 Properties** dialog box appears.

11. Click **Custom**.

    The **Custom** tab appears.

12. In the **Name** field, type Performance.

13. In the **Value** field, type Exceptions.

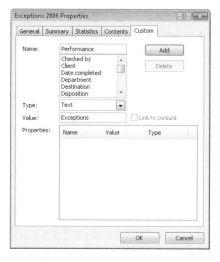

14. Click the **Add** button and then click **OK**.

    The **Exceptions 2006 Properties** dialog box disappears.

15. On the Quick Access Toolbar, click the **Save** button to save your work.

CLOSE the *Exceptions 2006* workbook.

# Modifying Workbooks

Most of the time, you create a workbook to record information about a particular business activity, such as the number of packages that a regional distribution center handles or the average time of the last delivery on a route. Each worksheet within that workbook should thus represent a subdivision of that activity. To display a particular worksheet, just click the worksheet's tab on the tab bar (just below the grid of cells).

In the case of Consolidated Messenger, the workbook used to track daily package volumes could have a separate worksheet for each regional distribution center. New Excel 2007 workbooks contain three worksheets; because Consolidated Messenger uses nine regional distribution centers, you need to create six new ones. To create a new worksheet, click the Insert Worksheet button at the right edge of the tab bar.

When you create a worksheet, Excel 2007 assigns it a generic name such as Sheet4, Sheet5, or Sheet6. After you decide what type of data you want to store on a worksheet, you should change the default worksheet names to something more descriptive. For example, you could change the name of Sheet1 in the regional distribution center tracking workbook to Northeast. When you want to change a worksheet's name, double-click the worksheet's tab on the tab bar to highlight the worksheet name, type the new name, and press Enter.

Another way to work with more than one workbook is to copy a worksheet from another workbook to the current workbook. One circumstance in which you might consider copying worksheets to the current workbook is if you have a list of your current employees in another workbook. You can copy worksheets from another workbook by right-clicking the tab of the sheet you want to copy and, from the shortcut menu that appears, clicking Move or Copy to display the Move Or Copy dialog box.

> **Tip** Selecting the Create a copy check box leaves the copied worksheet in its original workbook, whereas clearing the check box causes Excel 2007 to delete the worksheet from its original workbook.

After the worksheets are in the target workbook, you can change their order to make the data easier to locate within the workbook. To change a worksheet's location in the workbook, you drag its sheet tab to the desired location on the tab bar. If you want a worksheet to stand out in a workbook, you can right-click its sheet tab and use the menu that appears to change the tab's color. At the other end of the spectrum, you can hide the active worksheet by right-clicking the worksheet's tab on the tab bar and clicking Hide on the context menu that appears. When you want Excel 2007 to redisplay the worksheet, right-click any visible sheet tab and click Unhide. In the Unhide dialog box, click the sheet you want to display and click OK.

> **Note** If you copy a worksheet to another workbook, and the destination workbook has the same theme applied as the active workbook, the worksheet retains its tab color. If the destination workbook has another theme applied, the worksheet's tab color changes to reflect that theme.

If you determine that you no longer need a particular worksheet, such as one you created to store some figures temporarily, you can delete the worksheet quickly. To do so, right-click its sheet tab and then click Delete.

In this exercise, you will insert and rename a worksheet, change a worksheet's position in a workbook, hide and unhide a worksheet, copy a worksheet to another workbook, change a worksheet's tab color, and delete a worksheet.

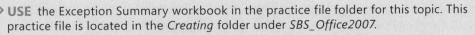

**USE** the Exception Summary workbook in the practice file folder for this topic. This practice file is located in the *Creating* folder under *SBS_Office2007*.
**OPEN** the *Exception Summary* workbook.

1. On the tab bar, click the **Insert Worksheet** button.

   A new worksheet appears.

2. Right-click the new worksheet's sheet tab and click **Rename**.

   Excel 2007 highlights the new worksheet's name.

3. Type 2007 and press [ Enter ].

4. On the tab bar, right-click the **Sheet1** sheet tab and click **Rename**.

5. Type 2006 and press Enter.

6. Right-click the **2006** sheet tab, point to **Tab Color**, and then, in the **Standard Colors** section of the color palette, click a green square.

   Excel 2007 changes the **2006** sheet's tab to green.

7. On the tab bar, drag the **2007** sheet tab to the left of the **Scratch Pad** sheet tab.

8. Right-click the **2007** sheet tab and then click **Hide**.

   Excel 2007 hides the **2007** worksheet.

9. Right-click the **2006** sheet tab and then click **Move or Copy**.

   The **Move or Copy** dialog box appears.

10. Click the **To Book** down arrow and click **New Book**.

11. Select the **Create a copy** check box.

12. Click **OK**.

    A new workbook appears; it contains only the worksheet you copied into it.

13. On the Quick Access Toolbar, click the **Save** button.

    The **Save As** dialog box appears.

14. In the **File name** field, type **2006 Archive** and press Enter.

    Excel 2007 saves the workbook, and the **Save As** dialog box disappears.

15. On the **View** tab, click the **Switch Windows** button, and then click **Exception Summary**.

    The **Exception Summary** workbook appears.

16. On the tab bar, right-click the **Scratch Pad** sheet tab and click **Delete**.

    The **Scratch Pad** worksheet disappears.

**17.** Right-click the **2006** sheet tab and then click **Unhide**.

The **Unhide** dialog box appears.

**18.** Click **2007** and then click **OK**.

The **Unhide** dialog box disappears, and the 2007 worksheet appears in the workbook.

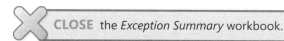

**CLOSE** the *Exception Summary* workbook.

# Modifying Worksheets

After you put up the signposts that make your data easy to find, you can take other steps to make the data in your workbooks easier to work with. For instance, you can change the width of a column or the height of a row in a worksheet by dragging the column or row's border to the desired position. Increasing a column's width or a row's height increases the space between cell contents, making it easier to select a cell's data without inadvertently selecting data from other cells as well.

> **Tip** You can apply the same change to more than one row or column by selecting the rows or columns you want to change and then dragging the border of one of the selected rows or columns to the desired location. When you release the mouse button, all the selected rows or columns change to the new height or width.

Modifying column width and row height can make a workbook's contents easier to work with, but you can also insert a row or column between the edge of a worksheet and the cells that contain the data to accomplish this. Adding space between the edge of a worksheet and cells, or perhaps between a label and the data to which it refers, makes the workbook's contents less crowded and easier to work with. You insert rows by clicking a cell and clicking the Home tab. Then, in the Cells group, click the Insert button's down arrow and click Insert Sheet Rows. Excel 2007 inserts a row above the row that contains the active cell. You insert a column in much the same way by choosing Insert Sheet Columns from the Insert button's drop-down list. When you do this, Excel 2007 inserts a column to the left of the active cell.

When you insert a row, column, or cell in a worksheet with existing formatting, the Insert Options button appears. Clicking the Insert Options button displays a list of choices you can make about how the inserted row or column should be formatted. The following table summarizes your options.

| Option | Action |
|---|---|
| Format Same as Above | Applies the format of the row above the inserted row to the new row. |
| Format Same as Below | Applies the format of the row below the inserted row to the new row. |
| Format Same as Left | Applies the format of the column to the left of the inserted column to the new column. |
| Format Same as Right | Applies the format of the column to the right of the inserted column to the new column. |
| Clear Formatting | Applies the default format to the new row or column. |

If you want to delete a row or column, right-click the row or column head and then, from the shortcut menu that appears, click Delete. You can temporarily hide a number of rows or columns by selecting those rows or columns and then, on the Home tab, in the Cells group, clicking the Format button, pointing to Hide & Unhide, and then clicking either Hide Rows or Hide Columns. The rows or columns you selected disappear, but they aren't gone for good, as they would be if you'd used Delete. Instead, they have just been removed from the display until you call them back. To return the hidden rows to the display, on the Home tab, in the Cells group, click the Format button, point to Hide & Unhide, and then click either Unhide Rows or Unhide Columns.

Likewise, you can insert individual cells into a worksheet. To insert a cell, click the cell that is currently in the position where you want the new cell to appear. On the Home tab, in the Cells group, click the Insert button down arrow and then click Insert Cells to display the Insert dialog box. In the Insert dialog box, you can choose whether to shift the cells surrounding the inserted cell down (if your data is arranged as a column) or to the right (if your data is arranged as a row). When you click OK, the new cell appears, and the contents of affected cells shift down or to the right, as appropriate. In a similar vein, if you want to delete a block of cells, select the cells, and on the Home tab of the user interface, in the Cells group, click the Delete button down arrow and then click

Delete Cells to display the Delete dialog box—complete with option buttons that enable you to choose how to shift the position of the cells around the deleted cells.

> **Tip** The Insert dialog box also includes option buttons you can select to insert a new row or column; the Delete dialog box has similar buttons that enable you to delete an entire row or column.

If you want to move the data in a group of cells to another location in your worksheet, select the cells you want to move and position the mouse pointer on the selection's border. When the mouse pointer changes to a four-way arrow, you can drag the selected cells to the desired location on the worksheet. If the destination cells contain data, Excel 2007 displays a dialog box asking if you want to overwrite the destination cells' contents. If you want to replace the existing values, click the OK button. If you don't want to overwrite the existing values, click the Cancel button and insert the required number of cells to accommodate the data you want to move.

In this exercise, you will insert a column and row into a worksheet, specify insert options, hide a column, insert a cell into a worksheet, delete a cell from a worksheet, and move a group of cells within the worksheet.

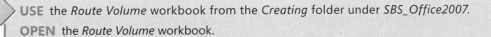

> **USE** the *Route Volume* workbook from the *Creating* folder under *SBS_Office2007.*
> **OPEN** the *Route Volume* workbook.

1. On the **May 12** worksheet, select cell A1.

2. On the **Home** tab, in the **Cells** group, click the **Insert** button down arrow and then click **Insert Sheet Columns**.

   A new column A appears.

3. On the **Home** tab, in the **Cells** group, click the **Insert** button down arrow and then click **Insert Sheet Rows**.

   A new row 1 appears.

4. Click the **Insert Options** button and click **Clear Formatting**.

   Excel 2007 removes the formatting from the new row 1.

5. Right-click the column header of column E and click **Hide**.

   Column E disappears.

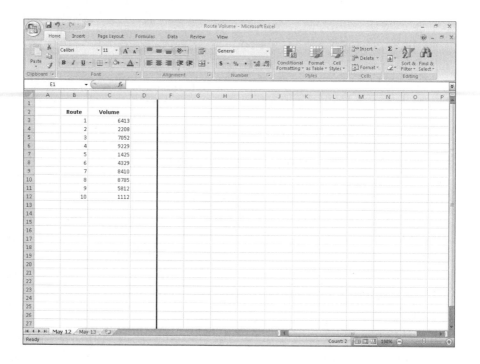

6. On the tab bar, click the **May 13** sheet tab.

   The worksheet named **May 13** appears.

7. Click cell B6.

8. On the **Home** tab, in the **Cells** group, click the **Delete** button down arrow and then click **Delete Cells**.

   The **Delete** dialog box appears.

9. If necessary, select the **Shift cells up** option button and then click **OK**.

   The **Delete** dialog box disappears and Excel 2007 deletes cell B6, moving the cells below it up to fill in the gap.

10. Click cell C6.

**11.** On the **Home** tab, in the **Cells** group, click the **Insert** button down arrow and then click **Insert Cells**.

The **Insert** dialog box appears.

**12.** If necessary, select the **Shift cells down** option button and then click **OK**.

The **Insert** dialog box disappears, and Excel 2007 creates a new cell C6, moving cells C6:C11 down to accommodate the inserted cell.

**13.** In cell C6, type 4499 and press ⌈Enter⌉.

**14.** Select cells E13:F13.

**15.** Point to the border of the selected cells. When your mouse pointer changes to a four-pointed arrow, drag the selected cells to cells B13:C13.

The dragged cells replace cells C13:D13.

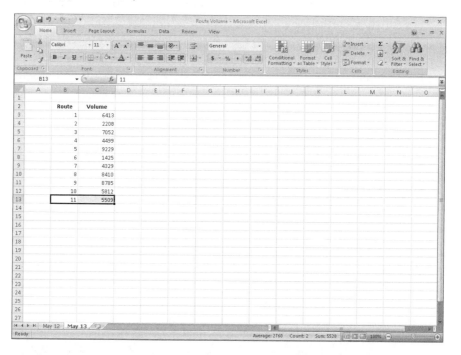

CLOSE the *Route Volume* workbook.

# Customizing the Excel 2007 Program Window

How you use Excel 2007 depends on your personal working style and the type of data collections you manage. The Excel 2007 product team interviews customers, observes how differing organizations use the program, and sets up the user interface so that you don't need to change it to work effectively. If you do find yourself wishing that you could change the Excel 2007 program window, including the user interface, you can. You can change how Excel 2007 displays your worksheets, zoom in on worksheet data, and add frequently used commands to the Quick Access Toolbar.

## Zooming In on a Worksheet

One way to make Excel 2007 easier to work with is to change the program's zoom level. Just as you can "zoom in" with a camera to increase the size of an object in the camera's viewer, you can use the Excel 2007 zoom setting to change the size of objects within the Excel 2007 program window. For example, if Peter Villadsen, the Consolidated Messenger European Distribution Center Manager, displayed a worksheet that summarized his distribution center's package volume by month, he could click the user interface's View tab and then, in the Zoom group, click the Zoom button to display the Zoom dialog box. The Zoom dialog box contains controls that enable him to select a preset magnification level or to type in a custom magnification level. He could also use the Zoom control at the lower-right corner of the Excel 2007 window.

Zoom out ⌐                          ⌐ Zoom in

Clicking the Zoom In control increases the size of items in the program window by 10 percent, whereas clicking the Zoom Out control decreases the size of items in the program window by 10 percent. If you want more fine-grained control of your zoom level, you can use the slider control to select a specific zoom level.

The View tab's Zoom group also contains the Zoom to Selection button, which fills the program window with the contents of any selected cells, up to the program's maximum zoom level of 400 percent.

> **Note**  The mimimum zoom level in Excel 2007 is 10 percent.

## Arranging Multiple Workbook Windows

As you work with Excel 2007, you will probably need to have more than one workbook open at a time. For example, you could open a workbook that contains customer contact information and copy it into another workbook to be used as the source data for a mass mailing you create in Microsoft Office Word 2007. When you have multiple workbooks open simultaneously, you can switch between them by clicking the user interface's View tab and then, in the Window group, clicking the Switch Windows button and clicking the name of the workbook you want to view.

You can arrange your workbooks within the Excel 2007 window so that most of the active workbook is shown, but the others are easily accessible by clicking the View tab and then, in the Window group, clicking the Arrange All button. Then, in the Arrange Windows dialog box, select the Cascade option.

Many Excel 2007 workbooks contain formulas on one worksheet that derive their value from data on another worksheet, which means you need to change between two work-sheets every time you want to see how modifying your data changes the formula's result. However, you can display two copies of the same workbook, displaying the worksheet that contains the data in the original window and displaying the worksheet with the formula in the new window. When you change the data in the original copy of the workbook, Excel 2007 updates the formula result in a new window. To display two copies of the same workbook, open the desired workbook and then, on the View tab's Window group, click New Window. Excel 2007 will open a second copy of the workbook. If the original workbook's name was ExceptionSummary, Excel 2007 displays the name ExceptionSummary:1 on the original workbook's title bar and ExceptionSummary:2 on the second workbook's title bar.

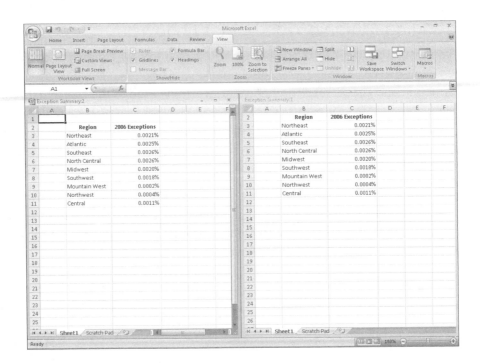

## Adding Buttons to the Quick Access Toolbar

As you continue to work with Excel 2007, you might discover that you use certain commands much more frequently than others. If your workbooks draw data from external sources, you might find yourself displaying the Data tab and then, in the Connections group, clicking the Refresh All button much more often than the program's designers might have expected. You can make any button accessible with one click by adding the button to the Quick Access Toolbar, located just to the right of the Microsoft Office Button at the upper-left corner of the Excel 2007 program window.

To add a button to the Quick Access Toolbar, click the Microsoft Office Button and then click Excel Options. In the Excel Options dialog box, click the Customize name, click the Choose Commands From down arrow, and then click the category from which you want to select the control to add. Excel 2007 displays the available commands in the list box below the Choose Commands From field. Click the control you want and then click the Add button. You can change a button's position on the Quick Access Toolbar by clicking its name in the lower-right pane and then clicking either the Move Up or Move Down button. To remove a button from the Quick Access Toolbar, click the button's name and then click the Remove button. When you're done making your changes, click the OK button.

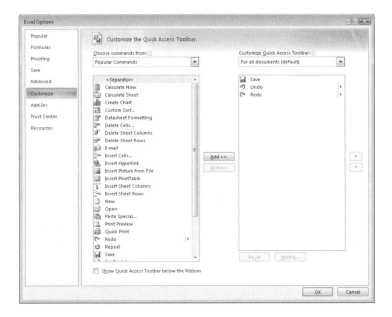

You can also choose whether your Quick Access Toolbar change affects all your workbooks or just the active workbook. To control how Excel 2007 applies your change, click the Customize Quick Access Toolbar field down arrow. Then either click For all documents (default) to apply the change to all of your workbooks or choose For workbookname.xlsx to apply the change to the active workbook only.

In this exercise, you will change your worksheet's zoom level, zoom in to emphasize a selected cell range, switch between multiple open workbooks, cascade multiple open workbooks within the Excel 2007 program window, and add a button to the Quick Access Toolbar.

 **USE** the Route Volume workbook and the Exception Summary workbook from the *Creating* folder under *SBS_Office2007*.
**OPEN** the *Route Volume* workbook.

1. In the **Exception Summary** workbook, display the **2006** worksheet.

2. In the lower-right corner of the Excel 2007 window, click the **Zoom In** control five times.

   The worksheet's zoom level changes to 150%.

3. Select cells B2:C11.

4. On the **View** tab, in the **Zoom** group, click the **Zoom to Selection** button.

   Excel 2007 displays the selected cells so they fill the program window.

| | A | B | C | D |
|---|---|---|---|---|
| 2 | | **Region** | **2006 Exceptions** | |
| 3 | | Northeast | 0.0021% | |
| 4 | | Atlantic | 0.0025% | |
| 5 | | Southeast | 0.0026% | |
| 6 | | North Central | 0.0026% | |
| 7 | | Midwest | 0.0020% | |
| 8 | | Southwest | 0.0018% | |
| 9 | | Mountain West | 0.0002% | |
| 10 | | Northwest | 0.0004% | |
| 11 | | Central | 0.0011% | |

5. On the **View** tab, in the **Zoom** group, click the **Zoom** button.

   The **Zoom** dialog box appears.

6. Select the **100%** option button and then click **OK**.

   The worksheet returns to its default zoom level.

7. On the **View** tab, in the **Window** group, click the **Switch Windows** button and then click **Route Volume**.

   The **Route Volume** workbook appears.

**8.** On the **View** tab, in the **Window** group, click the **Arrange All** button.

The **Arrange Windows** dialog box appears.

**9.** Select the **Cascade** option button and then click **OK**.

Excel 2007 cascades the open workbook windows within the Excel 2007 program window.

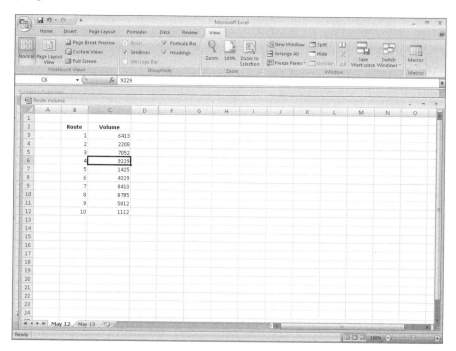

**10.** Click the **Microsoft Office Button** and then click **Excel Options**.

The **Excel Options** dialog box appears.

**11.** Click **Customize**.

The **Customize** tab appears.

**12.** Click the **Choose commands from** field down arrow and then click **Review Tab**.

The commands in the **Review Tab** category appear in the command list.

**13.** Click the **Spelling** command, and then click **Add**.

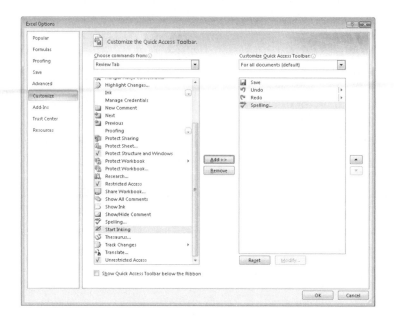

14. Click **OK**.

Excel 2007 adds the **Spelling** command to the Quick Access Toolbar.

 **CLOSE** Excel.

# Key Points

- Save your work whenever you do something you'd hate to have to do again.
- Assigning values to a workbook's properties makes it easier to find your workbook using the Windows search facility.
- Be sure to give your worksheets descriptive names.
- If you want to use a worksheet's data in another workbook, you can send a copy of the worksheet to that other workbook without deleting the original worksheet.
- You can delete a worksheet you no longer need, but you can also hide a worksheet in the workbook. When you need the data on the worksheet, you can unhide it.

- You can save yourself a lot of bothersome cutting and pasting by inserting and deleting worksheet cells, columns, and rows.

- Customize your Excel 2007 program window by changing how it displays your workbooks, zooming in on data, and adding frequently used buttons to the Quick Access Toolbar.

# Chapter at a Glance

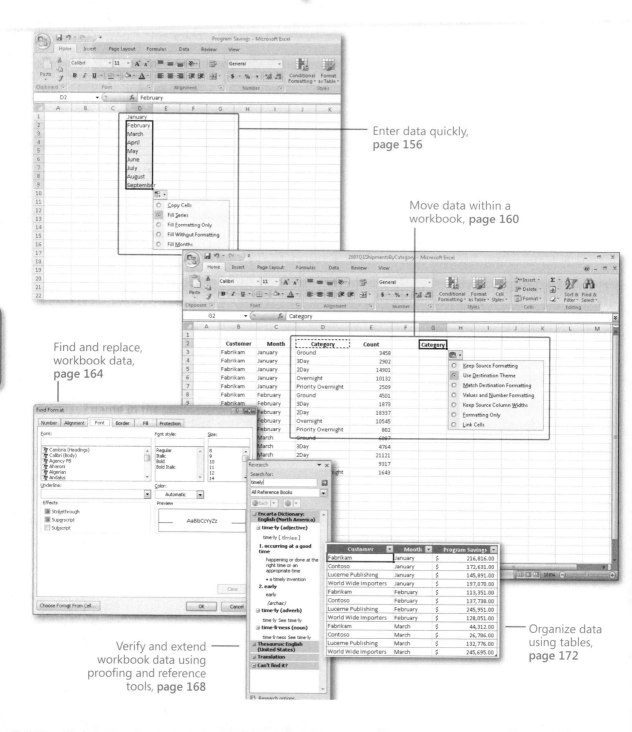

Enter data quickly,
**page 156**

Move data within a
workbook, **page 160**

Find and replace,
workbook data,
**page 164**

Organize data
using tables,
**page 172**

Verify and extend
workbook data using
proofing and reference
tools, **page 168**

# 6 Working with Data and Data Tables

---

**In this chapter, you will learn to:**

- ✔ Enter data quickly.
- ✔ Move data within a workbook.
- ✔ Find and replace workbook data.
- ✔ Verify and extend workbook data using proofing and reference tools.
- ✔ Organize your data using tables.

---

Microsoft Office Excel 2007 enables you to visualize and present information effectively using charts, graphics, and formatting, but the data is the most important part of any workbook. By learning to enter data efficiently, you will make fewer data entry errors and give yourself more time to analyze your data so you can make decisions about your organization's performance and direction.

Office Excel 2007 provides a wide variety of tools you can use to enter and manage worksheet data effectively. For example, Excel 2007 enables you to organize your data into tables, which enables you to analyze and store your data quickly and easily. Excel 2007 also enables you to enter a data series quickly; repeat one or more values; or control how Excel 2007 formats cells, columns, and rows moved from one part of a worksheet to another. And you can do so with a minimum of effort. Excel 2007 also enables you to check the spelling of worksheet text, look up alternative words using the Thesaurus, and translate words to foreign languages.

In this chapter, you will learn how to enter and revise Excel 2007 data, move data within a workbook, find and replace existing data, use proofing and reference tools to enhance your data, and organize your data by using Excel 2007 data tables.

**See Also** Do you need only a quick refresher on the topics in this chapter? See the Quick Reference entries at the beginning of this book.

> **Important**  Before you can use the practice sites provided for this chapter, you need to install them from the book's companion CD to their default location. See "Using the Book's CD" at the beginning of this book for more information.

# Entering and Revising Data

After you create a workbook, you can begin entering data. The simplest way to enter data is to click a cell and type a value, which is a method that works very well when you're entering a few pieces of data, but it is less than ideal when you're entering long sequences or series of values. For example, Craig Dewar, the VP of Marketing for Consolidated Messenger, might want to create a worksheet listing the monthly program savings that large customers can enjoy if they sign exclusive delivery contracts with Consolidated Messenger. To record those numbers, he would need to create a worksheet with the following layout.

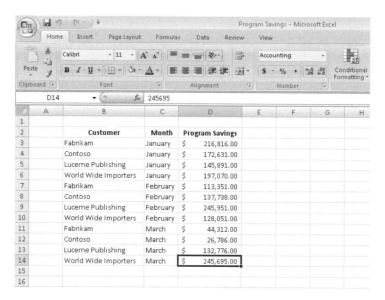

Entering the sequence January, February, March, and so on repeatedly can be handled by copying and pasting the first occurrence of the sequence, but there's an easier way to do it: use *AutoFill*. With AutoFill, you enter the first element in a recognized series, grab the **fill handle** at the lower-right corner of the cell, and drag the fill handle until the series extends far enough to accommodate your data. A similar tool, **FillSeries**, enables you to enter two values in a series and use the fill handle to extend the series in your worksheet. For example, if you want to create a series starting at 2 and increasing by 2, you can put 2 in the first cell and 4 in the second cell, select both cells, and then use the fill handle to extend the series to your desired end value.

You do have some control over how Excel 2007 extends the values in a series when you drag the fill handle. For example, if you drag the fill handle up (or to the left), Excel 2007 extends the series to include previous values. If you type January in a cell and then drag that cell's fill handle up (or to the left), Excel 2007 places *December* in the first cell, *November* in the second cell, and so on.

Another way to control how Excel 2007 extends a data series is by holding down the [Ctrl] key while you drag the fill handle. For example, if you select a cell that contains the value *January* and then drag the fill handle down, Excel 2007 extends the series by placing *February* in the next cell, *March* in the cell after that, and so on. If you hold down the [Ctrl] key, however, Excel 2007 repeats the value *January* in each cell you add to the series.

> **Tip**  Be sure to experiment with how the fill handle extends your series and how pressing the [Ctrl] key changes that behavior. Using the fill handle can save you a lot of time entering data.

Other data entry techniques you'll use in this section are **AutoComplete**, which detects when a value you're entering is similar to previously entered values; **Pick from Drop-down List**, which enables you to choose a value from existing values in a column; and [Ctrl]+[Enter], which enables you to enter a value in multiple cells simultaneously.

The following table summarizes these data entry techniques.

| Method | Action |
|---|---|
| AutoFill | Enter the first value in a recognized series and use the fill handle to extend the series. |
| FillSeries | Enter the first two values in a series and use the fill handle to extend the series. |
| AutoComplete | Type the first few letters in a cell, and if a similar value exists in the same column, Excel 2007 suggests the existing value. |
| Pick from Drop-down List | Right-click a cell, and from the shortcut menu that appears, choose Pick From Drop-down List. A list of existing values in the cell's column appears. Click the value you want to enter into the cell. |
| [Ctrl]+[Enter] | Select a range of cells to contain the same data, type the data in the active cell, and press [Ctrl]+[Enter]. |

> **Troubleshooting** If an AutoComplete suggestion doesn't appear as you begin typing a cell value, the option might be turned off. To turn on AutoComplete, click the Microsoft Office Button and click Excel Options. In the Excel Options dialog box, click the Advanced category. In the Editing Options section of the dialog box, select the Enable AutoComplete for cell values check box and click OK.

Another handy feature in the current version of Excel 2007 is the Auto Fill Options button that appears next to data you add to a worksheet using AutoFill.

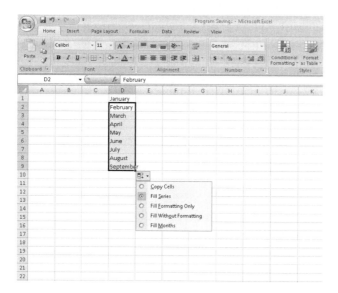

Clicking the Auto Fill Options button displays a list of actions Excel 2007 can take regarding the cells affected by your fill operation. The options in the list are summarized in the following table.

| Option | Action |
| --- | --- |
| Copy Cells | Copies the contents of the selected cells to the cells indicated by the Fill operation. |
| Fill Series | Fills the cells indicated by the Fill operation with the next items in the series. |
| Fill Formatting Only | Copies the format of the selected cell to the cells indicated by the Fill operation, but does not place any values in the target cells. |
| Fill Without Formatting | Fills the cells indicated by the Fill operation with the next items in the series, but ignores any formatting applied to the source cells. |

| Option | Action |
|--------|--------|
| **Fill** Days, Weekdays, **etc.** | Changes according to the series you extend. For example, if you extend the cells *Wed*, *Thu*, and *Fri*, Excel 2007 presents two options, Fill Days and Fill Weekdays, and enables you to select which one you intended. If you do not use a recognized sequence, the option does not appear. |

In this exercise, you will enter a data series by dragging the fill handle, enter data by accepting AutoComplete values, enter cell data by using Pick From Drop-down List, and control how Excel 2007 formats an extended data series by setting the program's Auto Fill Options.

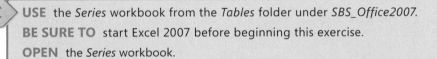

**USE** the *Series* workbook from the *Tables* folder under *SBS_Office2007*.
**BE SURE TO** start Excel 2007 before beginning this exercise.
**OPEN** the *Series* workbook.

1. On the **Monthly** worksheet, select cell B3 and then drag the fill handle down until it covers cells B3:B7.

   Excel 2007 repeats the value *Fabrikam* in cells B4:B7.

2. Select cell C3, hold down the ⌃ key, and drag the fill handle down until it covers cells C3:C7.

   Excel 2007 repeats the value *January* in cells C4:C7.

3. Select cell B8 and type the letter F.

   Excel 2007 displays the characters *abrikam* in reverse video.

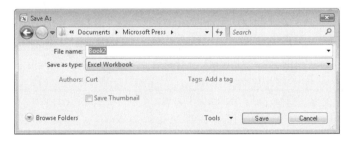

4. Press ⟦Tab⟧ to accept the value *Fabrikam* for the cell.

5. In cell C8, type **February**.

6. Right-click cell D8 and then click **Pick From Drop-down List**.

A list of values in column D appears below cell D8.

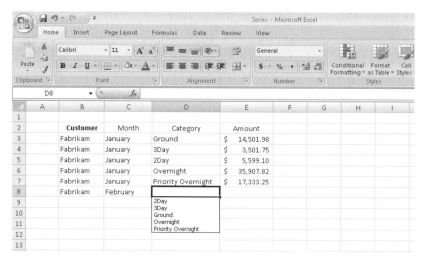

7. From the list that appeared, click **2Day**.

The value *2Day* appears in cell D8.

8. In cell E8, type **11802.14**.

The value *$11,802.14* appears in cell E8.

9. Select cell B2 and then drag the fill handle so that it covers cells C2:E2.

Excel 2007 replaces the values in cells C2:E2 with the value *Customer*.

10. Click the **Auto Fill Options** button and then click **Fill Formatting Only**.

Excel 2007 restores the original values in cells C2:E2 but applies the formatting of cell B2 to those cells.

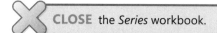 **CLOSE** the *Series* workbook.

# Moving Data Within a Workbook

You can move to a specific cell in lots of ways, but the most direct method is to click the cell to which you want to move. The cell you click will be outlined in black, and its contents, if any, will appear in the formula bar. When a cell is outlined, it is the

**active cell**, meaning that you can modify its contents. You use a similar method to select multiple cells (referred to as a **cell range**)—just click the first cell in the range and drag the mouse pointer over the remaining cells you want to select. After you select the cell or cells you want to work with, you can cut, copy, delete, or change the format of the contents of the cell or cells. For instance, Gregory Weber, the Northwestern Distribution Center Manager, might want to copy the cells that contain a set of column labels to a new page that summarizes similar data.

> **Important** If you select a group of cells, the first cell you click is designated the active cell.

You're not limited to selecting cells individually or as part of a range. For example, you might need to move a column of price data one column to the right to make room for a column of headings that indicate to which service category (ground, three-day express, two-day express, overnight, or priority overnight) a set of numbers belongs. To move an entire column (or entire columns) of data at a time, you click the column's header, located at the top of the worksheet. Clicking a column header highlights every cell in that column and enables you to copy or cut the column and paste it elsewhere in the workbook.

The Paste Options button appears next to data you copy from a cell and paste into another cell. Clicking the Paste Options button displays a list of actions that Excel 2007 can take regarding the pasted cells.

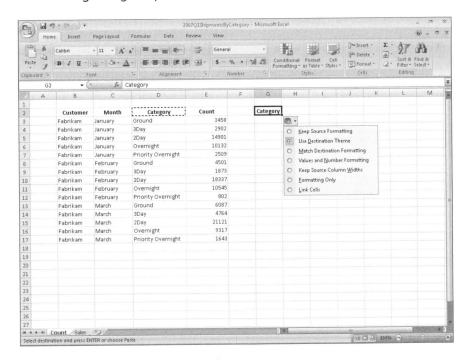

The options in the list are summarized in the following table.

| Option | Action |
| --- | --- |
| Use Destination Theme | Pastes the contents of the Clipboard (which holds the last information selected via Cut or Copy) into the target cells and formats the data using the theme applied to the target workbook. |
| Match Destination Formatting | Pastes the contents of the Clipboard into the target cells and formats the data using the existing format in the target cells, regardless of the workbook's theme. |
| Keep Source Formatting | Pastes a column of cells into the target column; applies the format of the copied column to the new column. |
| Values Only | Pastes the values from the copied column into the destination column without applying any formatting. |
| Values and Number Formatting | Pastes the contents of the Clipboard into the target cells, keeping any numeric formats. |
| Values and Source Formatting | Pastes the contents of the Clipboard into the target cells, retaining all the source cells' formatting. |
| Keep Source Column Widths | Pastes the contents of the Clipboard into the target cells and resizes the columns of the target cells to match the widths of the columns of the source cells. |
| Formatting Only | Applies the format of the source cells to the target cells, but does not copy the contents of the source cells. |

**Troubleshooting** If the Paste Options button doesn't appear, you can turn the feature on by clicking the Microsoft Office Button and then clicking Excel Options to display the Excel Options dialog box. In the Excel Options dialog box, click the Advanced category and then, in the Cut, copy, and paste section, select the Show Paste Options buttons check box. Click OK to close the dialog box and save your setting.

In this exercise, you will copy a set of column headers to another worksheet, move a column of data within a worksheet, and select paste options for copied data.

**USE** the *2007Q1ShipmentsByCategory* workbook from the *Data and Data Tables* folder under *SBS_Office2007*.

**OPEN** the *2007Q1ShipmentsByCategory* workbook.

1. On the **Count** worksheet, select cells B2:D2.

2.  On the **Home** tab, in the **Clipboard** group, click the **Copy** button.

    Excel 2007 copies the contents of cells B2:D2 to the Clipboard.

3.  On the tab bar, click the **Sales** sheet tab.

    The **Sales** worksheet appears.

4.  Select cell B2.

5.  On the **Home** tab, in the **Clipboard** group, click **Paste**.

    Excel 2007 pastes the header values into cells B2:D2.

6.  Click the **Paste Options** smart tag and then click **Keep Source Formatting**.

    Excel 2007 retains the cells' original formatting.

7.  Right-click the column header of column I and then click **Cut**.

    Excel 2007 outlines column I with a marquee.

8.  Right-click the header of column E and then click **Paste**.

    Excel 2007 pastes the contents of column I into column E.

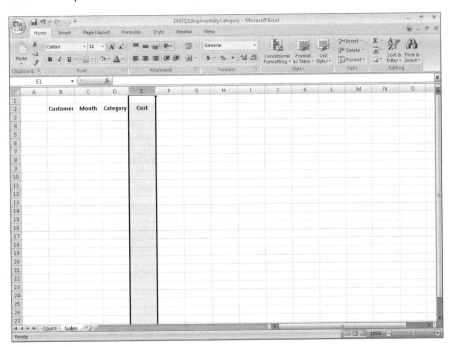

CLOSE the *2007Q1ShipmentsByCategory* workbook.

# Finding and Replacing Data

Excel 2007 worksheets can contain more than one million rows of data, so it's unlikely that you would have the time to move through a worksheet a row at a time to locate the data you want to find. You can locate specific data on an Excel 2007 worksheet by using the Find and Replace dialog box, which has two tabs (one named Find; the other named Replace) that enable you to search for cells that contain particular values. Using the controls on the Find tab finds the data you specify; using the controls on the Replace tab enables you to substitute one value for another. As an example, one of Consolidated Messenger's customers might change the company name. If that's the case, you can change every instance of the old name to the new name.

When you need more control over the data that you find and replace, such as if you want to find cells in which the entire cell value matches the value you're searching for, you can click the Options button to expand the Find and Replace dialog box.

One way you can use the extra options in the Find and Replace dialog box is to identify data that requires review using a specific format. As an example, Consolidated Messenger VP of Marketing Craig Dewar could make corporate sales plans based on a projected budget for the next year. After the executive board finalizes the numbers, he could use Find Format in the Find and Replace dialog box to locate the old prices and then change them by hand.

To change a value by hand, select the cell and then either type a new value in the cell or, on the Formula Bar, select the value you want to replace and type the new value.

The following table summarizes the Find and Replace dialog box controls' functions.

| Control | Function |
|---|---|
| **Find what** field | Contains the value you want to find or replace. |
| **Find All** button | Selects every cell that contains the value in the **Find what** field. |
| **Find Next** button | Selects the next cell that contains the value in the **Find what** field. |
| **Replace with** field | Contains the value to overwrite the value in the **Find what** field. |

| Control | Function |
|---|---|
| **Replace All** button | Replaces every instance of the value in the **Find what** field with the value in the **Replace with** field. |
| **Replace** button | Replaces the next occurrence of the value in the **Find what** field and highlights the next cell that contains that value. |
| **Options** button | Expands the **Find and Replace** dialog box to display additional capabilities. |
| **Format** button | Displays the **Find Format** dialog box, which you can use to specify the format of values to be found or to replace found values. |
| **Within** list box | Enables you to select whether to search the active worksheet or the entire workbook. |
| **Search** list box | Enables you to select whether to search by rows or by columns. |
| **Look in** list box | Enables you to select whether to search cell formulas or values. |
| **Match case** check box | When checked, requires that all matches have the same capitalization as the text in the **Find what** field (for example, cat doesn't match Cat). |
| **Match entire cell contents** check box | Requires that the cell contain exactly the same value as in the **Find what** field (for example, Cat doesn't match Catherine). |
| **Close** button | Closes the **Find and Replace** dialog box. |

In this exercise, you will find a specific value in a worksheet, replace every occurrence of a company name in a worksheet, and find a cell with a particular formatting.

> **USE** the *Average Deliveries* workbook from the *Data and Data Tables* folder under *SBS_Office2007*.
> **OPEN** the *Average Deliveries* workbook.

1. If necessary, click the **Time Summary** sheet tab.

   The **Time Summary** worksheet appears.

2. On the **Home** tab, in the **Editing** group, click **Find & Select** and then click **Find**.

   The **Find and Replace** dialog box appears with the **Find** tab displayed.

3. In the **Find what** field, type 114.

4. Click **Find Next**.

   Excel 2007 highlights cell B16, which contains the value *114*.

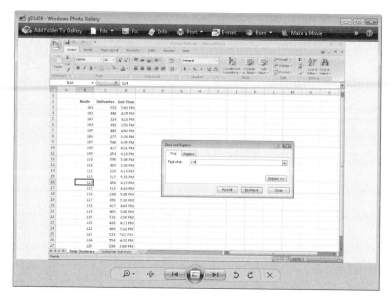

5. Delete the value in the **Find What** field and then click the **Options** button.

   The **Find and Replace** dialog box expands to display additional search options.

6. Click **Format**.

   The **Find Format** dialog box appears.

7. Click the **Font** tab.

   The **Font** tab appears.

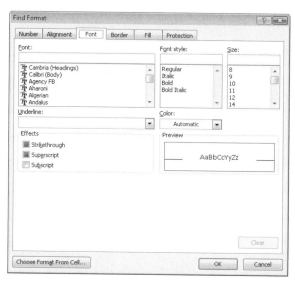

8. In the **Font Style** list, click **Italic**.

**9.** Click **OK**.

The **Find Format** dialog box disappears.

**10.** Click **Find Next**.

Excel 2007 highlights cell D25.

**11.** Click **Close**.

The **Find and Replace** dialog box disappears.

**12.** On the tab bar, click the **Customer Summary** sheet tab.

The **Customer Summary** worksheet appears.

**13.** On the **Home** tab, in the **Editing** group, click **Find & Select** and then click **Replace**.

The **Find and Replace** dialog box appears with the **Replace** tab displayed.

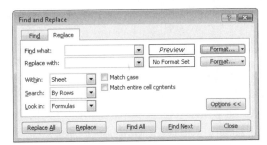

**14.** On the **Format** button to the right of the **Find what** field, click the **Format** button down arrow and then click **Clear Find Format**.

The format displayed next to the **Find what** field disappears.

**15.** In the **Find what** field, type Contoso.

**16.** In the **Replace with** field, type Northwind Traders.

**17.** Click **Replace All**.

**18.** Click **OK** to clear the message box that appears, indicating that Excel 2007 made three replacements.

**19.** Click **Close**.

The **Find and Replace** dialog box disappears.

**CLOSE** the *Average Deliveries* workbook.

# Correcting and Expanding Upon Worksheet Data

After you enter your data, you should take the time to check and correct it. You do need to verify visually that each piece of numeric data is correct, but you can make sure that the text is spelled correctly by using the Excel 2007 spelling checker. When the spelling checker encounters a word it doesn't recognize, it highlights the word and offers suggestions representing its best guess of the correct word. You can then edit the word directly, pick the proper word from the list of suggestions, or have the spelling checker ignore the misspelling. You can also use the spelling checker to add new words to a custom dictionary so that Excel 2007 will recognize them later, saving you time by not requiring you to identify the words as correct every time they occur in your worksheets. After you make a change, you can remove the change as long as you haven't closed the workbook in which you made the change. To undo a change, click the Undo button on the Quick Access Toolbar. If you decide you want to keep a change, you can use the Redo command to restore it.

If you're not sure of your word choice or if you use a word that is almost but not quite right for your meaning, you can check for alternative words by using the Thesaurus. A number of other research tools are also available, such as the Microsoft Encarta encyclopedia, which you can refer to as you create your workbook. To display those tools, on the Review tab of the user interface, in the Proofing group, click Research to display the Research task pane.

Finally, if you want to translate a word from one language to another, you can do so by selecting the cell that contains the value you want to translate, by displaying the Review tab, and then, in the Proofing group, by clicking Translate. The Research task pane appears (or changes if it's already open) and displays controls you can use to select the original and destination languages.

Caution Excel 2007 translates a sentence by using word substitutions, which means that the translation routine doesn't always pick the best word for a given context. The translated sentence might not capture your exact meaning.

In this exercise, you will check a worksheet's spelling, add two new terms to a dictionary, undo a change, search for an alternative word using the Thesaurus, and translate a word to French.

USE the *Service Levels* workbook from the *Data and Data Tables* folder under *SBS_Office2007*.
OPEN the *Service Levels* workbook.

1. On the **Review** tab, in the **Proofing** group, click **Spelling**.

   The **Spelling** dialog box appears with the misspelled word displayed in the **Not in Dictionary** field.

2. Verify that the word *shipped* is highlighted in the **Suggestions** pane and then click **Change**.

   Excel 2007 corrects the word and displays the next questioned word: *TwoDay*.

3. Click **Add to Dictionary**.

   Excel 2007 adds the word to the dictionary and displays the next questioned word: *ThreeDay*.

4. Click **Add to Dictionary**.

   Excel 2007 adds the word to the dictionary.

5. Click **Close**.

   The **Spelling** dialog box disappears, and a message box appears, indicating that the spell check is complete for the selected items.

6. Click **OK** to close the message box.

7. Click cell B6.

8. On the **Review** tab, in the **Proofing** group, click **Thesaurus**.

   The **Research** task pane appears and displays a list of synonyms and antonyms for the word *overnight*.

9. On the **Review** tab, in the **Proofing** group, click **Translate**.

   The **Research** task pane displays the translation tools.

10. If necessary, click the **From** list box down arrow and then click **English (United States).**

11. Click the **To** list box down arrow and then click **French (France).**

   The **Research** task pane displays French words that mean *overnight*.

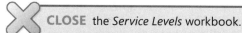

CLOSE the *Service Levels* workbook.

# Defining a Table

Excel has always enabled you to manage lists of data effectively, enabling you to sort your worksheet data based on the values in one or more columns, limit the data displayed by using criteria (for example, show only those routes with fewer than 100 stops), and create formulas that summarize the values in visible (that is, unfiltered) cells. Customer feedback indicated that many Excel 2007 users wanted a more robust structure within Excel 2007 that enabled users to perform those operations and more. Excel 2003 included a structure called a *data list* that has evolved into the *table* in Excel 2007.

To create a data table, type a series of column headers in adjacent cells and then type a row of data below the headers. Select the headers and data; on the Home tab, in the Styles group, click Format as Table; and then, from the gallery that appears, click the style you to apply to the table. When the Format as Table dialog box appears, verify that the cells in the Where is the data for your table? field reflect your current selection and that the My table has headers check box is selected, and then click OK.

Excel 2007 can also create a table from an existing data list as long as your data has a differently formatted header row, the list has no blank rows or columns within the data, and there is no extraneous data in cells immediately below or next to the list.

When you want to add data to a table, select a cell in the row immediately below the last row in the table or a cell in the column immediately to the right of the table; then type a value into the cell. After you enter the value and move out of the cell, the AutoCorrect Options smart tag appears. If you didn't mean to include the data in the table, you can click Undo Table AutoExpansion to exclude the cells from the table. If you never want Excel 2007 to include adjacent data in a table, click the Stop Automatically Expanding Tables option.

> **Tip** To stop Table AutoExpansion before it starts, click the Microsoft Office Button and then click Excel Options. In the Excel Options dialog box, click Proofing and then click the AutoCorrect Options button to display the AutoCorrect dialog box. Click the AutoFormat As You Type tab, clear the Include new rows and columns in table check box, and then click OK twice.

You can add rows and columns to a table, or remove them from a table, by dragging the resize handle at the table's lower-right corner. If your table's headers contain a recognizable series of values (such as *Region1*, *Region2*, and *Region3*), and you drag the resize handle to create a fourth column, Excel 2007 creates the column with the label *Region4*—the next value in the series.

Tables often contain data you can summarize by calculating a sum or average, or by finding the maximum or minimum value in a column. To summarize one or more columns of data, you can add a Total row to your table.

| Contoso | March | $ | 26,786.00 |
| Lucerne Publishing | March | $ | 132,776.00 |
| World Wide Importers | March | $ | 245,695.00 |
| **Total** | | $ | **1,807,068.00** |

When you add the Total row, Excel 2007 creates a formula that calculates the sum of the values in the rightmost table column. To change that summary operation or to add a summary operation to any other cell in the Total row, click the cell, click the down arrow that appears, and then click the summary operation you want to apply. Clicking the More Functions item displays the Insert Function dialog box, from which you can select any of the functions in Excel 2007.

**See Also** For more information about using the Insert Function dialog box, see "Creating Formulas to Calculate Values" in Chapter 7.

Much as it does when you create a new worksheet, Excel 2007 gives your tables generic names such as *Table1* and *Table2*. You can change a table name to something easier to recognize by clicking any cell in the table, clicking the Design contextual tab, and then, in the Properties group, editing the value in the Table Name field. Changing a table name might not seem important, but it helps make formulas that summarize table data much easier to understand. You should make a habit of renaming your tables so you can recognize the data they contain.

**See Also** For more information on referring to tables in formulas, see "Creating Formulas to Calculate Values" in Chapter 7.

If for any reason you want to convert your table back to a normal range of cells, click any cell in the table and then, on the Table Tools contextual tab, in the Tools group, click Convert to Range. When Excel 2007 displays a message box asking if you're sure you want to convert the table to a range, click OK.

In this exercise, you will create a data table from existing data, add data to a table, add a Total row, change the Total row's summary operation, and rename the table.

> **USE** the *Driver Sort Times* workbook in the practice file folder for this topic. This practice file is located in the *Data and Data Tables* folder under *SBS_Office2007*.
>
> **OPEN** the *Driver Sort Times* workbook.

1. Select cell B2.

2. On the **Home** tab, in the **Styles** group, click **Format as Table** and then select a table style.

   The **Format As Table** dialog box appears.

3. Verify that the range =$B$2:$C$17 appears in the **Where is the data for your table?** field and that the **My table has headers** check box is selected, and then click **OK**.

   Excel 2007 creates a table from your data and displays the **Design** contextual tab.

4. In cell B18, type D116, press ⒜⒝, type 100 in cell C18, and press Enter.

   Excel 2007 includes the data in your table.

5. Select a cell in the table and on the **Design** contextual tab, in the **Table Style Options** group, select the **Total Row** check box.

   A **Total** row appears in your table.

6. Select cell C19, click the down arrow that appears at the right edge of the cell, and then click **Average**.

   Excel 2007 changes the summary operation to Average.

| Drive | Sorting Minutes |
|---|---|
| D101 | 102 |
| D102 | 162 |
| D103 | 165 |
| D104 | 91 |
| D105 | 103 |
| D106 | 127 |
| D107 | 112 |
| D108 | 137 |
| D109 | 102 |
| D110 | 147 |
| D111 | 163 |
| D112 | 109 |
| D113 | 91 |
| D114 | 107 |
| D115 | 93 |
| D116 | 100 |
| Total | 119.4375 |

7. On the **Design** contextual tab, in the **Properties** group, type the value SortingSample01 in the **Table Name** field, and press Enter.

   Excel 2007 renames your table.

8. On the Quick Access Toolbar, click the **Save** button to save your work.

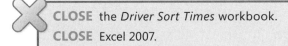

**CLOSE** the *Driver Sort Times* workbook.
**CLOSE** Excel 2007.

# Key Points

- You can enter a series of data quickly by entering one or more values in adjacent cells, selecting the cells, and then dragging the fill handle. To change how dragging the fill handle extends a data series, hold down the [Ctrl] key.

- Dragging a fill handle displays the Auto Fill Options button, which enables you to specify whether to copy the selected cells' values, extend a recognized series, or apply the selected cells' formatting to the new cells.

- Excel 2007 enables you to enter data by using a drop-down list, AutoComplete, and [Ctrl]+[Enter]. You should experiment with these techniques and use the one that best fits your circumstances.

- When you copy (or cut) and paste cells, columns, or rows, Excel 2007 displays the Paste Options smart tag. You can use its controls to determine which elements of the cut or copied elements Excel 2007 applies when they are pasted back into the worksheet.

- You can find and replace data within a worksheet by searching for specific values or by searching for cells that have a particular format applied.

- Excel 2007 provides a variety of powerful proofing and research tools, enabling you to check your workbook's spelling, find alternative words using the Thesaurus, and translate words between languages.

- Data tables, which are new in Excel 2007, enable you to organize and summarize your data effectively.

# Chapter at a Glance

Create formulas
to calculate values,
page 184

Name groups
of data,
page 180

Summarize data that
meets specific
conditions,
page 191

Find and
correct errors
in calculations,
page 195

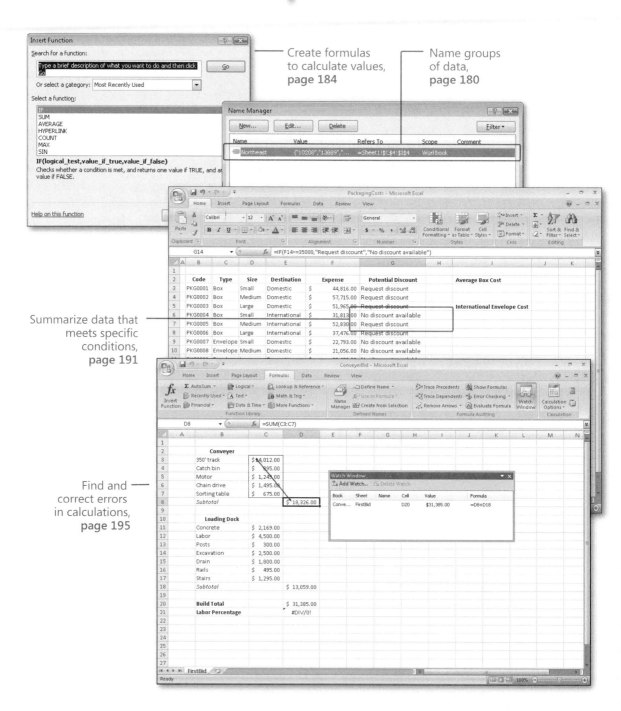

# 7 Performing Calculations on Data

In this chapter, you will learn to:

✔ Name groups of data.

✔ Create formulas to calculate values.

✔ Summarize data that meets specific conditions.

✔ Find and correct errors in calculations.

Microsoft Office Excel 2007 workbooks give you a handy place to store and organize your data, but you can also do a lot more with your data in Office Excel 2007. One important task you can perform is to calculate totals for the values in a series of related cells. You can also use Excel 2007 to find out other information about the data you select, such as the maximum or minimum value in a group of cells. By finding the maximum or minimum value in a group, you can identify your best salesperson, product categories you might need to pay more attention to, or suppliers that consistently give you the best deal. Regardless of your bookkeeping needs, Excel 2007 gives you the ability to find the information you want. And if you should make an error, you can find the cause and correct it quickly.

Many times you can't access the information you want without referencing more than one cell, and it's also often true that you'll use the data in the same group of cells for more than one calculation. Excel 2007 makes it easy to reference a number of cells at once, enabling you to define your calculations quickly.

In this chapter, you'll learn how to streamline references to groups of data on your worksheets and how to create and correct formulas that summarize Consolidated Messenger's business operations.

**See Also** Do you need only a quick refresher on the topics in this chapter? See the Quick Reference entries at the beginning of this book.

**Important** Before you can use the practice sites provided for this chapter, you need to install them from the book's companion CD to their default location. See "Using the Book's CD" at the beginning of this book for more information.

# Naming Groups of Data

When you work with large amounts of data, it's often useful to identify groups of cells that contain related data. For example, you can create a worksheet in which cells C4:I4 hold the number of packages Consolidated Messenger's Northeast processing facility handled from 5:00 PM to 12:00 AM on the previous day.

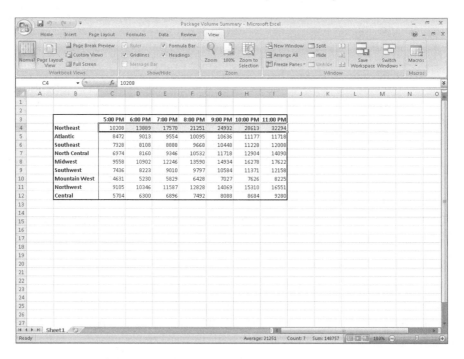

Instead of specifying the cells individually every time you want to use the data they contain, you can define those cells as a *range* (also called a *named range*). For instance, you can group the items from the preceding graphic into a range named *NortheastLastDay*.

Whenever you want to use the contents of that range in a calculation, you can simply use the name of the range instead of specifying each cell individually.

> **Note** Yes, you could just name the range *Northeast*, but if you use the range's values in a formula in another worksheet, the more descriptive range name tells you and your colleagues exactly what data is used in the calculation.

To create a named range, select the cells you want to include in your range, click the Formulas tab on the user interface, and then, in the Defined Names group, click Define Name to display the New Name dialog box. In the New Name dialog box, type a name in the Name field, verify that the cells you selected appear in the Refers to field, and then click OK. You can also add a comment about the field in the Comment field and select whether you want to make the name available for formulas in the entire workbook or just on an individual worksheet.

If the cells you want to define as a named range have a label you want to use as the range's name, you can display the Formulas tab and then, in the Defined Names group, click Create from Selection to display the Create Names from Selection dialog box. In the Create Names from Selection dialog box, select the check box that represents the label's position in relation to the data cells and then click OK.

A final way to create a named range is to select the cells you want in the range, click in the Name box next to the formula bar, and then type the name for the range. You can display the ranges available in a workbook by clicking the Name box down arrow.

To manage the named ranges in a workbook, display the Formulas tab on the ribbon and then, in the Defined Names group, click Name Manager to display the Name Manager dialog box.

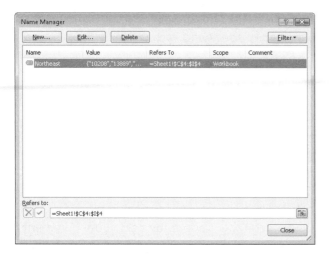

When you click a named range, Excel 2007 displays the cells it encompasses in the Refers to field. Clicking the Edit button displays the Edit Name dialog box, which is a version of the New Name dialog box, enabling you to change a named range's definition. You can also get rid of a name by clicking it, clicking the Delete button, and then clicking OK in the confirmation dialog box that appears.

> **Important** If your workbook contains a lot of named ranges, you can click the Filter button in the Name Manager dialog box and select a criterion to limit the names displayed in the Name Manager dialog box.

In this exercise, you will create named ranges to streamline references to groups of cells.

> **USE** the *VehicleMiles* workbook in the practice file folder for this topic. This practice file is located in the *Formulas* folder under *SBS_Office2007*.
>
> **BE SURE TO** start Excel 2007 before beginning this exercise.
>
> **OPEN** the *VehicleMiles* workbook from the *My Documents\Microsoft Press\Excel SBS\ Formulas* folder.

1. Select cells C4:G4.

2. In the **Name** box on the left of the formula bar, type V101LastWeek and press `Enter`.

   Excel 2007 creates a named range named *V101LastWeek*.

3. On the **Formulas** tab of the user interface, in the **Defined Names** group, click **Name Manager**.

   The **Name Manager** dialog box appears.

4. Click the **V101LastWeek** name.

   The cell range to which the **V101LastWeek** name refers appears in the **Refers to** field.

5. Edit the cell range in the **Refers to** field to =LastWeekMiles!$C$4:$H$4, click **OK**, and then click the check button next to the **Refers to** field.

   Excel 2007 changes the named range's definition.

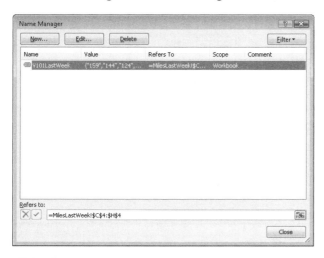

6. Click **Close**.

   The **Name Manager** dialog box disappears.

7. Select the cell range C5:H5.

8. On the **Formulas** tab, in the **Defined Names** group, click **Define Name**.

   The **New Name** dialog box appears.

9. In the **Name** field, type V102LastWeek.

10. Verify that the definition in the **Refers to** field is =LastWeekMiles!$C$5:$H$5.

11. Click **OK**.

    Excel 2007 creates the name and closes the **New Name** dialog box.

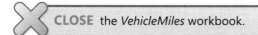

**CLOSE** the *VehicleMiles* workbook.

# Creating Formulas to Calculate Values

After you add your data to a worksheet and define ranges to simplify data references, you can create a *formula*, or an expression that performs calculations on your data. For example, you can calculate the total cost of a customer's shipments, figure the average number of packages for all Wednesdays in the month of January, or find the highest and lowest daily package volumes for a week, month, or year.

To write an Excel 2007 formula, you begin the cell's contents with an equal sign; when Excel 2007 sees it, it knows that the expression following it should be interpreted as a calculation, not text. After the equal sign, type the formula. For example, you can find the sum of the numbers in cells C2 and C3 using the formula =*C2+C3*. After you have entered a formula into a cell, you can revise it by clicking the cell and then editing the formula in the formula bar. For example, you can change the preceding formula to =*C3-C2*, which calculates the difference between the contents of cells C2 and C3.

> **Troubleshooting** If Excel 2007 treats your formula as text, make sure that you haven't accidentally put a space before the equal sign. Remember, the equal sign must be the first character!

Typing the cell references for 15 or 20 cells in a calculation would be tedious, but Excel 2007 makes it easy to handle complex calculations. To create a new calculation, click the Formulas tab on the ribbon and then, in the Function Library group, click Insert Function. The Insert Function dialog box appears, with a list of functions, or predefined formulas, from which you can choose.

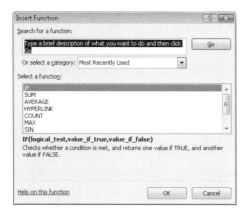

The following table describes some of the most useful functions in the list.

| Function | Description |
|----------|-------------|
| *SUM* | Finds the sum of the numbers in the specified cells |
| *AVERAGE* | Finds the average of the numbers in the specified cells |
| *COUNT* | Finds the number of entries in the specified cells |
| *MAX* | Finds the largest value in the specified cells |
| *MIN* | Finds the smallest value in the specified cells |

Two other functions you might use are the *NOW()* and *PMT()* functions. The *NOW()* function returns the time the workbook was last opened, so the value will change every time the workbook is opened. The proper form for this function is *=NOW()*. To update the value to the current date and time, just save your work, close the workbook, and then reopen it.

The *PMT()* function is a bit more complex. It calculates payments due on a loan, assuming a constant interest rate and constant payments. To perform its calculations, the *PMT()* function requires an interest rate, the number of months of payments, and the starting balance. The elements to be entered into the function are called *arguments* and must be entered in a certain order. That order is written *PMT(rate, nper, pv, fv, type)*. The following table summarizes the arguments in the *PMT()* function.

| Argument | Description |
|----------|-------------|
| rate | The interest rate, to be divided by 12 for a loan with monthly payments |
| nper | The total number of payments for the loan |
| pv | The amount loaned (pv is short for present value, or principal) |
| fv | The amount to be left over at the end of the payment cycle (usually left blank, which indicates 0) |
| type | 0 or 1, indicating whether payments are made at the beginning or at the end of the month (usually left blank, which indicates 0, or the end of the month) |

If Consolidated Messenger wanted to borrow $2,000,000 at a 6 percent interest rate and pay the loan back over 24 months, you could use the PMT() function to figure out the monthly payments. In this case, the function would be written =PMT(6%/12, 24, 2000000), which calculates a monthly payment of $88,641.22.

You can also use the names of any ranges you defined to supply values for a formula. For example, if the named range *NortheastLastDay* refers to cells C4:I4, you can calculate the average of cells C4:I4 with the formula *=AVERAGE(NortheastLastDay)*. In previous versions of Excel, you had to type the name into your formula by hand. Excel 2007 enables you to add functions, named ranges, and table references to your formulas more efficiently by using the new *Formula AutoComplete* capability. Just as AutoComplete offers to fill in a cell's text value when Excel 2007 recognizes that the value you're typing matches a previous entry, Formula AutoComplete offers to fill in a function, named range, or table reference while you create a formula.

As an example, consider a worksheet that contains a two-column table named Exceptions. The first column is labeled Route; the second is labeled Count.

| Route | Count |
|---|---|
| 101 | 7 |
| 102 | 0 |
| 103 | 4 |
| 104 | 6 |
| 105 | 18 |
| 106 | 12 |
| 107 | 3 |
| 108 | 3 |
| 109 | 8 |
| 110 | 9 |
| 111 | 8 |
| 112 | 18 |
| 113 | 12 |
| 114 | 16 |
| 115 | 12 |
| 116 | 9 |
| 117 | 10 |
| 118 | 6 |
| 119 | 10 |
| 120 | 4 |

You refer to a table by typing the table name, followed by the column or row name in square brackets. For example, the table reference *Exceptions[Count]* would refer to the Exceptions table's Count column.

To create a formula that finds the total number of exceptions by using the *SUM* function, you begin by typing =SU. When you type the letter S, Formula AutoComplete lists functions that begin with the letter *S*; when you type the letter U, Excel 2007 narrows the list down to the functions that start with the letters *SU*.

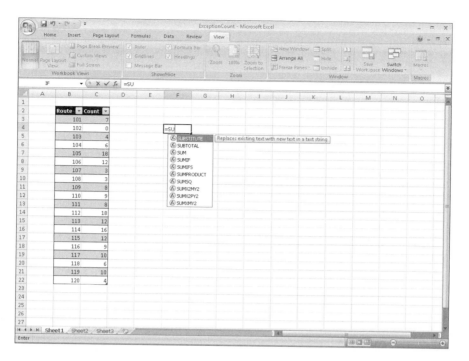

To add the *SUM* function (followed by an opening parenthesis) to the formula, click *SUM* and then press Tab. To begin adding the table column reference, type the letter E. Excel 2007 displays a list of available functions, tables, and named ranges that start with the letter *E*. Click Exceptions and press Tab to add the table reference to the formula. Then, because you want to summarize the values in the table's Count column, type [Count] to create the formula *=SUM(Exceptions[Count])*.

If you want to include a series of contiguous cells in a formula, but you haven't defined the cells as a named range, you can click the first cell in the range and drag to the last cell. If the cells aren't contiguous, hold down the Ctrl key and click the cells to be included. In both cases, when you release the mouse button, the references of the cells you selected appear in the formula.

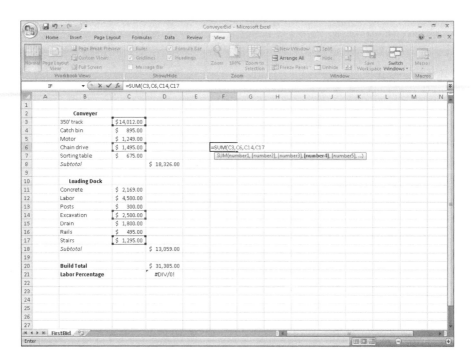

After you create a formula, you can copy it and paste it into another cell. When you do, Excel 2007 tries to change the formula so that it works in the new cells. For instance, suppose that you have a worksheet in which cell D8 contains the formula *=SUM(C2: C6)*. Clicking cell D8, copying the cell's contents, and then pasting the result into cell D16 writes *=SUM(C10:C14)* into cell D16. Excel 2007 has reinterpreted the formula so that it fits the surrounding cells! Excel 2007 knows it can reinterpret the cells used in the formula because the formula uses a *relative reference*, or a reference that can change if the formula is copied to another cell. Relative references are written with just the cell row and column (for example, *C14*). If you want a cell reference to remain constant when the formula using it is copied to another cell, you can use an absolute reference. To write a cell reference as an absolute reference, type $ before the row name and the column number. If you want the formula in cell D16 to show the sum of values in cells C10 through C14 regardless of the cell into which it is pasted, you can write the formula as =SUM($C$10:$C$14).

> **Tip** If you copy a formula from the formula bar, use absolute references or use only named ranges in your formula. Excel 2007 doesn't change the cell references when you copy your formula to another cell.

One quick way to change a cell reference from relative to absolute is to select the cell reference on the formula bar and then press ⟨F4⟩. Pressing ⟨F4⟩ cycles a cell reference through the four possible types of references:

- Relative columns and rows (for example, *C4*)
- Absolute columns and rows (for example, *$C$4*)
- Relative columns and absolute rows (for example, *C$4*)
- Absolute columns and relative rows (for example, *$C4*)

In this exercise, you will create a formula manually, revise it to include additional cells, create a formula that contains a table reference, create a formula with relative references, and change the formula so it contains absolute references.

> **USE** the *ITExpenses* workbook in the practice file folder for this topic. This practice file is located in the *Formulas* folder under *SBS_Office2007*.
>
> **OPEN** the *ITExpenses* workbook.

1. If necessary, display the **Summary** worksheet. Then, in cell F9, type =C4 and press ⟨Enter⟩.

   The value *$385,671.00* appears in cell F9.

2. Select cell F9 and then, on the formula bar, erase the existing formula and type =SU.

   Formula AutoComplete displays a list of possible functions to use in the formula.

3. In the Formula AutoComplete list, click **SUM** and then press ⟨Tab⟩.

   Excel 2007 changes the contents of the formula bar to *=SUM(*.

4. Select the cell range C3:C8, type a right parenthesis (the *)* character) to make the formula bar's contents *=SUM(C3:C8)* and then press ⟨Enter⟩.

   The value *$2,562,966.00* appears in cell F9.

5. In cell F10, type =SUM(C4:C5) and press ⟨Enter⟩.

6. Select cell F10 and then, on the formula bar, select the cell reference *C4* and press ⟨F4⟩.

   Excel 2007 changes the cell reference to *$C$4*.

7. On the formula bar, select the cell reference *C5*, press ⟨F4⟩, and then press ⟨Enter⟩.

   Excel 2007 changes the cell reference to *$C$5*.

8. On the tab bar, click the **JuneLabor** sheet tab.

   The **JuneLabor** worksheet appears.

9. In cell F13, type =SUM(J.

   Excel 2007 displays **JuneSummary**, the name of the table in the **JuneLabor** worksheet.

10. Press [Tab].

    Excel 2007 extends the formula to read =SUM(JuneSummary.

11. Type [, and then, in the Formula AutoComplete list, click **[Labor Expense]** and press [Tab].

    Excel 2007 extends the formula to read =SUM(JuneLabor[Labor Expense.

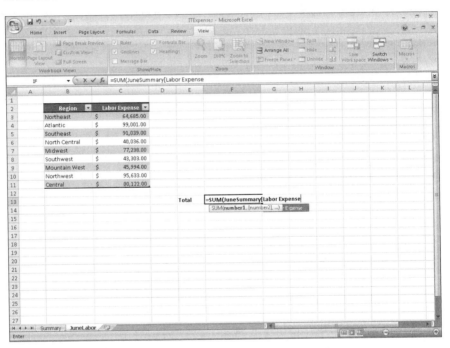

12. Type ]) to complete the formula and then press [Enter].

    The value $637,051.00 appears in cell F13.

**CLOSE** the *ITExpenses* workbook.

# Summarizing Data That Meets Specific Conditions

Another use for formulas is to display messages when certain conditions are met. For instance, Consolidated Messenger's VP of Marketing, Craig Dewar, might have agreed to examine the rates charged to corporate customers who were billed for more than $100,000 during a calendar year. This kind of formula is called a *conditional formula*, and it uses the *IF* function. To create a conditional formula, you click the cell to hold the formula and open the Insert Function dialog box. From within the dialog box, select *IF* from the list of available functions and then click OK. The Function Arguments dialog box appears.

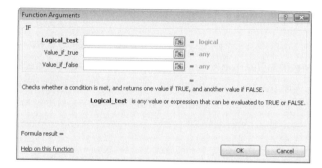

When you work with an *IF* function, the Function Arguments dialog box has three boxes: Logical_test, Value_if_true, and Value_if_false. The Logical_test box holds the condition you want to check. If the customer's year-to-date shipping bill appears in cell G8, the expression would be *G8>100000*.

Now you need to have Excel 2007 display messages that indicate whether Craig Dewar should evaluate the account for a possible rate adjustment. To have Excel 2007 print a message from an *IF* function, you enclose the message in quotes in the Value_if_true or Value_if_false box. In this case, you would type "High-volume shipper—evaluate for rate decrease." in the Value_if_true box and "Does not qualify at this time." in the Value_if_false box.

Excel 2007 also includes five new conditional functions with which you can summarize your data:

- *IFERROR*, which displays one value if a formula results in an error; another if it doesn't

- *AVERAGEIF*, which finds the average of values within a cell range that meet a given criterion

- *AVERAGEIFS*, which finds the average of values within a cell range that meet multiple criteria

- *SUMIFS*, which finds the sum of values in a range that meet multiple criteria

- *COUNTIFS*, which counts the number of cells in a range that meet multiple criteria

The *IFERROR* function enables you to display a custom error message instead of relying on the default Excel 2007 error messages to explain what happened. One example of an *IFERROR* formula is if you want to look up the CustomerID value from cell G8 in the Customers table by using the *VLOOKUP* function. One way to create such a formula is =IFERROR(VLOOKUP(G8,Customers,2,false),"Customer not found"). If the function finds a match for the CustomerID in cell G8, it displays the customer's name; if it doesn't find a match, it displays the text *Customer not found*.

The *AVERAGEIF* function is a variation on the existing *COUNTIF* and *SUMIF* functions. To create a formula using the *AVERAGEIF* function, you define the range to be examined, the criteria, and, if required, the range from which to draw the values. As an example, consider the following worksheet, which lists each customer's name, state, and total monthly shipping bill.

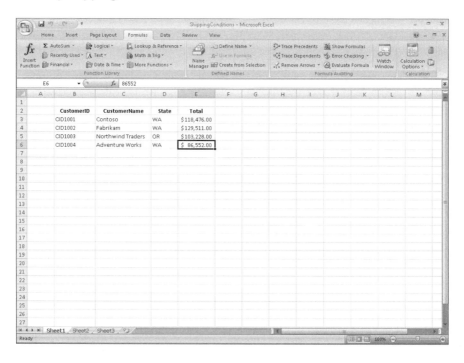

If you want to find the average order of customers from Washington State (abbreviated in the worksheet as WA), you can create the formula =AVERAGEIF(D3:D6,"=WA", E3:E6).

The AVERAGEIFS, SUMIFS, and COUNTIFS functions extend the capabilities of the AVERAGEIF, SUMIF, and COUNTIF functions to allow for multiple criteria. If you want to find the sum of all orders of at least $100,000 placed by companies in Washington, you can create the formula =SUMIFS(E3:E6, D3:D6, "=WA", E3:E6, ">=100000").

The AVERAGEIFS and SUMIFS functions start with a data range that contains values that the formula summarizes; you then list the data ranges and the criteria to apply to that range. In generic terms, the syntax runs =AVERAGEIFS(data_range, criteria_range1, criteria1[,criteria_range2, criteria2...]). The part of the syntax in square brackets is optional, so an AVERAGEIFS or SUMIFS formula that contains a single criterion works. The COUNTIFS function, which doesn't perform any calculations, doesn't need a data range—you just provide the criteria ranges and criteria. For example, you could find the number of customers from Washington billed at least $100,000 by using the formula =COUNTIFS(D3:D6, "=WA", E3:E6, ">=100000").

In this exercise, you will create a conditional formula that displays a message if a condition is true, find the average of worksheet values that meet one criterion, and find the sum of worksheet values that meet two criteria.

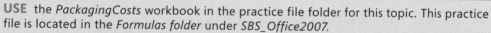

**USE** the *PackagingCosts* workbook in the practice file folder for this topic. This practice file is located in the *Formulas folder* under *SBS_Office2007.*
**OPEN** the *PackagingCosts* workbook.

1. In cell G3, type the formula =IF(F3>=35000,"Request discount","No discount available") and press `Enter`.

   Excel 2007 accepts the formula, which displays *Request discount* if the value in cell F3 is at least 35,000 and displays *No discount available* if not. The value *Request discount* appears in cell G3.

2. Click cell G3 and drag the fill handle down until it covers cell G14.

   Excel 2007 copies the formula in cell G3 to cells G4:G14, adjusting the formula to reflect the cells' addresses. The results of the copied formulas appear in cells G4:G14.

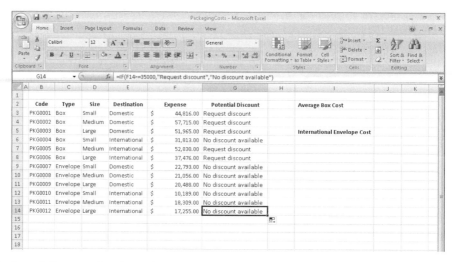

3.  In cell I3, type the formula =AVERAGEIF(C3:C14, "=Box", F3:F14) and press `Enter`.

The value *$46,102.50*, which represents the average cost per category of boxes, appears in cell I3.

4.  In cell I6, type  =SUMIFS(F3:F14, C3:C14, "=Envelope", E3:E14, "=International").

The value *$45,753.00*, which represents the total cost of all envelopes used for international shipments, appears in cell I6.

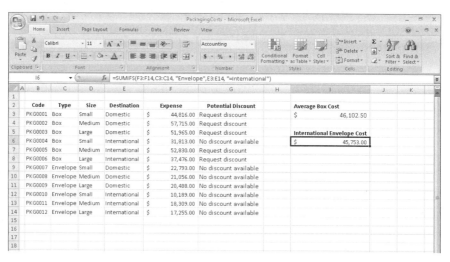

 **CLOSE** the *PackagingCosts* workbook.

# Finding and Correcting Errors in Calculations

Including calculations in a worksheet gives you valuable answers to questions about your data. As is always true, however, it is possible for errors to creep into your formulas. Excel 2007 makes it easy to find the source of errors in your formulas by identifying the cells used in a given calculation and describing any errors that have occurred. The process of examining a worksheet for errors in formulas is referred to as *auditing*.

Excel 2007 identifies errors in several ways. The first way is to fill the cell holding the formula generating the error with an *error code*. In the following graphic, cell F13 has the error code *#NAME?*.

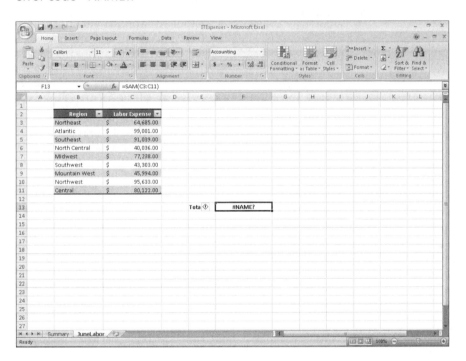

When a cell with an erroneous formula is the active cell, an Error button appears next to it. You can click the button down arrow to display a menu with options that provide information about the error and offer to help you fix it. The following table lists the most common error codes and what they mean.

| Error Code | Description |
| --- | --- |
| ##### | The column isn't wide enough to display the value. |
| #VALUE! | The formula has the wrong type of argument (such as text in which a *TRUE* or *FALSE* value is required). |
| #NAME? | The formula contains text that Excel 2007 doesn't recognize (such as an unknown named range). |
| #REF! | The formula refers to a cell that doesn't exist (which can happen whenever cells are deleted). |
| #DIV/0! | The formula attempts to divide by zero. |

Another technique you can use to find the source of formula errors is to ensure that the appropriate cells are providing values for the formula. For example, you might want to calculate the total number of deliveries for a service level, but you could accidentally create a formula referring to the service levels' names instead of their quantities. You can identify what kind of error has appeared by having Excel 2007 trace a cell's *precedents*, which are the cells with values used in the active cell's formula. Excel 2007 identifies a cell's precedents by drawing a blue tracer arrow from the precedent to the active cell.

You can also audit your worksheet by identifying cells with formulas that use a value from a given cell. For example, you might use one region's daily package total in a formula that calculates the average number of packages delivered per region on a given day. Cells that use another cell's value in their calculations are known as *dependents*, meaning that they depend on the value in the other cell to derive their own value. As with tracing precedents, you can click the Formulas tab on the user interface and then, in the Formula Auditing group, click Trace Dependents to have Excel 2007 draw blue arrows from the active cell to those cells that have calculations based on that value.

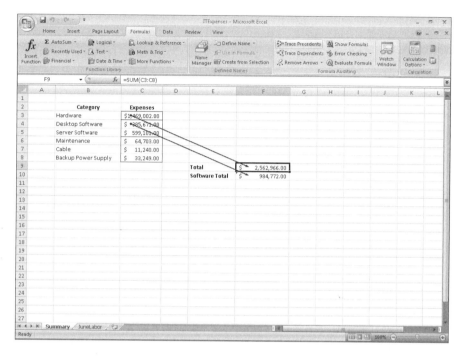

If the cells identified by the tracer arrows aren't the correct cells, you can hide the arrows and correct the formula. To hide the tracer arrows on a worksheet, display the Formulas tab and then, in the Formula Auditing group, click Remove Arrows.

If you prefer to have the elements of a formula error presented as text in a dialog box, you can use the Error Checking dialog box (which you can display by displaying the Formulas tab and then, in the Formula Auditing group, clicking the Error Checking button) to view the error and the formula in the cell in which the error occurs. You can also use the controls in the Error Checking dialog box to move through the formula one step at a time, to choose to ignore the error, or to move to the next or the previous error. If you click the Options button in the dialog box, you can also use the controls in the Excel Options dialog box to change how Excel 2007 determines what is an error and what isn't.

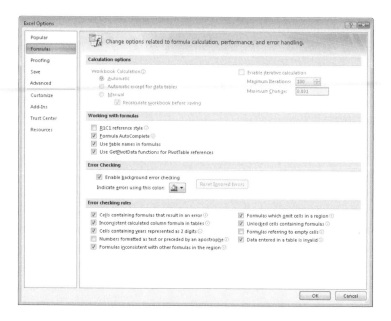

> **Tip** You can have the Error Checking tool ignore formulas that don't use every cell in a region (such as a row or column). If you clear the Formulas that omit cells in a region check box, you can create formulas that don't add up every value in a row or column (or rectangle) without Excel 2007 marking them as an error.

For times when you just want to display the results of each step of a formula and don't need the full power of the Error Checking tool, you can use the Evaluate Formula dialog box to move through each element of the formula. To display the Evaluate Formula dialog box, you display the Formulas tab and then, in the Formula Auditing group, click the Evaluate Formula button. The Evaluate Formula dialog box is much more useful for examining formulas that don't produce an error but aren't generating the result you expect.

Finally, you can monitor the value in a cell regardless of where in your workbook you are by opening a Watch Window that displays the value in the cell. For example, if one of your formulas uses values from cells in other worksheets or even other workbooks, you can set a watch on the cell that contains the formula and then change the values in the other cells. To set a watch, click the cell you want to monitor and then, on the Formulas tab, in the Formula Auditing group, click Watch Window. Click Add Watch to have Excel 2007 monitor the selected cell.

As soon as you type in the new value, the Watch Window displays the new result of the formula. When you're done watching the formula, select the watch, click Delete Watch, and close the Watch Window.

In this exercise, you use the formula-auditing capabilities in Excel 2007 to identify and correct errors in a formula.

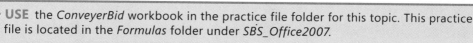

**USE** the *ConveyerBid* workbook in the practice file folder for this topic. This practice file is located in the *Formulas* folder under *SBS_Office2007*.

**OPEN** the *ConveyerBid* workbook.

1. Click cell D20.

2. On the **Formulas** tab, in the **Formula Auditing** group, click **Watch Window**.

   The **Watch Window** appears.

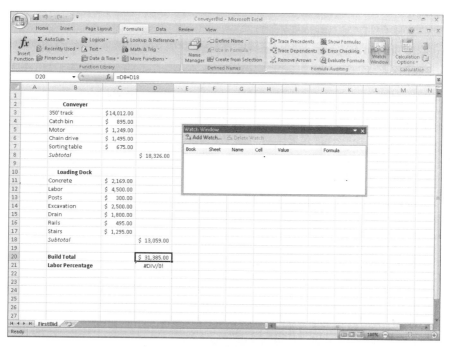

3. Click **Add Watch** and then, in the **Add Watch** dialog box, click **Add**.

   Cell *D20* appears in the **Watch Window**.

4. Click cell D8.

   *=SUM(C3:C7)* appears in the formula bar.

5. On the **Formulas** tab, in the **Formula Auditing** group, click **Trace Precedents**.

A blue arrow appears between cell D8 and the cell range C3:C7, indicating that the cells in the range C3:C7 are precedents of the value in cell D8.

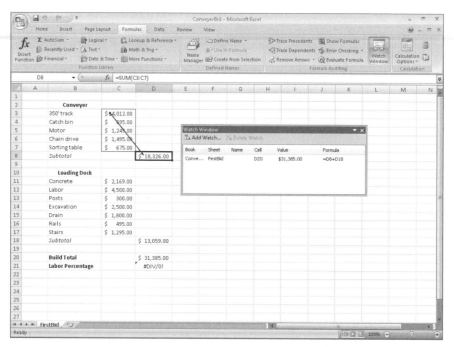

6. On the **Formulas** tab, in the **Formula Auditing** group, click **Remove Arrows**.

   The arrow disappears.

7. Click cell A1.

8. On the **Formulas** tab, in the **Formula Auditing** group, click the **Error Checking** button.

   The **Error Checking** dialog box appears.

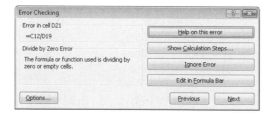

9. Click **Next**.

   Excel 2007 displays a message box indicating that there are no more errors in the worksheet.

10. Click **OK**.

The message box and the **Error Checking** dialog box disappear.

**11.** On the **Formulas** tab, in the **Formula Auditing** group, click the **Error Checking** button down arrow, and then click **Trace Error**.

Blue arrows appear, pointing to cell D21 from cells C12 and D19. These arrows indicate that using the values (or lack of values, in this case) in the indicated cells generates the error in cell D21.

**12.** On the **Formulas** tab, in the **Formula Auditing** group, click **Remove Arrows**.

The arrows disappear.

**13.** In the formula bar, delete the existing formula, type =C12/D20, and press ⏎.

The value *14%* appears in cell D21.

**14.** Click cell D21.

**15.** On the **Formulas** tab, in the **Formula Auditing** group, click the **Evaluate Formula** button.

The **Evaluate Formula** dialog box appears, with the formula from cell D21 displayed.

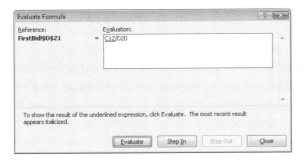

**16.** Click **Evaluate** three times to step through the formula's elements and then click **Close**.

The **Evaluate Formula** dialog box disappears.

**17.** In the **Watch Window**, click the watch in the list.

**18.** Click **Delete Watch**.

The watch disappears.

**19.** On the **Formulas** tab, in the **Formula Auditing** group, click **Watch Window**.

The **Watch Window** disappears.

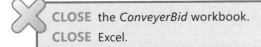

**CLOSE** the *ConveyerBid* workbook.
**CLOSE** Excel.

# Key Points

- You can add a group of cells to a formula by typing the formula and then, at the spot in the formula in which you want to name the cells, selecting the cells using the mouse.

- Creating named ranges enables you to refer to entire blocks of cells with a single term, saving you lots of time and effort. You can use a similar technique with table data, referring to an entire table or one or more table columns.

- When you write a formula, be sure you use absolute referencing ($A$1) if you want the formula to remain the same when it's copied from one cell to another or use relative referencing (A1) if you want the formula to change to reflect its new position in the worksheet.

- Instead of typing a formula from scratch, you can use the Insert Function dialog box to help you on your way.

- You can monitor how the value in a cell changes by adding a watch to the Watch Window.

- To see which formulas refer to the values in the selected cell, use Trace Dependents; if you want to see which cells provide values for the formula in the active cell, use Trace Precedents.

- You can step through the calculations of a formula in the Evaluate Formula dialog box or go through a more rigorous error-checking procedure using the Error Checking tool.

# Chapter at a Glance

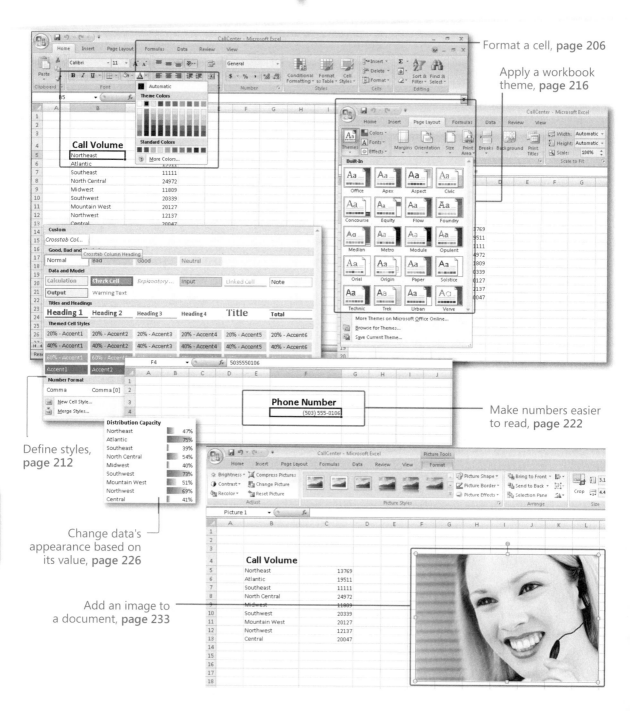

Format a cell, **page 206**

Apply a workbook theme, **page 216**

Make numbers easier to read, **page 222**

Define styles, **page 212**

Change data's appearance based on its value, **page 226**

Add an image to a document, **page 233**

# 8 Changing Document Appearance

---

## In this chapter, you will learn to:

✔     Format a cell.

✔     Define styles.

✔     Apply a workbook theme.

✔     Make numbers easier to read.

✔     Change data's appearance based on its value.

✔     Add an image to a document.

---

Entering data into a workbook efficiently saves you time, but you must also ensure that your data is easy to read. Microsoft Office Excel 2007 gives you a wide variety of ways to make your data easier to understand; for example, you can change the font, character size, or color used to present a cell's contents. Changing how data appears on a worksheet helps set the contents of a cell apart from the contents of surrounding cells. The simplest example of that concept is a data label. If a column on your worksheet has a list of days, you can set a label (for example, *Day*) apart easily by presenting it in bold type that's noticeably larger than the type used to present the data to which it refers. To save time, you can define a number of custom formats and then apply them quickly to the desired cells.

You might also want to specially format a cell's contents to reflect the value in that cell. For instance, Jenny Lysaker, the chief operating officer of Consolidated Messenger, might want to create a worksheet that displays the percentage of improperly delivered packages from each regional distribution center. If that percentage exceeds a threshold, she could have Office Excel 2007 display a red traffic light icon, indicating that the center's performance is out of tolerance and requires attention.

In addition to changing how data appears in the cells of your worksheet, you can also use headers and footers to add page numbers, current data, or graphics to the top and bottom of every printed page.

In this chapter, you'll learn how to change the appearance of data, apply existing formats to data, make numbers easier to read, change data's appearance based on its value, make printouts easier to follow, and position your data on the printed page.

**See Also** Do you need only a quick refresher on the topics in this chapter? See the Quick Reference entries at the beginning of this book.

**Important** Before you can use the practice sites provided for this chapter, you need to install them from the book's companion CD to their default location. See "Using the Book's CD" at the beginning of this book for more information.

# Formatting Cells

Office Excel 2007 spreadsheets can hold and process lots of data, but when you manage numerous spreadsheets it can be hard to remember from a worksheet's title exactly what data is kept in that worksheet. Data labels give you and your colleagues information about data in a worksheet, but it's important to format the labels so that they stand out visually. To make your data labels or any other data stand out, you can change the format of the cells in which the data is stored.

| | A | B | C | D | E |
|---|---|---|---|---|---|
| 1 | | | | | |
| 2 | | | | | |
| 3 | | | | | |
| 4 | | Call Volume | | | |
| 5 | | Northeast | 13769 | | |
| 6 | | Atlantic | 19511 | | |
| 7 | | Southeast | 11111 | | |
| 8 | | North Central | 24972 | | |
| 9 | | Midwest | 11809 | | |
| 10 | | Southwest | 20339 | | |
| 11 | | Mountain West | 20127 | | |
| 12 | | Northwest | 12137 | | |
| 13 | | Central | 20047 | | |
| 14 | | | | | |
| 15 | | | | | |
| 16 | | | | | |

Most of the tools you need to change a cell's format can be found on the user interface's Home tab. You can apply the formatting represented on a button by selecting the cells you want to apply the style to and then clicking the appropriate button. If you want to set your data labels apart by making them appear bold, click the Bold button. If you have already made a cell's contents bold, selecting the cell and clicking the Bold button will remove the formatting.

> **Tip** Deleting a cell's contents doesn't delete the cell's formatting. To delete a cell's formatting, select the cell and then, on the Home tab, in the Editing group, click the Clear button and then click Clear Formats.

Items in the Home tab's Font group that give you choices, such as the Font Color control, have a down arrow at the right edge of the control. Clicking the down arrow displays a list of options accessible for that control, such as the fonts available on your system or the colors you can assign to a cell.

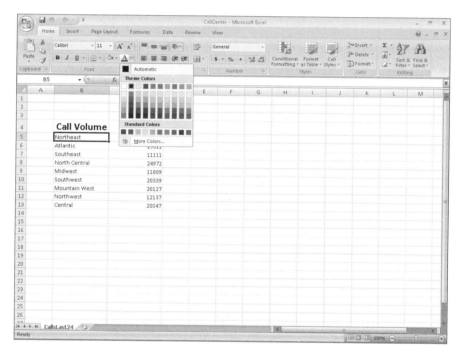

Another way you can make a cell stand apart from its neighbors is to add a border around the cell. To place a border around one or more cells, select the cells and then choose the border type you want by clicking the down arrow in the Font group's Border control and selecting the type of border to apply. Excel 2007 does provide more options—to display the full range of border types and styles, open the Border control's drop-down list and then click More Borders. The Border tab of the Format Cells dialog box contains the full range of tools you can use to define your cells' borders.

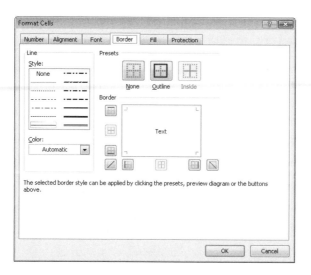

Another way you can make a group of cells stand apart from its neighbors is to change its shading, or the color that fills the cells. On a worksheet that tracks total package volume for the past month, Jenny Lysaker could change the fill color of the cells holding her data labels to make the labels stand out even more than by changing the formatting of the text used to display the labels.

> **Tip**  You can display the most commonly used formatting controls by right-clicking a selected range. When you do, a minitoolbar containing a subset of the Home tab formatting tools appears at the top of the shortcut menu.

If you want to change the attributes of every cell in a row or column, you can click the header of the row or column you want to format and then select your desired format.

One task you can't perform using the tools on the Home tab of the user interface is to change the standard font for a workbook, which is used in the Name box and on the formula bar. The standard font when you install Excel 2007 is Calibri, a simple font that is easy to read on a computer screen and on the printed page. If you want to choose another font, click the Microsoft Office Button and then click Excel Options. On the Popular page of the Excel Options dialog box, set the values in the Use this font and Font size list boxes to pick your new display font.

> **Important**  The new standard font doesn't take effect until you quit Excel 2007 and restart the program.

In this exercise, you emphasize a worksheet's title by changing the format of cell data, adding a border to a cell range, and then changing a cell range's fill color. After those tasks are complete, you change the default font for the workbook.

**USE** the *VehicleMileSummary* workbook in the practice file folder for this topic. This practice file is located in the *Appearance* folder under *SBS_Office2007*.

**BE SURE TO** start Excel 2007 before beginning this exercise.

**OPEN** the *VehicleMileSummary* workbook.

1. Click cell D2.

2. On the **Home** tab of the user interface, in the **Font** group, click the **Bold** button.

   Excel 2007 displays the cell's contents in bold type.

3. In the **Font** group, click the **Font Size** control down arrow and then click **18**.

   Excel 2007 increases the size of the text in cell D2.

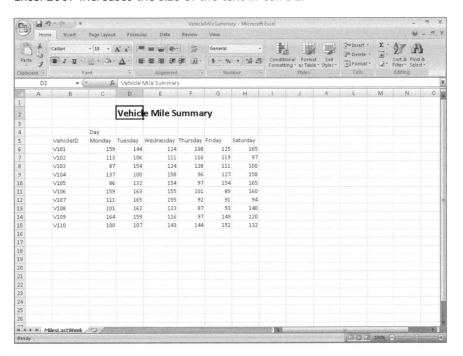

4. Select cells B5 and C4.

5. On the **Home** tab, in the **Font** group, click the **Bold** button.

   Excel 2007 displays the cells' contents in bold type.

6. Select the cell ranges B6:B15 and C5:H5.

**7.** On the **Home** tab, in the **Font** group, click the **Italic** button.

Excel 2007 displays the cells' contents in italic type.

| | A | B | C | D | E | F | G | H | I |
|---|---|---|---|---|---|---|---|---|---|
| 1 | | | | | | | | | |
| 2 | | | | | Vehicle Mile Summary | | | | |
| 3 | | | | | | | | | |
| 4 | | | Day | | | | | | |
| 5 | | VehicleID | Monday | Tuesday | Wednesday | Thursday | Friday | Saturday | |
| 6 | | V101 | 159 | 144 | 124 | 108 | 125 | 165 | |
| 7 | | V102 | 113 | 106 | 111 | 116 | 119 | 97 | |
| 8 | | V103 | 87 | 154 | 124 | 128 | 111 | 100 | |
| 9 | | V104 | 137 | 100 | 158 | 96 | 127 | 158 | |
| 10 | | V105 | 86 | 132 | 154 | 97 | 154 | 165 | |
| 11 | | V106 | 159 | 163 | 155 | 101 | 89 | 160 | |
| 12 | | V107 | 111 | 165 | 155 | 92 | 91 | 94 | |
| 13 | | V108 | 101 | 162 | 123 | 87 | 93 | 140 | |
| 14 | | V109 | 164 | 159 | 116 | 97 | 149 | 120 | |
| 15 | | V110 | 100 | 107 | 143 | 144 | 152 | 132 | |
| 16 | | | | | | | | | |
| 17 | | | | | | | | | |

**8.** Select the cell range C6:H15.

**9.** On the **Home** tab, in the **Font** group, click the **Border** control down arrow and then click **Outside Borders**.

Excel 2007 places a border around the outside edge of the selected cells.

**10.** Select the cell range B4:H15.

**11.** On the **Home** tab, in the **Font** group, click the **Border** control down arrow and then click **Thick Box Border**.

Excel 2007 places a thick border around the outside edge of the selected cells.

**12.** Select the cell ranges B4:B15 and C4:H5.

**13.** On the **Home** tab, in the **Font** group, click the **Fill Color** control down arrow and then, in the **Standard Colors** section of the color palette, click the yellow button.

Excel 2007 changes the selected cells' background color to yellow.

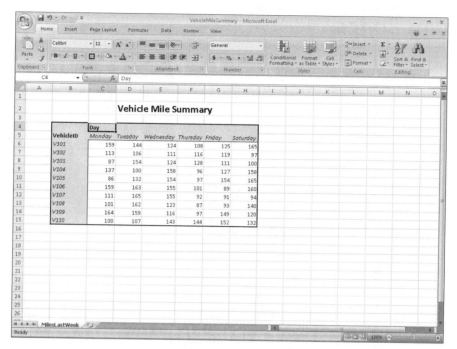

**14.** Click the **Microsoft Office Button** and then click **Excel Options**.

The **Excel Options** dialog box appears.

**15.** If necessary, click **Popular** to display the **Popular** tab.

**16.** In the **When creating new workbooks** section, click the **Use this font** field down arrow and then click **Verdana**.

*Verdana* appears in the **Use this font** field.

**17.** Click **Cancel**.

The **Excel Options** dialog box disappears without saving your change.

**CLOSE** the *VehicleMileSummary* workbook.

# Defining Styles

As you work with Excel 2007, you will probably develop preferred formats for data labels, titles, and other worksheet elements. Instead of adding the format's characteristics one element at a time to the target cells, you can have Excel 2007 store the format and re-call it as needed. You can find the predefined formats available to you by displaying the Home tab of the user interface and then, in the Styles group, clicking Cell Styles.

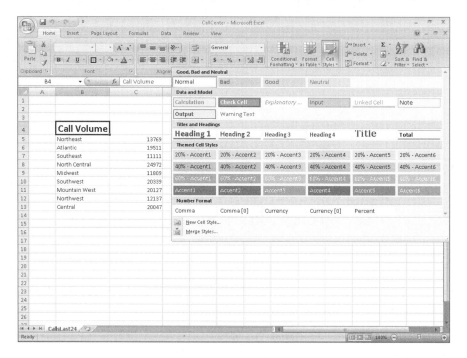

Clicking a style from the Cell Styles gallery applies the style to the selected cells, but Excel 2007 goes a step beyond previous versions of the program by displaying a live preview of a format when you hover your mouse pointer on it. If none of the exist-ing styles is what you want, you can create your own style by displaying the Cell Styles gallery and, at the bottom of the gallery, clicking New Cell Style to display the Style dialog box. In the Style dialog box, type the name of your new style in the Style name field and then click Format. The Format Cells dialog box appears.

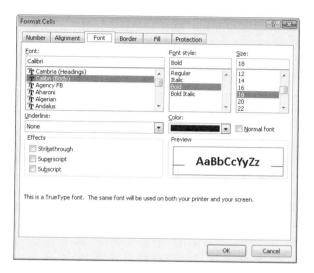

After you set the characteristics of your new style, click OK to make your style available in the Cell Styles gallery. If you ever want to delete a style, display the Cell Styles gallery, right-click the style, and then click Delete.

The Style dialog box is quite versatile, but it's overkill if all you want to do is apply formatting changes you made to a cell to the contents of another cell. To do so, use the Format Painter button, found in the Home tab's Clipboard group. Just click the cell that has the format you want to copy, click the Format Painter button, and select the target cells to have Excel 2007 apply the copied format to the target range.

In this exercise, you create a style, apply the new style to a data label, and then use the Format Painter to apply the style to the contents of another cell.

**USE** the *HourlyExceptions* workbook in the practice file folder for this topic. This practice file is located in the *Appearance* folder under *SBS_Office2007*.

**OPEN** the *HourlyExceptions* workbook.

1. On the **Home** tab, in the **Styles** group, click **Cell Styles** and then click **New Cell Style**.

   The **Style** dialog box appears.

2. In the **Style** name field, type Crosstab Column Heading.

3. Click the **Format** button.

   The **Format Cells** dialog box appears.

4. Click the **Alignment** tab.

   The **Alignment** tab of the **Format Cells** dialog box appears.

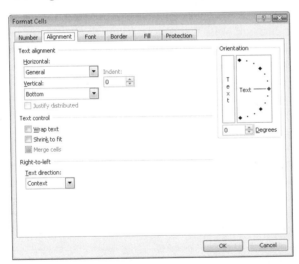

5. Click the **Horizontal** field down arrow and then click **Center**.

   *Center* appears in the **Horizontal** field.

6. Click the **Font** tab.

   The **Font** tab of the **Format Cells** dialog box appears.

7. In the **Font** style list, click **Italic**.

   The text in the **Preview** pane appears in italicized text.

   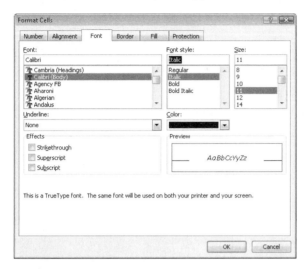

8. Click the **Number** tab.

   The **Number** tab of the **Format Cells** dialog box appears.

9. In the **Category** list, click **Time**.

   The available time formats appear.

10. In the **Type** pane, click **1:30 PM**.

11. Click **OK** to accept the default time format.

    The **Format Cells** dialog box disappears, and your new style's definition appears in the **Style** dialog box.

12. Click **OK**.

    The **Style** dialog box disappears.

13. Select cells C4:N4.

14. On the **Home** tab, in the **Styles** group, click **Cell Styles**.

    Your new style appears at the top of the gallery, in the **Custom** group.

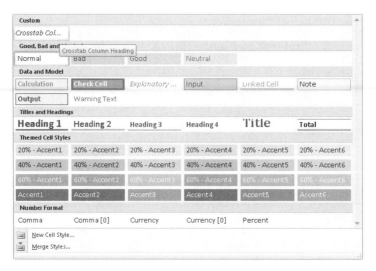

15. Click the **Crosstab Column Heading** style.

Excel 2007 applies your new style to the selected cells.

 **CLOSE** the *HourlyExceptions* workbook.

# Applying Workbook Themes and Table Styles

The 2007 Microsoft Office system includes powerful new design tools that enable you to create attractive, professional documents quickly. The Excel 2007 product team implemented the new design capabilities by defining workbook themes and table styles. A *theme* is a way to specify the fonts, colors, and graphic effects that appear in a workbook. Excel 2007 comes with many themes installed.

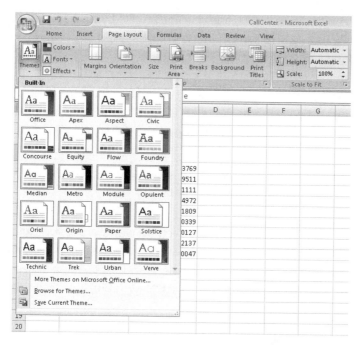

To apply an existing workbook theme, display the Page Layout tab of the user interface. Then, in the Themes group, click Themes and then click the theme you want to apply to your workbook. By default, Excel 2007 applies the Office theme to your workbooks.

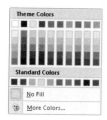

The theme colors appear in the top segment of the color palette—the standard colors and the More Colors link, which displays the Colors dialog box, appear at the bottom of the palette. If you format workbook elements using colors from the theme colors portion of the color palette, applying a different theme changes that object's colors.

You can change a theme's colors, fonts, and graphic effects by displaying the Page Layout tab on the user interface and then, in the Themes group, selecting new values by using the Colors, Fonts, and Effects buttons' drop-down lists. To save your changes as a new theme, display the Page Layout tab of the user interface, and then, in the Themes group, click Themes and then click Save Current Theme. Use the controls in the dialog box that appears to record your theme for later use. Later, when you click the Themes button, your custom theme will appear at the top of the gallery.

> **Note**  When you save a theme, you save it as an Office Theme file. You can apply the theme to Microsoft Office Word 2007 and Microsoft Office PowerPoint 2007 files as well.

Just as you can define themes and apply them to entire workbooks, you can apply and define table styles. You select a table's initial style when you create it; to create a new table style, display the Home tab of the user interface and then, in the Styles group, click Format as Table. In the Format as Table gallery, click New Table Style to display the New Table Quick Style dialog box.

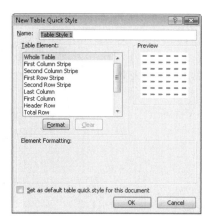

Type a name for the new style, select the first table element you want to format, and then click Format to display the Format Cells dialog box. Define the element's formatting and then click OK. When the New Table Quick Style dialog box reappears, its Preview pane displays the overall table style and the Element Formatting section displays the selected element's appearance. Also, in the Table Element list, Excel 2007 displays the element's name in bold to indicate it has been changed.

If you want to make your new style the default for any new tables created in the current workbook, select the Set as default table quick style for this document check box. When you click OK, Excel 2007 saves your custom table style.

**See Also**  For more information on creating Excel 2007 tables, see "Defining a Table" in Chapter 6.

In this exercise, you will create a new workbook theme, change a workbook's theme, create a new table style, and apply the new style to a table.

**USE** the *HourlyTracking* workbook in the practice file folder for this topic. This practice file is located in the *Appearance* folder under *SBS_Office2007*.
**OPEN** the *HourlyTracking* workbook.

1. If necessary, click any cell in the table.

2. On the **Home** tab of the ribbon, in the **Styles** group, click **Format as Table** and then click the style at the upper-left corner of the **Table Styles** gallery.

   Excel 2007 applies the style to the table.

3. On the **Home** tab of the user interface, in the **Styles** group, click **Format as Table** and then click **New Table Style**.

   The **New Table Quick Style** dialog box appears.

4. In the **Name** field, type Exception Default.

5. In the **Table Element** list, click **Header Row**.

6. Click **Format**.

   The **Format Cells** dialog box appears.

7. Click the **Fill** tab.

   The **Fill** tab appears.

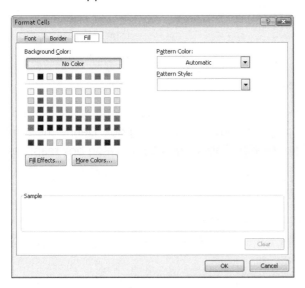

8. In the first row of color squares, just below the **No Color** button, click the third square from the left.

   The new background color appears in the **Sample** pane of the dialog box.

9. Click **OK**.

   The **Format Cells** dialog box disappears. When the **New Table Quick Style** dialog box reappears, the **Header Row** table element appears in bold, and the **Preview** pane's header row is shaded.

10. In the **Table Element** list, click **Second Row Stripe** and then click **Format**.

    The **Format Cells** dialog box appears.

11. Click the **No Color** button and click the third square from the left again.

    The new background color appears in the **Sample** pane of the dialog box.

12. Click **OK**.

    The **Format Cells** dialog box disappears. When the **New Table Quick Style** dialog box reappears, the **Second Row Stripe** table element appears in bold, and every second row is shaded in the **Preview** pane.

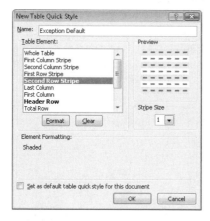

13. Click **OK**.

    The **New Table Quick Style** dialog box disappears.

14. On the **Home** tab, in the **Styles** group, click **Format as Table**. In the gallery that appears, in the **Custom** section, click the new format.

    Excel 2007 applies the new format.

15. On the **Page Layout** tab, in the **Themes** group, click the **Fonts** control down arrow and then click **Verdana**.

    Excel 2007 changes the theme's font to **Verdana**.

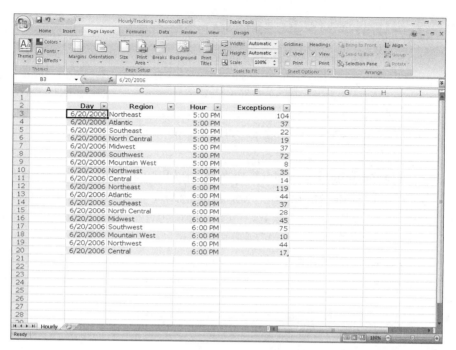

**16.** In the **Themes** group, click the **Themes** button and then click **Save Current Theme**.

The **Save Current Theme** dialog box appears.

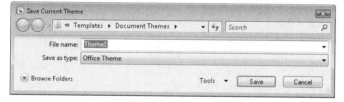

**17.** In the **File name** field, type Verdana Office and then click **Save**.

Excel 2007 saves your theme.

**18.** In the **Themes** group, click the **Themes** button and then click **Origin**.

Excel 2007 applies the new theme to your workbook.

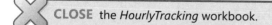

CLOSE the *HourlyTracking* workbook.

# Making Numbers Easier to Read

Changing the format of the cells in your worksheet can make your data much easier to read, both by setting data labels apart from the actual data and by adding borders to define the boundaries between labels and data even more clearly. Of course, using formatting options to change the font and appearance of a cell's contents doesn't help with idiosyncratic data types such as dates, phone numbers, or currency.

For example, consider U.S. phone numbers. These numbers are 10 digits long and have a 3-digit area code, a 3-digit exchange, and a 4-digit line number written in the form (###) ###-####. Although it's certainly possible to type a phone number with the expected formatting in a cell, it's much simpler to type a sequence of 10 digits and have Excel 2007 change the data's appearance.

You can tell Excel 2007 to expect a phone number in a cell by opening the Format Cells dialog box to the Number tab and displaying the formats under the Special category.

Clicking Phone Number from the Type list tells Excel 2007 to format 10-digit numbers in the standard phone number format. As you can see by comparing the contents of the active cell and the contents of the formula bar in the next graphic, the underlying data isn't changed, just its appearance in the cell.

| | F4 | | | $f_x$ | 5035550106 | | | | |
|---|---|---|---|---|---|---|---|---|---|
| | A | B | C | D | E | F | G | H | I | J |
| 1 | | | | | | | | | |
| 2 | | | | | | | | | |
| 3 | | | | | | **Phone Number** | | | |
| 4 | | | | | | (503) 555-0106 | | | |
| 5 | | | | | | | | | |
| 6 | | | | | | | | | |
| 7 | | | | | | | | | |

> **Troubleshooting**  If you type a nine-digit number in a field that expects a phone number, you won't see an error message; instead, you'll see a two-digit area code. For example, the number 425555012 would be displayed as (42) 555-5012. An 11-digit number would be displayed with a 4-digit area code.

Just as you can instruct Excel 2007 to expect a phone number in a cell, you can also have it expect a date or a currency amount. You can make those changes from the Format Cells dialog box by choosing either the Date category or the Currency category. The Date category enables you to pick the format for the date (and determine whether the date's appearance changes due to the Locale setting of the operating system on the computer viewing the workbook). In a similar vein, selecting the Currency category displays controls to set the number of places after the decimal point, the currency symbol to use, and the way in which Excel 2007 should display negative numbers.

> **Tip**  The new Excel 2007 user interface enables you to set the most common format changes by using the controls in the Home tab's Number group.

You can also create a custom numeric format to add a word or phrase to a number in a cell. For example, you can add the phrase *per month* to a cell with a formula that calculates average monthly sales for a year to ensure that you and your colleagues will recognize the figure as a monthly average. To create a custom number format, click the Home tab and then click the Number group's dialog expander to display the Format Cells dialog box. Then, if necessary, click the Number tab.

In the Category list, click Custom to display the available custom number formats in the Type list. You can then click the base format you want and modify it in the Type box. For example, clicking the 0.00 format causes Excel 2007 to format any number in a cell with two digits to the right of the decimal point.

> **Tip**  The zeros in the format indicate that the position in the format can accept any number as a valid value.

To customize the format, click in the Type box and add any symbols or text you want to the format. For example, typing a dollar sign to the left of the existing format and then typing "per month" to the right of the existing format causes the number 1500 to be displayed as *$1500.00 per month*.

> **Important**  You need to enclose any text in quotes so that Excel 2007 recognizes the text as a string to be displayed in the cell.

In this exercise, you assign date, phone number, and currency formats to ranges of cells in your worksheet. After you assign the formats, you test them by entering customer data.

**USE** the *ExecutiveSearch* workbook in the practice file folder for this topic. This practice file is located in the *Appearance* folder under *SBS_Office2007*.
**OPEN** the *ExecutiveSearch* workbook.

1. Click cell A3.

2. On the **Home** tab, in the **Font** group, click the dialog expander.

   The **Format Cells** dialog box appears.

3. If necessary, click the **Number** tab.

4. In the **Category** list, click **Date**.

   The **Type** list appears with a list of date formats.

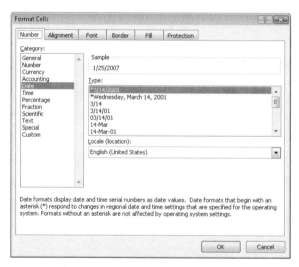

5. In the **Type** list, click **3/14/01**.

**Caution** Be sure to click the format without the asterisk in front of the sample date.

6. Click **OK**.

   Excel 2007 assigns the chosen format to the cell.

7. Click cell G3.

**8.** On the **Home** tab, in the **Font** group, click the dialog expander.

The **Format Cells** dialog box appears.

**9.** If necessary, click the **Number** tab.

The **Number** tab of the dialog box appears.

**10.** In the **Category** list, click **Special**.

The **Type** list appears with a list of special formats.

**11.** In the **Type** list, click **Phone Number** and then click **OK**.

The contents of the cell change to *(425) 555-0102*, matching the format you chose earlier, and the **Format Cells** dialog box disappears.

**12.** Click cell H3.

**13.** On the **Home** tab, in the **Font** group, click the dialog expander.

The **Format Cells** dialog box appears.

**14.** If necessary, click the **Number** tab.

The **Number** tab of the dialog box appears.

**15.** In the **Category** list, click **Custom**.

The contents of the **Type** list are updated to reflect your choice.

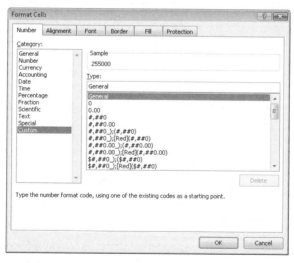

**16.** In the **Type** list, click the #,##0 item.

*#,##0* appears in the **Type** box.

**17.** In the **Type** box, click to the left of the existing format and type $ and then click to the right of the format and type "before bonuses".

18. Click **OK**.

The **Format Cells** dialog box disappears.

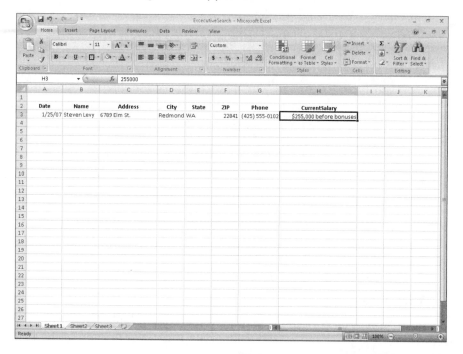

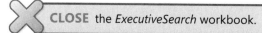

**CLOSE** the *ExecutiveSearch* workbook.

# Changing the Appearance of Data Based on Its Value

Recording package volumes, vehicle miles, and other business data in a worksheet enables you to make important decisions about your operations. And as you saw earlier in this chapter, you can change the appearance of data labels and the worksheet itself to make interpreting your data easier.

Another way you can make your data easier to interpret is to have Excel 2007 change the appearance of your data based on its value. These formats are called **conditional formats** because the data must meet certain conditions to have a format applied to it. For instance, if chief operating officer Jenny Lysaker wanted to highlight any Thursdays with higher-than-average weekday package volumes, she could define a conditional format that tests the value in the cell recording total sales, and that will change the format of the cell's contents when the condition is met.

In previous versions of Excel, you could have a maximum of three conditional formats. There's no such limit in Excel 2007; you may have as many conditional formats as you like. The other major limitation of conditional formats in Excel 2003 and earlier versions was that Excel stopped evaluating conditional formats as soon as it found one that applied to a cell. In other words, you couldn't have multiple conditions be true for the same cell! In Excel 2007, you can control whether Excel 2007 stops or continues after it discovers that a specific condition applies to a cell.

To create a conditional format, you select the cells to which you want to apply the format, display the Home tab of the user interface, and then, in the Styles group, click Conditional Formatting to display a menu of possible conditional formats. Excel 2007 enables you to create all the conditional formats available in previous versions of the program and offers many more conditional formats than were previously available. Prior to Excel 2007, you could create conditional formats to highlight cells that contained values meeting a certain condition. For example, you could highlight all cells that contain a value over 100, contain a date before 1/28/2007, or contain an order amount between $100 and $500. In Excel 2007, you can define conditional formats that change how the program displays data in cells that contain values above or below the average values of the related cells, that contain values near the top or bottom of the value range, or that contain values duplicated elsewhere in the selected range.

When you select which kind of condition to create, Excel 2007 displays a dialog box that contains fields and controls you can use to define your rule. To display all your rules, display the Home tab and then, in the Styles group, click Conditional Formatting. From the menu that appears, click Manage Rules to display the Conditional Formatting Rules Manager.

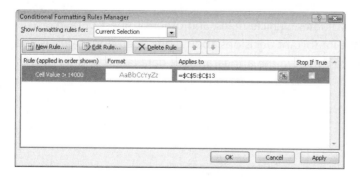

The Conditional Formatting Rules Manager, which is new in Excel 2007, enables you to control your conditional formats in the following ways:

- Creates a new rule by clicking the New Rule button
- Changes a rule by clicking the rule and then clicking the Edit Rule button
- Removes a rule by clicking the rule and then clicking the Delete Rule button
- Moves a rule up or down in the order by clicking the Move Up or Move Down button
- Controls whether Excel 2007 continues evaluating conditional formats after it finds a rule to apply by selecting or clearing a rule's Stop If True check box
- Saves any new rules and closes the Conditional Formatting Rules Manager by clicking OK
- Saves any new rules without closing the Conditional Formatting Rules Manager by clicking Apply
- Discards any unsaved changes by clicking Cancel

> **Note** Clicking the New Rule button in the Conditional Formatting Rules Manager displays the New Formatting Rule dialog box. The commands in the New Formatting Rule dialog box duplicate the options displayed when you click the Home tab's Conditional Formatting button.

After you create a rule, you can change the format applied if the rule is true by clicking the rule and then clicking the Edit Rule button to display the Edit Formatting Rule dialog box. In that dialog box, click the Format button to display the Format Cells dialog box. After you define your format, click OK.

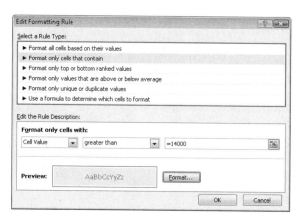

> **Important** Excel 2007 doesn't check to make sure that your conditions are logically consistent, so you need to be sure that you enter your conditions correctly.

Excel 2007 also enables you to create three new types of conditional formats: data bars, color scales, and icon sets. Data bars summarize the relative magnitude of values in a cell range by extending a band of color across the cell.

**Distribution Capacity**

| | | |
|---|---|---|
| Northeast | | 47% |
| Atlantic | | 75% |
| Southeast | | 39% |
| North Central | | 54% |
| Midwest | | 40% |
| Southwest | | 73% |
| Mountain West | | 51% |
| Northwest | | 69% |
| Central | | 41% |

Color scales compare the relative magnitude of values in a cell range by applying colors from a two- or three-color set to your cells. The intensity of a cell's color reflects the value's tendency toward the top or bottom of the values in the range.

**Distribution Capacity**

| | |
|---|---|
| Northeast | 47% |
| Atlantic | 75% |
| Southeast | 39% |
| North Central | 54% |
| Midwest | 40% |
| Southwest | 73% |
| Mountain West | 51% |
| Northwest | 69% |
| Central | 41% |

Icon sets are collections of three, four, or five images that Excel 2007 displays when certain rules are met.

**Distribution Capacity**

| | |
|---|---|
| Northeast | |
| Atlantic | |
| Southeast | |
| North Central | |
| Midwest | |
| Southwest | |
| Mountain West | |
| Northwest | |
| Central | |

When you click a color scale or icon set in the Conditional Formatting Rule Manager and then click the Edit Rule button, you can control when Excel 2007 applies a color or icon to your data.

> **Caution**  Be sure to not include cells that contain summary formulas in your conditionally formatted ranges. The values, which could be much higher or lower than your regular cell data, could throw off your formatting comparisons.

In this exercise, you create a series of conditional formats to change the appearance of data in worksheet cells displaying the package volume and delivery exception rates of a regional distribution center.

> **USE**  the *Dashboard* workbook in the practice file folder for this topic. This practice file is located in the *Appearance* folder under *SBS_Office2007*.
> **OPEN**  the *Dashboard* workbook.

**1.** Select cells C4:C12.

**2.** On the **Home** tab, in the **Styles** group, click **Conditional Formatting**. From the menu that appears, point to **Color Scales**, and then, in the top row of the palette that appears, click the second pattern from the left.

Excel 2007 formats the selected range.

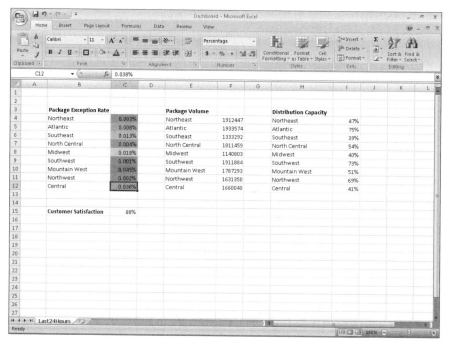

**3.** Select cells F4:F12.

4. On the **Home** tab, in the **Styles** group, click **Conditional Formatting**. From the menu that appears, point to **Data Bars**, and then click the light blue data bar format.

   Excel 2007 formats the selected range.

5. Select cells I4:I12.

6. On the **Home** tab, in the **Styles** group, click **Conditional Formatting**. From the menu that appears, point to **Icon Sets**, and then, in the left-hand column of the list of formats that appears, click the three traffic lights.

   Excel 2007 formats the selected cells.

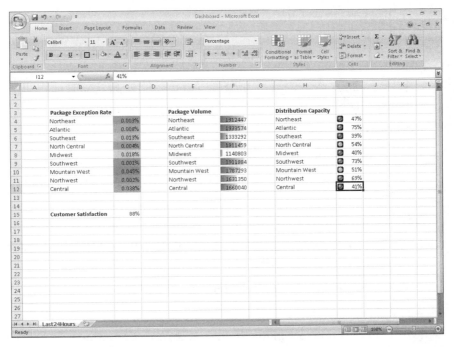

7. With the range I4:I12 still selected, on the **Home** tab, in the **Styles** group, click **Conditional Formatting**, and then click **Manage Rules**.

   The **Conditional Formatting Rules Manager** appears.

8. Click the icon set rule and then click **Edit Rule**.

   The **Edit Formatting Rule** dialog box appears.

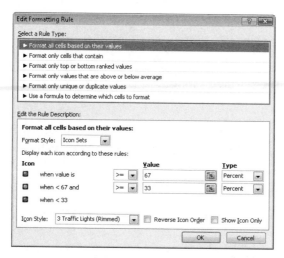

9. Select the **Reverse Icon Order** check box.

   Excel 2007 reconfigures the rules so the red light icon is at the top and the green light icon is at the bottom.

10. In the red light icon's row, click the **Type** field down arrow and then click **Percent**.

11. In the red light icon's **Value** field, type 80.

12. In the yellow light icon's row, click the **Type** field down arrow and then click **Percent**.

13. In the yellow light icon **Value** field, type 67.

14. Click **OK** twice to clear the **Edit Formatting Rule** dialog box and the **Conditional Formatting Rules Manager**.

    Excel 2007 formats the selected cell range.

15. Click cell C15.

16. On the **Home** tab, in the **Styles** group, click **Conditional Formatting**. From the menu that appears, point to **Highlight Cells Rules** and then click **Less Than**.

    The **Less Than** dialog box appears.

17. In the left field, type 96%.

18. Click the **With** field down arrow and then click **Red text**.

19. Click **OK**.

    The **Less Than** dialog box disappears, and Excel 2007 displays the text in cell C15 in red.

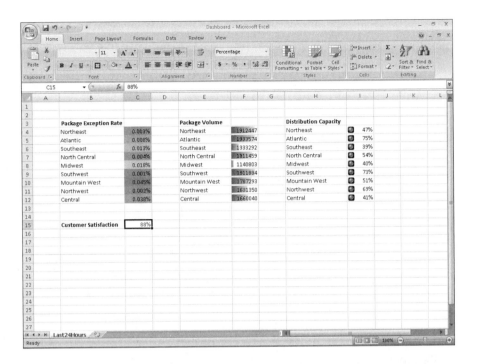

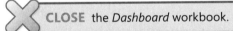

**CLOSE** the *Dashboard* workbook.

# Adding Images to a Document

Establishing a strong corporate identity helps customers remember your organization and the products and services you offer. Setting aside the obvious need for sound management, two important physical attributes of a strong retail business are a well-conceived shop space and an eye-catching, easy-to-remember logo. After you or your graphic artist has created a logo, you should add the logo to all your documents, especially any that might be seen by your customers. Not only does the logo mark the documents as coming from your company but it also serves as an advertisement, encouraging anyone who sees your worksheets to call or visit your company.

One way to add a picture to a worksheet is to display the Insert tab of the user interface and then, in the Illustrations group, click Picture. Clicking Picture displays the Insert Picture dialog box, which enables you to locate the picture you want to add from your hard disk. When you insert a picture, the Picture Tools contextual tab appears with the Format contextual tab right below it. You can use the tools on the Format contextual tab to change the picture's contrast, brightness, and so on. The controls in the Picture Styles group enable you to place a border around the picture, change the picture's shape, or change a picture's effects (such as shadow, reflection, or rotation in three dimensions). Other tools, found in the Arrange and Size groups, enable you to rotate, reposition, and resize the picture.

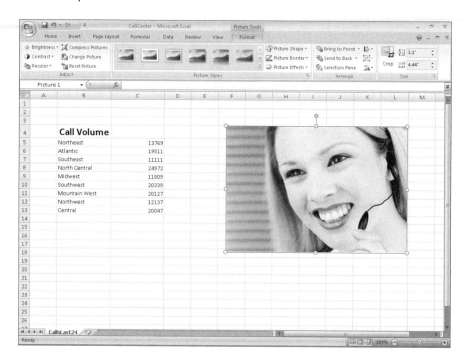

You can also resize a picture by clicking it and then dragging one of the handles that appear on the graphic. If you accidentally resize a graphic by dragging a handle, just click the Undo button to remove your change. If you want to generate a repeating image in the background of a worksheet, forming a tiled pattern behind your worksheet's data, you can display the Page Layout tab of the user interface and then, in the Page Setup group, click Background. In the Sheet Background dialog box, click the image that you want to serve as the background pattern for your worksheet and click OK.

> **Tip** To remove a background image from a worksheet, display the Page Layout tab of the user interface and then, in the Page Setup group, click Delete Background.

In this exercise, you add an image to an existing worksheet, change the graphic's location on the worksheet, reduce the size of the graphic, change the image's brightness and contrast, rotate and crop the image, delete the image, and then set the image as a repeating background for the worksheet.

**USE** the *CallCenter* workbook and the *callcenter.jpg* image file in the practice file folder for this topic. This practice file is located in the *Appearance* folder under *SBS_Office2007*.

**OPEN** the *CallCenter* workbook.

1. On the **Insert** tab, click **Picture**.

   The **Insert Picture** dialog box appears.

2. Browse to the *My Documents\Microsoft Press\Excel SBS\Appearance* folder and then double-click **callcenter.jpg**.

   The image appears on your worksheet.

3. Move the image to the upper-left corner of the worksheet, grab the handle at the lower-right corner of the image, and drag it up and to the left until it no longer obscures the Call Volume label.

4. On the **Page Layout** tab, in the **Page Setup** group, click **Background**.

   The **Sheet Background** dialog box appears.

5. Browse to the *My Documents\Microsoft Press\Excel SBS\Appearance* folder and then double-click **acbluprt.jpg**.

   Excel 2007 repeats the image to form a background pattern.

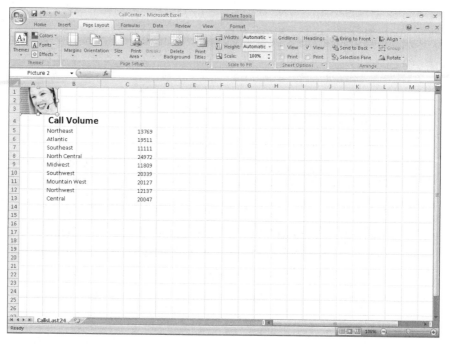

6. On the **Page Layout** tab, in the **Page Setup** group, click **Delete Background**.

Excel 2007 removes the background image.

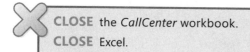

**CLOSE** the *CallCenter* workbook.
**CLOSE** Excel.

# Key Points

● If you don't like the default font in which Excel 2007 displays your data, you can change it.

● You can use cell formatting, including borders, alignment, and fill colors, to emphasize certain cells in your worksheets. This emphasis is particularly useful for making column and row labels stand out from the data.

● Excel 2007 comes with a number of existing styles that enable you to change the appearance of individual cells. You can also create new styles to make formatting your workbooks easier.

- If you want to apply the formatting from one cell to another cell, use the Format Painter to copy the format quickly.

- There are quite a few built-in document themes and table formats you can apply to groups of cells. If you see one you like, use it and save yourself lots of formatting time.

- Conditional formats enable you to set rules so that Excel 2007 changes the appearance of a cell's contents based on its value.

- Adding images can make your worksheets more visually appealing and make your data easier to understand.

# Part III

# Microsoft Office Access 2007

# Chapter at a Glance

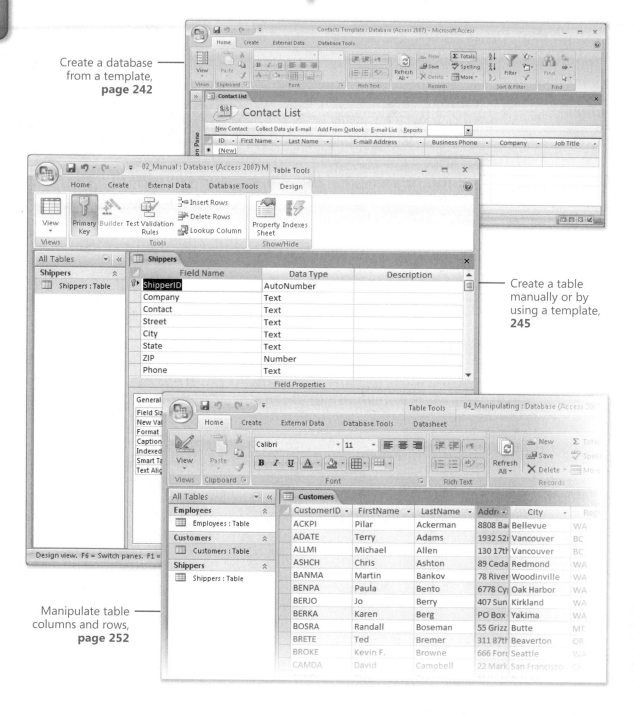

Create a database from a template, **page 242**

Create a table manually or by using a template, **245**

Manipulate table columns and rows, **page 252**

# 9 Creating a Database

In this chapter, you will learn to:

✔ Create a database from a template.

✔ Create a table manually or by using a template.

✔ Manipulate table columns and rows.

Creating the structure for a database is easy. But an empty database is no more useful than an empty document or worksheet. It is only when you fill, or *populate*, a database with data in tables that it starts to serve a purpose. As you add queries, forms, and reports, it becomes easier to use. If you customize it with a switchboard or custom categories and groups, it moves into the realm of being a *database application*.

Not every database has to be refined to the point that it can be classified as an application. Databases that only you or a few experienced database users will work with can remain fairly rough-hewn. But if you expect an administrative assistant to enter data or your company's executives to generate their own reports, spending a little extra time in the beginning to create a solid database application will save a lot of work later. Otherwise, you'll find yourself continually repairing damaged files or walking people through seemingly easy tasks.

Microsoft Office Access 2007 takes a lot of the difficult and mundane work out of creating and customizing a database by providing database applications in the form of *templates* that you modify and fill with your own information. Access 2007 also provides templates for common types of tables, and improved ways to import content from other applications to instantly create and populate tables. Using one of these methods to create something that is similar to what you need and then modifying your creation is generally easier than creating the same thing manually. If none of the templates or import methods match your needs, you can create tables manually—another process that has been improved in this version of Access.

In this chapter, you will create a database from a template, create a table manually, and create a single table from a template. Then, you'll adjust the display of a data table to fit your needs. By the end of this chapter, you will have a database containing three tables that will serve as the foundation for many of the exercises in this book.

**See Also** Do you need only a quick refresher on the topics in this chapter? See the Quick Reference entries at the beginning of this book..

**Important** Before you can use the practice files in this chapter, you need to install them from the book's companion CD to their default location. See "Using the Book's CD" at the beginning of this book for more information.

**Troubleshooting** Graphics and operating system–related instructions in this book reflect the Windows Vista user interface. If your computer is running Microsoft Windows XP and you experience trouble following the instructions as written, please refer to the "Information for Readers Running Windows XP" section at the beginning of this book.

# Creating a Database from a Template

A few years ago (the distant past in computer time), creating a database structure involved first analyzing your needs and then laying out the database design on paper. You would decide what information you needed to track and how to store it in the database. Creating the database structure could be a lot of work, and after you created it and entered data, making changes could be difficult. Templates have changed this process. Committing yourself to a particular database structure is no longer the big decision it once was. By using pre-packaged templates, you can create a dozen database applications in less time than it used to take to sketch the design of one on paper. Access templates might not create exactly the database application you want, but they can quickly create something very close that you can tweak to fit your needs.

In this exercise, you will open and explore a database application based on the Contacts template. This template is typical of those provided with Microsoft Office Access 2007, in that it looks nice and demonstrates a lot of the neat things you can do in a database, such as adding command buttons and embedded macros to link to other Office applications or Windows commands. Due to the complexity of these templates, you probably shouldn't try to modify them until you are comfortable working with simpler tables and forms in Design view. There are no practice files for this exercise.

> **BE SURE TO** start Access before beginning this exercise.

**1.** In the **Template Categories** list, click **Local Templates**.

> **Tip** When you are connected to the Internet, you can find additional templates and other resources in the From Office Online area of the Getting Started With Microsoft Office Access screen.

Access displays a list of the templates that are available from the default template location (*C:\Program Files\Microsoft Office\Templates\1033\Access*).

> **Tip** When you point to a template icon, Access displays a description of the database in a pop-up window, called a ScreenTip. For more information about these templates, search Access Help for *Guide to the Access 2007 templates*.

**2.** Click the **Contacts** template icon.

A description of the template appears on the right side of the program window, along with a box in which you can assign a name to the database and a folder button to browse to the place you want to store the database.

3. In the **File Name** box, type Contacts Template, and note the default path.

> **Tip** Naming conventions for Access database files follow those for Microsoft
> Windows files. A file name, including its path, can contain up to 260 characters,
> including spaces, but creating a file name that long is not recommended. File names
> cannot contain the following characters: \ / : * ? " < > |.
>
> The extension for an Access 2007 database file is *.accdb*, instead of the *.mdb* exten-
> sion used for previous versions. For information about the differences between the
> two formats, search Access Help for *accdb*.

4. Click the **Create** button.

   Access briefly displays a progress bar, and then your new database opens.

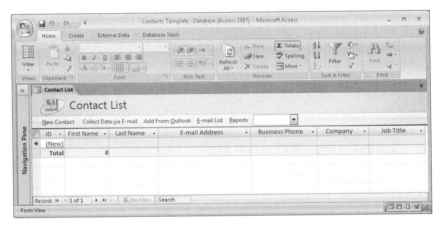

5. If the **Navigation Pane** is closed, press F11 to open it.

   Notice that the Navigation Pane displays a custom category named Contacts, and a
   custom group named Supporting Objects.

   Notice the commands above the column headers. These commands are examples
   of the embedded macros that make this an application rather than a database.

> **Tip** Access stores embedded macros as properties of the object to which they
> are attached. You can modify the design of the macro without worrying about
> other controls that might use the macro—each embedded macro is independent.
> Embedded macros are trusted because they are automatically prevented from
> performing certain potentially unsafe operations.

6. Enter your own contact information into the first record.

7. Explore the *Contacts Template* database on your own.

**CLOSE** the Contacts Template database.

**BE SURE TO** delete the Contacts Template database from the default storage location if you don't want to use it again.

---

**Tip** Access creates new databases in your Documents folder. You can change the location as you create each database, or change the default save location. To do so, click the Microsoft Office Button, click Access Options, and then on the Personalize page, under Creating Databases, click the Browse button. In the Default Database Path dialog box, browse to the folder you want to select as the default database storage folder. Then click OK in each of the open dialog boxes.

---

# Creating a Table Manually

In the previous exercise, you created a contact management database application based on an Access 2007 template. The database had all the tables, forms, reports, and code needed to import, store, and use basic information about people. But suppose you need to store different types of information for different types of contacts. For example, you might want to maintain different types of information about employees, customers, and suppliers. In addition to the standard information—such as names, addresses, and phone numbers—you might want to track these other kinds of information:

- Employee Social Security numbers, dates of hire, marital status, deductions, and pay rates
- Customer orders and account status
- Supplier contacts, current order status, and discounts

You could start with the template, add a lot of extra fields to the Contacts table, and then fill in just the ones you want for each contact type; but cramming all this information into one table would soon get pretty messy. In this instance, it's better to manually create a database that includes one table for each contact type: employee, customer, and supplier.

> **Important** With most computer programs, it is important to save your work frequently to avoid losing it if your computer crashes or the power goes out. With Access, it is not only *not* important to save your data, it is *not possible* to manually save it. When you move the insertion point out of a record after entering or editing information, Access saves that record. This means that you don't have to worry about losing your changes, but you do have to re-member that most data entry changes you make are permanent and can be undone only by editing the record again.
>
> Note, however, that changes to properties and layout are not saved automatically. If you create a new table, form, or report, or modify the properties or layout of an existing one, you will be prompted to save the changes before closing the object or the database.

**See Also** For information about ways of controlling table content, see Chapter 12, "Keeping Your Information Accurate."

In this exercise, you will open a blank database, create a table, manually add a record, and import some records. There are no practice files for this exercise.

**BE SURE TO** start Access before beginning this exercise.

1. On the **Getting Started with Microsoft Access** page, under **New Blank Database**, click **Blank Database**.

   Access displays information about the selected template on the right side of the program window.

Browse for a
location

2. In the **File Name** box, type 02_Manual, click the **Browse for a location** button and browse to the *Documents\MSP\SBS_Office2007\Chapter09* folder. Then click **OK**.

   > **Important** You can't create a blank database without saving it. If you don't provide a path and filename in the File Name box, Access saves the file in a default location and with a sequentially-numbered default name. The usual location is in the Documents folder, and the name is in the format *Database1.accdb*.

3. Click **Create** to create the blank database in the specified location.

   The database opens, displaying a new blank table named Table1, in a group named Table1.

**Tip** Notice that the first column is titled ID and the second is titled Add New Field. Access automatically creates the ID field—you can delete it if you don't need it. The ability to add fields to a table by simply typing data in the first row is new with Access 2007. As you enter information in the cells, Access adds fields to the table and guesses at the data type and other properties.

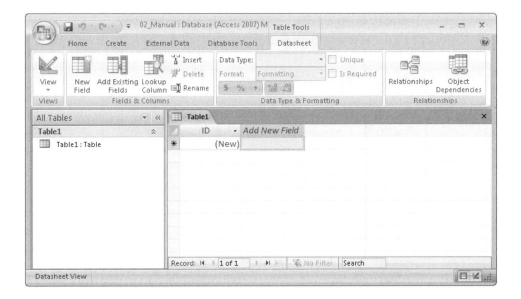

**Troubleshooting** At press time there was an unresolved bug in the process for adding the first record to a table. The result of the bug is that if you don't save the first record after adding the first field, and before adding the second field, then Access increments the record ID value for each field you add to the first record. If you add seven fields, Access assigns the value "7" to the ID field of the first record. To avoid this bug, simply click the record selector after adding a value to the first field of the first record in the table. This will save the record and Access will assign a value of "1" to the ID field. Then continue adding the rest of your fields.

**4.** Click in the empty cell below **Add New Field**, type Big Things Freight, and then press Tab to move to the next cell.

Access automatically assigns the value "1" to the ID field, assigns the name "Field1" to the first column, and moves the Add New Field heading to the third column. The **Unsaved Record icon in the Record Selector box** at the left of the record indicates that this record has not yet been saved.

5. Type the following information into the next six cells, pressing [Tab] after each entry.

John Woods

345 S. 34th St.

Ventura

CA

83003

805 555-0154

As the insertion point moves out of each cell, its name changes to *Field* followed by a number.

6. Double-click the **ID** column name, and then type ShipperID to rename it.

7. Repeat Step 6 for the other columns, changing the column names to the following:

| | |
|---|---|
| **Field1** | Company |
| **Field2** | Contact |
| **Field3** | Street |
| **Field4** | City |
| **Field5** | State |
| **Field6** | ZIP |
| **Field7** | Phone |

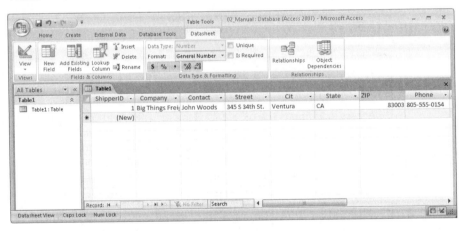

8. On the **View** toolbar in the lower-right corner of the program window, click the **Design View** button to switch to Design view.

Design View

> **Tip** The buttons displayed on the View toolbar change depending on the type of object that is active. They are a handy way to switch views if the pointer is near the bottom of the window. Most instructions to switch views in this book refer to the View button in the Views group on the Home tab.

Access prompts you to provide a name, because you need to save the table before changing to Design view.

**9.** In the **Save As** dialog box, type **Shippers**, and then click **OK**.

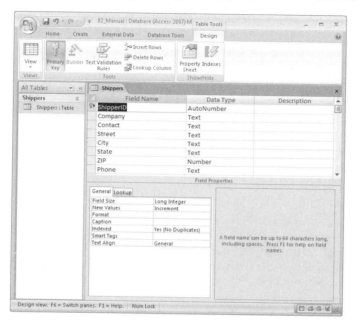

In Design view, the top portion of the window contains a list of the table's fields. The Field Name column contains the names you specified when you created the table. The Data Type column specifies the type of data that the field can contain. The Description column can contain a description of the field.

> **Tip** You can use field names that include spaces, but this can affect how queries and modules have to be written, so it is best not to do so.

Primary Key

Notice the Primary Key icon to the left of the ShipperID field. The value in the primary key field is used to uniquely identify each record; that is, no two records can have the same value in this field. You can enter this value yourself, or you can let Access help you with this chore. When the data type of a field is set to AutoNumber, as it is here, Access fills this field in every new record with the next available number.

> **Tip** If you no longer want the table to have a primary key, select the field designated as the primary key in the top portion of the window, and on the Design tab, click Primary Key. If you want to assign a different field as the primary key, select that field, and click Primary Key on the Design tab to make it the primary key and move the icon to that field.

10. Click the **Data Type** for the *ZIP* field, click the arrow that appears, and then in the list, click **Text**.

> **Tip** If you use only five-digit ZIP codes, the numeric data type would be fine. But setting it to Text is a good idea so users can enter ZIP codes in the ZIP + 4 format.

11. Click each field name in turn, and then in the **Field Properties** area, change the **Field Size** to the following:

| | |
|---|---|
| Company | 40 |
| Contact | 50 |
| Street | 50 |
| City | 50 |
| State | 2 |
| ZIP | 10 |
| Phone | 24 |

> **Troubleshooting** If you change any field properties that might cause data to be lost (for example, making the size of the field smaller), Access will warn you of this when you attempt to save the table.

 **CLOSE** the table, saving your changes, and then close the database.

# Creating a Table by Using a Template

Although manually creating a table is relatively easy, if one of the available table templates is close to what you want, using it might save you a little time and effort.

In this exercise, you will use a table template to add an Employees table to an existing database.

 **USE** the *03_TableTemplate* database. This practice file is located in the *Chapter09* subfolder under *SBS_Office2007*.
**OPEN** the *03_TableTemplate* database.

Table Templates ▾

1. On the **Create** tab, in the **Tables** group, click the **Table Templates** button to display the list of available templates, and then click **Contacts**.

   A new table opens. This table contains fields appropriate for many common kinds of contact information, but some aren't needed and you will need a few more.

2. On the **Datasheet** contextual tab, in the **Views** group, click the upper half of the **View** button. In the **Save As** dialog box that appears, type Employees, and then click **OK**.

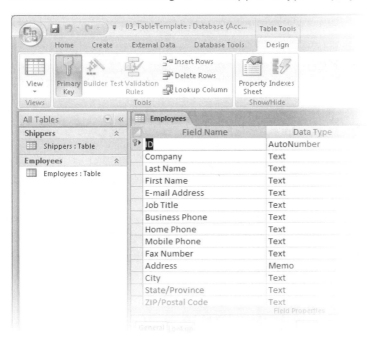

3. Right-click anywhere in the **Company** row, and then click **Delete Rows**.

4. Repeat the previous step to delete the E-Mail Address, Business Phone, Mobile Phone, Fax Number, Country, and Web Page rows.

> **Tip** You can select and delete adjacent records by clicking one and then shift-clicking another. You can't select multiple non-adjacent records.

5. In the **Job Title** field name, select *Job* and then press the [Del] key, so the field name is just *Title*.

6. Change the **ID** field name to EmployeeID.

Changing the name of the ID field makes it easier to differentiate the ID field of this table from the ID field of other tables.

7. Change the **Attachments** field name to Photograph.

The ability to store and display attachments in a database is new in Access 2007.

8. Click in the first blank **Field Name** cell and type BirthDate. Then press [Enter], type d to scroll the list to **Date/Time,** and press [Tab] twice.

The selection moves to the first column in the next row.

9. Repeat the previous step to add a field named DateHired.

10. On the **Quick Access Toolbar**, click the **Save** button.

Save

The Navigation pane now includes two tables, **Shippers** and **Employees**.

**CLOSE** the *03_TableTemplate* database.

# Manipulating Table Columns and Rows

When you refine a table's structure by adding fields and changing field properties, you affect the data that is stored in the table. But sometimes you will want to reorganize the table itself to get a better view of the data. If you want to look up a phone number, for example, but the names and phone numbers are several columns apart, you will have to scroll the table window to get the information you need. You might want to rearrange or hide a few columns to be able to see the fields you are interested in at the same time.

You can manipulate the columns and rows of an Access table without affecting the underlying data in any way. You can size both rows and columns, and you can also hide, move, and freeze columns. You can save your table formatting so that the table will look the same the next time you open it, or you can discard your changes without saving them.

In this exercise, you will open a table and manipulate its columns and rows.

**USE** the *04_Manipulating* database. This practice file is located in the *Chapter09* subfolder under *SBS_Office2007*.
**OPEN** the *04_Manipulating* database.

1. In the **Navigation Pane**, double-click the **Customers** table to open it in Datasheet view.

2. Drag the vertical bar at the right edge of the **Address** column header to the left until the column is about a half inch wide.

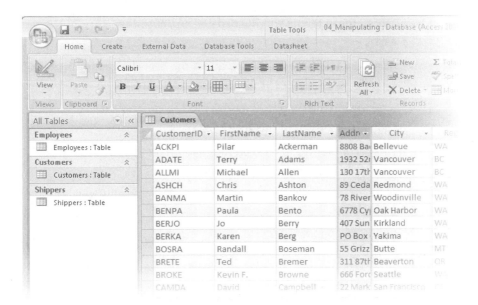

The column is too narrow to display the entire address.

**3.** Point to the vertical bar between the **Address** and **City** column headers, and when the pointer changes to a double-headed arrow, double-click the vertical bar.

Access resizes the column to the left of the vertical bar to the minimum width that will display all the text in that field in all records. This technique is particularly useful in a large table where you can't easily determine the length of a field's longest entry.

**4.** On the left side of the datasheet, drag the horizontal bar between any two record selectors downward to increase the height of all rows in the table.

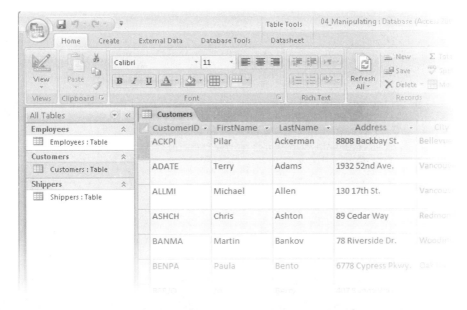

**5.** On the **Home** tab, in the **Records** group, click the **More** button, and then click **Row Height**.

**6.** In the **Row Height** dialog box, select the **Standard Height** check box, and then click **OK**.

Access resets the height of all rows to the default setting. (You can also set the rows to any other height in this dialog box.)

**7.** Click anywhere in the **First Name** column. In the **Records** group, click the **More** button, and then click **Hide Columns**.

The First Name column disappears, and the columns to its right shift to the left.

> **Tip** If you select several columns before clicking Hide Columns, they all disappear. You can select adjacent columns by clicking in the header of one, holding down the Shift key, and then clicking in the header of another. The two columns and any columns in between are selected.

**8.** To restore the hidden field, in the Records group, click the **More** button, and then click **Unhide Columns**.

The Unhide Columns dialog box opens.

**9.** In the **Unhide Columns** dialog box, select the **First Name** check box, and then click **Close**.

Access redisplays the First Name column.

10. Drag the right side of the database window to the left to reduce its size so that you cannot see all fields in the table.

11. Point to the **Customer ID** column header, hold down the mouse button, and drag through the **First Name** and **Last Name** column headers. With the three columns selected, click the **More** button in the **Records** group, and then click **Freeze**.

12. Scroll the window to the right.

    The first three columns remain in view.

13. In the **Records** group, click **More,** and then click **Unfreeze** to restore the columns to their normal condition.

> **Tip** The commands to hide, unhide, freeze, or unfreeze columns are available from the shortcut menu that appears when you right-click a column header.

 **CLOSE** the table without saving your changes, and then close the *04_Manipulating* database. If you are not continuing directly on to the next chapter, quit Access.

# Key Points

- Access 2007 includes templates to help you quickly and easily create databases and tables.

- In Design view, you can modify any object you created manually or from a template.

- Rather than storing all information in one table, you can create different tables for each type of information, such as employee, customer, and supplier contact information, or book, video, and CD catalog information.

- Properties determine what data can be entered in a field, and how the data will look on the screen. In Design view, you can change some properties without affecting the data stored in the table; but changing some might affect the data, so you must exercise caution when modifying properties.

- You can adjust the structure of a table—by manipulating or hiding columns and rows—without affecting the data stored in the table.

# Chapter at a Glance

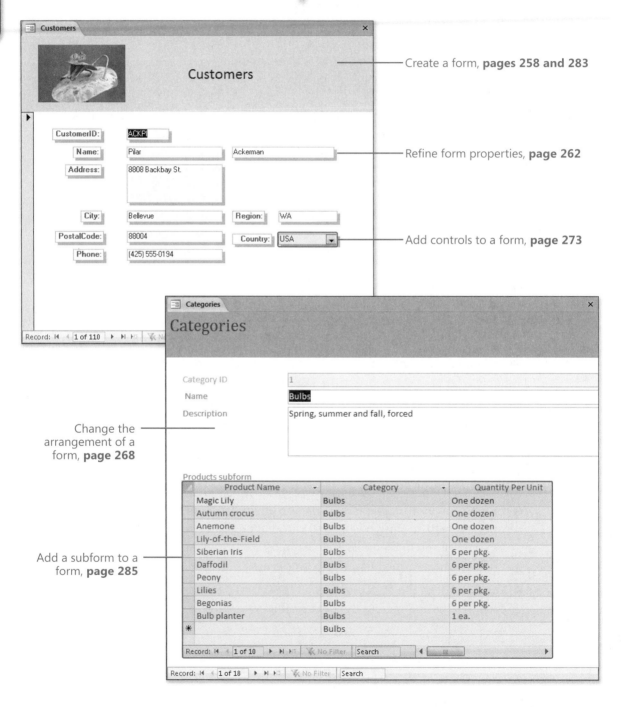

Create a form, **pages 258 and 283**

Refine form properties, **page 262**

Add controls to a form, **page 273**

Change the arrangement of a form, **page 268**

Add a subform to a form, **page 285**

# 10 Simplifying Data Entry by Using Forms

**In this chapter, you will learn to:**

✔ Create a form by using the Form tool.

✔ Refine form properties.

✔ Change the arrangement of a form.

✔ Add controls to a form.

✔ Enter data in a form by using VBA.

✔ Create a form by using an AutoForm.

✔ Add a subform to a form.

A database that contains the day-to-day records of an active company is useful only if it is kept current and if the information stored in it can be found quickly. Although Microsoft Office Access 2007 is fairly easy to use, entering, editing, and retrieving information in Datasheet view is not a task you would want to assign to someone who's not familiar with Access. Not only would these tasks be tedious and inefficient, but working in Datasheet view leaves far too much room for error, especially if details of complex transactions have to be entered into several related tables. The solution to this problem, and the first step in the conversion of this database to a database application in which you can efficiently manage information, is to create and use forms.

A form is an organized and formatted view of some or all of the fields from one or more tables or queries. Forms work interactively with the tables in a database. You use controls in the form to enter new information, to edit or remove existing information, or to locate information. Like printed forms, Access forms can include label controls that tell users what type of information they are expected to enter, as well as *text box controls* in which they can view or enter information. Unlike printed forms, Access forms can also include a variety of other controls, such as *option buttons* and *command buttons* that transform Access forms into something very much like a Microsoft Windows dialog box or wizard page.

> **Tip** You can also create forms to navigate among the features and functions of a database application and have little or no connection with its actual data. A *switchboard* is an example of this type of form.

As with other Access objects, you can create forms manually or with the help of a wizard. It is best to create navigational and housekeeping forms, such as switchboards, manually in Design view. However, you should always create forms that are based on tables by using a wizard, and then refine the form manually—not because it is difficult to drag the necessary controls onto a form, but because there is simply no point in doing it manually.

In this chapter, you will discover how easy it is to create forms—either by using the Form tool or by using the Form wizard—that you can modify to suit your needs, and how to present information from multiple tables in one form by using subforms. You will control a form's function and appearance by inserting controls and modifying the form and control properties. Then you will learn how to automatically enter data in a form by using Microsoft Visual Basic for Applications (VBA) when a user performs an action in the control, such as clicking or entering text.

**See Also** Do you need only a quick refresher on the topics in this chapter? See the Quick Reference entries at the beginning of this book.

> **Important** Before you can use the practice files in this chapter, you need to install them from the book's companion CD to their default location. See "Using the Book's CD" at the beginning of this book for more information.

> **Troubleshooting** Graphics and operating system–related instructions in this book reflect the Windows Vista user interface. If your computer is running Microsoft Windows XP and you experience trouble following the instructions as written, please refer to the "Information for Readers Running Windows XP" section at the beginning of this book.

# Creating a Form by Using the Form Tool

Before you begin creating a form, you need to know which database query or table to base it on, and have an idea of how the form will be used. After making these decisions, you can create a form in many ways. Remember that like almost any other object in

Access, after you create the form, you can customize it in Design view if it does not quite meet your needs.

The quickest way is to select a table or query in the Navigation Pane, and then click the Form button in the Forms group on the Create tab. This creates a simple form using all the fields in the table or query, and opens it in Layout view.

If there is one (and only one) other table in the database that has a one-to-many relationship with the table on which your form is based, then the Form tool adds a datasheet (called a subform) which displays all the records in the related table that pertain to the current record in the main form.

In this exercise, you will use the Form tool to create a form based on a table.

**USE** the *01_CreateFormTool* database. This practice file is located in the *Chapter10* subfolder under *SBS_Office2007*.

**BE SURE TO** start Access before beginning this exercise.

**OPEN** the *01_CreateFormTool* database.

1. In the **Navigation Pane**, under **Tables**, double-click **Customers**.

   The **Customers** table opens in Datasheet view.

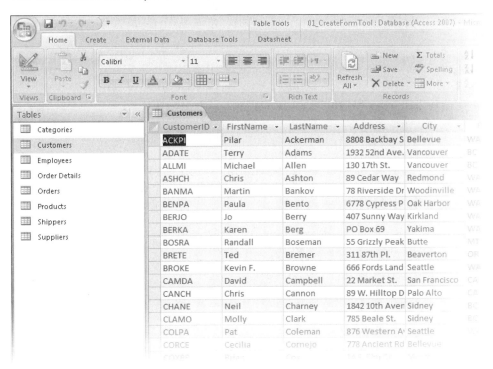

**2.** On the **Create** tab, in the **Forms** group, click the **Form** button

Access creates and displays a simple form based on the active table.

> **Tip** You don't have to open a table to create a form based on it. You can simply click the table in the Navigation Pane to select it, then click the Form button on the Create tab in the Forms group. But it is sometimes useful to have the table open behind the form in order to verify the form contents against the table contents.

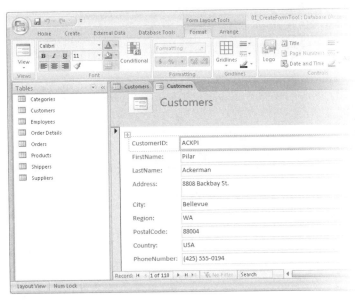

The Form tool automatically added a title (Customer) and a placeholder for a logo in the form header.

**3.** Scroll through a few of the records by using the navigation controls at the bottom of the form.

You can compare the information shown in the form to that in the datasheet view of the table by alternately clicking the Customers table tab and the Customers form tab in the database window to easily switch back and forth between views.

**CLOSE** the Customers form (without saving your changes) and the *01_CreateFormTool* database.

## Relationships

In Access, a *relationship* is an association between common fields in two tables. You can use this association to link information in one table to information in another table. For example, you can establish a relationship based on the CategoryID field between the Categories table and the Products table. Each product is in only one category, but each category can contain many products, so this type of relationship—the most common—is known as a *one-to-many relationship.*

Less common relationships include:

- *One-to-one relationships*, in which each record in one table can have one and only one related record in the other table.

  This type of relationship isn't commonly used because it is easier to put all the fields in one table. However, you might use two related tables instead of one to break up a table with many fields, or to track information that applies to only some of the records in the first table.

- *Many-to-many relationships*, which are really two one-to-many relationships tied together through a third table.

  You could see this relationship in a database that contains Products, Orders, and Order Details tables. The Products table has one record for each product, and each product has a unique ProductID. The Orders table has one record for each order placed, and each record in it has a unique OrderID. However, the Orders table doesn't specify which products were included in each order; that information is in the Order Details table, which is the table in the middle that ties the other two tables together. Products and Orders each have a one-to-many relationship with Order Details. Products and Orders therefore have a many-to-many relationship with each other. In plain language, this means that every product can appear in many orders, and every order can include many products.

If there is a one-to-many relationship between two tables in a database, an excellent way to display this is through the use of a form containing a *subform*. The main, or primary, form displays one record from the "one" side of the one-to-many relationship, and the subform lists all the pertinent records from the "many" side of the relationship.

# Refining Form Properties

As with tables, you can work with forms in multiple views. The two most common views are Form view, in which you view or enter data, and Design view, in which you add controls to the form or change the form's properties or layout.

When you create a form by using the Form tool or the Form wizard, every field included on the form is represented by a text box control and its associated label control. A form like the one you created earlier in this chapter is linked, or *bound*, to the table it's based on. Each text box is bound to a specific field in the table. The table is the *record source*, and the field is the *control source*. Each control has a number of *properties*, such as font, font size, alignment, fill color, and border. You can change the default values of these properties to improve the form's appearance.

A form inherits some of its properties from the table on which it is based. For instance, text box names on the form match field names in the source table, text box labels match the Caption property of each field, and the width of each text box is determined by the Field Size property. However, the properties of a form are not bound to their source. After you have created a form you can change the properties of the fields independently in the table and on the form.

In this exercise, you will edit the properties of a form.

> **USE** the *02_RefineProperties* database. This practice file is located in the *Chapter10* subfolder under *SBS_Office2007*.
>
> **OPEN** the *02_RefineProperties* database.

1. In the **Navigation Pane**, under **Forms**, right-click **Customers**, and then click **Design View**.

   The Customers form opens in Design view.

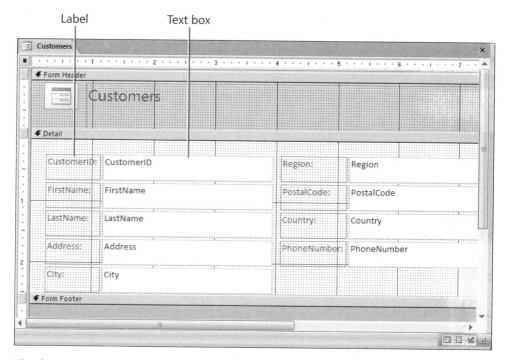

Label           Text box

The form is arranged in a Stacked layout that limits the extent of changes you can make to the form.

2. Click the top border of the blue **Form Footer** header and drag the Form Footer down about three inches to enlarge the Detail grid.

3. Click the **Detail** section of the form above the **Region** label, and then drag to draw a rectangle through some portion of all the controls on the right side of the form to select them.

4. Drag the selected group of controls down and to the left, positioning them just below the **City** label, then click any blank section of the grid to release the selection.

5. On the **Customers** form, click the **CustomerID** label (not its text box).

6. On the **Design** contextual tab, in the **Font** group, click the **Font** arrow, and then in the list, click **MS Sans Serif**.

7. With the label still selected, click the **Font Size** arrow, and then in the list, click **8**.

   The label text becomes slightly smaller.

8. If the **Property Sheet** pane is not visible, right-click the **CustomerID** text box (not its label), and then click **Properties**.

All the settings available in the Font group (plus a few more) are also available in the Property Sheet pane associated with each control. From this pane, you can display the properties of any object on the form, including the form itself.

You can display related types of properties by clicking the appropriate tab: Format, Data, Event, or Other, or display all properties by clicking the All tab.

9. In the **Property Sheet** pane, click the **Format** tab, scroll to the **Font Name** property, and change it to **MS Sans Serif**. Then set the **Font Size** property to **8**, and the **Font Weight** property to **Bold**.

The CustomerID text in the form reflects your changes.

> **Tip**  You can change the width of a task pane by dragging its edge, and you can *undock* it so it floats in the program window by dragging it by the title bar.

10. Click the arrow in the **Property Sheet** pane header, and then in the property list, click **Label3** to select the label to the left of the **FirstName** text box.

11. Repeat Step 9 to change the font of the text in the **FirstName** label box.

These different ways of selecting a control and changing its properties provide some flexibility and convenience, but it would be a bit tedious to make changes to a few dozen controls in a form. The next two steps provide a faster method.

12. Click anywhere in the **Detail** section of the form, and then drag diagonally to draw a rectangle through some portion of all the controls to select them.

> **Tip**  You can select all the controls in a form, including those in the header and footer, by pressing Ctrl+A.

Small handles appear around the selected controls. In the Property Sheet pane, the Selection type changes to *Multiple selection*, and the Objects box is blank. Only the Format settings that are the same for all the selected controls are displayed. Because the changes you made in the previous steps are not shared by all the selected controls, the Font Name, Font Size, and Font Weight settings are now blank.

**13.** Repeat Step 9 to set the same **Font Name**, **Font Size**, and **Font Weight** properties for all the selected controls.

**14.**  With all the controls still selected, on the **Format** tab of the **Property Sheet** pane, set the **Back Style** property to **Normal**.

The background of the labels is no longer transparent.

Ellipsis button

**15.** Click the **Back Color** property, and then click the **ellipsis** button that appears.

The Color Builder opens.

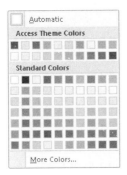

**16.** In the **Color** Builder, click the **yellow** square, and then press ⌈Enter⌉.

The background of all the controls changes to a bright yellow and the hexadecimal number representing this shade (#FFF200) appears in the **Back Color** property box.

> **Tip**  If the Color Builder doesn't include a color you want to use, click More Colors at the bottom of the gallery, select a color on the Standard or Custom tab of the Colors dialog box, and then click OK to set the color and add it to the list of recent colors at the bottom of the gallery.

**17.** In the **Back Color** property box, replace *#FFF200* with #FFFFCC.

The background color changes to a pale yellow.

**18.** Set the **Special Effect** property to Shadowed, and the **Border Color** property to green.

**19.** In the form, click away from the selected controls to release the selection (in other words, to *deselect* the controls).

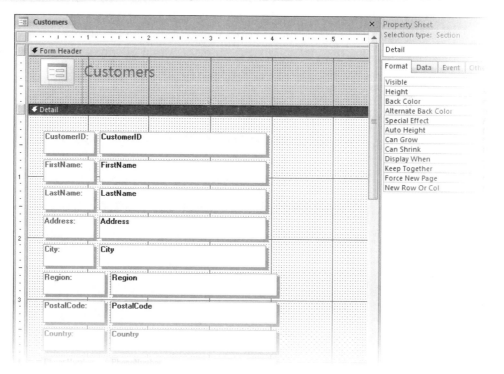

**20.** Click the **FirstName** label. In the **Property Sheet** pane, scroll up to the **Caption** property, change it from *FirstName* to Name, and then press Enter.

**21.** Repeat Step 20 to change *Phone Number* to Phone.

> **Tip** You can edit the Caption property of a label or the Control Source property of a text box by selecting it, clicking its text, and then editing the text as you would in any other Windows program. However, take care when editing the Control Source property, which defines where the content of the text box comes from.

**22.** Drag through all the controls on the form to select them. On the **Arrange** tab, in the **Control Layout** group, click the **Remove** button.

Removing the Stacked layout gives you more options for arranging the controls.

**23.** Click away from the selected controls to release the selection.

**24.** Click the label to the left of **LastName**, and then press the Del key.

**25.** Select all the labels, but not their corresponding text boxes, by holding down the
[Shift] key as you click each of them or by dragging through just the labels. Then in
the **Property Sheet** pane, set the **Text Align** property to **Right**.

Now let's size the bottom four label boxes to match the ones above, and line up
their associated text boxes.

**26.** Select the bottom four labels, but not their text boxes, and change their width
property to 0.8847″.

Size to Fit

**27.** Select all the labels again. On the **Arrange** contextual tab, in the **Size** group, click
the **Size to Fit** button to resize the labels to fit their contents, and then click anywhere in the form (but outside the controls) to release the selection.

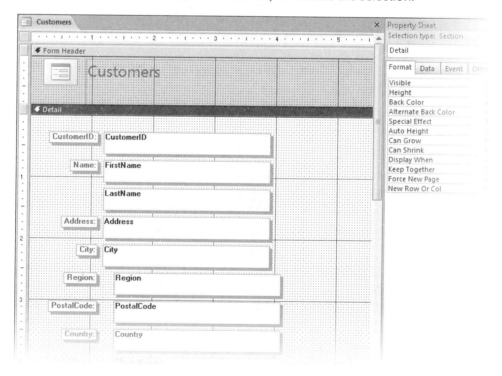

> **Tip** The order in which you make formatting changes, such as the ones you just
> made, can have an impact on the results. If you don't see the expected results, click
> the Undo button on the Quick Access Toolbar, or press Ctrl+Z, to step back through
> your changes. Then try again.

**28.** Select all the text boxes (but not their corresponding labels), and in the **Property
Sheet** pane, change the **Left** setting to 1.5″ to line up the text boxes and insert
space between them and the labels.

29. Change the **Font Weight** property to **Normal**, and then click anywhere in the form, but outside the controls, to deselect them.

Save

30. On the **Quick Access Toolbar**, click the **Save** button to save the design of the **Customers** form.

   **CLOSE** the *02_RefineProperties* database.

> **Tip**  Unless you close the Property Sheet pane, it remains open until you close all open forms.

# Changing the Arrangement of a Form

Both automatically-generated forms and forms created by a wizard are functional, not fancy. However, it's fairly easy to customize the layout to suit your needs and preferences. You can add and delete labels, move both labels and text controls around the form, add logos and other graphics, and otherwise improve the layout of the form to make it attractive and easy to use.

While you work with a form's layout, you should pay attention to the shape of the pointer, which changes to indicate the manner in which you can change the selected item. Because a text box and its label sometimes act as a unit, you have to be aware of the pointer's shape before making any change. The shape of the pointer indicates the action to be taken:

- **Four-headed arrow.** Drag to move both controls together, or independently if the pointer is over a large square in the upper-left corner of the control.

- **Pointing finger.** Drag to move just the control.

- **Vertical arrow.** Drag the top or bottom border to change the height.

- **Horizontal arrow.** Drag the right or left border to change the width.

- **Diagonal arrow.** Drag the corner to change both the height and width.

In this exercise, you will rearrange the label and text box controls in a form.

> **USE** the *03_RefineLayout* database. This practice file is located in the *Chapter10* subfolder under *SBS_Office2007*.
>
> **OPEN** the *03_RefineLayout* database.

1. In the **Navigation Pane**, under **Forms**, right-click **Customers**, and then click **Design View**.

   The form is divided into three sections: Form Header, Detail, and Form Footer. We are interested in only the Detail section right now.

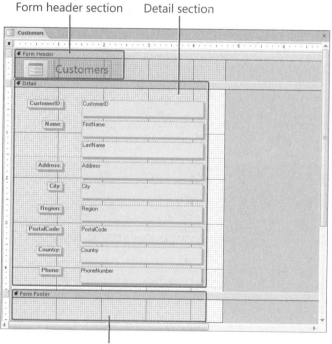

2. Point to the right edge of the **Detail** grid, and when the pointer changes to a double-headed arrow, drag the edge of the background to the right until you can see about seven full grid sections.

3. Click the **LastName** text box, and then slowly move the pointer around its border, from handle to handle, noticing how the pointer changes shape.

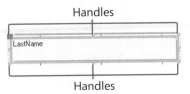

If a label or text box can be moved independently, then it will have a larger square in its upper-left corner.

4. Move the pointer over the **LastName** text box and when it changes to a four-headed arrow, drag it up and to the right of the **FirstName** text box.

> **Tip** If you can't move the label independently of the text box, the form is probably in Stacked layout. Drag through all the controls to select them, and then click the Remove button in the Control Layout group on the Arrange tab.

5. Resize each control and then move it to the location shown in the following graphic.

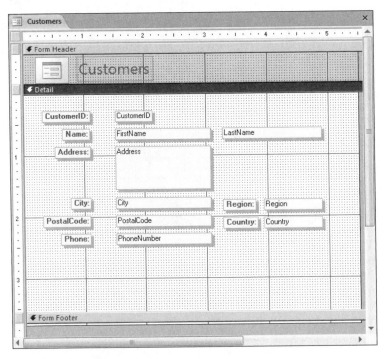

> **Tip** To fine-tune the position of a control, click it and then move the control by pressing the Up Arrow, Down Arrow, Left Arrow, or Right Arrow key. To move the control lesser distances, hold down the Ctrl key while pressing the arrow key. To fine-tune the size of a control, hold down the Shift key while pressing the arrow key.

**6.** On the **Arrange** contextual tab, in the **AutoFormat** group, click the **AutoFormat** button.

The **AutoFormat** gallery opens.

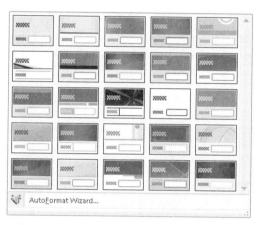

**7.** At the bottom of the **AutoFormat** gallery, click **AutoFormat Wizard**.

The **AutoFormat** dialog box opens.

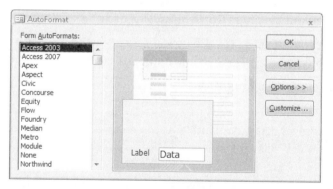

**8.** In the **AutoFormat** dialog box, click the **Customize** button.

The **Customize AutoFormat** dialog box opens.

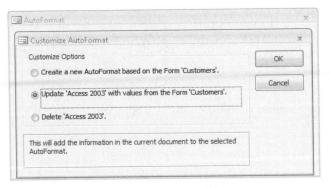

9. In the **Customize AutoFormat** dialog box, select the **Create a new AutoFormat based on the Form** 'Customers' option, and then click **OK**.

> **Tip** Form controls inherit whatever theme is set in the operating system. To change the theme, open Control Panel, click Appearance And Personalization, and then under Personalization, click Change The Theme. In the Theme Settings dialog box, select the theme you want, and then click OK.

The New Style Name dialog box opens.

10. In the **Style Name** box, type **Customers**, and then click **OK**.

In the AutoFormat dialog box, the new style appears in the Form AutoFormats list. This style will now be available in any database you open on this computer.

11. In the **AutoFormat** dialog box, click **OK**.

> **Tip** Access saves data automatically as you enter it, but you must manually save layout changes to any object.

**CLOSE** the Customers form, saving your changes, and then close the *03_RefineLayout* database.

# Adding Controls to a Form

Every form has three basic sections: Form Header, Detail, and Form Footer. When you use the Form tool or a wizard to create a form, they add a set of controls for each field that you select from the underlying table to the Detail section, add a logo placeholder and/or caption to the Form Header, and leave the Form Footer section blank. Because the Footer section is empty, Access collapses it, but you can resize the Footer section by dragging its *selector.* Although labels and text box controls are perhaps the most common controls found in forms, you can also enhance your forms with many other types of controls. For example, you can add groups of option buttons, check boxes, and list boxes to present people with choices instead of having them type entries in text boxes.

The controls that you can add to a form are located on the Design tab in the Controls group.

In this exercise, you will replace the logo and caption automatically placed in a form by the Form tool. You will also replace a text box control in the Detail section with a combo box control, and remove the record selector bar from the program window.

**USE** the *04_AddControls* database and the *04_CustomersFormLogo* graphic. These practice files are located in the *Chapter10* subfolder under *SBS_Office2007.*

**OPEN** the *04_AddControls* database. Then open the Customers form in Design view.

**1.** In the **Customers** form, point to the horizontal line between the **Form Header** section selector and the **Detail** section selector, and when the pointer changes to a double-headed arrow, drag the **Detail** section selector down a little more than an inch.

> **Tip** Use the rulers along the top and left side of the form as guides.

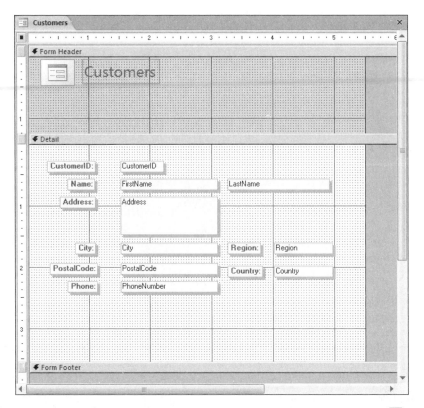

2. Select the logo and the caption in the **Form Header**, then press [Del].

Image

3. On the **Design** contextual tab, in the **Controls** group, click the **Image** button, and then, at the left end of the **Form Header** section, drag diagonally to draw a rectangle about 1 inch high and 1.5 inches wide.

   To view information about a control, point to its button in the **Controls** group. After a few seconds a ScreenTip is displayed.

   > **Tip** Access 2007 has a new Logo control that prompts you to enter a graphic name, and then automatically inserts the graphic in the form header.

4. In the Insert Picture dialog box, navigate to the *Documents\MSP\SBS_Office2007\Chapter10* folder, and then double-click the *04_CustomersFormLogo* graphic.

   > **Troubleshooting** If the practice file isn't visible, change the Files Of Type setting to Graphics Files.

   The logo appears inside the image control.

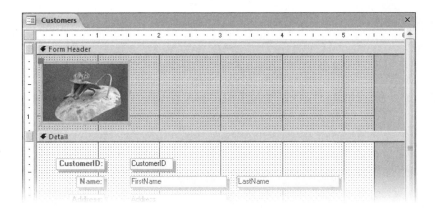

> **Tip** How an image fits into an image control is determined by the Size Mode property of the control. If the property is set to Clip and the control isn't large enough to display the entire image, the image is cropped. If the property is set to Stretch, you can enlarge the control to display the entire image. If the property is set to Zoom, the image will automatically resize to fit the control.

Label

**5.** In the **Controls** group, click the **Label** button, and then drag diagonally to draw another rectangle in the header section.

Access inserts a label control containing the insertion point, ready for you to enter a caption.

**6.** In the active label control, type **Customers**. Then press Enter.

The Customers label takes on the formatting of the other labels.

> **Troubleshooting** Access displays a Smart Tag next to the control, warning you that the label is not associated with any other control. You can ignore this, or click Ignore Error to make it go away.

**7.** If the **Property Sheet** pane is not already open, press F4 to open it.

> **Tip** You can toggle the display of the Property Sheet pane by pressing the F4 key.

**8.** Change the **Font Size** property to **18**, and the **Text Align** property to **Center**. Then close the **Property Sheet** pane.

Size to Fit

**9.** On the **Arrange** tab, in the **Size** group, click the **Size to Fit** button.

The size of the label control changes to fit the text.

**10.** Adjust the size and position of the image and label controls so that they are side-by-side.

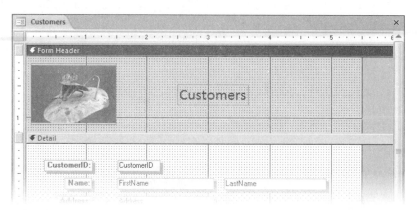

Use Control
Wizards

**11.** On the **Design** tab, in the Controls group, look at the **Use Control Wizards** button. If the button is active (orange), click it to deactivate it.

Turning off the Control Wizards feature enables you to add a control with all the default settings, without having to work through the wizard's pages.

Combo Box

**12.** In the **Controls** group, click the **Combo Box** button. Then drag diagonally to draw a rectangle just below the **Country** text box.

When you release the mouse button, Access displays a combo box control, which is *unbound* (not attached to a field in the Customers table).

> **Troubleshooting**  Access assigns a number to each control when it is created. Don't be concerned if the number displayed in your control is different from what you see in the graphics in this book.

Format Painter

**13.** Click the **Country** text box. In the **Font** group, click the **Format Painter** button and then click the combo box control.

Access copies the formatting of the text box to the combo box control and its label.

**14.** If the **Property Sheet** pane is not open, right-click the combo box, and then click **Properties**.

**15.** In the **Property Sheet** pane, on the **Data** tab, click the **Control Source** arrow, and then in the list, click **Country**.

**16.** In the **Row Source** box, type

SELECT DISTINCT Customers.Country FROM Customers;

There is a period (but no space) between *Customers* and *Country*, and a semicolon at the end of the text.

This line of code is a query that extracts one example of every country in the Country field of the Customers table and displays the results as a list when you click the Country arrow.

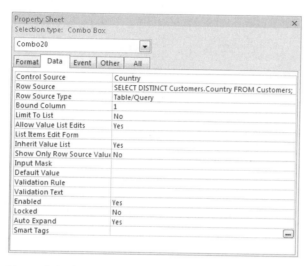

You might have to widen the Property Sheet pane to display the entire query.

> **Tip** If you need to add a customer from a country that is not in the list, you can type the country's name in the combo box. After the record is added to the database, that country shows up when the combo box list is displayed.

17. If it isn't already, set the **Row Source Type** to **Table/Query**.

18. Click the combo box label. (If you can't see the combo box label, move the **Property Sheet** pane.)

19. In the **Property Sheet** pane, on the **Format** tab, change the Caption to Country. Then close the **Property Sheet** pane.

20. Delete the original **Country** text box and its label, and then move the new combo box and label into their place, resizing them as needed.

21. On the **Home** tab, in the **Views** group, click the **View** button to see your form in Form view.

> **Tip** When a form is in Layout view or Design view, you can switch to Form view by clicking the View button.

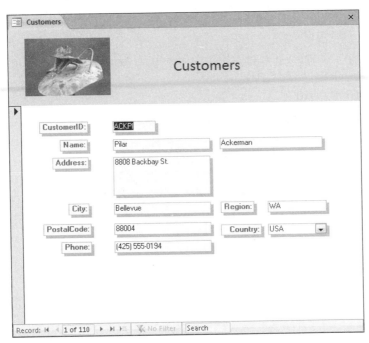

22. Scroll through a couple of records, and then click the combo box arrow to display the country list.

23. You don't need the *record selector*—the gray bar along the left edge of the form—for this exercise, so return to Design view and display the **Property Sheet** pane for the entire form by clicking the **Form** selector (the box at the junction of the horizontal and vertical rulers) and pressing F4 (if the sheet is not already displayed). Then on the **Format** tab, change **Record Selectors** to **No**, and **Scroll Bars** to **Neither**. Then press F4 again to close the **Property Sheet** pane.

24. Save the form's new design, and then switch to Form view for a final look.

**CLOSE** the *04_AddControls* database.

# Entering Data in a Form by Using VBA

As you might suspect by now, almost everything in Access, including the Access program itself, is an object. One of the characteristics of objects is that they can recognize and respond to *events*, which are essentially actions. Different objects recognize different events. The basic events, recognized by almost all objects, are Click, Double Click, Mouse

Down, Mouse Move, and Mouse Up. Most objects recognize quite a few other events. A text control, for example, recognizes 17 different events; a form recognizes more than 50.

> **Tip**  The events recognized by an object are listed on the Event tab in the object's Property Sheet pane.

While you use a form, objects are signaling events, or *firing events*, almost constantly. However, unless you attach a macro or VBA procedure to an event, the object is really just firing blanks. By default, Access doesn't do anything obvious when it recognizes most events. So without interfering with the program's normal behavior, you can use an event to specify what action should happen. You can even use an event to trigger a macro to run or a VBA procedure to perform a set of actions.

Sound complicated? Well, it's true that events are not things most casual Access users tend to worry about. But because knowing how to handle events can greatly increase the efficiency of objects such as forms, it is helpful to have an idea of what they're all about.

For example, while looking at customer records in one of the exercise databases, you might have noticed that the CustomerID is composed of the first three letters of the customer's last name and the first two letters of his or her first name, all in capital letters. This technique usually generates a unique ID for a new customer. If you try to enter an ID that is already in use, Access won't accept the new entry, and you'll have to add a number or change the ID in some other way to make it unique. Performing trivial tasks, such as combining parts of two words and then converting the results to capital letters, is some-thing a computer excels at. So rather than typing the ID for each new customer record that is added to the database, you can let VBA do it for you.

In this exercise, you will write a few lines of VBA code and attach the code to an event in a form. This is by no means an in-depth treatment of VBA, but this exercise will give you a taste of the power of VBA.

> **USE**  the *05_VBA* database and the *05_AftUpdate* text file. These practice files are located in the *Chapter10* subfolder under *SBS_Office2007*.
>
> **OPEN**  the *05_VBA* database. Then open the Customers form in Design view.

1. In the **Customers** form, click the **LastName** text box, and then if the **Property Sheet** pane isn't already open, press [F4] to open it.

2. Click the **Event** tab.

   This tab lists the events to which the LastName text box control can respond.

Ellipsis button

**3.** In the **Property Sheet** pane, click the **ellipsis button** to the right of the **After Update** property.

The Choose Builder dialog box opens, offering you the options of building an expression, a macro, or VBA code.

**4.** Click **Code Builder**, and then click **OK**.

The VBA Editor opens.

Project Explorer pane

Code window

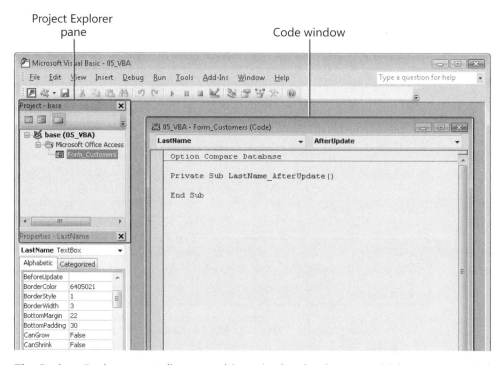

The Project Explorer pane lists any objects in the database to which you can attach code; in this case, only the Customers form (Form_Customers) appears in the list. New forms and reports appear here automatically.

The Code window displays a placeholder for the procedure that Access will use to handle the After Update event for the LastName text box control. This procedure is named *Private Sub LastName_AfterUpdate()*, and at the moment it contains only the Sub and End Sub statements that mark the beginning and end of any procedure.

5. Navigate to the *Documents\MSP\SBS_Office2007\Chapter10* folder, double-click the *05_AftUpdate* text file to open it in your default text editor, and then copy the following lines of text to the Clipboard.

```
'Create variables to hold first and last names
' and customer ID
Dim fName As String
Dim lName As String
Dim cID As String

'Assign the text in the LastName text box to
' the lName variable.
lName = Forms!customers!LastName.Text

'You must set the focus to a text box before
' you can read its contents.
Forms!customers!FirstName.SetFocus
fName = Forms!customers!FirstName.Text

'Combine portions of the last and first names
' to create the customer ID.
cID = UCase(Left(lName, 3) & Left(fName, 2))

'Don't store the ID unless it is 5 characters long
' (which indicates both names filled in).
If Len(cID) = 5 Then
    Forms!customers!CustomerID.SetFocus

    'Don't change the ID if it has already been
    ' entered; perhaps it was changed manually.
    If Forms!customers!CustomerID.Text = "" Then
        Forms!customers!CustomerID = cID
    End If
End If

'Set the focus where it would have gone naturally.
Forms!customers!Address.SetFocus
```

> **Important** A line of text beginning with an apostrophe is a comment that explains the purpose of the next line of code. In the VBA Editor, comments are displayed in green.

6. Switch back to the Code window, and then paste the copied text between the Private Sub LastName_AfterUpdate() and End Sub statements.

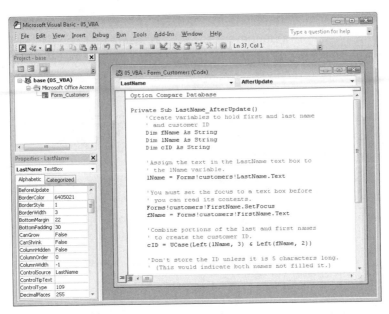

```
Option Compare Database

Private Sub LastName_AfterUpdate()
    'Create variables to hold first and last name
    ' and customer ID
    Dim fName As String
    Dim lName As String
    Dim cID As String

    'Assign the text in the LastName text box to
    ' the lName variable.
    lName = Forms!customers!LastName.Text

    'You must set the focus to a text box before
    ' you can read its contents.
    Forms!customers!FirstName.SetFocus
    fName = Forms!customers!FirstName.Text

    'Combine portions of the last and first names
    ' to create the customer ID.
    cID = UCase(Left(lName, 3) & Left(fName, 2))

    'Don't store the ID unless it is 5 characters long.
    ' (This would indicate both names not filled it.)
```

7. On the **File** menu, click **Save 05_VBA** to save your changes.

8. On the **File** menu, click **Close and Return to Microsoft Access** to return to the Access window. Then close the **Property Sheet** pane.

New Record

9. Switch to Form view. On the **Navigation** bar, click the **New Record** button.

   A blank Customers form appears.

10. In the new record, press the Tab key to move the insertion point to the **FirstName** box, type Chris, press Tab to move to the **LastName** box, type Sells, and then press Tab again.

    If you followed the above steps correctly, *SELCH* appears in the CustomerID box.

11. Change the first name to Dana and the last name to Birkby.

    Notice that the original CustomerID doesn't change, even when the names from which it was derived do.

12. Press the Esc key to remove your entry, and then try entering the last name first, followed by the first name.

    Access does not create a Customer ID. The code does what it was written to do, but not necessarily what you want it to do, which is to create an ID regardless of the order in which the names are entered. There are several ways to fix this problem. You could write a similar procedure to handle the After Update event in the FirstName text box, or you could write one procedure to handle both events and then jump to it when either event occurs. You won't do either in this exercise, but if you are interested, you can look at the code in the database file provided for the exercise in "Creating a Form by Using a Wizard" later in this chapter to see the second solution.

**13.** Press [Esc] to clear your entries.

> 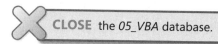 **CLOSE** the *05_VBA* database.

# Creating a Form by Using an AutoForm

Although a form doesn't have to include all the fields from the underlying table, when it is intended as the primary method of creating new records, it usually does. The quickest way to create a form that includes all the fields from one table is to use the Form button, as you did in the first exercise in this chapter. Another method, which provides more control over the creation of the form, is to use a wizard. In either case you can easily customize the forms created.

In this exercise, you will use a wizard to create a form that displays information about each of the product categories.

> **USE** the *06_CreateWizard* database. This practice file is located in the *Chapter10* subfolder under *SBS_Office2007*.
>
> **OPEN** the *06_CreateWizard* database. Then open the Categories table in Datasheet view.

 **More Forms ▾**

**1.** On the **Create** tab, in the **Forms** group, click the **More Forms** button and then in the list, click **Form Wizard**.

The Form wizard starts.

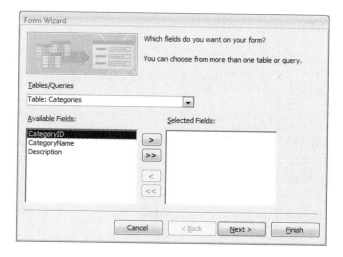

Move All

2. With the **Categories** table selected in the **Tables/Queries** list, click the **Move All** button to move all the table fields to the **Selected Fields** list, and then click **Next**.

    On the second page of the wizard, you choose the layout of the fields in the new form. When you select an option on the right side of the page, the preview area on the left side shows what the form layout will look like with that option applied.

3. With the **Columnar** option selected, click **Next**.

    On the third page of the wizard, you can select a style option to see how the style will look when applied to the form.

4. In the list of styles, click **Office**, and then click **Next**.

    Because this form is based on the Categories table, Access suggests *Categories* as the form's title.

5. With the **Open the form to view or enter information** option selected, click **Finish**.

    The new Categories form opens, displaying the first category record in the Categories table.

6. Scroll through a few records by using the navigation controls at the bottom of the form.

    > **Tip** To change the style of a form after you create it, switch to Design view, and on the Arrange tab, in the AutoFormat group, click AutoFormat. In the list displayed, click the style you would like to use.

7. Switch to Design view so that you can make a few more changes.

8. Delete the word *Category* from the **Category Name** label.

9.  You don't want to expose the CategoryID field to form users, because that value should never be changed. Click the **CategoryID** text box, and if the control's **Property Sheet** pane isn't open, press [F4] to display it.

10. In the **Property Sheet** pane, on the **Data** tab, change **Enabled** to **No**. Then press [F4] to close the **Property Sheet** pane.

    Disabling the CategoryID text box changes it, and the label text, to gray.

11. Switch to Form view, and then scroll through a few categories. Try to edit entries in the **CategoryID** field to confirm that you can't.

12. You don't need scroll bars or a record selector in this form, so return to Design view, and then display the form's **Property Sheet** pane by clicking the **Form selector** (the box in the upper-left corner) and pressing [F4].

13. In the **Property Sheet** pane, on the **Format** tab, change **Scroll Bars** to Neither and **Record Selectors** to No. Then close the **Property Sheet** pane.

14. Switch to Form view to see the effect of your changes.

**CLOSE** the Categories form, saving your changes, and then close the *06_CreateWizard* database.

# Adding a Subform to a Form

A form can display information (fields) from one or more tables or queries. If you want to display fields from several tables or queries in one form, you have to give some thought to the relationships that must exist between those objects.

In this exercise, you will add a subform to an existing form.

**USE** the *07_AddSubform* database. This practice file is located in the *Chapter10* subfolder under *SBS_Office2007*.

**OPEN** the *07_AddSubform* database. Then open the Categories form in Design view.

1.  Drag the **Form Footer** section selector down about 1 inch to give yourself some room to work in the Details section of the form. It should be about 3 inches high.

Use Control
Wizards

2.  On the **Design** tab, in the **Controls** group, make sure the **Use Control Wizards** button is active (orange).

Subform/
Subreport

**3.** In the **Controls** group, click the **Subform/Subreport** button, and then drag diagonally to draw a rectangle in the lower portion of the **Detail** section.

A white object appears in the form, and the SubForm wizard starts.

> **Tip** If prompted to do so, follow the instructions to install this wizard.

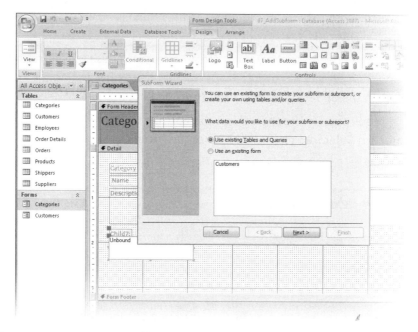

**4.** With the **Use existing Tables and Queries** option selected, click **Next**.

**5.** In the **Tables/Queries** list, click **Table: Products**.

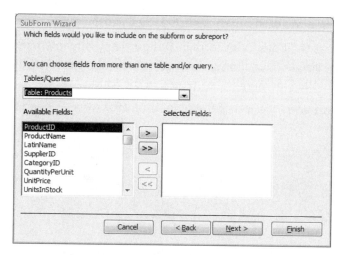

**6.** In the **Available Fields** list, double-click the **ProductName**, **CategoryID**, **QuantityPerUnit**, **UnitPrice**, and **UnitsInStock** fields to add them to the **Selected Fields** list. Then click **Next**.

Because the CategoryID field in the subform is related to the CategoryID field in the main form, the wizard selects Show Products For Each Record In Categories Using CategoryID as the Choose From A List option.

> **Tip** If the wizard can't figure out which fields are related, it selects the Define My Own option and displays list boxes in which you can specify the fields to be related.

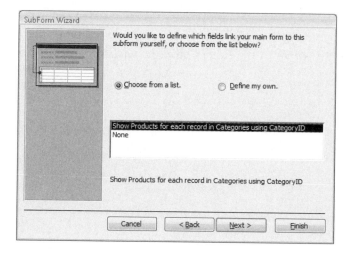

**7.** With the **Define my own** option selected, click **Finish**.

Access displays the Categories form in Design view, with an embedded Products subform. The size and location of the subform is determined by the size and location of the original rectangle you created in the form.

**8.** Adjust the size and location of the objects in your form as needed to view the entire subform.

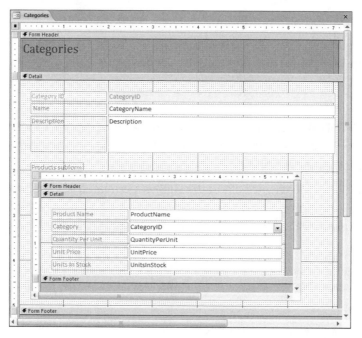

Form View

**9.** Notice the layout of the subform in Design view, and then on the View toolbar in the lower-right corner of the Access program window, click the **Form View** button to switch views.

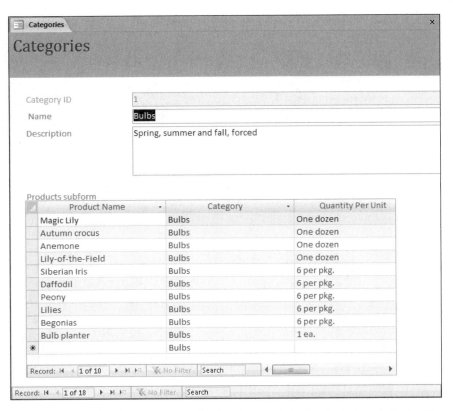

The format of the subform has totally changed. In Design view, it looks like a simple form, but in Form view, it looks like a datasheet.

**10.** Switch back to Design view, make any necessary size adjustments, and then open the **Property Sheet** pane if it isn't already open.

**11.** Click the **Form** selector in the upper-left corner of the subform twice.

The first click selects the Products subform control, and the second click selects the form. A small black square appears on the selector.

Products subform Form selector

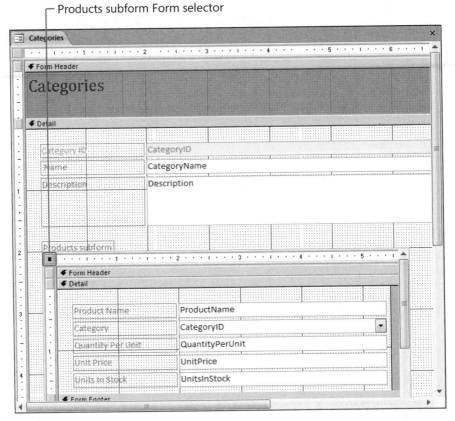

12. In the **Property Sheet** pane, on the **Format** tab, change the **Record Selectors** and **Navigation Buttons** properties to No.

While on this tab, notice the Default View property, which is set to Datasheet. You might want to return to this property and try the other options after finishing this exercise.

13. Close the **Property Sheet** pane, switch back to Form view, and then adjust the width of the columns by dragging the column dividers, until you can see all the fields.

| Product Name ▾ | Category ▾ | Quantity Per Unit ▾ | Unit Price ▾ | Units In ▾ |
|---|---|---|---|---|
| Magic Lily | Bulbs | One dozen | $40.00 | 40 |
| Autumn crocus | Bulbs | One dozen | $18.75 | 37 |
| Anemone | Bulbs | One dozen | $28.00 | 26 |
| Lily-of-the-Field | Bulbs | One dozen | $38.00 | 34 |
| Siberian Iris | Bulbs | 6 per pkg. | $12.95 | 30 |
| Daffodil | Bulbs | 6 per pkg. | $12.95 | 24 |
| Peony | Bulbs | 6 per pkg. | $19.95 | 20 |
| Lilies | Bulbs | 6 per pkg. | $10.50 | 18 |
| Begonias | Bulbs | 6 per pkg. | $18.95 | 12 |
| Bulb planter | Bulbs | 1 ea. | $6.95 | 6 |
| * | Bulbs | | $0.00 | 0 |

> **Tip**  You can quickly adjust the width of columns to fit their data by double-clicking the double arrow between column headings.

**14.** Scroll through several categories by using the navigation buttons.

As each category appears at the top of the form, the products in that category are listed in the datasheet in the subform.

First Record

**15.** Click the **First Record** button to return to the first category (Bulbs). In the subform click **Bulbs** in the **Category** column to the right of the first product (Magic Lily).

The arrow at the right end of the box indicates that this is a combo box.

**16.** Click the arrow to display the list of categories, and then change the category to **Cacti**.

Next Record

**17.** Click the **Next Record** navigation button to move to the Cacti category.

Magic Lily is now included in this category.

**18.** Display the category list to the right of Magic Lily and return it to the **Bulbs** category.

**19.** To prevent people from changing a product's category, return to Design view, click the **CategoryID** text box control in the subform, and then press [Del].

The CategoryID text box and its label no longer appear on the form.

> **Important**  You included the CategoryID field when the wizard created this subform because it is the field that relates the Categories and Products tables. The underlying Products table uses a combo box to display the name of the category instead of its ID number, so that combo box also appears in the subform.

**20.** Save the form, switch back to Form view, and then adjust the width of the subform columns and the size of the Form window until you can clearly see the fields.

| Product Name ⏷ | Quantity Per Unit ⏷ | Unit Price ⏷ | Units In ⏷ |
|---|---|---|---|
| Magic Lily | One dozen | $40.00 | 40 |
| Autumn crocus | One dozen | $18.75 | 37 |
| Anemone | One dozen | $28.00 | 26 |
| Lily-of-the-Field | One dozen | $38.00 | 34 |
| Siberian Iris | 6 per pkg. | $12.95 | 30 |
| Daffodil | 6 per pkg. | $12.95 | 24 |
| Peony | 6 per pkg. | $19.95 | 20 |
| Lilies | 6 per pkg. | $10.50 | 18 |
| Begonias | 6 per pkg. | $18.95 | 12 |
| Bulb planter | 1 ea. | $6.95 | 6 |
| * | | $0.00 | 0 |

**CLOSE** the *07_AddSubform* database.

## Simultaneously Creating Forms and Subforms

If you know when you create a form that you are going to add a subform, you can create the form and its subform by using the Form wizard. To do so:

1. On the **Create** tab, in the **Forms** group, click the **More Forms** button, and then in the list, click **Form Wizard**.

2. In the **Form** wizard, in the **Tables/Queries** list, click the table on which you want to base the form. Then click the **Move All** button to include all the table fields in the new form.

3. In the **Tables/Queries** list, click the table on which you want to base the subform.

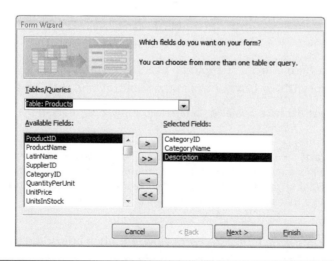

4. In the **Available Fields** list, double-click the fields you want to include in the subform to move them to the **Selected Fields** list, and then click **Next**.

> **Troubleshooting**  If the relationship between the selected tables has not been defined, Access displays a message containing a link to the Relationships window. If this occurs, you will need to define the relationship and then re-start the wizard.

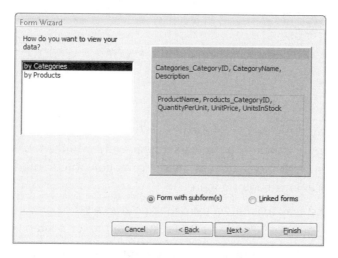

5. With your primary table and **Form with subform(s)** selected, click **Next**.

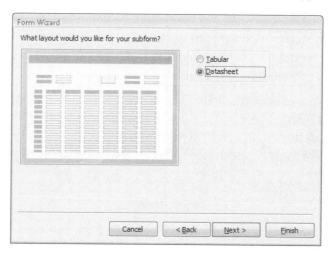

6. With **Datasheet** selected, click **Next**.

7. On the last page of the wizard, select a style and then click **Finish**.

   The wizard creates and opens the form and subform.

You can edit the form created by the Form wizard to suit your needs.

If there is only one one-to-many relationship between the tables you want to include in the form, and that relationship has been defined in the Relationships window, the fastest way to create the form and its subform is by using the Form tool. Simply select the primary table then on the Create tab, in the Forms group, click Form.

The Form tool creates and displays a form and subform, each containing all fields of its source table.

# Key Points

- A form is an organized and formatted view of some or all of the fields from one or more tables or queries. Forms work interactively with the tables in a database. You use controls in the form to enter new information, to edit or remove existing information, or to locate information.

- The quickest way to create a form that includes all the fields from one table is by using the Form tool. You can easily customize the form later in Design view.

- When you know what table to base your form on, and have an idea of how the form will be used, you can use the Form wizard to quickly create a form. You can make modifications to the form in Design view.

- The two most common views to work with forms in are Form view, in which you view or enter data, and Design view, in which you add controls, change form properties, and change the form layout.

- Each text box in a form is bound to a specific field in the underlying table. The table is the record source and the field is the control source. Each control has a number of properties, such as font style, font size, and font color, which you can change to improve a form's appearance.

- In Design view, you can resize the three basic sections of a form: the Form Header, Detail, and Form Footer. You can customize any section of your form's layout by adding and deleting labels, moving labels and text controls, and adding logos and other graphics. The most popular controls are available in the Controls group on the Design tab.

- The objects in your form can recognize and respond to events, which are essentially actions. But without a macro or VBA procedure attached to it, an event doesn't actually do anything. Knowing how to handle events can greatly increase the efficiency of objects, such as forms.

- If you want to display fields from several tables or queries in one form, you have to give some thought to the relationships that must exist between those objects. In Access, a relationship is an association between common fields in two tables, and you can relate the information in one table to the information in another table. There are three types of relationships that Access recognizes: one-to-one, one-to-many, and many-to-many.

- After you define a relationship between tables, you can add subforms to your forms. For example, for each category displayed in your main form, you might have a subform that displays all the products in that category.

# Chapter at a Glance

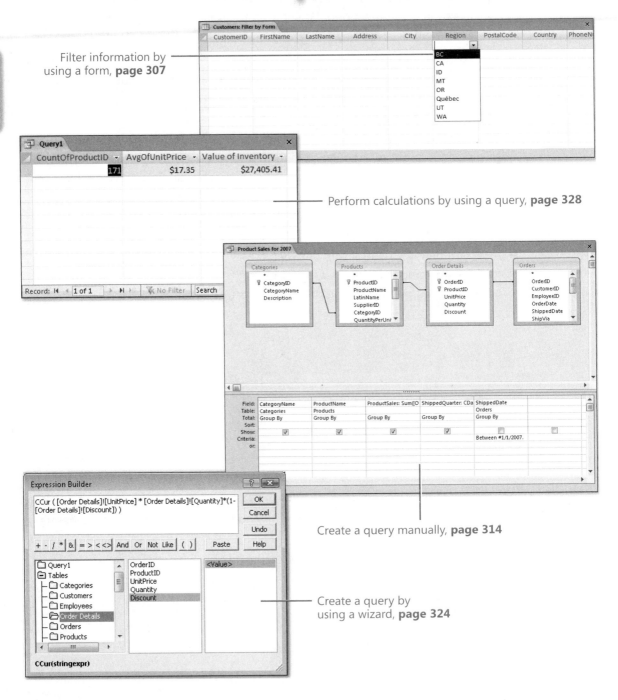

Filter information by using a form, **page 307**

Perform calculations by using a query, **page 328**

Create a query manually, **page 314**

Create a query by using a wizard, **page 324**

# 11 Locating Specific Information

In this chapter, you will learn to:

✔ Sort and filter information in a table.

✔ Filter information by using a form.

✔ Locate information that matches multiple criteria.

✔ Create a query manually or by using a wizard.

✔ Perform calculations by using a query.

A database is a repository for information. It might contain only a few records or thousands of records, stored in one table or multiple tables. No matter how much information a database contains, it is useful only if you can locate the information you need when you need it. In a small database you can find information simply by scrolling through a table until you find what you are looking for. But as a database grows in size and complexity, locating and analyzing information becomes more difficult.

Microsoft Office Access 2007 provides a variety of tools you can use to organize the display of information stored in a database and to locate specific items of information. Using these tools, you can organize all the records in a table by quickly *sorting* it based on any field or combination of fields, or you can *filter* the table so that information containing some combination of characters is displayed or excluded from the display. With a little more effort, you can create queries to display specific fields from specific records from one or more tables. You can save queries and run the saved queries to generate updated results when data changes.

In this chapter, you will learn how to sort and filter information in a table, display selected information in a form; and locate information that matches multiple criteria. Then you will create queries to locate information and to perform calculations.

**See Also** Do you need only a quick refresher on the topics in this chapter? See the Quick Reference entries at the beginning of this book.

**Important** Before you can use the practice files in this chapter, you need to install them from the book's companion CD to their default location. See "Using the Book's CD" at the beginning of this book for more information.

**Troubleshooting** Graphics and operating system–related instructions in this book reflect the Windows Vista user interface. If your computer is running Microsoft Windows XP and you experience trouble following the instructions as written, please refer to the "Information for Readers Running Windows XP" section at the beginning of this book.

# Sorting Information in a Table

You can sort the information stored in a table based on the values in one or more fields, in either ascending or descending order. For example, you could sort customer information alphabetically by last name and then by first name. This would result in the order found in telephone books.

| Last | First |
| --- | --- |
| Smith | Denise |
| Smith | James |
| Smith | Jeff |
| Thompson | Ann |
| Thompson | Steve |

Sorting a table groups all entries of one type together, which can be useful. For example, to qualify for a discount on postage, you might want to group customer records by postal code before printing mailing labels.

## How Access Sorts

The concept of sorting seems quite intuitive, but sometimes your computer's approach to such a concept is not so intuitive. Sorting numbers is a case in point. In Access, numbers can be treated as text or as numerals. Because of the spaces, hyphens, and punctuation typically used in street addresses, postal codes, and telephone numbers, the numbers in these fields are usually treated as text, and sorting them follows the logic applied to sorting all text. Numbers in a price or quantity field, on the other hand, are typically treated as numerals.

When Access sorts text, it sorts first on the first character in the selected field in every record, then on the next character, then on the next, and so on—until it runs out of characters. When Access sorts numbers, it treats the contents of each field as a single value, and sorts the records based on that value. This tactic can result in seemingly strange sort orders. For example, sorting the list in the first column of the following table as text produces the list in the second column. Sorting the same list as numerals produces the list in the third column.

| Original | Sort as text | Sort as numerals |
|---|---|---|
| 1 | 1 | 1 |
| 1234 | 11 | 3 |
| 23 | 12 | 4 |
| 3 | 1234 | 11 |
| 11 | 22 | 12 |
| 22 | 23 | 22 |
| 12 | 3 | 23 |
| 4 | 4 | 1234 |

If a field with the Text data type contains numbers, you can sort the field numerically by padding the numbers with leading zeros so that all entries are the same length. For example, 001, 011, and 101 are sorted correctly even if the numbers are defined as text.

In this exercise, you will sort records first by one field, and then by multiple fields.

1. In the **Navigation Pane**, under **Tables**, double-click **Customers**.

   The Customers table opens in Datasheet view.

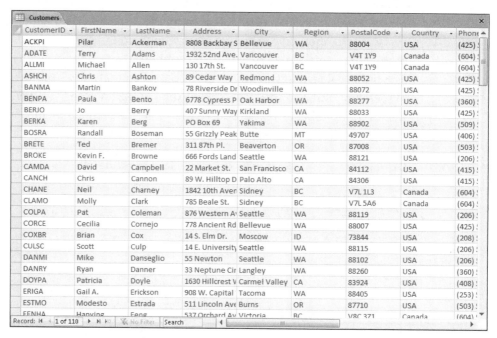

| CustomerID | FirstName | LastName | Address | City | Region | PostalCode | Country | Phone |
|---|---|---|---|---|---|---|---|---|
| ACKPI | Pilar | Ackerman | 8808 Backbay S | Bellevue | WA | 88004 | USA | (425) |
| ADATE | Terry | Adams | 1932 52nd Ave. | Vancouver | BC | V4T 1Y9 | Canada | (604) |
| ALLMI | Michael | Allen | 130 17th St. | Vancouver | BC | V4T 1Y9 | Canada | (604) |
| ASHCH | Chris | Ashton | 89 Cedar Way | Redmond | WA | 88052 | USA | (425) |
| BANMA | Martin | Bankov | 78 Riverside Dr | Woodinville | WA | 88072 | USA | (425) |
| BENPA | Paula | Bento | 6778 Cypress P | Oak Harbor | WA | 88277 | USA | (360) |
| BERJO | Jo | Berry | 407 Sunny Way | Kirkland | WA | 88033 | USA | (425) |
| BERKA | Karen | Berg | PO Box 69 | Yakima | WA | 88902 | USA | (509) |
| BOSRA | Randall | Boseman | 55 Grizzly Peak | Butte | MT | 49707 | USA | (406) |
| BRETE | Ted | Bremer | 311 87th Pl. | Beaverton | OR | 87008 | USA | (503) |
| BROKE | Kevin F. | Browne | 666 Fords Land | Seattle | WA | 88121 | USA | (206) |
| CAMDA | David | Campbell | 22 Market St. | San Francisco | CA | 84112 | USA | (415) |
| CANCH | Chris | Cannon | 89 W. Hilltop D | Palo Alto | CA | 84306 | USA | (415) |
| CHANE | Neil | Charney | 1842 10th Aven | Sidney | BC | V7L 1L3 | Canada | (604) |
| CLAMO | Molly | Clark | 785 Beale St. | Sidney | BC | V7L 5A6 | Canada | (604) |
| COLPA | Pat | Coleman | 876 Western A | Seattle | WA | 88119 | USA | (206) |
| CORCE | Cecilia | Cornejo | 778 Ancient Rd | Bellevue | WA | 88007 | USA | (425) |
| COXBR | Brian | Cox | 14 S. Elm Dr. | Moscow | ID | 73844 | USA | (208) |
| CULSC | Scott | Culp | 14 E. University | Seattle | WA | 88115 | USA | (206) |
| DANMI | Mike | Danseglio | 55 Newton | Seattle | WA | 88102 | USA | (206) |
| DANRY | Ryan | Danner | 33 Neptune Cir | Langley | WA | 88260 | USA | (360) |
| DOYPA | Patricia | Doyle | 1630 Hillcrest V | Carmel Valley | CA | 83924 | USA | (408) |
| ERIGA | Gail A. | Erickson | 908 W. Capital | Tacoma | WA | 88405 | USA | (253) |
| ESTMO | Modesto | Estrada | 511 Lincoln Ave | Burns | OR | 87710 | USA | (503) |
| FENHA | Hanying | Feng | 537 Orchard Av | Victoria | BC | V8C 371 | Canada | (604) |

Record: 1 of 110   No Filter   Search

2. Click the arrow at the right side of the **Region** column header, and then click **Sort A to Z**.

   Access rearranges the records in alphabetical order by region, and displays a narrow upward-pointing arrow at the right side of the column header to indicate the sort order.

Descending

3. To reverse the sort order by using a different method, on the **Home** tab, in the **Sort & Filter** group, click the **Descending** button.

   The sort order reverses. The records for customers living in Washington (WA) are now at the top of your list. In both sorts, the region was sorted alphabetically, but the City field was left in a seemingly random order.

Suppose that you want to see the records arranged by city within each region. You can do this by sorting the City column and then the Region column, or by moving the Region column to the left of the City column, selecting both, and then sorting them together.

> **Tip** Access can sort on more than one field, but it sorts consecutively from left to right. So the fields you want to sort must be adjacent, and they must be arranged in the order in which you want to sort them.

**4.** To sort the cities in ascending order within the regions, first click the **City** sort order arrow, and then click **Sort A to Z**.

Access sorts the records alphabetically by city.

**5.** To finish the process, right-click anyplace in the **Region** column, and then click **Sort A to Z**.

The two columns are now sorted so the cities in each region are listed in ascending order.

**6.** To sort both columns at the same time in descending order, move the **Region** field to the left of the **City** field by clicking its header to select the column, and then dragging the column to the left until a dark line appears between **Address** and **City**. Release the mouse button to complete the move operation.

**7.** With the **Region** column selected, hold down the ⌈Shift⌋ key and click the **City** header to extend the selection so that both the **Region** and **City** columns are selected.

**8.** In the **Sort & Filter** group, click the **Descending** button to arrange the records with the regions in descending order and the city names also in descending order within each region (or in this case, each state).

**9.** Experiment with various ways of sorting the records to display different results.

> **Tip** You can sort records while viewing them in a form. Click the field on which you want to base the sort, and then click the Sort command you want. You can't sort by multiple fields at the same time in Form view, but you can sort on one field then the next to achieve the same results.

 **CLOSE** the Customers table without saving your changes, and then close the *01_SortTable* database.

# Filtering Information in a Table

Sorting the information in a table organizes it in a logical manner, but you still have the entire table to deal with. To locate only the records containing (or not containing) specific information, filtering is more effective than sorting. For example, you could quickly create a filter to locate only customers who live in Seattle, only items that were purchased on January 13, or only orders that were not shipped by standard mail.

You can apply simple filters while viewing information in a table or form. To filter information by multiple criteria, you can apply additional filters to the results of the first one.

---

### Wildcards

If you want to locate records containing certain information but aren't sure of all the characters, or want your search to return multiple variations of a base character set, you can include *wildcard characters* in your search criteria. The most common wildcards are:

- \* (asterisk) represents any number of characters For example

  *LastName = Co\* returns entries including Colman and Conroy*

- ? (question mark) represents any single alphabetic character. For example

  *FirstName = er?? returns entries including Eric and Erma*

- # (number sign) represents any single numeric character. For example

  *ID = 1## returns any ID from 100 through 199*

  > **Tip** Access supports several sets of wildcards. For more information on these, search Access Help for *wildcards* and read the topic titled "Access wildcard character reference."

When searching for information in a text field, you can also use the Contains text filter to locate records containing words or character strings.

---

In this exercise, you will filter records by a single criterion and then by multiple criteria.

> **Tip** The Filter commands you will use in this exercise are available in the Sort & Filter group on the Home tab, on the column menu displayed when you click a column header arrow, and on the shortcut menu displayed when you right-click a column. However, not all Filter commands are available in each of these places.

**USE** the *02_FilterTable* database. This practice file is located in the *Chapter11* subfolder under *SBS_Office2007*.

**OPEN** the *02_FilterTable* database, and then open the Customers table in Datasheet view.

**1.** In the **City** field, click any instance of **Vancouver**.

**2.** On the **Home** tab, in the **Sort & Filter** group, click the **Selection** button, and then in the list, click **Equals "Vancouver"**.

The number of customers displayed in the table (and on the status bar at the bottom of the table) changes from *110* to *6*, because only six customers live in Vancouver.

Access displays a small filter icon at the right side of the City column header to indicate that the table is filtered by that field. The Toggle Filter button in the Sort & Filter group and the Filter status on the status bar changes to Filtered.

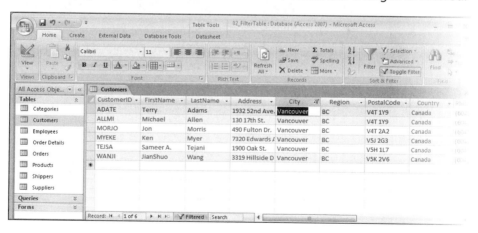

> **Important** When you filter a table, Access doesn't remove the records that don't match the filter; it simply hides them.

**3.** In the **Sort & Filter** group, click the **Toggle Filter** button.

Access removes the filter and displays all the records. If you click the Toggle Filter button again, the last filter used will be reapplied.

Suppose that you want a list of all customers with postal codes starting with *880*.

**4.** Click the **PostalCode** column header arrow, point to **Text Filters**, and then click **Begins With**.

> **Tip** The sort and filter options displayed when you click the column header arrow are determined by the field type. If this were a numeric field, then the submenu would be Number Filters and different options would be listed. U.S. Zip Codes and international postal codes are usually text fields to allow for the ZIP+4 codes.

The Custom Filter dialog box opens.

**5.** In the **PostalCode begins with** box, type *880*. Then click **OK**.

The filtered table includes 30 records that have postal codes starting with *880*.

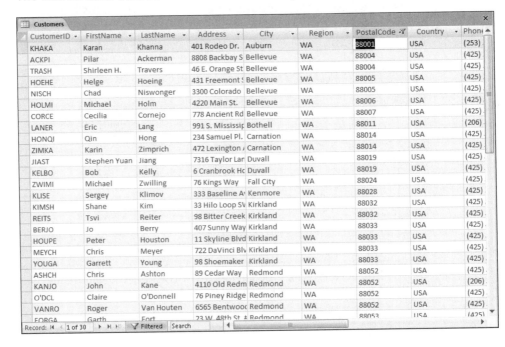

6. In the **Sort & Filter** group, click the **Toggle Filter** button to remove the filter and display all the records.

Suppose you want to display only those customers who live outside of the United States.

7. In the **Country** column, right-click any instance of **USA**, and then click **Does Not Equal "USA"**.

Access displays all the customers from countries other than the United States (in this case, only Canada).

8. Remove the filter, save and close the **Customers** table, and then open the **Orders** table in Datasheet view.

9. In the **EmployeeID** field, right-click **Emanuel, Michael**, and then click **Equals "Emanuel, Michael"**.

> **Troubleshooting** If you continued with the *01_SortTable* database from the previous exercise, the EmployeeID field does not list employee names. To complete this exercise, you must use the *02_FilterTable* database.

10. In the **OrderDate** field, right-click **2/1/2007**, and then click **On or After 2/1/2007**.

> **Tip** To see a list of the available options for date filters, right-click any cell in the OrderDate column and then point to Date Filters.

You now have a list of orders placed with the selected employee on or after the specified date. You could continue to refine the list by filtering on another field, or you could sort the results by a field.

> **Tip** After you locate the information you want, you can display the results in a form or report. To do so, on the Create tab, click the object you want to create.

 **CLOSE** the Orders table without saving changes, and then close the *02_FilterTable* database.

> **Tip** You can filter records while displaying them in a form by using the same commands as you do to filter forms in a table.

## Expressions

In Access lingo, *expressions* are synonymous with *formulas*. An expression is a combination of *operators*, *constants*, *functions*, and *control properties* that evaluates to a single value. Access builds formulas using the format *a=b+c*, where *a* is the *result* and *=b+c* is the expression. You can use an expression to assign properties to tables or forms, to determine values in fields or reports, as part of queries, and so on.

The expressions you use in Access combine multiple criteria to define a set of conditions that a record must meet to be included in the result of a filter or query. Multiple criteria are combined using logical, comparison, and arithmetic operators. Different types of expressions use different operators.

The most common *logical operators* are:

- And. This operator selects records that meet all the specified criteria.
- Or. This operator selects records that meet at least one of the criteria.
- Not. This operator selects records that don't match the criteria.

Common *comparison operators* include:

- < (less than)
- > (greater than)
- = (equal to)

You can combine these basic operators to form:

- <= (less than or equal to)
- >= (greater than or equal to)
- <> (not equal to)

The Like operator is sometimes grouped with the comparison operators and is used to test whether or not text matches a pattern.

You use *arithmetic operators* with numerals. The most common are:

- + (add)
- - (subtract)
- * (multiply)
- / (divide)

A related operator, & (a text form of +) is used to concatenate (combine) two text strings.

# Filtering Information by Using a Form

The Filter By Form command, available from the Advanced Filter Options list, provides a quick and easy way to filter a table based on the information in several fields. When you invoke this command within a table, Access displays a Look For tab containing a filtering form that looks like an empty datasheet. However, each of the blank cells is actually a combo box containing a list of all the entries in that field. You can select a filter criterion from the list, or enter a new one. Then you click the Toggle Filter button to display only the records containing your selected criteria.

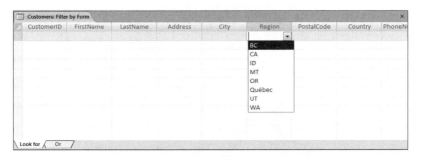

Using Filter By Form on a table that has only a few fields, such as the one shown above, is easy. But using it on a table that has a few dozen fields gets a bit cumbersome, and it is simpler to find information by using the Filter By Form command in the form version of the table. When you invoke this command within a form, Access filters the form in the same way it filters a table.

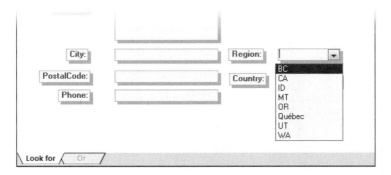

In a filtered form, you move between records by clicking the navigation buttons at the bottom of the form window.

> **Tip** Filter By Form offers the same features and techniques whether you are using it in a form or a table. Because defining the filter is sometimes easier in a form and viewing the results is sometimes easier in a table, you might consider creating a simple form based on the table, filtering the data within the form, and then switching to Datasheet view to display the results.

In this exercise, you will locate a record by using the Filter By Form command.

> **USE** the *03_FilterForm* database. This practice file is located in the *Chapter11* subfolder under *SBS_Office2007*.
>
> **OPEN** the *03_FilterForm* database.

1. In the **Navigation Pane**, under **Forms**, double-click **Customers**.

   The Customers form opens in Form view.

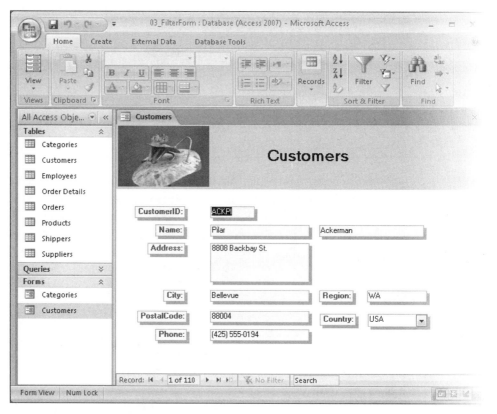

2. On the **Home** tab, in the **Sort & Filter** group, click the **Advanced** button, and then in the list, click **Filter By Form**.

   The Customers form, which displays the information from one record, is replaced by its Filter By Form version, which has a blank box for each field and the Look For and Or tabs at the bottom.

3. Click the second text box to the right of the **Name** label (the box intended to contain the surname), type s*, and then press Enter.

Access converts your entry to the proper format, or *syntax*, for this type of expression: *Like "s\*".*

4. In the **Sort & Filter** group, click the **Toggle Filter** button.

   Access displays all records including last names starting with *S*.

5. Click the **Filter By Form** button again to switch back to the filter form.

   Your filter criteria are still displayed. When you enter filter criteria using any method, they are saved as a form property and are available until they are replaced by other criteria.

6. Click the box to the right of **Region**, click the arrow that appears, and then in the list, click **CA**.

7. Click the **Toggle Filter** button to see only the customers living in California whose last names begin with *S*.

   Access replaces the filter window with the regular Customers form, and the status bar at the bottom of the form indicates that three filtered records are available.

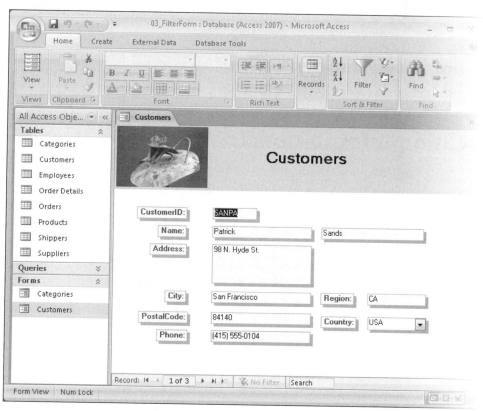

8. Click the **Filter By Form** button again to switch back to the filter form.

9. At the bottom of the form window, click the **Or** tab.

> **Tip** Criteria you enter on the Look For tab are joined with the And operator to reduce the number of possible hits in the underlying table. Criteria entered on the Or tabs tend to increase the number of hits.

This tab has the same blank cells as the Look For tab. You can switch between the two tabs to confirm that your criteria haven't been cleared.

> **Tip** When you display the Or tab, a second Or tab appears so that you can include a third criterion if you want.

10. Type s* in the **LastName** box, type or click WA in the **Region** box, and then click the **Toggle Filter** button.

You can scroll through the filtered Customers form to view the six records containing WA in the Region field.

 **CLOSE** the Customers form and the *03_FilterForm* database.

# Locating Information That Matches Multiple Criteria

The filtering methods discussed earlier in this chapter are quick and easy ways to narrow down the amount of information displayed, as long as your filter criteria are fairly simple. But suppose you need to locate something more complex, such as all the orders shipped to Midwest states between specific dates by either of two shippers. When you need to search a single table for records that meet multiple criteria, or with criteria based on complex expressions as criteria, you can use the Advanced Filter/Sort command, available from the Advanced Filter Options list.

You work with the Advanced Filter/Sort command in the *design grid*.

In this exercise, you will filter a table to display customers located in two states. Then you will experiment with the design grid to better understand its filtering capabilities.

> **USE** the *04_MultipleCriteria* database. This practice file is located in the *Chapter11* subfolder under *SBS_Office2007*.
>
> **OPEN** the *04_MultipleCriteria* database. Then open the Customers table in Datasheet view.

1. On the **Home** tab, in the **Sort & Filter** group, click the **Advanced Filter Options** button, and then in the list, click **Advanced Filter/Sort**.

   The CustomersFilter1 query window opens, displaying the Customers field list in a floating window at the top, and the design grid at the bottom.

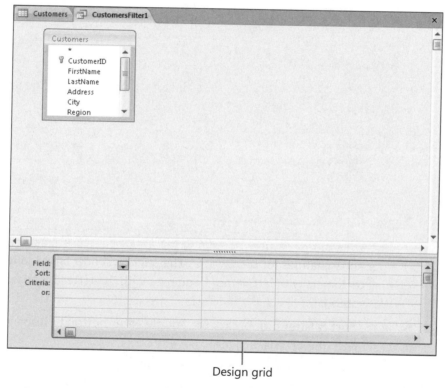

Design grid

2. In the **Customers** field list, double-click **LastName** to copy it to the **Field** cell in the first column of the design grid.

3. In the **Criteria** cell under **LastName**, type s*, and then press [Enter].

   Access changes the criterion to *Like "s*"*.

4. In the **Customers** field list, double-click **Region** to copy it to the next available column of the design grid.

5. In the **Criteria** cell under **Region**, type ca or wa, and then press [Enter].

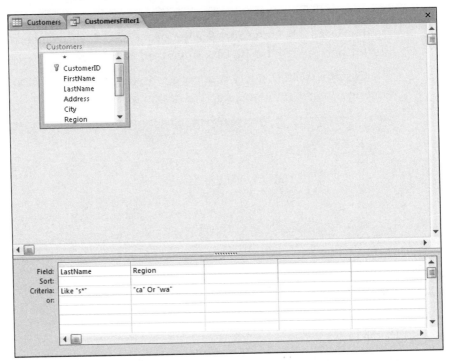

Your entry changes to *"ca" Or "wa"*. The query will now filter the table to display only customers with last names beginning with the letter *S* who live in California or Washington.

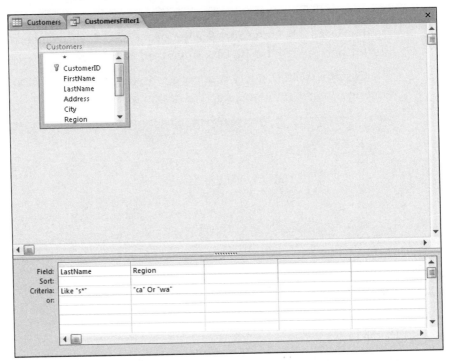 6. In the **Sort & Filter** group, click the **Toggle Filter** button to display only records that match the criteria.

   Access switches to the Customers table and displays the query results. There are six customers with last names beginning with *S* who live in either California or Washington.

7. Click the **CustomersFilter1** tab to switch to the filter window. In the **or** cell under **LastName**, type b*, and then press [Enter].

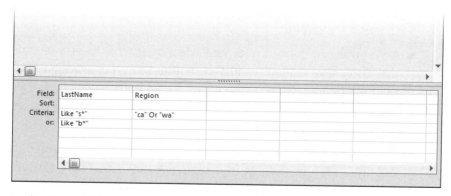

8. In the **Sort & Filter** group, click the **Toggle Filter** button.

   The result includes records for all customers with last names that begin with *s* or *b*, but some of the *b* names live in Montana and Oregon. If you look again at the design grid, you can see that the filter is formed by combining the fields in the Criteria row with the *And* operator, combining the fields in the "Or" row with the *And* operator, and then using the *Or* operator to combine the two rows. So the filter is searching for customers with names beginning with *s* who live in California or Washington, or customers with names beginning with *b*, regardless of where they live.

9. Switch to the filter window, type **ca or wa** in the **or** cell under **Region**, press [Enter], and then apply the filter to display only customers with last names beginning with *B* or *S* located in California and Washington.

 **CLOSE** the Customers table without saving your changes, and then close the *04_MultipleCriteria* database.

# Creating a Query Manually

A query can do more than simply return a list of records from a table. You can use functions in a query to perform calculations on the information in a table to produce the sum, average, count, and other mathematical values.

When you want to work with more than one table, you need to move beyond filters and into the realm of queries. Common types of queries include the following:

- A *select query* retrieves data from one or more tables and displays the results in a datasheet. You can also use a select query to group records and calculate sums, counts, averages, and other types of totals. You can work with the results of a select query in Datasheet view to update records in one or more related tables at the same time. This is the most common type of query.

- A *duplicate query* is a form of select query that locates records that have the same information in one or more fields that you specify. The Find Duplicates Query wizard guides you through the process of specifying the table and fields to use in the query.

- An *unmatched query* is a form of select query that locates records in one table that don't have related records in another table. For example, you could use this to locate people in the customer table who don't have an order in the order table. The Find Unmatched Query wizard guides you through the process of specifying the tables and fields to use in the query.

- A *parameter query* prompts you for information to be used in the query—for example, a range of dates. This type of query is particularly useful when used as the basis for a report that is run periodically.

- A *crosstab query* calculates and restructures data for easier analysis. You can use a crosstab query to calculate a sum, average, count, or other type of total for data that is grouped by two types of information—one down the left side of the datasheet and one across the top. The cell at the junction of each row and column displays the results of the query's calculation.

- An *action query* updates multiple records in one operation. It is essentially a select query that performs an action on the results of the selection process. Four types of actions are available:

  - *Delete queries*, which delete records from one or more tables
  - *Update queries*, which make changes to records in one or more tables
  - *Append queries*, which add records from one or more tables to the end of one or more other tables
  - *Make-table queries*, which create a new table from all or part of the data in one or more tables

> **Tip** In addition to these, you can create Structured Query Language (SQL) queries. SQL queries are beyond the scope of this book.

Access includes wizards that guide you through the creation of the common queries, but you create less common queries by hand in Design view, using the design grid.

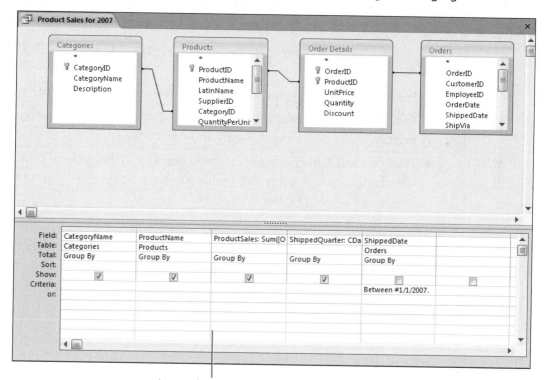

A complex query,
shown in Design view

The field lists (in the small windows at the top of the query window) list the fields in the four tables that can be included in this query. The lines connecting the tables indicate that they are related by virtue of common fields. The first row of the grid contains the names of the fields actually included in the query, and the second row shows which table each field belongs to. The third row (labeled *Total*) performs calculations on the field values, and the fourth row indicates whether the query results will be sorted on this field. A selected check box in the fifth row (labeled *Show*) means that the field will be displayed in the results datasheet. (If the check box isn't selected, the field can be used in determining the query results, but it won't be displayed.) The sixth row (labeled *Criteria*) contains criteria that determine which records will be displayed, and the seventh row (labeled *or*) sets up alternate criteria.

You can create a query by hand or by using a wizard. Regardless of what method you use to create the query, what you create is a statement describing the conditions that must be met for records to be matched in one or more tables. When you run the query, the matching records appear in a new datasheet.

---

### Filters and Sorts vs. Queries

The major differences between filtering a table, sorting a table, and querying a table are:

- The Filter and Sort commands are usually faster to implement than queries.
- The Filter and Sort commands are not saved, or are saved only temporarily. You can save a query permanently and run it again at any time.
- The Filter and Sort commands are applied only to the table or form that is currently open. A query can be based on multiple tables and on other queries, which don't have to be open.

---

In this exercise, you will create a form based on a select query that combines information from two tables into a datasheet and calculates the extended price of an item based on the unit price, quantity ordered, and discount.

USE the *05_QueryDesign* database. This practice file is located in the *Chapter11* sub-folder under *SBS_Office2007*.

**OPEN** the *05_QueryDesign* database.

**1.** On the **Create** tab, in the **Other** group, click the **Query Design** button.

A query window opens in Design view, and the Show Table dialog box opens. In this dialog box, you can specify which tables and saved queries to include in the current query.

**2.** In the **Show Table** dialog box, on the **Tables** tab, double-click **Order Details** and then **Products** to add each table to the query window. Then close the dialog box.

Each of the selected tables is represented in the top portion of the window by a small field list window with the name of the table—in this case, Order Details and Products—in its title bar.

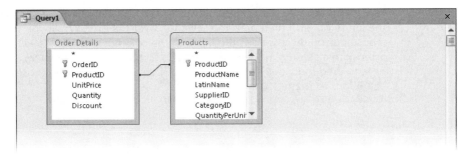

An asterisk at the top of each list represents all the fields in the list. The primary key field in each list is indicated by a key icon. The line from ProductID in the Order Details table to ProductID in the Products table indicates that these two fields are related.

> **Tip**  To add more tables to a query, reopen the Show Table dialog box by right-clicking a blank space in the top portion of the query window and then clicking Show Table, or by clicking the Show Table button in the Query Setup group on the Design contextual tab.

The lower area of the query window contains the design grid where you will specify the query's criteria.

3. Drag the following fields from the field lists to consecutive columns in the design grid:

| From this table | Drag this field |
|---|---|
| Order Details | OrderID |
| Products | ProductName |
| Order Details | UnitPrice |
| Order Details | Quantity |
| Order Details | Discount |

The query will include only the fields that are in the design grid.

> **Tip**  You can quickly copy a field to the next available column in the design grid by double-clicking the field.
>
> To copy all fields to the grid, double-click the title bar above the field list to select the entire list, and then drag the selection over the grid. When you release the mouse button, Access adds the fields to the columns in order. You can drag the asterisk to a column in the grid to include all the fields in the query, but you also have to drag individual fields to the grid if you want to sort on those fields or add conditions to them.

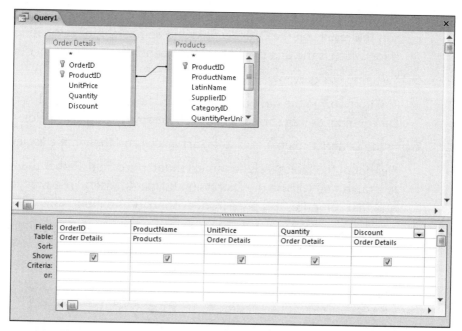

Run

**4.** On the **Design** contextual tab, in the **Results** group, click the **Run** button.

Access runs the query and displays the results in Datasheet view.

The results show that the query is working thus far. There are two things left to do: sort the results on the OrderID field and add a field for calculating the extended price, which is the unit price times the quantity sold minus any discount.

**5.** Switch to Design view.

The third row in the design grid is labeled Sort. You can select Ascending, Descending, or (not sorted) in this cell for any of the query fields.

**6.** In the **OrderID** column, click the **Sort** arrow, and then in the list, click **Ascending**.

Neither of the tables includes an extended price field. Rather than creating the field in a table, you will use the Expression Builder to insert an expression in the design grid that computes this price from existing information.

**7.** Right-click the **Field** cell in the first blank column in the design grid (the sixth column), and then click **Build**.

The Expression Builder dialog box opens.

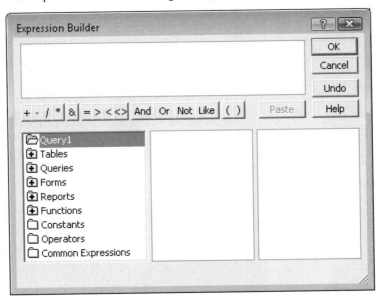

Here is the expression you will build:

```
CCur([Order Details]![UnitPrice]*[Order Details]![Quantity]*(1-[Order
Details]![Discount]))
```

The CCur function converts the results of the math inside its parentheses to currency format.

> **Tip** If you were to type this expression directly into the field, you could simplify it a bit to this:
> ExtendedPrice: CCur([Order Details]![UnitPrice]*[Quantity]*(1-[Discount]))
> The [Order Details]! part is required only with fields that appear in both tables. It tells the query which table to use.

8. In the first column of the elements area, double-click the **Functions** folder to display its contents, and then click **Built-In Functions**.

   Categories of built-in functions appear in the second column; actual functions within each category appear in the third column.

9. In the second column, click **Conversion** to limit the functions in the third column to those in that category. Then in the third column, double-click **Ccur**.

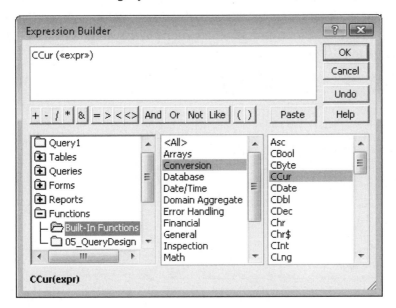

You've inserted the currency conversion function into the expression box. The *<<expr>>* inside the parentheses represents the other expressions that will eventually result in the number Access should convert to currency format.

10. In the expression box, click **<<expr>>** to select it so that the next thing you enter will replace it.

    The next element you want in the expression is the UnitPrice field from the Order Details table.

11. In the first column, double-click the **Tables** folder, and click **Order Details**. Then in the second column, double-click **UnitPrice**.

The insertion point is currently situated after UnitPrice, which is exactly where you want it. Now you want to multiply the amount in the UnitPrice field by the amount in the Quantity field.

Multiply

**12.** In the row of operator buttons below the expression box, click the **Multiply** button.

Access inserts the multiplication sign and another *<<Expr>>* placeholder.

**13.** In the expression box, click **<<Expr>>** to select it, and then in the second column, double-click **Quantity**.

What you have entered so far calculates the total cost by multiplying the price of an item by the quantity ordered. However, suppose the sale price is discounted due to quantity or another factor. The discount, which is stored in the Order Details table, is expressed as the percentage to deduct. But it is easier to compute the percentage to be paid than it is to compute the discount and subtract it from the total cost.

**14.** In the expression box, type *(1-. In the second column, double-click **Discount**, and type ). If the entire expression isn't visible in the window, widen the window by dragging its right edge.

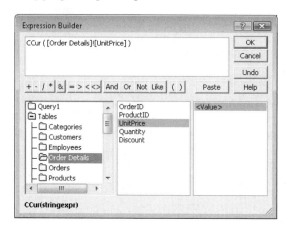

Although the discount is formatted in the datasheet as a percentage, it is actually stored in the database as a decimal number between 0 and 1. (For example, a discount displayed as 10% is stored as 0.1). So if the discount is 10%, the result of *(1-Discount) is *.9. In other words, the formula multiplies the unit price by the quantity and then multiplies that result by 0.9.

15. In the **Expression Builder** dialog box, click **OK**.

Access enters the expression in the design grid.

16. Press ⎡Enter⎤ to move the insertion point out of the field and complete the entry of the expression.

Access labels the expression Expr1, which isn't particularly meaningful.

> **Tip** You can quickly make a column in the design grid as wide as its contents by double-clicking the line in the gray selection bar that separates the column from the column to its right.

17. In the design grid, double-click **Expr1**, and then type ExtendedPrice as the label for the expression.

18. Switch to Datasheet view.

The orders are now sorted by the OrderID field, and the extended price is calculated in the last field.

19. Scroll down to see a few records with discounts.

If you check the math, you will see that the query calculates the extended price correctly.

20. Close the query window. In the **Microsoft Office Access** message box asking whether to save the query, click **Yes**. In the **Save As** dialog box, type Order Details Extended, and then click **OK**.

**CLOSE** the *05_QueryDesign* database.

> **Expression Builder**
>
> To create an expression as a filter or query option, you can either type the expression or use the Expression Builder. You can open the Expression Builder by clicking Build on a shortcut menu, clicking Builder in the Query Setup group, or clicking the Build button (which resembles an ellipsis) at the right end of a box that can accept an expression.
>
> The Expression Builder isn't a wizard; it doesn't lead you through the process of building an expression. But it does provide a hierarchical list of the most common elements that you can include in an expression. You can either type your expression in the expression box, or you can select functions, operators, and other elements to copy them to the expression box.

# Creating a Query by Using a Wizard

The process of creating a simple select query by using the Query wizard is almost identical to that of creating a form by using the Form wizard. Within the Query wizard, you can build a new query based on one or more fields from existing tables or queries. You can also create Crosstab, Find Duplicates, and Find Unmatched queries with the wizard.

For Access to work effectively with multiple tables, it must understand the relationships between the fields in those tables. If these relationships don't already exist.

**See Also**  For more information about creating relationships, see the sidebar "Relationships" in Chapter 10, "Simplifying Data Entry by Using Forms."

In this exercise, you will use the Query wizard to create a query that combines information from two tables related through common fields.

> **USE**  the *06_QueryWizard* database. This practice file is located in the *Chapter11* subfolder under *SBS_Office2007*.
> **OPEN**  the *06_QueryWizard* database.

1. On the **Create** tab, in the **Other** group, click the **Query Wizard** button.

   The New Query dialog box opens.

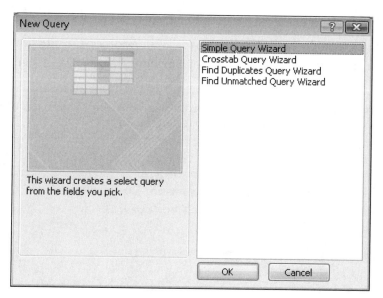

2. With **Simple Query Wizard** selected in the list, click **OK**.

   The Simple Query wizard starts.

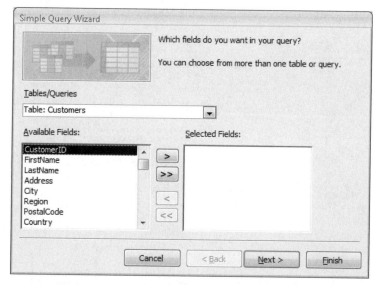

Move All

3. In the **Tables/Queries** list, click **Table: Orders**. Then click the **Move All** button to move all the fields from the **Available Fields** list to the **Selected Fields** list.

4. In the **Tables/Queries** list, click **Table: Customers.**

5. In the **Available Fields** list, double-click the **Address**, **City**, **Region**, **PostalCode**, and **Country** fields to move them to the **Selected Fields** list, and then click **Next**.

> **Tip** If the relationship between two tables hasn't already been established, you will be prompted to define it and then restart the wizard.

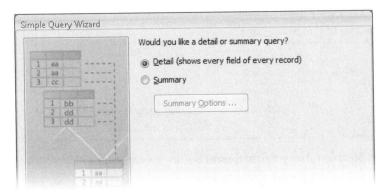

6. With the **Detail** option selected, click **Next**.

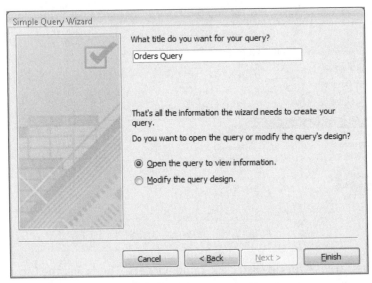

7. With the **Open the query to view information** option selected, click **Finish**.

   Access runs the query and displays the results in Datasheet view. You can scroll through the results and see that information is displayed for all the orders.

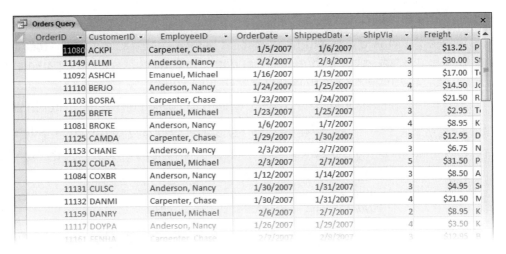

8. Switch to Design view.

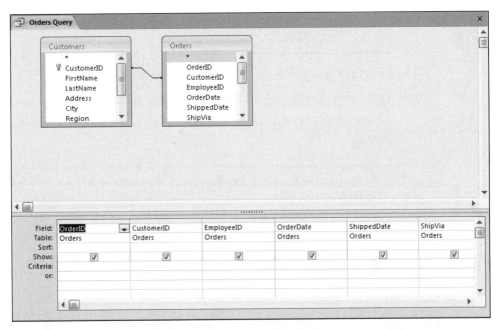

Notice that the Show check box is selected by default for each of the fields used in the query. If you want to use a field in a query—for example, to sort on, to set criteria for, or in a calculation—but don't want to see the field in the results datasheet, you can clear its Show check box.

9. Clear the **Show** check box for **OrderID**, **CustomerID**, and **EmployeeID**, and then switch back to Datasheet view.

The three fields have been removed from the results datasheet.

10. Switch to Design view.

   This query returns all records in the Orders table. To have the query match the records for a range of dates, you will convert it to a parameter query, which requests the date range each time you run it.

11. In the **OrderDate** column, type the following text in the **Criteria** cell, exactly as shown:

   Between [Type the beginning date:] And [Type the ending date:]

Run

12. On the **Design** contextual tab, in the **Results** group, click the **Run** button to run the query.

13. Enter a beginning date of 1/1/07, and then press Enter.

14. Enter an ending date of 1/31/07, and then press Enter.

   Access redisplays the datasheet, this time listing only orders between the specified dates.

**CLOSE** the datasheet, saving the changes to the query, and then close the *06_QueryWizard* database.

# Performing Calculations by Using a Query

You typically use a query to locate all the records that meet some criteria. But sometimes you are not as interested in the details of all the records as you are in summarizing them in some way. For example, you might want to know how many orders have been placed this year or the total dollar value of all orders placed. The easiest way to get this information is by creating a query that groups the necessary fields and does the math for you. To do this, you use *aggregate functions* in the query.

Access queries support the aggregate functions shown in the following table.

| Function | Calculates |
|----------|-----------|
| Sum | Total of the values in a field |
| Avg | Average of the values in a field |
| Count | Number of values in a field, not counting Null (blank) values |
| Min | Lowest value in a field |
| Max | Highest value in a field |
| StDev | Standard deviation of the values in a field |
| Var | Variance of the values in a field |

In this exercise, you will create a query that calculates the total number of products in an inventory, the average price of all the products, and the total value of the inventory.

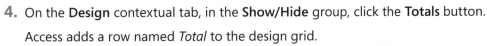
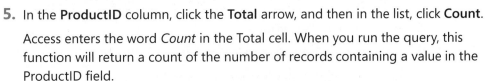

**USE** the *07_Calculate* database. This practice file is located in the *Chapter11* subfolder under *SBS_Office2007*.
**OPEN** the *07_Calculate* database.

Query Design

1. On the **Create** tab, in the **Other** group, click the **Query Design** button.

   Access opens the query window and the Show Table dialog box.

2. In the **Show Table** dialog box, double-click **Products**, and then click **Close**.

   Access adds the Products table to the query window and closes the Show Table dialog box.

3. In the **Products Items** field list, double-click **ProductID** and then **UnitPrice**.

   Access copies both fields to the design grid.

4. On the **Design** contextual tab, in the **Show/Hide** group, click the **Totals** button.

   Access adds a row named *Total* to the design grid.

Totals

5. In the **ProductID** column, click the **Total** arrow, and then in the list, click **Count**.

   Access enters the word *Count* in the Total cell. When you run the query, this function will return a count of the number of records containing a value in the ProductID field.

6. In the **UnitPrice** column, click the **Total** arrow, and then in the list, click **Avg**.

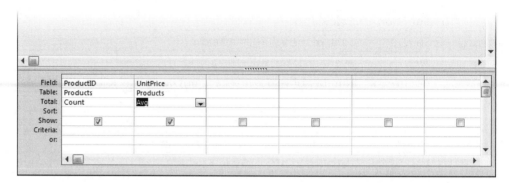

When you run the query, this function will return the average of all the UnitPrice values.

Run

7. In the **Results** group, click the **Run** button.

The query returns a single record containing the count and the average price.

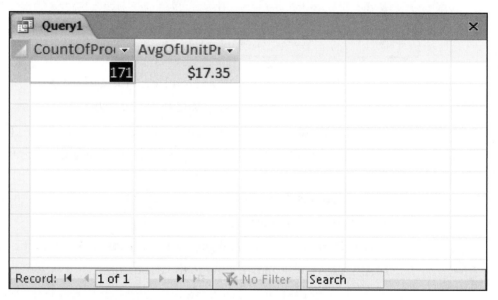

8. Switch back to Design view.

9. In the third column, in the **Field** cell, type UnitPrice*UnitsInStock, and press ⏎ Enter.

Access changes the expression you typed to

*Expr1: [UnitPrice]*[UnitsInStock]*

This expression will multiply the price of each product by the number of units in stock.

10. Select **Expr1** and type Value of Inventory to re-label the expression.

11. In the third column, click the **Total** arrow, and then in the list, click **Sum**.

Access will return the sum of all the values calculated by the expression.

12. On the **Design** tab, in the **Results group**, click the **Run** button.

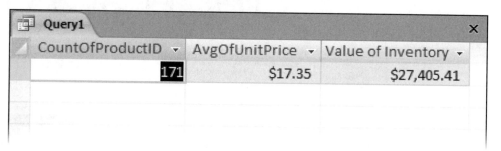

 **CLOSE** the query window without saving your changes, and then close the 07_Calculate database. If you are not continuing directly on to the next chapter, quit Access.

# Key Points

- Microsoft Office Access 2007 provides a variety of tools you can use to organize the display of information in a database and to locate specific items of information. These tools make it easy to search through and find information in your database, even as it grows in size and complexity.

- You can sort a table in either ascending or descending order, based on the values in any field (or combination of fields). In Access, numbers can be treated as text or numerals.

- You can filter a table so that information containing some combination of characters is displayed (or excluded from the display). You can apply simple filters while viewing information in a table or a form. These filters are applied to the contents of a selected field, but you can apply another filter to the results of the first one to further refine your search.

- The Filter By Form command filters a table or form based on the information in several fields.

- The Advanced Filter/Sort command searches a single table for records that meet multiple criteria or that require complex expressions as criteria.

- You can create queries to display specific fields from specific records from one or more tables, even designing the query to perform calculations for you. You can then save your queries for later use.

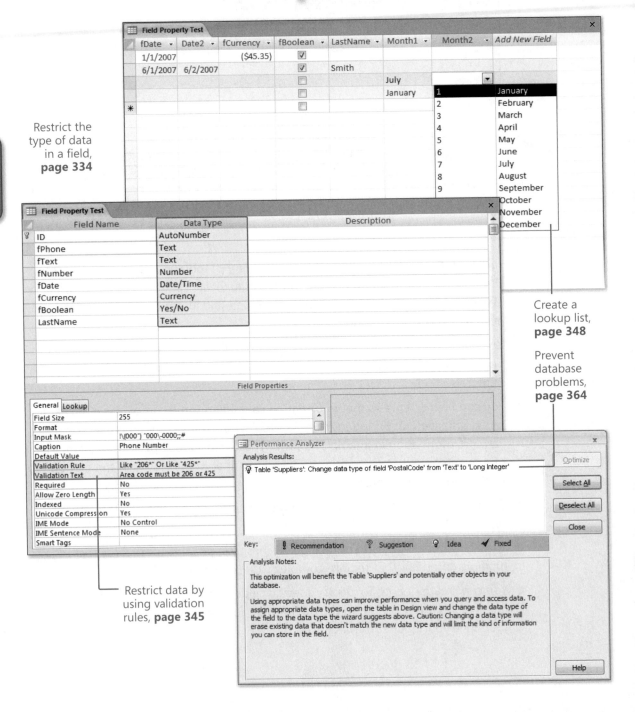

Restrict the type of data in a field, **page 334**

Create a lookup list, **page 348**

Prevent database problems, **page 364**

Restrict data by using validation rules, **page 345**

# 12 Keeping Your Information Accurate

---

**In this chapter, you will learn to:**

- ✔ Restrict the type and amount of data in a field.
- ✔ Specify the format of data in a field.
- ✔ Restrict data by using validation rules.
- ✔ Create a simple or multi-column lookup list.
- ✔ Update information in a table.
- ✔ Delete information from a table.
- ✔ Prevent database problems.

---

Depending on how much information you have and how organized you are, you might compare a database to an old shoebox or to a file cabinet, into which you toss items such as photographs, bills, receipts, and a variety of other paperwork for later retrieval. However, neither a shoebox nor a file cabinet restricts anything other than the physical size of what you can place in it or imposes any order on its content. It is up to you to decide what you store there and to organize it properly so that you can find it when you next need it.

When you create a database by using Microsoft Office Access 2007, you can set properties that restrict what can be entered and impose order on the database contents, thereby helping you to keep the database organized and useful. You would not, for example, want employees to enter text into a price field, or to enter a long text description in a field when a simple "yes" or "no" answer would work best.

To ensure the ongoing accuracy of a database, you can create and run *action queries* that quickly update information or delete selected records from a table. You could, for example, increase the price of all products in one category by a certain percentage, or remove all the elements of a specific product line. This type of updating is easy to do with an action query. Not only does using a query save time, but it helps to avoid errors.

In this chapter, you will restrict the type, amount, and format of data allowed in a field, and create a list from which a database user can choose a specific option. Then you will create and run an update query and a delete query.

**See Also** Do you need only a quick refresher on the topics in this chapter? See the Quick Reference entries at the beginning of this book.

**Important** Before you can use the practice files in this chapter, you need to install them from the book's companion CD to their default location. See "Using the Book's CD" at the beginning of this book for more information.

**Troubleshooting** Graphics and operating system–related instructions in this book reflect the Windows Vista user interface. If your computer is running Microsoft Windows XP and you experience trouble following the instructions as written, please refer to the "Information for Readers Running Windows XP" section at the beginning of this book.

# Restricting the Type of Data in a Field

The Data Type setting restricts entries in a field to a specific type of data, such as text, numbers, or dates. If, for example, the data type is set to Number and you attempt to enter text, Access refuses the entry and displays a warning.

The *field properties* you can set to control input are:

- Required
- Allow Zero Length
- Field Size
- Input Mask
- Validation Rule

The Required and Allow Zero Length properties are fairly obvious. If the Required property is set to *Yes*, the field can't be left blank. However, Access differentiates between a blank field (which it refers to as a Null field) and a field that looks blank, but contains an empty string. If Allow Zero Length is set to *Yes*, you can enter an *empty string* (two quotation marks with nothing in between), which looks like a blank field, but it is classified as empty rather than Null. This differentiation might seem silly, but if you are using programming code to work with an Access database, you will find that some commands produce different results for Null fields than they do for empty fields.

The Field Size, Input Mask, and Validation Rule properties are more complex, so the exercises in this chapter will focus on them.

> **Tip** Each field property has many options. For more information, search for *field property* in Access Help.

In this exercise, you will add fields of the most common data types to a table, and then use the Data Type setting and Field Size property to restrict the data that can be entered into the table.

> **USE** the *01_FieldTest* database. This practice file is located in the *Chapter12* subfolder under *SBS_Office2007.*
> **OPEN** the *01_FieldTest* database. Then display the Field Property Test table in Design view.

1. Click in the first available **Field Name** cell (below the automatically-generated ID field), type **fText,** and then press the [Tab] key to move to the **Data Type** cell.

   The data type defaults to **Text**.

2. In the second **Field Name** cell, type **fNumber,** and then press [Tab].

3. Click the **Data Type** arrow, and in the list, click **Number**.

   > **Tip** You can scroll the list to the data type you want by typing the first letter of its name in the cell.

4. Repeat Steps 2 and 3 to add the following fields:

| Field | Data type |
| --- | --- |
| fDate | Date/Time |
| fCurrency | Currency |
| fBoolean | Yes/No |

> **Tip** The data type referred to as *Yes/No* in Access is more commonly called *Boolean* (in honor of George Boole, an early mathematician and logistician). This data type can hold either of two mutually exclusive values, often expressed as *yes/no, 1/0, on/off,* or *true/false.*

**5.** Click the **fText** field name to select it.

Access displays the properties of the selected field in the lower portion of the dialog box.

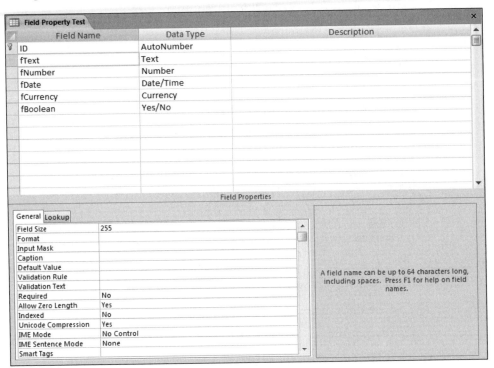

Save

Datasheet View

**6.** Repeat Step 5 to review the properties of each field, and then on the **Quick Access Toolbar**, click the **Save** button.

**7.** On the **View** toolbar, click the **Datasheet View** button.

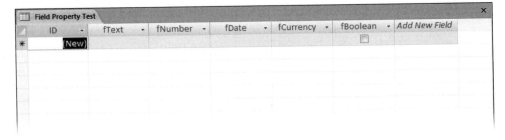

**8.** In the **fText** cell, type This entry is 32 characters long.

**9.** In the **fNumber** cell, type Five hundred.

The data type for this field is Number. Access does not accept your text entry, and displays a warning offering you several options.

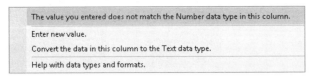

The value you entered does not match the Number data type in this column.

Enter new value.

Convert the data in this column to the Text data type.

Help with data types and formats.

**10.** In the **Microsoft Office Access** message box, click **Enter new value**. Then replace *Five Hundred* with 500.

**11.** In the **fDate** cell, type date, and then press Tab.

Access does not accept the unexpected data format.

**12.** In the **Microsoft Office Access** message box that appears, click **Enter new value**, type Jan 1, and then press Tab.

The fDate field accepts almost any entry that can be recognized as a date, and displays it in the default date format. Depending on the default format on your computer, Jan 1 might be displayed as *1/1/2007, 1/1/07*, or in some other format.

> **Tip** If you enter a month and day but no year in a date field, Access assumes the date is in the current year. If you enter a month, day, and two-digit year from 00 through 30, Access assumes the year is 2000 through 2030. If you enter a two-digit year that is greater than 30, Access assumes you mean 1931 through 1999.

**13.** In the **fCurrency** field, type the word currency, and then press Tab.

Access does not accept the unexpected data format.

**14.** In the **Microsoft Office Access** message box that appears, click **Enter new value**, type –45.3456, and then press Tab.

Access stores the number you entered but displays *($45.35)*, the default format for negative currency numbers.

> **Tip** Access uses the regional settings in the Windows Control Panel to determine the display format for date, time, currency, and other numbers. You can create custom formats to ensure that the correct currency symbol is always displayed with your values. Otherwise, the numbers won't change, but the currency symbol might, for instance from dollars to pounds, pesos, or euros.

**15.** In the **fBoolean** field, enter 123. Then click anywhere in the field to toggle the check box between **No** (not checked) and **Yes** (checked), finishing with the field in the checked state.

This field won't accept anything you type; you can switch only between two predefined values.

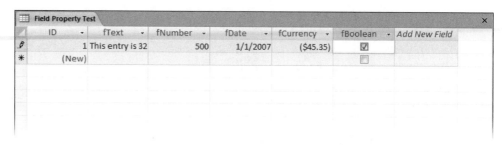

> **Tip** In Design view, you can open the Properties dialog box, and on the Lookup tab, set the Boolean field to display as a check box, text box, or combo box. You can set the Format property on the General tab to use True/False, Yes/No, or On/Off as the displayed values in this field (though the stored values will always be -1 and 0).

 **CLOSE** the table without saving your changes, and then close the *01_FieldTest* database.

# Restricting the Amount of Data in a Field

The Field Size property, which is valid for the Text, Number, and AutoNumber data types, restricts the number of characters that can be entered in a text field (from 0 to 255) and the number of digits that can be entered in a number or AutoNumber field. You can set number fields to any of the following values:

| Setting | Description |
| --- | --- |
| Byte | Stores whole numbers from 0 to 255 |
| Integer | Stores whole numbers from −32,768 to 32,767 |
| Long Integer | (The default.) Stores whole numbers from −2,147,483,648 to 2,147,483,647 |
| Single | Stores negative numbers from −3.402823E38 to −1.401298E−45 and positive numbers from 1.401298E−45 to 3.402823E38 |
| Double | Stores negative numbers from −1.79769313486231E308 to −4.94065645841247E−324 and positive numbers from 1.79769313486231E308 to 4.94065645841247E−324 |
| Decimal | Stores numbers from -10^28 -1 through 10^28 -1 |

AutoNumber fields are automatically set to Long Integer.

By setting the Field Size property to a value that allows the largest valid entry, you pre-vent the user from entering certain types of invalid information. If you try to type more characters in a text field than the number allowed by the Field Size setting, an audio alert sounds, and Access refuses to accept the entry. Likewise, Access rejects any value that is below or above the limits of a number field when you try to move out of the field.

In this exercise, you will change the Field Size property for several fields to see the impact this has on data already in the table and on new data that you enter.

**USE** the *02_Size* database. This practice file is located in the *Chapter12* subfolder under *SBS_Office2007*.

**OPEN** the *02_Size* database. Then open the Field Property Test table in Datasheet view.

1. Review the contents of the one record.

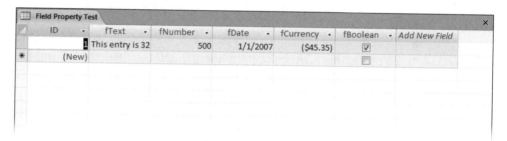

Design View

2. On the **View** toolbar, click the **Design View** button.

3. Click any cell in the **fText** row, and then in the **Field Properties** area, change the **Field Size** property from *255* to *12*.

4. Click any cell in the **fNumber** row, click the **Field Size** arrow, and then in the list, click **Byte**.

   Access restricts the number of characters that can be entered in the text field to 12, and the values that can be entered in the number field to the range from 0 to 255 (inclusive).

5. Switch to Datasheet view, clicking **Yes** when prompted to save the table.

   The table contains data that doesn't fit these new property settings, so Access displays a warning that some data might be lost.

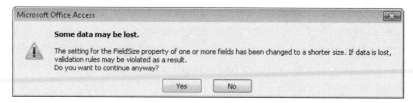

6. Click **Yes** to acknowledge the risk, and click **Yes** again to accept the deletion of the contents of one field.

fText now contains only 12 characters, rather than the 32 you entered. The other 20 characters have been permanently deleted. fNumber is empty because it is now limited to whole numbers from 0 through 255, and the value of 500 that you entered was deleted.

7. In the **fNumber** field, type 2.5, and then press the ⌷Enter⌷ key.

Access rounds the entered value to the nearest whole number.

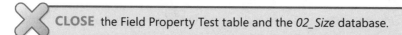

**CLOSE** the Field Property Test table and the *02_Size* database.

# Specifying the Format of Data in a Field

When you use *masks* in tables or forms, people entering information can see at a glance the format in which they should make entries and how long they should be. You can use the InputMask property to control how data is entered in text, number, date/time, and currency fields. This property has three sections, separated by semicolons, like the mask for a telephone number, shown here:

*!\(000") "000\-0000;1;#*

The first section contains characters that are used as placeholders for the information to be typed, as well as characters such as parentheses and hyphens. Together, all these characters control the appearance of the entry. The following table explains the purpose of the most common input mask characters:

| Character | Description |
| --- | --- |
| 0 | Required digit (0 through 9). |
| 9 | Optional digit or space. |
| # | Optional digit or space; blank positions are converted to spaces; plus and minus signs are allowed. |
| L | Required letter (A through Z). |
| ? | Optional letter (A through Z). |
| A | Required letter or digit. |
| a | Optional letter or digit. |
| & | Required character (any kind) or a space. |
| C | Optional character (any kind) or a space. |
| < | All characters that follow are converted to lowercase. |
| > | All characters that follow are converted to uppercase. |
| ! | Characters typed into the mask fill it from left to right. You can include the exclamation point anywhere in the input mask. |
| \ | Character that follows is displayed as a literal character. |
| "any text" | Access treats the string enclosed in double quotation marks as a literal string. |
| Password | Creates a password entry box. Any character typed in the box is stored as the character but displayed as an asterisk (*). |

Any characters not included in this list are displayed as literal characters. If you want to use one of the special characters in this list as a literal character, precede it with the \ (backslash) character.

The second and third sections of the input mask are optional. Including a 1 in the second section or leaving it blank tells Access to store only the characters entered; including a 0 tells it to store both the characters entered and the mask characters. Entering a character in the third section causes Access to display that character as a placeholder for each of the characters to be typed; leaving it blank displays an underscore as the placeholder.

The input mask *!\(000") "000\-0000;1;#* creates this display in a field in either a table or a form:

*(###) ###-####*

In this example, you are restricting the entry to ten digits—no more and no less. The database user does not enter the parentheses, space, or dash, nor does Access store those characters (although you could display them in your table, form, or report if you set the correct format property). Access stores only the ten digits.

In this exercise, you will use the Input Mask wizard to apply a predefined telephone number input mask to a text field, forcing entered numbers into the (XXX) XXX-XXXX format. You will then create a custom mask to force the first letter entered in another text field to be uppercase (a capital letter).

> **USE** the *03_Accurate* database. This practice file is located in the *Chapter12* subfolder under *SBS_Office2007*.
>
> **OPEN** the *03_Accurate* database. Then display the Field Property Test table in Design view.

1. In the first blank **Field Name** cell, type **fPhone**, and leave the data type set to *Text*.

2. Click the row selector to select the row, and then drag the selected field up to place it just below the ID field.

3. Save the table design, and with **fPhone** still selected, click **Input Mask** in the **Field Properties** area.

Ellipsis button

4. Click the **ellipsis** button to the right of the cell to start the **Input Mask** wizard and display the first page of the wizard. (If you are prompted to install this feature, click **Yes**.)

5. With **Phone Number** selected in the **Input Mask** list, click **Next**.

The second page of the wizard displays the input mask and gives you the opportunity to change the placeholder character that will indicate what to type. The exclamation point causes Access to fill the mask from left to right with whatever is typed. The parentheses and hyphen are characters that Access will insert in the specified places. The nines represent optional digits, and the zeros represent required digits. This allows you to enter a telephone number either with or without an area code.

> **Tip** Because Access fills the mask from left to right, you would have to press the Right Arrow key to move the insertion point past the first three placeholders to enter a telephone number without an area code.

**6.** Change *999* to *000* to require an area code, and then change the placeholder character to *#*.

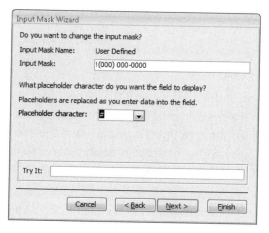

**7.** Click **Next**.

On the third page of the wizard, you specify whether you want to store the symbols with the data. If you store the symbols, the data will always be displayed in tables, forms, and reports in this format. However, the symbols take up space, meaning that your database will be larger.

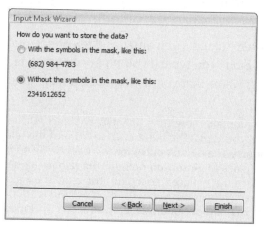

8. Accept the default selection—to store data without the symbols—by clicking **Finish**. Access closes the wizard and displays the edited mask as the Input Mask property.

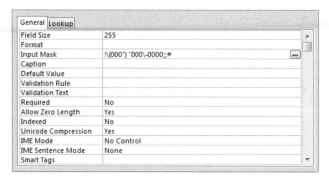

9. Press ⌊Enter⌋ to accept the mask.

   Access changes the format of the mask to *!\(000") "000\-0000;;#*. Notice the two semicolons that separate the mask into its three sections. Because you told Access to store data without the symbols, nothing is displayed in the second section of the mask. Notice also that Access added double quotation marks to ensure that the closing parenthesis and following space are treated as literals.

   > **Tip**  When you press Enter, a button appears in front of the Input Mask. This is the Property Update Options button, and if you click it, a list of options is displayed. In this case, the only options are to apply the input mask everywhere fPhone is used, and to provide help. This button disappears when you edit any other property or change to a different field.

10. Save your changes, and then switch to Datasheet view.

11. Press the ⌊↓⌋ key to move to the new record, then press the ⌊Tab⌋ key to move to the **fPhone** field. Type a series of numbers and letters to see how the mask works.

    Access formats the first ten numbers you enter as a telephone number, ignoring any letters or additional digits you type. If you type fewer than ten digits and then press Tab or Enter, Access warns that your entry doesn't match the input mask.

    > **Tip**  An input mask can contain more than only placeholders for the data to be entered. If, for example, you type "The number is" in front of the telephone number in the Input Mask property, the default entry for the field is *The number is (###) ###-####*. Then if you place the insertion point at the beginning of the field, the numbers you type replace the # placeholders, not the text. The Field Size setting is not applied to the characters in the mask, so if this setting is *15*, the entry is not truncated even though the number of displayed characters (including spaces) is 28.

12. Switch to Design view, and add a new field below **fBoolean**. Name it LastName. Leave the **Data Type** setting as the default, **Text**.

13. Select the new field, click **Input Mask**, type >L<?????????????????? (18 question marks), and press [Enter].

    The greater than symbol (>) forces all following text to be uppercase. The *L* requires a letter. The less than symbol ()< forces all following text to be lower-case. Each question mark allows any letter or no letter, and there is one fewer question mark than the maximum number of letters you want to allow in the field (19, including the leading capital letter). The Field Size setting must be greater than this maximum.

14. Save your changes, return to Datasheet view, type smith in the **LastName** field of one of the records, and press [Tab]. Try entering SMITH, and then McDonald.

    Regardless of how you type the name, only its the first letter appears in the record capitalized, This type of mask has its limitations, but it can be useful in many situations.

 **CLOSE** the Field Property Test table and the *03_Accurate* database.

> **Tip** You can create an input mask manually for text, number, date, or currency fields, or you can apply one of several standard masks for text and date fields by using the Input Mask wizard.

# Restricting Data by Using Validation Rules

A *validation rule* is an expression that can precisely define the information that will be accepted in one or several fields in a record. You might use a validation rule in a field containing the date an employee was hired to prevent a date in the future from being entered. Or if you make deliveries to only certain local areas, you could use a validation rule on the phone field or ZIP code field to refuse entries from other areas.

You can type validation rules in by hand, or you can use the *Expression Builder* to create them. At the field level, Access uses the rule to test an entry when you attempt to leave the field. At the table level, Access uses the rule to test the content of several fields when you attempt to leave the record. If an entry doesn't satisfy the rule, Access rejects the entry and displays a message explaining why.

In this exercise, you will create and test several field validation rules and one table validation rule.

**USE** the *04_Validate* database. This practice file is located in the *Chapter12* subfolder under *SBS_Office2007*.

**OPEN** the *04_Validate* database. Then display the Field Property Test table in Design view.

1. Select **fPhone**, and then click in the **Validation Rule** box.

   An ellipsis button appears at the end of the Validation Rule box. You can click this button to use the Expression Builder to create an expression, or you can type an expression in the box.

2. Type Like "206*" Or Like "425*" in the **Validation Rule** box, and press Enter.

   > **Troubleshooting** Be sure to include the asterisk after the 206 and 425.

3. In the **Validation Text** box, type Area code must be 206 or 425.

   A rule is set for the first three digits typed in the fPhone field including the text that Access should display if someone attempts to enter an invalid phone number.

4. In the **Caption** box, type Phone Number.

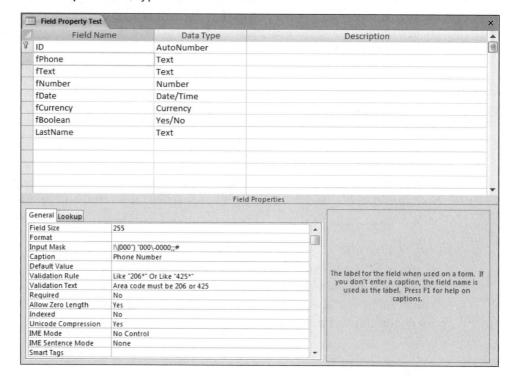

5. Save the table.

   Access warns that data integrity rules have changed. The table violates the new rule because it contains blank phone number fields.

6. Click **No** to close the message box without testing the data.

   > **Tip**  When displaying tables as overlapping windows (rather than tabbed documents), you can test the validation rules in a table at any time by right-clicking the title bar of the table in Design view and then clicking Test Validation Rules.

7. Return to Datasheet view, where the caption for the first field is now *Phone Number.*

8. Place the insertion point to the left of the first # of any **Phone Number** field, type 3605550109, and then press Enter.

   > **Tip**  To select the entire field, move the pointer to the left end of the Phone Number field, and when the pointer changes to a thick cross, click the field. The insertion point is then at the start of the area code when you begin typing.

   The Validation Rule setting causes Access to display an alert box, warning you that the area code must be either 206 or 425.

9. Click **OK** to close the alert box, type a new phone number with one of the allowed area codes, and press Enter.

10. Return to Design view, and add another date field. Type Date2 as the field name, set the data type to **Date/Time**, and drag the new field to just below **fDate**.

11. Right-click in the table window, and then click **Properties**.

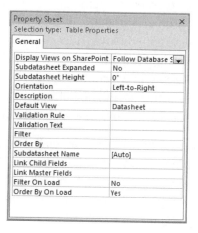

> **Tip** The purpose of this Property Sheet is to set properties that apply to more than one field in the table, as opposed to setting properties for a single field in the Field Properties area.

12. Click in the **Validation Rule** box, type [Date2]>[fDate], and press `Enter`.

13. In the **Validation Text** box, type Date2 must be later than fDate, and then close the sheet.

    A table validation rule is added that ensures that the second date is always later than the first one.

14. Save the table (click **No** to close the data-integrity alert box), and return to Datasheet view.

15. In any record, type 6/1/07 in **fDate** and 5/1/07 in **Date2**, and then click in another record.

    Access displays the Validation Text setting from the Table Properties dialog box, reminding you that Date2 must be later than fDate.

16. Click **OK**, change **Date2** to 6/2/2007, and then click in another record.

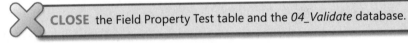

CLOSE the Field Property Test table and the *04_Validate* database.

# Creating a Simple Lookup List

It is interesting how many different ways people can come up with to enter the same items of information in a database. Asked to enter the name of their home state, for example, residents of the state of Washington will type *Washington*, *Wash*, or *WA*, plus various typographical errors and misspellings. If you ask a dozen sales clerks to enter the name of a specific product, customer, and shipper in an invoice, it is unlikely that all of them will type the same thing. In cases like this, in which the number of correct choices is limited (to actual product name, actual customer, and actual shipper), providing the option to choose the correct answer from a list will improve your database's consistency.

Minor inconsistencies in the way data is entered might not be really important to someone who later reads the information and makes decisions. For example, *Arizona* and *AZ* refer to the same state. But a computer is very literal, and if you tell it to create a list so that you can send catalogs to everyone living in *AZ*, the computer won't include anyone whose state is listed in the database as *Arizona*.

You can limit the options for entering information in a database in several ways:

- For only two options, you can use a Boolean field represented by a check box. A check in the box indicates one choice, and no check indicates the other choice.

- For several mutually exclusive options on a form, you can use option buttons to gather the required information.

- For more than a few options, a *combo box* is a good way to go. When you click the arrow at the right end of a combo box, a list of choices is displayed. Depending on the properties associated with the combo box, if you don't see the option you want, you might be able to type something else, adding your entry to the list of possible options displayed in the future.

- For a short list of choices that won't change often, you can have the combo box look up the options in a list that you provide. Although you can create a lookup list by hand, it is a lot easier to use the *Lookup wizard*.

In this exercise, you will use the Lookup wizard to create a list of months from which the user can choose.

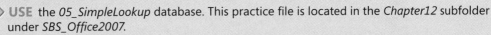

**USE** the *05_SimpleLookup* database. This practice file is located in the *Chapter12* subfolder under *SBS_Office2007*.

**OPEN** the *05_SimpleLookup* database. Then display the Field Property Test table in Design view.

1. Add a new field below **LastName**. Name it Month1, and set the data type to **Lookup Wizard**.

   The Lookup wizard starts.

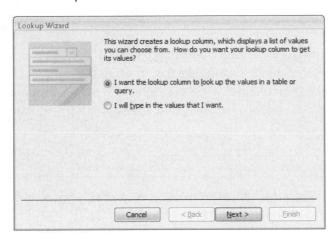

You can use the Lookup wizard to create a combo box that provides the entry for a text field. The combo box list can come from a table or query, or you can type the list in the wizard.

> **Tip** If a field has a lot of potential entries, or if they will change often, you can link them to a table. (You might have to create a table expressly for this purpose.) If a field has only a few possible entries that won't change, typing the list in the wizard is easier.

2. Select the **I will type in the values that I want** option, and then click **Next**.

3. Leave the number of columns set to *1*, and click in the **Col1** box.

4. Enter the 12 months of the year (January, February, and so on), pressing [Tab] after each one to move to a new row.

5. Click **Next**, and then click **Finish**.

6. In the **Field Properties** area, click the **Lookup** tab to view the Lookup information for the Month1 field.

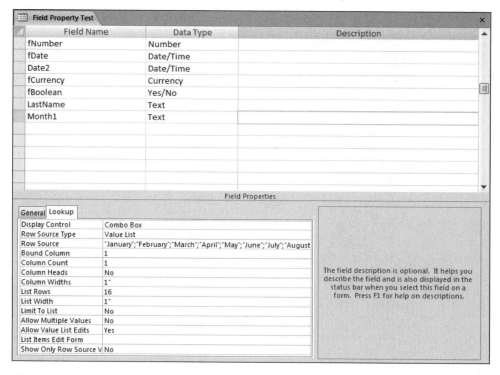

The wizard entered this information, but you can easily figure out what you would have to enter to create a lookup list by hand.

7. Switch to Datasheet view, clicking **Yes** to save your changes.

8. Double-click the vertical bars between the column headers to adjust the column widths so that you can see all the fields.

> **Tip** You can manually resize columns by dragging the vertical bars between the column headers.

9. Click in the **Month1** field of a record, and then click the arrow that appears to display the list of options.

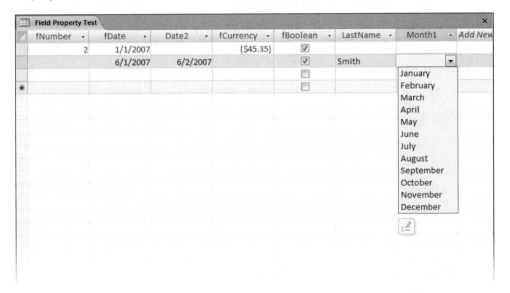

Notice the button below the Month1 options list. Clicking this button opens the Edit List Items dialog box. This feature is new with Access 2007. The database user can open the editor by clicking the button, or by entering text that is not in the list and answering Yes when asked whether she or he wants to edit the list. If you don't want users to be able to edit the list, you can disable this property, as we do later in this exercise.

10. If you opened it, close the **Edit List Items** dialog box and then click **February** to enter it in the field.

11. Click in the next **Month1** field, type Jan, and press Enter .

As soon as you type the *J*, the combo box displays *January*. If you had typed *Ju*, the combo box would have displayed *June*.

12. In the next **Month1** field, type jly, and press Enter .

    Even though the entry isn't in the list, it is accepted just as you typed it. Although there might be times when you want to allow the entry of information other than the items in the list, this isn't one of those times, so you need to change the field properties to limit what can be entered.

13. Return to Design view.

    The Limit To List property on the Lookup tab for Month1 is currently set to *No*, which allows people to enter information that isn't in the list.

14. Change **Limit To List** to **Yes**.

15. Change **Allow Value List Edits** to **No**.

16. Save the table, return to Datasheet view, type jly in a new **Month1** field, and then press Enter .

    Access informs you that the text you entered is not in the list, and refuses the entry.

17. In the **Microsoft Office Access** message box, click **OK**.

18. In the **Month1** list, click **July**.

    The month of July is displayed in the field.

**CLOSE** the *05_SimpleLookup* database, saving your changes.

# Creating a Multi-Column Lookup List

Selecting a month from a list of names is convenient for people, but if your computer has to deal with this information in some mathematical way, a list of the numbers associated with each month is easier for it to use.

In this exercise, you will use the Lookup wizard to create a two-column list of months from which the user can choose.

**USE** the *06_MulticolumnLookup* database. This practice file is located in the *Chapter12* subfolder under *SBS_Office2007*.

**OPEN** the *06_MulticolumnLookup* database. Then display the Field Property Test table in Design view.

1. Add a new field below **Month1**. Name it Month2, and set the data type to **Lookup Wizard**.

2. Select the **I will type in the values that I want** option, and then click **Next**.

3. Type 2 to add a second column, and then click in the **Col1** cell.

   Access adds a second column, labeled *Col2*.

4. Enter the following numbers and months in the two columns:

| Number | Month |
|--------|-------|
| 1 | January |
| 2 | February |
| 3 | March |
| 4 | April |
| 5 | May |
| 6 | June |
| 7 | July |
| 8 | August |
| 9 | September |
| 10 | October |
| 11 | November |
| 12 | December |

   It is not necessary to adjust the width of the columns in the Lookup wizard other than to make them visible within the wizard itself.

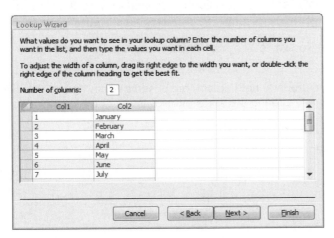

5. Click **Next**, and then click **Finish**.

6. In the **Field Properties** area, click the **Lookup** tab to view the Lookup information for the Month2 field.

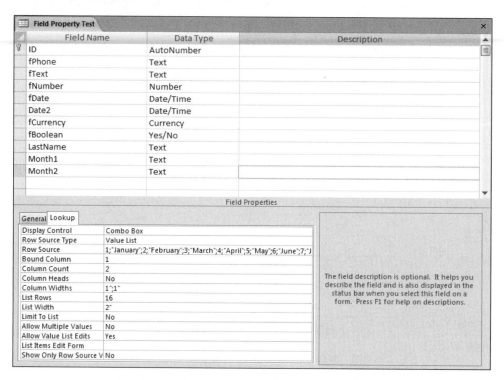

The wizard has inserted your column information into the Row Source box and set the other properties according to your specifications.

7. Change **Limit To List** to **Yes** and **Allow Value List Edits** to **No**.

> **Tip** When a property has two or more possible values, you can quickly cycle through them by double-clicking the value, rather than clicking the arrow to open the list.

8. Save your changes, switch to Datasheet view, and then click the arrow in a **Month2** field to display the list of options.

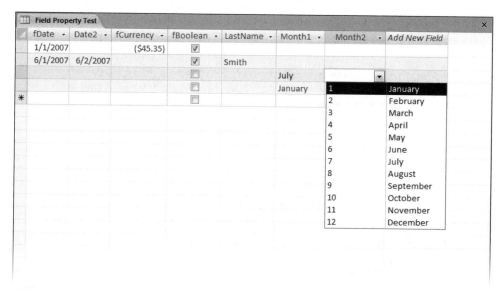

9. In the **Month2** list, click **January**.

Access displays the number *1* in the field, which is useful for the computer. However, people might be confused by the two columns and by seeing something other than what they clicked or typed.

10. Switch back to Design view, and in the **Column Widths** box—which appears as *1";1"*—change the width for the first column to *0* (you don't have to type the symbol for inches) to prevent it from being displayed.

11. Save your changes, return to Datasheet view, and as a test, in the remaining records set **Month2** to **February** in two records and to **March** in one record.

Only the name of the month is now displayed in the list, and when you click a month, that name is displayed in the field. However, Access actually stores the associated number from the list's first column.

12. Right-click any cell in the **Month2** column, point to **Text Filters**, and then click **Equals**.

13. In the **Custom Filter** box, type 2, and then press Enter .

Access now displays only the two records with February in the Month2 field.

14. Click the **Toggle Filter** button, and then repeat Steps 12 and 13, this time typing 3

 Toggle Filter    in the box to display the one record with March in the **Month2** field.

> **CLOSE** the *06_MulticolumnLookup* database, saving your changes.

# Updating Information in a Table

As you use a database and as it grows, you might discover that errors creep in or that some information becomes out of date. You can tediously scroll through the records looking for those that need to be changed, but it is more efficient to use a few of the tools and techniques provided by Access for that purpose.

If you want to find or replace multiple instances of the same word or phrase, you can use the Find and Replace commands on the Edit menu. This command works much like the same commands in Microsoft Office Word or Microsoft Office Excel.

If you want to change information stored in the database only under certain circumstances, you need the power of an *update query*, which is a select query that performs an action on the query's results.

> **Tip** Running an update query makes irreversible changes to the table; therefore, you should always create a backup copy of the table before running a query.
>
> You can quickly create a copy of a table by displaying the Tables list in the Navigation Pane, clicking the table you want to copy pressing Ctrl+C, and then pressing Ctrl+V to paste a copy. In the Paste Table As dialog box, type a name for the new table, and then click OK.

In this exercise, you will create an update query to increase the price of selected items by 10 percent.

> **USE** the *07_Update* database. This practice file is located in the *Chapter12* subfolder under *SBS_Office2007*.
>
> **OPEN** the *07_Update* database.

Query
Wizard

1. On the **Create** tab, in the **Other** group, click the **Query Wizard** button.

2. In the **New Query** dialog box, with **Simple Query Wizard** selected, click **OK**.

3. In the **Tables/Queries** list, click **Table: Categories**.

4. In the **Available Fields** list, double-click **CategoryName** to move it to the **Selected Fields** list.

5. In the **Tables/Queries** list, click **Table: Products**.

6. In the **Available Fields** list, double-click **ProductName** and **UnitPrice** to move them to the **Selected Fields** list.

7. In the **Simple Query Wizard** dialog box, click **Finish** to create the query using the default detail setting and title.

   Access displays the query results in a datasheet. Only the Category Name, Product Name, and Unit Price fields are displayed.

| Category Nam ▾ | Product Name ▾ | Unit Price ▾ |
|---|---|---|
| Bulbs | Magic Lily | $40.00 |
| Bulbs | Autumn crocus | $18.75 |
| Bulbs | Anemone | $28.00 |
| Bulbs | Lily-of-the-Field | $38.00 |
| Bulbs | Siberian Iris | $12.95 |
| Bulbs | Daffodil | $12.95 |
| Bulbs | Peony | $19.95 |
| Bulbs | Lilies | $10.50 |
| Bulbs | Begonias | $18.95 |
| Bulbs | Bulb planter | $6.95 |
| Cacti | Prickly Pear | •$3.00 |
| Ground covers | Crown Vetch | $12.95 |
| Ground covers | English Ivy | $5.95 |
| Ground covers | European Ginger | $6.25 |
| Ground covers | St. John's Wort | $9.75 |
| Ground covers | Fairies Fern | $9.95 |
| Grasses | The Best Bluegrass | $17.95 |
| Grasses | Decorator moss | $15.45 |
| Grasses | Colonial Bentgrass | $15.50 |
| Grasses | Creeping Bentgrass | $12.05 |
| Grasses | Red Fescue | $20.00 |
| Grasses | Perennial Ryegrass | $19.95 |
| Grasses | Redtop | $21.50 |
| Flowers | Lily-of-the-Valley | $33.00 |

Record: ◄ ◄ 1 of 189 ► ►► ► No Filter   Search

**8.** Display the query in Design view.

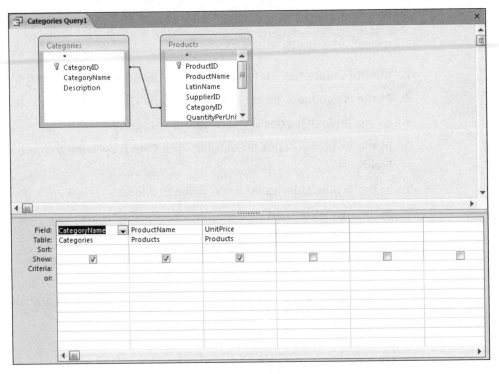

The current query results include the products in all categories. You want to raise the prices of only the products in the *bulbs* and *cacti* categories, so your next task is to change the query to select only those categories.

**9.** In the **Criteria** row, under **CategoryName**, type bulbs. Then in the **or** row, type cacti.

Run

**10.** Click the **Run** button to run the query to confirm that only bulbs and cacti are listed, and then return to Design view.

The query now selects only the records you want to change. But to actually make a change to the records, you have to use an update query.

> **Tip** You can't create an action query directly; you must first create a select query and then change the query to one of the action types. With an existing select query open in Design view, you can find the command to convert it to an action query in the Query Type group and on the shortcut menu that appears when you right-click the query window and then point to Query Type.

Update

11. Display the query in Design view. On the **Design** contextual tab, in the **Query Type** group, click the **Update** button.

Access converts the select query to an update query. In the design grid, the Sort and Show rows disappear and an Update To row appears.

12. In the **Update To** row, under **UnitPrice**, type [UnitPrice]*1.1.

> **Tip** Enclosing UnitPrice in brackets indicates that it is an Access object. If you use the Expression Builder to insert this expression, it looks like this: *[Products]![UnitPrice]*1.1*. Because this description of the field includes the table in which it is found, you can also insert this expression in other tables.

13. Display the query in Datasheet view.

In a select query, clicking the View button is the same as clicking the Run button. But in an update query, clicking the View button simply displays a list of the fields that will be updated. In this case, you see a list of unit prices that matches the ones shown earlier in the select query.

14. Switch to Design view. Then on the Query Tools **Design** contextual tab, in the **Results** group, click the **Run** button.

Access displays a warning that you can't undo the changes you are about to make, and asks you to confirm that you want to update the records.

View

15. In the **Microsoft Office Access** message box, click **Yes**. Then click the **View Datasheet** button to display the **UnitPrice** field, where all the prices have been increased by 10 percent.

16. Save and close the query.

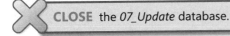
**CLOSE** the *07_Update* database.

# Deleting Information from a Table

Over time, some of the information stored in a database might become obsolete. The Products table in our sample database, for example, lists all the products the company currently offers for sale or has sold in the past. You can indicate that a product is no longer available for sale by placing a check mark in the Discontinued field. Discontinued products aren't displayed in the catalog or offered for sale, but they are kept in the database for a while in case it becomes practical to sell them again. A similar situation could exist with customers who haven't placed an order in a long time or who have asked to be removed from a mailing list but might still place orders.

To maintain an efficient database, it is a good idea to clean house and discard outdated records from time to time. You could scroll through the tables and delete records manually, but if all the records you want to delete match some pattern, you can use a delete query to quickly get rid of all of them.

> **Important** Keep in mind several things when deleting records from a database. First, you can't recover deleted records. Second, the effects of a delete query can be more far-reaching than you intend. If the table from which you are deleting records is linked to another table, and the Cascade Delete Related Records option for that relationship is selected, records in the second table will also be deleted. Sometimes this is what you want, but sometimes it isn't. For example, you probably don't want to delete records of previous sales at the same time you delete discontinued products.
>
> To safeguard against these problems, it is a good idea to back up your database before deleting the records, or to create a new table (perhaps named *Deleted<file name>*), and then move the records you want to delete to the new table, where you can review them before deleting them permanently.

In this exercise, you will create a delete query to remove all discontinued products from a database table.

 **USE** the *08_Delete* database. This practice file is located in the *Chapter12* subfolder under *SBS_Office2007*.

**OPEN** the *08_Delete* database.

Query
Design

1. On the **Create** tab, in the **Other** group, click the **Query Design** button.

   Access opens a new query object and the Show Table dialog box.

2. In the **Show Table** dialog box, double-click **Products** to add that table to the query window list area, and then click **Close**.

3. In the **Products** field list, double-click the asterisk to copy all the fields in the table to the query.

   *Products.** appears in the Field row of the first column of the design grid, and *Products* appears in the Table row.

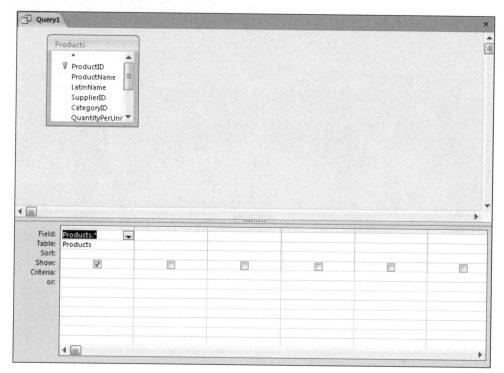

> **Important**  Double-clicking the asterisk in the field list is a quick way to move all the fields in a table to the query, without having each field appear in its own column. However, selecting multiple fields in this way prevents you from setting Sort, Show, and Criteria values for individual fields. To set these values, you have to add the specific fields to the design grid, thereby adding them twice. To avoid displaying the fields twice, clear the check mark in the Show row of the duplicate individual fields.

4. In the **Products** field list, double-click **Discontinued** to copy it to the next available column in the design grid.

Delete

5. In the **Query Type** group, click the **Delete** button to convert this select query to a delete query.

A Delete row appears in the design grid, and the Sort and Show rows disappear.

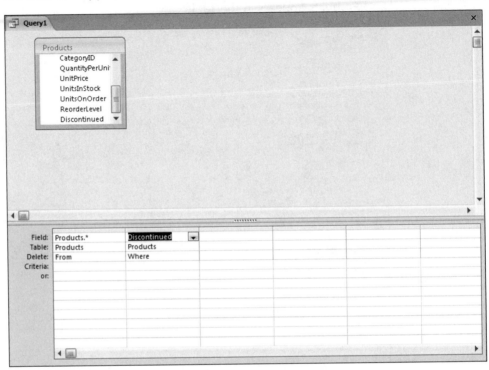

In the first column, which contains the reference to all fields in the Products table, the Delete row contains the word *From*, indicating that this is the table from which records will be deleted. When you add individual fields to the remaining columns, as you did with the Discontinued field, the Delete row displays *Where*, indicating that this field can include deletion criteria.

6. In the **Criteria** row, under **Discontinued**, type Yes.

The Discontinued field is set to the Boolean data type, which is represented in the datasheet as a check box that is selected to indicate Yes and cleared to indicate No. To locate all discontinued products, you need to identify records with the Discontinued field set to Yes.

7. To check the accuracy of the query, switch to Database view.

Testing the query results in a list of 18 discontinued products that would be deleted if you ran the query. Scroll to the right to verify that all records display a check mark in the Products.Discontinued field.

Run

8. Switch to Design view. Then on the **Design** contextual tab, in the **Results** group, click the **Run** button to run the delete query.

Access displays a warning to remind you of the permanence of this action.

> **Tip** Before actually deleting records, you might want to display the Relationships window by clicking the Relationships button in the Show/Hide Group on the Database Tools tab. If the table you are deleting data from has a relationship with any table containing information that shouldn't be deleted, right-click the relationship line, click Edit Relationship, and make sure that the Enforce Referential Integrity check box is selected and the Cascade Delete Related Records check box is *not* selected.

9. In the **Microsoft Office Access** message box, click **Yes** to delete the records.

10. Switch to Datasheet view and verify that all the records were deleted.

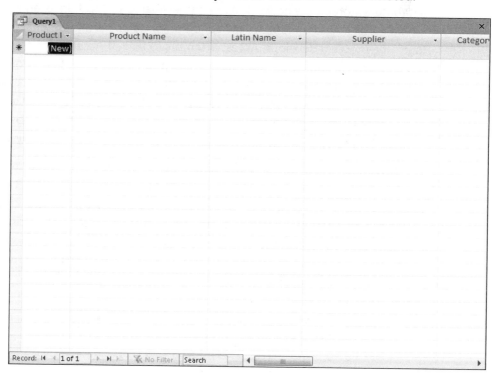

**11.** If you think you might run the same delete query in the future, save and name the query.

> **Tip** If you are concerned that someone might accidentally run a delete query and destroy records you weren't ready to destroy, change the query back to a select query before saving it. You can then open the select query in Design view and change it to a delete query the next time you want to run it.

 **CLOSE** the query and the *08_Delete* database.

# Preventing Database Problems

In the day-to-day use of an Access database—adding and deleting records, modifying forms and reports, and so on—various problems can develop. This is especially true if the database is stored on a network share, rather than on a local drive, and is accessed by multiple users. Access monitors the condition of database files as you open and work with them. If a problem develops, Access attempts to fix it. If Access can't fix the problem, it usually provides additional information that might help you to find a solution. But Access doesn't always spot problems before they affect the database; if this happens, you might notice that the database performance seems to slow down or become erratic. Even if no actual errors occur, normal database use causes the internal structure of a database to become fragmented, resulting in a bloated file and inefficient use of disk space.

You don't have to wait for Access to spot a problem. There are various things you can do to help keep your database healthy and running smoothly. Your first line of defense against damage or corruption in any kind of file is the maintenance of backups. Database files rapidly become too large to conveniently back up onto a floppy disk, but you have many other options: you can copy the file to another computer on the network or to removable media such as a USB flash drive, send it as an e-mail attachment to another location, create a tape backup, or burn a CD-ROM.

> **Tip** To back up a database in Access 2007, click the Microsoft Office Button, point to Manage, and then click Back Up Database.

You can use the following Access utilities to keep your database running smoothly:

- **Compact and Repair Database.** This utility first optimizes performance by re-arranging how the file is stored on your hard disk, and then attempts to repair corruption in tables, forms, reports, and modules.

- **Performance Analyzer.** This utility analyzes the objects in your database and offers three types of feedback: ideas, suggestions, and recommendations. You can instruct Access to optimize the file by following through on any of the suggestions or recommendations.

- **Database Documenter.** This tool produces a detailed report containing enough information to rebuild the database structure if that were ever necessary.

- **Analyze Table.** This wizard tests database tables for compliance with standard database design principles, suggests solutions to problems, and implements those solutions at your request.

- **Microsoft Office Diagnostics.** This command attempts to diagnose and repair problems with your Microsoft Office programs.

> **Important**  Take care when running the Microsoft Office Diagnostics utility, because it might change files and registry settings that affect all Office programs.

In this exercise, you will back up a database and then run the Compact And Repair Database, Performance Analyzer, and Database Documenter utilities.

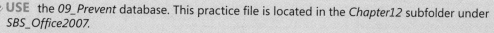

**USE** the *09_Prevent* database. This practice file is located in the *Chapter12* subfolder under *SBS_Office2007*.

**OPEN** the *09_Prevent* database. Do not display any of the database tables.

1. Click the **Microsoft Office Button**, point to **Manage**, and then click **Back Up Database**.

2. In the **Save As** dialog box, navigate to your *Documents\MSP\SBS_Office2007\ Chapter12* folder, and then click **Save**.

> **Tip** When you back up a database, Access appends the current date to the database file name in the following format: 09_Prevent_*2007-04-22.accdb*. You can change the file name to suit your needs.

Access creates a compacted copy of the database in the specified folder.

3. Click the **Microsoft Office Button**, point to **Manage**, and then click **Database Properties**.

The Database Properties dialog box opens, displaying information about your database on five tabs.

4. On the **General** tab, note the size of the database. Then click **OK** to close the dialog box.

5. Click the **Microsoft Office Button**, point to **Manage**, and then click **Compact and Repair Database**. Acknowledge the safety warning if prompted to do so.

The utility takes only a few seconds to run, and you will see no difference in the appearance of the database.

> **Troubleshooting** If you don't have enough space on your hard disk to store a temporary copy of the database, you don't have appropriate permissions, or another user also has the database open, the Compact And Repair Database function will not run.

6. Repeat Steps 3 and 4 to display the database size, and compare it to the original database size.

You can expect a 10 to 25 percent reduction in the size of the database if you have been using it for a while.

> **Tip** It is a good idea to compact and repair a database often. You can have Access do this automatically each time the database is closed. To do so, click the Microsoft Office Button, click the Access Options button, and then on the Current Database page, select the Compact On Close check box, and click OK.

7. On the **Database Tools** tab, in the **Analyze** group, click the **Analyze Performance** button.

The Performance Analyzer dialog box opens.

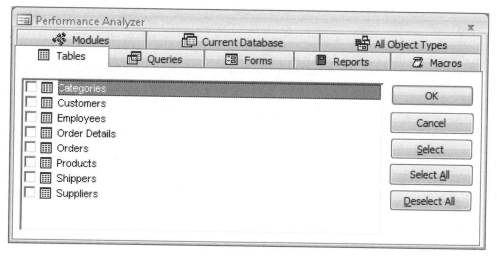

This dialog box contains a tab for each type of object the utility can analyze, and a tab displaying all the existing database objects.

8. On the **All Object Types** tab, click **Select All**, and then click **OK** to start the analyzer.

When it finishes, the Performance Analyzer displays its results. (The results you see might be different from those shown here.)

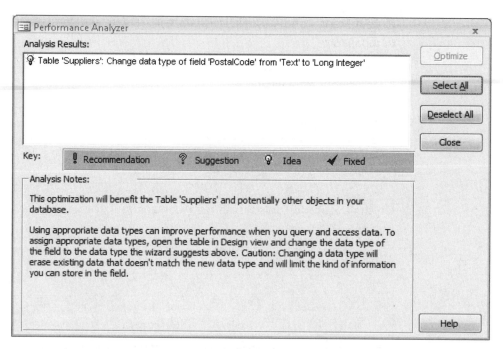

The icons in the left column of the Analysis Results list indicate the category of each entry: *Recommendation, Suggestion,* and *Idea.* (After you perform any of the optimizations, *Fixed* entries will also appear in the list.) Clicking an entry displays information about it in the Analysis Notes section.

9. Scroll through the list, clicking each entry in turn, and read all the analysis notes.

   Most of the suggestions are valid, though some, such as the one to change the data type of the PostalCode field to Long Integer, are not appropriate for this database.

10. Close the **Performance Analyzer** dialog box.

11. On the **Database Tools** tab, in the **Analyze** group, click the **Database Documenter** button.

   The Documenter dialog box opens. This dialog box is identical to the Performance Analyzer database. It contains a tab for each type of object the utility can document, and a tab displaying all the existing database objects.

**12.** On the **Tables** tab, click the **Options** button.

The Print Table Definition dialog box opens.

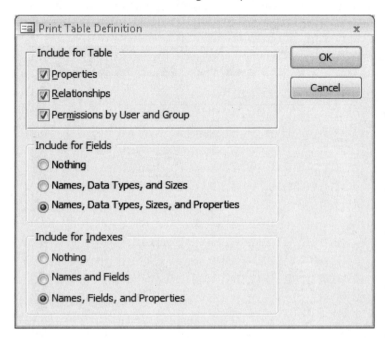

The dialog box offers print options associated with the objects on the selected dialog box tab. The options differ for each tab, but all are similar to these, in that you can use them to specify the documentation to include for each type of object.

**13.** In the **Print Table Definition** dialog box, click **Cancel**.

**14.** On the **All Object Types** tab, click **Select All**, and then click **OK** to start the documentation process.

> **Tip**  You can't save the report generated by the Documenter utility, but you can export it as a Word RTF file, Access database, text file, XML file, or HTML document. To do so, right-click the report, point to Export, and then click the format you want.

When the process finishes, Access displays a report in Print Preview. This report can run to hundreds of pages, so you probably don't want to print it. However, it is a good idea to create and save a report such as this for your own databases, in case you ever need to reconstruct them.

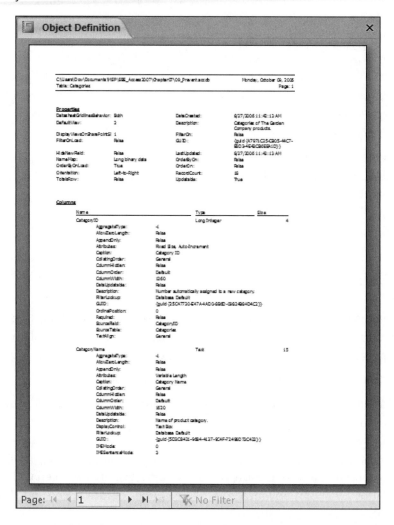

**CLOSE** the Object Definition report and the *09_Prevent* database. If you are not continuing directly on to the next chapter, quit Access.

# Key Points

- You can set properties that restrict the type and amount of data that can be entered into an Access database.

- You can replace specific words or phrases by using the Replace command, or quickly enact conditional changes by running an action query.

- The Data Type setting restricts entries to a specific type of data: text, numbers, dates, and so on. The Field Size property for the Text, Number, and AutoNumber data types restricts the number of characters allowed in a text field or the number of digits allowed in a number or AutoNumber field. The Input Mask property controls the format in which data can be entered.

- You can use a validation rule to precisely define the information that will be accepted in one or several fields in a record. At the field level, Access tests each entry against the rule when you attempt to leave a field. At the table level, Access tests the content of several fields against the rule when you attempt to leave a record. In both cases, Access rejects any entry that doesn't comply with the rule.

- For fields with a fixed set of possible entries, you can use a lookup field to ensure that users enter the right information. This helps prevent inconsistencies, thus making it easier to sort and search your data.

- You can use an update query to quickly perform an action, such as replacing the contents of a field, based on the results of a query.

- You can use a delete query to quickly delete records that meet specific criteria. You should always back up your database before running a delete query, and you must exercise caution when deleting records in this way. The effects of a delete query can be far-reaching, and you can't recover deleted records.

- There are several utilities that you can use to keep your database running smoothly—Compact And Repair Database, Performance Analyzer, Database Documenter, and Microsoft Office Diagnostics. You can keep your application healthy by taking advantage of these utilities before Access indicates there is a problem with your database.

# Part IV
# Microsoft Office PowerPoint 2007

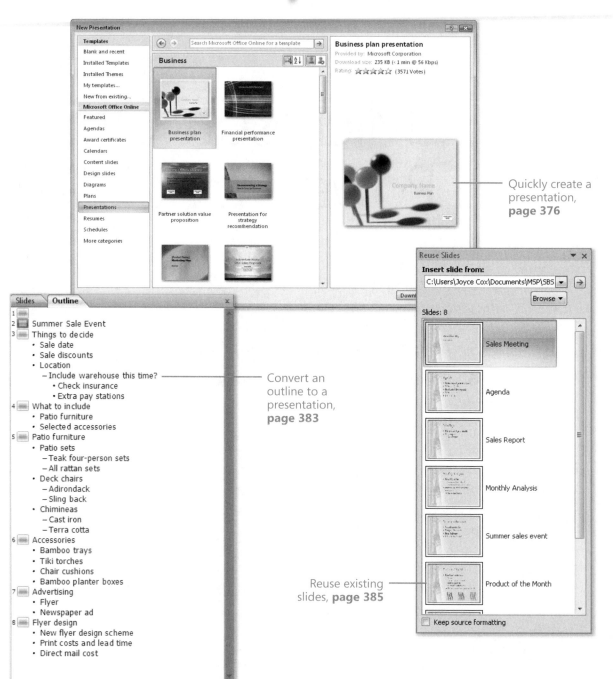

Quickly create a presentation, **page 376**

Convert an outline to a presentation, **page 383**

Reuse existing slides, **page 385**

# 13 Starting a New Presentation

---

**In this chapter, you will learn to:**

✔ Quickly create a presentation.

✔ Create a presentation based on a ready-made design.

✔ Convert an outline to a presentation.

✔ Reuse existing slides.

---

To work efficiently with Microsoft Office PowerPoint 2007, you must be able to decide the best way to start a presentation. The New Presentation window provides several options for creating a new presentation:

● If you need help with both the presentation's content and its look, you can download a complete presentation from Microsoft Office Online and then customize it to meet your needs.

● If you have already created a presentation that is close enough in content and design to be a good starting point, you can use that presentation as the basis for the new one.

● If you have content ready but need help with the look of the presentation, you can base your presentation on one of the design templates that comes with PowerPoint. These templates include graphics, colors, fonts, and styles. You can also base your presentations on your own custom templates.

● If you have created an outline of a presentation in Microsoft Office Word, you can import the outline into PowerPoint to create an instant slide show.

● If you know what your content and design will be and you want to build the presentation from scratch, you can start with a blank presentation.

This chapter will help you become familiar with these methods so that you can decide the best approach for each new presentation you create.

In this chapter, you will create several new presentations: one based on an example from Office Online, one based on a practice file stored on your hard disk, one based on a design template, and one based on a Word outline. You will also add slides to a presentation and insert slides from one presentation into another.

**See Also** Do you need only a quick refresher on the topics in this chapter? See the Quick Reference entries at the beginning of this book.

**Important**  Before you can use the practice files in this chapter, you need to install them from the book's companion CD to their default location. See "Using the Book's CD" at the beginning of this book for more information.

**Troubleshooting**  Graphics and operating system–related instructions in this book reflect the Windows Vista user interface. If your computer is running Microsoft Windows XP and you experience trouble following the instructions as written, please refer to the "Information for Readers Running Windows XP" section at the beginning of this book.

# Quickly Creating a Presentation

When you first start PowerPoint, a blank presentation is displayed in the presentation window, ready for you to enter text and design elements. If you want to create a presentation from scratch, this is the place to start.

**Tip**  If you are already working in PowerPoint, you can open a new blank presentation by clicking the Microsoft Office Button, clicking New, and then in the New Presentation window, double-clicking Blank Presentation.

However, creating presentations from scratch is time-consuming and requires quite a bit of skill and knowledge about PowerPoint. Even people with intermediate and advanced PowerPoint skills can save time by capitalizing on the work someone else has already done. In the New Presentation window, you can preview and download presentations that are available from Office Online and then customize these *templates* to meet your needs. You can also use any presentation that you have already created and saved on your hard disk as the basis for the new presentation.

When you create a new presentation based on a template, you are not opening the template; instead you are creating a new file that has all the characteristics of the template. The new file is temporary until you save it.

In this exercise, you will create two new presentations: one based on an example from Office Online, and the other based on a practice file stored on your hard disk.

> **Troubleshooting** Be sure your computer is connected to the Internet before starting this exercise. If it is not, you can read through the steps below but you won't be able to access the presentations available on Office Online.

> **USE** the *01_Creating* presentation. This practice file is located in the *Chapter13* subfolder under *SBS_Office2007*.
> **BE SURE TO** start PowerPoint before beginning this exercise.

Microsoft Office Button

1. Click the **Microsoft Office Button**, and then click **New**.

   The New Presentation window opens.

2. In the left pane, under **Microsoft Office Online**, click **Presentations**.

   The center pane now lists categories of presentations that are available from Office Online.

3. In the center pane, click Business.

   The center pane now displays images of all the ready-made business presentations that are available from Office Online. The selected presentation is indicated by an orange frame, and information about that presentation appears in the right pane.

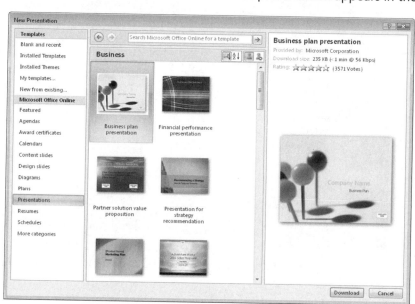

> **Troubleshooting** Don't be alarmed if your list of presentations is different than ours. New presentations are continually being added. In fact, it is worth checking Office Online frequently, just to see what's new.

4. Scroll the center pane, noticing the wide variety of presentations available.

5. About half way down the pane, click the **Company meeting presentation** image, and then in the lower-right corner of the window, click **Download**.

   A message box tells you that you can download templates from Office Online only if you are running a genuine version of PowerPoint.

6. Click **Continue**.

> **Tip** If you don't want this message box to appear every time you download a template, click the Do Not Show This Message Again check box before you click Continue.

After your version of PowerPoint is validated, a presentation based on the selected template opens on your screen in Normal view. The Slides tab shows thumbnails of the slides, and the title slide appears in the Slide pane.

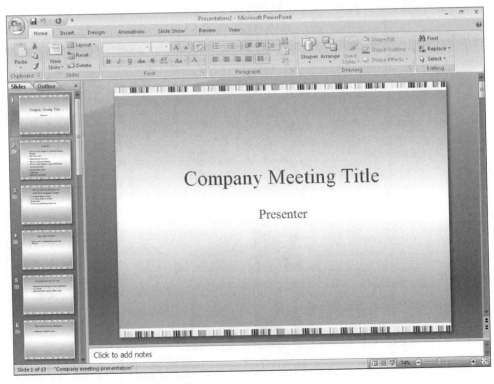

Next Slide

7. Below the scroll bar on the right side of the screen, click the **Next Slide** button repeatedly to display each slide of the presentation in turn.

The slides contain generic instructions about the sort of information that you might want to include in a presentation for a company meeting. You can replace these instructions with your own text.

Save

8. On the **Quick Access Toolbar**, click the **Save** button.

PowerPoint suggests the title of the first slide as the name of the file.

9. Navigate to your *Documents\MSP\SBS_Office2007\Chapter13* folder, and save the presentation with the name My Company Meeting.

The title bar now displays *My Company Meeting* as the name of the open presentation.

10. Display the **New Presentation** window again, and then in the left pane, under **Templates**, click **New from existing**.

The New From Existing Presentation dialog box opens.

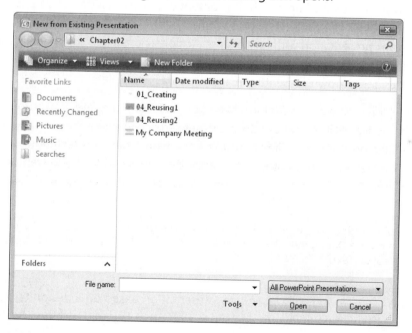

11. With the contents of the *Chapter13* subfolder displayed, double-click the **01_Creating** file.

A quick glance at the title bar tells you that instead of opening the *01_Creating* presentation, PowerPoint has opened a new presentation based on *01_Creating*.

12. On the **Quick Access Toolbar**, click the **Save** button.

Because this presentation is a new file, PowerPoint displays the Save As dialog box so that you can name the presentation.

13. Save the file in the **Chapter13** folder with the name My Sales Meeting.

The title bar now displays *My Sales Meeting* as the name of the active presentation.

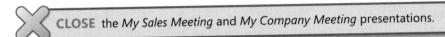 **CLOSE** the *My Sales Meeting* and *My Company Meeting* presentations.

# Creating a Presentation Based on a Ready-Made Design

When you don't need help with the content of a presentation but you do need help with its design, you can start a new presentation based on a *design template*. A design template is a blank presentation with formatting, a color scheme, and sometimes graphics already applied to it. You can base a presentation on a design template from Office Online, or you can design your own presentation and save it as a template.

When you create a presentation based on a design template, PowerPoint supplies a *title slide* and leaves it to you to add the other slides you need. You add a slide by clicking the Add Slide button in the Slides group on the Home tab. This technique adds a new slide with the default layout immediately after the current slide. If you want to add a slide with a different layout, you can select the layout you want from the Add Slide list.

> **Tip** You can also add new slides by pressing keyboard shortcuts while you are entering text on the Outline tab. For more information, see "Entering Text" in Chapter 14, "Working with Slide Text."

In this exercise, you will start a new presentation based on a design template, add a new slide with the default layout, add slides with other layouts, and then delete a slide. There are no practice files for this exercise.

 **BE SURE TO** start PowerPoint and close any open presentations before beginning this exercise.

Microsoft Office
Button

Back

1. Click the **Microsoft Office Button**, and then click **New**.

2. In the left pane of the **New Presentation** window, under **Microsoft Office Online**, click **Design slides**.

   The center pane now displays categories of ready-made designs.

3. In the center pane, click each category in turn, scroll through the thumbnails of the various design collections, and click the **Back** button at the top of the center pane to return to the list of categories.

4. In the center pane, click the **Business** category.

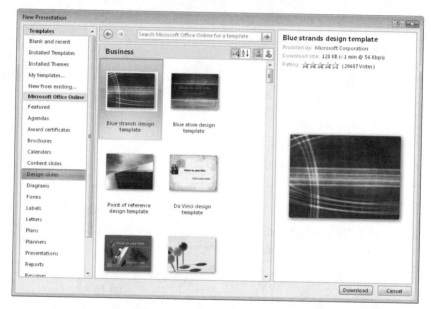

5. Scroll about a third of the way down the list of templates, and click the **Trust design template**. Then in the lower-right corner of the window, click **Download**, and if the **Microsoft Office Genuine Advantage** message box appears, click **Continue**.

   A new presentation with a single title slide opens on your screen in Normal view. The Slides tab shows a thumbnail of the slide, and the slide itself appears in the Slide pane. The PowerPoint Help window opens with information about how to use the Trust template.

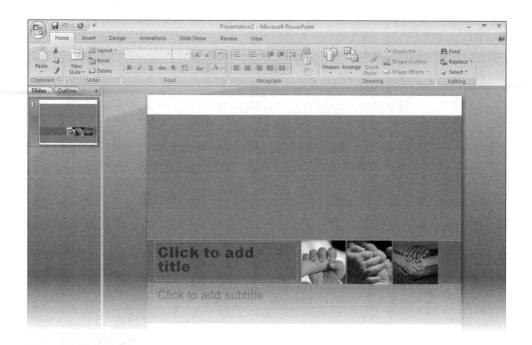

6. Read the information in the Help window, and then close it.

7. On the **Home** tab, in the **Slides** group, click the **New Slide** button (not its arrow).

   PowerPoint adds Slide 2 to the presentation with the default Title And Content layout. This layout is designed to accommodate a title and either text or graphic content—a table, chart, diagram, picture, clip art image, or movie clip.

New
Slide ▾

**8.** In the **Slides** group, click the **New Slide** arrow, and then in the list, click **Two Content**.

**9.** In the **Slides** group, click the **New Slide** button.

PowerPoint adds another slide with the Two Content layout. For all but the title slide, simply clicking the New Slide button adds a slide with the layout of the active slide.

**10.** Continue adding slides, selecting a different layout each time so that you can see what each one looks like.

**11.** At the top of the **Overview** pane, on the **Slides** tab, click **Slide 2**. Then in the **Slides** group, click the **Delete** button.

PowerPoint removes the slide from the presentation and renumbers all the subsequent slides.

  **CLOSE** the presentation without saving your changes.

# Converting an Outline to a Presentation

You can insert an outline created in another program into a PowerPoint presentation. The text can be a Word document (*.doc* or *.docx*) or a *Rich Text Format (RTF)* file (*.rtf*). PowerPoint uses the heading styles in the inserted document to create slide titles and bullet points.

In this exercise, you will convert a Word outline into a presentation.

USE the *03_Converting* document. This practice file is located in the *Chapter13* subfolder under *SBS_Office2007*.

OPEN a new blank presentation.

**New Slide ▾**

1. On the **Home** tab, in the **Slides** group, click the **New Slide** arrow, and then below the slide thumbnails, click **Slides from Outline**.

   The Insert Outline dialog box opens.

2. Navigate to your *Documents\MSP\SBS_Office2007\Chapter13* folder, and then double-click **03_Converting**.

3. After the outline is converted, in the **Overview** pane, click the **Outline** tab to get an idea of the content of the presentation.

   PowerPoint has converted each level-1 heading into a slide title, each level-2 heading into a bullet point, and each level-3 heading into a subpoint.

4. On the **Outline** tab, right-click the empty title of **Slide 1**, which is blank, and then click **Delete Slide**.

CLOSE the presentation without saving your changes.

**Tip** You can start a new presentation from a Word outline by using the Open command. Click the Microsoft Office Button, and then click Open. In the Open dialog box, click the All PowerPoint Presentations setting, and in the list of file types, click All Files. Then locate and double-click the outline document you want to use.

### Exporting a Presentation as an Outline

When you want to use the text from a presentation in another program, you can save the presentation outline as an RTF file. Many programs, including the Microsoft Windows and Macintosh versions of Word and older versions of PowerPoint, can import outlines saved in RTF with their formatting intact.

To save a presentation as an RTF file, follow these steps:

1. Click the **Microsoft Office Button**, and then click **Save As**.

   The Save As dialog box opens.

2. In the **File name** box, specify the name of the file.

3. Click the **Save as type** arrow, and then in the list, click **Outline/RTF**.

4. Navigate to the folder where you want to store the outline, and click **Save**.

   PowerPoint saves the presentation's outline in RTF format with the designated name in the designated folder.

# Reusing Existing Slides

If your presentations often include one or more slides that provide the same basic information, you don't have to recreate the slides for each presentation. For example, if you create a slide that shows your company's product development cycle for one new product presentation, you might want to use variations of that same slide in all new product presentations. You can easily tell PowerPoint to copy a slide and insert in a specific location in a different presentation. The slide will assume the formatting of its new presentation.

In this exercise, you will insert slides from a presentation stored on your hard disk into the active presentation.

**USE** the *04_Reusing1* and *04_Reusing2* presentations. These practice files are located in the *Chapter13* subfolder under *SBS_Office2007*.

**OPEN** the *04_Reusing1* presentation.

New
Slide ▾

1. On the **Slides** tab of the **Overview** pane, click **Slide 3**.

2. On the **Home** tab, in the **Slides** group, click the **New Slide** arrow, and then in the list, click **Reuse Slides**.

   The Reuse Slides task pane opens.

3. In the **Reuse Slides** task pane, click the **Open a PowerPoint File** link.

   PowerPoint displays the Browse dialog box with the contents of your *Documents* folder displayed.

4. Navigate to your *Documents\MSP\SBS_Office\Chapter13* folder, and then double-click the **04_Reusing2** presentation.

   Thumbnails of all the slides in the presentation appear in the Reuse Slides task pane.

**5.** Scroll the task pane, and click the seventh thumbnail, titled *Bamboo Product Line*.

PowerPoint inserts the selected slide from the *04_Reusing2* presentation as Slide 4 in the *04_Reusing1* presentation. The slide takes on the design of the presentation in which it is inserted.

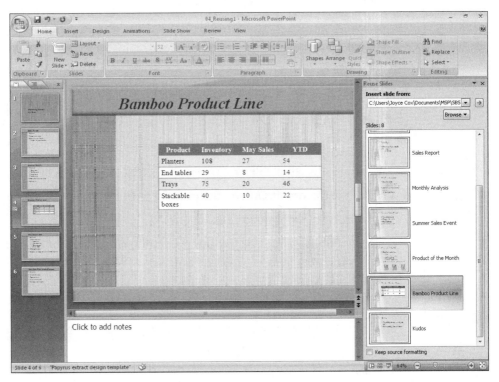

Close

**6.** Click the task pane's **Close** button.

CLOSE the *04_Reusing1* presentation without saving your changes.

## Working with a Slide Library

If your organization is running Microsoft Office SharePoint Server 2007 and has enabled *slide libraries*, you and your colleagues can store slides or even entire presentations in the library so that they are available for use in any presentation. You can then repurpose the slides instead of having to create them from scratch.

For example, suppose a graphically gifted person has developed a slide with a sophisticated chart showing the percentage of income derived from the sale of different categories of merchandise. He or she can store the slide in a slide library so that other people can use it in their presentations without having to take the time to develop a similar chart. Larger organizations might even have people on staff with responsibility for creating this type of slide, so that they can ensure that all slide shows convey the same information in the same professional way.

To store slides in a slide library:

1. Click the **Microsoft Office Button**, point to **Publish**, and then click **Publish Slides**. The Publish Slides dialog box opens.

2. In the **Publish Slides** dialog box, select the check box for the slide you want to store in the library.

   You can also right-click a slide that you want to publish and then click Publish Slides to display the dialog box with that slide already selected.

3. If the URL of your SharePoint slide library does not appear in the **Publish To** box, click the box, and type the URL.

4. Click **Publish** to store the slide in the slide library.

To insert a slide from a slide library:

1. Click the slide after which you want the new slide to appear.

2. On the **Home** tab, in the **Slides** group, click the **New Slide** arrow, and then in the list, click **Reuse Slides**.

3. In the **Reuse Slides** task pane, in the **Insert slide from** box, type the URL of your SharePoint slide library, and then click the **Go** arrow.

4. Double-click the thumbnail of the slide you want to insert in the active presentation.

# Key Points

- How you create a new presentation depends on whether you need help developing the content or the design.

- Office Online provides many presentation templates that you can customize to meet your needs.

- If you are required to use a particular design for a presentation, such as one with corporate colors and branding, it is often simpler to start with the design and then add your own content.

- Repurposing an existing presentation to fit the needs of a different audience is a useful technique that saves development time.

- Repurposing materials developed in other programs, such as Word, capitalizes on the compatibility of the 2007 Office system.

- Repurposing existing slides is another way to save time and ensure consistency.

# Chapter at a Glance

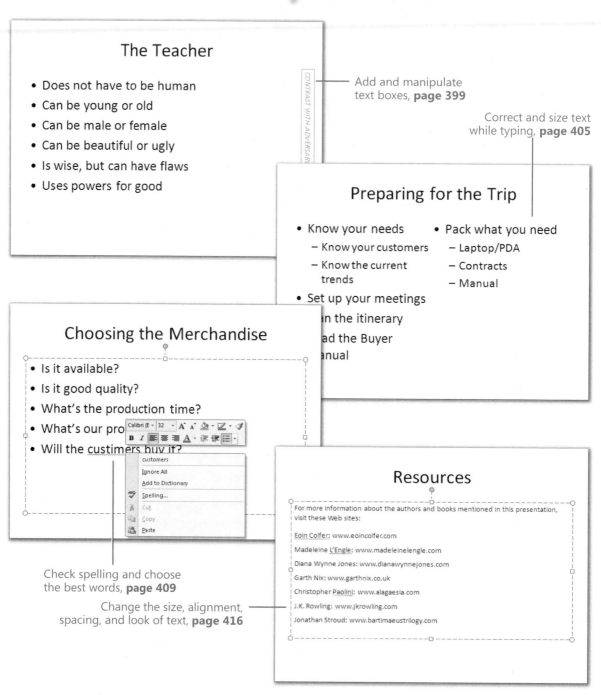

## The Teacher

- Does not have to be human
- Can be young or old
- Can be male or female
- Can be beautiful or ugly
- Is wise, but can have flaws
- Uses powers for good

CONTRAST WITH ADVERSARY

Add and manipulate text boxes, **page 399**

Correct and size text while typing, **page 405**

## Preparing for the Trip

- Know your needs
  - Know your customers
  - Know the current trends
- Set up your meetings
- n the itinerary
- ad the Buyer
- anual

- Pack what you need
  - Laptop/PDA
  - Contracts
  - Manual

## Choosing the Merchandise

- Is it available?
- Is it good quality?
- What's the production time?
- What's our pro
- Will the custimers buv it?

Calibri (E ▾ 32 ▾ A˄ A˅ ◇ ▾ ◇ ▾ ✦
B I ▐ ≡ ≡ A ▾ ⁆ ⁆ ≣ ▾

customers
Ignore All
Add to Dictionary
Spelling...
Cut
Copy
Paste

Check spelling and choose the best words, **page 409**

Change the size, alignment, spacing, and look of text, **page 416**

## Resources

For more information about the authors and books mentioned in this presentation, visit these Web sites:

Eoin Colfer: www.eoincolfer.com

Madeleine L'Engle: www.madeleinelengle.com

Diana Wynne Jones: www.dianawynnejones.com

Garth Nix: www.garthnix.co.uk

Christopher Paolini: www.alagaesia.com

J.K. Rowling: www.jkrowling.com

Jonathan Stroud: www.bartimaeustrilogy.com

# 14 Working with Slide Text

---

**In this chapter, you will learn to:**

- ✔ Enter text.
- ✔ Edit text.
- ✔ Add and manipulate text boxes.
- ✔ Correct and size text while typing.
- ✔ Check spelling and choose the best words.
- ✔ Find and replace text and fonts.
- ✔ Change the size, alignment, spacing, and look of text.

---

In later chapters of this book, we show you ways to add fancy effects to electronic slide shows to really grab the attention of your audience. But no amount of animation, jazzy colors, and supporting pictures will convey your message if the words on the slides are inadequate to the task. For most of your presentations, text is the foundation on which you build everything else, so this chapter shows you various ways to work with text to ensure that the words on your slides are accurate, consistent, and appropriately formatted.

In this chapter, you will learn how to enter and edit text on slides, on the Outline tab, and in text boxes. You will see how the AutoCorrect feature can help you avoid typographical errors, and how the spell-checking feature can help you correct misspellings after the fact. For those times when a word or phrase is correct but you want to substitute a different word or phrase, you will learn how to replace one word with another throughout a presentation by using the Find And Replace feature, which you also use to ensure the consistent use of fonts. Finally, you will vary the size, alignment, spacing, and look of words and phrases on individual slides.

**See Also** Do you need only a quick refresher on the topics in this chapter? See the Quick Reference entries at the beginning of this book.

> **Important** Before you can use the practice files in this chapter, you need to install them from the book's companion CD to their default location. See "Using the Book's CD" at the beginning of this book for more information.

> **Troubleshooting** Graphics and operating system–related instructions in this book reflect the Windows Vista user interface. If your computer is running Microsoft Windows XP and you experience trouble following the instructions as written, please refer to the "Information for Readers Running Windows XP" section at the beginning of this book.

# Entering Text

When you add a new slide to a presentation, the layout you select indicates the type and position of the objects on the slide with *placeholders*. For example, a Title And Content slide has placeholders for a *title* and either a bulleted list with one or more levels of *bullet points* (and subordinate levels called *subpoints*) or an illustration such as a table, chart, graphic, or movie clip. You can enter text directly into a placeholder on a slide in the Slide pane, or you can enter text on the Outline tab of the Overview pane, where the entire presentation is displayed in outline form.

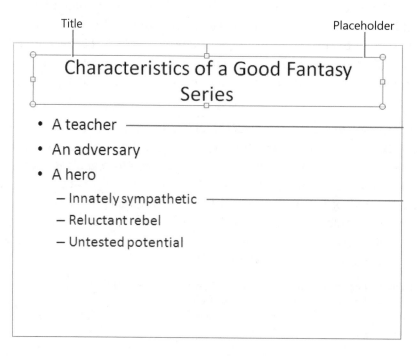

> **Tip** If you want to add text to a slide that has no text placeholder—for example, if you want to add an annotation to a graphic—you can create an independent text box and enter the text there. For information about creating text boxes, see "Adding and Manipulating Text Boxes" later in this chapter.

When you point to a placeholder on a slide or to text on the Outline tab, the pointer changes to an I-beam. When you click the placeholder or text, a blinking insertion point appears where you clicked to indicate where characters will appear when you type. As you type, the text appears both on the slide and on the Outline tab.

In this exercise, you will enter slide titles, bullet points, and subpoints, both directly in slides and on the Outline tab. There are no practice files for this exercise.

> **BE SURE TO** start PowerPoint before beginning this exercise.
>
> **OPEN** a new, blank presentation.

1. In the **Slide** pane, click the slide's **Click to add title** placeholder.

   A selection box surrounds the placeholder, and a blinking insertion point appears in the center of the box, indicating that the text you type will be centered in the placeholder.

2. Type **The Taguien Cycle**.

   Do not type the period. By tradition, slide titles have no periods. PowerPoint's spell-checking feature indicates with a red wavy underline that *Taguien* is a possible spelling error. This word is a proper name and is correct.

   > **Tip** If you make a typing error while working through this exercise, press Backspace to delete the mistake, and then type the correct text. For information about checking and correcting spelling, see "Checking Spelling and Choosing the Best Words" later in this chapter.

3. In the **Overview** pane, click the **Outline** tab, and notice that the text you typed also appears there.

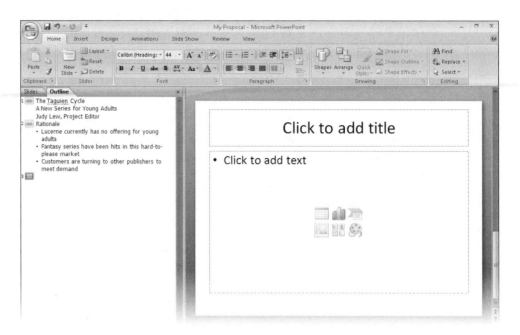

4. In the **Slide** pane, click the **Click to add subtitle** placeholder.

   The title placeholder is deselected, and the subtitle placeholder is selected.

5. Type A New Series for Young Adults, and then press ⏎ Enter to move the insertion point to a new line in the same placeholder.

6. Type Judy Lew, Project Editor.

   As you enter titles and bullet points throughout the exercises, don't type any ending punctuation marks.

Save

7. On the **Quick Access Toolbar**, click the **Save** button, and save the presentation in the **Chapter14** subfolder with the name My Proposal.

   We won't tell you to save your work again in this exercise. Suffice it to say that you should save often.

8. Add a new slide with the **Title and Content** layout.

   **See Also** For information about adding slides, see "Creating a Presentation Based on a Ready-Made Design" in Chapter 13, "Starting a New Presentation."

   PowerPoint creates a new slide with placeholders for a title and a bulleted list. The Outline tab now displays an icon for a second slide, and the status bar displays *Slide 2 of 2*.

9. Without clicking anywhere, type Rationale.

If you start typing on an empty slide without first selecting a placeholder, PowerPoint enters the text into the title placeholder. The title appears on both the slide and the Outline tab.

**10.** On the **Outline** tab, click to the right of *Rationale*, and then press Enter .

PowerPoint adds a new slide to the presentation, and an icon for Slide 3 appears in the Outline pane.

**11.** Press the Tab key.

The Slide 3 icon changes to a bullet on Slide 2. The bullet is gray until you enter text for the bullet point.

**12.** Type Lucerne currently has no offering for young adults, and then press Enter .

PowerPoint adds a new bullet at the same level.

**13.** Type Fantasy series have been hits in this hard-to-please market, and then press Enter .

**14.** Type Customers are turning to other publishers to meet demand, and then press Enter .

**15.** Press Shift + Tab .

On the Outline tab, the bullet changes into an icon for Slide 3. The new slide is displayed in the Slide pane.

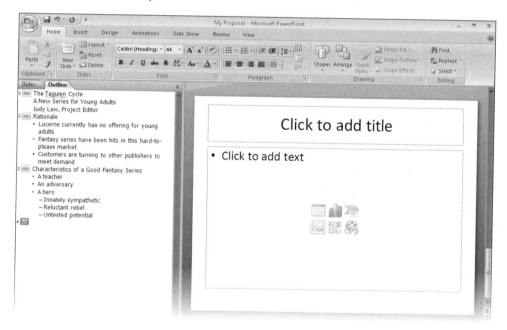

**16.** Type Characteristics of a Good Fantasy Series, press ⌷Enter⌷, and then press ⌷Tab⌷.

This slide title is too long to fit in the title placeholder at its default font size, so PowerPoint decreases the size to make it fit.

**See Also**  For more information about the AutoFit feature, see "Correcting Text While Typing" later in this chapter.

**17.** Type A teacher, press ⌷Enter⌷, type An adversary, press ⌷Enter⌷, type A hero, and then press ⌷Enter⌷.

Increase List
Level

**18.** On the **Home** tab, in the **Paragraph** group, click the **Increase List Level** button.

PowerPoint creates a subpoint.

> **Tip**  You can use the Increase List Level button to change slide titles to bullet points and bullet points to subpoints both on the slide and on the Outline tab. You can also use the Decrease List Level button to change subpoints to bullet points and bullet points to slide titles in both places. However, when you are entering text on the Outline tab, it is quicker to use keys—Tab and Shift+Tab—to perform these functions than it is to take your hands off the keyboard to use your mouse.

**19.** Type Innately sympathetic, press ⌷Enter⌷, type Reluctant rebel, press ⌷Enter⌷, and then type Untested potential.

**20.** Press ⌷Ctrl⌷+⌷Enter⌷.

Instead of creating another bullet, PowerPoint creates a new slide.

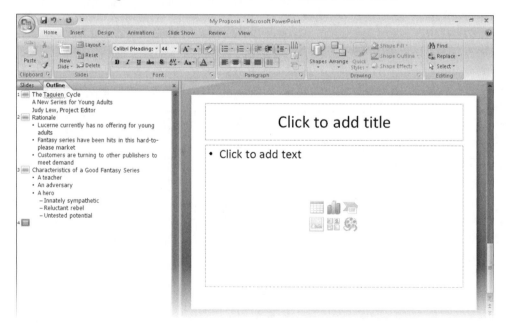

**21.** Save your work.

 **CLOSE** the My Proposal presentation.

# Editing Text

After you enter text, you can change it at any time. You can insert new text by clicking where you want to make the insertion and simply typing. Before you can change existing text, you have to *select* it by using the following techniques:

- Select an individual word by double-clicking it. The word and the space following it are selected. Punctuation following a word is not selected.

- Select adjacent words, lines, or paragraphs by dragging through them.

- Alternatively, position the insertion point at the beginning of the text you want to select, hold down the Shift key, and either press an arrow key to select characters one at a time or click at the end of the text you want to select.

- Select an entire slide title by clicking its slide icon on the Outline tab.

- Select an entire bullet point or subpoint by clicking its bullet on either the Outline tab or the slide.

- Select all the text in a placeholder by clicking inside the placeholder and then clicking Select and then Select All in the Editing group on the Home tab.

    **See Also** For more information about the Select feature, see "Finding and Replacing Text and Fonts" later in this chapter.

Selected text appears highlighted in the location where you made the selection—that is, on either the slide or the Outline tab. To replace a selection, you type the new text. To delete the selection, you press either the Delete key or the Backspace key.

To move a selection to a new location, you can simply drag it. You can also move and copy text by using the Cut or Copy and Paste buttons in the Clipboard group on the Home tab. You can work on the slide itself when moving or copying text within a slide, but it is more efficient to work on the Outline tab when moving or copying text between slides.

If you change your mind about a change you have made, you can reverse it by clicking the Undo button on the Quick Access Toolbar. If you undo an action in error, you can click the Redo button on the Quick Access Toolbar to reverse the change.

To undo multiple actions at the same time, you can click the earliest action you want to undo in the Undo list. You can undo actions only in the order in which you performed them—that is, you cannot reverse your fourth previous action without first reversing the three actions that followed it.

> **Tip** The number of actions you can undo is set to 20, but you can change that number by clicking the Microsoft Office Button, clicking PowerPoint Options, clicking Advanced, and then under Editing Options, changing the Maximum Number Of Undos setting.

In this exercise, you will delete and replace words, as well as move bullet points and subpoints around on slides and on the Outline tab.

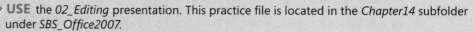

> **USE** the *02_Editing* presentation. This practice file is located in the *Chapter14* subfolder under *SBS_Office2007*.
>
> **OPEN** the *02_Editing* presentation.

1. On the **Outline** tab, in the **Slide 1** subtitle, double click the word **New**.

   When you select text on either the Outline tab or the slide, a small toolbar (called the *Mini toolbar*) containing options for formatting the text appears. If you ignore the Mini toolbar, it fades from view.

   **See Also** For information about using the Mini toolbar, see "Changing the Size, Alignment, Spacing, and Look of Text" later in this chapter.

2. Press the ⌈Del⌉ key.

3. In the **Slide 3** title, double-click **Good**, and then type **Hit** followed by a space.

   What you type replaces the selection. Notice that the text also changes in the Slide pane.

4. Press ⌈End⌉, and then press ⌈Backspace⌉ seven times to delete the word *Series*.

5. On the slide, click the bullet to the left of *Reluctant rebel*.

   The entire subpoint is selected, including the invisible paragraph mark at the end.

   > **Troubleshooting** When you want to work with a bullet point or subpoint as a whole, you need to ensure that the invisible paragraph mark at its end is included in the selection. If you drag across the text, you might miss the paragraph mark. As a precaution, hold down the Shift key and press End to be sure that the paragraph mark is part of the selection.

6. On the **Home** tab, in the **Clipboard** group, click the **Cut** button.

7. Click to the left of the word *Innately*, and then click the **Paste** button.

   The first two subpoints have effectively switched places.

8. On the **Outline** tab, click the bullet point to the left of *A hero* to select the bullet point and its subpoints.

9. Drag the selection up and to the left of *A teacher*.

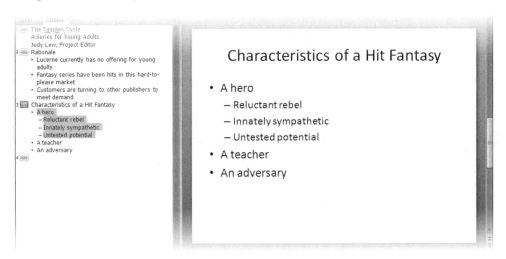

10. On the **Quick Access Toolbar**, click the **Undo** button to reverse your last editing action.

    The Redo button appears on the Quick Access toolbar, to the right of Undo. When you point to the Undo or Redo button, the name in the ScreenTip reflects your last editing action—for example, Redo Drag And Drop.

11. On the **Quick Access Toolbar**, click the **Redo** button to restore the editing action.

CLOSE the *02_Editing* presentation without saving your changes.

# Adding and Manipulating Text Boxes

The size and position of the placeholders on a slide are dictated by the slide's design. Every slide you create with a particular design has the same placeholders in the same locations, and the text you type in them has the same format.

When you want additional text to appear on the slide, such as annotations or minor points that do not belong in a bulleted list, you can create a *text box* by using the Text Box button in the Text group on the Insert tab. You can create a text box in two ways:

- You can click the Text Box button, click the slide where you want the text to appear, and then type. The text box grows to fit what you type on a single line, even expanding beyond the border of the slide if necessary.

- You can click the Text Box button, drag a box where you want the text to appear on the slide, and then type. When the text reaches the right boundary of the box, the height of the box expands by one line so that the text can wrap. As you continue typing, the width of the box stays the same, but the height grows as necessary to accommodate all the text.

When you click in a text box, an insertion point appears, and the box is surrounded by a dashed border. You can then edit the text—for example, you can add, delete, or correct words and punctuation. Clicking the dashed border changes it to a solid border. You can then manipulate the text box as a unit—for example, you can size, move, or copy it as a whole.

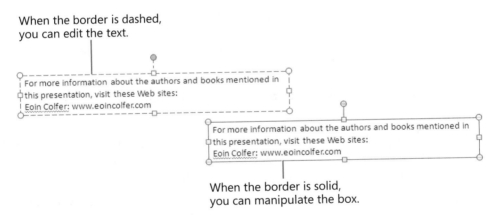

You can drag the *handles* around the border of the box to change its size and shape. By default, PowerPoint adjusts the box to fit the text within it. If you want to create a text box of a specific size or shape, you can right-click the box's border, click Format Shape, click Text Box in the Format Shape dialog box, and then change the settings. In this dialog box, you can also specify whether PowerPoint should shrink the text to fit the box if it won't all fit at the default size (18 points), and whether the text should wrap within the box.

> **Tip** If you want to change the size, shape, or behavior of a placeholder on an individual slide, you can use the same techniques as those you use with text boxes. If you want to make changes to the same placeholder on every slide, you should make the adjustments on the presentation's master slide."

Sometimes you will want the text in a text box to be oriented differently than the rest of the text on the slide. When a text box is selected, a green rotating handle is attached to its upper-middle handle. You can drag this handle to change the angle of the text.

> **Tip** You can also change the direction of text on the Text Box page of the Format Shape dialog box. In the Text Direction list, click one of the Rotate options. Or you can click the Stacked option to keep the individual characters horizontal but make them run from top to bottom in the box instead of from left to right.

When a text box is surrounded by a solid border, you can move or copy the text box anywhere on the slide. Dragging its border is the most efficient way to move a text box within a single slide, and you can copy it just as easily by holding down the Ctrl key while you drag it.

To deselect the text box, you click a blank area of the slide. The border then disappears. If you want a text box to have a border when it is not selected, you can display the Format Shape dialog box, and on the Line Color page, select either Solid Line or Gradient Line. You can then fine-tune the border's color or gradient to achieve the effect you want.

In this exercise, you will select and deselect a placeholder to see the effect on its border. You will create one text box whose height stays constant while its width increases and another whose width stays constant while its height increases. You will manipulate these text boxes by rotating and moving one of them and sizing the other. You will also make a text box border a solid line that is visible when the text box is not selected.

**USE** the *03_TextBoxes* presentation. This practice file is located in the *Chapter14* subfolder under *SBS_Office2007*.
**OPEN** the *03_TextBoxes* presentation.

1. Move to **Slide 2**, and then on the slide, click the slide title.

   The placeholder is selected for editing, as indicated by the blinking insertion point and the dashed border.

2. Point to the border of the placeholder, and when the pointer changes to a four-headed arrow, click the mouse button once.

   The placeholder is selected as a unit, as indicated by the solid border. Although you won't usually want to change the size or location of a text placeholder, while the placeholder has a solid border, you can size and move it just like any other text box. Your changes will affect only the placeholder on the current slide, not corresponding placeholders on other slides.

3. To deselect the placeholder, click outside it in a blank area of the slide.

4. Move to **Slide 5**, and then click the bulleted list placeholder.

Text
Box

5. On the **Insert** tab, in the **Text** group, click the **Text Box** button, and then point immediately below the lower-left handle of the placeholder for the bulleted list.

   The pointer changes shape to an upside-down T.

6. Click the slide to create a text box.

   A small, empty text box appears with a blinking insertion point inside it.

- Can be beautiful or ugly
- Is wise, but can have flaws
- Uses powers for good

7. Type **Contrast with Adversary on Slide 6**.

   The width of the text box increases to accommodate the text as you type it.

- Can be beautiful or ugly
- Is wise, but can have flaws
- Uses powers for good

   Contrast with Adversary on Slide 6

8. To rotate the text so that it reads vertically instead of horizontally, drag the green rotating handle that is attached to the upper-middle handle 90 degrees clockwise.

9. Point to the border of the box (not to a handle), and then drag the box to the right edge of the slide.

**10.** Right-click the border of the box, and then click **Format Shape**.

**11.** In the **Format Shape** dialog box, click **Line Color**.

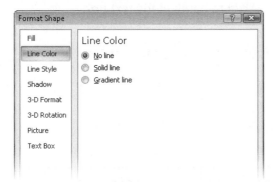

**12.** Click the **Solid line** option, click the **Color** arrow, and in the top row of the **Theme Colors** palette, click the orange box (**Orange, Accent 6**). Then click **Close**.

**13.** Click a blank area of the slide to deselect the text box, and then move to **Slide 2**.

**14.** On the **Insert** tab, in the **Text** group, click the **Text Box** button, point to the center of the area below the bulleted list, and drag approximately 2 inches to the right and ½ inch down.

No matter what height you make the box, it snaps to a standard height when you release the mouse button.

**15.** Type Need to decide whether to offer the series to one author or to multiple writers.

The width of the box does not change, but the box's height increases to accommodate the complete entry.

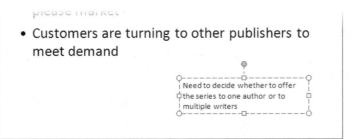

**16.** Click the border of the text box to select it as a unit, point to the solid border, and drag the box to the lower-left corner of the slide, so that its left border aligns with the text of the bullet points.

**17.** Point to the handle in the lower-right corner of the box, and drag up and to the right until the box is two lines high and the same width as the bullet points.

**18.** Click a blank area of the slide to deselect the text box.

> please market
>
> • Customers are turning to other publishers to meet demand
>
>   Need to decide whether to offer the series to one author or to multiple writers

 **CLOSE** the *03_TextBoxes* presentation without saving your changes.

## Changing the Default Font for Text Boxes

When you create a text box, PowerPoint applies default settings such as the font, size, and style—regular, bold, and italic—as well as other effects—underline, small capitals, embossing, and so on. To save yourself some formatting steps, you can change the default settings for the presentation you are working on. Here's how:

1. In a new, blank presentation, create a text box and enter some text in it.

2. Select the text, and then on the **Home** tab, click the **Font** Dialog Box Launcher.

3. Select the font, font style, size, color, underline style, and effects you want to apply to all the text boxes you create from now on in this presentation, and then click **OK**.

   You can also add other effects, such as a fill color, outline formatting, or a special effect.

4. Select the text box itself, right-click its border, and then click **Set as Default Text Box**.

5. Create another text box on the same slide, and then enter text in it.

   The text appears with the new default settings.

# Correcting and Sizing Text While Typing

We all make mistakes while typing test in a presentation. To help you ensure that these mistakes don't go uncorrected, PowerPoint uses the *AutoCorrect* feature to catch and automatically correct common capitalization and spelling errors. For example, if you type *teh* instead of *the* or *WHen* instead of *When*, AutoCorrect corrects the entry.

You can customize AutoCorrect to recognize misspellings you routinely type or to ignore text you do not want AutoCorrect to change. You can also create your own AutoCorrect entries to automate the typing of frequently used text. For example, you might customize AutoCorrect to enter the name of your organization when you type only an abbreviation.

In addition to using AutoCorrect to correct misspellings as you type, PowerPoint uses the AutoFit feature to size text to fit its placeholder. For example, if you type more text than will fit in a title placeholder, AutoFit shrinks the font size so that it all fits. The first time AutoFit changes the font size, it displays the AutoFit Options button to the left of the placeholder. Clicking this button displays a menu that gives you control over automatic sizing. For example, you can stop sizing text for the current placeholder while retaining your global AutoFit settings. You can also display the AutoCorrect dialog box, where you can change the AutoFit settings.

In this exercise, you will add an AutoCorrect entry and use AutoCorrect to fix a mis-spelled word. Then you will use AutoFit to size text so that it fits within its placeholder and to make a long bulleted list fit on one slide by converting its placeholder to a two-column layout.

> **USE** the *04_Correcting* presentation. This practice file is located in the *Chapter14* subfolder under *SBS_Office2007*.
>
> **OPEN** the *04_Correcting* presentation.

Microsoft Office
Button

1. Click the **Microsoft Office Button**, click **PowerPoint Options**, and then in the left pane of the **PowerPoint Options** window, click **Proofing**.

2. Under **AutoCorrect options**, click **AutoCorrect Options**.

   The AutoCorrect dialog box opens.

> **Troubleshooting** If the AutoCorrect tab is not active, click it to display its options.

3. In the lower part of the dialog box, scroll through the huge table of misspellings.

   When you type one of the entries in the first column, PowerPoint automatically substitutes the correct spelling from the second column.

4. In the **Replace** box above the table, type travil, and then press `Tab`.

5. In the **With** box, type travel, and then click **Add**.

Now if you type *travil* in any presentation, PowerPoint will replace it with *travel*.

6. Click **OK** to close the **AutoCorrect** dialog box, and then click **OK** again to close the **PowerPoint Options** window.

7. Move to **Slide 4**, click to the left of the word *advisories*, type travil, and then press `Space`.

PowerPoint corrects the word *travil* to *travel*.

8. Move to **Slide 3**, click to the right of the word *need* in the last bullet point, and then press `Enter`.

9. Press `Tab` to convert the new bullet point to a subpoint, type Laptop/PDA, and then press `Enter`.

10. Add Contracts and Manual as two additional subpoints, pressing `Enter` after each one.

PowerPoint makes the text of the bulleted list smaller so that all the bullet points and subpoints fit in the placeholder. The AutoFit Options button appears in the lower-left corner of the slide.

AutoFit Options

11. Click the **AutoFit Options** button to display a list of options.

12. Click **Change to Two Columns**.

The placeholder is instantly formatted to accommodate a two-column bulleted list, with the last bullet point and its subpoints at the top of the second column. All the bullet points in both columns increase in size.

13. Click a blank area of the slide to deselect the placeholder.

## Preparing for the Trip

- Know your needs
  - Know your customers
  - Know the current trends
- Set up your meetings
- Plan the itinerary
- Read the Buyer manual
- Pack what you need
  - Laptop/PDA
  - Contracts
  - Manual

**CLOSE** the *04_Correcting* presentation without saving your changes.

## Smart Tags

If you frequently use certain types of information, such as the date and time, names, street addresses, or telephone numbers, you can take advantage of the *Smart Tags* feature, which enables PowerPoint to recognize the information. When Smart Tags are turned on, PowerPoint displays a dotted line under the text to indicate that it has been flagged with a smart tag. Pointing to the underlined text displays the Smart Tag Actions button. You can click this button to display a menu of actions associated with that type of information.

You can check which types of information will be flagged with a smart tag by following these steps:

1. Click the **Microsoft Office Button**, click **PowerPoint Options**, click **Proofing**, and then click **AutoCorrect Options**.

2. In the **AutoCorrect** dialog box, click the **Smart Tags** tab.

To see what other Smart Tags available, you can click More Smart Tags and explore a Web site that features smart tags developed by Microsoft and other companies.

# Checking Spelling and Choosing the Best Words

The AutoCorrect feature is very useful if you frequently type the same misspelling. However, most misspellings are the result of erratic finger-positioning errors or memory lapses. You can use two different methods to ensure that the words in your presentations are spelled correctly in spite of these random occurrences:

- By default, PowerPoint's spelling checker checks the spelling of the entire presentation—all slides, outlines, notes pages, and handout pages—against its built-in dictionary. To draw attention to words that are not in its dictionary and that might be misspelled, PowerPoint underlines them with a red wavy underline. You can right-click a word with a red wavy underline to display a menu with a list of possible spellings. You can choose the correct spelling from the menu or tell PowerPoint to ignore the word. To turn off this feature, you can click the Microsoft Office Button, click PowerPoint Options, click Proofing, and then clear the Check Spelling As You Type check box.

- Instead of dealing with potential misspellings while you are creating a presentation, you can check the entire presentation in a single session by clicking the Spelling button in the Proofing group on the Review tab. PowerPoint then works its way through the presentation, and if it encounters a word that is not in its dictionary, it displays the Spelling dialog box. After you indicate how PowerPoint should deal with the word, it moves on and displays the next word that is not in its dictionary, and so on.

The English-language version of the 2007 Office release includes English, French, and Spanish dictionaries. If you use a word or phrase from a different language, you can mark it so that PowerPoint doesn't flag it as a misspelling.

You cannot make changes to PowerPoint's main dictionary, but you can add correctly spelled words that are flagged as misspellings to PowerPoint's supplemental dictionary (called CUSTOM.DIC). You can also create and use custom dictionaries and use dictionaries from other Microsoft programs.

PowerPoint can check your spelling, but it can't alert you if you are not using the best word. Language is often contextual—the language you use in a presentation to club members is different from the language you use in a business presentation. To make sure you are using words that best convey your meaning in any given context, you can use the *Thesaurus* to look up alternative words, or *synonyms*, for a selected word.

In this exercise, you will correct a misspelled word, mark a non-English word, and check the spelling of an entire presentation. You will then use the Thesaurus to replace a word on a slide with a more appropriate one.

**USE** the *05_Spelling* presentation. This practice file is located in the *Chapter14* subfolder under *SBS_Office2007.*

**OPEN** the *05_Spelling* presentation.

1. Move to **Slide 6**, add a fifth bullet point, and then type Will the custimers buy it?

   PowerPoint flags the word *custimers* as a possible error with a red wavy underline.

2. Right-click **custimers**.

   PowerPoint doesn't know whether you want to format the word or correct its spelling, so it displays both a Mini toolbar and a menu.

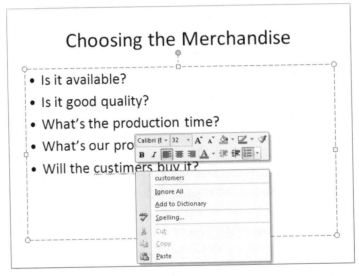

3. On the menu, click **customers** to replace the misspelled word.

4. Move to **Slide 5**.

   The Filipino word *Kumusta* has been flagged as a possible error.

5. Right-click **Kumusta**.

   The spelling checker suggests *Kumquats* as the correct spelling.

6. Press Esc to close the menu without making a selection.

7. With the insertion point still in **Kumusta**, on the **Review** tab, in the **Proofing** group, click the **Language** button.

   The Language dialog box opens.

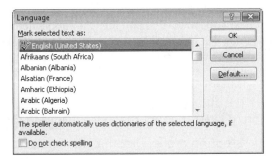

8. Scroll down the list of languages, click **Filipino**, and then click **OK**.

   Behind the scenes, PowerPoint marks *Kumusta* as a Filipino word, and the word no longer has a red wavy underline.

9. Move to **Slide 1**, and then on the **Review** tab, in the **Proofing** group, click the **Spelling** button.

   PowerPoint begins checking the spelling in the presentation. The spelling checker stops on the word *itinarary* and displays the Spelling dialog box.

10. In the **Spelling** dialog box, click **Change**.

    PowerPoint replaces *itinaray* with the suggested *itinerary* and then stops on the word *advizories*, suggesting *advisories* as the correct spelling.

> **Tip** You can click the AutoCorrect button in the Spelling dialog box to add the misspelling and the first suggested spelling of a word to the AutoCorrect substitution table.

11. Click **Change**.

    Next the spelling checker stops on *Dyck*. This term does not appear in the dictionary, but you know that it is a proper name that is spelled correctly.

12. Click **Add**.

    The term *Dyck* is added to the CUSTOM.DIC dictionary. A message box tells you that PowerPoint has finished the spelling check.

> **Tip** If you do not want to change a word or add it to the supplemental dictionary, you can click Ignore or Ignore All. The spelling checker then ignores that word or all instances of the word in the presentation in subsequent spell checking sessions.

**13.** Click **OK**.

**14.** On **Slide 5**, select the word **proper** (but not the space following the word).

**15.** On the **Review** tab, in the **Proofing** group, click the **Thesaurus** button.

The Research task pane opens, displaying a list of synonyms with equivalent meanings.

> **Tip** If you want to translate the selected word into a different language instead of find a synonym for it, you can click Translate in the Proofing group on the Review tab to display the Research task pane with a Translation area.

**16.** In the **Research** task pane, click the minus sign to the left of *polite* to bring more of the synonym list into view.

**17.** Under **good**, decide which word you want to substitute for the selection, point to the word until an arrow appears, click the arrow, and then click **Insert**.

If you don't see an obvious substitute for the selected word, you can click a word that is close in the Thesaurus list and synonyms for that word will be displayed.

18. Close the **Research** task pane.

 **CLOSE** the *05_Spelling* presentation without saving your changes.

> **Tip** For many words, there is a quicker way to find a suitable synonym. Right-click the word, and point to Synonyms. You can then either click one of the suggested words or click Thesaurus to display the Research task pane.

# Finding and Replacing Text and Fonts

You can locate and change specific text in a presentation by using the buttons in the Editing group on the Home tab to do the following:

- Click Find to locate each occurrence of a word, part of a word, or a phrase. In the Find dialog box, you enter the text, and then click Find Next. You can specify whether PowerPoint should locate matches with the exact capitalization or *case*— that is, if you specify *person*, PowerPoint will not locate *Person*—and whether it should locate matches for the entire text—that is, if you specify *person*, PowerPoint will not locate *personal*.

- Click Replace to locate each occurrence of a word, part of a word, or a phrase and replace it with something else. In the Replace dialog box, you enter the text you want to find and what you want to replace it with, click Find Next, and then click Replace to replace the found occurrence or Replace All to replace all occurrences. Again, you can specify whether to match capitalization and whole words.

  In the Replace list, click Replace Fonts to find and replace a font in a presentation. In the Replace Font dialog box, you specify the font you want to change and the font you want PowerPoint to replace it with.

- Click a text placeholder on a slide, click Select in the Editing group, and then click Select All to select all the text in that placeholder. If you select the placeholder itself, clicking Select and then Select All adds all the other objects on that slide to the selection. You can then work with all the objects as a unit. Clicking Select and then Selection Pane displays the Selection And Visibility task pane, where you can specify whether particular objects should be displayed or hidden.

> **Tip** You might want to hide an object if you are using the slide in similar presentations for two different audiences, one of which needs more detail than the other.

In this exercise, you will use the Replace feature to find and replace a word, and then you'll use Replace Fonts to find and replace a font. You will also display the Selection And Visibility task pane and hide an object on a slide.

> **USE** the *06_Finding* presentation. This practice file is located in the *Chapter14* subfolder under *SBS_Office2007.*
>
> **OPEN** the *06_Finding* presentation.

1. On the **Home** tab, in the **Editing** group, click the **Replace** button.

   The Replace dialog box opens.

   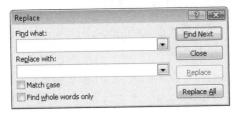

   > **Tip** You can move a dialog box on the screen so that it does not hide the text you are working with by dragging its title bar.

2. In the **Find what** box, type verdigris and press [Tab].

3. In the **Replace with** box, type Verdigris.

4. Select the **Match case** check box to locate text that exactly matches the capitalization you specified and replace it with the capitalization you specified.

5. Click **Find Next**.

   PowerPoint finds and selects the word *verdigris* on Slide 3.

6. Click **Replace**.

   PowerPoint replaces *verdigris* with *Verdigris*, and then locates the next match.

7. Click **Replace All**.

   An alert box tells you that PowerPoint has finished searching the presentation and that the Replace All operation changed two occurrences of the text.

8. Click **OK**, and then in the **Replace** dialog box, click **Close**.

9. Click a blank area of the current slide to release the selection.

10. In the **Editing** group, click the **Replace** arrow, and then in the list, click **Replace Fonts**.

    The Replace Font dialog box opens.

11. With **Arial** selected in the **Replace** list, click the **With** arrow, and then in the list, click **Calibri**.

12. Click **Replace**.

All the Arial text in the presentation changes to Calibri.

13. Click **Close** to close the **Replace Font** dialog box.

14. Move to **Slide 6**, and in the **Editing** group, click the **Select** button, and then click **Selection Pane**.

The Selection And Visibility task pane opens.

The task pane indicates that there are four objects on this slide, but a quick count reveals that only three of them are visible.

15. Under **Shapes on this Slide** in the task pane, click the box to the right of **Rectangle 4**.

An eye appears in the box to the right of Rectangle 4, and that object—a text box—is now displayed at the bottom of the slide.

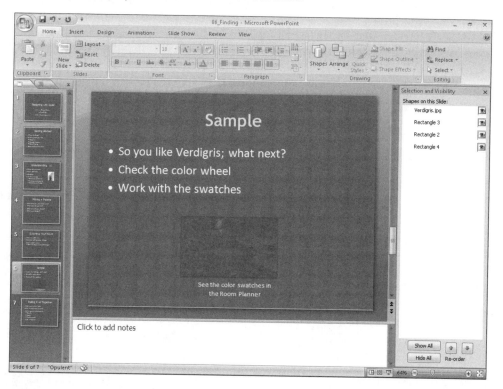

16. In the task pane, click the box to the right of **Rectangle 4** again.

The eye disappears, and the text box is now hidden again.

17. Close the **Selection and Visibility** task pane.

 **CLOSE** the *06_Finding* presentation without saving your changes.

# Changing the Size, Alignment, Spacing, and Look of Text

Earlier in this chapter we discussed the AutoFit feature, which shrinks the size of text that overflows a placeholder so that it fits in the allocated space. If you want to keep the size of the text in a presentation consistent, you can turn off this automatic text shrinking. You then have two ways to adjust the size of placeholders to fit their text:

● By manually dragging the handles around a selected placeholder.

● By using the Resize Shape To Fit Text option on the Text Box page of the Format Shape dialog box.

**See Also** For more information about AutoFit, see "Correcting Text While Typing" earlier in this chapter.

Of course, you can also manually control the size of text by using options in the Font group on the Home tab. You can either click the Increase Font Size or Decrease Font Size button or set a precise size in the Font Size box.

To control the way text is aligned within a placeholder, you can click the text and then click one of the following alignment buttons in the Paragraph group on the Home tab:

● The Align Text Left button aligns text against the placeholder's left edge. It is the usual choice for paragraphs.

● The Center button aligns text in the middle of the placeholder. It is often used for titles and headings.

● The Align Text Right button aligns text against the placeholder's right edge. It is not used much for titles and paragraphs, but you might want to use it in text boxes.

● The Justify button aligns text against both the left and right edges, adding space between words to fill the line.

You can adjust the vertical spacing between all the lines of text in the placeholder by clicking the Line Spacing button in the Paragraph group and making a selection. If you want to adjust the space before or after a paragraph, you need to display the Paragraph dialog box, either by clicking the Line Spacing button and then clicking More at the bottom of the menu or by clicking the Paragraph Dialog Box Launcher. You can then adjust the Before and After settings for the paragraph as a unit.

In addition to changing the look of paragraphs, you can also manipulate the look of individual words. After selecting the characters you want to format, you can make changes by using buttons in the Font group on the Home tab, as follows:

- You can change the font.
- You can apply attributes, including bold, italic, underlining, and shadow and strikethrough effects.
- You can increase or decrease the space between the letters in a selection.
- You can change the capitalization of the words—for example, you can change small letters to capital letters.
- You can change the color of the characters.

In this exercise, you will change the size of the text in a placeholder and then adjust the size of the placeholder both automatically and manually. You will experiment with text alignment, decrease line spacing, and increase paragraph spacing. Then you will use buttons in the Font group to format words so that they stand out and look attractive.

> **USE** the *07_Changing* presentation. This practice file is located in the *Chapter14* subfolder under *SBS_Office2007*.
>
> **OPEN** the *07_Changing* presentation.

1. Move to **Slide 2**, and in the **Slide** pane, click anywhere in the bulleted list.

2. On the **Home** tab, in the **Editing** group, click the **Select** button, and then click **Select All**.

   The note at the bottom of the slide is not selected because it was entered in a separate text box, not in the placeholder.

Decrease Font Size

3. On the **Home** tab, in the **Font** group, click the **Decrease Font Size** button twice.

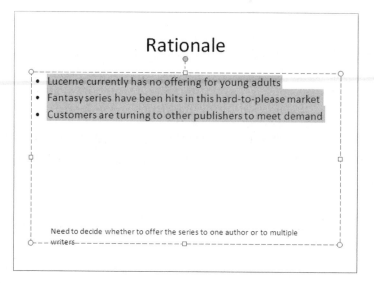

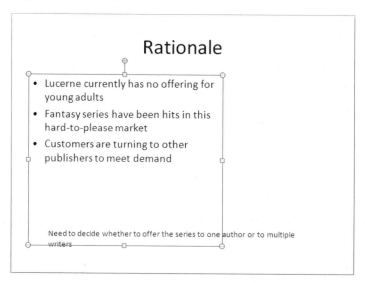

4. Experiment with the size by clicking the **Font Size** arrow, and then pointing to various sizes in the list to get a live preview of the effect.

5. Finish by clicking **24** in the list.

   Now suppose you want to make room for a graphic to the right of the bulleted list.

6. Point to the placeholder's right-middle handle, and when the pointer changes to a two-headed arrow, drag to the left until the right border of the placeholder is aligned with the right end of the slide title.

7. Right-click the placeholder's border, and then click **Format Shape**.

> **Troubleshooting** This command is available only if you right-click the placeholder's border while the pointer is a four-headed arrow. If you don't see the command, click away from the menu, and try again.

The Format Shape dialog box opens.

**8.** Click **Text Box**, select the **Resize shape to fit text** option, and then click **Close**.

The placeholder shrinks in size so that it is just big enough to hold its text.

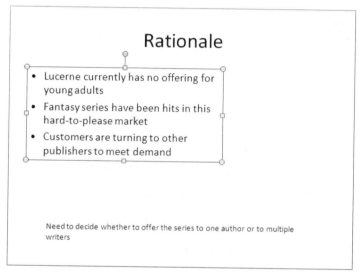

**9.** Move to **Slide 7**, and then click the text box containing the Web addresses.

If this text box contained only one paragraph, you could simply click the text box and then click a button in the Paragraph group to apply the paragraph formatting you want. However, the text box contains multiple paragraphs, and you first need to select them all.

**10.** On the **Home** tab, in the **Editing** group, click the **Select** button, and then click **Select All**.

Align Text Left

**11.** In the **Paragraph** group, click the **Align Text Left** button.

The text is now left-aligned and easier to read.

> **Tip** You want your slides to be as easy to read as possible, especially if you will be delivering your presentation to a large audience, some of whom might be sitting some distance away from the screen. Constantly evaluate whether the effects you apply to your slides enhance readability and understanding.

12. Select the seven Web site lines (not the first paragraph).

Line Spacing

13. In the **Paragraph** group, click the **Line Spacing** button, and then click **1.5**.

14. Click the first paragraph, and then click the **Paragraph** Dialog Box Launcher.

    The Paragraph dialog box opens.

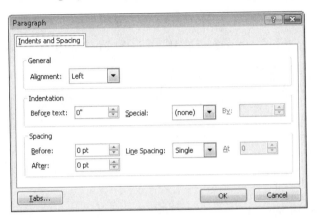

15. Under **Spacing**, change the **After** setting to **12**, and then click **OK**.

    The line spacing and paragraph spacing have both increased.

16. Move to **Slide 5**, and then select all the text in the text box at the right side of the slide.

17. In the **Font** group, click the **Change Case** arrow, and then in the list, click **UPPERCASE**.

The terms *lowercase* and *uppercase* come from the old days of typesetting, when individual letters were manually assembled into words, sentences, and paragraphs for printing. The small versions of the letters were kept in alphabetical order in the lower case, where they were easier for the typesetter to reach, and the capital versions were kept in the upper case.

Italic

**18.** With the text still selected, in the **Font** group, click the **Italic** button.

Font Color

**19.** Click the **Font Color** arrow, and then in the palette, point to each of the colors in the top **Theme Colors** row in turn.

As you point, the selected text changes color to give you a live preview of the effect.

**20.** At the right end of the top **Theme Colors** row, click the orange box (**Orange, Accent 6**).

**21.** Click a blank area of the slide to see the effect of your changes.

**CLOSE** the *07_Changing* presentation without saving your changes, and if you are not continuing on to the next chapter, quit PowerPoint.

# Key Points

- You can enter and edit text both on the Outline tab or directly on a slide, depending on which is most efficient at any particular time.

- Text in placeholders provides consistency across an entire presentation. But you are not limited to using placeholders. You can place text wherever you want it on a slide by using text boxes.

- PowerPoint provides assistance by correcting common spelling errors and adjusting the size of text so that it fits optimally on a slide.

- You can take advantage of the Find and Replace features to ensure consistent use of terms and fonts throughout a presentation.

- Although PowerPoint provides the structure for a presentation so that you can focus on your message, you can manually change the formatting, location, and size of text at any time.

# Chapter at a Glance

## Characteristics of a Hit Fantasy

- A hero
- An ally
- A teacher
- An adversary
- An innocent

- A problem
- A journey
- A skill or power
- A battle
- A twist

Change the layout
of a slide, **page 424**

Apply a theme,
**page 429**

## SALES MEETING
May Results

## Agenda

Review of key objectives
How did we do?
Organizational overview
Top issues facing the company
Review of our progress
Key spending areas
Headcount
Goals for the coming year

Switch to a different
color scheme, **page 431**

Add shading and texture
to the background of a
slide, **page 436**

## The Taguien Cycle

A Series for Young Adults
Judy Lew, Project Editor

# 15 Adjusting the Slide Layout, Order, and Look

**In this chapter, you will learn to:**

✔ Change the layout of a slide.

✔ Rearrange slides in a presentation.

✔ Apply a theme.

✔ Switch to a different color scheme.

✔ Use colors that are not part of the scheme.

✔ Add shading and texture to the background of a slide.

In Chapter 14, you looked at ways to work with the text on your slides. In this chapter, you will step back and focus on big-picture issues that can affect the success of a Microsoft Office PowerPoint 2007 presentation.

For each slide to accomplish its purpose, it needs to present its content in the most effective way. The layout of individual slides and the order of slides in the presentation contribute significantly to the logical development of your message. And an overall consistent look, punctuated by variations that add weight exactly where it is needed, can enhance the likelihood that your message will be well received and absorbed by your intended audience.

In this chapter, you will change the layout of a slide, rearrange slides in a presentation, and apply a theme to a presentation. You will also switch to a different color scheme and use colors that are not part of the scheme. Finally, you will add shading and texture to the background of a slide.

**See Also** Do you need only a quick refresher on the topics in this chapter? See the Quick Reference entries at the beginning of this book.

**Important** Before you can use the practice files in this chapter, you need to install them from the book's companion CD to their default location. See "Using the Book's CD" at the beginning of this book for more information.

**Troubleshooting** Graphics and operating system–related instructions in this book reflect the Windows Vista user interface. If your computer is running Microsoft Windows XP and you experience trouble following the instructions as written, please refer to the "Information for Readers Running Windows XP" section at the beginning of this book.

# Changing the Layout of a Slide

When you add a new slide to a presentation, you can specify which of several predefined layouts you want to use, or you can add a blank slide and create a custom layout. If you decide after you create a slide that you want it to have a different predefined layout, you can change the layout by displaying the slide, clicking the Layout button in the Slides group on the Home tab, and then making a selection.

**See Also** For information about adding slides, see "Creating a Presentation Based on a Ready-Made Design" in Chapter 13, "Starting a New Presentation."

If the slide already contains content, you can add the elements of a different layout to the existing layout without disturbing the existing content. For example, if you decide to add a chart to a slide that already contains a title and a bulleted list, clicking the Layout button and then clicking the Two Content layout adds a content placeholder to the right of the bulleted list placeholder.

If you make changes to the layout of a slide—for example, by sizing or moving a placeholder—but then decide you want to revert to the original layout, you can reapply the layout (without losing text you have already entered) by clicking the Reset button in the Slides group on the Home tab.

In this exercise, you will change the layout of a slide, change the size of the layout's placeholders, and then restore the layout.

1. Display **Slide 3**, and then on the **Home** tab, in the **Slides** group, click the **Layout** button.

   The Layout gallery includes the same layouts that are available for new slides.

2. Click the **Two Content** layout.

   PowerPoint adds a placeholder to the right of the bulleted list.

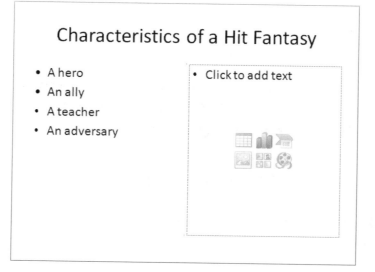

3. Click the bullet in the placeholder on the right side of the slide, and then type the following bullet points, pressing Enter after each one except the last:

   A problem

   A journey

   A skill or power

   A battle

   On the Outline tab, the bullet points are grouped to indicate that they appear in different placeholders.

4. Drag the bottom middle handle of the right placeholder upward until the placeholder is big enough only for its bullet points.

**5.** Repeat Step 4 for the left placeholder.

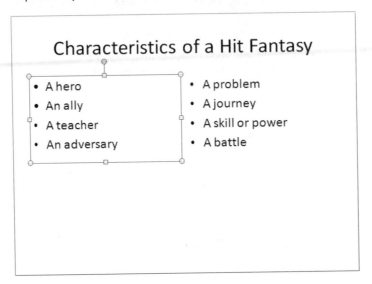

Now suppose you want to add more bullet points to each placeholder. You could manually enlarge the placeholders, but here's a quicker way.

**6.** On the **Home** tab, in the **Slides** group, click the **Reset** button.

The placeholders expand to their original size.

**7.** Click to the right of *adversary* in the left placeholder, press ⌷Enter⌷, and then type An innocent.

**8.** Click to the right of *battle* in the right placeholder, press ⌷Enter⌷, and then type A twist.

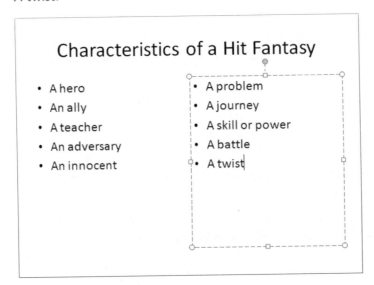

CLOSE the *01_Layout* presentation without saving your changes.

# Rearranging Slides in a Presentation

After you have created several slides, whether by adding them and entering text or
by importing them from another presentation, you might want to rearrange the order
of the slides so that they effectively communicate your message. You can rearrange a
presentation in two ways:

- On the Slides tab, you can drag slides up and down to change their order.
- To see more of the presentation at the same time, you can switch to Slide Sorter
  view. You can then drag slide thumbnails into the correct order.

In this exercise, you will use the Slides tab and Slide Sorter view to logically arrange the
slides in a presentation, and add a slide to a presentation.

USE the *02_Rearranging* presentation. This practice file is located in the *Chapter15*
subfolder under *SBS_Office2007.*

OPEN the *02_Rearranging* presentation.

1. On the **Outline** tab, move to **Slide 3**, and notice the order of the bullet points.

   This summary slide lists all the main players in the series on the left, and the main
   plot requirements on the right.

2. On the **Outline** tab of the **Overview** pane, scroll through the presentation, noticing
   that the slide order is different than that of the bullet points on Slide 3.

   > **Tip** On the Outline tab, you can collapse bullet points under slide titles so that
   > you can see more of the presentation at one time. Double-click the icon of the slide
   > whose bullet points you want to hide. Double-click again to redisplay the bullet
   > points. To expand or collapse the entire outline at once, right-click the title of a
   > slide, point to Expand or Collapse, and then click Expand All or Collapse All.

3. In the **Overview** pane, click the **Slides** tab, and then scroll so that you can see both
   Slide 5 and Slide 8.

4. Drag the thumbnail for **Slide 8** (*The Teacher*) upward to the space above the
   thumbnail for **Slide 6** (*The Problem*), but don't release the mouse button yet.

   The thumbnail itself remains in place, but a bar indicates where the slide will move
   to when you release the mouse button.

**5.** Release the mouse button.

PowerPoint moves the slide to its new location and renumbers the subsequent slides.

Slide Sorter

**6.** At the right end of the status bar, on the **View** toolbar, click the **Slide Sorter** button.

PowerPoint displays the presentation as a set of thumbnails. Because you have only 13 slides in this presentation, there is room to make the thumbnails bigger so that they are easier to read.

Zoom In

**7.** On the slider at the right end of the status bar, click the **Zoom In** button twice to change the Zoom percentage to 80%.

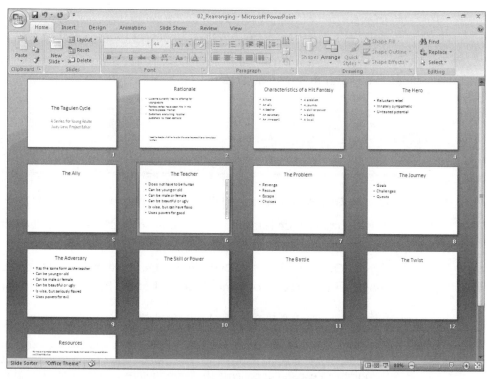

**8.** Drag **Slide 9** (*The Adversary*) to the left of **Slide 7** (*The Problem*).

Slide 9 moves to its new location, and again PowerPoint repositions and renumbers the subsequent slides in the presentation.

> **Tip** You can move slides from one open presentation to another in Slide Sorter view. Display both presentations in Slide Sorter view, and then on the View tab, in the Window group, click the Arrange All button. You can then drag slides from one presentation window to another.

If you check the results against Slide 3, you will see that the slide for *The Innocent* is missing. You can add a slide in Slide Sorter view, but you cannot enter or edit text in this view.

9. With **Slide 7** (*The Adversary*) still selected, add a **Title and Content** slide to the presentation.

   PowerPoint inserts the new slide after the selected slide.

10. Double-click **Slide 8**.

    PowerPoint returns to the previous view—in this case, Normal view—with Slide 8 active.

11. On the slide, click the title placeholder, and then type The Innocent.

 **CLOSE** the *02_Rearranging* presentation without saving your changes.

# Applying a Theme

When you create a presentation based on a template or a ready-made design, the presentation includes a theme—a combination of colors, fonts, formatting, graphics, and other elements that gives the presentation a coherent look. Even a presentation developed from scratch has a theme, albeit one that consists of only a white background and a very basic set of font styles and sizes.

If you want to change the theme applied to a presentation, you can choose a new one from the Themes group on the Design tab. With the live preview feature, you can easily try different effects until you find the one you want.

In this exercise, you will change the theme applied to a presentation that was created from a template. You will also apply a theme to a presentation that was created from scratch.

 **USE** the *03_Theme1* and *03_Theme2* presentations. These practice files are located in the *Chapter15* subfolder under *SBS_Office2007*.
**OPEN** the *03_Theme1* and *03_Theme2* presentations.

More

1. With *03_Theme1* active, on the **Design** tab, in the **Themes** group, click the **More** button to the right of the thumbnails.

   The Themes gallery opens, displaying all the available themes.

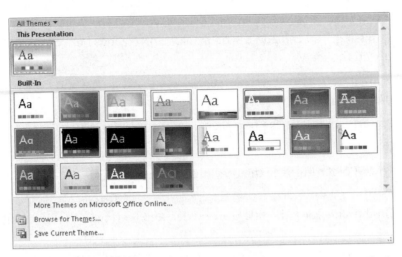

2. Point to each theme thumbnail in turn to see a live preview of what the presentation will look like with that theme applied.

3. Click the **Technic** thumbnail to apply that theme to the entire presentation.

   Instead of a blue background with text in the Times New Roman font, the presentation now has a tan striped background with text in the Franklin Gothic font.

4. Switch to the *03_Theme2* presentation, display the **Themes** gallery, and then click the **Apex** thumbnail.

   Instead of a white background with text in the Calibri font, the presentation now has a gray watermarked background with text in the Lucida and Book Antiqua fonts.

**CLOSE** the *03_Theme1* and *03_Theme2* presentations without saving your changes.

# Switching to a Different Color Scheme

Every presentation you create with PowerPoint 2007, even a blank one, has a set of colors associated with it. This *color scheme* consists of 12 complementary colors designed to be used for the following elements of a slide:

- Use the four Text/Background colors for dark or light text on a dark or light background.
- Use Accent 1 through Accent 6 for the colors of objects other than text.
- Use Hyperlink to draw attention to hyperlinks.
- Use Followed Hyperlink to indicate visited hyperlinks.

In the palette displayed in color galleries such as the Font Color gallery in the Font group on the Home tab, 10 of the 12 colors appear with light to dark gradients. (The two background colors are not represented in these palettes.)

Understanding color schemes can help you create professional-looking presentations that use an appropriate balance of color. You are not limited to using the colors in a presentation's color scheme, but because they have been selected by professional designers based on good design principles, using them ensures that your slides will be pleasing to the eye.

To view the color schemes you can apply to a presentation, you click the Colors button in the Themes group on the Design tab to display a Colors gallery with live preview capabilities. When you find the color scheme you want, click it to change the color scheme of the presentation.

If none of the color schemes is exactly what you are looking for, you can create your own by clicking Create New Theme Colors at the bottom of the Colors gallery and assembling colors in the Create New Theme Colors dialog box. After you save the scheme, you can apply it to one or all of the slides in a presentation.

In this exercise, you will examine the color scheme of a presentation, apply a different color scheme to an entire presentation, create your own scheme, and change the color scheme of only one slide.

> **USE** the *04_ColorScheme* presentation. This practice file is located in the *Chapter15* subfolder under *SBS_Office2007*.
>
> **OPEN** the *04_ColorScheme* presentation.

1. On the **Design** tab, in the **Themes** group, click the **Colors** button.

   The Colors gallery opens.

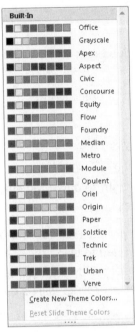

2. In the gallery, point to a few color schemes and watch the live preview effect on the active slide.

3. Click **Verve** to switch the color scheme of the theme applied to the presentation.

   Notice that the theme retains all its other characteristics, such as the font and background graphic; only the colors change. This color scheme is a good starting point.

4. In the **Themes** group on the **Design** tab, click the **Colors** button.

5. At the bottom of the **Colors** gallery, click **Create New Theme Colors**.

   The Create New Theme Colors dialog box opens, displaying the Verve theme colors.

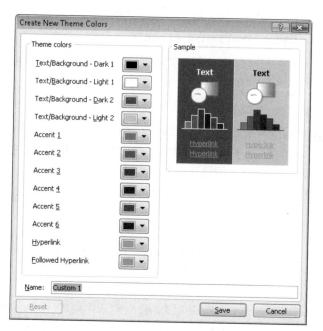

6. In the **Theme colors** area, click the **Text/Background – Dark 2** button.

   A gallery of colors related to the Verve theme colors opens.

7. In the **Theme Colors** palette, click the box in the third row of the range below the dark blue box.

   When you are pointing to the correct box, a ScreenTip labeled *Dark Blue, Accent 6, Lighter 40%* appears.

8. At the bottom of the dialog box, click **Save**.

   The dialog box closes and PowerPoint applies the new color scheme to the presentation, changing the background color of all the slides to bright blue.

9. Display **Slide 2**, and in the **Themes** group, click the **Colors** button.

   Notice that your new custom color scheme appears in the Custom area at the top of the Colors gallery.

10. Right-click the **Opulent** color scheme, and then click **Apply to Selected Slides**.

    PowerPoint applies the Opulent color scheme to only the selected slide, changing its background color to purple.

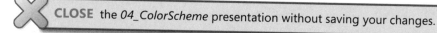

CLOSE the *04_ColorScheme* presentation without saving your changes.

### Changing a Theme's Fonts and Effects

In addition to changing a theme's color scheme, you can also change its fonts and effects by following these steps:

1. On the **Design** tab, in the **Themes** group, click the **Fonts** button.

   The Fonts gallery lists the combination of fonts that is used by each of the themes, in alphabetical order by theme. The top font in each combination is used for titles, and the bottom font is used for other slide text.

2. Click the font combination you want to use in the current presentation.

   **Tip** You can create a custom font combination by clicking Create New Theme Fonts at the bottom of the gallery and then specifying the font combination you want in the Create New Theme Fonts dialog box.

3. On the **Design** tab, in the **Themes** group, click the **Effects** button.

   Like the Fonts gallery, the Effects gallery displays the combination of effects that is applied to shapes by each of the themes.

4. Click the effect combination you want to use in the current presentation.

   Your changes are stored with the presentation and do not affect the default theme.

# Using Colors That Are Not Part of the Scheme

Although working with the 12 colors of a harmonious color scheme enables you to create presentations with a pleasing design impact, you might want to use a wider palette. You can add colors that are not part of the color scheme by selecting the element whose color you want to change and then choosing a standard color from the Colors palette or from the almost infinite spectrum of colors available in the Colors dialog box.

After you add a color, it becomes available on all the palettes that appear when you click a button that applies color—for example, the Font Color button in the Font group on the Home tab. The color remains on the palettes even if you change the theme applied to the presentation.

In this exercise, you will change the color of a slide title and will then apply the same color to other elements of the presentation.

USE the *05_OtherColors* presentation. This practice file is located in the *Chapter15* subfolder under *SBS_Office2007*.

OPEN the *05_OtherColors* presentation.

Font Color

1. On **Slide 1**, select the title of the presentation, and then on the **Home** tab, in the **Font** group, click the **Font Color** arrow.

   A color palette appears.

   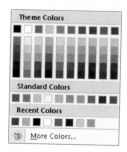

2. At the bottom of the color palette, click **More Colors**.

   The Colors dialog box opens.

3. In the **Colors** spectrum, click in the brightest green shade.

   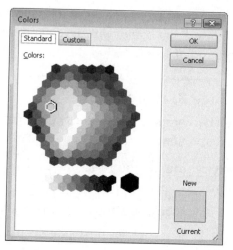

4. Click **OK**.

   The title changes to the selected shade of green, outlined in red.

5. Display **Slide 5**, select the text following the third bullet point, and then click the **Font Color** arrow.

   The color that you just applied appears at the left end of the Recent Colors palette and is now available for use throughout the presentation.

6. Under **Recent Colors**, click the **Green** box.

More

7. On the **Design** tab, in the **Themes** group, click the **More** button to display the Themes gallery, and then click **Median**.

The third bullet point retains the color you just applied even though you have switched themes.

> **CLOSE** the *05_OtherColors* presentation without saving your changes.

# Adding Shading and Texture to the Background of a Slide

In PowerPoint, you can customize the *background* of a slide by adding a solid color, a color gradient, a texture, or even a picture.

A color gradient is a visual effect in which a solid color gradually changes from light to dark or dark to light. PowerPoint offers several gradient patterns, each with several variations. You can also choose a preset arrangement of colors from professionally designed backgrounds in which the different colors gradually merge.

If you want something fancier than a gradient, you can give the slide background a texture, or you can use a picture. PowerPoint comes with several preset textures that you can easily apply to the background of slides.

---

### Adding a Picture to the Slide Background

You can add a picture to a slide's background, either as a single object or as a tiled image that fills the entire slide. Here's how:

1. On the **Design** tab, in the **Background** group, click the **Background Styles** button, and then click **Format Background**.

2. In the **Format Background** dialog box, click the **Picture or texture fill** option.

3. Click **File**, navigate to the folder that contains the picture you want to use, and then double-click the file name.

4. To make the picture fill the entire slide, select the **Tile picture as texture** check box.

5. To use the picture in the background of the current slide, click **Close**, or to use it in the background of all slides, click **Apply to All**.

In this exercise, you will add a shade to a slide background and then change the background from shaded to textured.

> **USE** the *06_Background* presentation. This practice file is located in the *Chapter15* subfolder under *SBS_Office2007*.
>
> **OPEN** the *06_Background* presentation.

1. On the **Design** tab, in the **Background** group, click the **Background Styles** button.

2. In the **Background** gallery, point to each style in turn to see a live preview of its effects.

3. Click the last thumbnail in the second row (**Style 8**).

4. Click the **Background Styles** button again, and then click **Format Background** at the bottom of the gallery.

   The Format Background dialog box opens.

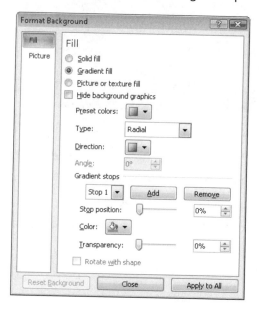

> **Tip** Clicking the Preset Colors button displays a gallery of professionally designed color gradients, which range from a single color to sets of several colors.

5. Click the **Type** arrow, and then in the list, click **Rectangular**.

6. Click the **Direction** button, and at the right end of the gallery, click the **From Corner** effect.

7. Under **Gradient stops**, drag the **Stop position** slider to the right until the adjacent setting is **80%**.

8. Click the **Color** button, and then in the **Theme Colors** palette, click the green color in the top row.

9. Click **Close**.

   PowerPoint applies the shaded background only to the current slide.

10. Click the **Background Styles** button again, and then click **Format Background**.

11. In the **Format Background** dialog box, select the **Picture or texture fill** option.

12. Click the **Texture** button, and then in the gallery, click **Denim**.

13. Click the **Apply to All** button, and then click **Close**.

    PowerPoint applies the textured background to the current slide and all the other slides in the presentation.

 **CLOSE** the *06_Background* presentation without saving your changes, and if you are not continuing on to the next chapter, quit PowerPoint.

# Key Points

- After you create a slide, you can easily modify its layout.
- If you manually change the layout of a slide, you can restore the default layout.
- You can change the order of slides by rearranging them on the Slides tab or in Slide Sorter view.
- You can easily change the look and feel of a presentation by switching from one predefined theme to another. If you like all the elements of a theme except its colors, you can apply a different color scheme.
- You can apply a color scheme to one or all the slides in a presentation.
- You can create your own color schemes, and you can add colors that aren't part of the current scheme to selected parts of a slide.
- To dress up the background of one slide or of all the slides in a presentation, you can apply a solid color, a color gradient, a texture, or a picture.

# Chapter at a Glance

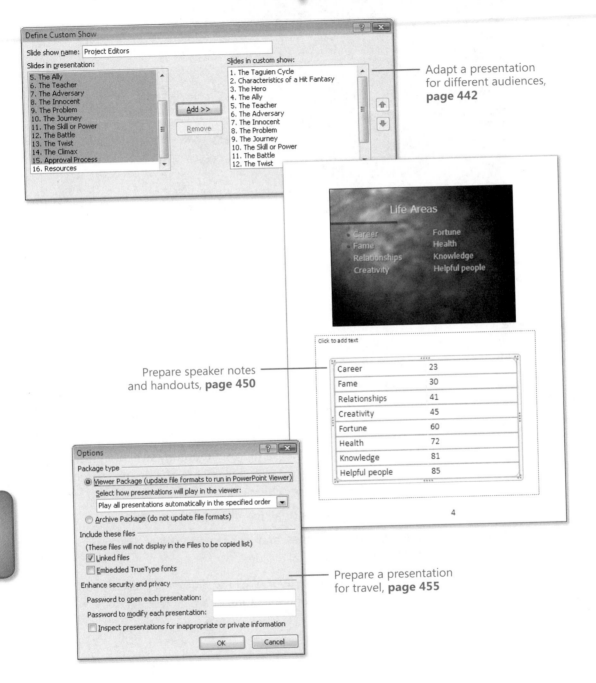

Adapt a presentation
for different audiences,
**page 442**

Prepare speaker notes
and handouts, **page 450**

Prepare a presentation
for travel, **page 455**

# 16 Delivering a Presentation Electronically

**In this chapter, you will learn to:**

✔ Adapt a presentation for different audiences.

✔ Rehearse a presentation.

✔ Prepare speaker notes and handouts.

✔ Prepare a presentation for travel.

✔ Show a presentation.

The goal of all the effort involved in creating a presentation is to be able to effectively deliver it to a specific audience. With Microsoft Office PowerPoint 2007, you can easily deliver a presentation from your computer as an electronic slide show. In Slide Show view, instead of the slide appearing in a presentation window within the PowerPoint program window, the slide occupies the entire screen.

Before you can deliver a presentation, you need to perform several tasks to ensure its success. You can hide individual slides to adapt the presentation for a specific audience, or if you know that you will be giving variations of the same presentation to different audiences, you can save a set of slides as a separate presentation that you will show only if appropriate. You can tailor the speed at which slides appear, to appropriately fit your presentation to the allotted time. To support your delivery of the presentation, you can prepare speaker notes, and to help your audience retain your message, you can prepare handouts. Finally, if you are delivering the presentation at a remote location, you will want to use the Package For CD feature to ensure that you take all the necessary files with you.

When you deliver a slide show from your computer, you navigate through slides by clicking the mouse button or by pressing the arrow keys. You can move forward and backward one slide at a time, and you can jump to specific slides as the needs of your audience dictate. During the slide show, you can mark up slides with an on-screen pen or highlighter to emphasize a point.

In this chapter, you will adapt a presentation for two audiences, first by creating a custom slide show, and then by hiding a slide. You will apply slide timings to a presentation, rehearse it, and have PowerPoint set the timings for you. You will enter speaker notes in both the Notes pane and in Notes Page view, customize the Notes master, and print speaker notes and handouts. Then you will save a presentation package on a CD and run it from the CD by using the presentation viewer that comes with PowerPoint. Finally, you will deliver a presentation and mark up slides while showing them.

**See Also**  Do you need only a quick refresher on the topics in this chapter? See the Quick Reference entries at the beginning of this book.

**Important**  Before you can use the practice files in this chapter, you need to install them from the book's companion CD to their default location. See "Using the Book's CD" at the beginning of this book for more information.

**Troubleshooting**  Graphics and operating system–related instructions in this book reflect the Windows Vista user interface. If your computer is running Microsoft Windows XP and you experience trouble following the instructions as written, please refer to the "Information for Readers Running Windows XP" section at the beginning of this book.

# Adapting a Presentation for Different Audiences

If you plan to deliver variations of the same presentation to different audiences, you should prepare a single presentation containing all the slides you are likely to need for all the audiences. Then you can select slides from the presentation that are appropriate for a particular audience and group them as a *custom slide show*. When you need to deliver the presentation for that audience, you open the main presentation and show the subset of slides by choosing the custom slide show from a list.

For example, suppose you need to pitch an idea for a new product or service to both a team of project managers and a company's executive team. Many of the slides would be the same for both groups, but the presentation to the executive team would include more in-depth competitive and financial analysis. You would develop the executive team's presentation first and then create a custom slide show for the project managers by using a subset of the slides in the executive presentation.

Sometimes you might want to be able to make an on-the-spot decision during a presentation about whether to display a particular slide. You can give yourself this flexibility by hiding the slide so that you can skip over it if its information doesn't seem useful to a particular audience. If you decide to include the slide's information in the presentation, you can display it by pressing the letter H or by using the Go To Slide command.

In this exercise, you will select slides from an existing presentation to create a custom slide show for a different audience. You will also hide a slide and then see how to display it when necessary.

**USE** the *01_Adapting* presentation. This practice file is located in the *Chapter16* subfolder under *SBS_Office2007.*

**BE SURE TO** start PowerPoint before beginning this exercise.

**OPEN** the *01_Adapting* presentation.

Custom
Slide Show ▾

1. On the **Slide Show** tab, in the **Start Slide Show** group, click the **Custom Slide Show** button, and then click **Custom Shows**.

   The Custom Shows dialog box opens.

2. Click **New**.

   The Define Custom Show dialog box opens. The default custom show name is selected in the Slide Show Name box.

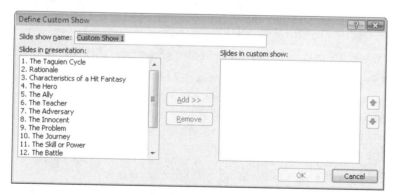

3. In the **Slide show name** box, type Project Editors.

4. In the **Slides in presentation** list, click **1. The Taguien Cycle**, and then click **Add**.

   Slide 1 appears as Slide 1 in the Slides In Custom Show box on the right.

5. In the **Slides in presentation** list, click **3. Characteristics of a Hit Fantasy**, scroll the list, hold down the [shift] key, and click **15. Approval Process**. Then click **Add**.

   The slides appear in sequential order in the Slides In Custom Show box on the right.

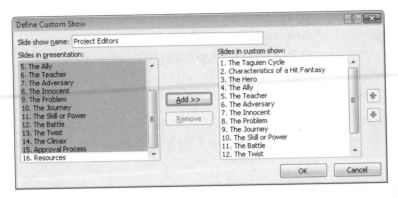

6. Click **OK**.

7. In the **Custom Shows** dialog box, click **Show** to start the custom slide show.

8. Click the mouse button to advance through all the slides, including the blank one at the end of the show.

9. In Normal view, on the **Slide Show** tab, in the **Start Slide Show** group, click the **Custom Slide Show** button.

   *Project Editors* has been added to the list. Clicking this option will run the custom slide show.

10. In the list, click **Custom Shows**.

11. In the **Custom Shows** dialog box, verify that **Project Editors** is selected, and then click **Edit**.

   The Define Custom Show dialog box opens.

12. At the bottom of the **Slides in custom show** box, click **14. Approval Process**, and then click **Remove**.

   PowerPoint removes the slide from the custom slide show, but not from the main presentation.

> **Tip** To change the order of the list, select a slide and click the Up arrow or the Down arrow to the right of the Slides In Custom Show box.

13. Click **OK** to close the **Define Custom Show** dialog box, and then click **Close** to close the **Custom Shows** dialog box.

14. In the **Overview** pane, scroll to the bottom of the **Slides** tab, right-click **Slide 12**, and then click **Hide Slide**.

   On the Slides tab, PowerPoint puts a box with a diagonal line around the number 12, and dims the slide contents to indicate that it is hidden.

> **Tip** In Slide Sorter view, you can select a slide and then on the Slide Show tab, in the Set Up group, click the Hide Slide button.

Slide Show

15. Display **Slide 11**, and on the **View** toolbar, click the **Slide Show** button. Then press `Space` to move to the next slide.

    Because Slide 12 is hidden, PowerPoint skips from Slide 11 to Slide 13.

16. Press the ← key to move back to Slide 11.

17. Right-click anywhere on the screen, point to **Go to Slide**, and then click **(12) The Battle**.

    The number is in parentheses because the slide is hidden. When you click it, the hidden slide appears in Slide Show view.

18. Press Esc to end the slide show.

**CLOSE** the *01_Adapting* presentation without saving your changes.

# Rehearsing a Presentation

When delivering a slide show, you can move from slide to slide in the following ways:

- **Manually.** You control when you move by clicking the mouse button, pressing keys, or clicking commands.

- **Automatically.** PowerPoint displays each slide for a predefined length of time and then displays the next slide.

The length of time a slide appears on the screen is controlled by its *slide timing*. By default slide timings are divided equally among the animations for each slide. So if a slide has a title and four bullet points that are all animated and you assign a timing of 1 minute to the slide, the five elements will appear at 12-second intervals.

To apply a timing to a single slide, to a group of slides, or to an entire presentation, you first select the slides, and then under Advance Slide in the Transition To This Slide group on the Animations tab, select the Automatically After check box and enter the number of minutes and/or seconds you want each slide to remain on the screen.

> **Tip** If you are delivering the presentation in Slide Show view and want to prevent PowerPoint from advancing to the slide according to a slide timing, press the letter S on your keyboard, or right-click the current slide and click Pause. To continue the presentation, press the letter S again, or right-click the slide and click Resume.

If you don't know how much time to allow for the slide timings of a presentation, you can rehearse the slide show while PowerPoint automatically tracks and sets the timings for you, reflecting the amount of time you spend on each slide during the rehearsal. During the slide show, PowerPoint displays each slide for the length of time you indicated during the rehearsal. In this way, you can synchronize an automatic slide show with a live narration or demonstration.

In this exercise, you will set the timing for one slide and then apply it to an entire presentation. Then you will rehearse the presentation and have PowerPoint set slide timings according to the amount of time you display each slide during the rehearsal.

> **USE** the *02_Rehearsing* presentation. This practice file is located in the *Chapter16* subfolder under *SBS_Office2007*.
>
> **OPEN** the *02_Rehearsing* presentation.

1. On the **Animations** tab, in the **Transition to This Slide** group, under **Advance Slide**, select the **Automatically After** check box, and then type or select **00:03**.

   Because both check boxes under Advance Slide are selected, the slide will advance either after three seconds or when you click the mouse button.

Slide Show

2. On the **View** toolbar, click the **Slide Show** button.

   Slide 1 is displayed for three seconds, and then PowerPoint moves to Slide 2.

Slide Sorter

3. Press [Esc] to end the show, and then on the **View** toolbar, click the **Slide Sorter** button.

   Below the lower-left corner of Slide 1 is the slide timing you just applied.

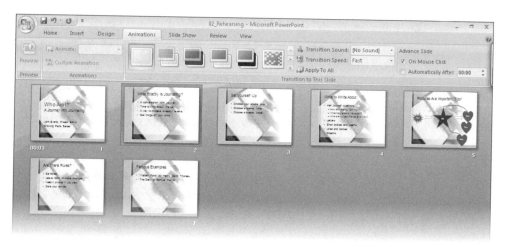

4. Click **Slide 1**, and then on the **Animations** tab, in the **Transition to This Slide** group, click the **Apply To All** button.

The slide timing you applied to Slide 1 is now applied to all the slides.

> **Important** When you click Apply To All, all the transition effects applied to the current slide are transferred to the other slides. If you have applied different transitions to different slides, those individually specified transitions are overwritten. So it's a good idea to apply all the effects that you want the slides to have in common first. Then you can select individual slides and customize their effects.

5. Switch to Slide Show view, watch as the slides advance, and then click the mouse button when the black screen is displayed.

6. Under **Advance Slide** in the **Transition to This Slide** group, clear the **Automatically After** check box, and then click **Apply To All**.

The slide timings disappear from below the slides.

7. With Slide 1 selected, on the **Slide Show** tab, in the **Set Up** group, click the **Rehearse Timings** button.

The screen switches to Slide Show view, starts the show, and displays the Rehearsal toolbar in the upper-left corner of the screen. A Slide Time counter is timing the length of time Slide 1 remains on the screen.

8. Wait about 10 seconds, and then on the **Rehearsal** toolbar, click the **Next** button.

Next

9. Work your way slowly through the slide show, clicking **Next** to move to the next slide.

Repeat

10. If you want to repeat the rehearsal for a particular slide, on the **Rehearsal** toolbar, click the **Repeat** button on the Rehearsal toolbar to reset the Slide Time for that slide to 0:00:00.

> **Tip** If you want to start the entire rehearsal over again, click the Rehearsal toolbar's Close button, and when a message asks whether you want to keep the existing timings, click No.

When you reach the end of the slide show, a message box displays the elapsed time for the presentation and asks whether you want to apply the recorded slide timings.

11. Click **Yes**.

The screen switches back to Slide Sorter view, where the recorded timings have been added below each slide.

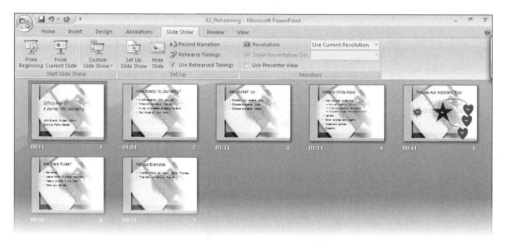

12. Click the **Animations** tab.

The timing for the active slide, Slide 1, appears in the Automatically After box under Advance Slide in the Transition To This Slide group.

13. If the **Automatically After** setting is not a whole second, click the Up arrow to adjust the time up to the next whole second.

You can manually adjust the timing of any slide by selecting it and changing the setting in this box.

14. On the **View** toolbar, click the **Slide Show** button.

The slides advance according to the recorded timings.

**15.** Press ⟨Esc⟩ at any time to stop the slide show.

 **CLOSE** the *02_Rehearsing* presentation without saving your changes.

## Creating a Self-Running Presentation

When slide timings have been applied to a PowerPoint presentation, the presentation can be set up to run automatically, either once or continuously. For example, you might want to set up a self-running presentation for a product demonstration in a store.

To set up a self-running presentation:

1. Open the presentation, and then on the **Slide Show** tab, in the **Set Up** group, click the **Set Up Slide Show** button.

   The Set Up Show dialog box opens.

2. In the **Show type** area, select the **Browsed at a kiosk (full screen)** option.

   When you select this option, the Loop Continuously Until 'Esc' check box in the Show Options area becomes unavailable so that you cannot clear it. Any narration or animation attached to the presentation will play with the presentation unless you select the Show Without Narration or Show Without Animation check box.

3. Click **OK**.

4. To test the show, display **Slide 1**, and on the **View** toolbar, click the **Slide Show** button.

   The presentation runs continuously, using its transitions, animations, and slide timings.

5. Press ⟨Esc⟩ to stop the slide show, and then save the presentation with a different name.

When you are ready to run the presentation, you can navigate to the folder where it is stored, and double-click it. The slide show opens in the view in which it was saved. Switch to Slide Show view to start the presentation. You can press Esc to stop the slide show at any time.

# Preparing Speaker Notes and Handouts

If you will be delivering your presentation before a live audience, you will probably need some speaker notes to guide you. Each slide in a PowerPoint presentation has a corresponding notes page. As you create each slide, you can enter notes that relate to the slide's content by simply clicking the Notes pane and typing. If you want to include something other than text in your speaker notes, you must switch to Notes Page view by clicking the Notes Page button in the Presentation Views group on the View tab. When your notes are complete, you can print them so that they are readily available to guide the presentation.

As a courtesy for your audience, you might want to supply handouts showing the presentation's slides so that people can take notes. You don't need to do anything special to create handouts. Printing them requires a few simple decisions, such as how many slides you want to appear on each page.

Notes and handouts have their own masters, and you can customize them by using the same techniques you use to customize slide masters. Usually, you will find that the default masters are more than adequate, but if you want to make changes, you click Notes Master or Handout Master in the Presentation Views group on the View tab to display the respective masters.

In this exercise, you will enter speaker notes for a couple of slides in the Notes pane. You will then switch to Notes Page view, insert a graphic in one note and a table in another, customize the Notes master, and then print speaker notes and handouts.

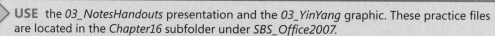

**USE** the *03_NotesHandouts* presentation and the *03_YinYang* graphic. These practice files are located in the *Chapter16* subfolder under *SBS_Office2007*.
**OPEN** the *03_NotesHandouts* presentation.

1. With Slide 1 selected, in the **Notes** pane, click the **Click to add notes** placeholder, type Welcome and introductions, and then press `Enter`.

2. Type Logistics, press `Enter`, and then type Establish knowledge level.

3. Display **Slide 2**, and in the **Notes** pane, type Talk about the main concepts.

4. Display **Slide 3**, and in the **Notes** pane, type Complementary energies, and then press `Enter` twice.

Notes
Page

5. On the **View** tab, in the **Presentation Views** group, click the **Notes Page** button.

Slide 3 is displayed in Notes Page view, with the view percentage set so that the entire page will fit in the window.

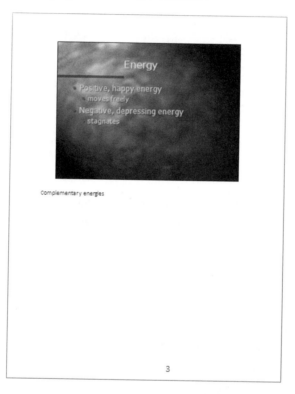

> **Tip** If you have trouble seeing the notes at this view percentage, click the Zoom button in the Zoom group on the View tab. Then when the Zoom dialog box opens, select or type a larger percentage, and click OK.

6. On the **Insert** tab, in the **Illustrations** group, click the **Picture** button.

7. In the **Insert Picture** dialog box, navigate to your *Documents\MSP\SBS_Office2007\Chapter16* folder, and then double-click the *03_YinYang* graphic.

8. Drag the image down below the note you typed in Step 4.

The picture is visible in Notes Page view.

Next Slide

9. At the bottom of the scroll bar, click the **Next Slide** button to move to Slide 4.

Table

10. On the **Insert** tab, in the **Tables** group, click the **Table** button, and then drag to create a table that is two columns wide and eight rows high.

**11.** Drag the table by its border down into the notes placeholder, and then on the **Design** contextual tab in the **Table Style Options** group, clear the **Header Row** and **Banded Rows** check boxes.

**12.** Enter the following information, pressing Tab to move from cell to cell and from row to row:

| | |
|---|---|
| Career | 23 |
| Fame | 30 |
| Relationships | 41 |
| Creativity | 45 |
| Fortune | 60 |
| Health | 72 |
| Knowledge | 81 |
| Helpful people | 85 |

The speaker notes now include the page numbers in a reference work where you can find additional information if required during the presentation.

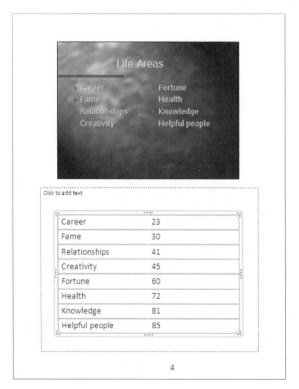

**13.** On the **View** tab, in the **Presentation Views** group, click the **Normal** button, and then drag the splitter bar above the Notes pane up to expand it.

Normal

The table is not visible in Normal view.

**14.** Drag the splitter bar down again. Then on the **View** tab, in the **Presentation Views** group, click the **Notes Master** button.

The Notes Master appears and the Notes Master tab is added to the Ribbon.

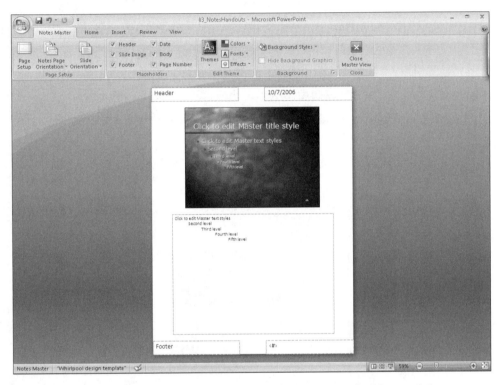

**15.** In the upper-left corner of the page, click the header placeholder, and then type Feng Shui.

**16.** In the lower-left corner of the page, click the footer placeholder, and then type Beginners' Class.

**17.** On the **View** toolbar, click the **Normal** button to return to Normal view.

**18.** Click the **Microsoft Office Button**, and then click **Print**.

The Print dialog box opens.

**19.** Click the **Print what** arrow, select **Notes Pages** in the list, and then click **OK**.

You now have a copy of the speaker notes to refer to during the presentation.

**20.** Display the **Print** dialog box again, and then change the **Print what** setting to **Handouts**.

You can print audience handouts in six formats: one, two, three, four, six, or nine slides per page. The default, six, is set on the Handout master, but you can change it in the Print dialog box.

**21.** Under **Handouts**, click the **Slides per page** arrow, and in the list, click **3**.

When you print three slides per page, PowerPoint adds lines for notes to the right of each slide, as shown in the diagram on the right side of the dialog box.

**22.** In the lower-left corner of the dialog box, click **Preview**.

The first page of the handouts appears in Print Preview.

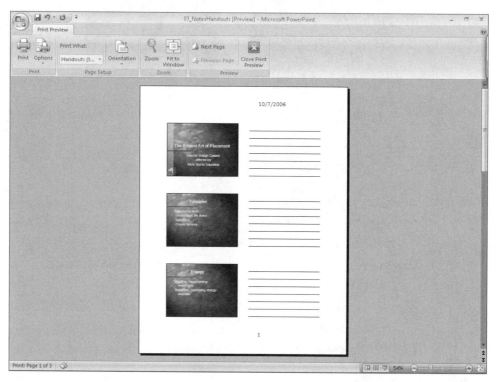

**23.** On the **Print Preview** tab, in the **Print** group, click the **Print** button, and then click **OK**.

Print

**24.** Return to Normal view.

CLOSE the *03_NotesHandouts* presentation without saving your changes.

# Preparing a Presentation for Travel

When you develop a presentation on the computer from which you will be delivering it, you will have all the fonts, linked objects, and other components of the presentation available when the lights go down and you launch your first slide. However, if you will deliver your presentation from a different computer, you need to make sure the fonts, linked objects, and any other necessary items are available.

With PowerPoint 2007, you can use the *Package for CD* feature to help you gather all the presentation components and save them to a CD or other type of removable media so that they can be transported to a different computer. Linked files are included in the presentation package by default. TrueType fonts are stored with the presentation if you select the Embedded TrueType Fonts option while creating the package. (When you include embedded fonts, the file size increases significantly.)

> **Tip** You can embed fonts when you package a presentation, or you can do it when you first save the presentation. In the Save As dialog box, click Tools, click Save Options, and on the Save page, select the Embed Fonts In The File check box. Then select the Embed Only The Characters Used In The Presentation option to embed only the characters in the font set that are actually used, or select the Embed All Characters option to embed the entire font set.

When you use Package For CD, by default the presentation will be set up to run automatically in the *Microsoft Office PowerPoint Viewer*. You can then send the CD containing the presentation package to people who do not have PowerPoint installed on their computers, and they will be able to view the presentation in the PowerPoint Viewer.

In this exercise, you will use Package For CD to create a presentation package on a CD. You will then run the presentation using the PowerPoint Viewer.

> **USE** the *04_Travel* presentation. This practice file is located in the *Chapter16* subfolder under *SBS_PowerPoint 2007*.
>
> **BE SURE TO** have a blank CD available. If your computer does not have a CD burner, you can follow along with the exercise but you will not be able to complete Steps 9 through 17.
>
> **OPEN** the *04_Travel* presentation.

MIcrosoft Office
Button

1. Click the **Microsoft Office Button**, click **Save As**, and then save the current presentation in the *Chapter16* subfolder under *SBS_Office2007*, with the name My Organization 101.

**2.** Click the **Microsoft Office Button**, point to **Publish**, and then click **Package for CD**.

A message box tells you that your file will be converted to the PowerPoint 97-2003 format so that it is compatible with the PowerPoint Viewer.

**3.** Click **OK**.

The Package For CD dialog box opens.

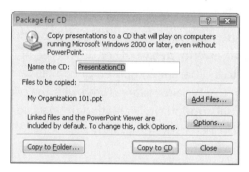

**4.** In the **Name the CD** box, type **Organization**.

The open presentation, its linked files, and the PowerPoint Viewer will be included in the presentation package by default, but you need to specifically include embedded fonts.

**5.** Click **Options**.

The Options dialog box opens.

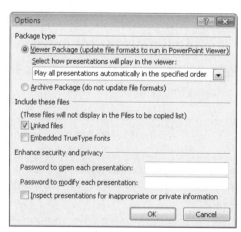

**6.** Under **Package type**, leave the **Viewer Package** option selected, but click the **Select how presentations will play in the viewer** arrow, and then in the list, click **Let the user select which presentation to view**.

Selecting the Viewer Package option includes the PowerPoint Viewer. If you select the Archive Package option, the package contains only the presentation.

7. Under **Include these files**, select the **Embedded TrueType fonts** check box, and then click **OK**.

> **Important** Be sure to select the Embedded TrueType Fonts check box if a presentation includes fonts that don't come with the version of Microsoft Windows running on the presentation computer or the 2007 Microsoft Office system programs. Then the presentation will look the same on a computer on which the fonts aren't installed as it does on your computer.

8. Insert a blank CD in your CD burner, and then click **Copy to CD**.

   If your computer does not have a CD burner, click Copy To Folder instead, and then select the folder in which you want to store the package.

> **Tip** PowerPoint 2007 does not support the direct burning of content to a DVD. If you prefer to burn to a DVD rather than a CD, first copy your presentation to a folder on your computer, and then use DVD-burning software to create the DVD.

9. When PowerPoint asks you to verify that you want to include linked content, click **Yes**.

10. When you see a message that the copy operation was successful, click **No** to indicate that you don't want to copy the same package to another CD.

11. Click **Close** to close the **Package for CD** dialog box.

Close

12. At the right end of the title bar, click the **Close** button to close the presentation and quit PowerPoint.

13. Remove the CD from your CD burner, and then re-insert it.

> **Troubleshooting** If you are running the package from your computer, navigate to the folder where the package is stored, and double-click the Organization folder (the name you assigned in Step 4). Then double-click PPTVIEW to start the Presentation Viewer.

After a few seconds, the PowerPoint Viewer starts. The first time you run this program, you need to click Accept to accept the terms of the program's license agreement. Then a dialog box opens in which you can select the presentation you want to run.

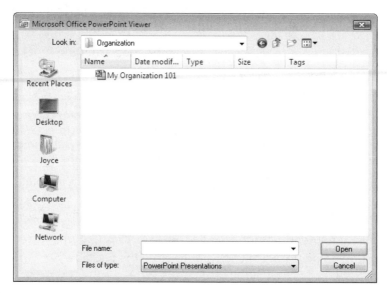

14. In the list of file and folder names, double-click **My Organization 101**.

    The PowerPoint Viewer displays the presentation's title slide.

15. Click the mouse button to advance through the slides in the PowerPoint Viewer, and then press the [Esc] key to end the presentation.

    The PowerPoint Viewer closes.

16. Close the **Microsoft Office PowerPoint Viewer** dialog box.

# Showing a Presentation

To start a slide show from Normal or Slide Sorter view, you click the Slide Show button to display the current slide full screen. Then the simplest way to move linearly from one slide to the next is to click the mouse button without moving the mouse. But you can also move around by using the keyboard:

- To move to the next slide, press the Spacebar, the Down Arrow key, or the Right Arrow key.
- To move to the previous slide, press the Page Up key or the Left Arrow key.
- To end the presentation, press the Esc key.

If you need to move to a slide other than the next one or the previous one, you can move the mouse pointer to display an inconspicuous toolbar in the lower-left corner of the slide. You can use this toolbar in the following ways:

- To move to the next slide, click the Next button.
- To move to the previous slide, click the Previous button.
- To jump to a slide out of sequence (even if it is hidden), click the Navigation button, click Go To Slide, and then click the slide.
- To display the slides in a custom slide show, click the Navigation button, click Custom Show, and then click the show.
- To display a list of keyboard shortcuts for carrying out slide show tasks click the Navigation button, and then click Help . For example, you can press the H key to show the next hidden slide, press the E key to erase pen annotations, or press the A key to show the pointer arrow.
- To end the presentation, click the Navigation button, and then click End Show.

> **Tip** You can also display the Navigation button's menu by right-clicking the slide.

During a presentation, you can reinforce your message by drawing on the slides with an electronic "pen" or changing the background behind text with a highlighter. You simply click the Pen button on the toolbar that appears when you move the mouse, click the tool you want, and then begin drawing or highlighting. You can change the pen or highlighter color to make it stand out on the slide by clicking the Pen button, clicking Ink Color, and then selecting the color you want.

In this exercise, you will move around in various ways while delivering a presentation. You'll also use a pen tool to mark up one slide, change the color, and mark up another.

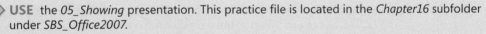

**USE** the *05_Showing* presentation. This practice file is located in the *Chapter16* subfolder under *SBS_Office2007*.
**OPEN** the *05_Showing* presentation.

Slide Show

1. With Slide 1 selected in Normal view, on the **View** toolbar, click the **Slide Show** button.

   The background of the first slide is displayed.

2. Click anywhere on the screen, and then click again.

   First the title moves onto the slide from the top, and then the subtitle moves onto the slide from the bottom.

3. Click the mouse button to advance to Slide 2.

   The slide contents move in from the left.

4. Press the ← key to display the previous slide, and then press the → key to display the next slide.

5. Move the mouse.

   The pointer appears on the screen, and the shadow toolbar appears in the lower-left corner.

> **Troubleshooting** If the pop-up toolbar doesn't appear, press the Esc key to end the slide show. Then click the Microsoft Office Button, click PowerPoint Options, click Advanced, and in the Slide Show section, select the Show Popup Toolbar check box, and click OK.

Next

6. On the toolbar, click the **Next** button (the button at the right end of the shadow toolbar) to display Slide 3.

7. Right-click anywhere on the screen, and then click **Previous** to redisplay Slide 2.

8. Right-click anywhere on the screen, point to **Go to Slide**, and then in the list of slide names, click **7 Pulling It All Together**.

Navigation

9. Display the toolbar, click the **Navigation** button, and then click **Next** to display Slide 8.

10. Use various navigation methods to move around the slide show until you are comfortable moving around.

11. Right-click anywhere on the screen, and then click **End Show**.

    Slide 8 appears in Normal view.

> **Tip** If you click all the way through to the end of the presentation, PowerPoint displays a black screen to indicate that the next click will return you to the previous view. If you do not want the black screen to appear at the end of a presentation, click the Microsoft Office Button, click PowerPoint Options, and click Advanced. Then in the Slide Show area, clear the End With Black Slide check box, and click OK. Then clicking while the last slide is displayed will return you to the previous view.

12. Display **Slide 5**, and switch to Slide Show view.

13. Right-click anywhere on the screen, point to **Pointer Options**, and click **Felt Tip Pen**.

    The pointer changes to resemble the tip of a felt tip pen.

> **Important** When the pen tool is active in Slide Show view, clicking the mouse does not advance the slide show to the next slide. You need to switch back to the regular pointer to use the mouse to advance the slide.

**14.** Draw a line under the word *Colorizing* in the title.

**15.** Right-click the screen, point to **Pointer Options**, and then click **Erase All Ink on Slide**. The line is erased.

**16.** Press [ Space ] to move to the next slide.

Pen

**17.** Display the toolbar, click the **Pen** button, point to **Ink Color**, and then in the palette, click a light purple color.

**18.** Draw circles around *color wheel* and *swatches*.

19. Right-click anywhere on the screen, point to **Pointer Options**, and then click **Arrow**.

    The pen tool changes back to the regular pointer, and you can now click the mouse button to advance to the next slide.

20. Press [Esc] to stop the slide show.

    A message asks whether you want to keep your ink annotations.

21. Click **Discard**.

    Slide 6 appears in Normal view.

**CLOSE** the *05_Showing* presentation without saving your changes, and if you are not continuing directly on to the next chapter, quit PowerPoint.

---

## Using Two Monitors

If your computer can support two monitors, or if you will be presenting a slide show from your computer through an overhead projector, you might want to check out Presenter view. In this view, you can control the slide show on one monitor while the audience sees the presentation in Slide Show view on the other monitor or the projector screen.

To deliver a slide show on one monitor and use Presenter view on another:

1. Open the PowerPoint presentation you want to set up.

2. On the **Slide Show** tab, in the **Set Up** group, click **Set Up Slide Show**.

   The Set Up Show dialog box opens.

3. Under **Multiple monitors**, click the **Display slide show on** arrow, and then in the list, click the name of the monitor you want to use to deliver the presentation.

   The slide show will run full-screen on the specified monitor.

4. Under **Multiple monitors**, select the **Show Presenter View** check box, and then click **OK**.

5. Switch to Slide Show view to start the slide show on the specified monitor.

6. On the other monitor, use the Presenter view navigation tools to control the presentation.

   You can see details about what slide or bullet point is coming next, see your speaker notes, jump directly to any slide, black out the screen during a pause in the presentation, and keep track of the time.

# Key Points

- When you don't want to include all the slides in a presentation for a particular audience, you can use a subset of the slides to create a custom slide show. You can also hide slides and then display them only if appropriate.

- You can assign timings to slides manually, or you can rehearse the presentation and record the slide timings from the rehearsal. The presentation automatically advances from one slide to the next have the specified time has elapsed.

- You can easily create speaker notes to ensure a smooth delivery or print handouts to ensure that your audience can easily follow along with your presentation.

- To run the presentation on a computer other than the one you developed the presentation on, you can create a presentation package. Including the PowerPoint Viewer in the package enables the presentation can run on a computer on which PowerPoint is not installed.

- Knowing how to use all the toolbar buttons, commands, and keyboard shortcuts to navigate in Slide Show view will ensure a smoother presentation delivery.

- To emphasize a point, you can mark up slides during a slide show by using different pen tools and different colors. You can save or discard these annotations.

# Part V

# Microsoft Office Outlook 2007

# Chapter at a Glance

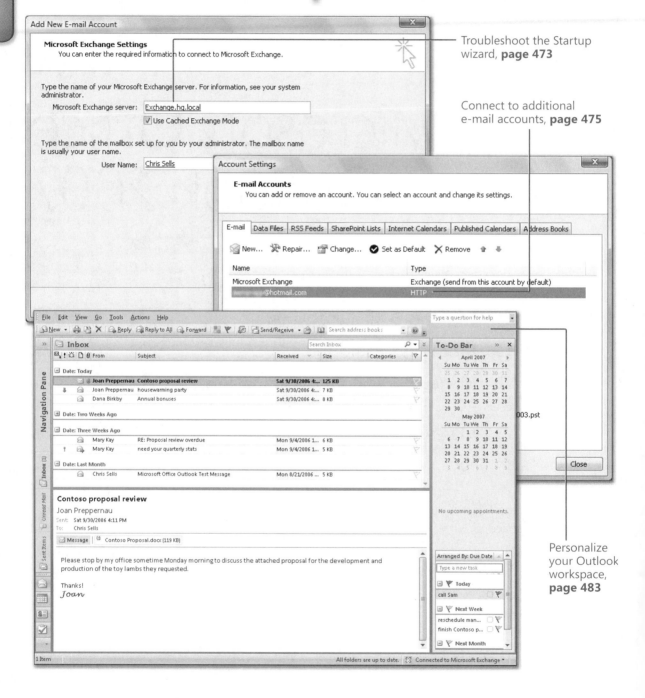

Troubleshoot the Startup wizard, **page 473**

Connect to additional e-mail accounts, **page 475**

Personalize your Outlook workspace, **page 483**

# 17 Getting Started with Outlook 2007

---

**In this chapter, you will learn to:**

✔ Connect to your primary e-mail account.

✔ Troubleshoot the Startup wizard.

✔ Connect to additional e-mail accounts.

✔ Create additional Outlook profiles.

✔ Personalize your Outlook workspace.

✔ Explore the Advanced toolbar.

---

Before you can begin using Outlook, you need to configure it to connect to your e-mail server, and thereby create your e-mail profile. Your profile consists of information about your e-mail account such as the user name, display name, server name, password, and where your Outlook data is stored. You can connect to more than one e-mail account,to manage all your e-mail communications through Outlook.

The Outlook user interface is organized in a manner intended to enable most people to easily view, locate, and link to information. You might find, though, that it is not perfectly suited for the way that you work on a day-to-day basis. Or perhaps you'd just like to try a different layout. There are many ways in which you can personalize the way Outlook appears and functions.

In this chapter, you will configure Outlook to connect to different types of e-mail accounts. You will also create additional Outlook profiles and personalize your Outlook workspace layout to suit your needs.

**See Also** Do you need only a quick refresher on the topics in this chapter? See the Quick Reference entries at the beginning of this book.

> **Important** No practice files are required to complete the exercises in this chapter. For more information about practice files, see "Using the Book's CD" at the beginning of this book.

**Troubleshooting** Graphics and operating system–related instructions in this book reflect the Windows Vista user interface. If your computer is running Microsoft Windows XP and you experience trouble following the instructions as written, please refer to the "Information for Readers Running Windows XP" section at the beginning of this book.

## Different Types of E-Mail Accounts

Outlook 2007 supports the following types of e-mail accounts:

- **Exchange Server.** If your organization runs Microsoft Exchange Server, you can send mail within or outside of your organization's network. Messages are usually stored on the e-mail server, but you can alternatively store them elsewhere (for example, on your computer or on a network share). By default, Outlook creates a local copy of your mailbox on your computer and synchronizes with the server when you're connected, so you can easily work offline if necessary.

- **Post Office Protocol 3 (*POP3*).** When connected to a POP3 account, Outlook downloads (copies) messages from your e-mail server to your computer. You can choose to remove the messages from the server or to leave them there for a specified amount of time. If you access your e-mail account from multiple computers, you will probably want to leave messages on the server to ensure that they're available to you.

- **Internet Message Access Protocol (*IMAP*).** When connected to an IMAP account, Outlook stores copies of messages on your computer, but leaves the originals on the e-mail server. You read and manage messages locally, and Outlook synchronizes with the server when connected.

- **Hypertext Transfer Protocol (*HTTP*).** Messages sent through an HTTP account (such as a Hotmail account), are in the form of Web pages that display within the message window.

You can add multiple POP3, IMAP, and HTTP accounts (but only one Exchange Server account) to your Outlook profile.

# Connecting to Your Primary E-Mail Account

The automatic setup functionality provided by the Outlook 2007 Startup wizard is a significant improvement over previous versions of Outlook, which required that you provide much more information. It might not work under all circumstances, but it generally does a very good job. In most cases, the only information you need is your e-mail address and password.

**See Also** If the Outlook automatic setup functionality doesn't work for you, see "Troubleshooting the Startup Wizard" later in this chapter.

In this exercise, you will start Outlook and configure it to connect to a Microsoft Exchange Server account. Although we demonstrate connecting to an Exchange Server account, you can follow the same basic process to connect to another type of e-mail server. There are no practice files for this exercise.

> **BE SURE TO** have your e-mail address and password available before beginning this exercise. If connecting to an Exchange Server account, you must be connected to your network. If you are working off-network, you might first need to establish a virtual private network (VPN) connection.

Start

1. On the taskbar, click the **Start** button.

2. On the **Start** menu, point to **All Programs**, click **Microsoft Office**, and then click **Microsoft Office Outlook 2007**.

> **Tip** If the E-mail link at the top of the Start menu specifies Microsoft Office Outlook as your default e-mail program, you can click that link instead.

Outlook 2007 starts. If Outlook hasn't yet been configured to connect to an e-mail account, the Outlook 2007 Startup wizard starts.

**See Also** If Outlook is already configured to connect to an e-mail account and you would like to configure a second account, see "Connecting to Additional E-Mail Accounts" later in this chapter.

3. On the welcome page, click **Next**.

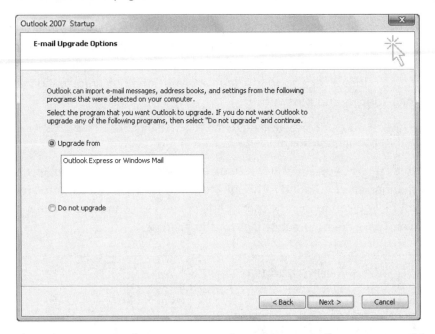

If you have an e-mail account set up in another e-mail program on this computer, Outlook offers the option of importing account information from that account. For the purposes of this exercise, we will not select that option, but you might find it convenient to do so when setting up your own account.

4. On the **E-mail Upgrade Options** page, select the **Do not upgrade** option, and then click **Next**.

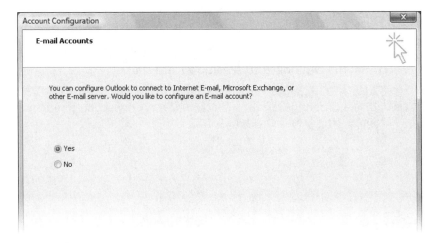

5. On the **E-mail Accounts** page, with the **Yes** option selected, click **Next**.

**6.** On the **Auto Account Setup** page, enter your name, e-mail address, and password in the corresponding text boxes.

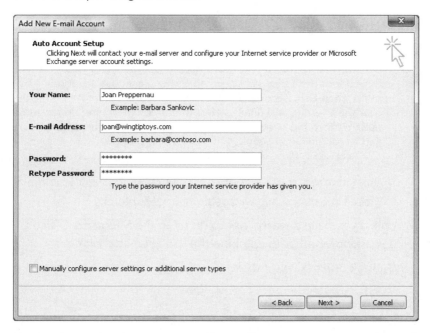

Notice the option here to manually configure your server settings. If you have trouble configuring Outlook by using the automatic setup tool, you can make manual changes by selecting this check box and then clicking Next.

**See Also**  For information about manually setting up Outlook, see "Troubleshooting the Startup Wizard" later in this chapter.

**7.** On the **Auto Account Setup** page, click **Next**.

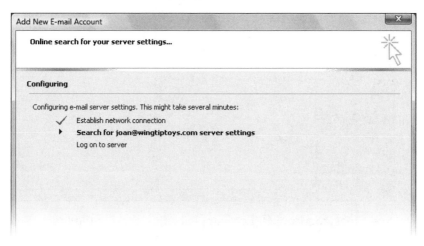

Provided it doesn't encounter any connection or security issues, Outlook uses the minimal information you provided to connect to your e-mail server and create your Outlook profile.

> **Tip** If this is the first time you have started a 2007 Microsoft Office System program, Office prompts you to enter your full name and initials. This information is used throughout the Office system when tracking changes, responding to messages, and so on. Then Office prompts you to select the type of information you want to share over the Internet, and finally, offers the option of signing up for automatic program updates from the Microsoft Update service. None of these options place you at risk, and all can be quite useful.

The first time you start Outlook, it asks whether you want to combine and synchronize RSS feeds in Outlook and Microsoft Internet Explorer.

8. Unless you have a reason not to do so, in the **Microsoft Office Outlook** message box asking whether to combine the RSS Feed lists, click **Yes**.

   Outlook displays your Inbox.

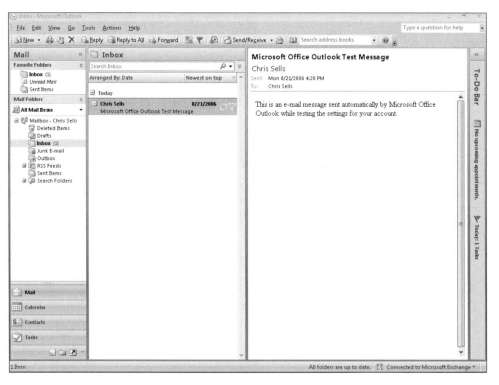

A test message from Outlook appears at the top of the Inbox. Your other e-mail messages will appear below the test message.

> **Tip**  What you see on your screen might not match the graphics in this book exactly. The screens in this book were captured on a monitor set to a resolution of 1024 by 768 pixels, with the Windows taskbar hidden to increase the display space.

# Troubleshooting the Startup Wizard

You are most likely to encounter problems with the automatic setup feature when configuring Outlook to connect to an Exchange Server account, especially if you are working away from your network. Here are some common error messages and problems you could encounter:

- **Server certificate does not match site.**  If Outlook encounters any security issues—for example, if the mail server's digital certificate does not match the name of your domain—Outlook notifies you of this problem and lets you choose whether to proceed.

  If a Security Alert message box appears, you can click the View Certificate button to see the digital certificate of the remote server and verify that you know and trust the company that issued the certificate. If you want, you can install the certificate on your computer by clicking the Install Certificate button and following the steps in the Certificate Import Wizard. When you are confident of the validity of the certificate, in the Security Alert message box, click Yes.

- **Encrypted connection not available.**  Outlook first attempts to establish an encrypted connection with the server. If this attempt is not successful, Outlook notifies you of this problem and asks whether you want to attempt to establish an unencrypted connection.

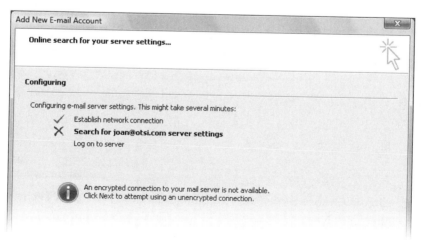

If you select this option, Outlook will most likely configure your Exchange Server account as an IMAP or POP3 account instead of as an Exchange Server account. This configuration will result in a loss of functionality—for instance, the To-Do Bar will not display your calendar and task information.

If you encounter either of these errors when connecting to your Exchange Server account, verify that your computer is connected to your network domain (locally or over a VPN connection, if you're not connecting by using HTTP) and using the correct internal server address method. For instance, if your e-mail address is *jane@adatum.com*, you might address your e-mail server as *mail.adatum.com* or by an internal address such as *ADATUMExchange.adatum.local*.

To successfully troubleshoot your connection issues, you will most likely need to manually configure your server settings. This process is similar to that of configuring an account in Outlook 2003.

1. Display the **Auto Account Setup** page of the **Outlook 2007 Startup** wizard.

2. Select the **Manually configure server settings** check box, and then click **Next**.

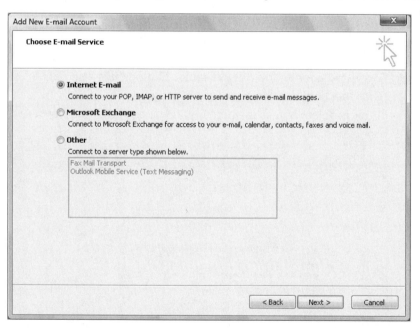

3. On the **Choose E-mail Service** page, select the **Microsoft Exchange** option, and then click **Next**.

4. On the **Microsoft Exchange Settings** page, enter the name or address of your Exchange Server and your user name, and then click the **Check Name** button.

5. If you didn't provide your password on the Auto Account Setup page, Outlook prompts you for it now. If the **Connect to** dialog box appears, enter your logon information, and then click **OK**.

   If you are connected to your network and the user name you enter matches the information on the server, the wizard replaces your user name with your display name (as recorded in your organization's Global Address List) and underlines it. (This is known as *resolving* the address.)

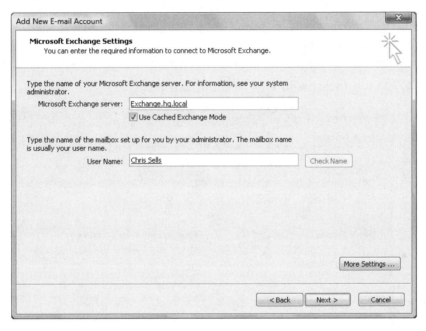

6. After your name appears underlined, click **Next**, and then on the final page of the wizard, click **Finish**.

# Connecting to Additional E-Mail Accounts

You can add e-mail accounts to the your primary Outlook profile. For example, if you want to check your work and personal e-mail accounts from the same Outlook profile, or if you monitor another e-mail alias, such as a support alias. Your profile may include only one Exchange Server account, but it may contain multiple HTTP, IMAP, and POP3 accounts.

> **Tip** If your profile includes multiple e-mail accounts, you can select the sending account each time you send an e-mail message. In the message header, click the Account button, and then in the list, click the account from which you want to send the message. The Account button is visible only when multiple accounts are configured within a profile.

**See Also** For information about connecting to additional Exchange Server accounts, see "Creating Additional Outlook Profiles" later in this chapter.

In this exercise, you will add an HTTP, IMAP, or POP3 e-mail account to your Outlook profile. There are no practice files for this exercise.

> **BE SURE TO** have the logon information for your HTTP, IMAP, or POP3 account available before beginning this exercise.

1. On the **Tools** menu, click **Account Settings**.

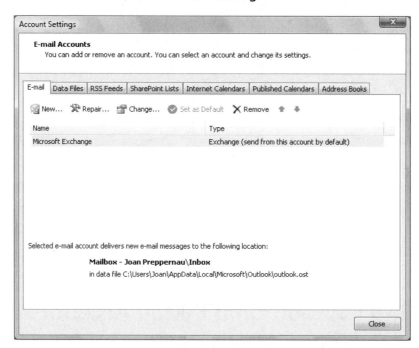

2. On the **E-mail** tab of the **Account Settings** dialog box, click the **New** button.

   The Add New E-mail Account wizard starts.

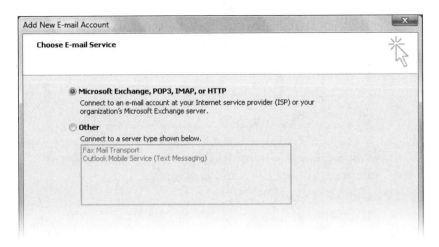

Although Microsoft Exchange Server is shown as an option, you can't configure more than one Exchange Server account per profile.

3. On the **Choose E-mail Service** page, with the **Microsoft Exchange Server, POP3, IMAP, or HTTP** option selected, click **Next**.

4. On the **Auto Account Setup** page, enter the account display name, the e-mail address, and the password of the account you want to add to your profile. Then click **Next**.

Outlook establishes a network connection and searches for the server settings. After locating the server and validating your user name and password, Outlook displays a confirmation message.

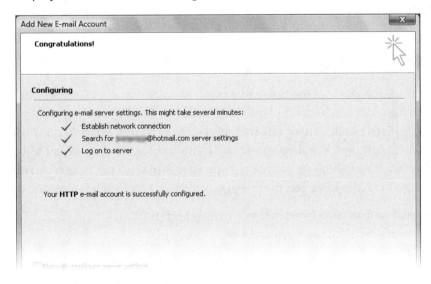

5. Click **Finish** to complete the account setup.

The new account appears on the E-mail tab of the Account Settings dialog box and in the All Mail Folders list.

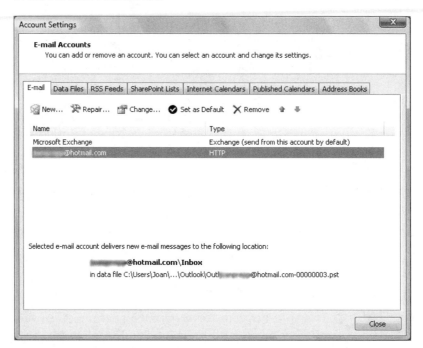

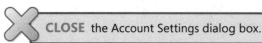
**CLOSE** the Account Settings dialog box.

# Creating Additional Outlook Profiles

In the same way that multiple users of a computer running Windows Vista or Windows XP can have individual user profiles, you can have more than one e-mail profile on your computer. Each profile can include multiple e-mail accounts, but only one Exchange Server account. Most people will have only one e-mail profile, but if you want to connect to multiple Exchange accounts—for instance, if you have e-mail accounts with two companies that you access from the same computer—you can do so only through a second e-mail profile.

E-mail profiles are stored in the Windows registry. You create additional profiles from Windows, rather than from Outlook.

If you have multiple e-mail profiles, you can instruct Outlook to log on to one by default or to prompt you to select a profile each time it starts. If you're planning to regularly access more than one profile, the latter is the easiest solution.

## Outlook with Business Contact Manager

Microsoft Office Outlook 2007 with Business Contact Manager integrates complete small business contact-management capabilities into Outlook so that you can easily manage prospect and customer information and track sales and marketing activities all in one place.

- **Organize your customer information in one place.** Track your prospects, leads, and customers from initial contact through closing and after the sale.

- **Manage sales leads and opportunities.** Monitor opportunities by type, sales stage, projected amount of sale, and probability of closing, and then easily re-assign leads.

- **Review important sales metrics.** Use the summaries in the new central information dashboard to help you make decisions and prioritize tasks.

- **Distribute personalized marketing communications.** Create filtered mailing lists, and then use the improved mail merge integration functionality with Microsoft Office Publisher, Microsoft Office Word, or HTML to personalize print and e-mail marketing materials.

- **Track marketing campaign activities.** Evaluate the success of your campaign so that you can target your marketing budget more effectively in the future.

- **Centralize project information.** Organize project information and follow up on project-related tasks, including activities, e-mail messages, meetings, notes, and attachments.

When using Outlook with Business Contact Manager you can easily access all of your customer communications history in one place within the familiar Outlook environment. The Business Contact Manager toolbar at the top of the Outlook window contains commands for managing Accounts, Business Contacts, Opportunities, Business Projects, Project Tasks, and Marketing Campaigns. The Business Contact Manager home page, or dashboard, is your central point for managing your company's important business contact and opportunity information.

Outlook 2007 with Business Contact Manager is available in the Microsoft Office Professional 2007 and Microsoft Office Small Business 2007 product suites, or through volume licensing programs. For more information about Outlook 2007 with Business Contact Manager, visit

*www.microsoft.com/office/outlook/contactmanager/prodinfo/*

> **Tip** You can't switch between profiles while Outlook is running. If you don't select the option to have Outlook prompt you for a profile, you can change the default profile from the Windows Control Panel.

In this exercise, you will create a second Outlook profile and configure Outlook so that you can choose which profile to log on to each time you start Outlook. There are no practice files for this exercise.

> **BE SURE TO** configure Outlook to connect to at least one account before beginning this exercise.

1. Exit Outlook if it is running.

2. On the **Start** menu, click **Control Panel**.

3. In the left pane, click **Classic View** to display the individual module icons.

4. In **Control Panel**, double-click the **Mail** icon. If the **User Account Control** message box requesting permission to continue appears, click **Continue**.

> **Troubleshooting** The Mail icon appears only after you have completed the initial Outlook account configuration.

The Mail Setup dialog box opens. You can set up e-mail accounts and data files from this dialog box or from Outlook.

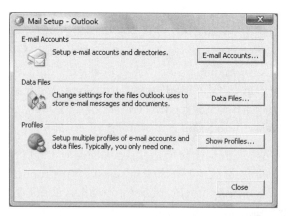

5. In the **Mail Setup** dialog box, click **Show Profiles**.

The Mail dialog box opens, listing the mail profiles set up on your computer under your user account profile. Other people's mail profiles are not visible to you.

Outlook created the *Outlook* profile the first time you configured Outlook to connect to an e-mail account.

**6.** In the **Mail** dialog box, click **Add**.

The New Profile dialog box opens.

**7.** In the **Profile Name** box, type a name to identify your second profile.

> **Tip** You cannot change the name of a profile after you create it. If you want to work under a different profile name you must create a new profile.

You should make this name obvious—for instance, the name of the company or e-mail account the profile applies to.

**8.** Click **OK**.

The Add New E-mail Account wizard starts.

**9.** If the **Choose E-mail Service** page appears, select the **Internet E-mail or Microsoft Exchange** option, and then click **Next**.

**10.** On the **Auto Account Setup** page, enter the display name, e-mail address, and password of the e-mail account you want to associate with the new profile in the corresponding text boxes, and then click **Next**.

**11.** After Outlook connects to the e-mail account, click **Finish**.

> **Troubleshooting** If Outlook isn't able to successfully connect to your account, see "Troubleshooting the Startup Wizard" earlier in this chapter.

The new profile appears in the Mail dialog box.

**12.** In the **Mail** dialog box, select the **Prompt for a profile to be used** option, and click **OK**.

**13.** Start Outlook.

The Choose Profile dialog box opens.

**14.** Click the **Profile Name** arrow, and in the list, click the profile you want to connect to.

If you want to stop this box from appearing in the future, you can click Options, and then select the Set As Default Profile check box. You can select an alternate default profile or have Outlook prompt you by returning to the Mail dialog box in Control Panel.

**CLOSE** Outlook. If you want to change the Outlook profile options before continuing, display Control Panel, display the Mail dialog box, and then adjust your settings.

# Personalizing Your Outlook Workspace

The Outlook program window includes six areas or elements in which you work with Outlook or with your Outlook items (e-mail messages, contact records, calendar entries, tasks, or notes).

Menu bar        Toolbar                                      To-Do Bar

Navigation Pane   Message content pane            Reading Pane

You might find that this is an ideal arrangement for the way you work. But if you're viewing the program window on a low-resolution screen, don't need all the available tools, or would like more space for the main work area, you can easily change the appearance and layout of the workspace in the following ways:

- **Menu bar.** When working in the Outlook program window, you can access commands from the menus displayed here. You can't hide the menu bar, but you can move it, docking it on any side of the program window or floating it anywhere on your screen.

- **Toolbars.** The buttons on the Standard toolbar, which is shown by default, represent frequently used commands in the File, Edit, and Actions categories. You can also display the Advanced toolbar and the Web toolbar. To display or hide a toolbar, right-click anywhere on the menu bar or toolbar area, and then click the name of the toolbar.

  **See Also** For information about the Advanced toolbar, see "Exploring the Advanced Toolbar" later in this chapter.

- **Navigation Pane.** This view pane appears on the left side of the Outlook window. Its contents change depending on the module you're viewing—it might display the module organizational structure, view options, links to external content or Help topics, and so on.

  - You can minimize or expand the Navigation Pane by clicking the left- or right-facing chevrons at the top of the pane.

  - You can change the width of the Navigation Pane by dragging the vertical frame divider to its right.

  - You can change the number and size of the module buttons.

    To display more buttons at the bottom of the Navigation Pane, drag the handle above the module buttons to increase the available space, or click the Configure Buttons button in the lower-right corner of the Navigation Pane, and then click Show More Buttons. To display buttons in a small format or allocate more space to the Navigation Pane folders and options, drag the handle to decrease the available space, or click the Configure Buttons button and then click Show Less Buttons.

- **Module content pane.** This view pane appears in the center of the window, and displays the content of the selected module—your e-mail messages, calendar, contacts, and so on. You can display and organize content in this pane in many ways. These options are covered in this book as part of the individual module discussions.

- **Reading Pane.** When displayed, you can preview a selected message, appointment, attached document, and so on in this view pane. You can display the pane to the right of or below the content pane, or close it entirely.

- **To-Do Bar.** On the right side of the Outlook window, this view pane displays the monthly calendar previously found in the Date Navigation Pane of the Outlook Calendar. It also displays your upcoming appointments and your task list. You can hide or display the pane, change the number of calendar months and appointments shown, and arrange the task list in different ways. You can change the size of the module content pane by minimizing or maximizing the To-Do Bar—the minimized pane bar displays your next appointment and the number of active and completed tasks due today.

All of these window elements are available from every Outlook module, but the Reading Pane and To-Do Bar are not always displayed by default. The following table indicates whether they appear by default in each module.

| Module | Reading Pane | To-Do Bar |
|---|---|---|
| Mail | Yes | Yes |
| Calendar | No | No |
| Contacts | No | Yes |
| Tasks | Yes | Yes |
| Notes | No | Yes |

> **Tip** We refer to each of the above as modules. You might also think of them as folders—because each is represented in the Navigation Pane as a folder.

You can display or hide any of the workspace elements (other than the menu bar, which can't be changed) from the View menu. Your Outlook environment preferences are preserved from session to session. When you start Outlook, the Navigation Pane, To-Do Bar, and Calendar will appear the same way they did when you last exited.

When you first start Outlook, the Mail module appears and displays your Inbox. The Navigation Pane displays the folder structure of your mailbox (e-mail account). When connecting to any type of e-mail account, four folders are visible:

- **Deleted Items.** Outlook items that you delete from other folders are held in this folder, and not deleted permanently until you empty the folder.

- **Inbox.** Outlook delivers new messages to this folder.

- **Junk E-mail.** Outlook delivers messages held by the spam filter to this folder.
- **Sent Items.** When you send a message, Outlook stores a copy of it in this folder.

In Exchange Server account mailboxes, these four folders are also visible:

- **Drafts.** Temporary copies of in-progress messages are stored in this folder.

    **See Also**   For information about creating and working with drafts, see "Creating and Sending Messages" in Chapter 18, "Sending E-Mail Messages."

- **Outbox.** Messages that you send are held in this folder until Outlook establishes a connection to your mail server.
- **RSS Feeds.** Web site information feeds you subscribe to are available from this folder. When you first start Outlook, you might find information feeds recommended by Microsoft here.
- **Search Folders.**  These virtual folders track messages matching specific search criteria.

When you click the Folder List button at the bottom of the Navigation Pane, these six folders appear in Exchange Server mailboxes:

- **Calendar.**  Displays the Outlook Calendar module.
- **Contacts.**  Displays the Outlook Contacts module.
- **Journal.**  Displays the Outlook Journal.
- **Notes.**  Displays the Outlook Notes module.
- **Sync Issues.**  Tracks conflicts and communication failures on your mail server or in your mailbox.
- **Tasks.**  Displays the Outlook Tasks module.

You can display any of the modules—Mail, Calendar, Contacts, Tasks, or Notes—by clicking the corresponding button at the bottom of the Navigation Pane, by clicking the module name on the Go menu, or by holding down the Ctrl key and then pressing the function key representing the module you want to display:

| Module | Keyboard shortcut |
| --- | --- |
| Mail | Ctrl+1 |
| Calendar | Ctrl+2 |
| Contacts | Ctrl+3 |
| Tasks | Ctrl+4 |
| Notes | Ctrl+5 |

The Navigation Pane contents differ depending on the displayed module. We discuss each module's Navigation Pane in the related chapters of this book.

In this exercise, you will change the space allocated to the module content pane, change the content displayed on the To-Do Bar, and learn how to move the menu bar and move or hide the toolbars. There are no practice files for this exercise.

**BE SURE TO** start Outlook and display the Inbox before beginning this exercise.

Minimize the
Navigation Pane

1. At the top of the **Navigation Pane**, click the **Minimize the Navigation Pane** button.

   The Navigation Pane contracts to display only a vertical bar on the left side of the program window. In the Mail module, buttons on the minimized Navigation Pane give you one-click access to the folders included in your Favorite Folders list.

2. Click the **Navigation Pane** bar at the top of the pane.

   Outlook displays your Favorite Folders and Mail Folders in a slide-out window.

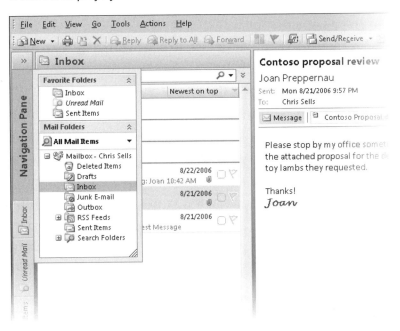

3. Click away from the slide-out window to collapse it.

4. At the top of the **To-Do Bar**, click the **Maximize the To-Do Bar** button.

Maximize the
To-Do Bar

   The To-Do Bar expands to display the current month's calendar, your next three appointments, and your task list.

> **Tip** You can close the To-Do Bar completely by clicking the Close button in the upper-right corner of the expanded To-Do Bar. To redisplay the To-Do Bar after closing it, point to To-Do Bar on the View menu, and then click Normal or Minimized.

5. On the **View** menu, point to **To-Do Bar**, and then click **Options**.

   The To-Do Bar Options dialog box opens.

6. Change the **Date Navigator** setting to display 2 months and the **Appointments** setting to display 4 appointments. Then click **OK**.

7. On the **View** menu, point to **Reading Pane**, and then click **Bottom**.

   The Reading Pane moves from the side of the content pane to the bottom.

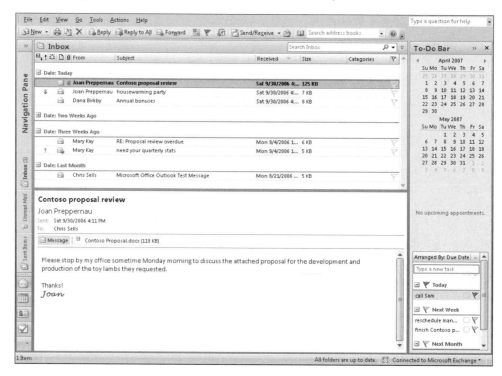

8. On the **View** menu, point to **Reading Pane**, and then click **Off** to close the Reading Pane entirely.

> **Tip** You can close the Reading Pane by pointing to Reading Pane on the View menu, and then clicking Off.

9. At the top of the Outlook window, point to the move handle (the vertical line of four dots) to the left of the **File** menu.

   The mouse pointer changes to a four-headed arrow.

10. Drag the menu bar to the right side of the Outlook program window. (Release the menu bar when it changes to a vertical orientation.)

    The menu names rotate to follow the window edge, but clicking any menu name displays the menu at the normal angle. You can use the same drag-and-drop technique to move any of the displayed toolbars.

11. Drag the menu bar by the move handle to the content pane.

    The menu bar becomes a *floating toolbar*.

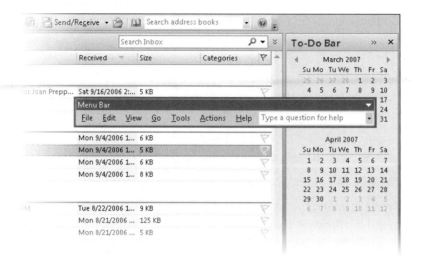

> **Tip** When the Outlook window is not maximized, you can place a floating toolbar inside or outside of the program window.

**12.** Right-click the floating menu bar or the toolbar area at the top of the Outlook window.

On the toolbar shortcut menu, you can select the toolbars you want to display.

**13.** Using the techniques discussed in this topic, rearrange the Outlook window elements to your liking.

> **Troubleshooting** Changes you implement might make your Outlook window appear different from those shown in this book. We depict the Outlook window with the menu bar and Standard toolbar at the top of the window, the Navigation Pane and To-Do Bar maximized, and the Reading Pane displayed on the right side of the window.

# Exploring the Advanced Toolbar

The Outlook program window has three toolbars: the Standard toolbar, the Advanced toolbar, and the Web toolbar. Even people who use Outlook on a daily basis might find that they have never displayed the Advanced toolbar or used any of the commands available on it.

> **Tip** You can access Internet resources and interact with Internet Explorer from the Web toolbar. Because the Web toolbar functionality is not specific to Outlook, we don't discuss it in this book.

We don't make use of the Advanced toolbar in this book, but you can experiment with it on your own—you might find it very useful to have its commands available to you. To display the Advanced toolbar, right-click the menu bar or toolbar and then click Advanced.

Current View lis

In the Mail module, the features and commands available from the Advanced toolbar include:

- **Outlook Today.** The Outlook Today page, which in a previous version of Outlook appeared by default when you started the program, presents information from your Calendar and Tasks list along with a count of the unread messages in your Inbox and all the messages in your Drafts folder and Outbox. If you would like to see this overview page when you start Outlook, display the Outlook Today page, click the Customize Outlook Today button, select the When Starting, Go Directly To Outlook Today check box, and then click Save Changes. On the Customize Outlook Today page, you can also configure what is shown in the message, calendar, and tasks areas, and choose between five page layouts and themes.

- **Back, Forward, and Up One Level.** You can quickly move between folders by using these commands.

- **Reading Pane.** Toggles the display of the Reading Pane on the right side of the window.

- **Print Preview.** Previews the currently selected item as it would be printed using the default settings.

- **Undo.** Reverts your most recent change. For instance, if you delete an e-mail message and then click the Undo button, the message moves back to the original folder.

- **Rules and Alerts.** Opens the Rules And Alerts dialog box, where you can create and manage rules for incoming e-mail and RSS feeds, and alerts.

- **Current View list.** This drop-down list includes all available views of the current folder.

- **Group By Box.** Toggles the display of a box in the content pane header from which you can choose how Outlook groups the displayed content.

- **Field Chooser.** Toggles the display of the Field Chooser window, from which you can specify the item fields you want to display in the content pane, by dragging fields between the Field Chooser window and the content pane header.

- **AutoPreview.** Toggles the display of the first three lines of message text within the content pane. AutoPreview is specific to the folder in which you select it, so you can choose to display extra message text in only certain folders.

In the Calendar module, the Advanced toolbar also includes:

- **Plan a Meeting.** Opens the Plan A Meeting dialog box in which you can view prospective attendees' schedules. This is similar to the Scheduling page of a meeting window. After you enter information in the Plan A Meeting dialog box, Outlook displays a meeting window in which you can enter the meeting subject and location before sending invitations.

In the Contacts module, the Advanced toolbar also includes:

- **New Meeting Request to Contact.** Opens a meeting window addressed to the currently selected contact(s).

- **New Task for Contact.** Opens a task window assigned to the currently selected contact.

- **Explore Web Page.** Displays the Web page listed in the currently selected contact record in your default Internet browser.

When you display the Advanced toolbar it is available (in its different forms) from any module.

# Key Points

- You can configure Outlook 2007 to connect to most e-mail accounts automatically. You need to provide only your e-mail address and account password.

- You can configure multiple e-mail accounts within one Outlook profile, but you can have only one Exchange Server account per profile. To connect to multiple Exchange Server accounts from the same computer, you must log on to each through its own profile.

- You can rearrange the Outlook window to suit your working preferences. Any of the Outlook view panes—the Navigation Pane, To-Do Bar, and Reading Pane—as well as the Advanced toolbar can be displayed in any Outlook module. Outlook preserves changes to the default arrangement from session to session.

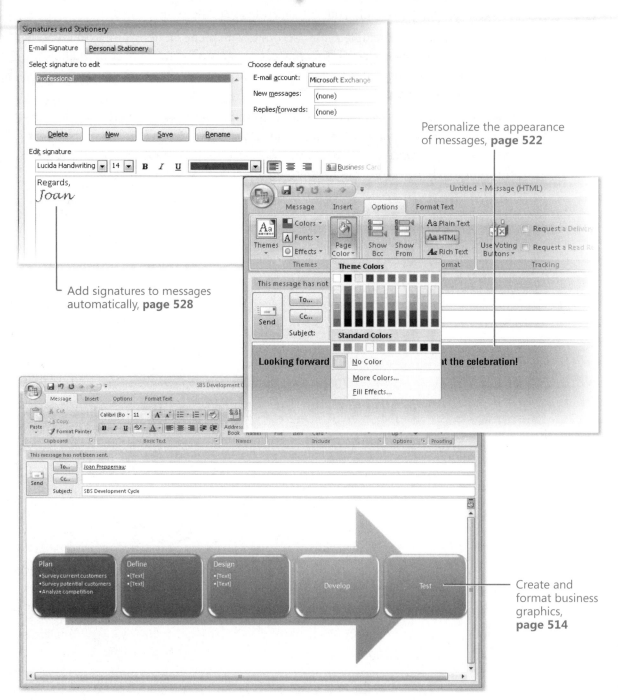

Personalize the appearance of messages, **page 522**

Add signatures to messages automatically, **page 528**

Create and format business graphics, **page 514**

# 18 Sending E-Mail Messages

**In this chapter, you will learn to:**

✔ Work in the message window.

✔ Create and send messages.

✔ Attach files to messages.

✔ Create and format business graphics.

✔ Personalize the appearance of messages.

✔ Add signatures to messages automatically.

Although Microsoft Office Outlook 2007 includes useful components for managing your calendar, contacts, tasks, and notes, the primary reason most people use Outlook is to send and receive e-mail messages. Over the past decade, *e-mail* (short for electronic mail) has become an accepted and even required form of business communication. And of course, many people use e-mail to keep in touch with friends and family, either from work or from home. Outlook makes it easy to connect to multiple e-mail accounts, either on a business network or over the Internet, and provides all the tools you need to send, respond to, organize, filter, sort, find, and otherwise manage e-mail messages.

> **Tip** In this chapter and throughout this book, we might refer to e-mail messages simply as *messages*.

When sending messages from Outlook, you can:

● Include attachments such as documents, spreadsheets, or business graphics.

● Personalize your messages by using colors, fonts, backgrounds, electronic signatures, and electronic business cards.

● Set message options such as voting buttons, importance, sensitivity, and reminders.

● Request electronic receipts when a message is delivered to the recipient's mailbox or opened by the recipient.

In this chapter, you will look at elements of the item window interface. You will create and send messages, learn various ways of addressing messages to recipients, and practice sending messages with and without attachments. Then you will create and format a business graphic using the exciting new SmartArt feature provided in Outlook as well as in Microsoft Office PowerPoint 2007 and Microsoft Office Word 2007. Finally, you will experiment with the various ways you can personalize a message, including changing the font and background and adding a signature.

> **Important** You will use the messages you create in this chapter as practice files for exercises in later chapters of this book.

**See Also** Do you need only a quick refresher on the topics in this chapter? See the Quick Reference entries at the beginning of this book.

> **Important** Before you can use the practice files in this chapter, you need to install them from the book's companion CD to their default location. See "Using the Book's CD" at the beginning of this book for more information.

> **Troubleshooting** Graphics and operating system–related instructions in this book reflect the Windows Vista user interface. If your computer is running Microsoft Windows XP and you experience trouble following the instructions as written, please refer to the "Information for Readers Running Windows XP" section at the beginning of this book.

# Working in the Message Window

Outlook displays e-mail messages in the Mail module. When you create or respond to an e-mail message, it opens in a *message window*. The message window has its own set of commands separate from those in the Outlook program window. You can format and modify outgoing e-mail messages by using the message window commands.

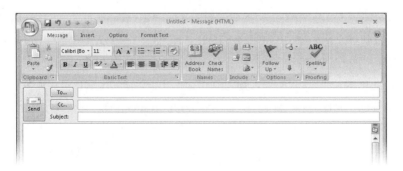

Commands related to managing messages (such as saving, printing, securing, and sharing a message) are available from the Office menu.

In this exercise, you will take a tour of the message item window elements that differ from the contact window elements. There are no practice files for this exercise.

**BE SURE TO** start Outlook and display the Inbox before beginning this exercise.

New Mail
Message

1. On the Standard toolbar, click the **New Mail Message** button.

   An untitled message window opens.

Customize Quick Access
Toolbar button

Title bar displaying
message subject

View Ruler
button

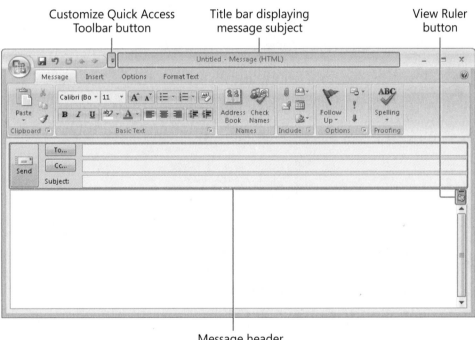

Message header

> **Important** Depending on your screen resolution and the size of the message window that opens, you might see more or fewer buttons in each of the groups, or the buttons you see might be represented by larger or smaller icons than those shown in this book. Experiment with the size of the message window to understand the effect on the appearance of the command interface tabs.

Microsoft Office
Button

2. In the upper-left corner of the message window, click the **Microsoft Office Button**.

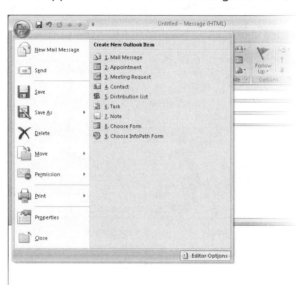

Notice that although you are working in the message window, you can create any type of Outlook item from the Office menu. We'll review the commands available from the Office menu in other chapters of this book.

**See Also** For information about the Permission commands, see the sidebar "Restricting Message Permissions" later in this chapter.

3. Click away from the **Office** menu to close it.

Customize Quick
Access Toolbar

4. Click the **Customize Quick Access Toolbar** button.

A menu of commonly used commands and customization options appears.

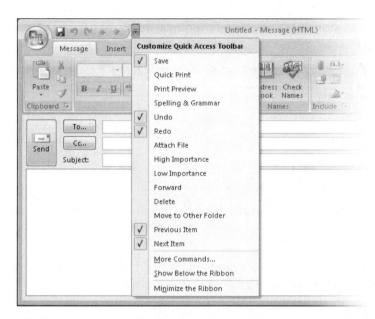

Clicking a command in the first menu section adds it to the Quick Access Toolbar.

**5.** On the **Customize Quick Access Toolbar** menu, click **Show Below the Ribbon**.

The Quick Access Toolbar moves to a position between the tabs and the *message header*. You might find this position useful if you place many additional commands on the Quick Access Toolbar and it crowds the text shown in the message title bar.

Alternate Quick Access
Toolbar location

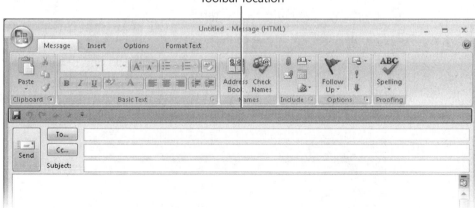

**6.** On the **Customize Quick Access Toolbar** menu, click **Show Above the Ribbon** to return the Quick Access Toolbar to its original location.

The message window commands are organized in groups on four tabs:

- Message
- Insert
- Options
- Format Text

> **Tip** Depending on what programs you have installed on your computer, tabs and groups other than those described here might also appear on the Ribbon.

The Message tab is active by default. Buttons representing commands related to creating messages are organized on this tab in six groups:

- Clipboard
- Basic Text
- Names
- Include
- Options
- Proofing

You can compose and send any standard e-mail message by using only the commands available on this tab.

**7.** Double-click the **Message** tab.

Double-clicking the active tab hides the Ribbon and provides more space for the message.

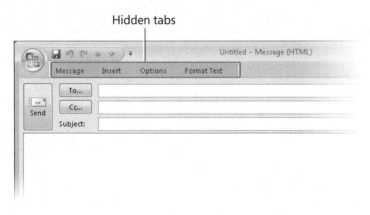

Hidden tabs

**8.** Click the **Insert** tab.

The Ribbon reappears, with the Insert tab active.

> **Tip** If you click away from the Ribbon (for instance, in the content pane) the Ribbon hides again. This behavior is the default until you again double-click a tab.

Buttons representing commands related to items you can insert are organized on this tab in six groups:

- Include
- Tables
- Illustrations
- Links
- Text
- Symbols

**9.** Click the **Options** tab.

Buttons representing commands related to the format, appearance, and actions of messages are organized on this tab in five groups:

- Themes
- Fields
- Format
- Tracking
- More Options

**10.** Click the **Format Text** tab.

Command buttons related to the appearance of message content are organized on this tab in six groups:

- Clipboard
- Font
- Paragraph
- Styles
- Zoom
- Editing

Many of the commands on this tab also appear on the Message tab.

 **CLOSE** the message window.

---

## Outlook Message Formats

Outlook can send and receive e-mail messages in three message formats:

- *Hypertext Markup Language (HTML)* supports paragraph styles (including numbered and bulleted lists), character styles (such as fonts, sizes, colors, weight), and backgrounds (such as colors and pictures). Most (but not all) e-mail programs support the HTML format—those that don't display HTML messages as Plain Text.

- *Rich Text Format (RTF)* supports more paragraph formatting options than HTML, including borders and shading, but is compatible with only Outlook and Microsoft Exchange Server. Outlook converts RTF messages to HTML when sending them outside of your Exchange network.

- *Plain Text* does not support the formatting features available in HTML and RTF messages, but is supported by all e-mail programs.

# Creating and Sending Messages

Regardless of the type of e-mail account you have, as long as you have an Internet connection you can send e-mail messages to people within your organization and around the world. You can personalize your messages by using an individual font style or color, and by inserting your contact information in the form of an e-mail signature or business card. (You can apply other formatting, such as themes and page backgrounds, but these won't always appear to e-mail recipients as you intend them to, and they can make your communications appear less professional.) You can format the text of your message to make it more readable, by including headings, lists, or tables, and represent information graphically by including charts, pictures, clip art, and other types of graphics. You can attach files to your message and link to other information such as files or Web pages.

**See Also** For more information about formatting messages, see "Personalizing the Appearance of Messages" later in this chapter.

## Addressing Messages

Addressing an e-mail message is as simple as typing the intended recipient's e-mail address into the To box. If you want to send a message to more than one person, indicate a different level of involvement for certain recipients, or include certain people without other recipients knowing, here are some tips.

By default, Outlook requires that you separate multiple e-mail addresses with semicolons. If you prefer, you can instruct Outlook to accept both semicolons and commas. To do this:

1. On the **Tools** menu, click **Options**.
2. In the **Options** dialog box, on the **Preferences** tab, click the **E-mail Options** button.
3. In the **E-mail Options** dialog box, click the **Advanced E-mail Options** button.
4. In the **When sending a message** area, select the **Allow comma as address separator** check box, and then click **OK** in each of the three open dialog boxes.

As you type a name or an e-mail address into the To, Cc, or Bcc box, Outlook displays matching addresses in a list below the box. Select a name or e-mail address from the list and then press Tab or Enter to insert the entire name or address in the box.

If your e-mail account is part of an Exchange Server network, you can send messages to another person on the same network by typing only his or her e-mail alias (for instance, *joan*)—the at symbol (@) and domain name aren't required.

If a message recipient's address is in your address book, you can type the person's name and Outlook will look for the corresponding e-mail address. (You can either wait for Outlook to validate the name or press Ctrl+K to immediately validate the names and addresses in the address boxes.) By default, Outlook searches your Global Address List and main address book. To have Outlook also search other address books:

1. On the **Tools** menu, click **Address Book**.

2. In the **Address Book** window, on the **Tools** menu, click **Options**.

3. In the **Addressing** dialog box, click **Add**.

4. In the **Add Address List** dialog box, click the address list you want to add, click **Add**, and then click **Close**.

5. In the **Addressing** dialog box, click **OK**, and then close the **Address Book** window.

If the address book does not contain an entry for a name that you type in the To, Cc, or Bcc box of a new message, when you send the message, Outlook prompts you to select an address book entry or provide a full e-mail address.

## Sending Courtesy Copies

To send a courtesy copy of a message to a person, enter his or her e-mail address in the Cc box. This is commonly referred to as "CCing" a person. You might CC someone to provide him or her with information but indicate that you don't require his or her involvement in the conversation. To send a message to a person without making it known to other recipients, enter the person's e-mail address in the Bcc box to send a "blind" courtesy copy (also known as "BCCing" a person). Outlook does not display the Bcc field by default. To display the Bcc field:

1. Display a message window.

2. On the **Options** tab, in the **Fields** group, click the **Show Bcc** button.

Addresses entered in the Bcc box can't be seen by other message recipients. They also aren't included in any replies to the original message.

## Saving Message Drafts

Until you save or send a message, Outlook maintains a temporary copy of it in your Drafts folder. If you close Outlook (or a problem causes Outlook to close or your computer to shut down) before you send the message, the *draft* retains most or all of your work. When the first draft of a message is saved (either automatically or manually), a banner appears in the message header with the notation "This message has not been sent."

You can save a message draft at any time by clicking the Save button on the Quick Access Toolbar in the message window, or by closing the message window and then clicking Yes in the Microsoft Office Outlook message box asking whether to keep the draft. (If you click No, Outlook deletes the draft.) To restart work on a draft message, display the Mail module, click the Drafts folder in the Navigation Pane, and then double-click the message you want to open.

> **Troubleshooting** Some users running Adobe Acrobat version 6 or 7 might experience problems when creating new messages or responding to messages in Outlook 2007. If you have Adobe Acrobat installed and experience these types of problems, try uninstalling the Adobe Outlook add-ins.

In this exercise, you will compose and send a new e-mail message. There are no practice files for this exercise.

> **BE SURE TO** start Outlook and display the Inbox before beginning this exercise.

New Mail
Message

**1.** On the Standard toolbar, click the **New Mail Message** button.

A new message window opens.

> **Tip** By clicking the New Mail Message arrow, you can choose to create other types of Outlook items such as appointments, contacts, tasks, notes, or faxes, as well as organizational items such as folders and data files.

Message header                              Content pane

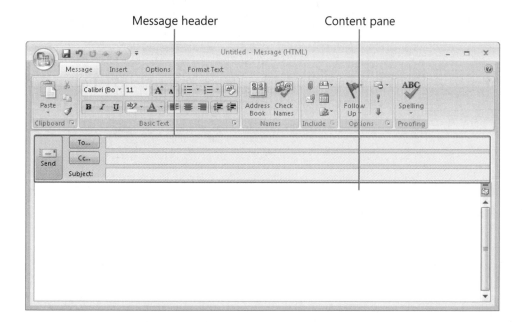

> **Tip** Only those commands that can be performed on the currently selected message element are active.

2. In the **To** box, type your own e-mail address.

3. In the **Subject** box, type SBS Tradeshow Schedule.

> **Important** The subject of this message begins with *SBS* so that you can easily differentiate it from other messages in your Inbox and Sent Items folders.

4. In the content pane, type The following people will be working at the tradeshow: and press the [Enter] key twice. Then type the following names, pressing [Enter] once after each of the first four names, and twice at the end: Anna, Barry, Carl, Denis, Emma.

Bullets

5. Select the list of names. Then on the **Message** tab, in the **Basic Text** group, click the **Bullets** button (not its arrow).

> **Tip** The Bullets button is also available in the Paragraph group on the Format Text tab.

Outlook converts the list of names to a simple bulleted list.

> **Tip** In this book, when we give instructions to implement a command, we tell you on what tab and in which group the command button appears. When directing you to use multiple command buttons on the same tab, we might omit the tab name to avoid needless repetition.

6. With the bulleted list still selected, in the **Basic Text** group, click the **Bullets** arrow.

Outlook has saved a
draft of this message

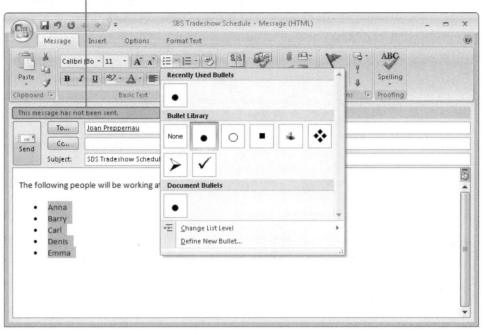

Notice the types of bullets available in the Bullet Library. You can change the list to
use any of these bullets by clicking the bullet you want.

7. In the **Bullets** gallery, point to **Change List Level**.

You can demote (or promote) a list item to any of nine levels, differentiated by the
bullet character and indent level.

8. Press `Esc` twice to close the Bullets gallery without making changes.

9. Press `Ctrl`+`End` to move the insertion point to the end of the message. Type
Giveaways are: and then press `Enter` twice.

10. On the **Insert** tab, in the **Tables** group, click the **Table** button.

Table

**11.** On the **Insert Table** menu, point to the third cell in the second row.

A preview of the table appears in the message window behind the Insert Table menu. This is a display of the new live preview functionality available in many parts of Outlook and other programs in the 2007 Microsoft Office system. You can use live preview to see the effect of an option before you actually select it.

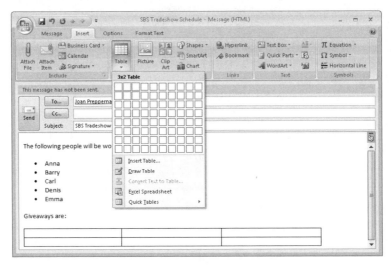

**12.** Click the selected cell to insert the table in the message.

The Table Tools contextual tabs, *Design* and *Layout*, appear on the Ribbon. Contextual tabs appear only when the element they control is active (selected). Contextual tabs are differentiated from standard tabs by color: the contextual group name is highlighted and the active tab is colored. Contextual groups are differentiated from each other by color.

Contextual tabs related to
managing the active table

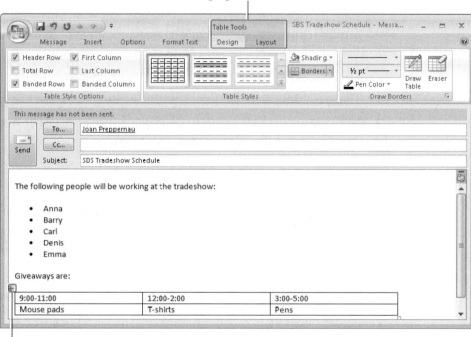

Table selector

13. Enter the following information in the table:

| 9:00-11:00 | 12:00-2:00 | 3:00-5:00 |
| --- | --- | --- |
| Mouse pads | T-shirts | Pens |

14. In the message header, click the **Send** button.

Outlook closes the message window and sends the message. When you receive the message in your Inbox, leave it there for use in a later exercise.

**Resending and Recalling Messages**

If you want to send a new version of a message you've already sent, for example, a weekly status report, you can *resend* the message. Resending a message creates a new version of the message with none of the extra information that might be attached to a forwarded message. To resend a message:

1. From your **Sent Items** folder, open the message you want to resend.

2. On the **Message** tab, in the **Actions** group, click the **Other Actions** button, and then in the list, click **Resend This Message**.

Outlook creates a new message form identical to the original. You can change the message recipients, subject, attachments, or content if you want before sending it.

If, after sending a message, you realize that you shouldn't have sent it (for example, if the message contained an error or was sent to the wrong people), you can *recall* it by instructing Outlook to delete or replace any unread copies of the message. To recall a message:

1. From your **Sent Items** folder, open the message you want to recall.

2. On the **Message** tab, in the **Actions** group, click the **Other Actions** button, and then click **Recall This Message**.

3. In the **Recall This Message** dialog box, select the option to delete unread copies of the message or the option to replace unread copies with a new message, and then click **OK**.

Message recall is available only for Exchange Server accounts.

# Attaching Files to Messages

A convenient way to distribute a file (such as a Microsoft Office Word document, Microsoft Office Excel spreadsheet, or Microsoft Office PowerPoint presentation) to other people is by attaching the file to an e-mail message. The message recipient can save the file to his or her hard disk, open the file from the message, or if he or she is using Outlook 2007, preview the file in the Reading Pane.

You can send a file as a regular attachment or—if your organization has a collaboration site built on Microsoft SharePoint products and technologies—as a *shared attachment*. When you send a shared attachment, Outlook creates a *document workspace* for the attached file and, rather than sending a copy of the file to each message recipient, sends an invitation to visit the workspace.

**See Also**  For information about creating a shared workspace for a file attachment, see "Creating a Document Library from Outlook" in Chapter 10, "Collaborating with Other People."

In this exercise, you will send a Word document and a PowerPoint presentation as attachments to an e-mail message.

> **USE** the *03_Attaching* document and the *03_Attaching* presentation. These practice files are available in the *Chapter18* subfolder under *SBS_Office2007*.
>
> **BE SURE TO** start Outlook and display the Inbox before beginning this exercise.

New Mail
Message

1. On the Standard toolbar, click the **New Mail Message** button.

2. In the **To** box of the new message window, type your own e-mail address.

> **Tip**  If you completed the previous exercise, Outlook will display your e-mail address in a list as you begin typing. You can insert the address by pressing the Down Arrow key to select it (if necessary) and then pressing Enter.

3. In the **Subject** box, type SBS First Draft.

4. In the content pane, type Here is some information for your review. Then press `Enter` to move to the next line.

5. On the **Message** tab, in the **Include** group, click the **Attach File** button.

Attach
File

> **Tip**  A larger version of the Attach File button is available in the Include group on the Insert tab.

The Insert File dialog box opens, displaying the contents of your Documents folder.

6. Browse to the practice file folder for this chapter (*Documents\MSP\SBS_Office2007\ Chapter18*), click the *03_Attaching* document, hold down the [Ctrl] key, click the *03_ Attaching* presentation, and then click **Insert**.

> **Troubleshooting** By default, Windows does not display file extensions in Explorer windows or dialog boxes. You can usually differentiate file types by their icons—for example, the Word icon precedes the *03_Attaching* document name. However, the icon preceding a PowerPoint 2007 presentation is an image of the first slide in the presentation, and in the default Small Icons view, you will probably see only the slide background.
>
> You can display the file type by clicking Details on the Views list, or you can display larger icons by clicking Extra Large Icons, Large Icons, Medium Icons, or Tiles on the Views list. In these views, you can see that the PowerPoint icon appears in the lower-right corner of the icon image. If you want Windows to display file extensions, display a folder (such as your Documents folder) in Explorer, click Search And Folder Options on the Organize menu, and then on the View tab of the Folder Options dialog box, clear the Hide Extensions For Known File Types check box, and click Apply or OK.

The files appears in the Attach box in the message header.

**7.** In the message header, click the **Send** button.

Outlook closes the message window and sends the message. When you receive the message in your Inbox, leave it there for use in a later exercise.

---

### Sending Contact Information

You can send your own or someone else's contact information from your address book to another Outlook user by attaching the contact's Outlook business card to an e-mail message. The recipient can then save the contact information in his or her own address book.

To send a business card:

**1.** In the message window, on the **Message** tab, in the **Include** group, click the **Insert Business Card** button, and then in the list, click **Other Business Cards**.

> **Tip** Business cards that you've previously sent appear in the Insert Business Card list. You can insert a card in the message by selecting it from the list.

**2.** In the **Insert Business Card** dialog box listing all your contacts, select the card or cards you want to send, and then click **OK**. If you have multiple address books, you can display a different address book in the dialog box by clicking it in the Look In list.

To select multiple sequential cards, click the first card, hold down the Shift key, and then press the Up Arrow or Down Arrow key to select additional cards. To select multiple non-sequential cards, click the first card, hold down the Ctrl key, click the next card, and so on.

The message recipient can add the contact to his or her main address book by dragging the business card from the received message to the Contacts module or by opening the card from the message and then clicking the Save & Close button.

> **Tip** Readers of a previous edition of this book wrote to us asking how to create mail-merge e-mail messages from Outlook. This is actually a function of Word, rather than Outlook.
>
> For information about creating e-mail messages to multiple recipients by using mail-merge, refer to *Microsoft Office Word 2007 Step by Step* (ISBN 0-7356-2302-3) by Joyce Cox and Joan Preppernau (Microsoft Press, 2007).

# Creating and Formatting Business Graphics

The saying that "a picture is worth a thousand words" is especially true in business communications, when you need to clearly explain facts or concepts, particularly to an increasingly global audience. Several programs in the 2007 Office system include a new feature called *SmartArt*. This tool is very useful for creating professional business graphics within documents, spreadsheets, presentations, and messages. You can easily create lists and diagrams depicting relationships, processes, cycles, and hierarchies and so on in your e-mail messages. When sending a message, Outlook converts any SmartArt graphics within the message to static graphics.

In this exercise, you will create a SmartArt diagram within an e-mail message. There are no practice files for this exercise.

> **BE SURE TO** display the Inbox before beginning this exercise.
> **OPEN** a new message window.

1. Maximize the message window, and then click to position the insertion point in the content pane.

 2. On the **Insert** tab, in the **Illustrations** group, click the **SmartArt** button.

   The Choose A SmartArt Graphic dialog box opens, displaying the many types of graphics available. You can view the graphic types by category by clicking the category names in the left pane, and preview an individual graphic type by clicking it in the center pane.

3. Scroll the center pane of the dialog box for an overview of the available SmartArt graphics. You can display the name of a graphic by pointing to it.

4. In the left pane, click **Process**, and then in the center pane, click the last icon in the top row (**Alternating Flow**).

   A preview of the selected SmartArt graphic appears in the right pane. This is a process diagram showing the details of a three-step process.

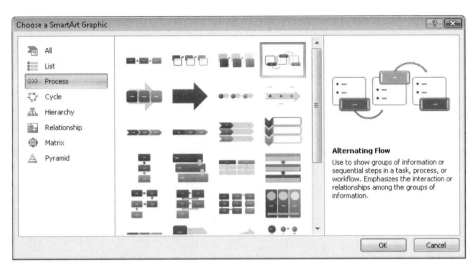

5. In the **Choose a Smart Art Graphic** dialog box, click **OK**.

Outlook inserts the selected process diagram in the content pane. It looks similar to the preview graphic, but without the colors and three-dimensional aspects. (You select formatting options later.) The SmartArt Tools contextual tabs, *Design* and *Format*, appear on the Ribbon.

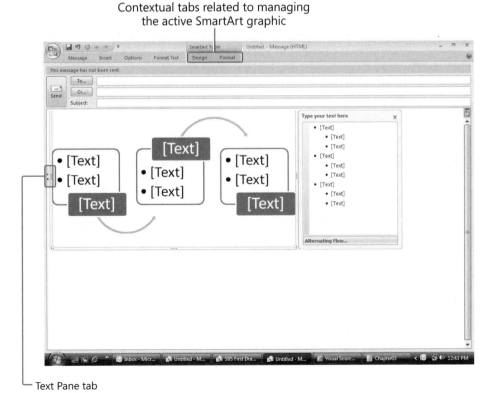

Contextual tabs related to managing
the active SmartArt graphic

Text Pane tab

6.  Click the Text Pane tab on the left side of the diagram.

> **Tip**  You can display or hide the Text Pane for any SmartArt diagram by clicking the diagram and then clicking the Text Pane button in the Create Graphic group on the Design contextual tab, or by clicking the Text Pane tab on the left side of the diagram drawing area.

The Text Pane appears, clearly illustrating the hierarchy of the text contained in the diagram.

You can enter text in the Text Pane or directly in the diagram—selecting a diagram element or positioning the insertion point within the bulleted list also selects the corresponding element in the diagram or Text Pane. The diagram type appears at the bottom of the Text Pane; pointing to it displays a ScreenTip describing the purpose of the selected type of diagram.

7.  In the **Text Pane**, click the **[Text]** placeholder to the right of the first bullet, and then type Plan.

As you type in the pane, the text appears in the diagram.

8.  Click the **[Text]** placeholder to the right of the first second-level bullet, and type Survey current customers. Press the ↓ key to move to the next second-level bullet, and then type Survey potential customers.

The font size in the diagram adjusts to fit the available space.

9.  Press Enter to create another second-level bullet in the Text Pane and in the diagram, and then type Analyze competition.

10. In the diagram, click the second solid blue box to select the placeholder, and then type Define.

As you type, the text also appears in the second first-level bullet in the Text Pane.

11. In the third solid blue box, type Design.

**12.** On the **Design** contextual tab, in the **Create Graphic** group, click the **Add Shape** arrow (not the button), and then in the list, click **Add Shape After**.

An additional item appears at the right end of the diagram and in the Text Pane. You can add shapes above, below, before, or after the selected shape, depending on the diagram layout.

**13.** In the new solid blue box, type Develop.

**14.** In the **Text Pane**, click at the end of the word *Develop*, and then press [ Enter ].

A first-level bullet and additional shape appear.

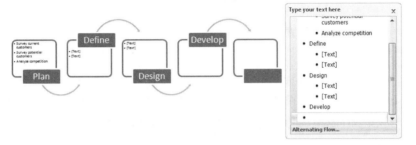

Close

**15.** Type Test, and then in the **Text Pane**, click the **Close** button.

At its current size, the text within the diagram is very difficult to read.

**16.** Point to the move handle on the right side of the diagram until the pointer becomes a double-headed arrow. Drag the move handle to the right to fill the message window.

More

**17.** In the **Layouts** group, click the **More** button.

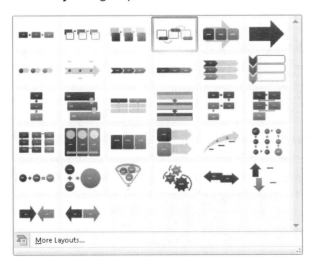

**18.** In the **Layouts** gallery, point to a few of the diagram layouts to display live previews. Then click the fifth icon in the first row (**Continuous Block Process**).

The process diagram layout changes but the contents remain the same.

**19.** In the **SmartArt Styles** group, click the **More** button.

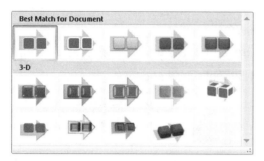

**20.** In the **SmartArt Styles** gallery, point to a few of the diagram styles to display live previews. Then under **3-D**, click the first icon (**Polished**).

**21.** In the **SmartArt Styles** group, click the **Change Colors** button.

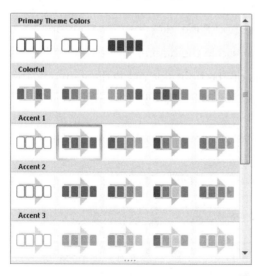

The color schemes displayed in the Colors gallery are variations of the current theme, and are organized in groups reflecting the six thematic accent colors. Changing the theme also changes the color schemes in the gallery.

**22.** Point to a few of the diagram styles to display live previews. Then under **Colorful**, click the second icon (**Colorful Range – Accent Colors 2 to 3**).

**23.** Enter your own e-mail address in the **To** box, and type SBS Development Cycle in the **Subject** box.

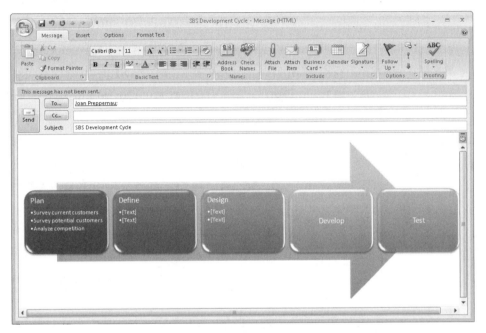

**24.** Send the message, and then display your Inbox.

**25.** When you receive the message, the diagram is visible in the Reading Pane. Open the message, and click the diagram.

The diagram is no longer an active SmartArt graphic; it has been converted to a static image. If you open the message from your Sent Items folder, you will find that the same is true of the diagram in that message.

**CLOSE** the message window, and retain the message in your Inbox for use in a later exercise.

## Changing Message Settings and Delivery Options

When sending a message, you can optionally include visual indicators of the importance, sensitivity, or subject category of a message, restrict other people from changing or forwarding message content, provide a simple feedback mechanism in the form of voting buttons, and specify message delivery options to fit your needs.

Common message settings and delivery options include:

● **Importance.** You can indicate the urgency of a message by setting its *importance* to High or Low. A corresponding banner appears in the message header and, if the Importance field is included in the view, an importance icon appears in the Inbox or other message folder..

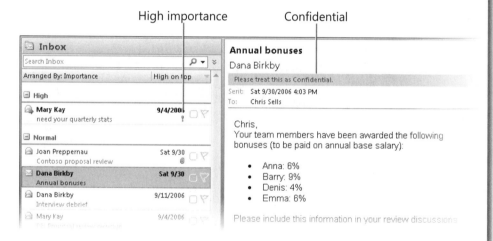

High importance          Confidential

You can easily sort and group messages based on importance by clicking Importance in the Arranged By list.

● **Sensitivity.** You can indicate that a message should be kept private by setting its *sensitivity* to Confidential, Personal, or Private). No indicator appears in the message folder, but a banner appears in the message header to indicate a sensitivity other than Normal. You can choose to include the sensitivity as one of the message attributes shown in the Inbox pane, but if you do, it replaces the message subject, which isn't very helpful.

- **Security.** If you have a digital ID, you can digitally sign the message; or you can encrypt the contents of the message.

- **Voting options.** If you and your message recipients have Exchange Server accounts, you can add *voting buttons* to your messages to enable recipients to quickly select from multiple-choice response options.

- **Tracking options.** You can track messages by requesting delivery receipts and read receipts. These receipts are messages automatically generated by the recipient's e-mail server when it delivers the message to the recipient and when the recipient reads the message.

- **Categories.** You can assign a message to a color category that will be visible to the recipient if he or she views the message in Outlook.

The most commonly used options are available in the Options group on the Message tab of the message window. You can access other options from the Message Options dialog box, which you open by clicking the Dialog Box Launcher in the lower-right corner of the Options group.

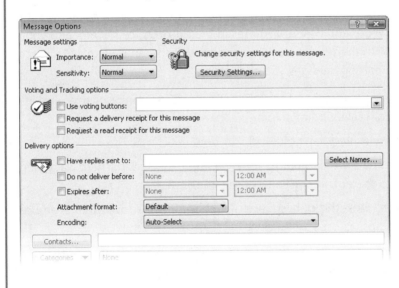

You can limit the actions other people can take with messages they receive from you by restricting the message permissions. For example, you can prevent recipients from forwarding or printing the message, copying the message content, or changing the content when they forward or reply to the message. (Restrictions apply also to message attachments.) Within a message window, permission options are available both on the Office menu and in the Options group on the Message tab.

# Personalizing the Appearance of Messages

By default, the content of an Outlook message appears in black, 10-point Calibri (a very readable *sans serif* font that is new in this release of the Office system), arranged in left-aligned paragraphs on a white background. You can change the appearance of a message either by applying *local formatting* (text or paragraph attributes) or *global formatting* (a theme or style).

The local formatting options available in Outlook 2007 are largely the same as those available in Word and other programs in the 2007 Office system, and you might already be familiar with them from working with those programs. Here's a quick review of the types of formatting changes you can make:

- **Font, size, and color.** More than 220 fonts in a range of sizes and in a virtually unlimited selection of colors.
- **Font style.** Regular, bold, italic, or bold italic.
- **Underline style and color.** Plain, multiple, dotted, dashed, wavy, and many combinations thereof, in any color of the rainbow.
- **Effects.** Strikethrough, superscript, subscript, shadow, outline, emboss, engrave, small caps, all caps, or hidden.
- **Character spacing.** Scale, spacing, position, and kerning.
- **Paragraph attributes.** Alignment, indentation, and spacing.

The global formatting options are sets of local formatting that you can apply with a couple of clicks. You use a theme to apply a pre-selected combination of several formatting options to the entire message. In addition, the 2007 Office system introduces a handy new set of formatting options called *Quick Styles* that you can apply to individual elements of a message.

You are more likely to use Quick Styles when working in Word documents than in messages, but we'll give you an overview and you can investigate further on your own. Within a message window, Quick Styles are available in the Styles group on the Format Text tab.

They include a number of standard styles for titles, headings, lists, quotes, emphasis, and so on. You can see a live preview of the effect of a style on your text by pointing to the style in the Quick Styles gallery.

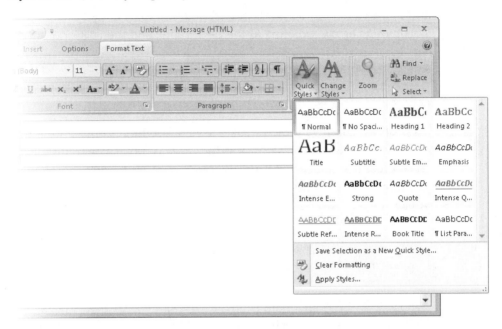

You can change the appearance of all the styles in the Quick Styles gallery by selecting any of the 11 available style sets (or creating your own). Selecting a style set changes the appearance of all the text in the current document, as well as the appearance of the icons in the Quick Style gallery. You can select or preview a style set, color scheme, or font set by clicking the Change Styles button in the Styles group on the Format Text tab and then pointing to Style Set, Colors, or Fonts.

**See Also**  For more information about Quick Styles, style sets, color schemes, and font sets, refer to *Microsoft Office Word 2007 Step by Step* (ISBN 0-7356-2302-3) by Joyce Cox and Joan Preppernau (Microsoft Press, 2007).

In this exercise, you will experiment with some of the formatting features that are new or improved in this version of Outlook while changing the font and background color of an e-mail message. Then you will apply a theme to the same message, overwriting the local formatting. There are no practice files for this exercise.

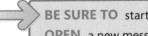
**BE SURE TO**  start Outlook and display the Inbox before beginning this exercise.

**OPEN**  a new message window.

1.  In the content pane, type

    Looking forward to seeing you next week at the celebration!

2.  Select the sentence you just typed by pointing to its left edge until the pointer becomes an arrow (pointing at the paragraph), and then clicking once.

    The *Mini toolbar* appears.

    This context-sensitive toolbar makes several common formatting options immediately available when you select a letter, word, or phrase by using the mouse. When the toolbar first appears, it is nearly transparent, and it disappears in a short time if you don't activate it by pointing to it.

Font

3.  On the **Mini toolbar**, click the **Font** arrow.

    > **Tip** If the Mini toolbar is not visible, you can find the Font box in the Basic Text group on the Message tab, and in the Font group on the Format Text tab.

    Many more fonts are available in Outlook 2007 than in previous versions of Outlook. The name of each font appears in the list in that font, so you can easily select a font that appeals to you.

    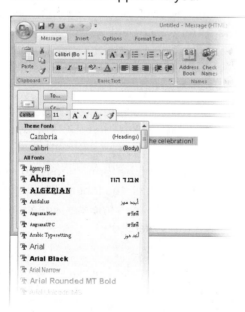

4.  Scroll the **Font** list, noting the many available fonts, and then click **Franklin Gothic Medium**.

    The font of the selected text changes.

Font Size

Font Color

**5.** On the Mini toolbar or in the Font group on the Format Text tab, click the **Font Size** arrow, and in the list, click **12**.

The size of the selected text changes.

**6.** Click once in the word *next*, without selecting any letters. Then on the **Format Text** tab, in the **Font** group, click the **Font Color** arrow.

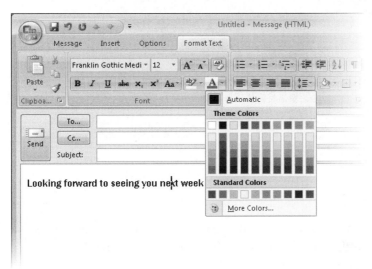

Outlook 2007 offers a new palette of theme colors (which change depending on the selected theme) and standard colors.

**7.** In the **Font Color** gallery, under **Standard Colors**, click the **Red** box.

The font color of the word *next* changes to red. Notice that the entire word changes even though you didn't select it. This is a new feature of Outlook 2007.

Format Painter

**8.** Double-click the word *next*, and on the **Mini toolbar** (or in the **Clipboard** group), click the **Format Painter** button. Then click once in the word *week*.

Outlook copies the formatting of the word *next* to the word *week*. By using the Format Painter, you can copy formatting from one item to any other item. To copy formatting to multiple items, double-click the Format Painter button to turn it on and then click it again to turn it off after you're finished applying the formatting.

Page Color ▾

**9.** On the **Options** tab, in the **Themes** group, click the **Page Color** button.

The Page Color gallery includes the same theme colors and standard colors as the Font Color gallery.

10. In the **Page Color** gallery, point to any color.

    Outlook displays a live preview of the color in the message window.

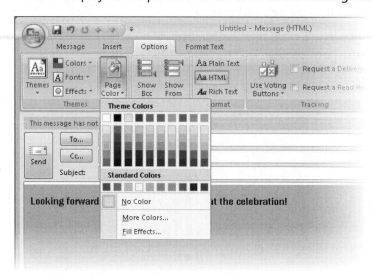

11. In the **Page Color** gallery, in the color gradient area, click the second shade down in the fifth column from the left (**Accent 1, Lighter 60%**).

    The message background changes to the selected color.

12. In the **Themes** group, click the **Themes** button.

    Outlook displays a gallery of themes. In each theme icon, the theme colors appear across the bottom, and the presentation background appears on the right.

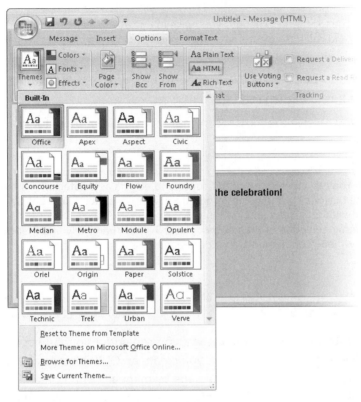

13. In the **Themes** gallery, click **Oriel**.

    The message background and font change to those of the theme.

    Notice that the colors displayed on the Colors button in the Themes group have changed.

14. In the **Themes** group, click the **Page Color** button. In the list, compare the new page background to the new set of colors displayed in the color gradient area. The page background color is still *Accent 1, Lighter 60%* (the color you selected in Step 11).

> **Tip** The formatting changes you make in this exercise apply only to the active message, and will not be automatically applied to other messages.

**15.** Enter your own e-mail address in the **To** box; type SBS Festival Reminder in the **Subject** box, and then send the message.

When you receive the message in your Inbox, leave it there for use in a later exercise.

> **Tip** You can change the colors, fonts, and effects associated with a theme by clicking those buttons in the Themes group on the Options tab. You might want to experiment with different combinations on your own. However, Outlook offers such an extensive selection of themes that you will more than likely find that one of these ready-made combinations fits your needs.

# Adding Signatures to Messages Automatically

When you create a paper-based message, you can add a signature at the end of the message by writing your name. When you create an Outlook message, you can add an *e-mail signature* at the end of the message by manually or automatically inserting a predefined block of text (with optional graphics). An e-mail signature provides consistent information to message recipients. You can include any text or graphics you want in your e-mail signature; you would commonly include your name and contact information, but depending on your own situation you might also include information such as your company name, job title, a legal disclaimer, a corporate or personal slogan, a photo, and so on. When using Outlook 2007, you can choose to include your electronic business card as part or all of your e-mail signature.

You can create different signatures for use in different types of messages. For instance, you might create a formal business signature for client correspondence, a casual business signature for interoffice correspondence, and a personal signature for messages sent from a secondary account. Or you might create a signature containing more information to send with original e-mail messages, and a signature containing less information to send with message replies. You can format the text of your e-mail signature in the same ways that you can format message text.

In this exercise, you will create an e-mail signature and then instruct Outlook to insert the signature in all the new messages you create. There are no practice files for this exercise.

**BE SURE TO** start Outlook and display the Inbox before beginning this exercise.

1. On the **Tools** menu, click **Options**.

   The Options dialog box opens.

2. On the **Mail Format** tab, click **Signatures**.

   The Signatures And Stationery dialog box opens.

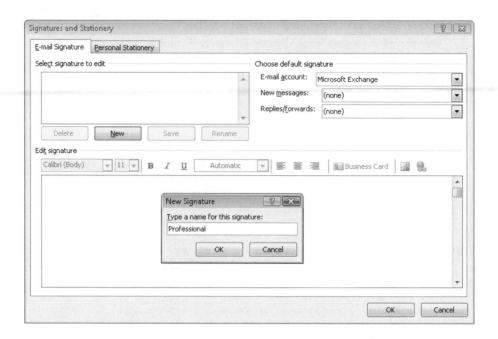

3. On the **E-mail Signature** tab, click **New**.

4. In the **New Signature** dialog box, type Professional as the name of your new e-mail signature, and then click **OK**.

   The Professional signature appears and is selected in the Select Signature To Edit list.

5. In the signature content area, type Regards followed by a comma, press the Enter key, and then type your name.

6. Select your name, click the **Font** arrow, and then in the list, click **Lucida Handwriting** (or any other font you like).

7. Click the **Font Size** arrow, and then in the list, click **14**.

8. Click the **Font Color** arrow, and then under **Standard Colors**, click the **Purple** box. Then click away from your name to see the results of your changes.

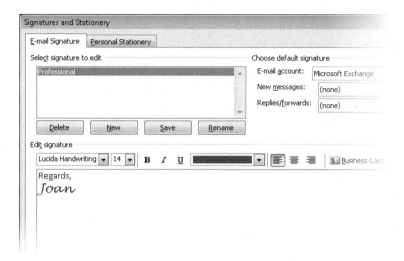

9. Apply any other types of formatting you want.

> **Tip** If you would like to include your electronic business card as part of your signature, click the Business Card button. Then in the Insert Business Card dialog box, locate and click your name, and click OK.

You can manually insert any signature you create in an e-mail message, but it is more common to instruct Outlook to automatically insert it for you.

10. In the **Choose default signature** area, click the **New messages** arrow, and then in the list, click **Professional**.

Outlook will now insert your signature into all new e-mail messages you send from this account, but not into replies or forwarded messages.

> **Tip** If you have more than one e-mail account set up in Outlook, you can instruct Outlook to insert a different signature in messages sent from each account. To do so, click the account in the E-mail Account list, click the signature you want to use with that account in the New Messages and/or Replies/Forwards list, and then click OK.

11. Make any other changes you want, and then click **OK** in the two open dialog boxes.

New Mail
Message

12. On the Standard toolbar, click the **New Mail Message** button.

A new message opens, with your e-mail signature in the content pane.

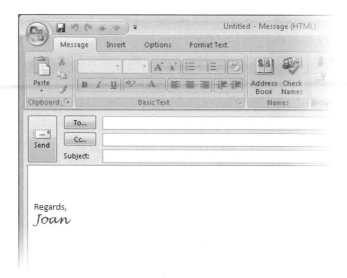

**CLOSE** the message window.

**BE SURE TO** reset the New Messages signature to <none> if you don't want to use the *Professional* signature you created in this exercise.

## Key Points

- All the commands you need when creating a message in Outlook 2007 are available on the Ribbon at the top of the message window, grouped on tabs by function.
- You can easily create e-mail messages that include text, hyperlinks, and attachments.
- You can send messages in a variety of formats. Some message formats support more formatting options than others. Recipients using e-mail programs that don't support HTML or Rich Text Formatting will see the message in plain text.
- You can format the text and background of your messages, either by choosing individual formatting options and styles or by applying a theme.

- You can create professional business graphics by using the new SmartArt feature available in Outlook 2007, Word 2007, and PowerPoint 2007.

- You can automatically insert contact information in e-mail messages by using an electronic signature. You can create different signatures for different purposes and instruct Outlook to insert a specific signature depending on the e-mail account and message type.

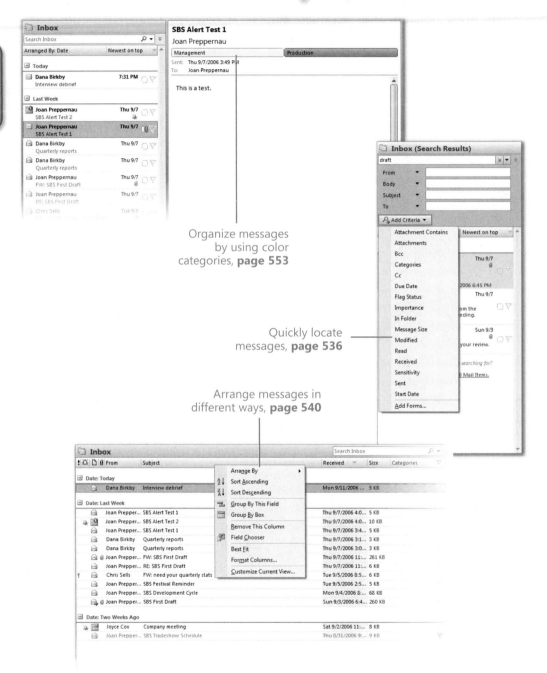

Organize messages
by using color
categories, **page 553**

Quickly locate
messages, **page 536**

Arrange messages in
different ways, **page 540**

# 19 Managing Your Inbox

---

**In this chapter, you will learn to:**

✔ Quickly locate messages.

✔ Arrange messages in different ways.

✔ Organize messages by using color categories.

✔ Organize messages in folders.

✔ Archive messages.

---

So far in this book, we've discussed the basic mechanics of sending and receiving messages, and the Outlook components used for those purposes. Now we'll tackle the task that heavy e-mail users spend a lot of time on—managing the messages you receive. This is where Microsoft Office Outlook 2007 really stands apart from its competitors.

In addition to providing ways to organize messages in subfolders within the Inbox and to archive messages, Outlook 2007 includes a number of new features that simplify the process of managing messages and other Outlook items. The greatest of these is the new Instant Search capability, which filters messages as you type the keywords you want to search for, highlighting the search terms within each message. Another useful tool is Color Categories, which combines the named categories available in earlier versions of Outlook with colored labels to provide quick visual recognition and search capabilities.

In this chapter, you will filter and find messages by using Instant Search, display the messages in your Inbox in a variety of arrangements, and use Search Folders. Then you will organize messages by assigning color categories and by organizing them in folders within the Inbox. Finally, you will look at the default archive settings and manually archive an e-mail folder.

**See Also** Do you need only a quick refresher on the topics in this chapter? See the Quick Reference entries at the beginning of this book.

> **Important** The exercises in this chapter require practice files created in earlier chapters; none are supplied on the book's CD. For more information about practice files, see "Using the Book's CD" at the beginning of this book.

> **Troubleshooting** Graphics and operating system–related instructions in this book reflect the Windows Vista user interface. If your computer is running Microsoft Windows XP and you experience trouble following the instructions as written, please refer to the "Information for Readers Running Windows XP" section at the beginning of this book.

# Quickly Locating Messages

Although you can use Instant Search in the Calendar, Contacts, and Tasks modules, you will most often use it to locate messages in your Inbox and other mail folders. You can search a particular mail folder or search all mail folders.

**See Also** For information about mail folders, see "Organizing Messages in Folders" later in this chapter.

As you define the criteria for a search, Outlook filters out all messages that don't match, making it easy to find exactly what you're looking for. And here's the neat thing: Outlook searches not only the content of the e-mail message header and the message itself, but also the content of message attachments. So if the search term you're looking for is in a Microsoft Office Word document attached to a message, the message will be included in the search results.

> **Tip** You can't instantly filter content in a Public Folder (if your organization uses these) but you can enter the search criteria and then click the Search button to get the same results as you would in your inbox.

Instant Search is based on the new Desktop Search Engine from Microsoft, which also drives the search functionality in Windows Vista. With this very powerful search engine, you can find any file on your computer containing a specified search term—whether in the file or folder name, in document or spreadsheet content, in an e-mail message

within Outlook, in a message attachment, in a picture, music, or video file, and so on..
As a matter of fact, if you prefer to do so you can conduct all of your Outlook searches
from the Windows Vista Start menu.

**See Also** For information about Windows Vista search features, refer to *Windows Vista Step by Step* (ISBN 0-7356-2269-8) by Joan Preppernau and Joyce Cox (Microsoft Press, 2007).

If the search term you enter produces more than 200 results, the Search Results pane
displays this information bar:

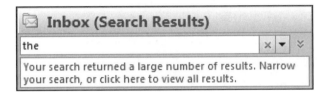

You can display all the results for the current search term by clicking the message bar,
or you can narrow the results by expanding the search term or by specifying other
search criteria, such as the sender, the recipient (whether the message was addressed
or only copied to you), whether the message contains attachments, and so on.

In this exercise, you will use the Instant Search feature to locate a specific message in
your Inbox. There are no practice files for this exercise.

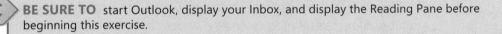

**BE SURE TO** start Outlook, display your Inbox, and display the Reading Pane before
beginning this exercise.

1. In the **Search** box in the Inbox header, type one or more words likely to appear in
   messages in your Inbox.

   As you type, Outlook filters the contents of your Inbox to display only those items
   containing the characters, word, or words you enter, and highlights the search term
   in the displayed messages.

Search term

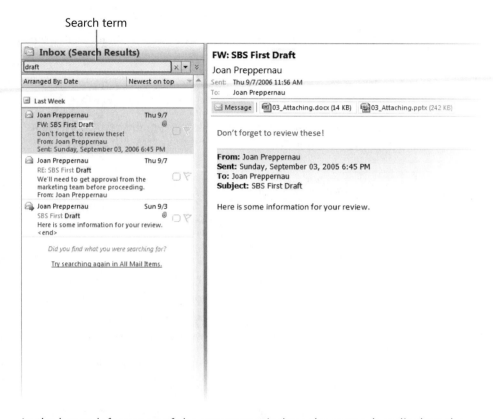

In the lower-left corner of the program window, the status bar displays the number of messages included in the search results. The search results include only messages contained in the Inbox folder and not in any of its subfolders or any other mailbox folders.

**2.** To the right of the **Search** box, click the **Expand the Query Builder** button.

Expand the
Query Builder

The search pane expands to include text boxes in which you can specify the sender, a term that appears in the message body, a term that appears in the message subject, or a primary recipient of the message.

**3.** In the expanded **Search Results** pane, click **Add Criteria** to display a list of additional criteria.

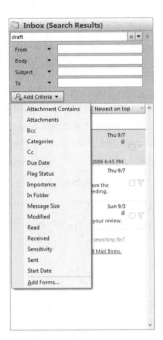

Selecting a field from this list adds the field to the search criteria section. Alternatively, you can click the arrow to the right of any of the default criteria and select a different field.

**4.** In the **Add Criteria** list, click **Attachments** to add that field to the search pane.

**5.** Click the **Attachments** arrow, and then in the list, click **Yes**.

Notice that your search criteria are also described in the search term box.

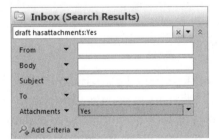

Outlook instantly updates the search results to display only the messages in your Inbox that contain the search term and one or more attachments.

6. To expand the search to include all the folders in your mailbox, at the end of the list of results shown in the Search Results pane, click **Try searching again in All Mail Items**.

   Outlook displays the expanded search results grouped by the folder in which they appear. You can open, delete, and process a message from the Search Result pane as you would from any other. If, however, you change a message so that it no longer fits the search criteria—for instance, if you search for flagged messages and then mark the message task as complete, the message no longer appears in the Search Results pane. (It does still appear in whatever folder it is in).

Clear Search

7. Experiment with locating information by specifying criteria. When you finish, click the **Clear Search** button to remove the filter and redisplay the Inbox message list.

# Arranging Messages in Different Ways

As the number of messages in your Inbox increases, it can be challenging to prioritize them. You can customize how you view, arrange, sort, and group messages in Outlook to help you quickly determine which are the most important, decide which can be deleted, and locate any that need an immediate response. You can view only certain groups of messages, such as messages received in the last seven days, unread messages, or messages sent to a certain person or distribution list. You can also view a timeline of all your received messages. Outlook 2007 offers eight predefined *views*, and you can customize any of these to fit your needs.

| **Category views** | **List views** | **Other views** |
|---|---|---|
| Messages | Messages with AutoPreview | Message Timeline |
| Sent To | Last Seven Days | |
| Outlook Data Files | Unread Messages in This Folder | |
| Documents | | |

In category views, the Inbox header includes only the arrangement and sort order, the Reading Pane is visible by default, and the message header information is grouped on multiple lines. In list views, information appears in columns; the Reading Pane is not displayed by default, but you can display it if you want. To experiment with different views, point to Current View on the View menu, and then click the view option you want.

> **Tip** For one-click access to the various views available in the Mail module, on the View menu, point to Navigation Pane, and then click Current View Pane (if a check mark appears before the command, this feature is already in use). You can then switch views by selecting the view option you want from the list.
>
> The Current View pane is displayed by default in the Contacts, Tasks, and Notes modules but not in the Mail and Calendar modules.

You can also group messages by the contents of any field—by the sender of the message, for instance, or by the subject. You can arrange messages by conversation.

By default, Outlook displays messages in the order you receive them, with the newest messages at the top of your Inbox. Messages received during the current week are grouped by day. Earlier messages are grouped by week or by longer periods. You can easily change the order in which messages and other items (such as meeting requests and task assignments) appear in the Inbox or any other mail folder. You can arrange items by:

- **Attachments.** Messages are grouped by whether they have attachments, and secondarily by date received.

- **Category.** Messages are arranged by the category to which they are assigned. Messages without a category appear first. Messages assigned to multiple categories appear in each of those category groups.

- **Conversation.** This grouped view is similar to sorting messages by subject except that each series of related messages is grouped together, and messages within the group appear in a *threaded* conversation order. This arrangement is particularly useful when you want to find a response to a specific version of a message in a multi-person *e-mail trail*. In conversations with multiple messages, Outlook displays only unread or flagged messages, indicating additional messages by a small arrow to the left of the conversation title. Click the arrow to display all the messages in the conversation.

- **Date.** Messages are arranged by date of receipt in order from newest to oldest. Outlook groups messages received on each of the past four days, each of the previous four weeks, the previous month, and those more than one month old.

- **E-mail Account.** Messages are grouped by the e-mail account to which they were sent. This is useful if you receive messages for more than one e-mail account in your Inbox (for instance, if you receive messages sent to your POP3 account within your Microsoft Exchange Server mailbox).

- **Importance.** Messages are grouped by priority: High (indicated by a red exclamation point), Normal (the default), or Low (indicated by a blue arrow).

- **Recipient (To).** Messages are grouped alphabetically by the primary recipients—the addresses or names on the To line. The group name exactly reflects the order in which addresses appear on the To line. Therefore, a message addressed to *Bart Duncan; Lukas Keller* will not be grouped with a message addressed to *Lukas Keller; Bart Duncan.*

- **Sender (From).** Messages appear in alphabetical order by the message sender's display name. If you receive messages from a person who uses two different e-mail accounts, or who sends messages from two different e-mail clients (for example, from Outlook and Microsoft Outlook Express), the messages will not necessarily be grouped together.

- **Size.** Messages are grouped by the size of the message, including any attachment. Groups include Huge (1–5 MB), Very Large (500KB–1 MB), Large (100–500 KB), Medium (25–100 KB), Small (10-25 KB), and Tiny (less than 10 KB). This feature is useful if you work for an organization that limits the size of your Inbox, because you can easily locate large messages and delete them or move them to a personal folder.

- **Start date or due date.** Unflagged messages and messages without specific schedules appear first. Messages that you've added to your task list with specific start or due dates are grouped by date.

- **Subject.** Messages are arranged alphabetically by their subject lines and secondarily by date. This is similar to arranging by conversation except that the messages aren't threaded.

- **Type.** Items in your Inbox (or other folder) are grouped by the type of item; for instance, messages, encrypted messages, message receipts, meeting requests and meeting request responses, tasks, Microsoft InfoPath forms, and server notifications.

When viewing messages in a category view, the Arranged By bar in the Inbox header indicates how the messages are arranged and in what order. Clicking the order indicator reverses the order; for instance, from Newest On Top to Oldest On Top. Regardless of what order you choose, group headers divide the messages into groups that you can collapse or expand.

Arrangement   Groups   Order

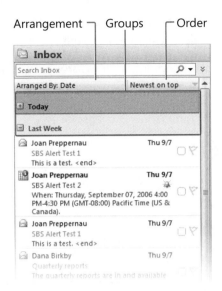

To experiment with the *arrangement* options, on the View menu, point to Arrange By, and then click the arrangement option you want.

Regardless of the view and arrangement you choose, you can sort messages by any visible field simply by clicking its column heading (and reverse the sort order by clicking the column heading a second time). You can change the displayed fields from the Show Fields dialog box, which you display by pointing to Arrange By on the View menu, and then clicking Custom.

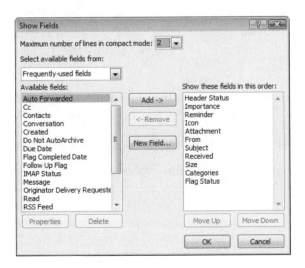

Outlook displays the selected fields in the order shown in the right column. If displaying all the fields requires more space than is available, only some of the fields will be visible.

If necessary, you can change the number of lines shown to accommodate more fields. However, it is likely that one of the standard views will fit your needs.

In a list view, you can control the message arrangement, sorting, grouping, visible fields, and other settings from the context menu that appears when you right-click any column header.

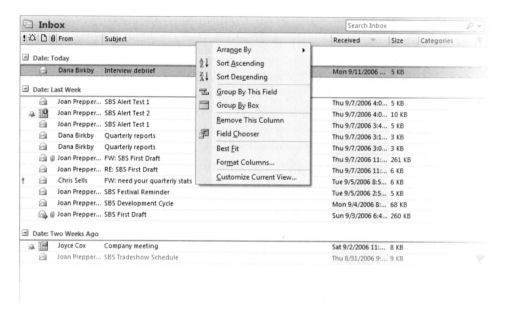

In this exercise, you will change the display, arrangement, sort order, and grouping of messages in your Inbox. Then you will filter the Inbox content, add and remove fields, and change the appearance of the Inbox. Finally, you will restore the default settings. There are no practice files for this exercise.

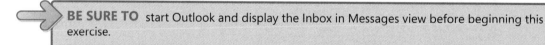

**BE SURE TO** start Outlook and display the Inbox in Messages view before beginning this exercise.

1. If there are no unread messages in your Inbox, right-click a message, and then click **Mark as Unread**.

The message header will change to bold, and its icon will change from an open envelope to a closed envelope.

> **Tip** Unread items are distinguished from read items by their bold type and closed-envelope icons.

2. On the **View** menu, point to **Navigation Pane**, and then if a check mark doesn't appear to the left of it, click **Current View Pane**.

The basic view options appear at the bottom of the Navigation Pane.

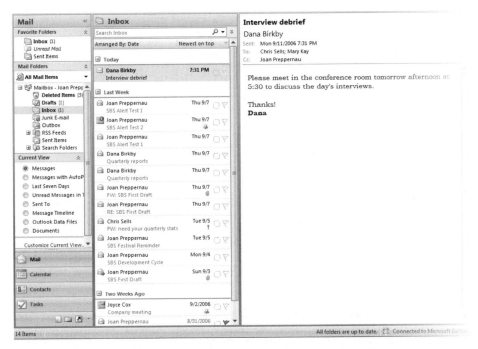

3. On the **View** menu, if the icon to the left of it is not shaded, click **AutoPreview**.

The first three lines of each unread message appear in the Inbox below the message header.

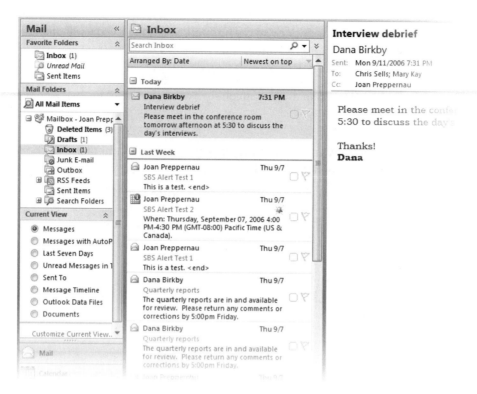

4. On the **View** menu, point to **Arrange By**, and then click **From**.

   Outlook rearranges and groups the messages in your Inbox alphabetically by sender.

5. In the Inbox header, click **A on Top**.

   Outlook reverses the order of the messages.

6. In the Inbox header, click the **Arranged By** bar, and then click **Subject**.

   Outlook groups the messages by subject.

7. On the **View** menu, point to **Expand/Collapse Groups**, and then click **Collapse All Groups**.

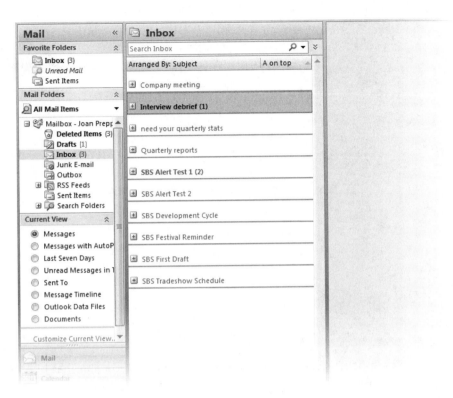

Notice that the number of unread items in each group (if there are any) is indicated in parentheses following the conversation subject.

You can use this method to expand or collapse all groups. You can expand or collapse individual groups by clicking the Expand (+) or Collapse (-) button to the left of the group name. You can collapse the group containing the currently selected item by pressing the ← key and expand a selected group by pressing the → key.

8. In the **Current View** pane, select the **Unread Messages in This Folder** option.

   Outlook filters the Inbox to display only unread messages.

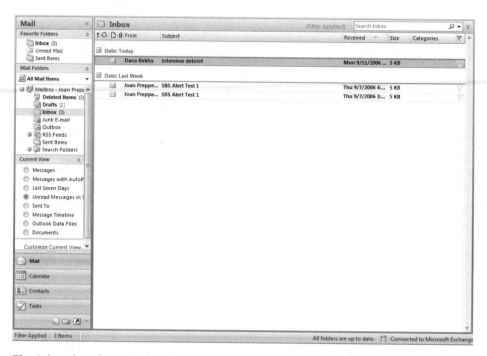

The Inbox header and the status bar indicate that a filter has been applied. (If you have no unread messages in your Inbox, it will appear to be empty.)

9. In the **Current View** pane, select the **Messages with AutoPreview** option.

   Outlook removes the filter and displays a list view of the messages, with the first lines of each unread message visible.

10. Experiment with the available arrangement, sorting, and grouping options if you want. Then on the **View** menu, point to **Current View**, and click **Customize Current View**.

    The Customize View dialog box opens.

> **Tip** If the Reset Current View button is active, your view is currently customized and you can reset the view to its default settings by clicking the button.

**11.** Click **Fields**.

The Show Fields dialog box shown earlier opens.

**12.** In the **Available fields** list, click **Sensitivity**, and then click **Add**.

The Sensitivity field moves to the bottom of the list of columns to be shown in this view.

**13.** In the **Show these fields in this order** list, drag **Sensitivity** to appear below **Importance**.

While you drag the field, red arrows indicate where it will appear when you release the mouse button.

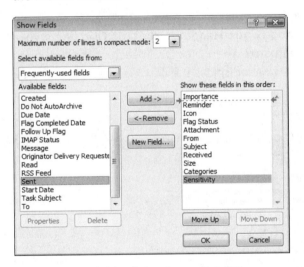

**14.** In the **Show Fields** dialog box, click **OK**.

> **Tip** To change the order of columns in any list view, simply drag the column headings to the locations you prefer. While you are dragging a column heading, red arrows indicate where the column will appear when you release the mouse button.

**15.** In the **Customize View** dialog box, click **Other Settings**.

The Other Settings dialog box opens.

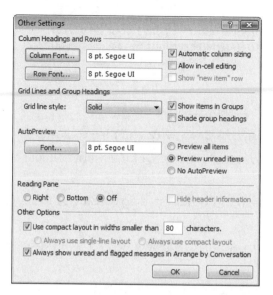

15. Under **Grid Lines and Group Headings**, click the **Grid line style** arrow, and then in the list, click **Small dots**. Then click **OK** in each of the two open dialog boxes to return to the Inbox, which displays the new view settings.

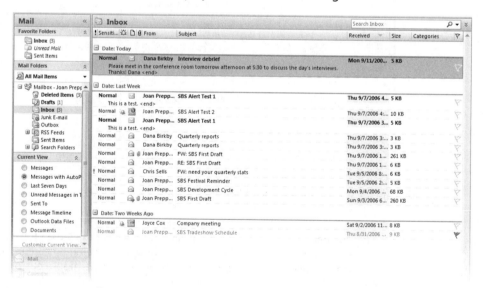

16. Drag the **Sensitivity** column heading downward into the message list, and release the mouse button when a large black X appears over the heading.

Outlook removes the Sensitivity column from the view.

**17.** On the **View** menu, point to **Current View**, and then click **Define Views**.

The Custom View Organizer dialog box opens, with the current view selected.

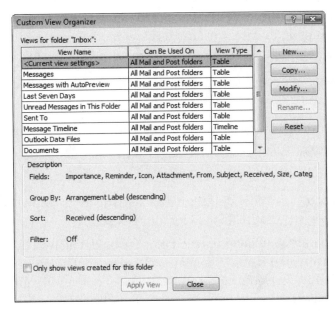

**18.** In the **Custom View Organizer** dialog box, click the **Reset** button. In the **Microsoft Office Outlook** message box asking whether you want to reset the current view to its original settings, click **OK**.

**19.** In the **View Name** list, click each view in turn.

If the view settings have been changed from the default, the Reset button becomes active.

**20.** Repeat Step 18 to reset any customized views you want. When you finish, click the **Messages** view, and then click **Apply View**.

The Inbox is restored to its default view.

**BE SURE TO** restore the default view settings before continuing, if you want them to match those shown in the rest of this book.

## Using Search Folders

A Search Folder is a *virtual folder* that displays all the messages in your mailbox that match a specific set of search criteria, no matter which folders the messages are actually stored in. When you create a Search Folder, it becomes part of your mailbox and is kept up to date. The Search Folder module is located in the All Mail Items list under your top-level mailbox, at the same level as the Inbox.

The For Follow Up folder displays messages flagged for future For Follow Up folder displays messages flagged for future action.

- The Categorized Mail folder displays messages assigned to a category.
- The Large Mail folder displays messages larger than 100 kilobytes (KB).
- The Unread Mail folder displays messages that are marked as unread.
- The For Follow Up folder displays messages flagged for future For Follow Up folder displays messages flagged for future action.

The names of folders containing unread items are bold, followed by the number of unread items in parentheses. The names of folders containing items flagged for follow up are bold, followed by the number of flagged items in square brackets. The names of folders whose contents are not up to date are italic. To update a Search Folder, click the folder name.

Each message in your mailbox is stored in only one folder (such as your Inbox), but it might appear in many Search Folders. Changing or deleting a message in a Search Folder changes or deletes the message in the folder where it is stored.

If you want quick access to messages that fit a specific set of criteria, you can create a custom Search Folder. To do so:

1. In the **Navigation Pane**, expand the Search Folders folder to display the default Search Folders.

2. Right-click the **Search Folders** folder, and then click **New Search Folder**.

3. In the **New Search Folder** dialog box, select the type of Search Folder you want to create, and then click **OK**.

    You can choose from the standard options presented or click Custom to specify other search options.

You can make changes to the contents of an existing Search Folder by right-clicking the folder and then clicking Customize This Search Folder.

# Organizing Messages by Using Color Categories

Assigning messages to categories can help you more easily locate information. Outlook 2007 introduces Color Categories, which combine named categories with color bars to provide an immediate visual cue when viewing messages in your Inbox.

You can apply color categories to messages, calendar items, contacts, tasks, and notes. You can apply color categories several ways:

Categorize

- In any folder, you can select one or more items, click the **Categorize** button on the Standard toolbar, and then click the category you want.

> **Troubleshooting**  The Categorize button might not appear on the toolbar until you select one or more items.

- In any folder, you can right-click a single item or a selection of multiple items, point to Categorize, and then click the category you want.

Category bar

- In any mail folder, you can right-click the **Category** bar that appears when the Reading Pane is displayed, and then click the category you want.

- If you frequently use a particular category, you can assign it as your Quick Click category. You can then apply the Quick Click category to a message by clicking its Category bar.

To quickly view the messages belonging to a category, you can group your messages by category or include the category as a search criterion in the Query Builder. On the To-Do Bar, you can arrange your flagged messages and tasks by category.

> **Tip**  To help you easily distinguish messages received from certain people, you can color-code message headers. For example, you might show all messages from your boss in red and all messages from the finance department in green. You can also choose to have messages that were sent only to you displayed in a different color than messages sent to multiple people or a distribution list. You apply color-coding on a per-folder basis. To experiment with color-coding, click Organize on the Tools menu, and then click the Using Colors tab.

In this exercise, you will display the default color categories, rename and create categories, change the color associated with a category, categorize a message, and sort the Inbox contents by category.

> **USE** For this exercise, take any message in your Inbox and forward it to your Inbox with the new subject line SBS Alert Test 1.
>
> **BE SURE TO** start Outlook and display your Inbox in the default Messages view before beginning this exercise.

1. In the Inbox, click the *SBS Alert Test 1* message.

Categorize

2. On the Standard toolbar, click the **Categorize** button.

> **Troubleshooting** If the Categorize button is not visible or active, click any message in the Inbox to activate it.

The Category list displays the standard and currently assigned categories. Notice that you can remove all categorizations from a message by clicking Clear All Categories.

3. In the **Category** list, click **All Categories**.

The Color Categories dialog box opens, displaying the current color-to-category assignments. You can rename any of the standard color categories or create new color categories.

4. In the **Color Categories** dialog box, click the **Blue Category** name (not the check box), and then click **Rename**. With the category name selected for editing, type Management, and then press [Enter].

The category name changes.

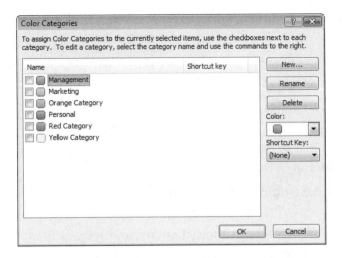

> **Tip** If you haven't renamed a color category, Outlook gives you the option of re-naming the category the first time you use it.

5. With the **Management** category still selected, click the **Color** arrow, and then in the color palette, click the **Yellow** square.

   The color associated with the Management category changes from Blue to Yellow.

6. In the **Color Categories** dialog box, click **New**.

   The Add New Category dialog box opens.

7. In the **Name** box, type Marketing. Click the **Color** arrow, and then in the color palette, click the **Red** square. Then click the **Shortcut Key** arrow.

   Notice that you can assign keyboard shortcuts to up to 11 color categories. You might want to implement this feature if you frequently use multiple categories.

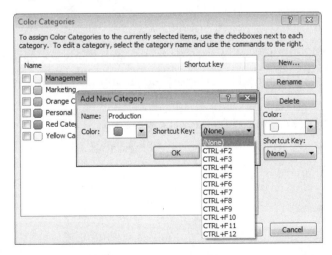

8. In the **Shortcut Key** list, click **None**. Then in the **Add New Category** dialog box, click **OK**.

   The new category appears at the bottom of the Color Categories list. Its check box is selected, indicating that it has been assigned to the currently selected message.

9. In the **Color Categories** dialog box, click **OK**.

   In the message list, a red square appears in the Category bar of the selected message, and in the Reading Pane, a red bar with the category name *Production* appears at the top of the message.

10. In the message list, right-click the **Category** bar of the *SBS Alert Test 1* message, and then in the list, click **Management**.

    The Category bar changes to display both red and yellow icons, indicating that the message is assigned to two categories. You can assign a message to an unlimited number of categories, but only the three most recently assigned appear in the Category bar.

    The Reading Pane displays two colored bars of equal size. Up to three categories can be displayed in one row; additional categories are displayed in additional rows.

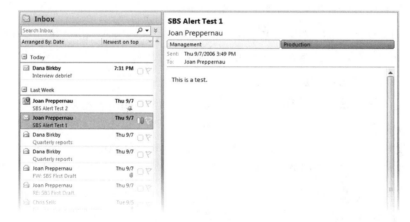

11. In the Inbox header, click the **Arranged By** bar, and then click **Categories**.

    The messages are arranged by category, beginning with the uncategorized messages.

12. To the right of the **Arranged By** bar, click **A on top**.

    The order reverses so that the categorized messages are displayed at the top of the list.

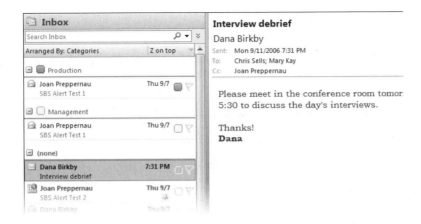

**BE SURE TO** sort the Inbox by date before continuing to the next exercise.

# Organizing Messages in Folders

After you've read and responded to messages, you might want to keep some for future reference. You can certainly choose to retain them all in your Inbox if you want, but as the number of messages in your Inbox increases to the hundreds and then into the thousands, it might quickly become overwhelming. To keep your Inbox content low and avoid an accumulation of unrelated messages, you can organize messages into folders.

Popular personal-organization gurus advocate various folder structures as an important part of an organizational system. You can apply any of these physical folder structures to Outlook, or you can use any other structure that works for you. For example, you might create a folder for each project you're working on and store all messages regarding a particular project in its own folder, no matter who sent them. Or you might create a folder to store all messages from a particular person, such as your manager, no matter what they are about.

You can move messages to folders manually, or if your organization is running Exchange Server, you can have Outlook move them for you. You can automatically move messages to another folder by creating a rule; for instance, you can instruct Outlook to automatically move all messages received from your manager to a separate folder. You can set up different rules that go into effect when you're away from the office.

In this exercise, you will create a folder and then move messages to it.

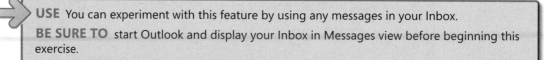

**USE** You can experiment with this feature by using any messages in your Inbox.

**BE SURE TO** start Outlook and display your Inbox in Messages view before beginning this exercise.

**1.** On the Standard toolbar, click the **New** arrow, and then in the list, click **Folder**.

The Create New Folder dialog box opens.

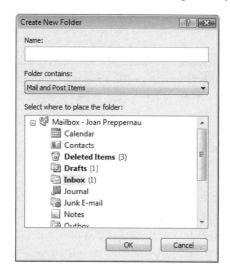

> **Troubleshooting** If your default data file (the file where your messages are stored) is a personal folder on your hard disk, the first item in the Select Where To Place The Folder box is Personal Folders.

**2.** In the **Name** box, type SBS Practice Messages, and then click **OK**.

> **Important** The name of this folder begins with *SBS* so that you can easily differentiate it from other folders in your mailbox.

Because you created this folder from the Inbox, Outlook creates the new folder as a subfolder of the Inbox, and formats it to contain mail items.

New fold

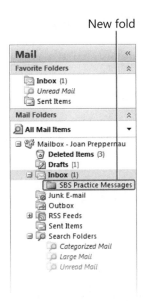

3. In the **Navigation Pane**, locate the *RE: SBS First Draft* and *FW: SBS First Draft* messages.

4. Drag the *RE: SBS First Draft* message to the **SBS Practice Messages** folder in the Navigation Pane.

   The message disappears from the Inbox.

5. Right-click the *FW: SBS First Draft* message, and then click **Move to Folder**.

   The Move Items dialog box opens.

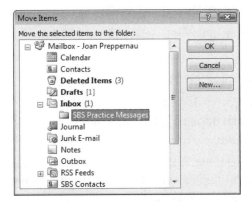

6. In the **Move the selected items to the folder** list, click **SBS Practice Messages** (if it isn't already selected). Then click **OK**.

   The message disappears from the Inbox.

**7.** In the **Navigation Pane**, under the **Inbox** folder, click the **SBS Practice Messages** folder.

The two messages appear in the new folder.

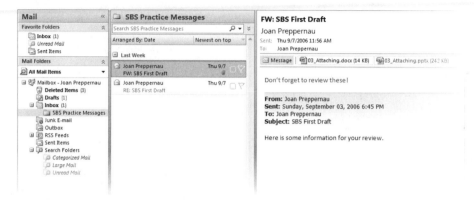

> **BE SURE TO** move the messages back to your Inbox if you used your own messages rather than the practice messages.

## Creating a OneNote Page from an E-Mail Message

If your 2007 Office system installation includes Microsoft Office OneNote, you can send or link items you create in Outlook, such as e-mail messages, contact records, and meeting invitations, to your OneNote notebook.

To send the content of an e-mail message to OneNote:

1. Display the Inbox, and then select the message (or messages) you want to send.

2. On the Standard toolbar, click the **Send to OneNote** button.

   Send to OneNote

   OneNote starts and, for each selected message, creates a page in your Unfiled Notes section. Each page contains the full text of the original message and links to any attachments.

You can move pages from the Unfiled Notes section to a notebook section by dragging it, or by right-clicking the page tab, and then clicking Move Page To, Another Section, and the target notebook section.

# Archiving Messages

As messages accumulate in your Inbox and other message folders, you might need to consider other ways to store them in order to cut down on the amount of storage space you're using. For example, you might want to *archive* all messages sent or received before a certain date. Archiving messages in a separate Outlook message file helps you manage clutter and the size of your primary data file, while still allowing easy access to the archived messages from within Outlook.

By default Outlook automatically archives messages in all your folders at regular intervals to a location determined by your operating system—usually an Archive data file you can access from the Navigation Pane. You can change the default *AutoArchive* settings, such as the archive frequency and location, and you can specify unique archive settings for individual folders.

If you are working on an Exchange Server network, your archival options might be limited by retention policies set by your network administrator. For instance, your company might have a policy that you may retain items for no more than a certain number of days.

> **Tip** You can use the Mailbox Cleanup feature to see the size of your mailbox, find and delete old items or items that are larger than a certain size, manually archive your mail, empty your Deleted Items folder, and delete conflicting versions of items stored on your computer or on the server. To use this feature, click Mailbox Cleanup on the Tools menu.

In this exercise, you will learn how to set the default automatic archive options, how to manually archive a folder, and how to set the archive options for an individual folder. There are no practice files for this exercise.

 **BE SURE TO** start Outlook and display the Inbox before beginning this exercise.

1. On the **Tools** menu, click **Options**.

   The Options dialog box opens.

2. In the **Options** dialog box, click the **Other** tab.

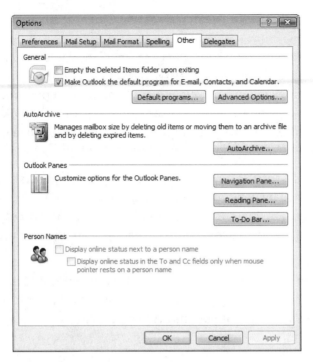

3. In the **AutoArchive** area, click **AutoArchive**.

The AutoArchive dialog box opens.

**4.** Review your AutoArchive settings—particularly note how often Outlook will start the archival process, the age at which items will be archived, and the location in the **Move old items to** box.

If the Prompt Before AutoArchive Runs check box is selected, Outlook requests your approval each time it runs the AutoArchive process. If you decline, the process doesn't start again until the next scheduled time.

Notice that you have the option to permanently delete old items. If you make changes to your AutoArchive settings or want to standardize settings across all folders, you can apply the changes to all the folders in your mailbox by clicking the Apply These Settings To All Folders Now button.

**5.** If you want to make changes to your AutoArchive settings, do so, and then click **OK** in each of the open dialog boxes. Otherwise, click **Cancel** in each of the dialog boxes to close them without initiating any changes.

**6.** With the Inbox active, on the **File** menu, point to **Folder**, and then click **Properties for "Inbox"**.

The Inbox Properties dialog box opens.

**7.** Click the **AutoArchive** tab.

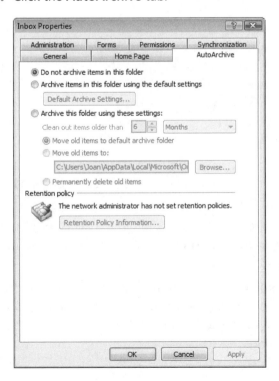

You can set the archive options for each folder individually from the AutoArchive tab of the folder's Properties dialog box.

- If you select the Archive Items In This Folder Using The Default Settings option, you can view and modify the default settings in the AutoArchive dialog box shown earlier by clicking the Default Archive Settings button.

- If you select the Archive This Folder Using These Settings option, you can specify a unique archival age and location for the items in this folder.

8. If you want to make changes to the Inbox AutoArchive settings, do so, and then click **OK**. Otherwise, click **Cancel** to close the dialog box without initiating any changes.

9. On the **File** menu, click **Archive**.

The Archive dialog box opens.

From this dialog box, you can manually start the archive process for your entire mailbox or for selected folders.

10. If you want to initiate the archive process for your mailbox now, select the **Archive all folders according to their AutoArchive settings** option, and then click **OK**. Otherwise, click **Cancel**.

If you click OK, Outlook displays the progress of the archive process on the status bar in the lower-right corner of the program window. You can cancel an archive process by clicking the Archiving button on the status bar and then in the list, clicking Cancel Archiving.

The first time Outlook archives messages, it creates an Archive Folders data file that you can access from the Navigation Pane. The data file contents are organized in the same folder structure as the original contents, and are stored in a separate file on your computer.

> **Tip** You can restore archived Outlook items from the Archive Folders data file to your mailbox by dragging or moving them to the mailbox folder.

 **BE SURE TO** review your AutoArchive settings and ensure they are set the way you want.

# Key Points

- You can filter and locate messages in your mailbox by using the new Instant Search function. You can create virtual Search Folders that automatically update to display messages meeting certain criteria.

- You can group and sort messages by sender, time, subject, size, category, or any other field.

- You can assign color-coded categories to messages, tasks, appointments, and other Outlook items, and then group and sort items by color category. You can use the default Outlook categories or tailor them to fit your needs.

- You can create folders to organize your mail, and move items to folders manually or automatically.

- Outlook automatically archives old and expired items to a separate data file. You can specify the AutoArchive frequency, location, and other settings on a global and per-folder basis.

# Chapter at a Glance

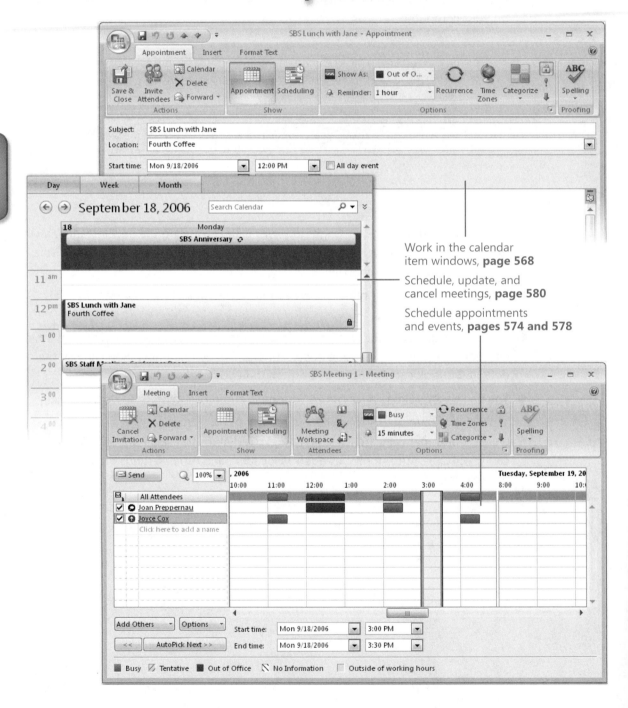

Work in the calendar
item windows, **page 568**

Schedule, update, and
cancel meetings, **page 580**

Schedule appointments
and events, **pages 574 and 578**

# 20 Managing Appointments, Events, and Meetings

---

**In this chapter, you will learn to:**

✔ Work in the calendar item windows.

✔ Schedule and change appointments and events.

✔ Schedule, update, and cancel meetings.

✔ Respond to meeting requests.

---

You might find that your Microsoft Office Outlook Calendar runs your life—but that isn't necessarily a bad thing! Using the Calendar effectively can help you to stay organized, on task, and on time. You can schedule and track appointments, meetings, and events. Because Outlook 2007 maps your scheduled tasks to your calendar, you can look at your calendar in Day view or Week view to see the tasks that need to be completed that day, and you can track your progress by marking tasks as complete when you finish them.

In this chapter, you will record different types of information in your Outlook calendar, scheduling an appointment and an event on your own calendar and then scheduling a meeting with another person. If your organization is running Microsoft Exchange Server, you will learn methods of determining meeting times during which other people are available—these vary depending on the version of Exchange Server. Then you will learn about responding to, updating, and canceling meeting requests.

**See Also** Do you need only a quick refresher on the topics in this chapter? See the Quick Reference entries at the beginning of this book.

> **Important** No practice files are required to complete the exercises in this chapter. For more information about practice files, see "Using the Book's CD" at the beginning of this book.

> **Troubleshooting** Graphics and operating system–related instructions in this book reflect the Windows Vista user interface. If your computer is running Microsoft Windows XP and you experience trouble following the instructions as written, please refer to the "Information for Readers Running Windows XP" section at the beginning of this book.

# Working in the Calendar Item Windows

We refer to the window in which you create or respond to an appointment as the *appointment window*, to a meeting as the *meeting window*, and to an event as the *event window*; collectively we refer to these windows as the *calendar item windows*. Like the contact and message windows, the calendar item windows contain their own commands, arranged on the new Office Ribbon instead of on menus and toolbars.

In this exercise, you will take a tour of the calendar item window elements that differ from the contact and message window elements discussed in earlier chapters, and you'll learn about the differences between the types of calendar items. There are no practice files for this exercise.

 **BE SURE TO** start Outlook before beginning this exercise.

 1. In the **Navigation Pane**, click the **Calendar** button to display the Calendar module.

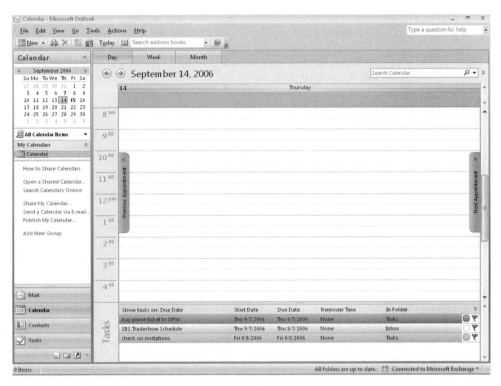

New

New
Appointment

**2.** On the Standard toolbar, click the **New Appointment** button.

An untitled appointment window opens.

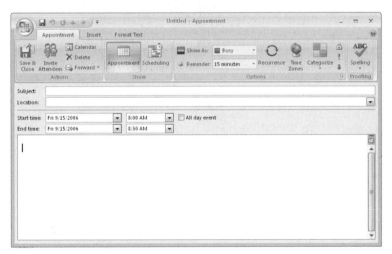

> **Important** Depending on your screen resolution and the size of the appointment window that opens, you might see more or fewer buttons in each of the groups, or the buttons you see might be represented by larger or smaller icons than those shown in this book. Experiment with the size of the appointment window to understand the effect on the appearance of the Ribbon.

Microsoft Office
Button

**3.** In the upper-left corner of the appointment window, click the **Microsoft Office Button**.

Commands related to managing appointments (such as creating, saving, deleting, and printing) are available from the Office menu that appears.

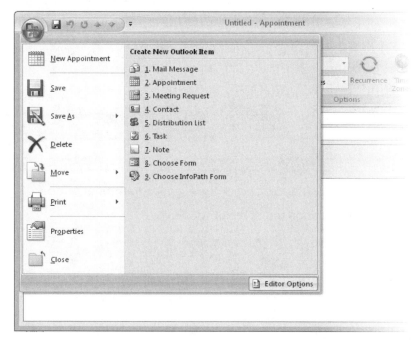

**4.** Click away from the Office menu to close it.

The appointment window commands are organized in groups on three tabs:

● Appointment

● Insert

● Format Text

> **Tip** Depending on what programs you have installed on your computer, tabs and groups other than those described here might also appear on the Ribbon. For example, if Microsoft Office OneNote is installed on your computer, a OneNote group appears on the Appointment tab.

The Appointment tab is active by default. Buttons representing commands related to creating appointments are organized on this tab in four groups:

- Actions
- Show
- Options
- Proofing

You can create a simple appointment by using only the commands available on this tab.

**5.** Click the **Insert** tab.

Buttons representing commands related to items you can insert are organized on this tab in six groups:

- Include
- Tables
- Illustrations
- Links
- Text
- Symbols

**6.** Click the **Format Text** tab.

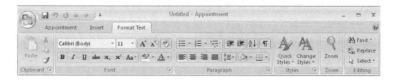

Buttons representing commands related to the appearance of message content are organized on this tab in six groups:

- Clipboard
- Font
- Paragraph
- Styles
- Zoom
- Editing

**7.** On the **Appointment** tab, in the **Options** group, click the **Time Zones** button.

A new field displaying the time zone for each of the start and end times appears. With this useful Outlook 2007 feature, you can schedule an appointment that crosses time zones—for instance, a flight from Los Angeles to New York.

**See Also** For more information about configuring Outlook for different time zones, see the sidebar "Configuring Outlook for Multiple Time Zones" in Chapter 21, "Managing Your Calendar."

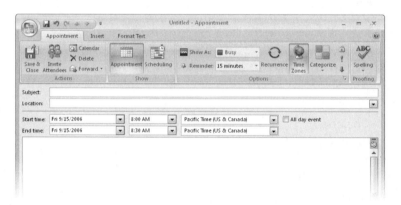

**8.** In the **Start time** area, select the **All day event** check box.

The window changes from an appointment window to an event window. The contents of the Format Text and Insert tabs don't change, but an Event tab replaces the Appointment tab.

**9.** Click the **Event** tab.

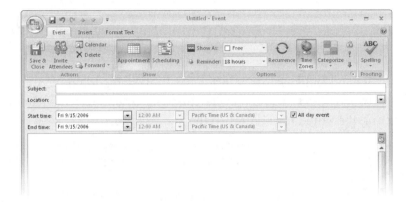

The Event tab contents are nearly identical to the Appointment tab contents—the only change is that on the Event tab, in the Options group, by default your time is shown as Free rather than Busy, and the reminder is set to display 18 hours prior to the event rather than 15 minutes.

**10.** In the **Start time** area, clear the **All day event** check box to change the event to an appointment.

Invite
Attendees

**11.** In the **Actions** group, click the **Invite Attendees** button.

The window changes from an appointment window to a meeting window. The contents of the Format Text and Insert tabs don't change, but a Meeting tab that includes two additional groups replaces the Appointment tab:

- Send
- Attendees

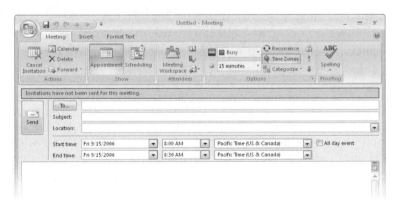

> **Tip** You can invite people to an event in the same way you do to a meeting, by clicking the Invite Attendees button from within an event window.

The meeting window header includes a To field in addition to the standard Subject and Location fields. You can invite attendees by entering them in the To field or by clicking the Scheduling button in the Show group.

**BE SURE TO** click the Time Zones button to hide the time zone settings, if you don't want to display them.

**CLOSE** the meeting window without saving your changes.

# Scheduling and Changing Appointments

*Appointments* are blocks of time you schedule for only yourself (as opposed to meetings, to which you invite other people). If an appointment recurs at specific intervals, such as every Tuesday and Thursday, every other week or every month, you can set it up in your Outlook calendar as a *recurring* appointment; doing so creates multiple instances of the appointment in your calendar at the time interval you specify. Recurring appointments are linked. When making changes to recurring appointments, you can choose to update all occurrences or only an individual occurrence of the appointment.

When creating an appointment, you can show your time on the calendar as Free, Tentative, Busy, or Out Of Office. This information is available to other people on your network, and also when you send your schedule information to other people in an e-mail message or share your calendar. You can include information such as driving directions or Web site links in the Notes field, and attach related files so that they are easily available to you at the time of the appointment.

**See Also** For information about sending your schedule information via e-mail, see "Sending Calendar Information in an E-Mail Message' in Chapter 21, "Managing Your Calendar."

When Outlook is running, it displays a *reminder* message 15 minutes before the appointment start time—you can change the reminder time or turn it off completely if you want to. If you synchronize your Outlook installation with a mobile device such as a BlackBerry or a mobile phone running Microsoft Windows Mobile, you can also receive reminders on your device. This is very convenient when you are away from your computer.

**See Also**  For information about assigning appointments to categories, see "Organizing Messages by Using Color Categories" in Chapter 19, "Managing Your Inbox."

In this exercise, you will schedule an appointment and a recurring appointment. There are no practice files for this exercise.

 **BE SURE TO** display the Calendar before beginning this exercise.

**Troubleshooting**  The default Calendar display is Day view. If your calendar does not look like the one shown in this exercise, click the Day button on the Standard toolbar.

1. In the **Navigation Pane**, in the **Date Navigator**, click tomorrow's date.

   **Tip**  The Date Navigator displays six weeks at a time, including the selected month. The days of the selected month are black; days of the previous and next months are gray, but you can still select them in the Date Navigator.

   Outlook displays tomorrow's schedule.

2. In the Calendar pane, point to the **1:00 P.M.** time slot (or, if you already have an appointment scheduled at 1:00 P.M., to another time when you have 30 minutes available).

   Click To Add Appointment appears in the time slot.

3. Click once to activate the time slot.

   In this mode, you can enter basic appointment details directly in the Calendar pane.

4. Type SBS Lunch with Jane, and then press $\boxed{\text{Enter}}$.

   **Important**  The subject of each appointment, meeting, or event we have you create while working through the exercises in this book begins with *SBS* so that you can easily differentiate the practice files from other items on your calendar.

   Outlook creates a half-hour appointment beginning at 1:00 P.M.

5. Drag the appointment from the 1:00 P.M. time slot to the **12:00 P.M.** time slot (or, if you already have an appointment scheduled at noon, to another time when you have an hour available).

   Outlook changes the appointment start time.

6. Point to the bottom border of the appointment, and when the pointer becomes a double-headed arrow, drag down so that the appointment ends at **1:00 P.M.**

   You can add more details to the appointment and vary from the default settings from within the appointment window.

7. Double-click the **SBS Lunch with Jane** appointment.

   The appointment window opens. The subject, start time, and end time are set according to the information you entered in the Calendar pane.

8. In the **Location** box, type Fourth Coffee.

9. On the **Appointment** tab, in the **Options** group, click the **Show As** arrow, and then in the list, click **Out of Office**.

   > **Tip** In this book, when we give instructions to implement a command, we tell you on what tab and in which group the command button appears. When directing you to use multiple command buttons on the same tab, we might omit the tab name to avoid needless repetition.

10. In the **Options** group, click the **Reminder** arrow, and then in the list, click **1 hour**.

11. In the **Options** group, click the **Private** button.

Private

   Marking an appointment, event, or meeting as Private hides the details from anyone you share your calendar with.

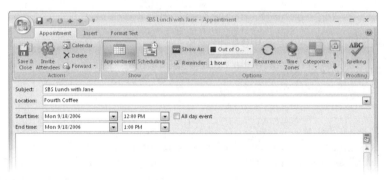

12. In the **Actions** group, click the **Save & Close** button.

Save & Close

   Outlook adds a purple stripe at the left side of the appointment to indicate you will be out of the office, and displays the location. The lock icon in the lower-right corner indicates that the appointment has been marked as private.

13. Double-click the **2:00 P.M.** time slot.

   Outlook opens an appointment window with the appointment start time set to 2:00 P.M. and the end time set 30 minutes later.

**14.** In the **Subject** box, type SBS Staff Meeting. In the **Location** box, type Conference Room.

**15.** On the **Appointment** tab, in the **Options** group, click the **Recurrence** button.

The Appointment Recurrence dialog box opens.

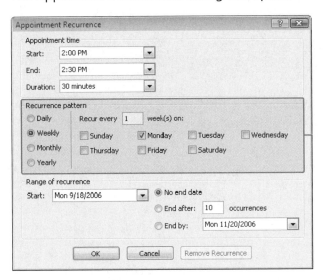

The default appointment recurrence is weekly on the currently selected day of the week. You can set the appointment to recur until further notice, or to end after a certain number of occurrences or by a certain date.

**16.** In the **Range of recurrence** area, select the **End after** option, and then in the box, replace *10* with *2*.

**17.** To create a 30-minute appointment beginning at 2:00 P.M. on the selected day of the week, this week and next week only, click **OK**.

The appointment window title bar changes to reflect that this is now a recurring appointment, the Appointment tab changes to a Recurring Appointment tab, and the frequency (labeled *Recurrence*) appears in the header.

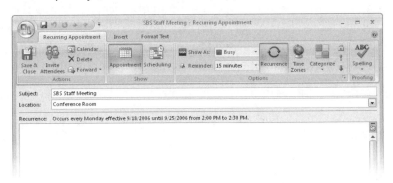

18. On the **Recurring Appointment** tab, in the **Actions** group, click the **Save & Close** button.

    The appointment appears on your calendar. The circling arrow icon at the right end of the time slot indicates the recurrence.

Private appointment

| 18 | Monday |
| --- | --- |
| 11 <sup>am</sup> | |
| 12 <sup>pm</sup> | SBS Lunch with Jane<br>Fourth Coffee |
| 1 <sup>00</sup> | |
| 2 <sup>00</sup> | SBS Staff Meeting; Conference Room |
| 3 <sup>00</sup> | |
| 4 <sup>00</sup> | |

Recurring appointment

19. In the **Date Navigator**, click the day of the appointment, in each of the next two weeks, to verify that the appointment appears on your calendar the next week, but not the following week.

**See Also**  For information about creating a OneNote page linked to an appointment, see the sidebar "Creating a OneNote Page Linked to an Appointment, an Event, or a Meeting" in Chapter 21, "Managing Your Calendar."

# Scheduling and Changing Events

*Events* are day-long blocks of time that you schedule on your Outlook calendar—for example, a birthday, a payroll day, or anything else occurring on a particular day but not at a specific time. In all other respects, events are identical to appointments, in that you can specify a location, indicate recurrence, indicate your availability, invite attendees, and attach additional information to the event item.

You can create an event when viewing your calendar in Day view, Week view, or Month view.

In this exercise, you will schedule an event and convert it to a recurring event. There are no practice files for this exercise.

> **BE SURE TO** display the Calendar in Day view before beginning this exercise.

1. In the **Date Navigator**, click tomorrow's date.

2. In the Calendar pane, point to the blank space below the day header and above the delineated time slots.

   Click To Add Event appears in the space.

3. Click once to activate the event slot.

   In this mode, you can enter basic event details directly in the Calendar pane.

4. Type **SBS Anniversary**, and then press ⌈Enter⌋.

   Outlook creates a one-day event. You can add more details to the event and vary from the default settings from within the event window.

5. Double-click the **SBS Anniversary** event.

   The event window opens. The subject and date are set according to the information you entered in the Calendar pane.

6. On the **Event** tab, in the **Options** group, click the **Recurrence** button.

   The Appointment Recurrence dialog box shown earlier in this chapter opens. The default recurrence for events is the same as for appointments—weekly on the currently selected day of the week.

7. In the **Recurrence pattern** area, select the **Yearly** option.

   You can schedule an annual event to recur on a specific date or on a selected (first, second, third, fourth, or last) day of the month.

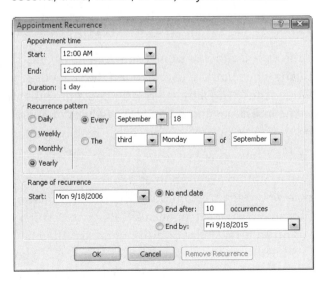

**8.** To create a recurring annual appointment on the same date each year, click **OK**.

The event window title bar changes to reflect that this is now a recurring event, the Event tab changes to a Recurring Event tab, and the frequency appears in the header.

Save & Close

**9.** On the **Recurring Event** tab, in the **Actions** group, click the **Save & Close** button.

The event appears at the top of the Calendar pane. The circling arrow icon at the right end indicates the recurrence.

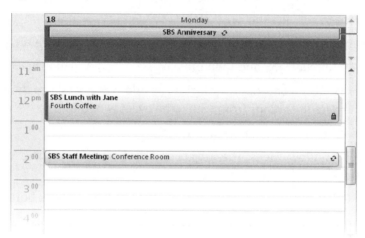

# Scheduling, Updating, and Canceling Meetings

Scheduling meetings through Outlook is significantly simpler than scheduling meetings manually, particularly when you are coordinating the schedules of several people. A primary difficulty when scheduling a meeting is finding a time that works for everyone. Outlook displays the individual and collective schedules of people within your own organization, and of people outside of your organization who have published their availability to the Internet.

You can send a meeting invitation (referred to as a *meeting request*) to any e-mail account (even to people who don't use Outlook). You can inform non-critical attendees of the meeting by marking their attendance as Optional. You can invite entire groups of people by using an e-mail alias or distribution list. The meeting request can include text and Web links, as well as file attachments. This is a convenient way of ensuring that meeting attendees have specific information available to them. Outlook automatically tracks responses from attendees and those responsible for scheduling the resources you requested, so you always have an up-to-date report of how many people will be attending your meeting.

If your organization is running Microsoft Exchange Server and the Exchange Server directory includes shared resources such as conference rooms or presentation equipment, you can request these resources by inviting them to the meeting. Resource requests may be automatically approved, or an individual may be assigned the responsibility of approving each resource request.

You might find it necessary to change the date, time, or location of a meeting—for example, because of a schedule conflict. You can change any information in a meeting request at any time, including adding or deleting invited attendees, or canceling the meeting. After you make changes, Outlook sends an updated meeting request to the invited attendees to keep them informed. If the only change you make is to the attendee list, Outlook gives you the option of sending an update only to the affected attendees.

In this exercise, you will create and send a meeting request. There are no practice files for this exercise.

> **BE SURE TO** display the Calendar and inform a coworker or friend that you are going to practice inviting him or her to a meeting.

1. In the **Date Navigator**, click tomorrow's date. Then in the Calendar pane, click the **3:00 P.M.** time slot (or if you have a conflicting appointment, click a time when you have 30 minutes available).

New
Appointment

2. On the Standard toolbar, click the **New Appointment** arrow, and then in the list, click **Meeting Request**.

   An untitled meeting window opens.

   > **Troubleshooting** If the active selection in the Calendar pane is an event, Outlook will create an Invited Event request instead; if this happens, clear the All Day Event check box to convert the Invited Event to a Meeting.

3. In the **To** box, type the e-mail address of someone within your organization, or if you aren't working on an Exchange Server network, type any e-mail address, for instance, adam@contoso.com.

4. In the **Subject** box, type SBS Meeting 1.

5. In the **Location** box, type Test – please accept to indicate to the person you are inviting that the meeting request is for testing purposes only.

**6.** On the **Meeting** tab, in the **Show** group, click the **Scheduling** button.

The All Attendees list on the Scheduling page includes you and the e-mail address (or if the person is in your address book, the associated name) you entered in the To box. The black icon next to your name indicates that you are the meeting organizer. The red icon next to the sole attendee's name indicates that he or she is a required attendee. You can click an attendee's icon to switch between Required Attendee and Optional Attendee status, or to indicate a resource rather than a person.

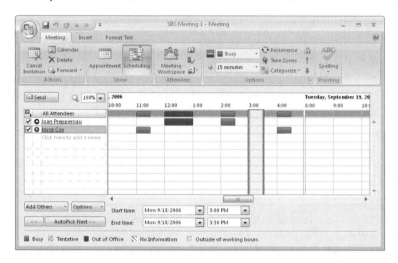

> **Tip** You can enter additional attendees in the To box on the Appointment page or in the All Attendees list on the Scheduling page. If you prefer, you can organize a meeting directly from a Scheduling page-like interface by clicking Plan A Meeting on the Actions menu.

Outlook indicates the suggested meeting time with green (start time) and red (end time) vertical bars. If free/busy information is available for meeting invitees, their time is shown as white (Available), blue (Busy), or purple (Out of Office). Tentative bookings are indicated by light-blue diagonal stripes. If no information is available (either because Outlook can't connect to a person's calendar or because the proposed meeting is further out than the scheduling information stored on the server), Outlook indicates this by gray diagonal stripes. The gray row at the top of the schedule indicates the collective schedule of all the invitees.

You can change the time and duration of the meeting to work with the displayed schedules by selecting from the lists at the bottom of the Scheduling page, by dragging the green and red vertical bars in the schedule area, or by clicking the time you want in the schedule area.

## Using the Exchange Server 2007 Smart Scheduling Feature

If your organization is running Exchange Server 2007, Outlook simplifies even further the process of selecting a suitable meeting time by presenting you with a list of meeting times of any duration you specify, and indicating for each time the number of required and optional attendees who are available.

The Scheduling Assistant page is similar to the Scheduling page displayed when organizing a meeting on an Exchange Server 2003 network.

Smart Scheduling features ─┐

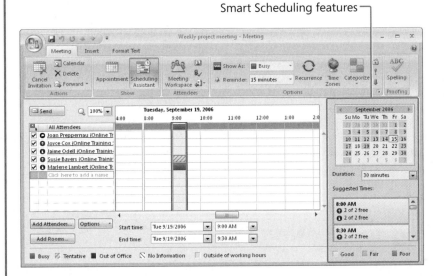

The calendar on the right side of the window indicates the collective availability of the group by color:

- Days when all attendees are available are white (Good)

- Days when most attendees are available are light blue (Fair)

- Days when most attendees are not available are medium blue (Poor)

- Dates that occur in the past and non-working days are shaded; scheduling suggestions are not provided for those days.

In the Suggested Times list, Outlook displays attendee availability for appointments of the length specified in the Duration list. The availability of required attendees is shown separately from that of optional attendees and resources.

You can select a date in the calendar to display the suggested meeting times for that day. Clicking a meeting time in the Suggested Times list updates the meeting request.

7. In the lower-right corner of the **Scheduling** page, click the **AutoPick Next** button.

   The green Start Time and red End Time lines move to the next available half-hour time slot.

   You can change the Show As and Reminder settings, create recurrences, assign color categories, and make any other changes you want. The availability specified in the Show As list will apply to all attendees who accept your meeting request.

Appointment

8. After you select the meeting time you want, click the **Appointment** button in the **Show** group to display the Appointment page.

Send

9. Verify the meeting details, and then click the **Send** button in the meeting request header.

   The meeting appears in your calendar on the specified date and in the specified time slot.

> **Tip** To send an e-mail message to everyone you've invited to a meeting, first open the meeting window, and then on the Meeting tab, in the Attendees group, click the Message To Attendees button.

# Responding to Meeting Requests

When you receive a meeting request from another Outlook user, the meeting appears on your calendar with your time scheduled, but shown as Tentative. Until you respond to the meeting request, the organizer doesn't know whether you plan to attend. You can respond in one of four ways:

- You can accept the request. Outlook deletes the meeting request and shows your time scheduled on your calendar as the meeting organizer indicated in the meeting request.

- You can tentatively accept a request, indicating that you might be able to attend the meeting but are undecided. Outlook deletes the meeting request and shows your time on your calendar as tentatively scheduled.

- You can propose a new meeting time. Outlook sends your request to the meeting organizer for confirmation and shows the original time on your calendar as tentatively scheduled.

- You can decline the request. Outlook deletes the meeting request and removes the meeting from your calendar.

Meeting
response
options

Display your calendar
for the proposed
meeting date

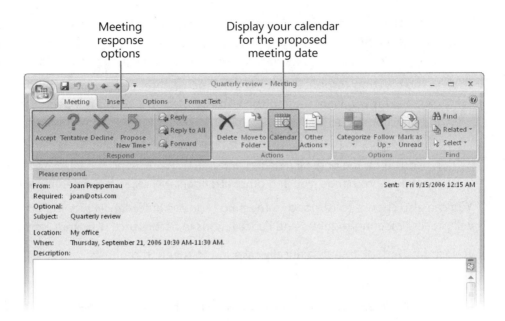

If you don't respond to a meeting request, the meeting remains on your calendar, with your time shown as tentatively scheduled.

If you're unsure whether a meeting time works for you, you can click the Calendar button within the meeting request window to open your Outlook calendar for the suggested meeting day in a separate window, so you can view any conflicting appointments.

When accepting or declining a meeting, you can choose whether to send a response to the meeting organizer. If you don't send a response, your acceptance will not be tallied in the Meeting form, and the organizer and other attendees will not know whether you are planning to attend the meeting. If you do send a response, you can add information to the response before sending it, if you want to convey a message to the meeting organizer.

To manually respond to a meeting request:

1. In the meeting request window, in the Reading Pane, or on the shortcut menu that appears when you right-click the meeting request, click **Accept**, **Tentative**, or **Decline**.

2. Choose whether to send a standard response, a personalized response, or no response at all.

To propose a new time for a meeting:

1. In  the meeting request window, in the Reading Pane, or on the shortcut menu that appears when you right-click the meeting request, click **Propose New Time**.

2. In the schedule area of the **Propose New Time** dialog box, similar to the Scheduling page of the meeting request window shown earlier, change the meeting start and end times to the times you want to propose, and then click the **Propose Time** button.

3. In the meeting response window that opens, enter a message to the meeting organizer if you want to, and then on the **Meeting** tab, in the **Send** group, click the **Send** button.

   Outlook sends your response and adds the meeting to your calendar as tentatively scheduled for the original meeting time. After the meeting organizer approves the meeting time change, you and other attendees will receive updated meeting requests.

You can also choose to respond to meeting requests automatically. If you do, Outlook will process meeting requests and cancellations in accordance with your instructions.

To instruct Outlook to automatically respond to meeting requests:

1. On the **Tools** menu, click **Options**.

2. On the **Preferences** tab of the **Options** dialog box, click the **Calendar Options** button.

3. In the **Calendar Options** dialog box, click the **Resource Scheduling** button.

4. In the **Resource Scheduling** dialog box, select the **Automatically accept meeting requests and process cancellations** check box.

5. Select the **Automatically decline conflicting meeting requests** and/or the **Automatically decline recurring meeting requests** check boxes if you want Outlook to do this.

6. Click **OK** in each of the open dialog boxes.

## Creating a Meeting Workspace

If your organization has a Microsoft Windows SharePoint site, such as a team site, on which you have permission to create document libraries, you can create a *meeting workspace* (a shared site for planning a meeting and tracking related tasks and results) at the same time that you schedule the meeting. You can also create a meeting workspace for a meeting that you previously scheduled; after you change the meeting request to include the meeting workspace information, Outlook sends an updated request containing the information to all attendees.

To create a meeting workspace in a new or existing meeting request:

1. In the meeting window, on the **Meeting** tab, in the **Attendees** group, click the **Meeting Workspace** button.

2. In the **Meeting Workspace** pane that opens on the right side of the meeting window, click the **Select a location** arrow, and then in the list, click the SharePoint site where you want to create the meeting workspace. (If this is the first time you've used the Meeting Workspace pane, you might first need to click **Change settings**.) If you haven't previously set up a meeting workspace or document library on the SharePoint site you want to use, click **Other** in the **Select a location** list, enter the SharePoint site address in the **Other Workspace Server** dialog box that opens, and then click **OK**.

3. In the **Select a workspace** area, select the template language and meeting workspace template you want to use, and then click **OK**. Or if you want to link to an existing meeting workspace, select that option, click the **Select the workspace** arrow, and then in the list, click the existing workspace.

4. In the **Meeting Workspace** pane, click **OK**.

Attendees can link to the meeting workspace from the meeting request or from the meeting item on their calendars.

# Key Points

- You can create and manage appointments and all-day events in your calendar.

- You can use Outlook to set up meetings, invite participants, and track their responses. Outlook can help you choose a meeting time based on participants' schedules.

- Other people in your organization can see your free, busy, and out-of-office time that you indicate in your calendar. You can personalize the display of your available working hours, and mark appointments as private to hide the details from other people.

- If your organization has a SharePoint collaboration site, you can create a meeting workspace to accompany a meeting request. Meeting workspaces provide a central location for sharing information and files among meeting attendees.

- If you organization is running Exchange Server 2007, you can use the Smart Scheduling feature to quickly identify meeting times of a specific duration during which your planned attendees are available.

# Chapter at a Glance

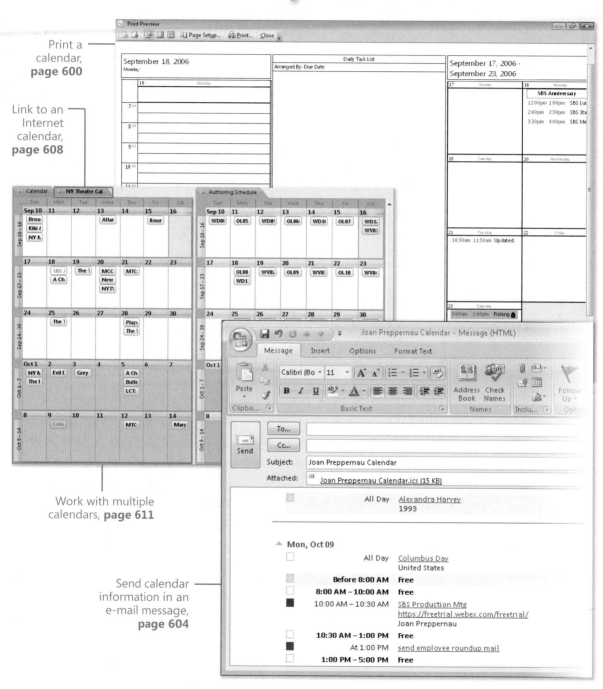

Print a calendar, **page 600**

Link to an Internet calendar, **page 608**

Work with multiple calendars, **page 611**

Send calendar information in an e-mail message, **page 604**

# 21 Managing Your Calendar

**In this chapter, you will learn to:**

✔ Display different views of a calendar.

✔ Define your available time.

✔ Print a calendar.

✔ Send calendar information in an e-mail message.

✔ Link to an Internet calendar.

✔ Work with multiple calendars.

Using the Microsoft Office Outlook 2007 Calendar is a big step toward efficient time management. Earlier in this book, you learned how to enter and update various types of appointments in your calendar. To make your calendar work more effectively for you, and to simplify the process of finding the information you need, you can refine the default calendar settings.

In this chapter, you will learn about the different ways you can display calendar information. Then you will print daily and monthly calendars and attach calendar information to an e-mail message. Finally, you will link to a public calendar on the Internet and experiment with the different ways you can display and move between calendars. You also learn how to add region-specific holidays to your calendar, configure Outlook for use in multiple time zones, save information from your Calendar as a Web page, and create a OneNote page linked to a Calendar item, as well as ways in which you can delegate control of your calendar to another person or manage a calendar on behalf of another person.

**See Also** Do you need only a quick refresher on the topics in this chapter? See the Quick Reference entries at the beginning of this book.

> **Important** No practice files are required to complete the exercises in this chapter. For more information about practice files, see "Using the Book's CD" at the beginning of this book.

> **Troubleshooting** Graphics and operating system–related instructions in this book reflect the Windows Vista user interface. If your computer is running Microsoft Windows XP and you experience trouble following the instructions as written, please refer to the "Information for Readers Running Windows XP" section at the beginning of this book.

# Displaying Different Views of a Calendar

In the Calendar module, the Navigation Pane includes the *Date Navigator*, lists of calendars you can connect to, and links to open, search, share, send, and publish calendars. To help you stay on top of your schedule, you can view your calendar in a variety of ways:

- **Day/Week/Month view.** A calendar view displaying one of the following:

    - Day view, displaying one day at a time separated into half-hour increments.

    - Work Week view, displaying your work week, which by default is defined as Monday through Friday from 8:00 A.M. to 5:00 P.M. You can define your work week as whatever days and hours you want.

    **See Also** For information about modifying the work week show in Outlook, see "Defining Your Available Time" later in this chapter.

    - Week view, displaying one week (Sunday through Saturday) at a time.

    - Month view, displaying five weeks at a time.

    You switch among time periods by clicking the buttons at the top of the Calendar pane. In Month view, you can click the week tab at the left edge of a week to display only that week. In Week view, you can switch between displays of the work week and the full seven-day week. In either view, you can double-click a day to display only that day.

- **All Appointments view.** A list view displaying all appointments (but not events) grouped by frequency of recurrence (none, Daily, Weekly, Monthly, or Yearly).

- **Active Appointments view.** A list view displaying all appointments starting on or after the current day, grouped by frequency of recurrence.

- **Events view.** A list view displaying only day-long events, grouped by frequency of recurrence.

- **Annual Events view.** A list view displaying only events that recur yearly.

- **Recurring Appointments view.** A list view displaying only recurring appointments and events, grouped by frequency of recurrence.

- **By Category view.** A list view displaying all calendar items grouped by Color Category. Items assigned to multiple categories appear in each of the assigned category groups.

- **Outlook Data Files view.** A list view displaying all calendar items grouped by Outlook Data File and then by frequency of recurrence.

By default, Outlook displays your calendar in Day view. To change the view, select the view option you want in the Current View list in the Navigation Pane, or click the view you want on the View menu. To return to the current Day view from any other view, click the Today button on the Standard toolbar.

You can display the previous or next time periods by clicking the Back or Forward button next to the date or date range, or you can display a specific day, week, or month by selecting it in the Date Navigator.

- To display a month, click the current month name and then in the list, click the month you want to display. To scroll beyond the seven-month range displayed by default, point to the top or bottom of the month list.

- To display a week, click the margin to the left of that week. Or, if you display week numbers in the Date Navigator and Calendar, click the week number to display that week.

> **Tip** Week numbers are used in some countries to reference events, vacations, and the like. Week 1 is the calendar week (Sunday through Saturday) in which January 1st falls, Week 2 is the following week, and so on through to the end of the year. Because of the way the weeks are numbered, a year can comprise Weeks 1 through 53. To display week numbers, click Tools on the Options menu, click the Calendar Options button, and then select the Show Week Numbers In The Month View And Date Navigator check box. Then click OK in the open dialog boxes.

- To display a day, click that day.

> **Tip** If you've made changes to any view (such as the order in which information appears) and want to return to the default settings, point to Current View on the View menu, click Customize Current View, and then in the Customize View dialog box, click Reset Current View. If the Reset Current View button is unavailable, the view already displays the default settings.

In calendar views that include the Date Navigator, increasing the width of the Navigation Pane also increases the number of months shown in the Data Navigator. You can allocate up to 50% of the program window to the Navigation Pane.

You can use the Outlook 2007 Instant Search feature to quickly locate appointments, events, meetings, or holidays by searching on any text within the calendar item.

**See Also** For more information about Instant Search, see "Quickly Locating Messages" in Chapter 19, "Managing Your Inbox."

In this exercise, you will display different periods of time in the Date Navigator and in your calendar, and display different views of your schedule.

**BE SURE TO** start Outlook before beginning this exercise.

**USE** the calendar items you created in Chapter 20, "Managing Appointments, Events, and Meetings." If you did not complete the exercises in that chapter, you can complete them now, or use any appointments, meetings, or events in your own calendar.

1. In the **Navigation** pane, click the **Calendar** button to display the Calendar module.

   By default, Outlook displays your calendar for the current day, which is indicated in the Date Navigator by a red outline. Tasks due today are listed in the Tasks area at the bottom of the Calendar pane.

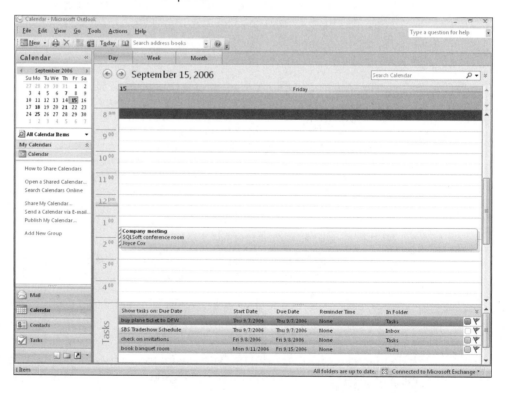

> **Tip** To reset your calendar to the default display settings, point to Current View on the View menu, click Customize Current View, and then in the Customize View dialog box, click Reset Current View. Then click OK in the message box requesting confirmation, and in the open dialog box.

2. In the **Date Navigator**, click a bold date to display your calendar for a day on which you have scheduled appointments or meetings.

   Dates with scheduled events (but no appointments or meetings) do not appear bold.

3. At the top of the Calendar pane, click **Week**.

   Outlook displays your calendar for the work week of the selected date, and high-lights the corresponding days in the Date Navigator. The Tasks area displays tasks due each day.

4. At the top of the Calendar pane, select the **Show full week** option.

   Outlook displays the full seven-day week. Time that falls outside of your defined work week appears shaded.

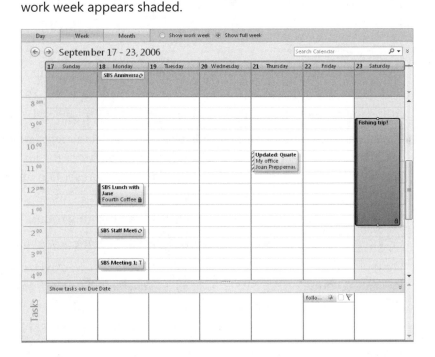

5. At the top of the Calendar pane, click **Month**.

   Outlook displays your calendar for the month. Alternating months are shaded to provide an obvious visual indicator of the change. The Tasks area is not available in Month view.

Week labels

| | Day | Week | Month | Details: ○ Low ○ Medium ◉ High | | |
|---|---|---|---|---|---|---|

September 2006

Search Calendar

| | Sunday | Monday | Tuesday | Wednesday | Thursday | Friday | Saturday |
|---|---|---|---|---|---|---|---|
| Aug 27 - Sep 2 | Aug 27 | 28 | 29 | 30 | 31 | Sep 1 | 2 |
| Sep 3 - 9 | 3 | 4 | 5 | 6 | 7 — SBS Alert Test 2; / SBS Tradeshow S | 8 | 9 |
| Sep 10 - 16 | 10 | 11 | 12 | 13 | 14 | 15 — Company meetin | 16 |
| Sep 17 - 23 | 17 | 18 — SBS Anniversary / SBS Lunch with J / SBS Staff Meetin / SBS Meeting 1; T | 19 | 20 | 21 — Updated: Quarte | 22 | 23 — Fishing trip! |
| Sep 24 - 30 | 24 | 25 — SBS Staff Meetin | 26 | 27 | 28 | 29 | 30 |

You can display a different month by scrolling the Calendar pane or by clicking the month you want to view, in the Date Navigator.

**6.** At the top of the Calendar pane, to the right of **Details**, select the **Medium** option.

The calendar changes to display only events as readable items; appointments and meetings appear as horizontal lines, with the width of the line indicating the amount of time scheduled for that item. The lines representing items assigned to color categories appear in the assigned color.

**7.** Select the **Low** option to hide appointments and meetings entirely.

**8.** Click one of the week labels that appears along the left edge of the Calendar pane.

Outlook displays the selected week in the most recent week view (Work Week or Full Week) you selected. No detail level is available in Day or Week view; Outlook shows all the calendar items.

Forward

**9.** To the left of the date range in the calendar header, click the **Forward** button.

The calendar moves forward one week.

**10.** Click one of the day labels that appears in the calendar header.

Outlook displays the selected day in Day View.

**11.** On the Standard toolbar, click **Today** to return to the default view.

## Adding and Removing Local Holidays

You can add the national holidays of any country to your Outlook calendar.

To add the holidays of one or more countries to your calendar:

1. On the **Tools** menu, click **Options**.
2. On the **Preferences** tab of the **Options** dialog box, click **Calendar Options**.
3. In the **Calendar Options** dialog box, click **Add Holidays**.

4. In the **Add Holidays to Calendar** dialog box, select the check boxes of the countries whose holidays you want to add to your calendar, and then click **OK**.
5. After Outlook adds the selected country's holidays to your calendar, click **OK** in each of the open dialog boxes.

Outlook 2007 assigns a color category named *Holiday* to all holidays in your calendar. If the only holidays in your calendar were added in Outlook 2007, you can view a list of holidays by displaying the calendar in By Category view and then scrolling to the Holiday category. You can then remove all holidays from your calendar by selecting the Categories: Holiday group header and pressing the Delete key.

If your calendar includes holidays created in a previous version of Outlook, or if you want to remove only the holidays of a specific country, follow these steps to remove the holidays:

1. Display the Calendar in **All Appointments** view.
2. On the **View** menu, point to **Current View**, and then click **Customize Current View**.
3. In the **Customize View** dialog box, click the **Group By** button.
4. In the **Group By** dialog box, clear the **Automatically group according to arrangement** check box if it is selected. Then click the **Group items by** arrow, and in the list, click **Location**.

5. Ensure that all the **Then by** lists display **(none)**, and then click **OK** in each of the open dialog boxes.

6. In the **Calendar** pane, collapse the displayed groups or scroll the pane until the **Location** group of the holidays you want to remove (for instance, Location: Sweden) is visible.

7. To remove all the holidays of the displayed country, click the **Location** group header, and then press the ⌨Del key. If a Outlook displays a message box warns you that this action will apply to all items in the selected group, click **OK**.

8. To remove selected holidays, click the holiday(s) you want to delete (hold the ⌨Ctrl key to select multiple holidays), and then press ⌨Del.

# Defining Your Available Time

You can tell Outlook what your work schedule is so that other people can make appointments with you only during the times that you plan to be available. This defined time is called your *work week*.

By default, Outlook defines the work week as Monday through Friday from 8:00 A.M. to 5:00 P.M. You can change this to suit your needs—for instance, if you work a late shift or on weekends. Your work week is colored differently in your calendar and by default is the only time displayed to other people on your network who look at your calendar.

In this exercise, you will view and change your work week. There are no practice files for this exercise.

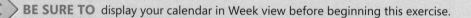

**BE SURE TO** display your calendar in Week view before beginning this exercise.

1. At the top of the **Calendar** pane, select the **Show work week** option.

> **Troubleshooting** If your work week does not match the default days and times described here, work through this exercise using your own settings.

**2.** Scroll the calendar page so that you can see the beginning or end of the work day, indicated by a change in shading.

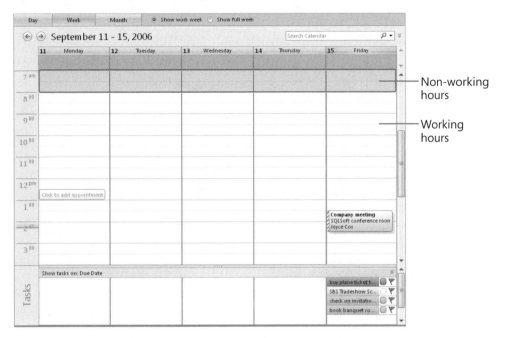

**3.** On the **Tools** menu, click **Options**.

**4.** On the **Preferences** tab of the **Options** dialog box, click **Calendar Options**.

The Calendar Options dialog box opens.

**5.** In the **Calendar work week** area, select the **Sun** and **Sat** check boxes, and clear the **Tue**, **Wed**, and **Thu** check boxes.

The work week is now set to Friday through Monday.

**6.** Click the **Start time** arrow, and in the list, click **3:00 PM**. Then click the **End time** arrow, and in the list, click **11:00 PM**.

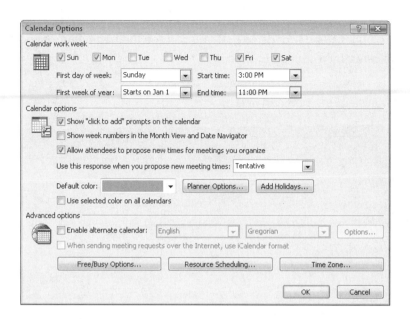

> **Troubleshooting** Outlook doesn't allow you to define a workday that crosses midnight, or to define different start and end times for different days.

**7.** Click **OK** in each of the open dialog boxes.

Your calendar displays your new work week settings.

**BE SURE TO** set up your work week the way you want it before continuing.

## Configuring Outlook for Multiple Time Zones

If you frequently travel to locations outside of your usual time zone, you will find it helpful to change the time zone on your computer. You can do this from Microsoft Windows or from Outlook. When you change the time zone, information such as the receipt time of e-mail messages and appointment times changes to match the new time zone, and if you display the clock in the Windows taskbar notification area, the time shown there also changes.

To change the time zone:

1. On the **Tools** menu, click **Options**.

2. On the **Preferences** tab of the **Options** dialog box, click the **Calendar Options** button.

3. In the **Advanced Options** area of the **Calendar Options** dialog box, click the **Time Zone** button.

4. In the **Time Zone** dialog box, click the **Time zone** arrow, and in the list, click the time zone you want. Then click **OK** in each of the open dialog boxes.

When preparing to travel or if you schedule meetings involving participants in different time zones, you might want to configure Outlook to display two time zones in your calendar. Outlook then displays the time zones in Day view in two columns to the left of the Calendar pane.

To simultaneously display two time zones in your calendar:

1. On the **Tools** menu, click **Options**.

2. In the **Options** dialog box, on the **Preferences** tab, click the **Calendar Options** button.

3. In the **Calendar Options** dialog box, click the **Time Zone** button.

4. In the **Time Zone** dialog box, select the **Show an additional time zone** check box. Then in the second **Time zone** list, click the additional time zone you want to display.

5. Type a label for each time zone (such as *San Diego* and *Copenhagen*) in the corresponding **Label** box.

6. Click **OK** in each of the open dialog boxes.

If you have already set up two time zones in your Outlook calendar, you can quickly switch between time zones by clicking the Swap Time Zones button in the Time Zone dialog box.

# Printing a Calendar

From time to time, you might find it convenient to print a day, week, month, or other period of your calendar; for instance, if you're traveling without a laptop or want to have your weekly schedule quickly available in your briefcase. You can easily print any time period of your calendar. The amount of detail that appears depends on the period you print.

Outlook offers several built-in print styles, and you can create others if you want. The available print styles vary based on what view you're in when you choose the Print command. The default print styles include:

- **Daily Style.** Prints the selected date range with one day per page. Printed elements include the date, day, TaskPad, and reference month calendar, along with an area for notes.

- **Weekly Style.** Prints the selected date range with one calendar week per page, including reference calendars for the selected and following months.

- **Monthly Style.** Prints a page for each month in the selected date range. Each page includes the six-week range surrounding the month, along with reference calendars for the selected and following months.

- **Tri-fold Style.** Prints a page for each day in the selected date range. Each page includes the daily schedule, weekly schedule, and TaskPad.

- **Calendar Details Style.** Lists your appointments for the selected date range, as well as the accompanying appointment details.

You can select the date or range of dates to be printed and modify the page setup options to fit your needs.

In this exercise, you will learn two ways of selecting print styles as you preview and optionally print your calendar in the Daily and Tri-fold styles. There are no practice files for this exercise.

> **Important** To complete this exercise, you must have a printer installed. If you don't have a printer installed, you can preview the various print options, but not print. To install a printer, click the Start button and then click Control Panel. In Control Panel, under Hardware And Sound, click Printers, and then click Add A Printer. If you are working on a network, your administrator can provide the information you need to install a printer.

> **BE SURE TO** display your calendar in Day view before beginning this exercise. For best results, display a day on which one or more appointments, meetings, or events appear on the calendar.

Print

**1.** On the Standard toolbar, click the **Print** button.

The Print dialog box opens, with the Daily Style format and today's date selected.

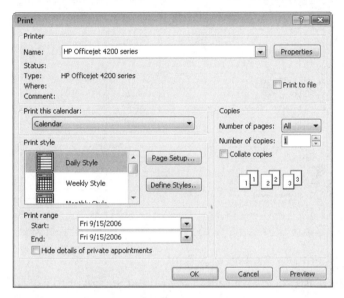

**2.** In the **Print** dialog box, click **Preview**.

Outlook displays a Print Preview window depicting how your calendar will appear when printed.

Actual Size

**3.** On the Print Preview window toolbar, click the **Actual Size** button to magnify the calendar page so it is legible.

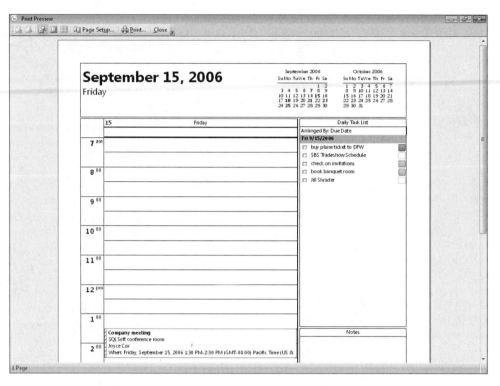

4. On the Print Preview toolbar, click **Print**.

5. In the **Print** dialog box, ensure that the printer you want to use is selected in the **Printer** area, and then click **OK**.

   Outlook prints today's schedule in the Daily Style format, which approximates the calendar Day view.

6. On the **File** menu, point to **Page Setup**, and then click **Tri-fold Style**.

   The Page Setup dialog box opens, displaying a preview of the Tri-fold print style. In the Options area, you can select the calendar elements you want to print in each of the three panes

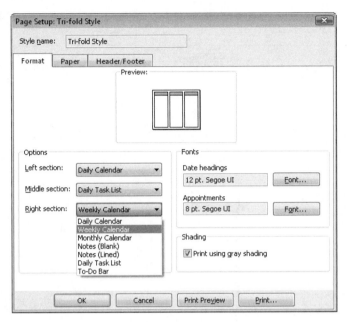

7.  In the **Page Setup** dialog box, click **Print**.

    Note that Outlook doesn't retain your settings from one print session to the next.

8.  In the **Print range** area of the **Print** dialog box, click the **End** arrow, and then in the list, click the date two days from today. Then click **Preview**.

    The Print Preview window displays the tri-fold calendar as it will appear when printed. The insertion point changes to a magnifying glass.

9.  Click once near the center of the previewed page to magnify the calendar page.

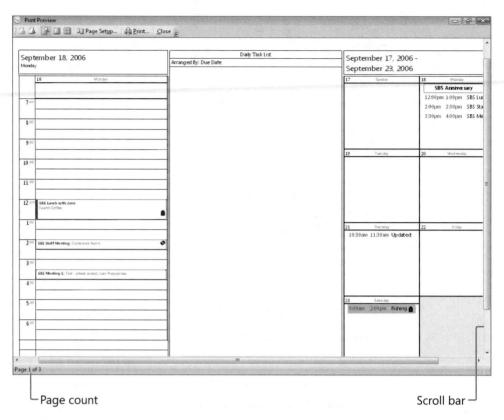

Page count          Scroll bar

In the lower-left corner of the Print Preview window, the status bar indicates that you are viewing the first of three pages, to match the date range you selected. With the default options, each page displays the daily calendar on the left, your task list for that day in the center, and the weekly calendar on the right. You can preview the second and third pages by clicking the down arrow on the vertical scroll bar on the right side of the window.

**10.** On the Print Preview toolbar, click **Print**, and then in the **Print** dialog box, click **OK**.

Outlook prints three pages—one page for each day of the selected date range—and then closes the Print Preview window.

**11.** Experiment with different print styles and date ranges, previewing the results of each.

# Sending Calendar Information in an E-Mail Message

You might frequently find it necessary to share information about your schedule with colleagues, friends, or family members. With Outlook 2007, you can easily embed selected calendar information as a static image in an e-mail message that you can send to any person who uses an HTML-capable e-mail program (not only people who use Outlook).

You can choose the period of time for which you want to share information (Today, Tomorrow, Next 7 Days, Next 30 Days, or Whole Calendar, or you can specify a custom date range) and the level of detail you want to share:

- **Availability only.** Includes only your availability (Free, Busy, Tentative, or Out Of Office) during scheduled time periods.
- **Limited details.** Includes only your availability and the subjects of calendar items.
- **Full details.** Includes your availability and the full details of calendar items.

The details of calendar items marked as Private will not be shown unless you specifically choose to do so.

**See Also**  For information about private appointments, see "Scheduling and Changing Appointments" in Chapter 20, "Managing Appointments, Events, and Meetings."

In this exercise, you will embed information about your schedule in an e-mail message. There are no practice files for this exercise.

**BE SURE TO** display your calendar before beginning this exercise.

1. In the **Navigation Pane**, click **Send a Calendar via E-mail**.

   Outlook opens a new message window and the Send A Calendar Via E-mail dialog box.

2. In the **Advanced** area, click **Show** to display all the options.

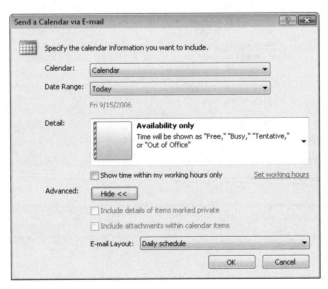

If you have multiple calendar folders in Outlook, you can choose which calendar you want to send information from.

3. Click the **Date Range** arrow, and then in the list, click **Next 7 days**.

4. Click the **Detail** arrow, and then in the list, click **Full details**.

You can choose whether to include private appointment details and attachments, and whether to present schedule information as a daily schedule or only a list of events.

5. With **Daily schedule** selected in the **E-mail Layout** list, click **OK**.

Outlook embeds the selected calendar information in the e-mail message window and also attaches the same information as an *.ics* file. You can send the e-mail message to any recipient. A recipient using an e-mail program that supports *.ics* files can add your calendar information to his or her calendar list.

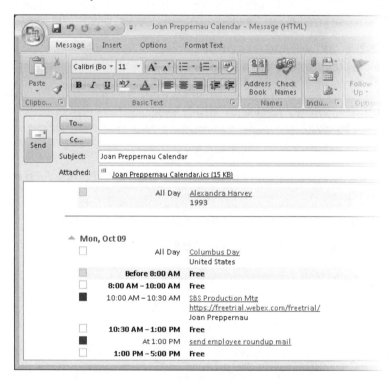

6. Scroll the e-mail to view its contents. Then experiment with other time periods, details, and layout options on your own.

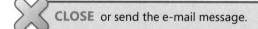 **CLOSE** or send the e-mail message.

## Saving Calendar Information as a Web Page

You can share your schedule with co-workers by publishing it as a Web page on an intranet site, or with a larger group of people by publishing it as a Web page on an Internet site. Outlook provides a simple method of saving selected calendar information as a static HTML page.

To save calendar information as a Web page:

1. Display your calendar. Then on the **File** menu, click **Save as Web Page**.

   The Save As Web Page dialog box opens.

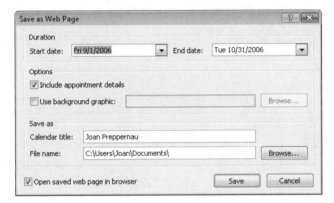

2. Enter the start and end dates for which you want to publish your calendar information.

3. In the **Options** area, select whether to include appointment details or a background graphic.

4. In the **Save as** area, append a file name (the extension is unnecessary) at the end of the path shown in the **File name** box. You can change the title that will be displayed on the Web page, and change the location where Outlook saves it.

   By default, Outlook saves calendar Web pages in your Documents folder.

5. With the **Open saved web page in browser** check box selected, click **Save**.

6. If Outlook displays a security notice asking you to confirm that you trust the link to the Web page you just created, click **Yes**.

7. If Outlook displays a message box asking you whether to open or save the Web page, click **Open**.

   The page opens in your default Web browser. (The browser loads the file from your computer, not from the Internet—you haven't yet published the schedule to the Internet.)

8. Review the calendar. If an Information Bar appears at the top of the window, click it, click **Allow Blocked Content**, and then in the **Security Warning** message box, click **Yes** to allow Windows to run a Microsoft ActiveX control in order to display nicely formatted content.

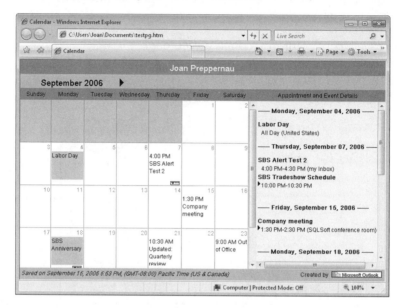

You can publish the calendar Web page to any intranet or Internet site that you have authoring permissions on.

# Linking to an Internet Calendar

A variety of specialized calendars tracking professional sports schedules, holidays, entertainment, scientific data, and so on are available from the Microsoft Office Online Web site. You can link to these Internet calendars from the Calendar module so that you have up-to-date information conveniently available, in the same place as your own scheduling information.

After you link to an Internet calendar, you can display or hide the linked calendar at any time by selecting or clearing its check box in the Other Calendars section of the All Calendar Items list. You can display Internet calendars within the Calendar module as you would any other, viewing them independently or next to another calendar, or displaying a combined view of information from multiple calendars. You can remove the linked calendar from your list of available calendars by right-clicking the calendar's tab and then clicking Delete.

In this exercise, you will link to an Internet calendar. There are no practice files for this exercise.

**Important** This exercise requires an active Internet connection.

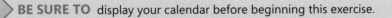

**BE SURE TO** display your calendar before beginning this exercise.

1. At the bottom of the **Navigation Pane**, click **Search Calendars Online**.

   The Internet Calendars page of the Office Online Web site opens in your default Internet browser.

2. Scroll the page to display the **Subscribe to a Free Internet Calendar** section.

3. In the **Entertainment** list, click **New York theater events** (or click any other Internet calendar that interests you).

4. If an **Internet Explorer Security** message box appears prompting you to allow Outlook to open Web content, click the **Allow** button.

5. In the **Microsoft Office Outlook** message box asking whether you want to add the calendar to Outlook and subscribe to updates, click **Yes**.

Outlook adds the selected Internet calendar to your Other Calendars list, and displays it in the Calendar pane, side by side with your own calendar.

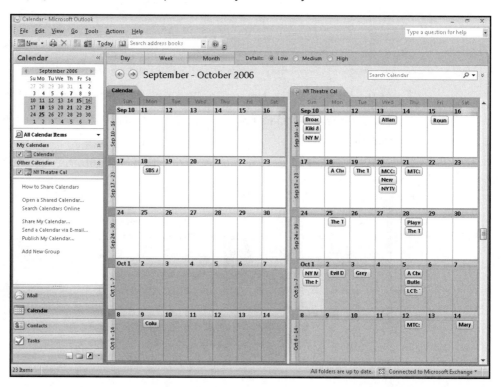

The linked calendar also appears (as *NY Theatre*) in the Other Calendars list in the Navigation Pane. Any calendars you link to that aren't your own—for example, SharePoint calendars, calendars of coworkers, and so on, appear in this list.

**BE SURE TO** retain the linked Internet calendar for use in the next exercise.

### Creating a OneNote Page Linked to an Appointment, an Event, or a Meeting

If your 2007 Office system installation includes Microsoft Office OneNote, you can link calendar entries from Outlook to your OneNote notebook.

To link one or more calendar entries to OneNote:

1. Display the Calendar, and select the item (or items) you want to link.

2. On the Standard toolbar, click the **Notes About This Item** button.

   Notes About
   This Item

   OneNote starts (if it isn't already running) and, in its Unfiled Notes section, creates a page for each of the selected calendar items. Each page contains the appointment, event, or meeting information and a link that opens the original Outlook calendar item from within OneNote.

You can move pages from the Unfiled Notes section to a notebook section by dragging or by right-clicking the page tab, pointing to Move Page To, and then clicking Another Section. In the Move Or Copy Pages dialog box, click the target notebook section, and then click Move.

## Working with Multiple Calendars

It is often useful to have more than one Outlook calendar, and it's easy to create secondary calendars.

The process of creating a secondary calendar is the same as that of creating an address book or mail folder—you simply create a folder designated to hold calendar items.

You can display calendars individually, or you can display more than one calendar at a time. For instance, you might want to display a team project calendar in addition to your own calendar, or you might have separate business and personal calendars and want to view them together.

With Outlook 2007, you can view multiple calendars next to each other, or you can overlay them to display a composite view of the separate calendars. When you view and scroll multiple calendars, they all display the same date or time period.

You can drag appointments and events from one calendar to another, and copy items between calendars by dragging with the right mouse button and then clicking Copy on the shortcut menu.

In this exercise, you will view multiple calendars next to each other and then as a composite. There are no practice files for this exercise.

> **BE SURE TO** display your calendar and complete the previous exercise, "Linking to an Internet Calendar," before beginning this exercise.

1. In the **Navigation Pane**, in the **My Calendars** or **Other Calendars** list, select the check box for at least one other calendar.

> **Tip** If you just completed the previous exercise, a second calendar is already visible.

By default, Outlook displays multiple calendars next to each other. Each calendar is a different color.

View in Overlay Mode buttons

In Side-By-Side mode, the title bar tab of each calendar other than your own calendar displays a View In Overlay Mode button.

2. On the title bar tab of the **NY Theatre** calendar (or any other secondary calendar), click the **View in Overlay Mode** button.

View in Overlay Mode

The secondary calendar overlaps your own calendar (or whichever calendar is active). Appointments on the overlapped calendar appear in a muted font; those on the top calendar appear normally.

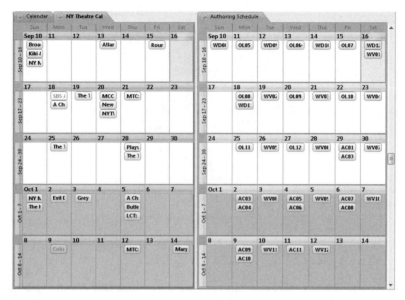

3. Click the **Calendar** tab to display your calendar on top of the Internet calendar.

4. On either of the overlaid calendars, click the **View in Side-By-Side Mode** button to return to the standard display.

View in Side-By-Side Mode

> **BE SURE TO**  clear the Internet Calendar check box in the Other Calendars list to display only your own calendar, before continuing to the next exercise.

---

## Delegating Control of Your Calendar

You can delegate control of your calendar (or any other Outlook module) to a coworker so that he or she can create and respond to meeting requests on your behalf. To do so:

1. On the **Tools** menu, click **Options**.

2. On the **Delegates** tab of the **Options** dialog box, click **Add**.

3. In the **Add Users** dialog box, click the person you want to delegate control to, click **Add**, and then click **OK**.

   You can delegate control to multiple people.

4. In the **Delegate Permissions** dialog box, click the **Calendar** arrow, and then in the list, click the level of permission you want to delegate.

5. Select any other permissions you want to delegate.

6. Select the **Automatically send a message to delegate summarizing these permissions** check box, and then click **OK**.

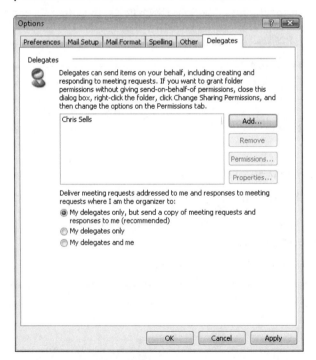

7. In the **Options** dialog box, select whether you would like to receive copies of meeting requests and responses. Then click **OK**.

From this time forward, meeting requests sent to you are automatically delivered to your delegate rather than to you. You receive copies of the meeting requests and copies of your delegate's responses, but you don't have to respond to meeting requests. Your delegate can create meeting requests on your behalf (that is, they appear to come from you).

# Key Points

- You can display a traditional calendar view of your schedule by the day, work week, full week, or month. You can display multiple list views of calendar items.

- You can display multiple time zones, change your calendar as you travel between time zones, and schedule appointments or meetings that start and end in different time zones.

- You can print selected schedule information in a number of different layout styles.

- You can share schedule information by sending it in an e-mail message or by publishing it to a Web site.

- You can subscribe to many types of calendars available from the Internet. Internet calendar information is automatically updated.

- You can view two or more calendars next to each other or as a composite. Outlook displays each calendar in a different color so you can easily tell them apart.

# Glossary

from a table. See also *crosstab query*, *select query*, and *parameter query*.

**active cell** The cell that is currently selected and open for editing.

**aggregate function** A function, such as Sum, Avg, or Count, that groups fields and performs calculations on the field values.

**append query** A query that adds, or appends, records from one or more tables to the end of one or more tables.

**Appointment** A block of time you schedule on your calendar that has a defined start time and end time, and to which you do not invite other attendees.

**appointment window** The program window displaying the form in which you enter information about an appointment.

**Archiving** Moving older or unused items to a secondary location for the purpose of backing up or long-term storage.

**Arguments** The specific data a function requires to calculate a value.

**arithmetic operator** An operator that is used with numerals: + (addition), - (subtraction), * (multiplication), or / (division).

**Arrangement** The order in which Microsoft Office Outlook displays messages or other items.

**Attribute** Individual items of character formatting, such as style or color, which determine how text looks.

**Auditing** The process of examining a worksheet for errors.

**AutoArchive** An Outlook feature that automatically archives items meeting specific age and location criteria at regular intervals.

**action query** A type of query that quickly updates information or deletes selected records

**AutoComplete** The ability to complete data entry for a cell based on similar values in other cells in the same column.

**AutoCorrect** A feature that corrects common capitalization and spelling errors (such as changing as *teh* to *the*) as you type them.

**AutoFill** The ability to extend a series of values based on the contents of a single cell.

**Background** The underlying scheme, including colors, shading, texture, and graphics, that appears behind the text and objects on a slide.

**Bound** Linked, as when a text box is linked to a specific field in a table.

**building blocks** Frequently used text saved in a gallery, from which it can be inserted quickly into a document.

**bullet point** An item in a list in which each list entry is preceded by a symbol, rather than by a number.

**calendar item windows** Collectively refers to the program windows displaying the forms in which you enter information about appointments, meetings, and events.

**Case** The capitalization (uppercase or lowercase) of a word or phrase. In title case, the first letter of all important words is capitalized. In sentence case, only the first letter of the first word is capitalized.

**Cell** A box at the intersection of a column and row in a table or worksheet.

**cell address** The location of a cell, expressed as its column letter and row number, as in A1.

**cell range** A group of cells.

**character formatting** The collection of attributes applied to text.

**character spacing** The space between characters, which can be expanded or contracted so that characters are pushed apart or pulled together.

**character style** A variation of a font, such as bold or italic.

**Click and Type** A feature that allows you to double-click a blank area of a document to position the insertion point in that location, with the appropriate paragraph alignment already in place.

**Clipboard** A storage area shared by all Office programs where cut or copied items are stored.

**color scheme** A set of 12 complementary colors used for different elements of a PowerPoint slide. A color scheme consists of a background color, a color for lines and text, and additional colors balanced to provide a professional look.

**column** In a chart, a vertical representation of plotted data from a table or worksheet. In page layout, the area between margins where text is allowed to flow. (Pages can have a single column or multiple columns.)

**column break** A break inserted in the text of a column to force the text below it to move to the next column.

**combo box** A control that displays a list of choices when you click the arrow on its right side. It might also allow you to enter a different choice from those available on the list.

**command button** A control that appears as a button, which performs an action when clicked.

**comparison operator** An operator that compares values: < (less than), > (greater than), and = (equal to). These operators can also be combined, as in <= (less than or equal to), >= (greater than or equal to), and <> (not equal to).

**conditional formula** A formula that calculates a value using one of two different expressions, depending on whether a third expression is true or false.

**constant** A part of an expression that represents a constant value.

**control property** A setting, accessible through the Properties dialog box, that determines a control's appearance, and what kind of data it can display.

**control source** The Access object, such as a field, table, or query, to which a control is bound. See also *record source*.

**crosstab query** A query that calculates a sum, average, count, or other type of total for data that is grouped by two types of information. See also *action query*, *parameter query*, and *select query*.

**custom slide show** A set of slides extracted from a presentation to create a slide show for an audience that doesn't need to see the entire presentation.

**database application** A database that is made easier to use by the inclusion of queries, forms, reports, a switchboard, custom categories and groups, and various other tools.

**Date Navigator** The small calendar that appears next to the appointment area in the Outlook Calendar. The Date Navigator provides a quick and easy way to change and view dates.

**delete query** A query that deletes records that match a specified pattern from one or more tables.

**demote** In an outline, the process of changing a heading to a lower-level heading or body text.

**dependents** The cells with formulas that use the value from a particular cell.

**deselect** Clicking away from selected data or controls to release the selection.

**design grid** In Design view, the grid in which you can manually work with advanced filters and queries.

**design template** A presentation file containing only design elements that can be used as a basis for creating new presentations.

**desktop publishing** A process that creates pages by combining text and objects such as tables and graphics in a visually appealing way.

**destination file** A file into which you insert an object created in another program.

**Dialog Box Launcher** A button that launches a dialog box containing options for refining a command.

**digital signature** A security mechanism used on the Internet that relies on two keys, one public and one private, that are used to encrypt messages before transmission and to decrypt them on receipt.

**Document Map** A pane that displays a linked outline of a document's headings and allows you to jump to a heading in the document by clicking it in the Document Map.

**document window** The window that provides a workspace for an open document.

**document workspace** A temporary space, usually on a Microsoft SharePoint site, dedicated to a single document. It provides a forum where everyone can work from a single location.

**draft** A temporary copy of a message that has not yet been sent, located in the Drafts folder.

**Draft view** A view that displays the content of a document with a simplified layout.

**drag-and-drop editing** A way of moving or copying selected text by dragging it with the mouse pointer.

**dragging** A way of moving objects by pointing to them, holding down the mouse button, moving the mouse pointer to the desired location, and releasing the button.

**duplicate query** A type of select query that finds records containing identical information in one or more specified fields.

**e-mail** Short for *electronic mail*; messages sent between defined entities over the Internet.

**e-mail signature** A block of text that is appended to the end of a message you send.

**e-mail trail** An e-mail message and all responses to that message. When an individual message receives multiple responses, the e-mail trail can branch into multiple trails. You can view all the branches of an e-mail trail in Conversation view.

**embedded object** An object that is created in a different program but that is incorporated into a Word document.

**empty string** An Access field that has two quotation marks with nothing in between. Access is able to differentiate between an empty string and a Null (blank) field.

**error code** A brief message that appears in a worksheet cell, describing a problem with a formula or a function.

**event** An action, including Click, Double Click, Mouse Down, Mouse Move, and Mouse Up, to which code can be attached. The events recognized by an object are listed on the Event tab in the object's Property Sheet pane.

**event window** The program window displaying the form in which you enter information about an event.

**expression** A combination of functions, field values, constants, and operators that can be used to assign properties to tables or forms, to determine values in fields or reports, as a part of a query, and in many other places. Also known as a *formula*.

**Expression Builder** A tool with which you can quickly create expressions (formulas) in queries, forms, and reports.

**field** A placeholder that tells Word to supply the specified information in the specified way.

Also, the set of information of a specific type in a data source, such as all the last names in a contacts list.

**field property** A property that controls what can be put into a field and how it can be placed there.

**fill handle** The square at the lower right corner of a cell you drag to indicate other cells that should hold values in the series defined by the active cell.

**Fill Series** The ability to extend a series of values based on the contents of two cells, where the first cell has the starting value for the series and the second cell shows the increment.

**filtering** A way to organize information so that some combination of characters is displayed or excluded from the display.

**firing event** The phrase used to describe when objects signal events in a form.

**floating toolbar** A toolbar that is not docked on any side of the program window. You can move a floating toolbar to any location on your screen, within or outside of the program window.

**flow** The way text continues from the bottom of one column to the top of the next column.

**font** A complete set of characters that all have the same design.

**font color** One of a range of colors that can be applied to text.

**font effect** An attribute, such as superscript, small capital letters, or shadow, that can be applied to a font.

**font size** The size of the characters in a font, in points.

**font style** An attribute that changes the look of text. The most common font styles are regular (or plain), italic, bold, and bold italic.

**formula** An expression used to calculate a value.

**Formula AutoComplete** The ability to enter a formula quickly by selecting functions, named ranges, and table references that appear when you begin to type the formula into a cell.

**Full Screen Reading view** A view that displays as much of the content of the document as will fit in the screen at a size that is comfortable for reading.

**function** A named procedure or routine in a program, often used for mathematical or financial calculations.

**gallery** A grouping of thumbnails that display options visually.

**global formatting** A theme or style applied to an entire document.

**gridlines** Lines that visually clarify the information in a chart.

**group** A category of buttons on a tab.

**hover** To pause the pointer over an object, such as a menu name or button, for a second or two to display more information, such as a submenu or ScreenTip.

**Hypertext Markup Language (HTML)** In Outlook, an e-mail message format that supports paragraph styles, character styles, and backgrounds. Most e-mail programs support the HTML format.

**Hypertext Transfer Protocol (HTTP)** A protocol used to access Web pages from the Internet.

**Importance** The property defining the urgency of a message or other Outlook item. The default setting is Normal; you can optionally change the setting for an individual item or for all items to High or Low.

**indent marker** A marker on the horizontal ruler that controls the indentation of text from the left or right side of a document.

**Internet Message Access Protocol (IMAP)** An e-mail–handling protocol that organizes messages on the server, and you choose messages to download by viewing their headers.

**justify** To make all lines of text in a paragraph or column fit the width of the document or column, with even margins on each side.

**landscape** The orientation of a horizontal page whose width is larger that its height.

**line break** A manual break that forces the text that follows it to the next line. Also called a text.

**linked object** An object that exists in a source file and that is inserted in a document with a link to that source file.

**live preview** A feature of a thumbnail that displays what an option will look like if applied to a document.

**local formatting** Formatting applied at the text or paragraph level.

**Lookup wizard** An Access wizard with which you can easily create a lookup list.

**make-table query** A query that combines all or part of the data from one or more tables into a new table.

**many-to-many relationship** Two one-to-many relationships tied together through a third table. See also *one-to-many relationship*; *one-to-one relationship*.

**margin** Blank space around the column in which text can flow on the page.

**message header** Basic information identifying an e-mail message, such as the date, time, sender, subject, and size. When working on a slow connection, you can download message headers and, based on the header information, decide whether to download the entire message.

**message window** The program window displaying the form in which you create or respond to an e-mail message.

**meeting window** The program window displaying the form in which you enter information to place a meeting on your calendar.

**meeting request** A message generated by Outlook to invite people to attend a meeting.

**meeting workspace** A shared site for planning a meeting and tracking related tasks and results.

**Microsoft Office Button** A button that provides access to a menu with commands that manage Word and Word documents as a whole (rather than document content).

**Microsoft Office PowerPoint Viewer** A viewer with which you can display presentations on a computer that does not have PowerPoint installed.

**Microsoft Office Word Help button** A button with a question mark (?) at the right end of the Ribbon that can be clicked to open the Word Help window.

**Mini toolbar** A toolbar of formatting commands that appears when you select text. named range A group of related cells defined by a single name.

**nested table** A table that is positioned inside another table.

**object** An item, such as a graphic, video clip, sound file, or worksheet, that can be inserted in a Word document and then selected and modified.

**Office menu** A menu that contains commands related to managing documents (such as creating, saving, and printing). This menu takes the place of the File menu that appeared in previous versions of Word.

**one-to-many relationship** A relationship in which each record in one table is linked to multiple records in another table. See also *many-to-many relationship*; *one-to-one relationship*.

**one-to-one relationship** A relationship in which each record in one table has one and only one associated record in the other table. See also *many-to-many relationship*; *one-to-many relationship*.

**operator** See *arithmetic operator*; *comparison operator*.

**option button** A form control with which users can choose preselected settings.

**orientation** The direction—horizontal or vertical—in which a page is laid out.

**Outline view** A view that shows headings and body text and can be used to evaluate and reorganize the structure of a document.

**Package for CD** A feature to help you gather all the components of a presentation and store them to a CD or another type of removable media so that they can be transported to a different computer.

**paragraph** In word processing, a block of text of any length that ends when you press the Enter key.

**paragraph formatting** Collectively, the settings used to vary the look of paragraphs.

**paragraph style** A set of formatting that can be applied to the paragraph containing the insertion point by selecting the style from a list.

**parameter query** A query that prompts for the information to be used in the query, such as a range of dates. This type of query is useful when used as the basis for a report that is run periodically. See also *action query*, *crosstab query*, and *select query*.

**parent folder** The folder in which another folder is contained.

**placeholder** An area on a slide into which you should enter a specific type of content.

**Plain Text** An e-mail message format that does not support character or paragraph formatting. All e-mail programs support Plain Text.

**point** The unit of measure for expressing the size of characters in a font, where 72 points equals 1 inch.

**populate** To add data to a table or other object.

**portrait** The orientation of a vertical page whose width is smaller that its height.

**Post Office Protocol 3 (POP3)** A common protocol used to retrieve e-mail messages from an Internet e-mail server.

**precedents** The cells that are used in a formula.

**Print Layout view** A view that shows how document will look when printed.

**property** A setting applied to an object that can determine its content, such as the Required and Input Mask properties, and appearance, such as the Font and Alignment properties.

**promote** In an outline, to change body text to a heading, or to change a heading to a higher level heading.

**Quick Access Toolbar** A toolbar that displays the Save, Undo, and Repeat buttons by default, but can be customized to show other commands.

**Quick Styles** Formatting options that you can apply to individual elements of a message.

**quick table** A table with sample data.

**range** A group of related cells.

**read-only** Available for viewing but protected from alterations.

**recall** Instructing Outlook to delete or replace any unread copies of a message already sent.

**record selector** The gray bar along the left edge of a table or form. You can select an entire record by clicking the record selector next to it.

**record source** The source from which the data in a bound record originates. See also *control source*.

**recurring** Repeating on a regular basis. You can specify an appointment, meeting, or event as recurring, and specify the frequency of recurrence. Outlook then creates a series of items based on your specifications.

**relationship** An association between common fields in two or more tables.

**relative reference** A cell reference in a formula, such as =B3, that refers to a cell that is a specific distance away from the cell that contains the formula. For example, if the formula =B3 were in cell C3, copying the formula to cell C4 would cause the formula to change to =B4.

**reminder**  An optional message displayed by Outlook a specific amount of time prior to an appointment, meeting, event, or task milestone. You can dismiss the reminder, reset it for a later time, or open the item from the reminder window.

**resend**  Creating a new version of an original message.

**resolving**  The process of matching a user name to the information on a network server, resulting in the user name being replaced by a display name and the name underlined.

**result**  In an Access formula, the *result* equals the outcome of the equation.

**Ribbon**  An area across the top of the screen that makes almost all the capabilities of Word available in a single area.

**Rich Text Format (RTF)**  A text format that can be opened by many programs and that is used to export presentation content as an outline.

**sans serif**  A style of typeface with no ornamentation on the upper or lower end of the character.

**ScreenTip**  Information displayed in a small window when you rest the pointer over a button or window element.

**select**  To make an object, graphic, or text active, usually by clicking it with the mouse, so that it can be moved or modified.

**selector**  A small box attached to an object that you click to select the object, and drag to resize it.

**select query**  A query that retrieves, or selects, data matching specified criteria from one or more tables and displays the results in a datasheet. See also *action query*, *crosstab query*, and *parameter query*.

**selection area**  An area in a document's left margin in which you can click and drag to select blocks of text.

**sensitivity**  An optional setting that indicates, by icons or words, that an item is Personal, Private, or Confidential.

**shared attachments**  Attachments saved on a SharePoint document workspace Web site, where a group can collaborate to work on f les and discuss a project.

**slide library**  A place on a SharePoint site where co-workers store slides that other people can use.

**slide timing**  The time a slide will be displayed on the screen before PowerPoint moves to the next slide.

**SmartArt**  A technology first introduced by Microsoft with the 2007 Office system, with which you can easily create professional business graphics within documents, spreadsheets, presentations, and messages.

**smart tag**  A flag that identifies a certain type of information, such as date and time, names, street addresses, or telephone numbers, so that you can perform actions associated with that type of information.

**sorting**  Arranging information so that it's based on any field or combination of fields.

**source file**  A file containing an object that is inserted in a destination file.

**status bar**  An area across the bottom of the program window that gives information about the current document.

**subform**  A form contained within another form.

**subpoint**  A subordinate item below a bullet point in a list.

**switchboard**  A hierarchy of pages containing buttons that the user can click to open additional pages, display dialog boxes, present forms for viewing and entering data, preview and print reports, and initiate other activities.

**syntax** The required format in which expressions must be entered.

**tab** An area on the Ribbon that contains buttons organized in groups.

**tab leader** A repeating character (usually a dot or dash) that separates text before the tab from text or a number after it.

**tab stop** A location in the text column where text will align after you press the Tab key to insert a tab character.

**tabular list** A list that arranges text in simple columns separated by left, right, centered, or decimal tab stops. can customize.

**template** A pattern used as the basis for creating the slides, handouts, and speaker notes in a PowerPoint presentation.

**text box** A box drawn independently on a slide to contain text that is not part of any placeholder.

**text box control** A control on a form or report in which text can be entered or edited.

**text wrapping break** A manual break that forces the text that follows it to the next line. Also called a *line break*.

**theme** A predefined format that can be applied to a worksheet.

**Thesaurus** A feature that looks up alternative words, or synonyms, for a word.

**threaded** A series of messages that have been sent as replies to each other.

**thumbnail** A picture representation of choices available in a gallery; or of pages in a document.

**title** A name you designate for a slide in the Title placeholder.

**title bar** An area at the top of the program window that displays the name of the active document

**title slide** The introductory slide in a presentation.

**unmatched query** A select query that locates records in one table without any related records in another table.

**update query** A select query that performs an action on the query's results in some way, such as by changing a field.

**validation rule** A field property that ensures entries contain only the correct types of information.

**View toolbar** A toolbar on the right end of the status bar that contains tools for adjusting the view of document content.

**views** Different ways in which the Outlook window can be arranged for viewing messages.

**virtual folder** Folder that looks like and links to an original folder.

**voting buttons** Used in conjunction with an Exchange Server account, this feature enables recipients to respond to a poll by clicking a button corresponding to a specific response option. Responses return to the sender in a format that allows easy collating and tabulation.

**Web Layout view** A view that shows how a document will look when viewed in a Web browser.

**wildcard characters** When using the Find and Replace dialog box, characters that serve as placeholders for a single character, such as *?ffect* for *affect* and *effect*, or for multiple characters.

**wildcard character** A placeholder, such as an asterisk (*) or question mark (?) representing an unknown character or characters in search criteria.

**word processing** The writing, editing, and formatting of documents in a word processor.

**word wrap** The automatic breaking of a line of text when it reaches the page margin.

**work week** The days and times you define within Outlook as available for work-related activities.

# Index

## Symbols

## A

# F

# What do you think of this book?

# We want to hear from you!

Do you have a few minutes to participate in a brief online survey?

Microsoft is interested in hearing your feedback so we can continually improve our books and learning resources for you.

To participate in our survey, please visit:

**www.microsoft.com/learning/booksurvey/**

...and enter this book's ISBN-10 number (appears above barcode on back cover*).
As a thank-you to survey participants in the United States and Canada, each month we'll randomly select five respondents to win one of five $100 gift certificates from a leading online merchant. At the conclusion of the survey, you can enter the drawing by providing your e-mail address, which will be used for prize notification only.

Thanks in advance for your input. Your opinion counts!

**\* Where to find the ISBN-10 on back cover**

ISBN-13: 000-0-0000-00000
ISBN-10: 0-0000-00000

0 000000 000000

Example only. Each book has unique ISBN.

**Microsoft**
*Press*

# welcome to the ribbon

## Your quick reference to the new user interface in Microsoft® Office

**Microsoft® Office**

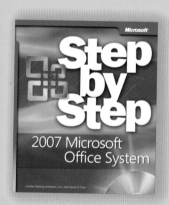

Microsoft
**Step by Step**
2007 Microsoft Office System

Online Training Solutions, Inc., and Curtis D. Frye

See more learning resources at
**microsoft.com/mspress**

# Customizing Your Workspace

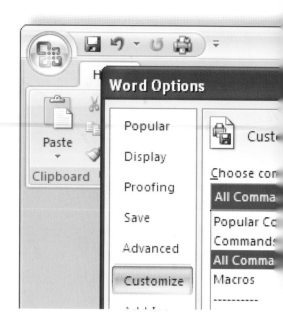

## Add frequently used commands to the Quick Access Toolbar

1. Click the **Microsoft® Office Button** and then click **Options**.

2. In the list at the left, click **Customize** then choose your commands.

   or

1. Right-click a command or command group on the Ribbon.

2. Click **Add to Quick Access Toolbar**.

## Collapse the Ribbon

To reduce the Ribbon to a single line of tabs, press **CTRL +F1** or click **Customize Quick Access Toolbar** and then click **Minimize the Ribbon**.

Clicking on a tab while the Ribbon is minimized will temporarily restore the Ribbon. After you have made your selection, it will collapse again.

## Use keyboard shortcuts to access commands

1. Press and release the **ALT** key.

   KeyTips are displayed for each Tab on the Ribbon, as well as the **Microsoft Office Button** and the **Quick Access Toolbar**.

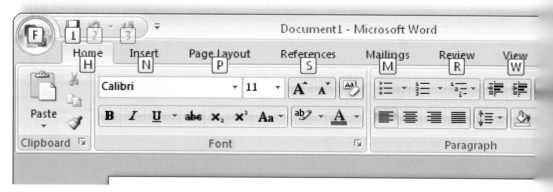

2. Type the letter(s) shown in the KeyTip for the feature you want to use. Typing the letter associated with a Tab will display KeyTips for every command on that Tab.